DATE DUE			

SAMUEL RICHARDSON

Born at Derby in 1689, the son of a joiner.
Came to London at seventeen, and entered
the printing trade, eventually purchasing
the moiety of the patent of King's Printer.
Died in London in 1761.

SAMUEL RICHARDSON

Pamela

IN TWO VOLUMES · VOLUME ONE

INTRODUCTION BY

M. KINKEAD-WEEKES
B.A. (*Capetown*), M.A. (*Oxon*)

*Lecturer in the Faculty of
English Literature and Rhetoric
in the University of Edinburgh*

DENT: LONDON
EVERYMAN'S LIBRARY
DUTTON: NEW YORK

© Introduction, J. M. Dent & Sons Ltd, 1962
All rights reserved
Made in Great Britain
at the
Aldine Press · Letchworth · Herts
for
J. M. DENT & SONS LTD
Aldine House · Bedford Street · London
First included in Everyman's Library 1914
Last reprinted 1966

NO. 683

INTRODUCTION

IN 1740, at the age of fifty-one, Richardson was merely a prosperous printer whose few editorial performances only proved him an intelligent man of his trade with an eye to a new venture. Fourteen years later he reached the peak of his profession as Master of the Stationers' Company; but he had also written three novels which were to earn him a readership and literary influence spread across Europe. He had become arguably the greatest English novelist of his century, and certainly the inventor of a whole new way of writing—one of the most fruitful 'kinds' of the novel.

The transformation began when two booksellers asked him to compile a letter-writer—a collection of letters which could both be entertaining and serve as models in all sorts of situations. The task was still humble; yet in several of the situations there was a new challenge to his dramatic imagination, his ability to put himself into the minds and the language of very different kinds of people. He also discovered how subtly the letter form can reveal character. In one situation, moreover, the correspondence of a father and a daughter whose master has tried to seduce her, there were dramatic and moralistic possibilities too fascinating to be confined to the letter-writer. So he laid it aside, and in only two months of intense creativity amongst all his everyday business he finished *Pamela: or Virtue Rewarded*, and published it anonymously. The story of the virtuous servant who resists her wicked master and is rewarded by his reformation and his hand may be based on fact, as Richardson himself claimed; but the novel which embodies it in a collection of letters and a journal was a brilliantly original invention.

It became one of the century's best sellers, going through five editions in its first year and being rapidly translated into most European languages. Fashionable ladies displayed copies in public places, and held fans painted with pictures of its best-loved scenes. *Pamela* became a play, an opera, even a waxwork; and in a society suspicious of fiction had the distinction of a recommendation from a London pulpit. Yet the triumph was not unmixed. Even at its height harsher voices objected to the book's moral tendencies, and denounced its heroine as a sly minx far less innocent than she appears. Outstanding among these was Henry Fielding, first in the outrageously amusing and malicious parody *An Apology for the Life of Mrs Shamela Andrews*, and then in his novel *Joseph Andrews*. By mid-century opinion was sharply divided all over Europe. A Danish writer speaks of 'two different parties, Pamelists and Antipamelists. . . . Some look on this young Virgin as an example for ladies to follow. . . . Others, on the contrary, discover in it the behaviour of an hypocritical, crafty girl . . . who understands the Art of bringing a man to her lure'.

In our own time the Antipamelists seem to have won the day, *Shamela* is vindicated, and there is widespread agreement that Pamela's conduct is hypocritical, whether consciously so or not. Indeed, critics are less concerned to proclaim this now than to point to the psychological realism of Richardson's creation, and to seek the source of both this and the moral confusion in his unquestioning identification with his heroine. By tapping her author's unconscious, on this view, *Pamela* reveals to us not only Richardson's confusions, but a typical and significant ambivalence in the whole Puritan ethos. As Steele pointed out, prude and coquette are alike in that they have 'the distinction of sex in all their thoughts, words and actions'—this is why Pamela can seem to be either. The more indeed the moralist and his heroine proclaim their rejection of sexuality, the more they can be seen to be obsessed by it. We may also recall Mrs Peachum's observation that 'by keeping men off, you keep them on'.

Yet only four years later Richardson completed *Clarissa*, about whose power and moral stature there is no less widespread agreement; and while there is much evidence of technical development, the moral and spiritual concerns of the two novels are remarkably similar. There is certainly no evidence of re-thinking deep enough to account for the radical discrepancy the critics discover between them. Disturbing, too, is the assumption that Richardson was an unconscious artist with little idea what he was doing, when it is coupled with a failure to examine the implications and complications of the new form he invented. For although Richardson wrote no formal essay on his art, he did scatter through his published and unpublished letters a large number of statements which show a surprisingly acute understanding of his problems.

What he invented was the dramatic novel, not merely the idea of writing in letters. The epistolary form is a means, not an end. It is an attempt to gain something of the immediacy of a playgoer's experience; of getting to know characters directly, not through a narrative filter, and of watching an action unfold now, while one looks and listens. Richardson called his invention 'writing to the moment'. As often as he could he made his characters write during the crises of their affairs. Where this was impossible they write immediately afterwards; either in letters largely composed of dialogue and description of action and gesture, to convey the effect of watching a dramatic scene; or in letters of immediate self-analysis like extensions of dramatic soliloquy. Because these are written 'to the moment' and not collectedly later, consciousness can be caught on the wing, and one can discover things about the characters that they do not yet know themselves.

Drama, moreover, is not merely a technique of writing. It is a kind of imaginative vision that is quite different from other kinds. In narrative the author tells you directly in his own words what he has conceived. In drama he has to see and communicate indirectly, by projecting his imagination into characters who reveal themselves without his mediation. The author himself is not there at all—he has become all his characters. Some are obviously closer to him than others, but we can only establish his own views when we understand the whole meaning that results from the conflicts he has created. The moment we identify him with one character, we begin to blind ourselves to that meaning.

Since we are given no direct guidance, it is more than ever important that we become alive to the full implications of the conflicts; that we enter the 'points of view' of all the characters; and that we build up a much fuller understanding than any of them possesses. Indirect forms are much more difficult than direct ones, and demand closer, more subtle and sensitive reading. This is particularly so with Richardson because his moral world is one in which the minutiae of speech, dress and behaviour may be important revelations of the state of the heart and mind that prompts them. We have also to be sensitive to the implications of different styles, for 'styles differ, too, as much as faces, and are indicative, generally beyond the power of disguise, of the mind of the writer'.

We should also be very wary of treating dramatic characters as though they were real people. It is ironic that the more successful a dramatist is in putting one directly inside the minds of his characters the greater becomes the danger of distortion through analysing them as one would an acquaintance. For we tend to forget how crucially our knowledge is limited by and dependent on the method and form of the work of art. It may be unjustified to see incurable vanity in Pamela's continual repetition of the praise she receives; or evidence that her delicacy about sex is hypocritical when she details the attempts made on her, or passes on dubious jokes; or morbid introspection in her prolonged and brooding self-analysis. For these are all *formal* matters. There are several dramatic points of view, but only one of them 'writes' the novel; so Pamela has to tell us all there is to tell and carry the whole burden of analysis. We on the other hand ought to distinguish what is genuinely self-revelatory from what is narrative or analytic, and know when psychological inferences are appropriate and when they are not. We may point to the formal crudity which creates such difficulties, but this is quite a different criticism. (It is here that Richardson's great formal development, the multiplication of foci in *Clarissa*, itself removes many of what had appeared to be moral objections to *Pamela*.) Again, our knowledge of characters must be controlled by the development of a novel's formal patterning, the artful relationship between its scenes. However artless Richardson may look, his scenes are carefully related, often in cycles each of which reorchestrates its predecessor. So the gift of clothes on which the novel opens is related to the important 'clothes scene' of Letter XXIV. This in turn is parodied by B. in Letter XXVII, redeveloped in the 'bundle scene' of Letter XXIX, given a new symbolic twist in Pamela's garments floating on the pond, another reorchestration on page 270, and a final pointing on page 449. Examples could be multiplied, but in all the psychological speculation about Pamela and her creator the meaning of this patterning has played no part.

Most important of all, the fact that the dramatic 'kind' is the most exploratory type of novel has not been understood. As well as formal crudities there are several crudities of attitude and value in *Pamela*. Yet what is really significant is not that these exist, but that in so many cases Richardson is able, in developing his novel, to feel his way towards far deeper and finer values which he carried over and extended in *Clarissa*. While we identify him with his heroine, and pay no attention to the structural and textural development of his work, we shall fail to see that its significance and its achievement lie precisely in its *criticism* of the mental and moral world of the little girl of fifteen we meet at the beginning, even if—as may be the case—that world was Richardson's when he began to write. For a dramatic writer not only has to become several very different points of view; he also is forced to imagine how these look to one another, and has to try to resolve the conflicts that arise. Whatever values he may have held are likely to go through what Blake called the fire of thesis and antithesis; they are tested, realized, criticized—and they change.

The novel's first movement, up to the abduction of Pamela, is concerned with the day-to-day fluctuations of her struggle with her master. In this first conflict Richardson obviously uses her values to expose the implications of B.'s amoral world of pride and power; but in the process he discovers dangerous weaknesses in Pamela too. Hypocrisy is not one of them. Richardson saw the possibility of such a charge perfectly clearly—it is actually made by B. in Letter XXIV. But to Richardson this could only spring from a failure to understand how diametrically opposed to the world of the sex war with its laws of attraction and seduction the behaviour of Pamela is, as soon as one grasps what her new clothes symbolize. In that letter B.'s moral sensibility begins to be awakened. We have to be alive to the implications of what B. says and does to realize what is happening, but when we do the charge of hypocrisy is effectively refuted. What Richardson does discover about his heroine are the dangers that lie in her innate suspiciousness, which blinds her to the complex realities of other people; in her calculating prudence; and in her vanity and her inability to achieve real humility, social, moral or spiritual.

In the second movement Pamela is imprisoned. This is a period of 'persecutions, oppressions and distress', but it is also a period of spiritual growth. It lasts, pointedly, for forty days and forty nights, and the presence of biblical language in the prayer which opens it, and in the scene by the pond at its heart, should indicate that the new conflict within Pamela herself has a religious dimension. Her greatest temptation in the wilderness has indeed nothing to do with B. Behind all her faults there lies a stubborn pride and self-reliance, and to be like this, for Richardson, is to court despair when one's human fallibility is inevitably exposed. Pamela's battles against despair, her struggles to regain true faith not only in God but in Man, lie at the very centre of the novel's meaning. At the first scene by the pond she discovers in her temptation to suicide the core of a new self-knowledge and humility. 'And how do I know, but that God, who sees all the lurking vileness of my heart, may have permitted these sufferings on that very score, and to make me rely solely on his grace and assistance, who, perhaps, have too much prided myself in a vain dependence on my own foolish contrivances.' In the carefully related second pond scene she adds faith in Man to faith in God, even though this means acting imprudently. For the first time she and her persecutor really meet and communicate as human beings.

Pamela's suspicion and timidity are not overcome in a day, but her happiness will depend on her ability to continue in her new-won faith. At first she fails disastrously. Her fear of a mock marriage makes her reject a genuine proposal from B., and at last she is given what she has constantly begged for, and is angrily dismissed to her parents. Now, however, she discovers (what the competent reader should have known from innumerable hints long before) the depth of her feeling for her persecutor. When he begs her to return, against all the dictates of pride and prudence, she does so in love and faith and makes her happiness and his regeneration possible.

Apart from the angry scenes with Lady Davers and the discovery of B.'s illegitimate daughter, the drama ends here. The rest of the novel consists mainly of social visiting, in which the happy pair discuss their history in public while Pamela is deluged with choric praise and blessing; and of long discussions of the duties and proper behaviour of man and wife—or, rather, largely of wife. This spinning out of the novel is further evidence that Richardson was not primarily interested in pursuit and capture, but one can see why readers find it tedious. Yet it was important, for Richardson, to demonstrate the consistency and integrity of Pamela's behaviour before and after her marriage; and also to enforce the validity of her values over a wider field than her struggles with B. could provide. The novel becomes a 'Whole Duty of Woman'; a fictional counterpart to the *Whole Duty of Man* which Pamela sends to Farmer Jones. Her humility and obedience, her piety, her capacity for love, forgiveness and gratitude, her charities, and the regulation of her married life all throw out the challenge of an old-fashioned morality to a frivolous and lax society. The scenes of choric praise enact Richardson's hopes for the educative power of his story. They also prefigure the idea of moral community which is central to *Sir Charles Grandison*. The living example and the public discussion of virtue awaken the latent good nature and moral sensibility of all who meet them. All are 'improved'; and in joining the concord of praise all find their true selves, and the true sense of fellowship binding them to their neighbours.

It remains unfortunately true that it is not merely the overt didacticism of all this that prevents Richardson's readers from making the same response. For the novel, although it is not a case-study of hypocrisy, still fails in several important ways.

The most central of these concerns not Pamela but B. Once one has learned to read with the sensitivity to implications that Richardson demands, it becomes clear that after markedly crude beginnings B. does become a complex character in the grip of acute conflict. But if Pamela and B. are both on the stage, and we are required to understand and judge them both in their opposition, the fact remains that we live always in her mind and never in his because the novel is told from a single point of view. Not only is it fatally easy to miss the exact fluctuations of B.'s conflict through superficial reading, but we inhabit so continuously a mind in which he appears simply as a 'black-hearted wretch' that we tend to oversimplify him too. (It is always a danger in point-of-view writing that we are tempted to adopt the viewpoint of one character instead of holding them all against our own greater knowledge.) At important points we need the same direct experience of B.'s heart and mind that we have of Pamela's; but the single focus cannot provide this. The result is disastrous when we come to B.'s reformation. If we are reading carefully enough we should understand perfectly clearly why and how it happens, but we cannot *experience* it. It is not proved on our pulses, it cannot have the imaginative reality of Pamela's transformation. If we do not grasp the technical origin of this, or are reading carelessly anyway, our response is likely to register itself in doubts of the quality of Pamela's forgiveness, her return, her gratitude and meekness, which ought never to have arisen. Critics who believe that it is not the man she objected to all along, but his terms, ought to be discussing not Pamela but B., and not B. as Richardson intended him, but his realization. Yet, however technical, this is a serious failure that affects one's whole response to the novel.

There are also flaws which are the result of crude moral vision, and most have to do with Richardson's attitude to sex. He is frequently accused of prurience. Any honest reader knows, however, that the sexual scenes are anything but inflammatory. Yet there is something strange about them, and this is that they are not *about* sex at all. They are intensifications of a study of pride, theatrical attempts of the male to subjugate, and they result in humiliation. They remain unsatisfactory, not because Richardson gives too much treatment to sex, but too little; because he treats it too narrowly in its brutally egotistic and violating aspects, and sees too little of its full human potential and significance. There are, however, once again interesting signs in Pamela's reactions to her wedding night, and in her attitude towards Sally Godfrey and her child, of the dawnings of more liberal attitudes.

Again, in putting virtue on trial in a sexual arena, Richardson has a tendency to confuse virtue with physical virginity. Towards the end Pamela becomes clear that her integrity would be untouched by violation, but earlier Richardson had allowed her to speak of the attempts at rape as though these had been her worst trials. This could only be true physically and emotionally; the hardest tests of her whole being come in the scenes where her own unacknowledged love and B.'s gentleness combine to trouble her. In these scenes Richardson's vision is clean and sure; but his tendency to give undifferentiated praise to her 'resistance' too often leaves the assumption open that he places as much emphasis on resistance to force and finance as on the far deeper values which first send Pamela into the wilderness, and then bring her back to her master in love and faith. There is a similar crudity, less of the imaginative creation than of the author's attitude towards it, in the concept of virtue rewarded which gives *Pamela* its subtitle. Though calculating prudence is one of Pamela's faults, perhaps the greatest achievement of the novel is the way in which the fault is transcended. Yet in his subtitle and the moral summary he appended, Richardson does fall back into crudity, and appears to argue as though the reasons for being virtuous had something to do with the calculation of rewards. Pamela is not a hypocritical politician, but she could legitimately blame her creator if readers are tempted to foist upon her the idea that virginity is the best policy.

Indeed Richardson's value is vitally dependent on his dramatic imagination. The significance of *Pamela* is precisely the way in which he was able to feel his way imaginatively towards deeper and finer attitudes. Flaws remain, but they are less important than the growth. Yet the sequel to the novel shows again how fatally easy it was for him to relapse as soon as his dramatic imagination no longer predominated. He had finished his work, but to meet the challenge of an unscrupulous hack who advertised a sequel, he forced himself to continue. Apart from some technical experiment and a wholly proper realization that the reformation of B. had come rather too easily, the book is a product of the didactic will rather than the creative imagination. It shows all too clearly the pressure of the rigid, calculating morality he had inherited. Yet it also shows, by contrast with the first novel, the great value of the imagination which had enabled him to transcend himself as long as it continued to operate. What we watch in *Pamela*, despite its flaws, is the invention of a kind of novel which can help its author to find his way to a deeper sense of human integrity and a nobler idea of how human beings can attain true relationship with one another and with God. This seems more important than the faults of his first attempt.

M. KINKEAD-WEEKES.

1962.

SELECT BIBLIOGRAPHY

NOVELS. *Pamela: or Virtue Rewarded*, 2 vols., 1740; with sequel, 4 vols., 1741; *Clarissa, Or, The History of a Young Lady*, 7 vols.,1747–8; *The History of Sir Charles Grandison*, 7 vols., 1753–4.

OTHER WORKS. *Letters Written to and for particular friends, Directing the Requisite Style and Form to be Observed in writing Familiar Letters*, 1741; ed. B. W. Downs (as *Familiar Letters on Important Occasions*), 1928; *The Case of Samuel Richardson, of London, Printer*, 1753; *An Address to the Public, on the Treatment which the Editor of the History of Sir Charles Grandison has met with*, 1754; *A Collection of the Moral and Instructive Sentiments, Maxims, Cautions, and Reflexions contained in the Histories of Pamela, Clarissa, and Sir Charles Grandison*, 1755; *The Paths of Virtue delineated: or, the History in Miniature of the Celebrated Pamela, Clarissa Harlowe, and Sir Charles Grandison, familiarised and adapted to the capacities of Youth*, 1756.

Richardson also edited Defoe's *Tour Thro' Great Britain*, 3 vols., 1738; Aesop's *Fables*, 1740; and *The Negotiations of Sir Thomas Roe in his Embassy to the Ottoman Porte*, 1740.

COLLECTED EDITIONS. (1) *Novels:* Sir Walter Scott, with a memoir, 3 vols., 1824; Austin Dobson, with prefatory note (Life and Introduction by W. Lyon Phelps), 19 vols., 1902; Ethel M. M. McKenna, with Introduction, 20 volumes, 1902; Shakespeare Head edition, 19 vols., 1930. (2) *Correspondence:* Mrs A. L. Barbauld, with Life, 6 vols., 1804. (3) *Works:* E. Mangin, with sketch of Life and writings, 19 vols., 1811; Leslie Stephen, with prefatory chapter of biographical criticism, 12 vols., 1883–4.

BIOGRAPHY AND CRITICISM. Miss C. L. Thomson, *Samuel Richardson: a Biographical and Critical Study*, 1900; A. Dobson, *Samuel Richardson*, 1902; B. W. Downs, *Richardson*, 1928; P. Dottin, *Samuel Richardson, Imprimeur, de Londres*, 1931; A. D. McKillop, *Samuel Richardson, Printer and Novelist*, 1936, and *The Early Masters of English Fiction*, 1956; D. Daiches, *Literary Essays*, 1956; I. Watt, *The Rise of the Novel*, 1957; R. F. Brissenden, *Samuel Richardson*, 1958; B. Kreissman, *Pamela-Shamela*, 1960.

PAMELA

LETTER I

DEAR FATHER AND MOTHER,

I have great trouble, and some comfort, to acquaint you with. The trouble is that my good lady died of the illness I mentioned to you, and left us all much grieved for the loss of her : she was a dear good lady, and kind to all us her servants. Much I feared, that as I was taken by her ladyship to wait upon her person, I should be quite destitute again, and forced to return to you and my poor mother, who have enough to do to maintain yourselves; and, as my lady's goodness had put me to write and cast accounts, and made me a little expert at my needle, and otherwise qualified above my degree, it was not every family that could have found a place that your poor Pamela was fit for : but God, whose graciousness to us we have so often experienced, put it into my good lady's heart, just an hour before she expired, to recommend to my young master all her servants, one by one; and when it came to my turn to be recommended (for I was sobbing and crying at her pillow), she could only say—" My dear son ! " and so broke off a little; and then recovering, " remember my poor Pamela." —And these were some of her last words. O how my eyes run ! Don't wonder to see the paper so blotted.

Well, but God's will must be done ! And so comes the comfort, that I shall not be obliged to return back to be a clog upon my dear parents ! For my master said, " I will take care of you all, my good maidens. And for you, Pamela," (and took me by the hand; yes, he took my hand before them all), " for my dear mother's sake, I will be a friend to you, and you shall take care of my linen." God bless him ! and pray with me, my dear father and mother, for a blessing upon him; for he has given mourning and a year's wages to all my lady's servants, and I having no wages as yet (my lady having said she would do for me as I deserved), he ordered the housekeeper to give me mourning with the rest; and gave me with his own hand four golden guineas, and some silver, which were in my old lady's pocket when she died; and said, if I was a good girl,

I

and faithful and diligent, he would be a friend to me, for his mother's sake. And so I send you these four guineas for your comfort, for Providence will not let me want: and so you may pay some old debt with part, and keep the other part to comfort you both. If I get more, I am sure it is my duty, and it shall be my care, to love and cherish you both; for you have loved and cherished me when I could do nothing for myself. I send them by John our footman, who goes your way: but he does not know what he carries, because I seal them up in one of the little pill-boxes, which my lady had, wrapped close in paper, that they mayn't chink; and be sure don't open it before him.

I know, dear father and mother, I must give you both grief and pleasure: and so I will only say, pray for your Pamela; who will ever be your most dutiful daughter.

I have been scared out of my senses; for just now, as I was folding up this letter in my late lady's dressing-room, in comes my young master! How was I frightened! I went to hide the letter in my bosom; and he seeing me tremble, said, smiling, "To whom have you been writing, Pamela?" I said, in my confusion, "Pray, your honour, forgive me!—only to my father and mother." He said, "Well, then, let me see how you are come on in your writing." O how ashamed I was! He took it, without saying more, and read it through, and then gave it me again; and I said, "Pray, your honour, forgive me!" Yet I know not for what: for he was always dutiful to his parents; and why should he be angry that I was so to mine! And indeed he was not angry; for he took me by the hand, and said, "You are a good girl, Pamela, to be kind to your aged father and mother. I am not angry with you for writing such innocent matters as these; though you ought to be wary what tales you send out of a family. Be faithful and diligent; and do as you should do, and I like you the better for this." And then he said, "Why, Pamela, you write a very pretty hand, and spell tolerably too. I see my good mother's care in your learning has not been thrown away upon you. She used to say, you loved reading; you may look into any of her books to improve yourself, so you take care of them." I did nothing but curtsey and cry, and was all in confusion at his goodness. Indeed he is the best of gentlemen, I think: but I am making another long letter; so will only add to it, that I shall ever be your dutiful daughter,

PAMELA ANDREWS.

LETTER II

In answer to the preceding

DEAR PAMELA,

Your letter was a great trouble, and some comfort, to me and your poor mother. We are troubled for your good lady's death, who took such care of you, and gave you learning, and for three or four years past has always been giving you clothes and linen, and every thing that a gentlewoman need not be ashamed to appear in. But our chief trouble is, and a very great one, for fear you should be brought to any thing dishonest or wicked, by being set so above yourself. Every body talks how you have come on, and what a genteel girl you are; and some say you are very pretty : and six months since, when I saw you last, I should have thought so myself, if you was not our child. But what avails all this, if you are to be ruined and undone? My dear Pamela, we begin to be in great fear for you; for what signify all the riches in the world, with a bad conscience, and to be dishonest? We are, it is true, very poor, and find it hard enough to live; though once, as you know, it was better with us. But we would sooner live upon the water, and, if possible, the clay of the ditches I dig, than live better at the price of our child's ruin.

I hope the good squire has no design; but when he has given you so much money, and speaks so kindly to you, and praises your coming on; and, oh! that fatal word, that he would be kind to you, if you would do *as you should do,* almost kills us with fears.

I have spoken to good old widow Mumford about it, who, you know, has formerly lived in good families; and she put us in some comfort; for she says, it is not unusual, when a lady dies, to give what she has about her person to her waiting-maid, and to such as sit up with her in her illness. But then why should he smile so kindly upon you? why should he take such a poor girl as you by the hand, as your letter says he has done twice? Why should he stoop to read your letter to us, and commend your writing and spelling? And why should he give you leave to read his mother's books? Indeed, my dearest child, our hearts ache for you : and then you seem so full of *joy* at his goodness, so *taken* with his kind expressions, (which, truly, are very great favours, if he means well) that we *fear*—yes, my dear child, we *fear*—you should be *too* grateful, and reward him with that jewel, your virtue, which no riches, nor favour, nor any thing in this life, can make up to you.

3

I, too, have written a long letter, but will say one thing more; and that is, that in the midst of our poverty and misfortunes, we have trusted in God's goodness, and been honest, and doubt not to be happy hereafter, if we continue to be good, though our lot is hard here : but the loss of our dear child's virtue would be a grief that we could not bear, and would bring our gray hairs to the grave at once.

If, then, you love *us*, if you wish for *God's* blessing and *your own* future happiness, we both charge you to stand upon your guard : and if you find the least attempt made upon your virtue, be sure you leave every thing behind you, and come away to us; for we had rather see you all covered with rags, and even follow you to the churchyard, than have it said, a child of our's preferred any worldly convenience to her virtue.

We accept kindly of your dutiful present; but, till we are out of pain, cannot make use of it, for fear we should partake of the price of our poor daughter's shame : so have laid it up in a rag among the thatch, over the window, for awhile, lest we should be robbed. With our blessings, and our hearty prayers for you, we remain, *your careful, but loving father and mother,*

JOHN AND ELIZABETH ANDREWS.

LETTER III

DEAR FATHER,

I must say, your letter has filled me with trouble : it has made my heart, which was overflowing with gratitude for my master's goodness, suspicious and fearful; yet I hope I shall never find him act unworthy of his character; for what could he get by ruining such a young poor creature as me? But that which gives me most trouble is, that you seem to mistrust the honesty of your child. No, my dear father and mother, be assured, that, by God's grace, I never will do any thing that shall bring your gray hairs with sorrow to the grave. I will die a thousand deaths rather than be dishonest any way. Of that be assured, and set your hearts at rest; for although I have lived above myself for some ages past, yet I can be content with rags, poverty, and bread and water, and will embrace them, rather than forfeit my good name, let who will be the tempter. Of this pray rest satisfied, and think better of *your dutiful daughter till death.*

My master continues to be very affable to me. As yet I see no cause to fear any thing. Mrs. Jervis the housekeeper too is very civil to me, and I have the love of every body. Sure they cannot all have designs against me, because they are civil! I hope I shall always behave so as to be respected by every one; and that nobody would do me more hurt than I am sure I would do them. Our John so often goes your way that I will always get him to call, that you may hear from me either by writing (for it brings my hand in), or by word of mouth.

LETTER IV

DEAR MOTHER,

For the last was to my father, in answer to his letter, and so I will write to you, though I have nothing to say but what will make me look more like a vain hussey than any thing else : however, I hope I shan't be so proud as to forget myself. Yet there is a secret pleasure one has to hear one's self praised. You must know that my Lady Davers, who, I need not tell you, is my master's sister, has been a month at our house, and has taken great notice of me, and given me good advice to keep myself to myself. She told me I was a very pretty wench, and that every body gave me a very good character, and loved me; and bid me take care to keep the fellows at a distance; and said, *that* I might do, and be more valued for it, even by themselves.

But what pleased me much was what I am going to tell you; for at table, as Mrs. Jervis says, my master and her ladyship talking of me, she told him she thought me the prettiest wench she ever saw; and that I was too pretty to live in a bachelor's house, since no lady he might marry would care to continue me with her. He said, I was vastly improved, and had a good share of prudence and sense above my years : it would be a pity that what was my merit should be my misfortune. "No," says my good lady, "Pamela shall come and live with me, I think." He said, with all his heart; he should be glad to have me so well provided for. "Well," said she, "I'll consult my lord about it." She asked how old I was? and Mrs. Jervis said I was fifteen last February. "O!" says she, "if the wench" (for so she calls all us maiden servants) "takes care of herself, she'll improve yet more and more, as well in her person as her mind."

Now, my dear father and mother, though this may look too vain to be repeated by me, yet are you not rejoiced, as well as I, to see my master so willing to part with me? This shews that he has nothing bad in his heart. But John is just going away : and so I have only to say, that I am, and will always be, *your honest, as well as dutiful, daughter.*

Pray make use of the money. You may do it safely.

5

My dear Father and Mother,

  John being to go your way, I am willing to write, because he is so willing to carry any thing for me. He says it does him good at his heart to see you both, and to hear you talk. He says you are both so sensible, and so honest, that he always learns something from you to the purpose. It is a thousand pities, he says, that such worthy hearts should not have better luck in the world; and wonders that you, my father, who are so well able to teach, and write so good a hand, succeeded no better in the school you attempted to set up, but was forced to go to hard labour. But this is more pride to me, that I am come of such honest parents, than if I had been born a lady.

I hear nothing yet of going to Lady Davers; and I am very easy at present here : for Mrs. Jervis uses me as if I were her own daughter; and is a very good woman, and makes my master's interest her own. She is always giving me good counsel, and I love her, next to you two, I think, best of any body. She keeps so good rule and order, she is respected by us all; and takes delight to hear me read to her : and all she loves to hear read is good books, which we read whenever we are alone : so that I think I am at home with you. She heard one of our men, Harry, who is no better than he should be, speak freely to me; I think he called me his pretty Pamela, and took hold of me, as if he would have kissed me, for which you may be sure I was very angry : and she took him to task, and was as angry at him as could be; and told me she was very well pleased to see my prudence and modesty, and that I kept all the fellows at a distance. And I am sure I am not proud, and carry it civilly to every body; but yet, methinks, I cannot bear to be looked at by these men-servants, for they seem as if they would look one through : and, as I generally breakfast, dine, and sup with Mrs. Jervis, (so good is she to me) I am very easy that I have so little to say to them. Not but they are very civil to me for Mrs. Jervis's sake, who they see loves me; and they stand in awe of her, knowing her to be a gentlewoman born, though she had misfortunes.

I am going on again with a long letter, for I love writing, and shall tire you. But when I began, I only intended to say, that I am quite fearless of any danger now; and cannot but wonder at myself, (though your caution to me was your watchful love) that I should be so foolish as to be so uneasy as I have been : for I am sure my master would not demean himself so as to think upon such a poor girl as I for my harm. For such a thing would ruin his credit as well as mine, you know; who, to be sure, may expect one of the best ladies in the land. So no more at present, but that I am *your ever-dutiful daughter.*

LETTER VI

DEAR FATHER AND MOTHER,

My master has been very kind since my last; for he has given me a suit of my late lady's clothes, and half a dozen of her shifts, and six fine handkerchiefs, and three of her cambric aprons, and four Holland ones. The clothes are fine silk, and too rich and too good for me, to be sure. I wish it was no affront to him to make money of them, and send it to you; it would do me more good.

You will be full of fears, I warrant now, of some design upon me, till I tell you, that he was with Mrs. Jervis when he gave them me; and he gave her a mort of good things at the same time, and bid her wear them in remembrance of her good friend, my lady, his mother. And when he gave me these fine things, he said, " These, Pamela, are for you; have them made fit for you, when your mourning is laid by, and wear them for your good mistress's sake. Mrs. Jervis gives you a very good word, and I would have you continue to behave as prudently as you have hitherto done, and every body will be your friend."

I was so surprised at his goodness, that I could not tell what to say. I curtseyed to him, and to Mrs. Jervis, for her good word; and said, I wished I might be deserving of his favour, and her kindness; and nothing should be wanting in me to the best of my knowledge. O how amiable a thing is doing good! It is all I envy great folks for.

I always thought my young master a fine gentleman, as every body says he is: but he gave these good things to us with such a graciousness, as I thought he looked like an angel.

Mrs. Jervis says, he asked her if I kept the men at a distance; for, he said, I was very pretty: and to be drawn in to have any of them might be my ruin, and make me poor and miserable betimes. She never is wanting to give me a good word, and took occasion to launch out in my praise, she says. But I hope she has said no more than I shall try to deserve, though I mayn't at present. I am sure I will always love her, next to you and my dear mother. So I rest *your ever-dutiful daughter.*

7

LETTER VII

Dear Father,

Since my last, my master gave me more fine things. He called me up to my late lady's closet, and pulling out her drawers, he gave me two suits of fine Flanders laced head-clothes; three pair of fine silk shoes, two hardly the worse, and just fit for me (for my lady had a very little foot,) and the other with wrought silver buckles in them, and several ribbands and top-knots of all colours; four pair of white cotton stockings, three pair of fine silk ones, and two pair of rich stays. I was quite astonished, and unable to speak for a while; but yet I was inwardly ashamed to take the stockings, for Mrs. Jervis was not there: if she had, it would have been nothing. I believe I received them very awkwardly; for he smiled at my awkwardness, and said, "Don't blush, Pamela; dost think I don't know pretty maids should wear shoes and stockings?"

I was so confounded at these words, you might have beat me down with a feather. For you must think there was no answer to be made to this: so, like a fool, I was ready to cry, and went away curtseying and blushing, I am sure, up to the ears; for, though there was no harm in what he said, yet I did not know how to take it. But I went and told all to Mrs. Jervis, who said, God put it into his heart to be good to me; and I must double my diligence. It looked to her, she said, as if he would fit me in dress for a waiting-maid's place on Lady Daver's own person.

But still your kind fatherly cautions came into my head, and made all these gifts nothing near to me what they would have been. But yet, I hope, there is no reason; for what good could it do to him to harm such a simple maiden as me? Besides, to be sure no lady would look upon him, if he should so disgrace himself. So I will make myself easy; and, indeed, I should never have been otherwise, if you had not put it into my head, for my good, I know very well. But may be, without these uneasinesses to mingle with these benefits, I might be too much puffed up: so I conclude all that happens is for our good; and God bless you, my dear father and mother: I know you constantly pray for a blessing upon me, who am, and shall always be, *your dutiful daughter.*

LETTER VIII

Dear Pamela,

I cannot but renew my cautions on your master's kindness, and his free expressions about the stockings. Yet there may not be, and I hope there is not, any thing in it. But when I reflect, that there *possibly* may, and that if there should, no less depends upon it than my child's everlasting happiness in this world and the next, it is enough to make one fearful for you. Arm yourself, my dear child, for the worst, and resolve to lose your life sooner than your virtue. Though the doubts I filled you with lessen the pleasure you would have had in your master's kindness; yet what signify the delights that arise from a few fine clothes, in comparison with a good conscience?

These are very great favours he heaps upon you, but so much the more to be suspected; and when you say he looked so amiable and like an angel, how afraid I am that they should make too great an impression upon you! For, though you are blessed with sense and prudence above your years, yet I tremble to think what a sad hazard a poor maiden of little more than fifteen years of age stands against the temptations of this world, and a designing gentleman, if he should prove so, who has so much *power* to oblige, and has a kind of *authority* to command as your master.

I charge you, my dear child, on both our blessings, poor as we are, to be on your guard : there can be no harm in that. And since Mrs. Jervis is so good a gentlewoman, and so kind to you, I am easier a great deal, and so is your mother; and we hope you will hide nothing from her, and take her counsel in every thing. So, with our blessings and assured prayers for you, more than for ourselves, we remain *your loving father and mother.*

Be sure you don't let people's telling you, you are pretty, puff you up; for you did not make yourself, and so can have no praise due to you for it. It is virtue and goodness only that make the true beauty. Remember that, Pamela.

LETTER IX

DEAR FATHER AND MOTHER,

I am sorry to write you word, that the hopes I had of going to wait on Lady Davers are quite over. My lady would have had me, but my master, as I heard, would not consent to it. He said, her nephew might be taken with me, and I might draw him in, or be drawn in by him; and he thought, as his mother loved me, and committed me to his care, he ought to continue me with him; and Mrs. Jervis would be a mother to me. Mrs. Jervis tells me, the lady shook her head, and said,

9

" *Ah! Brother!* " and that was all. And as you have made me fearful by your cautions, my heart at times misgives me. But I say nothing yet of your caution or my own uneasiness to Mrs. Jervis, not that I mistrust her, but for fear she should think me presumptuous, vain, and conceited, to have any fears about the matter, from the great distance between such a gentleman and so poor a girl. But yet Mrs. Jervis seemed to build something upon Lady Davers's shaking her head, and saying, " *Ah! Brother!* " and no more. God, I hope, will give me his grace; and so I will not, if I can help it, make myself too uneasy; for I hope there is no occasion. But every little matter that happens, I will acquaint you with, that you may continue to me your good advice, and pray for *your sad-hearted*,

PAMELA.

LETTER X

DEAR MOTHER,

You and my good father may wonder you have not had a letter from me in so many weeks : but a sad, sad scene has been the occasion of it. For, to be sure, now, it is too plain, that all your cautions were well-grounded. O, my dear mother! I am miserable, truly miserable !—But yet, don't be frighted, I am honest—God, of his goodness, keep me so !

O this angel of a master ! this fine gentleman ! this gracious benefactor to your poor Pamela ! who was to take care of me at the prayer of his good dying mother; who was so apprehensive for me lest I should be drawn in by Lord Davers's nephew, that he would not let me go to Lady Davers's : this very gentleman (yes, I *must* call him gentleman, though he has fallen from the merit of that title,) has degraded himself to offer freedoms to his poor servant ! He has now shewed himself in his true colours, and, to *me*, nothing appears so black, and so frightful.

I have not been idle; but had writ, from time to time, how he, by sly mean degrees, exposed his wicked views; but somebody stole my letter, and I know not what has become of it. It was a very long one. I fear, he that was mean enough to do bad things, in one respect, did not stick at *this*. But be it as it will, all the use he can make of it will be, that he may be ashamed of *his* part; I not of *mine :* for he will see I was resolved to be virtuous, and gloried in the honesty of my poor parents.

I will tell you all the next opportunity; for I am watched very narrowly; and he says to Mrs. Jervis, " This girl is always a scribbling; I think she may be better employed." And yet

I work all hours with my needle upon his linen, and the fine linen of the family; and am, besides, about flowering him a waistcoat. But oh! my heart's broke almost; for what am I likely to have for my reward, but shame and disgrace, or else ill words and hard treatment! I'll tell you all soon, and hope I shall find my long letter. *Your most afflicted daughter*.

May-be, I *he* and *him* him too much: but it is his own fault if I do. For why did he lose all his dignity with me?

LETTER XI

DEAR MOTHER,

Well, I can't find my letter, and so I'll try to recollect it all, and be as brief as I can. All went on well enough in the main for some time after my last letter but one. At last I saw some reason to *suspect*; for he would look upon me, whenever he saw me, in such a manner as shewed not well. One day he came to me, as I was in the summer house in the little garden, at work with my needle; Mrs. Jervis was just gone from me; and I would have gone out, but he said, "No, don't go, Pamela; I have something to say to you: and you always fly me when I come near you, as if you were afraid of me."

I was much out of countenance, you may well think; but said at last, "It does not become your poor servant to stay in your presence, Sir, without your business required it; and I hope I shall always know my place."

"Well," says he, "my business does require it sometimes, and I have a mind you should stay to hear what I have to say to you."

I stood still confounded, and began to tremble, and the more when he took me by the hand; for now no soul was near us.

"My sister Davers," said he, (and seemed, I thought, to be as much at a loss for words as I) "would have had you live with *her;* but she would not do for you what I am resolved to do, if you continue faithful and obliging. What say'st thou, my girl?" said he, with some eagerness, "hadst thou not rather stay with me, than go to my sister?" He looked so as filled me with affrightment: I don't know how; wildly, I thought.

I said, when I could speak, "Your honour will forgive me; but as you have no lady for me to wait upon, and my good lady has been now dead this twelvemonth, I had rather, if it would not displease you, wait upon Lady Davers, *because*——" I was proceeding, and he said a little hastily, "*Because* you are

11

a little fool, and know not what's good for yourself. I tell you I will make a gentlewoman of you, if you be obliging, and don't stand in your own light;" and so saying, he put his arm about me, and kissed me !

Now, you will say, all his wickedness appeared plainly. I struggled and trembled, and was so benumbed with terror, that I sunk down, not in a fit, and yet not myself; and I found myself in his arms, quite void of strength, and he kissing me two or three times with frightful eagerness. At last I burst from him, and was getting out of the summer-house, but he held me back, and shut the door.

I would have given my life for a farthing. And he said, " I'll do you no harm, Pamela; don't be afraid of me." I said, " I won't stay."—" You won't, hussey !" said he : " do you know whom you speak to?" I lost all fear and all respect, and said, " Yes, I do, Sir, too well ! Well may I forget that I am your servant, when you forget what belongs to a master."

I sobbed and cried most sadly—" What a foolish hussey you are !" said he; " have I done you any harm?"—" Yes, Sir," said I, " the greatest harm in the world : you have taught me to forget myself, and what belongs to me, and have lessened the distance that fortune has made between us, by demeaning yourself, to be so free to a poor servant. Yet, Sir, I will be bold to say, I am honest, though poor : and if you was a prince I would not be otherwise."

He was angry, and said, " Who would have you otherwise, you foolish slut ! Cease your crying. I own I have demeaned myself ! but it was only to try you : if you can keep this matter secret, you'll give me a better opinion of your prudence, and here's something," said he, putting some gold in my hand, " to make you amends for the fright I put you in. Go, take a walk in the garden, and don't go in till your crying is over; and I charge you to say nothing of what is past, and all shall be well, and I'll forgive you."

" I won't take the money, indeed, Sir," said I, " poor as I am, I won't take it." For, to say the truth, I thought it looked like taking earnest, and so I put it upon the bench, and as he seemed vexed and confused at what he had done, I took the opportunity to open the door, and went out of the summer-house.

He called to me, and said, " Be secret, I charge you, Pamela, and don't go in yet, as I told you."

O how poor and mean must those actions be, and how little must they make the best of gentlemen look, when they offer such things as are unworthy of themselves, and put it into the power of their inferiors to be greater than they!

I took a turn or two in the garden, but in sight of the house, for fear of the worst; and breathed upon my hand to dry my eyes, because I would not be disobedient. My next shall tell you more.

Pray for me, my dear father and mother, and don't be angry I have not yet run away from this house, so late my comfort and delight, but now my terror and anguish. I am forced to break off hastily. *Your dutiful and honest daughter.*

LETTER XII

Dear Mother,

Well, I will proceed with my sad story. After I had dried my eyes, I went in, and began to ruminate what I had best do. Sometimes I thought I would leave the house and go to the next town, and wait an opportunity to get to you; but then I was at a loss to resolve whether to take away the things he had given me or no, and how to take them away: sometimes I thought to leave them behind me, and only go with the clothes on my back; but then I had two miles and a half, and a bye-way, to the town; and being pretty well dressed, I might come to some harm, almost as bad as what I would run away from; and then, thought I, "it will be reported I had stolen something, and so was forced to run away: and to carry a bad name back with me to my dear parents, would be a sad thing!"—O how I wished for my gray russet again, and my poor dress with which you fitted me out, (and hard enough too it was for you to do it!) for going to this place, when I was not twelve years old, in my good lady's days! Sometimes I thought of telling Mrs. Jervis, and taking her advice, and only feared his command to be secret; for, thought I, he may be ashamed of his actions, and never attempt the like again: and as poor Mrs. Jervis depended upon him, through misfortunes that had attended her, I thought it would be a sad thing to bring his displeasure upon her for my sake.

In this quandary, considering, crying, and not knowing what to do, I passed the time in my chamber till evening: when, desiring to be excused going to supper, Mrs. Jervis came up to me, and said, "Why must I sup without you, Pamela? Come, I see you are troubled at something: tell me what is the matter."

I begged I might be permitted to lie with her on nights; for I was afraid of spirits, and they would not hurt such a good person as she. "That was a silly excuse," she said; "for why was you not afraid of spirits before?" Indeed I did not think of that. "But you shall be my bedfellow with all my heart," added she, "let your reason be what it will; only come down to supper." I begged to be excused, "For," said I, "I have been crying so, that it will be taken notice of by my fellow-servants: and I will hide nothing from you, Mrs. Jervis, when we are alone."

She was so good as to indulge me; but made haste to bed; and told the servants that I should lie with her, because she could not rest well, and would get me to read her to sleep; for she knew I loved reading, she said.

When we were alone, I told her all that had passed; for I thought, though he had bid me not, yet if he should come to know I had told, it would be no worse; for to keep a secret of such a nature, would be, as I apprehended, to deprive myself of the good advice which I never wanted more; and might encourage him to think I did not resent it as I ought, and would keep worse secrets, and so make him do worse by me. Was I right, my dear mother?

Mrs. Jervis could not help mingling tears with my tears; for I cried all the time I was telling her my story, and begged her to advise me what to do; and I shewed her my dear father's two letters, and she praised the honesty and inditing of them, and said pleasing things to me of you both. But she begged I would not think of leaving my service; "For," says she, "in all likelihood, you behaved so virtuously that he will be ashamed of what he has done, and never offer the like to you again: though, my dear Pamela," said she, "I fear more for your prettiness than for any thing else; because the best man in the land might love you:" so she was pleased to say.—She wished it was in her power to live independent; then she would take a little private house, and I should live with her like her daughter.

And so, as you ordered me to take her advice, I resolved to tarry to see how things went, except he was to turn me away; although, in your first letter, you ordered me to come away the moment I had any reason to be apprehensive. So, dear father and mother, it is not disobedience, I hope, that I stay; for I could not expect a blessing, or the good fruits of your prayers for me, if I was disobedient.

All the next day I was very sad, and began my long letter. He saw me writing, and said (as I mentioned) to Mrs. Jervis, "That girl is always scribbling; methinks she might find

14

something else to do," or to that purpose. And when I had finished my letter, I put it under the toilet, in my late lady's dressing-room, whither nobody comes but myself and Mrs. Jervis, besides my master; but when I came up again to seal it, to my great concern, it was gone; and Mrs. Jervis knew nothing of it; and nobody knew of my master's having been near the place in the time; so I have been sadly troubled about it : but Mrs. Jervis, as well as I, thinks he has it, for he appears cross and angry, and seems to shun me, as much as he said I did him. It had better be so than worse !

But he has ordered Mrs. Jervis to bid me not pass so much time in writing; which is a poor matter for such a gentleman as he to take notice of, as I am not idle other-ways, if he did not resent what I wrote upon. And this has no very good look.

But I am a good deal easier since I lie with Mrs. Jervis; though, after all the fears I live in on one side, and his frowning and displeasure at what I do on the other, make me more miserable than enough.

O that I had never left my little bed in the loft, to be thus exposed to temptations on one hand, or disgusts on the other ! How happy was I awhile ago ! How contrary now ! Pity and pray for *your afflicted*   PAMELA.

LETTER XIII

MY DEAREST CHILD,

Our hearts bleed for your distress, and the temptations you are exposed to. You have our hourly prayers; and we would have you flee this evil great house and man, if you find he renews his attempts. You ought to have done it at first, had you not had Mrs. Jervis to advise with. We can find no fault with your conduct hitherto : but it makes our hearts ache for fear of the worst. O my child ! temptations are sore things; but yet, without them, we know not ourselves, nor what we are able to do.

Your danger is great: you have riches, youth, and a fine gentleman to withstand; but how great will be your honour to withstand them ! When we consider your past conduct, your virtuous education, and that you have been bred to be more ashamed of dishonesty than poverty, we trust in God, that he will enable you to overcome. Yet, as we cannot see but your life must be a burden to you, through the great apprehensions always upon you; and it may be presumptuous to

15

trust too much to your own strength; you are but very young, and the devil may put it into his heart to use some stratagems, of which great men are full, to decoy you; I think you had better come home to share our poverty with safety, than live with so much discontent in a plenty that may be dangerous. God direct you for the best! While you have Mrs. Jervis for an adviser and bedfellow, (and, O my dear child, that was prudently done of you!) we are easier than we should be, and so, committing you to the Divine Protection, remain *your truly loving, but careful, father and mother.*

LETTER XIV

DEAR FATHER AND MOTHER,

Mrs. Jervis and I have lived very comfortably together for this fortnight; my master was all that time at his Lincolnshire estate, and at his sister's the Lady Davers. He came home yesterday, and had some talk with Mrs. Jervis soon after, mostly about me. He said to her, "Well, Mrs. Jervis, I know Pamela has your good word; but do you think her of any use in the family?" She told me, she was surprised at the question, but said, that I was one of the most virtuous and industrious young creatures she ever knew. "Why that word *virtuous*," said he, "I pray you? Was there any reason to suppose her otherwise; or has any body taken it into his head to *try* her?" —"I wonder, Sir," says she, "you ask such a question! Who dare offer any thing to her in such an orderly and well-governed house as yours, and under a master of so good a character for virtue and honour?"—"Your servant, Mrs. Jervis," said he, "for your good opinion; but pray, if any body *did*, do you think Pamela would let *you* know of it?"—"Why, Sir," said she, "she is a poor innocent young creature, and I believe has so much confidence in me, that she would take my advice as soon as she would her mother's."—"*Innocent!* again; and *virtuous*, I warrant! Well, Mrs. Jervis, you abound with your epithets; but I take her to be an artful young baggage; and had I a young handsome butler or steward, she'd soon make her market of one of them, if she thought it worth while to snap at him for a husband."—"Alack-a-day, Sir?" said she, "'tis early days with Pamela; and she does not yet think of a husband, I dare say: and your steward and butler are both men in years, and think nothing of the matter."—"No," said he; "if they were younger, they'd have more wit than to think of such a girl.

16

I'll tell you my mind of her, Mrs. Jervis: I don't think this same favourite of your's, so very artless a girl as you imagine." —" I am not to dispute with your honour," said Mrs. Jervis: " but I dare say, if the men will let her alone, she'll never trouble herself about them."—" Why, Mrs. Jervis," said he, " are there any men that will not let her alone, that you know of? "—" No, indeed, Sir," said she; " she keeps herself so much to herself, and yet behaves so prudently, that they all esteem her, and shew her as great respect, as if she was a gentlewoman born."— " Aye," says he, " that's her art that I was speaking of. But, let me tell you, the girl has vanity and conceit, and pride too, or I am mistaken; and perhaps I could give an instance of it." " Sir," said she, " you can see farther than such a poor silly woman as I am; but I never saw any thing but innocence in her."—" And *virtue* too, I'll warrant ye!" said he. " But suppose I could give you an instance, where she has talked a little too freely of the kindnesses that have been shewn her from a *certain quarter;* and has had the vanity to impute a few kind words, uttered in mere compassion to her youth and cir- cumstances, into a design upon her, and even dared to make free with names which she ought never to mention but with reverence and gratitude; what would you say to that? "—" Say, Sir!" said she; " I cannot tell what to say. But I hope Pamela incapable of such ingratitude."

" Well, no more of this silly girl," says he. " You may only advise her, as you are her friend, not to give herself too much licence upon the favours she meets with; and, if she stays here, that she will not write the affairs of my family purely for an exercise to her pen and her invention. I tell you, she is a subtle, artful gipsey, and time will shew it you."

Was ever the like heard, my dear father and mother? It is plain he did not expect to meet with such a repulse, and mis- trusts that I have told Mrs. Jervis, and has my long letter too, that I intended for you; and so is vexed to the heart. But I can't help it. I had better be thought artful and subtle, than be so, in *his* sense: and as light as he makes of the word *virtue* and *innocence* in me, he would have made a less angry con- struction, had I less deserved that he should do so; for then, may be, my *crime* would have been my *virtue* with him; naughty gentleman as he is!—

I will soon write again, but must end with saying, that I am, and shall always be, *your honest daughter.*

DEAR MOTHER,

I broke off abruptly my last letter; for I feared he was coming; and so it happened. I put the letter in my bosom, and took up my work, which lay by me; but I had so little of the *artful*, as he called it, that I looked as confused as if I had been doing some great harm.

"Sit still, Pamela," said he, "and mind your work, for all me.—You don't tell me I am welcome home, after my journey to Lincolnshire."—"It would be hard, Sir," said I, "if you was not always welcome to your honour's own house."

I would have gone; but he said, "Don't run away, I tell you. I have a word or two to say to you." Good Sirs, how my heart went pit-a-pat! "When I was a *little kind* to you," said he, "in the summer-house, and you carried yourself so *foolishly* upon it, as if I had intended to do you great harm, did I not tell you you should take no notice of what passed, to any creature? and yet you have made a common talk of the matter, not considering either my reputation or your own."—"I made a common talk of it, Sir!" said I: "I have nobody to talk to, hardly."

He interrupted me and said, "*Hardly!* you little equivocator! what do you mean by *hardly?* Let me ask you, have not you told Mrs. Jervis for one?"—"Pray, your honour," said I, all in agitation, "let me go down: for it is not for me to hold an argument with your honour."—"Equivocator, again!" said he, and took my hand, "what do you talk of an *argument?* Is it holding an argument with me to answer a plain question? Answer me what I asked."—

"O, good Sir," said I, "let me beg you will not urge me farther, for fear I forget myself again, and be saucy!"

"Answer me, then, I bid you!" says he: "have you not told Mrs. Jervis? It will be saucy in you, if you don't answer me directly to what I ask."—"Sir," said I, and fain would have pulled my hand away, "perhaps I should be for answering you by another question, and that would not become me."—"What is it you would say?" replies he; "speak out."

"Then, Sir," said I, "why should your honour be so angry, I should tell Mrs. Jervis, or any body else, what passed, if you intended no harm?"

"Well said, pretty *innocent* and *artless!* as Mrs. Jervis calls you," said he; "and it is thus you taunt and retort upon me, insolent as you are! But still I will be answered directly to my question."—"Why, then, Sir," said I, "I will not tell a lie

18

for the world : I *did* tell Mrs. Jervis; for my heart was almost broken : but I opened not my mouth to any other."—"Very well, bold-face," said he, "and equivocator again; you did not open your *mouth* to any other; but did you not write to some other ? "—" Why now, and please your honour," said I, (for I was quite courageous just then) " you could not have asked me this question, if you had not taken from me my letter to my father and mother, in which, I own, I opened my mind freely to them, and asked their advice, and poured forth my griefs ! "

" And so I am to be exposed, am I," said he, " *in* my own house, and *out* of my house, to the whole world, by such a saucebox as you ? "—" No, good Sir," said I ; " and I hope your honour won't be angry with me : it is not I that expose you, if I say nothing but the truth."—" So, taunting again ! Assurance as you are ! " said he, " I will not be thus talked to ! "

" Pray, Sir," said I, " of whom can a poor girl take advice, if it must not be of her father and mother, and such a good woman as Mrs. Jervis ? "—" Insolent ! " said he, and stamped with his foot, " am I to be questioned thus by such a one as you ? " I fell down on my knees, and said, " For heaven's sake, your honour, pity a poor creature, that knows nothing of her duty, but how to cherish her virtue and good name ! I have nothing else to trust to; and, though poor and friendless, yet I have always been taught to value honesty above my life."— " Here's ado with your honesty," said he, " foolish girl ! Is it not one part of honesty to be dutiful and grateful to your master, do you think ? "—" Indeed, Sir," said I, " it is impossible I should be ungrateful to your honour, or disobedient, or deserve the names of Bold-face and Insolent, which you call me, but when your commands are contrary to that first duty which shall ever be the principle of my life."

He seemed to be moved, and rose up, and walked into the great chamber two or three turns, leaving me on my knees; I threw my apron over my face, and laid my head on a chair, and cried as if my heart would break, having no power to stir.

At last he came in again; but, alas ! with mischief in his heart, and raising me up, he said, " Rise, Pamela, rise; you are your own enemy. Your perverse folly will be your ruin. I tell you this, that I am very much displeased with the freedoms you have taken with my name to my housekeeper, as also to your father and mother; and you may as well have *real* cause to take these freedoms with me, as to make my name suffer for *imaginary* ones." And saying so, he offered to take me on his knee, with some force. O now I was terrified! I said, like as I had read in a book a night or two before, " Angels and saints, and all the host of heaven, defend me! And may I never survive, one moment, that fatal one in which I shall forfeit my innocence."—" Pretty fool!" said he, " how will you forfeit your innocence, if you are obliged to yield to a force you cannot withstand? Be easy," said he: " for, let the worst happen that can, *you'll* have the merit, and *I* the blame; and it will be a good subject for letters to your father and mother, and a tale into the bargain for Mrs. Jervis."

He by force kissed my neck and lips; and said, " Who ever blamed Lucretia! All the shame lay on the ravisher only: and I am content to take all the blame upon me; as I have already borne too great a share for what I have deserved."— " May I," said I, " Lucretia-like, justify myself with my death, if I am used barbarously?"—" O, my good girl," said he, tauntingly, " you are well read, I see; and we shall make out between us, before we have done, a pretty story in romance I warrant ye."

He then put his hand in my bosom, and indignation gave me double strength, and I got loose from him by a sudden spring, and ran out of the room; and the next chamber being open, I entered it, shut to the door, and it locked after me: but he followed me so close, he got hold of my gown, and tore a piece off, which hung without the door; for the key was on the inside.

I just remember I got into the room; for I knew nothing further of the matter till afterwards; for I fell into a fit with my terror, and there I lay, till he, as I suppose, looking through the keyhole, espied me upon the floor, stretched out at length, on my face; and then he called Mrs. Jervis to me, who, by his assistance, bursting open the door, he went away, seeing me coming to myself; and bid her say nothing of the matter, if she was wise.

Poor Mrs. Jervis thought it was worse, and cried over me like as if she was my mother; and I was two hours before I came to myself; and just as I got a little upon my feet, he coming in, I fainted away again with the terror; and so withdrew; but he staid in the next room to let nobody come near us, that his foul proceedings might not be known.

Mrs. Jervis gave me her smelling bottle, and had cut my laces, and set me in a great chair, when he called her to him.

" How is the girl?" said he: " I never saw such a fool in my life. I did nothing to her." Mrs. Jervis could not speak for crying. " So," he said, " she has told you, it seems, that I was kind to her in the summer-house, though I'll assure you, I was quite innocent then as well as now : and I desire you to keep this matter to yourself, and let *me* not be named in it."—" O, Sir," said she, " for your honour's sake, and for Christ's sake ! " But he would not hear her, and said, " For *your own sake*, I tell you, Mrs. Jervis, say not a word more. I have done her no harm. And I won't have her stay in my house ; prating, perverse fool, as she is ! But since she is so apt to fall into fits, or at least pretend to do so, prepare her to see me to-morrow after dinner, in my mother's closet ; do you be with her, and you shall hear what passes between us."

And so he went out in a pet, and ordered his chariot and four to be got ready, and went a visiting somewhere.

Mrs. Jervis then came to me ; I told her all that had happened, and said I was resolved not to stay in the house : and she replying—" He seemed to threaten as much ; " I said, " I am glad of that ; then I shall be easy." So she told me all he had said to her, as above. Mrs. Jervis is very loath I should go ; and yet, poor woman, she begins to be afraid for herself ; but would not have me ruined for the world. She says, to be sure he means no good ; but may be, now he sees me so resolute, he will give over all attempts : and that I shall better know what to do after to-morrow, when I am to appear before a very bad judge, I doubt.

O how I dread this to-morrow's appearance ! But be assured, my dear parents, of the honesty of your poor child, as I am of your prayers for *your dutiful daughter*.

O this frightful to-morrow ! how I dread it !

LETTER XVI

My dear Parents,

I know you longed to hear from me soon ; and I send you as soon as I could.

Well, you may believe how uneasily I passed the time till his appointed hour came. Every minute, as it grew nearer, my terrors increased ; and sometimes I had great courage, and sometimes none at all ; and I thought I should faint when it came to the time my master had dined. I could neither eat nor drink, for my part ; and do what I could, my eyes were swelled with crying.

At last he went up to the closet, which was my good lady's dressing-room ; a room I once loved, but then as much hated. Don't your heart ache for me ? I am sure mine fluttered about like a new caught bird in a cage. " O Pamela," said I to myself, " why art thou so foolish and fearful? Thou hast done no harm! What, if thou fearest an unjust judge, when thou art innocent, wouldst thou do before a just one, if thou wert guilty? Have courage, Pamela; thou knowest the worst! And how easy a choice poverty and honesty is, rather than plenty and wickedness."

So I cheered myself, but yet my poor heart sunk, and my spirits were quite broken. Every thing that stirred, I thought was to call me to my account. I dreaded it, and yet I wished it to come.

Well, at last he rung the bell; " O," thought I, " that it was my passing bell!" Mrs. Jervis went up, with a full heart enough, poor good woman! He said, "Where's Pamela! Let her come up; and do you come with her." She came to me: I was ready to go; but my heart was with my dear father and mother, wishing to share your poverty and unhappiness. I went up, however.

O how can wicked men seem so steady and untouched with such black hearts, while poor innocents stand like malefactors before them!

He looked so stern that my heart failed me, and I wished myself any where but there, though I had before been summoning up all my courage.

" Good heaven," said I to myself, " give me courage to stand before this naughty master! O soften him, or harden me!"

" Come in, fool!" said he, angrily, (and snatched my hand with a pull;) " you may well be ashamed to see me after your noise and nonsense, and exposing me as you have done."—" I ashamed to see *you!*" thought I: " very pretty, indeed!" But I said nothing.

" Mrs. Jervis," said he, " here you are both together. Do you sit down; but let her stand, if she will."—" Aye," thought I, " if I *can;*" for my knees beat one against the other. " Did you not think, when you saw the girl in the way you found her, that I had given her the greatest occasion for complaint that could possibly be given to a woman? And that I had actually ruined her, as she calls it? Tell me, *could* you think any thing less?"—" Indeed," said she, " I feared so at first."—" Has she told you what I did to her, and *all* I did to her, to occasion all this folly, by which my reputation might have suffered in your opinion, and in that of all the family; inform me what she has told you?"

She was a little too much frightened, as she owned afterwards,

22

at his sternness, and said, " Indeed she told me you *only* pulled
her on your knee, and kissed her."

Then I plucked up my spirit a little. " *Only !* Mrs. Jervis ? "
said I ; " and was not that enough to shew me what I had to
fear ? When a master of his honour's degree demeans himself
to be so free as *that* to such a poor servant as me, what is the
next to be expected ? But your honour went further ; and
threatened me what you would do, talked of Lucretia and her
hard fate. Your honour knows you went too far for a master
to a servant, or even to his equal ; and I cannot bear it." So I
fell a crying most sadly.

Mrs. Jervis began to excuse me, and to beg he would pity a
poor maiden, that had such a value for her reputation. He
said, " I think her very pretty, and I thought her humble,
and one that would not grow upon my favours, or the notice
I took of her ; but I abhor the thought of forcing her to any
thing. I know myself better," said he, " and what belongs
to me : and to be sure I have enough demeaned myself to take
notice of such a one as she ; but I was bewitched by her, I think,
to be freer than became me ; though I had no intention to carry
the jest farther."

What poor stuff was all this, my dear mother, from a man
of his sense ! but, see how a bad cause and bad actions confound
the greatest wits ! it gave me a little more courage then ; for
innocence, I find, in a low fortune, and weak mind, has many
advantages over guilt, with all its riches and wisdom.

So I said, " Your honour may call this jest, or sport, or what
you please ; but, Sir, it is not a jest that becomes the distance
between a master and servant."—" Do you hear, Mrs. Jervis,"
said he, " the pertness of this creature ? I had a good deal
of this sort before in the summer-house, and yesterday too,
which made me rougher with her than, perhaps, I had otherwise been."—Says Mrs. Jervis, " Pamela, don't be so pert to
his honour : you should know your distance ; you see his honour
was only in jest."—" O dear Mrs. Jervis," said I, " don't *you*
blame me too. It is very difficult to keep one's distance to the
greatest of men, when they won't keep it themselves to their
meanest servants."

" See again ! " said he : " could you believe this of the young
baggage, if you had not heard it ? "—" Good, your honour," said
Mrs. Jervis, " pity and forgive the poor girl ; she is but a girl,
and her virtue is very dear to her : I will pawn my life for her,
she will never be pert to your honour, if you will be so good
as to molest her no more, nor frighten her again. You saw,

Sir, by her fit, she was in terror; she could not help it: and though your honour intended her no harm, yet the apprehension was almost death to her; and I had much ado to bring her to herself again."—"O the little hypocrite," said he; "she has all the arts of her sex; they were *born* with her; I told you awhile ago you did not know her. But this was not the reason principally of my calling you before me together: I find I am likely to suffer in my reputation by the perverseness and folly of this girl. She has told you all, and perhaps more than all; I make no doubt of it; and she has written letters (for I find she is a mighty letter-writer) to her father and mother, and others, as far as I know; in which, representing herself as an angel of light, she makes her kind master and benefactor a devil incarnate."—(O how people will sometimes, thought I, call themselves by their right names!)—"And all this," added he, "I won't bear; and so am resolved she shall return to the distress and poverty she was taken from; and let her be careful how she uses my name with freedom when she is gone from me."

I was brightened up with these welcome words; I threw myself upon my knees at his feet, with a most sincere glad heart, and said, "May your honour be for ever blessed for your resolution! Now I shall be happy. Permit me, on my bended knees, to thank you for all the benefits and favours you have heaped upon me; for the opportunities I have had of improvement and learning, through my good lady's means and yours. I will now forget all your honour has offered to me; and I promise you, that I will never let your name pass my lips but with reverence and gratitude. God Almighty bless your honour for ever and ever, *Amen!*"

Then rising from my knees, I went away with another-guise sort of heart than I came into his presence with: and so I fell to writing this letter. And thus all is happily over.

And now, my dearest father and mother, expect to see soon your poor daughter, with an humble and dutiful mind, returned to you; and don't fear but I know to be as happy with you as ever; for I will lie in the loft, as I used to do; and pray let my little bed be got ready. I have a small matter of money, which will buy me a suit of clothes fitter for my condition than what I have; and I will get Mrs. Mumford to help me to some needle-work; and fear not that I shall be a burden to you, if my health continues. I know I shall be blessed, if not for my own sake, for both *your* sakes, who have, in all your trials and misfortunes, preserved so much integrity, as makes every body speak well of you both. But I hope he will let good Mrs. Jervis give me a character, for fear it should be thought I was turned away for dishonesty.

And so, my dear parents, may you be blest for me, and I for you. And I will always pray for my master and Mrs. Jervis. So good night; for it is late, and I shall soon be called to bed.

I hope Mrs. Jervis is not angry with me. She has not called me to supper; though I could eat nothing if she had. But I make no doubt I shall sleep purely to-night, and dream that I am with you in my dear, dear happy loft once more.

So good night again, my dear father and mother, says *your poor honest daughter.*

Perhaps I mayn't come this week, because I must get up the linen, and leave in order every thing belonging to my place. Send me a line if you can, to let me know if I shall be welcome, by John, who will call for it as he returns. But say nothing of my coming away to him as yet: for it will be said I blab every thing.

LETTER XVII

MY DEAREST DAUGHTER,

Welcome, welcome, ten times welcome, shall you be to us; for you come to us innocent, happy, and honest: you are the staff and the comfort of our old age. And though we cannot do for you as we would, yet, fear not, we shall live happily together: what with my diligent labour, your poor mother's spinning, and your needle-work, I make no doubt we shall do better and better. Only your poor mother's eyes begin to fail her: though, I bless God, I am as strong and able, and willing to labour as ever; and, O, my dear child ! your virtue has made me, I think, stronger and better than I was before. What blessed things are trials and temptations, when we have the strength to resist and subdue them.

But I am uneasy about those four guineas : I think you should give them back again to your master; and yet I have broken them. Alas ! I have only three left; but I will borrow the fourth, if I can, part upon my wages, and part of Mrs. Mumford, and send the whole sum back that you may return it against John comes next, if he comes again before you.

I want to know how you come. I fancy honest John will be glad to bear you company part of the way, if your master is not so cross as to forbid him. If I know time enough, your mother will go one five miles, and I will go ten on the way, or till I meet you, as far as one holiday will go; for that I can get leave to make on such an occasion; and we shall receive you with more pleasure than we had at your birth, or than we ever had in our lives.

And so God bless you, till the happy time comes, say both your mother and I; which is all at present, from *your truly loving parents*.

LETTER XVIII

DEAR FATHER AND MOTHER,

I thank you a thousand times for your goodness to me, expressed in your last letter. I now long to get my business done, and come to my old loft again, as I may call it. I have been quite another thing since my master has turned me off; and as I shall come to you an honest daughter, what pleasure it is to what I should have had if I could not have seen you but as a guilty one. Well, my writing-time will soon be over; so I will make use of it now, and tell you all that has happened since my last letter.

I wondered Mrs. Jervis did not call me sup with her, and feared she was angry; and when I had finished my letter I longed for her coming to bed. At last she came up, but seemed shy and reserved; I said, " My dear Mrs. Jervis, I am glad to see you; you are not angry with me, I hope." She said, she was sorry things had gone so far; that she had a great deal of talk with my master after I was gone; that he seemed moved at what I said, and at my falling on my knees to him, and my prayer for him at going away. He said, I was a strange girl; he knew not what to make of me. " And is she gone ? " said he. " I intended to have said something else to her; but she behaved so oddly, that I had not power to stop her." She asked, if she should call me again. He said, " Yes;" and then "No : let her go; it is best for her and me too : she shall go, now I have given her warning. Where she had it, I can't tell; but I never met with the fellow of her in my life." She said, he had ordered her not to tell me all : but she believed he never would offer any thing to me again; and I might stay, she fancied, if I would beg it as a favour, though she was not sure.

" I stay ! dear Mrs. Jervis," said I; " why 'tis the best news that could have come to me, that he will let me go. I long to go back again to my *poverty* and *distress*, as he threatened I should; for though I am sure of the poverty, I shall not have half the distress I have had for some months past, I assure you."

Mrs. Jervis, dear good soul, wept over me, and said, "Well, well, Pamela, I did not think I had shewn so little love to you, as that you should express so much joy upon leaving me. I am sure I never had a child half so dear to me as you are."

I wept to hear her so good to me, as indeed she has always been; and said, "What would you have me *do*, dear Mrs. Jervis? I love you next to my own father and mother; and to leave you is the chief concern I have at quitting this place; but I am sure it is certain ruin if I stay. After such offers, such threatenings, and his comparing himself to a wicked ravisher in the very time of his last offer; and turning it into a jest, that we should make a pretty story in romance; can I stay and be safe? Has he not demeaned himself twice? It behoves me to beware of the third time, for fear he should lay his snares surer; for, perhaps, he did not expect a poor servant would resist her master so much. And must it not be looked upon as a sort of warrant for such actions, if I stay after this? For, I think, when one of our sex finds she is attempted, it is an encouragement to the attempter to proceed, if one puts one's self in the way of it, when one can help it: it is neither more nor less, than inviting him to think one forgives what, in short, ought *not* to be forgiven; which is no small countenance to foul actions, I'll assure you."

She hugged me to her, and said, "*I'll assure you!* Pretty face, where gottest thou all thy knowledge, and thy good notions, at these years? Thou art a miracle for thy age, and I shall always love thee. But do you resolve to leave us, Pamela?"

"Yes, my dear Mrs. Jervis," said I; "for as matters stand, how can I be otherwise?—But I'll finish the duties of my place first, if I may; and I hope you'll give me a character, as to my honesty, that it may not be thought I was turned away for any harm."—"Aye, that I will," said she; "I will give thee such a character as never a girl at thy years deserved."—"I am sure," said I, "I will always love and honour you, as my third best friend, wherever I go, or whatever becomes of me." So we went to bed, and I never waked till it was time to rise; which I did, as blythe as a bird, and went about my business with great pleasure.

I believe my master is angry with me; for he passed by me two or three times, and would not speak to me: towards evening he met me in the passage going into the garden, and said

27

such a word to me as I never heard from him, to man, woman, or child; for he first said, "This creature's always in the way." I said, standing up as close as I could (and the entry was wide enough for a coach), "I hope I shan't be long in your honour's way."—"D—n you," said he (that was the hard word,) "for a little wretch; I have no patience with you."

I profess I trembled to hear him say so; but I *saw* he was vexed; and as I am going away I minded it the less. Well, I see, my dear parents, that when a person will do wicked things, it is no wonder he will speak wicked words. May God keep out of the way of them both *your dutiful daughter*.

LETTER XIX

Dear Father and Mother,

Our John having an opportunity to go your way, I write again, and send both letters at once. I cannot say yet when I shall get away, or how I shall come; because Mrs. Jervis shewed my master the waistcoat I am flowering for him, and he said, "It looks well enough; I think the creature had best stay till she has finished it."

There is some private talk carried on betwixt him and Mrs. Jervis, that she don't tell me of; but yet she is very kind to me, and I don't mistrust her: I should be very base if I did. But, to be sure, she must oblige him, and keep all his lawful commands; and other, I dare say, she won't keep; she is too good, and loves me too well: but *she* must stay, when I am gone, and so must get no ill-will.

She has been at me again to ask me to stay, and humble myself. "But what have I done, Mrs. Jervis?" said I. "If I have been a Sauce-box, a Bold-face, a Pert, and a Creature, as he calls me, have I not had reason? Do you think I should ever have forgot *myself*, if he had not forgot to act as my *master?* Tell me from your own heart, dear Mrs. Jervis, if you think I could stay and be safe: what would *you* think or how would *you* act, in *my* case?"

"My dear Pamela," said she, and kissed me, "I don't know how I should act, or what I should think. I hope I should act as *you* do. But I know nobody else that would. My master is a fine gentleman; he has a great deal of wit and sense, and is admired, as I know, by half a dozen ladies, who would think themselves happy in his addresses. He has a noble estate; and

28

yet I believe he loves you, though his servant, better than all the ladies in the land; he has tried to overcome it, because you are so much his inferior; and it is my opinion he finds he can't; and that vexes his proud heart, and makes him resolve you shan't stay: and so he speaks so cross to you when he sees you by accident."

"Well, but, Mrs. Jervis," said I, "let me ask you, if he can stoop to like such a poor girl as me, as perhaps he may (for I have read of things almost as strange, from great men to poor damsels), what can it be *for*? He may condescend, perhaps, to think I may be good enough for his harlot; and those things don't disgrace men, that ruin poor women, as the world goes. And so, if I was wicked enough, he would keep me till I was undone, and till his mind changed; for even wicked men, I have read, soon grow weary of wickedness with the same person, and love variety. Then poor Pamela must be turned off and looked upon as a vile abandoned creature; and every body would despise her, and *justly* too, Mrs. Jervis; for she that can't keep her virtue, ought to live in disgrace. But, Mrs. Jervis," continued I, "let me tell you that I hope, if I was sure he would always be kind to me, and never turn me off at all, that I shall have so much grace, as to hate and withstand his temptations, were he not only my master, but my king; and that for the *sin's* sake. This my poor dear parents have always taught me: and I should be a sad wicked creature, if, for the sake of riches or favour, I should forfeit my good name; yea, and worse than any other young body of my sex; because I can so contentedly return to my poverty again, and think it a less disgrace to be obliged to wear rags, and live upon rye-bread and water, as I used to do, than to be a harlot to the greatest man in the world."

Mrs. Jervis lifted up her hands, and had her eyes full of tears. "God bless you, my dear love!" said she: "you are my admiration and delight.—How shall I do to part with you?"

"Well, good Mrs. Jervis," said I, "let me ask you now:— You and he have had some talk; and you *mayn't* be suffered to tell me all: but do you think if I was to ask to stay, that he is sorry for what he has done?—aye, and *ashamed* of it too; for I am sure he ought, considering his high degree, and my low degree, and that I have nothing in the world to trust to but my honesty. Do you think, in *your own* conscience, (pray answer me truly) that he would never offer any thing to me again, and that I could be safe?"

"Alas! my dear child," said she, "don't put thy home questions to me, with that pretty becoming earnestness in thy look.

29

I know this, that he is vexed at what he has done; he was vexed the *first* time, more vexed the *second* time."

"Yes," said I, "and so he will be vexed, I suppose, the *third* and the *fourth* time too, till he has quite ruined your poor maiden; and who will have cause to be vexed then?"

"Nay, Pamela," said she, "don't imagine that I would be accessory to your ruin for the world. I only can say, that he has yet done you no hurt; and 'tis no wonder he should love you, you are so pretty, though so much beneath him: but I dare swear he never will offer you any force."

"You say," said I, "that he was sorry for his *first* offer in the summer-house. Well, and how long did his sorrow last? Only till he found me by myself: and then he was worse than before; and so became sorry *again*. And if he has designed to love me, and you say can't *help* it, why, he can't *help* it neither, if he should have an opportunity, a *third* time to distress me. And I have read, that many a man has been ashamed of his wicked attempts, when he has been repulsed, that would never have been ashamed of them, had he succeeded. Besides, Mrs. Jervis, if he really intends to offer no *force*, what does that mean? While you say he can't *help* liking me—for *love* it cannot be—does it not imply that he hopes to ruin me by my own *consent?* I *think*," said I (and I hope I should have grace to *do* so), "that I should not give way to his temptations on *any* account; but it would be very presumptuous in me to rely upon my own strength against a gentleman of his qualifications and estate, who is my *master*, and thinks himself entitled to call me Bold-face, and what not, only for standing on my defence, and that too, where the good of my soul and body, my duty to God and my parents, are all concerned. How then, Mrs. Jervis," said I, "can I *ask* or *wish* to stay?"

"Well, well," says she, "as he seems very desirous you should *not* stay, I hope it is from a good motive—for fear he should be tempted to disgrace himself as well as you."—"No, no, Mrs. Jervis," said I; "I have thought of that too; for I would be glad to consider him with that duty which becomes me; but then he would have let me go to Lady Davers, and not have hindered my preferment; he would not have said, I should return to my *poverty* and *distress*, when, by his mother's goodness, I had been lifted out of it; but he intended to fright and *punish* me, as he thought, for not complying with his wickedness; and this shews what I have to expect from his future goodness, except I will deserve it at his own dear price."

She was silent; and I added, "Well, there's no more to be

30

said; I must go, that's certain; all my concern will be how to part with *you*, and, after you, with *every body*; for all my fellow-servants have loved me: you and they will often cost me a sigh, and a tear too." So I fell a crying, I could not help it: for it is a pleasant thing to be in a house, among a great many fellow-servants, and be beloved by them all.

Nay, I should have told you before now, how kind and civil Mr. Longman, our steward, is; vastly courteous, indeed, on all occasions! He said once to Mrs. Jervis he wished he was a young man for my sake; I should be his wife, and he would settle all he had upon me on marriage: and you must know he is reckoned worth a power of money.

I take no pride in this; but bless God, and your good examples, my dear parents, that I have been enabled so to carry myself, as to have every body's good word: not but our cook, one day, who is a little cross sometimes, said once to me, " Why, this Pamela of *ours* goes as fine as a lady. See what it is to have a fine face!—I wonder what the girl will come to at last." She was hot with her work; and I went away; for I seldom go down into the kitchen. I heard the butler say, " why, Jane, nobody has your good word: what has Pamela done to you? I am sure she offends nobody."—" And what," said the peevish wench, " have I said to her, *footatum*, but that she was pretty?" They quarrelled afterwards, I heard: I was sorry for it, but troubled myself no more about it. Forgive this silly prattle, from *your dutiful daughter*.

Oh! I forgot to say, that I would stay to finish the waistcoat, if I might with safety: Mrs. Jervis tells me I certainly may. I never had a prettier piece of work; and I am up early and late to get it over; for I long to be with you.

LETTER XX

DEAR FATHER AND MOTHER,

I did not send my last letters so soon as I hoped, because John (whether my master mistrusts or not, I can't say) had been sent to Lady Davers's instead of Isaac, who used to go; and I could not be so free with, nor so well trust Isaac, though he is very civil to me. So I was forced to stay till John returned.

As I may not have opportunity to send again soon, and as I know you keep my letters, and read them over and over (so

John told me) when you have done work (so much does your kindness make you love all that comes from your poor daughter), and as it may be some little pleasure to me to read them myself, when I am come to you, to remind me of what I have gone through, and how great God's goodness has been to me (which, I hope, will farther strengthen my good resolutions, that I may not hereafter, from my bad conduct, have reason to condemn myself from my own hand, as it were): for all these reasons I will write as I have time, and as matters happen, send the scribble to you as I have opportunity; and if I do not every time, in form, subscribe as I ought, I am sure you will always believe that it is not for want of duty. So I will begin where I left off; about the talk between Mrs. Jervis and me, for me to ask to stay.

Unknown to Mrs. Jervis, I put a project, as I may call it, in practice. I thought with myself some days ago—" Here I shall go home to my poor father and mother, and have nothing on my back that will be fit for my condition; for how would your poor daughter look with a silk nightgown, silken petticoats, cambric head-clothes, fine Holland linen, laced shoes, that were my lady's, and fine stockings! And how, in a little while, must these have looked, like old cast-offs, and I looked so for wearing them! People would have said (for poor folks are envious as well as rich), "See there Goody Andrews's daughter, turned home from her fine place! What a tawdry figure she makes! How well that garb becomes her poor parents' circumstances!" How would they look upon me, thought I to myself, when they should come to be thread-bare, and worn out! And how should I look even if I could purchase home-spun clothes, to dwindle into them, one by one, as I got them? —May be, an old silk gown, and linsey-woolsey petticoat, and the like. So, thought I, I had better get myself equipped in the dress that will become my condition. And though it may look but poor to what I have been used to wear of late days, yet it will serve me, when I am with you, for a good holiday and Sunday suit, and what, by a blessing on my industry, I may, perhaps, make shift to keep up to. So, as I was saying, unknown to any body, I bought of Farmer Nichol's wife and daughters, a good sad-coloured stuff, of their own spinning, enough to make me a gown and two petticoats; and I made robings and facing of a pretty bit of printed calico I had by me.

I had a pretty good camblet quilted coat that I thought might do tolerably well; and I bought two flannel undercoats, not so good as my swan-skin and fine linen ones, but what will keep me warm, if any neighbour should get me to help them to milk, as sometimes I used to do formerly; for I am resolved to do all your good neighbours what kindness I can, and hope to make myself as much beloved about you as I am here.

I got some Scots cloth, and made me, at mornings and nights, when nobody saw me, two shirts; I have enough left for two shirts and two shifts for you, my dear father and mother. When I come home, I'll make them for you, and desire your acceptance.

Then I bought of a pedlar two pretty round-eared caps, a little straw-hat, and a pair of knit-mittens turned up with white calico, and two pair of blue worsted hose with white clocks, that make a smartish appearance, I'll assure you; and two yards of black ribband for my shift sleeves, and to serve as a necklace. When I had them all come home, I went and looked at them once in two hours for two days together: for you must know, though I lie with Mrs. Jervis, I keep my own apartment for my clothes, and nobody goes thither but myself. You'll say I was no bad house-wife to have saved so much money; but my dear good lady was always giving me something.

I believed myself the more obliged to do this, because as I was turned away for what my master thought want of duty; and as he expected other returns for his presents than I intended to make him; I thought it was but just to leave his presents behind me when I went away; for, you know, if I would not earn his wages, why should I have them?

Don't trouble yourself about the four guineas, nor borrow to make them up; for they were given to me, with some silver, as a perquisite, being what my lady had about her when she died; and, as I expect no wages, I am so vain as to think I have deserved all that money in the fourteen months since my lady's death: for she, good soul, overpaid me before, in learning and other kindnesses. Had *she* lived, none of these things might have happened! But I ought to be thankful it is no worse. Every thing will turn out for the best; that's my confidence.

So, as I was saying, I have provided a new and more suitable dress, and I long to appear in it, more than ever I did in any new clothes in my life; for then I shall be soon after with you, and at ease in my mind—But mum! Here he comes, I believe——

I am, &c.

33

My dear Father and Mother,

I was forced to break off; for I feared my master was coming; but it proved to be only Mrs. Jervis. She said, " I can't endure you should be so much by yourself, Pamela."—" I," said I, " dread nothing so much as company; for my heart was up at my mouth now, for fear my master was coming. But I always rejoice to see dear Mrs. Jervis." Said she, " I have had a world of talk with my master about you."—" I am sorry for it," said I, " that I am made of so much consequence as to be talked of by him."—" O," said she, " I must not tell you all; you are of more consequence to him than you think for."—" Or *wish* for," said I; " for the fruits of being of consequence to him, would make me of none to myself, or any body else."

Said she, " Thou art as witty as any lady in the land : I wonder where thou gottest it." But they must be poor ladies, with such great opportunities, I am sure, if they have no more wit than I. But let that pass. " I suppose," said I, " that I am of so much consequence, however, as to vex him, if it be but to think he can't make a fool of such a one as I; and that is nothing but a rebuke to the pride of his high condition, which he did not expect, and knows not how to put up with."

" There is something in that may-be," said she; " but, indeed, Pamela, he is very angry with you *too;* and calls you twenty perverse things; wonders at his own folly, to have shewn you so much favour, as he calls it; which he was first inclined to, he says, for his mother's sake, and would have persisted to shew you for your own, if you was not your own enemy."

" Nay, now I shan't love you, Mrs. Jervis," said I; " you are going to persuade me to ask to stay, though you know the hazards I run."—" No," said she, " he says you *shall* go : for he thinks it won't be for his reputation to keep you; but he wished (don't speak of it for the world, Pamela) that he knew a lady of birth, just such another as yourself, in person and mind, and he would marry her to-morrow."

I coloured up to the ears at this word : but said, " Yet if I was the lady of birth, and he would offer to be rude first, as he has twice done to poor me, I don't know whether I should have him; for *she* that can bear an insult of that kind, I should think not worthy to be a gentleman's wife, any more than *he* would be a gentleman that would offer it."

" Nay, now, Pamela," said she, " thou carriest thy notions a great way."—"Well, dear Mrs. Jervis," said I, very seriously, for I could not help it, "I am more full of fears than ever. I have only to beg of you, as one of the best friends I have in the world, to say nothing of my asking to stay. To say my master likes me, when I know what end he aims at, is abomination to my ears; and I shan't think myself safe till I am at my poor father's and mother's."

She was a little angry with me, till I assured her that I had not the least uneasiness on her account, but thought myself safe under her protection and friendship. And so we dropt the discussion for that time.

I hope to have finished the ugly waistcoat in two days; after which, I have only some linen to get up, and shall then let you know how I contrive as to my passage; for the heavy rains will make it sad travelling on foot: but may-be I may get a place to ——, which is ten miles of the way, in Farmer Nichols's close cart; for I can't sit a horse well at all, and may-be nobody will be suffered to see me on upon the way. But I hope to let you know more, *from*, &c.

LETTER XXII

My dear Father and Mother,

All my fellow-servants have now some notion that I am to go away; but can't imagine for what. Mrs. Jervis tells them, that my father and mother, growing in years, cannot live without me; and so I go home to them to comfort their old age, but they seem not to believe it.

What they found it out by, was, the butler heard him say to me, as I passed by him, in the entry leading to the hall, "Who's that?"—"Pamela, Sir," said I.—"Pamela!" said he, "how long are *you* to stay here?"—"Only, please your honour," said I, "till I have done the waistcoat; and it is almost finished."—"You might," says he very roughly, "have finished that long ago."—"Indeed, and please your honour," said I, "I have worked early and late upon it: there is a great deal of work in it."—"*Work in it!*" said he; "you mind your pen more than your needle; I don't want such idle sluts to stay in my house."

He seemed startled when he saw the butler as he entered the hall, where Mr. Jonathan stood. "What do *you* here?" said he. The butler was as much confounded as I; for, never having been taxed so roughly, I could not help crying sadly; and got

35

out of both their ways to Mrs. Jervis, and told my complaint. "This love," said she, "is the d—l! In how many shapes does it make people shew themselves! And in some the farthest from their hearts."

So one, and then another, has been since whispering, "Pray, Mrs. Jervis, are we to lose Mrs. Pamela?" as they call me. "What has she done?" and then she tells them as above, about going home to you.

She said afterwards to me, "Well, Pamela, you have made our master, from the sweetest tempered gentleman in the world, one of the most peevish. But you have it in your power to make him as sweet tempered as ever; though I hope you'll never do it on his terms." This was very good of Mrs. Jervis, but it intimated, that she thought as ill of his designs as I; and, as she knew his mind more than I, it convinced me that I ought to get away as fast I could.

My master came in, just now, to speak to Mrs. Jervis about household matters, having some company to dine with him to-morrow; I stood up, and having been crying at his roughness in the entry, I turned away my face. "You may well," said he, "turn away your cursed face; I wish I had never seen it!—Mrs. Jervis, how long is she to be about this waistcoat?"

"Sir," said I, "if your honour had pleased, I would have taken it with me; and, though it would be now finished in a few hours, I will do so still, and remove this hated poor Pamela out of your house and sight for ever."—"Mrs. Jervis," said he, not speaking to me, "I believe this little slut has the power of witchcraft, if ever there was a witch; for she enchants all that come near her. She makes even *you*, who should know better what the world is, think her an angel."

I offered to go away; for I believe he wanted me to ask to stay in my place, for all this his great wrath; and he said, "Stay here, stay here, when I bid you!" and snatched my hand. I trembled, and said, "I will! I will!" for he hurt my fingers he grasped me so hard.

He seemed to have a mind to say something to me; but broke off abruptly, and said, "Be gone!" And away I tripped as fast as I could; and he and Mrs. Jervis had a deal of talk, as she told me; and, among the rest, he expressed himself vexed to have spoken in Mr. Jonathan's hearing.

Now you must know, that Mr. Jonathan, our butler, is a very grave good sort of old man, with his hair as white as silver; and an honest worthy man he is. I was hurrying out with a flea in my ear, as the saying is, and going down stairs

36

into the parlour, met him. He took hold of my hand (in a gentler manner, though, than my master) with both his: and he said, "Ah! sweet, sweet Mrs. Pamela! what is it I heard but just now? I am sorry at my heart; but I am sure I will sooner believe *any body* in fault than *you*."—"Thank you, Mr. Jonathan," said I, "but, as you value your place, don't be seen speaking to such a one as me." I cried too; and slipt away as fast as I could from him, for his own sake, lest he should be seen to pity me.

And now I will give you an instance how much I am in Mr. Longman's esteem also.

I had lost my pen, some how; and my paper being written out, I stepped to Mr. Longman's our steward's office, to beg him to give me a pen or two, and a sheet or two of paper. He said, "Aye, that I will, my sweet maiden!" and gave me three pens, some wafers, a stick of wax, and twelve sheets of paper; and coming from his desk, where he was writing, he said, "Let me have a word or two with you, my sweet little mistress" (for so these two good old gentlemen often call me; for I believe they love me dearly); "I hear bad news; that we are going to lose you: I hope it is not true?"—"Yes, it is, Sir," said I, "but I was in hopes it would not be known till I went away."

"What the d—l," said he, "ails our master of late! I never saw such an alteration in any man in my life! He is pleased with nobody, as I see; and by what Mr. Jonathan tells me just now, he was quite out of the way with you. What could *you* have done to him, tro? Only Mrs. Jervis is a very good woman, or I should have feared *she* had been your enemy."

"No," said I, "nothing like it. Mrs. Jervis is a just good woman, and, next to my father and mother, the best friend I have in the world."—"Well, then," said he, "it must be worse. Shall I guess! You are too *pretty*, my sweet mistress, and maybe too *virtuous*. Ah! have I not hit it?"—"No, good Mr. Longman," said I, "don't think any thing amiss of my master; he is cross and angry with me, indeed, that's true; but I may have given him occasion for it, possibly; and because I am desirous to go to my father and mother, rather than stay here, perhaps he may think me ungrateful. But, you know, Sir," said I, "that a father and mother's comfort is the dearest thing to a good child that can be."—"Sweet excellence!" said he, "this becomes *you;* but I know the world and mankind too well; though I must hear and see, and say nothing! And so a blessing attend my little sweeting," said he, "wherever you go!" And away I went, with a curtsey and thanks.

Now this pleases me, my dear father and mother, to be so beloved. How much better it is, by good fame and integrity, to get every one's good word but *one*, than by *pleasing that one*, to make *every one else* one's enemy, and be an execrable creature besides! I am, &c.

LETTER XXIII

MY DEAR FATHER AND MOTHER,

We had a great many neighbouring gentlemen, and their ladies, this day at dinner; and my master made a fine entertainment for them: Isaac, Mr. Jonathan, and Benjamin, waited at table: and Isaac tells Mrs. Jervis that the ladies will by and by come to see the house, and have the curiosity to see me; for, it seems, they said to my master, when the jokes flew about, "Well, Mr. B——, we understand you have a servant-maid who is the greatest beauty in the county; and we promise ourselves to see her before we go."

"The wench is well enough," said he, "but no such beauty as you talk of, I'll assure ye. She was my mother's waiting-maid, who, on her death-bed, engaged me to be kind to her. She is young, and every thing is *pretty* that is *young*."

"Ay, ay," said one of the ladies, "that's true; but if your mother had *not* recommended her so strongly, there is so much merit in beauty, that I make no doubt such a fine gentleman would have wanted no inducement to be kind to it."

They all laughed at my master: and he, it seems, laughed for company; but said, "I don't know how it is, but I see with different eyes from other people; for I have heard much more talk of her prettiness than I think it deserves: she is well enough, as I said; but her greatest excellence is, that she is humble and courteous, and faithful, and makes all her fellow-servants love her: my housekeeper, in particular, doats upon her; and you know, ladies, she is a woman of discernment: and, as for Mr. Longman and Jonathan here, if they thought themselves young enough, I am told they would fight for her. Is it not true, Jonathan?"—"Troth, Sir," said he, "an't please your honour, I never knew her peer, and all your honour's family are of the same mind."—"Do you hear now?" said my master.—"Well," said the ladies, "we will make a visit to Mrs. Jervis, by-and-by, and hope to see this paragon."

I believe they are coming; and will tell you the rest by-and-by.

I wish they had come, and were gone. Why can't they make their game without me?

Well, these fine ladies have been here, and are gone back again. I would have been absent if I could, and did step into the closet : but they saw me when they came in. There were four of them : Lady Arthur, at the great white house on the hill, Lady Brooks, Lady Towers, and the other, it seems, a countess, of some hard name, I forget what.

"So, Mrs. Jervis," says one of the ladies, "how do you do? We are all come to enquire after your health."—"I am much obliged to your ladyships," said Mrs. Jervis : "will your ladyships please to sit down?"—"But," said the countess, "we are not *only* come to ask after Mrs. Jervis's health, but we are come to see a rarity besides."—"Ah," says Lady Arthur, "I have not seen your Pamela these two years, and they tell me she is grown wondrous pretty in that time."

Then I wished I had not been in the closet; for when I came out, they must needs know I heard them : but I have often found, that bashful bodies owe themselves a spite, and frequently confound themselves more by endeavouring to avoid confusion.

"Why, yes," says Mrs. Jervis, "Pamela is very pretty indeed ; she's but in the closet there.—Pamela, pray step hither." I came out all covered with blushes, and they smiled at one another.

The countess took me by the hand. "Why, indeed," she was pleased to say, "report has not been too lavish, I'll assure you.—Don't be ashamed, child" (and stared full in my face), "I wish I had just such a face to be ashamed of." O how like a fool I looked !

Lady Arthur said, "Ay, my good Pamela," I say as her ladyship says : "don't be so confused ; though it becomes you too. I think your good departed lady made a sweet choice of such a pretty attendant. She would have been mighty proud of you, as she was always praising you, had she lived till now."

"Ah, Madam !" said Lady Brooks, "do you think that so *dutiful* a son as our neighbour, who always *admired* what his mother *loved*, does not pride himself, for all what he said at table, in such a pretty maiden?" She looked with such a malicious sneering countenance, I can't abide her.

Lady Towers said, with a freer air (for it seems she is called a wit), "Well, Mrs. Pamela, I can't say I like you so well as these ladies do ; for I should never care, if you were *my* servant, to have *you* and your *master* in the same house together." Then

39

they all set up a great laugh. I know what I could have said, if I durst. But they are ladies—and ladies may say any thing.

Says Lady Towers, " Can the pretty image speak, Mrs. Jervis? I vow she has speaking eyes! O you little rogue," said she, and tapped me on the cheek, " you seem born to undo, or to be undone ! "—" God forbid, an' please your ladyship," said I, " it should be *either*. I beg," said I, " to withdraw; for the sense I have of my unworthiness renders me unfit for such a presence."

I then went away with one of my best curtsies: and Lady Towers said, as I went out, " Prettily said, I vow ! " And Lady Brooks said, " See that shape ! I never saw such a face and shape in my life; why, she must be better descended than you have told me ! "

And so they ran on for half an hour more, in my praises, as I was told; and glad I was when I got out of the hearing of them !

But, it seems, they went down with *such* a story to my master, and so full of *me*, that he had much ado to stand it; but, as it was very little to my reputation, I am sure I could take no pride in it; and I feared it would make no better for me. This gives me another cause for wishing myself out of this house.

This is Thursday morning, and next Thursday I hope to set out; for I have finished my task, and my master is horrid cross ! I am vexed his crossness affects me so. If ever he had any kindness towards me I believe he now hates me heartily.

Is it not strange that love borders so much upon hate? But this wicked love is not like the true virtuous love, to be sure: *that* and *hatred* must be far off as *light* and *darkness*. And how must this hate have been increased if he had met with a base compliance, after his wicked will had been gratified?

Well, we may see by a little what a great deal means. For if *innocence* cannot attract common civility, what must *guilt* expect, when novelty has ceased to have its charms, and change-ableness has taken place of it? Thus we read in holy writ, that wicked Amnon, when he had ruined poor Tamar, hated her more than ever he had loved her, and would have turned her out of doors.

How happy am I to be turned out of doors with that sweet companion, my innocence ! O may that be always my companion ! And while I presume not upon my own strength, and am willing to avoid the tempter, I hope the Divine Grace will assist me.

Forgive me, that I repeat in my letter part of my hourly

prayer. I owe every thing next to God's goodness to your piety
and good examples, my dear parents, my dear *poor* parents!
I say that word with pleasure: for your *poverty* is my *pride*,
as your integrity shall be my imitation.

As soon as I have dined, I will put on my new clothes. I
long to have them on. I know I shall surprise Mrs. Jervis
with them; for she shan't see me till I am full dressed. John
is come back, and I'll soon send you some of what I have written.
I find he is going early in the morning; and so I'll close here
that I am *your most dutiful daughter.*

Don't lose your time in meeting me: because I am so uncertain. It is hard if I can't get a passage to you. But may-be
my master won't refuse to let John bring me. I can ride behind
him, I believe, well enough; for he is very careful, and very
honest; you know John as well as I; he loves you both. Besides,
may-be, Mrs. Jervis can put me in some way.

LETTER XXIV

DEAR FATHER AND MOTHER,

I shall write as long as I stay, though I shall have nothing
but silliness to write; for I know you divert yourselves on
nights with what I write, because it is mine. John tells me how
much you long for my coming; but he says, he told you he hoped
something would happen to hinder it.

I am glad you did not tell him the occasion of my coming
away; for *if* my fellow-servants should guess, it were better
so, than to have it from you or me; besides, I really am concerned
that my master should cast away a thought upon such a poor
creature as me; for, besides the disgrace, it has quite turned
his temper; and I begin to believe what Mrs. Jervis told me,
that he likes me, and can't help it; and yet strives to conquer
it, and so finds no way but to be cross to me.

Don't think me presumptuous and conceited; for it is more
my concern than my pride to see such a gentleman so demean
himself, and lesson the regard he used to have in the eyes of
all his servants, on my account.—But I am to tell you of my
new dress to-day.

And so when I had dined, up stairs I went, and locked myself
up in my little room. There I dressed myself in my new garb,
and put on my round-eared ordinary cap, but with a green knot,
my home-spun gown and petticoat, and plain leather shoes,

but yet they are what they call Spanish leather; and my ordinary hose, ordinary I mean to what I have been lately used to, though I should think good yarn may do very well for every day, when I come home. A plain muslin tucker I put on, and my black silk necklace, instead of the French necklace my lady gave me; and put the ear-rings out of my ears. When I was quite equipped, I took my straw hat in my hand, with its two blue strings, and looked in the glass, as proud as any thing. To say truth, I never liked myself so well in my life.

O the pleasure of descending with ease, innocence, and resignation!—Indeed there is nothing like it! An humble mind, I plainly see, cannot meet with any very shocking disappointment, let Fortune's wheel turn round as it will.

So I went down to look for Mrs. Jervis, to see how she liked me. I met, as I was upon the stairs, our Rachel, who is the housemaid; she made me a low curtsey, and I found did not know me. I smiled, and went to the housekeeper's parlour: there sat good Mrs. Jervis at work, making a shift: and, would you believe it? she did not know me at first; but rose up, pulled off her spectacles, and said, "Do you want *me* forsooth?" I could not help laughing, and said, "Hey-day! Mrs. Jervis, what, don't you know me? She stood all in amaze, and looked at me from top to toe: "Why, you surprise me," said she. "What, Pamela! thus metamorphosed! How came this about?"

As it happened, in stepped my master; and my back being to him, he thought it was a stranger speaking to Mrs. Jervis, and withdrew again; and did not hear her ask if his honour had any commands for her. She turned me about and about, and I shewed her all my dress, to my under petticoat; she said, sitting down, "Why, I am amazed! I must sit down. What can all this mean?" I told her I had no clothes suitable to my condition when I returned to my father's; and so it was better to begin here, as I was soon to go away, that all my fellow-servants might see I knew how to suit myself to the state I was returning to.

"Well," said she, "I never knew the like of thee. But this sad preparation for going away (for now I see you are quite in earnest) is what I know not how to get over. O my dear Pamela, how can I part with you?"

My master rung in the back-parlour, and so I withdrew, and Mrs. Jervis went to attend him. He said to her, "I was coming in to let you know that I shall go to Lincolnshire, and possibly to my sister Davers's, and be absent some weeks. But, pray, what pretty neat damsel was with you?" She says she smiled, and asked if his honour did not know who it was. "No," said he; "I never saw her before. Farmer Nichols, or farmer Brady, have neither of them such a tight prim lass for a daughter, have they?—Though I did not see her face, neither," said he. "If your honour won't be angry," said she, "I will introduce her into your presence; for I think she outdoes our Pamela."

Now, I did not thank her for this, as I told her afterwards (for it brought a great deal of trouble upon me as well as crosses, as you shall hear). "That can't be," he was pleased to say; "but if you can find an excuse for it, let her come in."

At that she stepped to me, and told me I must go in with her to my master; "But," said she, "for goodness' sake, let him find you out, for he don't know you."—"O fie, Mrs. Jervis," said I, "how could you serve me so? Besides, it looks too free both *in me*, and *to him*."—"I tell you," said she, "you *shall* come in; and pray don't reveal yourself till he finds you out."

So I went in, foolish as I was: though I must have been seen by him another time, if I had not then. And she would make me take my straw hat in my hand.

I dropt a low curtsey, but said never a word. I dare say he knew me as soon as he saw my face; but was as cunning as Lucifer. He came up to me, and took me by the hand, and said, "Whose pretty maiden are you? I dare say you are Pamela's sister, you are so like her. So neat, so clean, so pretty! Why, child, you far surpass your sister Pamela!"

I was all confusion, and would have spoken, but he took me about the neck: "Why," said he, "you are very pretty, child: I would not be so free with your *sister*, you may believe; but I must kiss *you*."—"O Sir," said I, "I am Pamela, indeed I am: indeed I am Pamela, *her own-self!*"

He kissed me for all I could do: and said, "Impossible! you are a lovelier girl by half than Pamela; and sure I may be innocently free with *you*, though I would not do her so much favour."

This was a sad trick upon me indeed, and what I could not expect; and Mrs. Jervis looked like a fool as much as I, for her officiousness. At last I got away, and ran out of the parlour, most sadly vexed, as you may well think.

He talked a good deal to Mrs. Jervis, and at last ordered me to come in to him. "Come in," said he, "you little villain!" for so he called me. Good Sirs, what a name was there! "Who

43

is it you put your tricks upon? I was resolved never to honour your unworthiness," said he, " with so much notice again; and so you must disguise yourself to attract me, and yet pretend, like an hypocrite as you are——"

I was out of patience then : " Hold, good Sir," said I; " don't impute disguise and hypocrisy to me, above all things : for I hate them both, mean as I am. I have put on no disguise."— " What a plague," said he, for that was his word, " do you mean then by this dress?"—" Why, and please your honour," said I, " I mean one of the honestest things in the world. I have been in disguise, indeed, ever since my good lady your mother took me from my poor parents. I came to her ladyship so poor and mean, that these clothes I have on are a princely suit to those I had then : and her goodness heaped upon me rich clothes, and other bounties : and as I am now returning to my poor parents again so soon, I cannot wear those good things without being hooted at : and so have bought what will be more suitable to my degree, and be a good holiday-suit too, when I get home."

He then took me in his arms, and presently pushed me from him. " Mrs. Jervis," said he, " take the little witch from me; I can neither bear nor forbear her !"—Strange words these !— " But stay; you shan't go !—Yet begone !—No, come back again."

I thought he was mad; for he knew not what he would have. I was going, however, but he stept after me, and took hold of my arm, and brought me in again : I am sure he made my arm black and blue, for the marks are upon it still. " Sir, Sir," said I, " pray have mercy; I will, I will come in !"

He sat down, and looked at me, and, as I thought afterwards, as sillily as such a poor girl as I. At last he said, " Well, Mrs. Jervis, as I was telling you, you may permit her to stay a little longer, till I see if my sister Davers will have her; if, meantime, she humble herself, and ask this as a favour, and is sorry for her pertness, and the liberty she has taken with my character, in and out of the house."—" Your honour told me so," said Mrs. Jervis : " but I never found her inclinable to think herself in a fault."—" Pride and perverseness," said he, " with a vengeance ! Yet this is your doating-piece ! Well, for once, I'll submit myself to tell you, hussy," said he to me, " you may stay a fortnight longer, till I see my sister Davers : do you hear what I say to you, statue? Can you neither speak nor be thankful?"—" Your honour frights me so," said I, " that I can hardly speak : but I will venture to say, that I have only

to beg, as a favour, that I may go to my father and mother."—
"Why, fool," said he, "won't you like to go to wait on my
sister Davers?"—"Sir," said I, "I was once fond of that
honour: but you were pleased to say, I might be in danger
from her ladyship's nephew, or he from me."—"D—d impertinence!" said he; "do you hear, Mrs. Jervis; do you hear how
she retorts upon me? Was ever such matchless assurance?"

I then fell a weeping; for Mrs. Jervis said, "Fie, Pamela,
fie." And I said, "My lot is very hard indeed. I am sure I
would hurt nobody; and I have been, it seems, guilty of indis-
cretions, which have cost me my place, and my master's favour,
and so have been turned away; and when the time is come,
that I should return to my poor parents, I am not suffered to
go quietly. Good your honour, and what have I done, that I
should be used worse than if I had robbed you?"—"Robbed
me!" said he, "why so you have, hussy; you *have* robbed
me."—"Who, I, Sir?" said I; "have I robbed you? Why
then you are a justice of peace, and may send me to gaol, if
you please, and bring me to a trial for my life! If you can
prove that I have robbed you, I am sure I ought to die."

Now, I was quite ignorant of his meaning; though I did not
like it, when it was afterwards explained, neither: "And, well,"
thought I, "what will this come to at last, if poor Pamela is
esteemed a thief!" Then I thought in an instant, how I
should shew my face to my honest poor parents, if I was but
suspected.

"But, Sir," said I, "let me ask you but one question, and
pray don't let me be called names for it; for I don't mean
disrespectfully: why, if I have done amiss, am I not left to be
discharged by your housekeeper, as the other maids have been?
And if Jane, or Rachel, or Hannah, were to offend, would your
honour stoop to take notice of them? And why should you so
demean yourself to take notice of me? Pray, Sir, if I have
not been worse than others, why should I suffer more than
others? Why should I not be turned away, and there's an end
of it? For indeed I am not of consequence enough for my
master to concern himself, and be angry about such a creature
as me."

"Do you hear, Mrs. Jervis," cried he again, "how pertly I
am interrogated by this saucy slut? Why, sauce-box," says
he, "did not my good mother desire me to take care of you?
And have you not been always distinguished by me above a
common servant? And does your ingratitude upbraid me for
this?"

45

I said something mutteringly, and he vowed he would hear it. I begged excuse, but he insisted upon it. " Why, then," said I, " if your honour must know, I said, that my good lady did not desire your care to extend to the *summer-house* and her *dressing-room.*"

Well, this was a little saucy, you'll say—And he flew into such a passion, that I was forced to run for it; and Mrs. Jervis said it was happy I got out of the way.

Why, what makes him provoke one so, then? I'm almost sorry for it; but I would be glad to get away at any rate. For I begin to be more fearful now.

Just now Mr. Jonathan sent me these lines—— (Bless me! what shall I do?)

" DEAR MRS. PAMELA,
       " Take care of yourself; for Rachel heard my master say to Mrs. Jervis, who, she believes, was pleading for you,— ' Say no more, Mrs. Jervis, for, by G—, I will have her.' Burn this instantly."

O pray for your poor daughter. I am called to go to bed by Mrs. Jervis, for it is past eleven, and I am sure she shall hear of it; for all this is owing to her, though she did not mean any harm. But I have been, and am, in a strange fluster; and I suppose, too, she'll say I have been full pert.

O my dear father and mother, power and riches never want advocates! But, poor gentlewoman, she cannot live without him : and he has been very good to her. So good-night. May-be I shall send this in the morning; but may-be not; so won't conclude, though I can't say too often, that I am (though with great apprehension) *your most dutiful daughter.*

LETTER XXV

MY DEAR PARENTS,
       O let me take up my complaint, and say, " Never was poor creature so unhappy, and so barbarously used as poor Pamela." Indeed, my dear father and mother, my heart's just broke ! I can neither write as I should, nor let it alone : to whom but you can I vent my griefs, and keep my poor heart from bursting? Wicked, wicked man !—I have no patience when I think of him !—But yet, don't be frighted, for I hope I am honest !—If my head and my hand will let me you shall

hear all. Is there no constable or head-borough, to take me out of his house? I am sure I can safely swear the peace against him: but, alas! he is greater than any constable: he is a justice: from such a justice deliver me!—But God Almighty, I hope, in time will right me; for he knows the innocence of my heart!

John went your way in the morning; but I have been too much distracted to send by him; and have seen nobody but Mrs. Jervis, or Rachel, and one I hate to see or be seen by; and indeed I hate now to see any body. Strange things I have to tell you, that happened since last night, that good Mr. Jonathan's letter, and my master's harshness, put me in such a fluster; but I will not keep you in suspense.

I went to Mrs. Jervis's chamber; and, O dreadful! my wicked master hid himself, base man as he is, in her closet, where she has a few books, a chest of drawers, and such like. I little suspected it; though I used, till this night, always to look into that closet, and another in the room, also under the bed, ever since the summer-house trick, but never found any thing; therefore I did not do it then, being resolved to be angry with Mrs. Jervis for what had happened in the day, so thought of nothing else.

I sat myself down on one side of the bed, and she on the other; we began to undress ourselves; but she on that side next the wicked closet that held the worst heart in the world. "So," said Mrs. Jervis, "you won't speak to me, Pamela! I find you are angry with me."—"Why, Mrs. Jervis," said I, "I am a little; 'tis a folly to deny it. You see what I have suffered by your forcing me in to my master: a woman of your years and experience must needs know, that it was not fit for me to pretend to be any body else for my own sake, nor with regard to my master."

"But," said she, "who would have thought it would have turned out so?"—"Aye," said I, little thinking who heard me, "Lucifer always is ready to promote his own work and workmen. You see what use he makes of it, pretending not to know me, on purpose to be free with me. And when he took upon himself to know me, to quarrel with me, and use me hardly: and you too," said I, "to cry, 'Fie, fie, Pamela!' cut me to the heart."

"Do you think, my dear," said she, "that I would encourage him? I never said so to you before; but since you forced it from me, I must tell you, that ever since you consulted me, I have used my utmost endeavours to divert him from his wicked

47

purposes; and he has promised fair; but, to say all in a word, he doats upon you; and I begin to see it is not in his power to help it."

I luckily said nothing of the note from Mr. Jonathan: I began to suspect all the world: but I said, to try Mrs. Jervis, "Well, then, what would you have me do? You see he is for having me wait on Lady Davers now."

"Why, I'll tell you freely, my dear Pamela," said she, "and I trust to your discretion to conceal what I say: my master has been often desiring me to put you upon asking him to let you stay——"

"Yes," said I, "Mrs. Jervis, let me interrupt you; I will tell you why I could not think of that: it was not the pride of my *heart*; but the pride of my *honesty*; for what must have been the case? Here my master has been very rude to me, once and twice: and you say he cannot help it, and is sorry for it: he has given me warning to leave my place, and uses me very harshly; perhaps, to frighten me to his purposes, as he supposes I would be fond of staying (as indeed I should, if I could be safe; for I love you and all the house, and value him, if he would act as my master). Well, then, as I know his designs, and that he owns he cannot help it, must I have asked to stay, knowing he would attempt me again? For all you could assure me of was, he would do nothing by *force*; so I, a poor weak girl, was to be left to my own strength! Was not this to *allow* him to tempt me, as one may say? and to encourage him to go on in his wicked devices!—How, then, Mrs. Jervis, could I ask or wish to stay?"

"You say well, my dear child," says she; "and you have a justness of thought above your years, and for all these considerations, and for what I have heard this day, after you ran away, (and I am glad you went as you did,) I cannot persuade you to stay; I should be glad (which is what I never thought I could have said) that you were well at your father's; for if Lady Davers will entertain you, she may as well have you from thence as here."—"There's my good Mrs. Jervis!" said I; "God will bless you for your good counsel to a poor maiden, that is hard beset. But pray, what did he say, when I was gone?"—"Why," says she, "he was very angry with you,"—"But he would hear it!" said I; "I think it was a little bold; but then he provoked me to it. And had not my honesty been in the case, I would not by any means have been so saucy. Besides, Mrs. Jervis, consider it was the truth; if he does not love to hear of the *summer-house* and the *dressing-room*, why

48

should he not be ashamed to continue in the same mind?"—
"But," said she, "when you had muttered this to yourself,
you might have told him any thing else."—"Well," said I,
"I cannot tell a wilful lie, and so there's an end of it. But I
find you now give him up, and think there's danger in staying.
Lord bless me! I wish I was well out of the house; so it
was at the bottom of a wet ditch, on the wildest common in
England."

"Why," says she, "it signifies nothing to tell you all he said;
but it was enough to make me fear you would not be as safe as
I could wish: and, upon my word, Pamela, I don't wonder
he loves you; for, without flattery, you are a charming girl!
I never saw you look more lovely in my life than in that new
dress of yours. And then it was such a surprise upon us all!
I believe truly you owe some of your danger to the lovely
appearance you made."—"Then," said I, "I wish the clothes
in the fire: I expected *no* effect from them; but if *any*, a quite
contrary one.

"Hush!" said I, "Mrs. Jervis, did you not hear something
stir in the closet?"—"No, silly girl," said she; "your fears
are always awake."—"But," said I, "I think I heard something
rustle."—"May-be," says she, "the cat may be got there;
but I hear nothing."

I was hush; but she said, "Pr'ythee, my good girl, make haste
to bed. See if the door be fast." I did, and was thinking to
look into the closet; but, hearing no more noise, thought it needless, and so went again and sat myself down on the bed-side,
and went on undressing myself. And Mrs. Jervis, being by this
time undressed, stepped into bed, and bid me hasten, for she
was sleepy.

I don't know what was the matter, but my heart sadly misgave me: indeed, Mr. Jonathan's note was enough to make
it do so, with what Mrs. Jervis had said. I pulled off my stays,
and my stockings, and all my clothes to an under-petticoat;
then hearing a rustling again in the closet, "Heaven protect
us! But before I say my prayers I must look into this closet."
And so was going to it slip-shod, when, O dreadful! out rushed
my master in a rich silk and silver morning-gown.

I screamed, ran to the bed, and Mrs. Jervis screamed too; he
said, "I'll do you no harm if you forbear this noise; but otherwise take what follows."

Instantly he came to the bed (for I had crept into it, to Mrs.
Jervis, with my coat on and my shoes), and taking me in his arms,
said, "Mrs. Jervis, rise, and just step up stairs, to keep the

49

maids from coming down at this noise : I'll do no harm to this rebel."

"O for Heaven's sake ! for pity's sake ! Mrs. Jervis," said I, "if I am not betrayed, don't leave me ; and, I beseech you raise all the house."—"No," said Mrs. Jervis, "I will not stir, my dear lamb ; I will not leave you. I wonder at you, Sir," said she ; and kindly threw herself upon my coat, clasping me round the waist. "You shall not hurt this innocent," said she ; "for I will lose my life in her defence. Are there not," said she, "enough wicked ones in the world, for your base purpose, but you must attempt such a lamb as this ? "

He was desperate angry, and threatened to throw her out of the window ; and turn her out of the house the next morning. "You need not, Sir," said she ; "for I will not stay in it. God defend my poor Pamela till to-morrow, and we will both go together."—Says he, "Let me but expostulate a word or two with you, Pamela."—"Pray, Pamela," said Mrs. Jervis, "don't hear a word, except he leaves the bed, and goes to the other end of the room."—"Aye, out of the room," said I, "expostulate to-morrow, if you must expostulate ! "

I found his hand in my bosom, and when my fright let me know it, I was ready to die ; I sighed, screamed and fainted away. And still he had his arms about my neck ; Mrs. Jervis was about my feet, and upon my coat. And all in a cold dewy sweat was I. "Pamela ! Pamela ! " says Mrs. Jervis, as she tells me since, "—Oh ! " and gave another shriek, "my poor Pamela is dead for certain ! " And so I was for a time ; for I knew nothing more of the matter, one fit followed another, till about three hours after, I found myself in bed, and Mrs. Jervis sitting up on one side, with her wrapper about her, and Rachel on the other ; but no master, for the wicked wretch was gone. I was so overjoyed that I hardly could believe myself ; I said, which were my first words, "Mrs. Jervis—Mrs. Rachel, can I be *sure* it is you ? Tell me, can I ?—Where have I been ? " —"Hush, my dear," said Mrs. Jervis ; "you have been in fit after fit. I never saw any body so frightful in my life ! "

By this I judged Rachel knew nothing of the matter ; and it seems my wicked master had, upon Mrs. Jervis's second noise on my fainting away, slipped out ; and, as if he had come from his own chamber, disturbed by the screaming, went up to the maids' room (who, hearing the noise, lay trembling, afraid to stir), bid them go down and see what was the matter with Mrs. Jervis, and me. He charged Mrs. Jervis, and promised to forgive her for what she had said and done, if she would conceal the matter. So the maids came down; and all went up again, when I came to myself a little, except Rachel, who staid to sit up with me, and bear Mrs. Jervis company. I believe they all guess the matter to be bad enough; though they dare not say any thing.

When I think of my danger, and the freedoms he actually took, though I believe Mrs. Jervis saved me from worse, and she says she did, (though what can I think, who was in a fit and knew nothing of the matter?) I am almost distracted.

At first I was afraid of Mrs. Jervis, but I am fully satisfied she is very good, and I should have been lost but for her; she takes on grievously about it. What would have become of me, had she gone out of the room, to still the maids, as he bid her? He'd certainly have shut her out; then, mercy on me! what would have become of your poor Pamela?

I must leave off a little; for my eyes and my head are sadly bad. This was a dreadful trial! This was the worst of all! Oh! that I was out of the power of this dreadfully wicked man! Pray for *your distressed daughter.*

LETTER XXVI

MY DEAR FATHER AND MOTHER,

I did not rise till ten o'clock, and I had all the concerns and wishes of the family, and multitudes of enquiries about me. My wicked master went out early to hunt! but left word that he would be in to breakfast. And so he was. He came up to our chamber about eleven, and had nothing to do to be sorry, for he was our *master*, and so put on sharp anger at first. I had great emotions at his entering the room, and threw my apron over my head, and fell a crying, as if my heart would break.

"Mrs. Jervis," said he, "since I know *you*, and you *me* so well, I don't know how we shall live together for the future."—"Sir," said she, "I will take the liberty to say, what I think is best for both. I have so much grief, that you should attempt to do any injury to this poor girl, and especially in my chamber, that I should think myself accessory to the mischief, if I was not to take notice of it. Though my ruin may depend upon it, I desire not to stay; but pray let poor Pamela and me go together."—"With all my heart," said he, "and the sooner the better." She fell a crying. "I find," says he, "this girl has

made a party of the whole house in her favour against me."—
" Her innocence deserves it of us all," said she very kindly :
" and I never could have thought that the son of my dear good
lady departed, could have so forfeited his honour, as to endeavour
to destroy a virtue he ought to protect."—" No more of this,
Mrs. Jervis ! " said he ; " I will not bear it. As for Pamela,
she has a lucky knack of falling into fits when she pleases. But
the cursed yellings of you both made me not myself. I intended
no harm to her, as I told you both, if you'd have left your
squallings : and I did no harm neither, but to myself ; for I
raised a hornet's nest about my ears, that, as far as I know,
may have stung to death my reputation."—" Sir," said Mrs.
Jervis, " then I beg Mr. Longman may take my accounts,
and I will go away as soon as I can. As for Pamela, she
is at her liberty, I hope, to go away next Thursday, as she
intends ? "

I sat still ; for I could not speak nor look up, and his presence
discomposed me extremely ; but I was sorry to hear myself
the unhappy occasion of Mrs. Jervis's losing her place, and hope
it may still be made up.

" Well," said he, " let Mr. Longman make up your accounts
as soon as you will ; and Mrs. Jewkes " (who is his housekeeper
in Lincolnshire) " shall come hither in your place, and won't
be less obliging, I dare say, than *you* have been." She said, " I
have never disobliged you till now ; and let me tell you, Sir, if
you knew what belonged to your own reputation or honour——"
—" No more, no more," said he, " of these antiquated topics.
I have been a friend to you ; I shall always esteem you, though
you have not been so faithful to my secrets as I could have
wished, and have laid me open to this girl, which has made
her more afraid of me than she had occasion."—" Well, Sir,"
said she, " after what passed yesterday, and last night, I think
I went rather too far in favour of your injunctions than otherwise ; I should have deserved every body's censure, as the basest
of creatures, had I been capable of contributing to your lawless
attempts."—" Still, Mrs. Jervis, still reflecting upon me, and
all for imaginary faults ! what harm have I done the girl ! I
won't bear it, I'll assure you. But yet, in respect to my mother,
I am willing to part friendly with you : though you ought both
to reflect on the freedom of your conversation, in relation to
me ; which I should have resented more than I do, but that I
am conscious I had no business to demean myself so as to be
in your closet, where I might have expected to hear much
impertinence between you."

" Well, Sir," said she, " you have no objection, I hope, to Pamela's going away on Thursday next ? "—" You are mighty solicitous," said he, " about Pamela : but no, not I ; let her go as soon as she will : she is a naughty girl, and has brought all this upon herself ; and upon me more trouble than she can have had from me : but I have overcome it all, and I will never concern myself about her."

" I have had a proposal made me," added he, " since I have been out this morning, that I shall go near to embrace ; and so wish only that a discreet use may be made of what is past ; and there's an end of every thing with me, as to Pamela, I'll assure you."

I clasped my hands together through my apron, overjoyed at this, though I was soon to go away : for, naughty as he has been to me, I wish his prosperity with all my heart, for my good old lady's sake.

" Well, Pamela," said he, " you need not now be afraid to speak to me ; tell me what you lifted up your hands at ? " I said not a word. Says he, " If you like what I have said, give me your hand upon it." I held my hand up through my apron ; for I could not speak to him ; and he took hold of it, and pressed it, though less hard than he did my arm the day before. " What does the little fool cover her face for ? " said he : " pull your apron away, and let me see how you look, after your freedom of speech of me last night. No wonder you're ashamed to see me. You know you were very free with my character."

I could not stand this barbarous insult, as I took it to be, considering his behaviour to me ; and I then spoke and said, " Oh ! the difference between the minds of thy creatures, good God ! How shall some he cast down in their innocence, while others can triumph in their guilt ! "

And so saying, I went up stairs to my chamber, and wrote all this ; for though he vexed me at his taunting, yet I was pleased to hear he was likely to be married, and that his wicked intentions were so happily overcome as to me ; and this made me a little easier. I hope I have passed the worst ; or else it is very hard. And yet I shan't think myself quite at ease, till I am with you : for, methinks, after all, his repentance and amendment are mighty suddenly resolved upon. But the Divine Grace is not confined to space ; and remorse may, and I hope has, smitten him to the heart at once, for his injuries to poor me ! Yet I won't be too secure neither.

Having opportunity, I send now what I know will grieve you

53

to the heart. But I hope I shall bring my next scribble myself; and so conclude, though half broken-hearted, *your ever dutiful daughter.*

LETTER XXVII

DEAR FATHER AND MOTHER,

I am glad I desired you not to meet me, and John says you won't; for he told you, he is sure I should get a passage well enough, either behind some of my fellow-servants on horseback, or by Farmer Nichols's means; but as to the chariot he talked to you of, I can't expect that favour, to be sure; and I should not care for it, because it would look so much above me. But Farmer Brady, they say, has a chaise with one horse, and we hope to borrow that, or hire it rather than fail; though money runs a little lowish, after what I have laid out; but I don't care to say so here; though I warrant I might have what I would of Mrs. Jervis, or Mr. Jonathan, or Mr. Longman; but then how shall I pay it, you'll say: and besides, I don't like to be beholden.

But the chief reason I'm glad you don't set out to meet me, is the uncertainty; for it seems I must stay another week still, and hope certainly to go Thursday after. For poor Mrs. Jervis will go at the same time, she says, and can't be ready before.

Oh! that I was once well with you!—though he is very civil to me at present, and not so cross as he was; and yet he is as vexatious another way, as you shall hear. For yesterday he had a rich suit of clothes brought home, which they call a birthday suit; for he intends to go to London against next birth-day, to see the court, and our folks will have it he is to be made a lord. I wish they may make him an honest man, as he was always thought; but I have not found it so, alas for me!

And so, as I was saying, he had these clothes come home, and he tried them on. And before he pulled them off, he sent for me, when nobody else was in the parlour with him: "Pamela," said he, " you are so neat and so nice in your own dress " (Alack-a-day, I didn't know I was!) " that you must be a judge of ours. How are these clothes made? Do they fit me? "—" I am no judge," said I, " and please your honour; but I think they look very fine."

His waistcoat stood on end with silver lace, and he looked very grand. But what he did last has made me very serious, and I could make him no compliments. Said he, " Why don't you wear your usual clothes?—Though I think every thing looks well upon you:" (for I still continue in my new dress,) I said, "I have no clothes, Sir, I ought to call my own, but these: and it is no matter what such a one as I wears." Said he, "Why, you look very serious, Pamela. I see you can bear malice." —"Yes, so I can, Sir," said I, "according to the occasion!" —"Why," said he, "your eyes always look red, I think. Are you not a fool to take my last freedom so much to heart? I am sure you and that fool Mrs. Jervis, frightened me by your hideous squalling, as much as I could frighten you."— "That is all we had for it," said I; "and if you could be so afraid of your own servants knowing of your attempts upon a poor unworthy creature, that is under your protection while I stay, surely your honour ought to be more afraid of God Almighty, in whose presence we all stand, in every action of our lives, and to whom the greatest, as well as the least, must be account-able, let them think what they will."

He took my hand in a kind of good-humoured mockery, and said, "Well urged, my pretty preacher! When my Lincolnshire chaplain dies, I'll put thee on a gown and cassock, and thou'lt make a good figure in his place."—"I wish," said I, a little vexed at his jeer, "your honour's conscience would be your preacher, and then you would need no other chaplain."—"Well, well, Pamela," said he, "no more of this unfashionable jargon. I did not send for you so much for your opinion of my new suit, as to tell you, you are welcome to stay, since Mrs. Jervis desires it, till she goes."—"I welcome!" said I; "I shall rejoice when I am out of the house!"

"Well," said he, "you are an ungrateful baggage; but I am thinking it would be a pity, with these fair soft hands, and that lovely skin" (as he called it, and took hold of my hand), "that you should return again to hard work, as you must, if you go to your father's; and so I would advise her to take a house in London, and let lodgings to us members of Parliament, when we come to town; and such a pretty daughter as you may pass for, will always fill her house, and she'll get a great deal of money."

I was sadly vexed at his barbarous joke; but being ready to cry before, the tears gushed out, and (endeavouring to get my hand from him, but in vain,) I said, "I can expect no better: your behaviour, Sir, to me, has been just of a piece with these words: nay, I will say't, though you were to be ever so angry." —"I angry, Pamela! No, no," said he, "I have overcome all that; and as you are to go away, I look upon you now as Mrs.

55

Jervis's guest while you both stay, and not as my servant; and so you may say what you will. But, I'll tell you, Pamela, why you need not take this matter in such high disdain! You have a pretty romantic turn for virtue, and all that. And I don't suppose but you'll hold it still, and nobody will be able to prevail upon you. But, my girl" (fleeringly he spoke it), "do but consider what a fine opportunity you will then have, for a tale every day to good mother Jervis, and what subjects for letter-writing to your father and mother, and what pretty preachments you may hold forth to the young gentlemen. Ad's my heart! I think it would be the best thing you and she could do."

"You do well, Sir," said I, "to even your wit to such a poor girl as me; but, permit me to say, that if you were not rich and great, and I poor and little, you would not insult me thus. Let me ask you, Sir, if you think this becomes your fine clothes, and a master's station?"—"Why so serious, my pretty Pamela?" said he: "why so grave?" And would kiss me; but my heart was full, and I said, "Let me alone; I *will* tell you, if you were a king, and insulted me as you have done, that you have forgot to act like a gentleman; and I won't stay to be used thus: I will go to the next farmer's, and there wait for Mrs. Jervis, if she must go: I'd have you know, Sir, that I can stoop to the ordinariest work of your scullions, for all these nasty soft hands, sooner than hear such ungentlemanly imputations."

"I sent for you," said he, "in good humour; but 'tis impossible to hold it with such impertinence: however, I'll keep my temper. But while I see you here, pray don't put on those dismal grave looks: why, girl, you should forbear them, if it were but for your pride-sake; for the family will think you are grieving to leave the house."—"Then, Sir," said I, "I'll try to convince them of the contrary, as well as your honour; for I will endeavour to be more cheerful while I stay, for that very reason."

"Well," replied he, "I will set this down by itself, as the first time that ever what I had advised had any weight with you." —"And I will add," said I, "as the first advice you have given me of late, that was fit to be followed."—"I wish," said he, (I'm almost ashamed to write it, impudent gentleman as he is!) "I wish I had thee as *quick another way*, as thou art in thy repartees." And he laughed, and I snatched my hand from him, and I tripped away as fast as I could. Ah! thought I, married! I'm sure 'tis time you were married, or at this rate no honest maiden ought to live with you.

Why, dear father and mother, to be sure he grows quite a rake! How easy it is to go from bad to worse, when once people give way to vice!

How would my poor lady, had she lived, have grieved to see it! But may-be he would have been better *then!* Though it seems he told Mrs. Jervis he had an eye upon me in his mother's life-time: and he intended to let me know as much by-the-bye, he told her!—Here's shamelessness for you! Sure the world must be near at an end; for all the gentlemen here are as bad as he, as far as I can hear! And see the fruits of such bad examples! There is 'Squire Martin, in the Grove, has had three lyings-in, it seems, in his house, in three months past; one by himself, one by his coachman, and one by his woodman, yet he has turned none of them away. Indeed, how can he, when they but follow his own vile example?—There is he, and two or three more such as he, within ten miles of us; who keep company, and hunt with our fine master, truly; and I suppose he's never the better for their examples. But, Heaven bless me, say I, and send me out of this wicked house.

But, dear father and mother, what sort of creatures must the women-kind be, do you think, to give way to such wickedness? Why, this it is that makes every one to be thought of alike: and, a-lack-a-day! what a world we live in! for it is grown more a wonder that the men are *resisted,* than that the women *comply.* This, I suppose, makes me such a Sauce-box, and Bold-face, and a creature; and all because I won't be a Sauce-box and Bold-face indeed.

But I am sorry for these things; one don't know what arts and stratagems men may devise to gain their vile ends; and so I will think as well as I can of these poor undone creatures, and pity them. For you see, by my sad story, and narrow escapes, what hardships poor maidens go through whose lot it is to go out to service, especially to houses where there is not the fear of God, and good rule kept by the heads of the family.

You see I am quite grown grave and serious; indeed it becomes the present condition of *your dutiful daughter.*

LETTER XXVIII

DEAR FATHER AND MOTHER,

John says you wept when you read my last letter, that he carried. I am sorry you let him see that; for they all mistrust already how matters are; and, as it is no credit that I have been *attempted*, though it is that I have *resisted*; yet I am sorry they have cause to think so evil of my master from any of us.

Mrs. Jervis has made up her accounts with Mr. Longman, and will stay in her place. I am glad of it for her own sake, and for my master's; for she has a good master of him: so indeed all have, but poor me; and he has a good housekeeper in her.

Mr. Longman, it seems, took upon him to talk to my master, how faithful and careful of his interests she was, and how exact in her accounts; and he told him there was no comparison between her accounts and Mrs. Jewkes's, at the Lincolnshire estate.

He said so many fine things, it seems, of Mrs. Jervis, that my master sent for her in Mr. Longman's presence, and said Pamela might come along with her; I suppose to mortify me, that I must go, while she was to stay: but as, when I go away, I am not to go with her, nor was she to go with me; so it did not matter much; only it would have been creditable to such a poor girl that the housekeeper would bear me company, if I went.

Said he to her, "Well, Mrs. Jervis, Longman says you have made up your accounts with him, with your usual fidelity and exactness. I had a good mind to make you an offer of continuing with me, if you can be a little sorry for your hasty words, which, indeed, were not so respectful as I have deserved at your hands." She seemed at a sad loss what to say, because Mr. Longman was there, and she could not speak of the occasion of those words, which was *me*.

"Indeed," said Mr. Longman, "I must needs say, before your face, that since I have known my master's family, I have never found such good management in it, nor so much love and harmony. I wish the Lincolnshire estate was as well served!" —"No more of that," said my master: "but Mrs. Jervis may stay, if she will: and here, Mrs. Jervis, pray accept of this, which, at the close of every year's accounts, I will present you with, besides your salary, as long as I find your care so useful and agreeable." He gave her five guineas.—She made him a low curtsey, and thanking him, looked to me, as if she would have spoken to me.

He took her meaning, I believe; for he said, "Indeed, I love to encourage merit and obligingness, Longman: but I can never be equally kind to those who don't deserve it at my hands, as to those who do;" and then he looked full at me. "Longman," continued he, "I said that the girl might come in with Mrs. Jervis, because they love to be always together. For Mrs. Jervis is very good to her, and loves her as well as if she was her daughter. But else——" Mr. Longman, interrupting him, said, "*Good* to Mrs. Pamela! Ay, Sir, and so she is to be sure! But every body must be good to her; for——"

He was going on, but my master said, "No more, no more, Mr. Longman. I see old men are taken with pretty young girls, as well as other folks; and fair looks hide many a fault, where a person has the art to behave obligingly."—"Why, and please your honour," said Mr. Longman; "every body——" and was going on, I believe, to say something more in my praise; but he interrupted him, and said, "Not a word more of this Pamela; I can't let her stay, I'll assure you, not only for her own freedom of speech, but her letter-writing of all the secrets of my family."—"Ay," said the good old man: "I'm sorry for that too!—But, Sir——" —"No more, I say," said my master; "for my reputation's so well known" (mighty fine! thought I,) "that I care not what anybody writes or says of *me*; but to tell you the truth (not that it need go any further), I think of changing my condition soon; and, you know, young ladies of birth and fortune will choose their own servants, and that's my chief reason why Pamela can't stay. As for the rest," said he, "the girl is a good sort of body, take her altogether; though I must say, a little pert, since my mother's death, in her answers, and gives me two words for one, which I can't bear; nor is there reason I should, you know, Longman."—"No, to be sure, Sir," said he; "but 'tis strange she should be so mild and meek to every one of us in the house, and forget herself so where she should shew most respect!"—"Very true, Mr. Longman," said he; "but so it is, I'll assure you; and it was from her pertness, that Mrs. Jervis and I had the words: and I should mind it the less, but that the girl (there she stands, I say it to her face,) has wit and sense above her years, and knows better."

I was in great pain to say something, but yet I knew not what, before Mr. Longman; and Mrs. Jervis looked at me, and walked to the window to hide her concern for me. At last, I said, "It is for you, Sir, to say what you please; and for *me* only to say, God bless your honour!"

Poor Mr. Longman faltered in his speech, and was ready to cry. Said my insulting master to me, "Why, pr'ythee, Pamela, now shew thyself as thou art, before Longman. Canst not give him a specimen of that pertness which thou hast exercised upon me sometimes?" Did he not, my dear father and mother, deserve all the truth to be told? Yet I overcame myself so far as to say, "Your honour may play upon a poor girl, that you know *can* answer you, but *dare* not."

"Why, pr'ythee now, insinuator," said he, "say the worst you *can* before Longman and Mrs. Jervis. I challenge the utmost of thy impertinence; and, as you are going away, and have the love of every body, I would be a little justified to my family, that you have no reason to complain of hardships from me, as I have of pert saucy answers from you, besides exposing me by your letters."

"Surely, Sir," said I, "I am of no consequence equal to this, in your honour's family, that such a great gentleman as you should need to justify yourself about me. I am glad Mrs. Jervis stays with your honour; and I know I have *not deserved* to stay; and, more than that, I don't *desire* to stay."

"Ads-bobbers," said Mr. Longman, and ran to me, "don't say so, don't say so, dear Mrs. Pamela! We all love you dearly; and pray down on your knees, and ask his honour pardon, and we will all become pleaders in a body, and I, and Mrs. Jervis too, at the head of it, to beg his honour's pardon, and to continue you, at least, till his honour marries."—"No, Mr. Longman," said I, "I cannot ask; nor will I stay, if I might. All I desire is, to return to my poor father and mother; though I love you all, I won't stay."—"O well-a-day, well-a-day!" said the good old man, "I did not expect this!—When I had got matters thus far, and had made all up for Mrs. Jervis, I was in hopes to have got a double holiday of joy for all the family in your pardon too."—"Well," said my master, "this is a little specimen of what I told you, Longman. You see there's a spirit you did not expect."

Mrs. Jervis told me, after, that she could stay no longer to hear me so hardly used; and must have spoken, had she staid, what would never have been forgiven her; so she went out. I looked after her, to go too; but my master said, "Come, Pamela, give another specimen, I desire you, to Longman: I am sure you must, if you will but *speak*."—"Well, Sir," said I, "since it seems your greatness wants to be justified by my lowness, and I have no desire you should suffer in the sight of your family, I will say, on my bended knees," (and so I kneeled down,) "that I have been a very faulty, and a very ungrateful creature, to the *best* of masters; I have been very perverse and saucy; and have deserved nothing at your hands, but to be

60

turned out of your family with shame and disgrace. I therefore have nothing to say for myself, but that I am not *worthy* to stay, and so cannot wish to stay, and will not stay : so God Almighty bless you—and you, Mr. Longman—and good Mrs. Jervis—and every living soul of the family ! and I will pray for you as long as I live."—And so I rose up, and was forced to lean upon my master's elbow-chair, or I should have sunk down.

The poor old man wept more than I, and said, " Ads-bobbers, was ever the like heard ! 'tis too much, too much, I can't bear it. As I hope to live, I am quite melted.—Dear Sir, forgive her, the poor thing prays for you : she prays for us all : she owns her fault ; yet *won't* be forgiven ! I profess I know not what to make of it."

My master himself, hardened wretch as he was, seemed a little moved, and took his handkerchief out of his pocket, and walked to the window. " What sort of a day is it ? " said he. And then getting a little more hard-heartedness, he said, " Well, you may be gone from my presence, thou strange medley of inconsistence ! but you shan't stay after your time in the house."—" Nay, pray, Sir, pray, Sir," said the good old man, " relent a little. Adsheartlikins, you young gentlemen are made of iron and steel, I think : I'm sure," said he, " my heart's turned into butter, and is running away at my eyes. I never felt the like before." Said my master with an imperious tone, " Get out of my presence, hussy ; I can't bear you in my sight." —" Sir," said I, " I am going as fast as I can."

But, indeed, my dear father and mother, my head was so giddy, and my limbs trembled so, that I was forced to go holding by the wainscot all the way with both my hands, and thought I should not have got to the door : but when I did, as I hoped this would be my last interview with this terrible hard-hearted master, I turned about, and made a low curtsey, and said, " God bless you, Sir !—God bless *you*, Mr. Longman ! " and I went into the lobby leading to the great hall, and dropt into the first chair ; for I could get no farther a good while.

I leave all these things to your reflection, my dear parents ; but I can write no more. My poor heart's almost broken. Indeed it is.—O when shall I get away ? Send me, good God, in safety, once more, to my poor father's peaceful cot ! and there the worst that can happen will be joy in perfection to what I now bear. O pity *your distressed daughter.*

LETTER XXIX

My dear Father and Mother,

I must write, though I shall come so soon : for now I have hardly any thing else to do. I have finished all that lay upon me, and only wait the good time of setting out. Mrs. Jervis said, I must be low in pocket for what I had laid out; and so would have presented me with two guineas of her five; but I could not take them of her, because, poor gentlewoman, she pays old debts for her children that were extravagant, and wants them herself. This was very good in her.

I am sorry I shall have but little to bring with me; but I know *you* won't, you are so good ! and I will work the harder when I come home, if I can get a little plain work or any thing to do. But all your neighbourhood is so poor, that I fear I shall want work, except may-be Dame Mumford help me to something from any good family she is acquainted with !

Here what a sad thing it is ! I have been brought up wrong, as matters stand. For, you know, my good lady, now in Heaven, loved singing and dancing; and, as she would have it I had a voice, she made me learn both; and often and often has she made me sing her an innocent song, and a good psalm too, and dance before her. And I must learn to flower and draw to, and to work fine-work with my needles; why all this too I have got pretty tolerably at my fingers' end, as they say; and she used to praise me, and was a good judge of such matters.

Well now, what is all this to the purpose, as things have turned out ?

Why, no more nor less, than that I am like the grasshopper in the fable, which I have read of in my lady's book, as follows : [1]

" As the ants were airing their provisions one winter, a hungry grasshopper (suppose it was poor me) begged charity of them. They told him, he should have wrought in summer, if he would not want in winter. 'Well,' says the grasshopper, ' but I was not idle, for I sung the whole season.'—' Then,' said they, ' you'll e'en do well to make a merry year of it, and dance in winter to the tune you sung in summer.' "

I shall make a fine figure with my singing and dancing when I come home ! I shall be unfit even for a *May-day* holiday; for these minuets, rigadoons, and French dances, that I have been practising, will make me but ill company for my milk-

---

[1] See the Æsop's Fables which have lately been selected and reformed from those of Sir R. L'Estrange, and the most eminent mythologists.

maid companions that are to be. I had better, as things are, have learned to wash, scour, brew, bake, and such like. But I hope, if I can't get work, and can meet with a place, to learn these soon, if any body will have the goodness to bear with me till I am able : for, notwithstanding what my master says, I hope I have an humble and teachable mind ; and, next to God's grace, that is all my comfort, for I shall think nothing too mean that is honest. It may be a little hard at first ; but woe to my proud heart if I find it so on trial ! I will make it bend to its condition, or break it.

I have read of a good bishop that was to be burnt for his religion : he tried how he could bear it, by putting his fingers into the lighted candle : so I, the other day, tried, when Rachel's back was turned, if I could not scour a pewter plate she had begun. I could do it by degrees ; it only blistered my hands in two places.

All the matter is, if I could get plain work enough, I need not spoil my fingers ; but if I can't, I hope to make my hands as red as a blood-pudding, and as hard as a beechen trencher to accommodate them to my condition. I must break off ; here's somebody coming.—'Tis only our Hannah, with a message from Mrs. Jervis.—But hold, here is somebody else.—It is only Rachel.

I am as much frighted as were the city mouse and country mouse, in the same book of fables, at every thing that stirs. I have a power of these things to entertain you with in winter evenings, when I come home. If I can but get work, with a little time for reading, I hope we shall be very happy, over our peat fires. What made me hint to you that I should bring but little with me, is this :

You must know, I did not intend to do, as I have this after-noon ; that is, I took all my clothes and linen, and divided them into three parcels, as I had before told Mrs. Jervis I intended to do ; and said, " It is now Monday, Mrs. Jervis ; I am to go away on Thursday morning by times : though I know you don't doubt my honesty, I beg you will look over my things, and let every one have what belongs to them ; for you know I am resolved to take with me only what I can properly call my own."

Said she (I did not know her drift then ; to be sure she meant well ; but I did not thank her for it, when I did know it), " Let your things be brought down into the green-room, and I will do anything you would have me."

" With all my heart," said I, " green-room, or any where ; but I think you might step up, and see 'em as they lie." However, I fetched 'em down, and laid them in three parcels, as before; when done, I went down to call her up to look at them.

Now, it seems she had prepared my master for this scene, unknown to me; and in this green-room was a closet, with a sash-door and a curtain before it; for there she puts her sweet-meats and such things. She did it, it seems, to turn his heart, knowing what I intended, as I suppose, that he should make me take the things; for, if he had, I should have made money of them, to help us when we got together; for I could never have appeared in them.

Well, as I was saying, he had got, unknown to me, into this closet; I suppose while I went to call Mrs. Jervis: and she since owned to me, it was at his desire, when she told him something of what I intended, or else she would not have done it: though I have reason to remember the last closet-work.

So I said, when she came up, " Here, Mrs. Jervis, is the first parcel: I will spread it all abroad. These are the things my good lady gave me. In the first place,"—and so I went on describing the clothes and linen my lady had given me, mingling blessings as I proceeded, for her goodness to me: when I had turned over that parcel, I said, " Well, so much for the first parcel, Mrs. Jervis; that was my lady's gifts.

" Now I come to the presents of my dear virtuous master: hey, you know, *closet* for that, Mrs. Jervis." She laughed and said, " I never saw such a comical girl in my life: but go on." —" I will, Mrs. Jervis," said I, " as soon as I have opened the bundle; " for I was as brisk and as pert as could be, little thinking who heard me.

" Now here," said I, " are my ever-worthy master's presents; " and then I particularised all those in the second bundle. After which I turned to my own, and said—

" Now comes poor Pamela's bundle: and a little one it is to the others. First, here is a calico night-gown, that I used to wear o' mornings. 'Twill be rather too good for me when I get home; but I must have something. Then, there is a quilted calimanco coat, a pair of stockings I bought of the pedlar, my straw hat with blue strings; and a remnant of Scotch cloth, which will make two shirts and two shifts, the same I have on, for my poor father and mother. And here are four other shifts, one the fellow to that I have on; another pretty good one, and the other two old fine ones, that will serve me to turn and wind with at home, for they are not worth leaving behind me; and here are two pair of shoes; I have taken the lace off, which I will burn, and may-be will fetch me some little matter at a pinch, with an old silver buckle or two.

"What do you laugh for, Mrs. Jervis?" said I. "Why, you are like an April day; you cry and laugh in a breath.

"Well, let me see: here's a cotton handkerchief I bought of the pedlar; there should be another somewhere. O here it is; and here are my new-bought knit mittens; this is my new flannel coat, the fellow to that I have on: and in this parcel, pinned together, are several pieces of printed calico, remnants of silk, and such-like, that, if good luck should happen, and I should get work, would serve for robings and facings, and such-like uses. Here too are a pair of pockets; they are too fine for me; but I have no worse. Bless me, I did not think I had so many good things.

"Well, Mrs. Jervis," said I, "you have seen all my store, and I will now sit down, and tell you a piece of my mind."

"Be brief, then," said she, "my good girl;" for she was afraid, she said afterwards, that I should say too much.

"Why then the case is this: I am to enter upon a point of equity and conscience, Mrs. Jervis; and I must beg, if you love me, you'd let me have my own way. Those things there of my lady's, I can have no claim to, so as to take them away; for she gave them me, supposing I was to wear them in her service, and to do credit to her bountiful heart. But, since I am to be turned away, you know, I cannot wear them at my poor father's; for I should bring all the little village upon my back; and so I resolve not to have *them*.

"Then, Mrs. Jervis," said I, "I have far less right to these of my worthy master's: for you see what was his intention in giving them to me. So they were to be the price of my shame; and if I *could* make use of them, I should think I should never prosper with them; and besides you know, Mrs. Jervis, if I would not do the good gentleman's work, why should I take his wages? So in conscience, in honour, in every thing, I have nothing to say to thee, thou *second wicked* bundle !

"But," said I, "come to my arms, my dear *third* parcel, the companion of my poverty, and the witness of my honesty; and may I never deserve the least rag that is contained in thee, when I forfeit a title to that innocence, that I hope will ever be the pride of my life; and I am sure it will be my highest comfort at my death, when all the riches and pomps of the world will be worse than the vilest rags that can be worn by beggars !" And so I hugged my *third* bundle. "But," said I, "Mrs.

Jervis," (and she wept to hear me,) "one thing more I have to trouble you with, and that's all.

" There are four guineas, you know, that came out of my good lady's pocket, when she died, that, with some silver, my master gave me : now these four guineas I sent to my poor father and mother, and they have broken them; but would make them up, if I would : and if you think it should be so, it shall. But pray tell me honestly your mind; as to the three years before my lady's death, do you think, as I had no wages, I may be supposed to be quits?—By quits I cannot mean that my poor services should be equal to my lady's goodness; for that's impossible. But as all her learning and education of me, as matters have turned, will be of little service to me now : it had been better to have been brought up to hard labour, for that I must turn to at last, if I can't get a place, (and you know, in places too, one is subject to such temptations as are dreadful,) I say, by quits, as I return all the good things she gave me, whether I may not set my little services against my keeping; because my learning is not now in the question, and I am sure my dear good lady would have thought so, had she lived; but that is now out of the question. Well then, if so, I would ask, whether in above this year that I have lived with my master, as I am resolved to leave all his gifts behind me, I may not have earned, besides my keeping, these four guineas, and these poor clothes here upon my back, and in my third bundle? Now tell me your mind freely, without favour or affection."

" Alas! my dear girl," said she, "you make me unable to speak to you at all : it will be the highest affront that can be offered, to leave any of these things behind you; and you must take all your bundles, or my master will never forgive you."

" Well, Mrs. Jervis," said I, "I don't care; I have been too much used to be snubbed and hardly treated by my master, of late. I have done him no harm; I shall always pray and wish him happy. But I don't deserve these things; I can't wear them if I should take them; so they can be of no use to me; I trust I shall not want the poor pittance, that is all I desire, to keep life and soul together. Bread and water I can live upon with content. Water I shall get any where; and if I can't get bread, I will live, like a bird in winter, upon hips and haws, and at other times upon pig-nuts, potatoes, or turnips. So what occasion have I for these things?—But all I ask is about these four guineas, if you think I need not return them; that is all I want to know."—" To be sure, my dear, you need not," said

66

she; "you have well earned them by that waistcoat only."—
"No, I think not *so*, in that only; but in the linen, and other
things, do you think I have?"—"Yes, yes," said she, "and
more."—"And my keeping allowed for, I mean," said I, "and
these poor clothes on my back, besides? Remember that,
Mrs. Jervis."—"Yes, my dear, no doubt you have."—"Well
then," said I, "I am as happy as a princess. I am quite as
rich as I wish to be: and, once more, my dear third bundle,
I will bring thee to my bosom. I beg you'll say nothing of this
till I am gone, that my master mayn't be so angry, but that I
may go in peace; for my heart, without other matters, will be
ready to break to part with you all.

"Now, Mrs. Jervis," said I, "as to one matter more, and that
is my master's last usage of me, before Mr. Longman." Said
she—"Pr'ythee, dear Pamela, step to my chamber, and fetch
me a paper I left on my table.—I have something to shew you
in it."—"I will," said I, and stepped down; but that was
only an excuse to take orders of my master, I found. He said
he thought two or three times to have burst out upon me;
but he could not stand it, and wished I might not know he was
there. But I tript up again so nimbly (for there was no paper),
that I just saw his back, as if coming out of that green-room,
and going into the next to it, the first door that was open, I
whipped in, shut the door, and bolted it.—"O Mrs. Jervis,"
said I, "what have you done by me;—I see I can't confide in
any body. I am beset on all hands. Wretched, wretched
Pamela! where shalt thou expect a friend, if Mrs. Jervis joins
to betray thee thus?" She made so many protestations,
(telling me all, and that he owned I had made him wipe his eyes
two or three times, and said she hoped it would have a good
effect, and remembered me, that I had said nothing but what
would rather move compassion than resentment,) that I forgave her. But O! that I was safe from this house; for never
poor creature sure was so flustered as I have been so many
months together! I wonder what will next befal *your dutiful
daughter*.

Mrs. Jervis says, she is sure I shall have the chariot to carry
me home to you. Though this will look too great for me, yet
it will shew as if I was not turned away quite in disgrace. The
travelling chariot is come from Lincolnshire, and I fancy I shall
go in that; for the other is quite grand.

My dear Father and Mother,

I write again, though, may-be, I shall bring it to you in my pocket: for I shall have no writing, or writing-time, I hope, when I come to you. This is Wednesday morning, and I shall, I hope, set out to you to-morrow morning; but I have had more trials, and more vexations; but of another complexion, though all from the same quarter.

Yesterday my master, after he came from hunting, sent for me. I went with great terror; for I expected he would storm and be in a passion with me, for my freedom of speech; so I resolved to begin first, with submission, to disarm his anger; and I fell upon my knees, as soon as I saw him, and said—" Good Sir, let me beseech you as you hope to be forgiven yourself and for the sake of my dear good lady, your mother, who recommended me to you with her last words, to forgive me all my faults; and only grant me this favour, the last I shall ask you, that you will let me depart your house with peace and quietness of mind, that I may take such a leave of my dear fellow-servants as befits me; and that my heart be not quite broken."

He took me up in a kinder manner than ever I had known; and he said—" Shut the door, Pamela, and come to me in my closet: I want to have a little serious talk with you."—" How can I, Sir," said I; " how can I!" and wrung my hands. " O pray, Sir, let me go out of your presence, I beseech you."—" By the God that made me," said he, " I'll do you no harm. Shut the parlour door, and come to me in my library."

He then went into his closet, which is his library, and full of rich pictures besides : a noble apartment, though called a closet, and next the private garden, into which it has a door that opens. I shut the parlour door, as he bid me, but stood at it irresolute.— " Place some confidence in me," said he : " surely you may, when I have spoken thus solemnly." So I crept towards him with trembling feet, and my heart throbbing through my hand-kerchief. " Come in," said he, " when I bid you." I did so. " Pray, Sir," said I, " pity and spare me !"—" I will," said he, " as I hope to be saved." He sat down upon a rich settee, and took hold of my hand, and said—" Don't doubt me, Pamela. From this moment I will no more consider you as my servant; and I desire you'll not use me with ingratitude for the kindness I am going to express towards you." This a little emboldened me; he said, holding both my hands between his—" You have

68

too much good sense not to discover, that I, in spite of my heart, and all the pride of it, cannot but love you. Look up to me, my sweet-faced girl! I *must* say I love you: and have put on a behaviour to you, that was much against my heart, in hopes to frighten you from your reservedness. You see I own it ingenuously: and don't play your sex upon me for it." I was unable to speak; and he seeing me too much oppressed with confusion to go on in that strain, said—" Well, Pamela, let me know in what situation of life is your father: I know he is a poor man: but is he as low and as honest as he was when my mother took you?"

Then I could speak a little; and with a down look (and I felt my face glow like fire) I said—" Yes, Sir, as *poor* and as *honest* too: and that is my pride."—Says he, " I will do something for him, if it be not your fault, and make all your family happy." —" Ah, Sir!" said I, " he is happier already than ever he can be, if his daughter's innocence is to be the price of your favour; and I beg you will not speak to me on the *only* side that can wound me."—" I have no design of that sort," said he. " O Sir," said I, " tell me not so, tell me not so!"—" 'Tis easy," said he, " to be the making of your father, without injuring *you*."—" Well, Sir," said I, " if this can be done, let me know how; and all I can do with innocence shall be the study and practice of my life. But, what can such a poor creature as I do?"—" I would," said he, " have you stay a week or a fortnight only, and behave yourself with kindness to me; I stoop to beg it of you: you shall see all shall turn out beyond your expectations. I see," said he, " you are going to answer otherwise than I would have you; and I begin to be vexed I should thus meanly sue. Your behaviour before honest Longman, when I used you as I did, and you could so well have vindicated yourself, has quite charmed me. And though I am not pleased with all you said yesterday while I was in the closet, yet you have moved me more to admire you than before; I see more worthiness in you, than ever I saw in any lady in the world. All the servants, from the highest to the lowest, doat upon you, instead of envying you; and look upon you in so superior a light, as speaks what you ought to be. I have seen more of your letters than you imagine; (this surprised me!) and am quite overcome with your charming manner of writing; so free, so easy, and many of your sentiments so much above your years; all which put together, makes me love you to extravagance. Now, Pamela, as I have stooped to acknowledge this, oblige me only to stay another week or fortnight, to give me time to bring about certain affairs, and you shall see how much you may find your account in it."

I trembled to find my poor heart giving way. " O good Sir," said I, " spare a poor girl that cannot look up to you, and speak. My heart is full; and why should you wish to undo me? "—" Only oblige me," said he, " to stay a fortnight longer, and John shall carry word to your father, that I will see him in the mean time, either here, or at the Swan, in his village."— " O Sir," said I, " my heart will burst, but, on my bended knees, I beg you to let me go to-morrow, as I designed; and don't offer to tempt a poor creature, whose will would be yours, if my virtue would permit."—" It shall permit it," said he; " for I intend no injury to you, God is my witness! "—" Impossible! " said I: " I cannot, Sir, believe you, after what has passed: how many ways are there to undo poor creatures! Good God, protect me, this *one* time, and send me but to my dear father's cot in safety! "—" Strange, damned fate! " says he, " that when I speak so solemnly, I can't be believed! "—" What *should* I believe, Sir? " said I, " what *can* I believe? What have you said, but that I am to stay a fortnight longer? and what then is to become of me? "—" My pride of birth and fortune, (damn them both! " said he, " since they cannot obtain credit with you, but only add to your suspicions) will not let me descend all at once: I therefore ask you but a fortnight's stay, that, after this declaration, I may pacify those proud demands upon me." O how my heart throbbed! and I begun (for I did not know what I did) to say the Lord's Prayer. " None of your beads to me, Pamela! " said he; " thou art a perfect nun." But I said aloud, with my eyes lifted up to Heaven, " *Lead me not into temptation, but deliver me from evil*, O my good God! " He hugged me in his arms, and said, " Well, my dear girl, then you stay this fortnight, and you shall see what I will do for you. I'll leave you a moment, and walk into the next room, to give you time to think of it, and to shew you I have no design upon you." Well, this, I thought, did not look amiss.

He went out, and I was tortured with twenty different doubts in a minute; sometimes I thought, that to stay a week or fortnight longer in this house, to obey him, while Mrs. Jervis was with me, could do no great harm: " But then," thought I, " how do I know what I may *be able* to do? I have withstood his *anger;* but may I not relent at his *kindness?* How shall I stand *that?*—Well, I hope, by the same protecting grace in which I will always confide.—But then, what has he promised? Why, he will make my poor father and mother's life comfortable. O!" said I to myself, "that is a rich thought; but let me not dwell upon it, for fear I should indulge it to my ruin. What can he do for *me*, poor girl as I am?—What can his greatness stoop to? He talks," thought I, "of his pride of heart, and pride of condition: O these are in his *head*, and in his heart too, or he would not confess them to me at *such* an instant. Well, then," thought I, "this can be only to seduce me. He has promised nothing." But I am to *see* what he will do, if I stay a fortnight. "And this fortnight is no such great matter: and I shall see in a few days how he carries it." But then when I again reflected upon the distance between him and me, and his now open declaration of love, as he called it; and that after this he would talk with me on this subject *more plainly* than ever, and I should be *less* armed, may-be, to withstand him; and then I bethought myself, "Why, if he meant no dishonour, he should not speak before Mrs. Jervis;" and the odious, frightful closet came into my head, and my narrow escape upon it; and how easy it might be for him to send Mrs. Jervis, and the maids out of the way; that all the mischief he designed me might be brought about in less than that time; I resolved to go away, and trust all to Providence, and nothing to myself. And how ought I to be thankful for this resolution! as you shall hear.

But just as I have writ to this place, John sends me word, that he is going this minute your way; and so I will send you as far as I have written, and hope by to-morrow night to ask your blessings, at your own poor, but happy abode, and tell you the rest by word of mouth: and so I rest, till then, and for ever, *your dutiful daughter.*

LETTER XXXI

DEAR FATHER AND MOTHER,

I will continue my writing still, because, may-be, I shall like to read it, when I am with you, to see what dangers I have been enabled to escape; although I bring it along with me.

I told you my resolution, my happy resolution, as I have reason to think it; and just then he came in again, with great kindness in his looks, and said, "I make no doubt, Pamela, you will stay this fortnight to oblige me." I knew not how to frame my words so as to deny, and yet not make him storm. "But," said I, "forgive, Sir, your poor distressed servant. I know I cannot possibly deserve any favour at your hands, consistent with virtue; and I beg you will let me go to my poor father."— " Why," said he, " thou art the greatest fool that I ever knew. I tell you I will see your father; I'll send for him hither to-morrow, in my travelling chariot, if you will; and I'll let him know what I intend to do for *him* and *you*."—" What, Sir, can that be? Your honour's noble estate may easily make *him* happy, and not unuseful, perhaps, to you, in some respect or other. But what price am I to pay for all this?"—" You shall be happy as you can wish," said he, " I do assure you: here, I will give you this purse, in which are fifty guineas, which I will allow your father yearly, and find an employ suitable to his liking, to deserve *that* and *more*: Pamela, he shall never want, depend upon it. I would have given you still more for him, but that perhaps you'd suspect I intended it as a design upon you."—" O Sir," said I, " take back your guineas; I will not touch one, nor will my father, I am sure, till he knows what is to be done *for* them, and particularly what is to become of *me*."—" Why, then, Pamela," said he, " suppose I find a man of probity, and genteel calling, for your husband, that shall make you a gentlewoman as long as you live!"—" I want no husband, Sir," said I; for now I began to see him in all his black colours; yet, being so much in his power, I thought I would a little dissemble. " But," said he, " you are so pretty, that, go where you will, you can never be free from the designs of some or other of our sex; and I shall think I don't answer the care of my dying mother for you, who committed you to me, if I don't provide you a husband to protect your virtue, and your innocence; and a worthy one I have thought of for you."

" O black, perfidious creature!" thought I, " what an implement art thou in the hands of Lucifer, to ruin this innocent heart!"—Yet still I dissembled; for I feared much both him and the place I was in. " But whom, pray, Sir, have you thought of?"—" Why," said he, " young Mr. Williams, my chaplain, in Lincolnshire, who will make you happy."—" Does he know, Sir," said I, " anything of your honour's intentions?"—" No, my girl," said he, and kissed me, (much against my will; for his very breath was now poison to me:) " but his dependence upon my favour, and your beauty and merit, will make him rejoice at my kindness to him."—" Well, Sir," said I, " then it is time enough to consider of this matter; and it cannot hinder me from going to my father's; for what will staying a fortnight longer signify to this? Your honour's care and goodness may extend to me *there*, as well as *here*; and Mr. Williams, and all the world, shall know that I am not ashamed of my father's poverty."

He would kiss me again; and I said, "If I am to think of Mr. Williams, or any body, I beg *you* will not be so free with me; that is not pretty, I'm sure."—" Well," said he, " but you stay this next fortnight, and in that time I'll have both Williams and your father here; for I will have the match concluded in my house : and when I have brought it in, you shall settle it as you please together. Meantime take and send these fifty pieces to your father, as an earnest of my favour, and I'll make you all happy." "Sir," said I, " I beg at least two hours to consider of this."—" I shall," said he, " be gone out in one hour; and I would have you write to your father what I propose; and John shall carry it on purpose; and he shall take the purse with him for the good old man, if you approve of it."—" Sir," said I, " I will then let you know, in one hour, my resolution."— " Do so," said he; and gave me another kiss, and let me go.

O how I rejoiced I had got out of his clutches!—So I write you this, that you may see how matters stand; for I am resolved to come away, if possible. Base, wicked, treacherous gentleman, as he is !

Here was a trap laid for your poor Pamela ! I tremble to think of it ! O what a scene of wickedness was here laid down for all my wretched life ! Black-hearted wretch ! how I hate him !—For at first, as you'll see by what I have written, he would have made me believe other things; and this of Mr. Williams, I suppose, came into his head after he walked out of his closet, to give himself time to think how to delude me better : but the covering was now too thin, and easy to be seen through.

I went to my chamber, and the first thing I did was to write to him; for I thought it was best not to see him again, if I could help it; and I put it under his parlour-door, after I had copied it, as follows :

" HONOURED SIR,

" Your last proposal to me convinces me that I ought not to stay, but to go to my father, if it were but to ask his advice about Mr. Williams. And I am so set upon it, that I am not to be persuaded. So, honoured Sir, with a thousand thanks for all favours, I will set out to-morrow early; and the honour you designed me, as Mrs. Jervis tells me, of your chariot, there will be no occasion for; because I can hire, I believe, Farmer Brady's chaise. So, begging you will not take it amiss, I shall ever be *your dutiful servant.*

73

" As to the purse, Sir, my poor father, to be sure, won't forgive me, if I take it, till he can know how to deserve it : which is impossible."

So he has just now sent Mrs. Jervis to tell me, that since I am resolved to go, go I may, and the travelling chariot shall be ready; but it shall be worse for me; for that he will never trouble himself about me as long as he lives. Well, so I get out of the house, I care not; only I should have been glad I could, with innocence, have made you, my dear parents, happy.

I cannot imagine the reason of it, but John, who I thought was gone with my last, is but now going; and he sends to know if I have any thing else to carry. So I break off, to send you this with the former.

I am now preparing for my journey, and about taking leave of my good fellow-servants : and if I have not time to write, I must tell you the rest, when I am so happy as to be with you.

One word more : I slip in a paper of verses, on my going— Sad poor stuff : but as they come from me, you'll not dislike them, may-be. I shewed them to Mrs. Jervis and she liked them, and took a copy; and made me sing them to her, and in the green-room too; but I looked into the closet first. I will only add, that I am *your dutiful daughter*.

Let me just say, that he has this moment sent me five guineas, by Mrs. Jervis, as a present for my pocket; so I shall be very rich; for as *she* brought them, I thought I might take them. He says he won't see me : and I may go when I will in the morning; and Lincolnshire Robin shall drive me : but he is so angry, he orders that nobody shall go out at the door with me, not so much as into the coach-yard. Well ! I can't help it, not I ! But does not this expose himself, more than me ?

But John waits, and I would have brought this and the other myself; but he says he has put it up among other things, and so can take both as well as one.

John is very good and very honest : I am under many obligations to him. I'd give him a guinea, now I'm so rich, if I thought he'd take it I hear nothing of my lady's clothes, and those my master gave me : for I told Mrs. Jervis I would not take them; but I fancy, by a word or two that was dropped, they will be sent after me. Dear Sirs ! what a rich Pamela you'll have, if they should ! But as I can't wear them, if they do, I don't desire them; and if I have them, will turn them into money, as I can have opportunity. Well, no more—I'm in a fearful hurry.

74

VERSES ON MY GOING AWAY

My fellow-servants dear, attend
To these few lines, which I have penn'd.
I'm sure they're from your honest friend;
 And wisher-well, poor Pamela.

I, from a state of low degree,
Was plac'd in this good family:
Too high a fate for humble me,
 The helpless, hopeless Pamela.

Yet though my happy lot was so,
Joyful, I homeward from it go,
No less content, when poor and low,
 Than here you find your Pamela.

For what indeed is happiness,
But conscious innocence and peace?
And that's a treasure I possess;
 Thank Heav'n that gave it Pamela.

My future lot I cannot know:
But this I'm sure, wher'er I go,
Whate'er I am, what'er I do,
 I'll be the grateful Pamela.

No sad regrets my heart annoy,
I'll pray for all your peace and joy,
From master high to scullion boy,
 For all your loves to Pamela.

One thing or two I've more to say;
God's holy will, be sure, obey,
And for our master always pray,
 As ever shall poor Pamela.

For, Oh! we *pity* should the great,
Instead of envying their estate;
Temptations always on 'em wait,
 Exempt from which are such as we.

Their riches, gay deceitful snares,
Enlarge their fears, increase their cares;
Their servants' joy surpasses theirs;
 At least, so judges Pamela.

Your parents and relations love:
Let them your duty ever prove;
And you'll be blest by Heaven above,
 As will, I hope, poor Pamela.

For if asham'd I e'er could be
Of my dear parents' low degree,
What lot had been too mean for me,
 Unbless'd, unvirtuous Pamela.

Thrice happy may you ever be
Each one in his and her degree;
And, Sirs, whene'er you think of me,
    Pray for content to Pamela.

Pray for her wish'd content and peace;
And rest assur'd she'll never cease
To pray for all your joy's increase,
    While life is lent to Pamela.

On God all future good depends;
Serve Him. And so my sonnet ends,
With thank ye, thank ye, honest friends,
    For all your loves to Pamela.

Here it is necessary the reader should know that the fair
Pamela's trials were not yet over; but the worst were to come,
at a time she thought them at an end, and that she was returning
to her father: for when her master found her virtue was not
to be subdued, and he had in vain tried to conquer his passion
for her, being a gentleman of pleasure and intrigue, he had
ordered his Lincolnshire coachman to bring his travelling chariot
from thence, not caring to trust his Bedfordshire coachman,
who, with the rest of the servants, so greatly loved and honoured
the fair damsel; and having given him instructions accordingly,
and prohibited the other servants, on pretence of resenting
Pamela's behaviour, from accompanying her any part of the
road, he drove her five miles on the way to her father's; and
then turning off, crossed the country, and carried her onwards
towards his Lincolnshire estate.

It is also to be observed, that the messenger of her letters to
her father, who so often pretended business that way, was an
implement in his master's hands, and employed by him for that
purpose; and always gave her letters first to him, and his master
used to open and then read them, and send them on; by which
means, as he hints to her (as she observes in one of her letters,
page 69), he was no stranger to what she wrote. Thus every
way was the poor virgin beset; and the whole will shew the base
arts of designing men, to gain their wicked ends; and how much
it behoves the fair sex to stand upon their guard against artful
contrivances, especially when riches and power conspire against
innocence and a low estate.

A few words more will be necessary to make the sequel better
understood. The intriguing gentleman thought fit, however, to
keep back from her father her three last letters; in which she
mentions his concealing himself to hear her partitioning out her
clothes, his last effort to induce her to stay a fortnight, his

76

pretended proposal of the chaplain, and her hopes of speedily seeing them, as also her verses; and to send himself a letter to her father, which was as follows:

" GOODMAN ANDREWS,
        " You will wonder to receive a letter from me. But I think I am obliged to let you know, that I have discovered the strange correspondence carried on between you and your daughter, so injurious to my honour and reputation, and which, I think, you should not have encouraged, till you knew there were sufficient grounds for those aspersions which she so plentifully casts upon me. Something possibly there might be in what she has written from time to time; but, believe me, with all her pretended simplicity and innocence, I never knew so much romantic invention as she is mistress of. In short, the girl's head is turned by romances, and such idle stuff, to which she has given herself up, ever since her kind lady's death. And she assumes airs, as if she was a mirror of perfection, and every body had a design upon her.
        " Don't mistake me, however; I believe her very honest, and very virtuous; but I have found out, also, that she is carrying on a sort of correspondence, or love affair, with a young clergyman that I hope in time to provide for; but who, at present, is destitute of any subsistence but my favour: and what would be the consequence, can you think, of two young folks, who have nothing in the world to trust to of their own, to come together, with a family multiplying upon them, before they have bread to eat?
        " For my part, I have too much kindness to them both, not to endeavour to prevent it, if I can; and for this reason I have sent her out of his way for a little while, till I can bring them both to better consideration; and I would not, therefore, have you be surprised you don't see your daughter as soon as you might possibly expect.
        " Yet I do assure you, upon my honour, that she shall be safe and inviolate; and I hope you don't doubt me, notwithstanding any airs she may have given herself, upon my jocular pleasantry to her, and perhaps a little innocent romping with her, so usual with young folks of the two sexes, when they have been long acquainted, and grown up together; for pride is not my talent.
        " As she is a mighty letter-writer, I hope she has had the duty to apprise you of her intrigue with the young clergyman; and I know not whether it meets with your countenance: but

now she is absent for a little while, (for I know he would have followed her to your village, if she had gone home; and there perhaps they would have ruined one another by marrying,) I doubt not I shall bring him to see his interest, and that he engages not before he knows how to provide for a wife; and when that can be done, let them come together in God's name, for me.

" I expect not to be answered on this head, but by your good opinion, and the confidence you may repose in my honour; being *your hearty friend to serve you.*

" P.S. I find my man John has been the manager of the correspondence, in which such liberties have been taken with *me.* I shall soon, in a manner that becomes me, let the saucy fellow know how much I resent his part of the affair. It is a hard thing, that a man of my character in the world should be used thus freely by his own servants."

It is easy to guess at the poor old man's concern upon reading this letter, from a gentleman of so much consideration. He knew not what course to take, and had no manner of doubt of his poor daughter's innocence, and that foul play was designed her. Yet he sometimes hoped the best, and was ready to believe the surmised correspondence between the clergyman and her, having not received the letters she wrote, which would have cleared up that affair.

But, after all, he resolved, as well to quiet his own as her mother's uneasiness, to undertake a journey to the squire's; and leaving his poor wife to excuse him to the farmer who employed him, he set out that very evening, late as it was; and travelling all night, found himself, soon after daylight, at the gate of the gentleman, before the family was up : and there he sat down to rest himself till he should see somebody stirring.

The grooms were the first he saw, coming out to water their horses; and he asked, in so distressful a manner, what was become of Pamela, that they thought him crazy; and said, " Why, what have you to do with Pamela, old fellow? Get out of the horses' way."—" Where is your master? " said the poor man : " pray, gentlemen, don't be angry : my heart's almost broken."—" He never gives any thing at the door, I assure you," says one of the grooms; " so you lose your labour."—" I am not a beggar *yet*," said the poor old man. " I want nothing of him, but my Pamela : O my child ! my child ! "

" I'll be hanged," says one of them, " if this is not Mrs. Pamela's father."—" Indeed, indeed," said he, wringing his hands, " I am ; " and weeping, " Where is my child? where is my Pamela?"—"Why, father," said one of them, "we beg your pardon; but she is gone home to you: how long have you been come from home?"—"But last night," said he; "I have travelled all night.—Is the squire at home, or is he not?"—"Yes, but he is not stirring though," said the groom, "as yet."—"Thank God for that!" said he; "thank God for that! Then I hope I may be permitted to speak to him anon." They asked him to go in, and he stepped into the stable, and sat down on the stairs there, wiping his eyes, and sighing so sadly, that it grieved the servants to hear him.

The family was soon raised, with a report of Pamela's father coming to enquire after his daughter; and the maids would fain have had him go into the kitchen. But Mrs. Jervis, having been told of his coming, arose, and hastened down to her parlour; and took him in with her, and there heard all his sad story, and read the letter. She wept bitterly, but yet endeavoured before him to hide her concern; and said, "Well, Goodman Andrews, I cannot help weeping at your grief; but I hope there is no occasion. Let nobody see this letter, whatever you do. I dare say your daughter is safe."

"Well, but," said he, "I see, *you*, Madam, know nothing about her:—if all was right, so good a gentlewoman as you are, would not have been a stranger to this. To be sure, you thought she was with me!"

Said she, "My master does not always inform his servants of his proceedings; but you need not doubt his honour. You have his hand for it: and you may see he can have no design upon her, because he is not from hence, and does not talk of going hence."—"O that is all I have to hope for," said he; "that is all, indeed!—But," said he—and was going on, when the report of his coming had reached the squire, who came down in his morning-gown and slippers, into the parlour, where he and Mrs. Jervis were talking.

"What's the matter, Goodman Andrews," said he; "what's the matter?"—"O my child!" said the good old man; "give me my child! I beseech you, Sir."—"Why, I thought," says the squire, "that I had satisfied you about her: sure you have not the letter I sent you, written with my own hand."—"Yes, yes, but I have, Sir," said he; "and that brought me hither; and I have walked all night."—"Poor man," returned he, with great seeming compassion, "I am sorry for it, truly! Why, your daughter has made a strange racket in my family; and if I thought it would have disturbed you so much, I would have e'en let her gone home; but what I did was to serve *her*, and

79

you too. She is very safe, I do assure you, Goodman Andrews; and you may take my honour for it, I would not injure her for the world. Do you think I would, Mrs. Jervis?"—"No, I hope not, Sir," said she.—"*Hope not!*" said the poor man; "so did I: but pray, Sir, give me my child; that's all I desire; and I'll take care no clergyman shall come near her."

"Why, London is a great way off," said the squire, "and I can't send for her back presently."—"What then," said he, "have you sent my poor Pamela to London?"—"I would not have it said so," replied the squire; "but I assure you, upon my honour, she is quite safe and satisfied, and will quickly inform you of it by letter. She is in a reputable family, no less than a bishop's, and is to wait on his lady, till I get the matter over that I mentioned to you."

"O how shall I know this?" replied he.—"What!" said the squire, pretending anger, "am I to be doubted?—Do you believe I can have any view upon your daughter? And if I had, do you think I would take such methods as *these* to effect it?—Why, surely, man, thou forgettest whom thou talkest to!"—"O, Sir," said he, "I beg your pardon; but consider, my dear child is in the case: let me know but what bishop, and where; and I will travel to London on foot, to see my daughter, and then shall be satisfied."

"Why, Goodman Andrews, I think thou hast read romances as well as thy daughter: thy head is turned with them. May I not have my word taken? Do you think I would offer any thing dishonourable to your daughter? Is there any thing looks like it? Pr'ythee, man, recollect a little who I am; and if I am not to be believed, what signifies talking?"—"Why, Sir," said he, "pray forgive me: but there is no harm to say, what bishop's, or whereabouts?"—"What, and so you'd go troubling his lordship with your impertinent fears and stories? Will you be satisfied, if you have a letter from her within a week, it may be less, if she be not negligent, to assure you all is well with her?"—"Why that," said the poor man, "will be some comfort."—"Well, then," said the gentleman, "I can't answer for her negligence, if she don't write; and if she should send a letter to you, Mrs. Jervis, (for I desire not to see it; I have had trouble enough about her already,) be sure you send it by a man and horse the moment you receive it."—"To be sure I will," answered she. "Thank your honour," said the good man: "and then I must wait with as much patience as I can for a week, which will be a year to me."

"I tell you," said the gentleman, "it must be her own fault

if she don't write : for 'tis what I insisted upon for my own reputation : and I shan't stir from this house, I assure you, till she is heard from, and that to satisfaction."—" God bless your honour," said the poor man, " as you say and mean truth." —" *Amen, Amen*, Goodman Andrews," said he : " you see I am not afraid to say *Amen*.—So, Mrs. Jervis, make the good man as welcome as you can ; and let me have no uproar about the matter."

He then, whispering her, bid her give him a couple of guineas to bear his charges home ; telling him he should be welcome to stay there, till the letter came, if he would ; and be a witness that he intended honourably.

The poor old man staid and dined with Mrs. Jervis, with some tolerable ease of mind, in hopes to hear from his beloved daughter in a few days : and then accepting the present, returned for his own house, and resolved to be as patient as possible.

Meantime Mrs. Jervis, and all the family, were in the utmost grief for the trick put upon poor Pamela ; and she and the steward represented it to their master in as moving terms as they durst ; but were forced to rest satisfied with his general assurances of intending her no harm ; which, however, Mrs. Jervis little believed, from the pretence he had made in his letter, of the correspondence between Pamela and the young parson ; which she knew to be all mere invention, though she durst not say so.

But the week after, they were made a little more easy by the following letter, brought by an unknown hand, and left for Mrs. Jervis ; which, how procured, will be shewn in the sequel :

" DEAR MRS. JERVIS,

" I have *been vilely tricked*, and, instead of being driven by Robin to my dear father's, I *am* carried off, to where I have no liberty to tell. However, I am at present not used hardly, *in the main ;* and I write to beg of you to let my dear father and mother (whose hearts must be well nigh broken) know that I am well, and that I am, and by the grace of God, ever will be, their honest as well as dutiful daughter, and *your obliged friend,*   PAMELA ANDREWS.

" I must neither send date nor place : but have most solemn assurances of honourable usage. *This is the only time my low estate has been troublesome to me, since it has subjected me to the frights I have undergone. Love to your good self, and all my dear fellow-servants.—Adieu ! Adieu ! but pray for poor*
                                                                        " PAMELA."

This, though it quieted not entirely their apprehensions, was shewn to the whole family, and to the gentleman himself, who pretended not to know how it came. Mrs. Jervis sent it away to the good old folks, who at first suspected it was forged, and not their daughter's hand; but, finding the contrary, they were a little easier to hear she was alive and honest: and having enquired of all their acquaintance what could be done, and no one being able to put them in a way how to proceed, on so extraordinary an occasion, against so rich and resolute a gentleman; and being afraid to make matters worse (though they saw plainly that she was in no bishop's family, and so mistrusted all the rest of his story), they applied themselves to prayers for their poor daughter, and for an happy issue to an affair that almost distracted them.

We shall now leave the honest old pair, praying for their dear Pamela, and return to the account she herself gives of all this; having written it journalwise, to amuse and employ her time in hopes some opportunity might offer to send it to her friends, and, as was her constant view, that she might afterwards thankfully look back upon the dangers she had escaped, when they should be happily over-blown, as in time she hoped they would be; and that then she might examine, and either approve or repent of her conduct in them.

LETTER XXXII

O MY DEAREST FATHER AND MOTHER,

Let me write and bewail my miserable hard fate, though I have no hope that what I write can be conveyed to you. I have now nothing to do but write, and weep, and pray! But yet, what can I hope for, when I seem to be devoted as a victim to the will of a wicked violater of all the laws of God and man?— " But, gracious heaven, forgive my rashness and despondency! O let me not sin against thee; for thou best knowest what is fittest for thy poor handmaid! And as thou sufferest not thy poor creatures to be tempted above what they can bear, I will resign myself to thy good pleasure!" Still, I hope, desperate as my condition seems, that, as these trials are not of my own seeking, nor the effects of my presumption and vanity, I shall be enabled to overcome them, and, in God's own good time, be delivered from them.

Thus do I pray imperfectly, as I am forced by my distracting

fears and apprehensions: O join with me, my dear parents!
But, alas! how can you know, how can I reveal to you, the
dreadful situation of your poor daughter! The unhappy
Pamela may be undone (which God forbid, and sooner deprive
me of life!) before you can know her hard lot!

O the unparalleled wickedness, stratagems, and devices, of
those who call themselves gentlemen, yet pervert the designs
of Providence in giving them ample means to do good, to their
own everlasting perdition, and the ruin of poor oppressed
innocence!

Now I will tell you what has befallen me; but yet, how shall
you receive it? Here is no honest John to carry my letters to
you! And, besides, I am watched in all my steps, and no
doubt shall be, till my hard fate may ripen his wicked projects
for my ruin. I will every day, however, write my sad state;
and some way, perhaps, may be opened to send the melancholy
scribble to you. But, alas! when you know it, what will it
do but aggravate your troubles? For what can the abject
poor do against the mighty rich, when they are determined to
oppress?

Well, but I must proceed to write what I had hoped to tell
you in a few hours, when I believed I should receive your
grateful blessings, on my return to you from so many hardships.

I will begin with my account from the last letter I wrote you,
in which I inclosed my poor stuff of verses; and continue it as
I have opportunity, though, as I said, I know not how it can
reach you.

The long-hoped-for Thursday morning came, when I was
to set out. I had taken my leave of my fellow-servants overnight: a mournful leave it was to us all; for men as well as
women servants wept much to part with me; and, for *my* part, I
was overwhelmed with tears, at the affecting instances of their
esteem. They all would have made me little presents, as
tokens of their love; but I would not take any thing from
the lower servants. But Mr. Longman would have me accept
of several yards of Holland, a silver snuff-box, and a gold ring,
which he desired me to keep for his sake; he wept over me,
but said—"I'm sure so good a maiden God will bless; and
though you return to your poor father again, and his low estate,
yet Providence will find you out: remember I tell you so; and
one day, though I mayn't live to see it, you will be rewarded."

I said—"O dear Mr. Longman, you make me too rich, and
too mody; yet I must be a beggar before my time; for I shall
want often to be scribbling," (little thinking it would be my

only employment so soon,) " and I will beg you, Sir, to favour me with some paper; and as soon as I get home, I will write you a letter, to thank you all for your kindness to me; and a letter for good Mrs. Jervis too."

This was lucky; for I should have had none else, but at the pleasure of my rough-natured governess, as I may call her: but now I can write to ease my mind, though I can't send it to you; and write what I please, for she knows not how well I am provided; for good Mr. Longman gave me above forty sheets of paper, a dozen pens, and a little phial of ink, which last I wrapped in paper, and put in my pocket, with some wax and wafers.

" O dear Sir," said I, " you have set me up; how shall I requite you?" He said—" By a kiss, my fair girl." And I gave it very willingly, for he is a good old man.

Rachel and Hannah cried sadly, when I took my leave; Jane, who sometimes used to be a little crossish, and Cicely too, wept sadly, and said they would pray for me; but poor Jane, I doubt, will forget *that*, for she seldom says her prayers for herself: more's the pity! Arthur the gardener, Robin the coachman, and little Lincolnshire Robin too, who was to carry me, were very civil: both had tears in their eyes; which I thought then very good-natured in Lincolnshire Robin, because he knew but little of me. But since, I find, he might well be concerned; for he had then his instructions, and knew how he was to be a means to entrap me.

Our other three footmen, Harry, Isaac, and Benjamin, and the grooms and helpers, were very much affected likewise; and the poor little scullion boy, Tommy, was oppressed with grief.

They had got altogether over night, expecting to be differently employed in the morning; they all begged to shake hands with me. I kissed the maidens, and prayed to God to bless them all; and thanked them for all their love and kindnesses to me: I was forced to leave them sooner than I would, because I could not stand it: indeed I could not. Harry (I could not have thought it, for he is a little wildish, they say) cried considerably. Poor honest John was not then come back from you. But as for the butler, Mr. Jonathan, he could not stay in company.

I thought to have told you a deal about this, but I have worse things to employ my thoughts.

Mrs. Jervis, good Mrs. Jervis, cried all night long, and I comforted her as well as I could; she made me promise, that if my master went to London, to attend Parliament, or to

Lincolnshire, I would come and stay a week with her: and she would have given me money, but I would not take it.

Well, next morning came, and I wondered I saw nothing of honest John, for I waited to take leave of him, and thank him for all his civilities to me and you: but I suppose he was sent farther by my master, and could not return, so I desired to be remembered to him.

When Mrs. Jervis told me, with a sad heart, the chariot was ready with four horses to it, I was just upon sinking into the ground, though I wanted to be with you.

My master was above stairs, and never asked to see me. I was glad of it in the main; but he knew, false-heart as he is! that I was not to be out of his reach.—O preserve me, Heaven, from his power, and from his wickedness!

The servants were not suffered to go with me one step, as I writ to you before; for he stood at the window to see me go. And in the passage to the gate, out of his sight, there they stood, all of them, in two rows; and could say nothing on both sides but "God bless you!" and "God bless you!" But Harry carried my own bundle, my third bundle, as I used to call it, to the coach, and some plumb-cake, and diet-bread, made for me over night, some sweet-meats, and six bottles of Canary wine, which Mrs. Jervis would make me take in a basket, to cheer our hearts when we got together, she said. I kissed all the maids again; but Mr. Jonathan and Mr. Longman were not there; I tripped down the steps to the chariot, Mrs. Jervis crying most sadly.

I looked up when I got to the chariot, and saw my master at the window, in his gown; I curtseyed three times to him very low, and prayed for him with my hands lifted up; for I could not speak; indeed I was not able; and he bowed his head to me, which made me very glad he would take such notice of me; and in I stept. I was ready to burst with grief; and could only, till Robin began to drive, wave my white handkerchief to them, wet with my tears; at last, away we drove, Jehu-like, as they say, out of the court-yard. And I too soon found I had cause for greater and deeper grief.

"Well," said I to myself, "at this rate I shall soon be with my dear father and mother;" till I had got, as I supposed, half way, I thought of the good friends I had left: and when, on stopping to bait the horses, Robin told me I was near half way, I thought it was high time to wipe my eyes, and think to whom I was going. So I began to ponder what a meeting I should have with you; how glad you'd be to see me come

85

safe and innocent to you, after all my dangers; so I began to comfort myself, and to banish the other gloomy sight from my mind, though it returned now and then, for I should be ungrateful not to love them for their love.

I believe I set out about eight o'clock in the morning; I wondered, when it was about two, as I saw by a church-dial in a little village, as we passed through, that I was still more and more out of my knowledge. "Hey day!" thought I, "to drive this strange pace, and be so long a going a little more than twenty miles, is very odd! But, to be sure," thought I, "Robin knows the way."

At last he stopped and looked about him, as if he was at a loss for the road. I said—"Mr. Robert, sure you are out of the way!"—"I am afraid I am," said he; "but it can't be much; I'll ask the first person I see."—"Pray do," said I; and he gave his horses a mouthful of hay; and I gave him some cake, and two glasses of Canary wine. We stopped about half an hour in all. Then he drove on very fast again.

I had so much to think of, of the dangers I now doubted not I had escaped, and of the loving friends I had left, as also of my best friends I was going to, and the many things I had to relate, that I the less thought of the way, till I was startled out of my meditations by the sun beginning to set, and still the man driving on, and his horses sweating and foaming; then I began to be alarmed all at once, and called to him; he said he had horrid ill-luck, for that he had come several miles out of the way, but was now right, and should get in before it was quite dark.—My heart then began to misgive me a little, and I was very much fatigued; for I had no sleep for several nights before, to signify; at last I said: "Pray, Mr. Robert, there is a town before us, what do you call it? If we are so much out of the way, we had better put up there, for the night comes on apace." Lord protect me, thought I, I shall have new dangers, mayhap, to encounter with the *man*, who have escaped the *master*,—little thinking of the base contrivance of the latter. Says he—"I am just there: 'tis but a mile on one side of the town before us."—"Nay," said I, "I may be mistaken; for it is a good while since I was this way: but I am sure the face of the country here is nothing like what I remember it."

He pretended to be much out of humour with himself for mistaking the way, and at last stopped at a farm-house, about two miles beyond the village we had passed; it was then almost dark, and he alighted, and said—"We must make shift here: for I am quite out."

Lord, thought I, be good to poor Pamela!—More trials still!—What will befall me next?

The farmer's wife, maid, and daughter, came out; the wife said—"What brings you this way at this time of night, Mr. Robert? And with a lady too?" Then I began to be frightened out of my wits; and, laying middle and both ends together, I fell a crying, and said—"God give me patience! I am undone for certain!—Pray, mistress," said I, "do you know Squire B——, of Bedfordshire?"

The wicked coachman would have prevented her answering me: but the simple daughter said—"Know his worship! yes, surely; why he is my father's landlord."—"Well," said I, "then I am undone, undone for ever!—O wicked wretch! what have I done to you," said I to the coachman, "to serve me thus?—Vile tool of a wicked master!"—"Faith," said the fellow, "I am sorry this task was put upon me: but I could not help it. But make the best of it now; here are very civil, reputable folks; and you'll be safe here, I'll assure you."— "Let me get out," said I, "and I'll walk back to the town we came through, late as it is: for I will not enter here."

The farmer's wife said—"You'll be very well used here, I'll assure you, young gentlewoman, and have better conveniences than any where in the village."—"It matters not conveniences," said I, "I am betrayed and undone! As you have a daughter of your *own* pity me. Let me know, if your landlord, as you call him, be here?"—"No, I'll assure you he is not," said she.

And then came the farmer, a good-like sort of man, grave, and well behaved; he spoke in such a way as made me a little pacified; and, seeing no help for it, I went in: the wife immediately conducted me up stairs to the best apartment, and told me that was mine, as long as I staid; and nobody should come near me, but when I called. I threw myself on the bed in the room, tired and frightened to death almost; and gave way to the most excessive fit of grief I ever had.

The daughter came up, and said, Mr. Robert had given her a letter to give me; and there it was. I raised myself, and saw it was the hand and seal of the wicked wretch, my master, directed to me. This was a little better than to have him here; though if he had, he must have been brought through the air: for I thought I was.

The good woman (for I began to see things about a little reputable, and no guile appearing in them, but rather a face of grief for my grief) offered me a glass of some cordial water, which I accepted, for I was ready to sink; I then sat up in a chair a little, though very faint. They brought me two candles, lighted a brush-wood fire, and said, if I called, I should be waited on instantly; so left me to ruminate on my sad condition, and to read my letter, which I was not able to do presently. After I had a little come to myself, I found it to contain these words:

" DEAR PAMELA,

" The passion I have for you, and your obstinacy, have constrained me to act by you in a manner that, I know, will occasion you great trouble and fatigue, both of mind and body. Yet, forgive me, my dear girl; for, although I have taken these steps, I will, by all that's good and holy, use you honourably. Suffer not your fears to transport you to a behaviour that will be disreputable to us both; for the place where you'll receive this, is a farm that belongs to me; and the people civil, honest, and obliging.

" You will by this time be far on your way to the place I have allotted for your abode for a few weeks, till I have managed some affairs, that will make me shew myself to you in a much different light, than you may possibly apprehend from this rash action; and to convince you that I mean no harm, I assure you, that the house you are going to shall be so much at your command, that even I myself will not approach it without leave from you. So make yourself easy; be discreet and prudent; and a happier turn shall reward these your troubles, than you may at present apprehend.

" Meantime I pity the fatigue you will have, if this come to your hand in the place I have directed: and will write to your father to satisfy him, that nothing but what is honourable shall be offered to you, by *your passionate admirer (so I must style myself,)*
                                                   " _____ "

" Don't think hardly of poor Robin: you have so possessed all my servants in your favour, that I find they had rather serve you than me; and 'tis reluctantly the poor fellow undertook the task; I was forced to submit to assure him of my honourable intentions to you, which I am fully resolved to make good, if you compel me not to a contrary conduct."

I but too well apprehended, that the letter was only to pacify me for the present; but as my danger was not so immediate as I had reason to dread, and he had promised to forbear coming to me, and to write to you, my dear parents, to quiet your concern, I was a little more easy than before: I made a shift to eat a little bit of boiled chicken, and drank a glass of my sack, and made each of them do so too.

But after I had so done, I was again a little flustered : for in came the coachman with the look of a hangman, I thought, and *madam'd* me up strangely ; telling me, he would beg me to get ready to pursue my journey by five in the morning, or else he should be late in. I was quite grieved at this ; for I began not to dislike my company, considering how things stood ; and was in hopes to get a party among them, and so to put myself into any worthy protection in the neighbourhood, rather than go forward.

When he withdrew, I began to tamper with the farmer and his wife. But, alas ! they had had a letter delivered to them at the same time I had : so securely had Lucifer put it into his head to do his work : they only shook their heads, and seemed to pity me ; so I was forced to give over that hope.

However, the good farmer shewed me his letter ; which I copied as follows : for it discovers the deep arts of this wicked master ; and how resolved he seems to be on my ruin, by the pains he took to deprive me of all hopes of freeing myself from his power.

" FARMER NORTON,

" I send to your house, *for one night only*, a young gentle-woman, much against her will, who has deeply embarked in a love affair, which will be her ruin, as well as the person's to whom she wants to betroth herself. I have, *to oblige her father*, ordered her to be carried to one of my houses, where she will be well used, to try if, by absence, and expostulation with both, they can be brought to know their own interest : I am sure you will use her kindly for my sake ; for excepting this matter, *which she will not own*, she does not want prudence and discretion. I will acknowledge any trouble you shall be at in this matter, the first opportunity, and am

" *Your friend and servant.*"

He had said, too cunningly for me, that I would not *own* this pretended love affair : so that he had provided them not to believe me, say what I would ; and as they were his tenants, who all love him, (for he has some amiable qualities, so he had need !) I saw all my plot cut out, and was forced to say the less.

I wept bitterly, for I found he was too hard for me, as well in his contrivances as riches ; so I had recourse again to my only refuge, comforting myself, that God never fails to take the innocent heart into his protection, and is alone able to baffle and confound the devices of the mighty. The farmer was so prepossessed with the contents of his letter, that he began to praise his care and concern for me, and to advise me against entertaining addresses without my friends' advice and consent, and made me the subject of a lesson for his daughter's improvement. So I was glad to stop this discourse, as I was not likely to be believed. I sent to tell my driver, that I was so fatigued, I could not set out so soon the next morning. But he insisted upon it, and said, it would make my day's journey the lighter; and I found he was a more faithful servant to his master, notwithstanding what he wrote of his reluctance, than I could have wished: so I saw, still more and more, that all was deep dissimulation, and contrivance worse and worse.

I might have shewn them his letter to me, as a full confutation of his to them; but I saw no probability of engaging them in my behalf: and so thought it signified little, as I was to go away so soon, to enter more particularly into the matter with them; besides, I saw they were not inclinable to let me stay longer, for fear of disobliging him: so I went to bed, but had very little rest: they would make their servant-maid bear me company in the chariot five miles early in the morning, and she was to walk back.

I had contrived in my thoughts, when I was on my way in the chariot, on Friday morning, that when we came into some town to bait, as he must do for the horses' sake, I would, at the inn, apply myself to the mistress of the house, tell her the case, and refuse to go farther, having nobody but this wicked coachman to contend with.

Well, I was very full of this project, and in great hopes to extricate myself this way. But the artful wretch had provided for even this last refuge of mine; for when we came to put up at a large inn on the way, to partake of a dinner, and I was fully resolved to execute my project, who should be at the inn, but the wicked Mrs. Jewkes, expecting me! And her sister-in-law was the mistress of it; and she had provided a little entertainment for me. And this I found, when I desired, as soon as I went in, to speak with the mistress of the house. She came to me, and I said—" I am a poor unhappy young body that want your advice and assistance; you seem to be a good sort of gentlewoman, that would assist an oppressed innocent person." —" Yes, madam," said she, " I hope you guess right: and I have the happiness to know something of the matter before you speak. Pray call my sister Jewkes." Jewkes! Jewkes! thought I, I have heard of that name, I don't like it.

Then the wicked creature appeared, whom I had never seen but once before; I was terrified out of my wits. No stratagem, thought I, not *one!* for a poor innocent girl; but every thing to turn out against me; that is hard indeed. So I began to pull in my horns, as they say; for I saw I was now worse off than at the farmer's.

The naughty woman came up to me with an air of confidence, and kissed me! "See, sister," said she, "here's a charming creature! Would she not tempt the best lord in the land to run away with her?"—O frightful! thought I; here's an avowal of the matter at once. I am now gone, that's certain; and was quite silent and confused. Seeing no help for it, (for she would not part with me out of her sight) I was forced to set out with her in the chariot: for she came thither on horseback, with a man-servant, who rode by us the rest of the way, leading her horse. I now gave over all thoughts of redemption, and was in a desponding condition.

Well, I thought, here are strange pains taken to ruin a poor innocent, helpless, and *worthless* young body.—This plot is laid too deep, and has been to long hatching, to be baffled, I fear. I put my trust in God, who I knew was able to do every thing for me, when all other possible means should fail: and in him I was resolved to confide.

You may see what sort of woman this Mrs. Jewkes is, compared to good Mrs. Jervis, by this: every now-and-then she would be staring in my face, in the chariot, and squeezing my hand, saying—"Why, you are very pretty, my silent dear!" And once she offered to kiss me. But I said—"I don't like this sort of carriage, Mrs. Jewkes; it is not like two persons of one sex." She fell a laughing very confidently, and said—"That's prettily said, I vow! Then thou hadst rather be kissed by the other sex! I-fackins, I commend thee for that."

I was sadly teazed with her impertinence and bold way; but no wonder; she was an inn-keeper's house-keeper, before she came to my master; and those sort of creatures don't want confidence, you know: and indeed she made nothing to talk boldly on twenty occasions, and said two or three times, when she saw the tears every now-and-then, as we rid, trickle down my cheeks, "I was sorely hurt, truly, to have the handsomest and finest young gentleman in five counties in love with me!"

So I find I have got into the hands of a wicked procuress; and if I was not safe with good Mrs. Jervis, and where every body loved me, what a dreadful prospect have I now before me, in the hands of a woman that seems to delight in filthiness!

91

What shall I do! what shall I do!—Surely I shall never be equal to all these things.

About eight at night we entered the court-yard of this handsome, large, old, and lonely mansion, that looks made for solitude and mischief, as I thought, by its appearance, with all its brown nodding horrors of lofty elms and pines about it. Here, said I to myself, I fear is to be the scene of my ruin unless God protect me, who is all-sufficient!

I was very sick at entering it, partly from fatigue, and partly from dejection of spirits: Mrs. Jewkes got me some mulled wine, and seemed mighty officious to welcome me hither. While she was absent, ordering the wine, wicked Robin came in to me, and said, "I beg a thousand pardons for my part in this affair, since I see your grief and distress; and I do assure you, I am sorry it fell to my task."

"Mighty well, Mr. Robert!" said I; "I never saw an execution but once; and then the hangman asked the poor creature's pardon, wiped his mouth as you do, pleaded his duty, and then calmly tucked up the criminal. But I am no criminal, as you all know; if I could have thought it my duty to obey a wicked master in his unlawful commands, I had saved you all the merit of this vile service."

"I am sorry," said he, "you take it so; but every body don't think alike."—"Well," said I, "you have done *your* part, Mr. Robert, towards my ruin very faithfully; and will have cause to be sorry, may-be, at the long run, when you shall see the mischief that comes of it. Your eyes were open; you knew I was to be carried to my father's, and that I was barbarously tricked and betrayed. I can only, once more, thank you for your part of it. God forgive you!"

He went away a little sad. "What have you said to Robin, Madam?" said Mrs. Jewkes, who came in as he went out; "the poor fellow is ready to cry."—"I need not be afraid of *your* following his example, Mrs. Jewkes," said I; "I have been telling him he has done *his* part to my ruin: and he now can't help it! So his repentance does *me* no good: I wish it may *him*."

"I'll assure you, Madam," said she, "I should be as ready to cry as he, if I should do you any harm."—"It is not in *his* power to help it now," said I; "but *your* part is to come: you may choose whether you'll contribute to my ruin or not."—"Why, look ye, Madam," said she: "I have a great notion of doing my duty to my master, you may depend upon it, if I can do *that*, and serve *you*, I will; but you must think, if *your*

92

desire and *his* will clash, I shall do as he bids me, let it be what it will."

"Pray, Mrs. Jewkes," said I, "don't *Madam* me so : I am but a silly poor girl, set up by the gambol of Fortune, for a May-game; and now am to be something, and now nothing, just as Fortune thinks fit to sport with me. Let you and me talk upon a footing together : for I am a servant inferior to you, and so much the more, as I am turned out of place."

"Ay, ay," says she; "I understand something of the matter : you have so great power over my master, that you may be soon mistress of us all; and so I would oblige you if I could. I must and will call you Madam; for I am instructed to shew you all respect, I'll assure you."

"Who instructed you to do so?" said I.—"Who! my master, to be sure," said she.—"Why," said I, "how can that be? You have not seen him lately."—"That's true," said she; "but I have been expecting you here some time." (O the deep-laid wickedness, thought I.) "And, besides, I have a letter of instructions by Robin; but, may-be, I should not have said so much."—"If you would shew them to me," said I, "I should be able to judge how far I could, or could not, expect favour with you, consistent with your duty to our master."— "I beg your pardon, fair mistress, for that," said she; "I am sufficiently instructed; and you may depend upon it, I will observe my orders; and so far as they will let me, so far will I oblige you; and there's an end of it."

"Well," said I, "you will not, I hope, do an unlawful or wicked thing, for any master in the world."—"Look ye," said she, "he is my master; and if he bids me do any thing I *can* do, I think I *ought* to do it : and let him, who has power to command me, look to the *lawfulness* of it."—"Why," said I, "suppose he should bid you cut my throat, would you do it?" —"There's no danger of that," said she; "but to be sure I would not; for then I should be hanged, for that would be murder."—"Well," said I, "and suppose he should resolve to ensnare a poor young creature, and ruin her, would you assist him in that? For to rob a person of her virtue is worse than cutting her throat."

"Why, now," says she, "how strangely you talk!—Are not the two sexes made for one another? And is it not natural for a gentleman to love a pretty woman? And suppose he can obtain his desires, is that so bad as cutting her throat?" And then the wretch fell a laughing, and talked most impertinently, and shewed me that I had nothing to expect from her virtue or

93

conscience ; and this gave me great mortification ; for I was in hopes of working upon her by degrees.

So we ended our discourse here, and I bid her shew me where I must lie.—" Why," said she, " lie where you list, Madam ; I can tell you, I must lie with you for the present."—" *For the present !* " said I, and torture then wrung my heart ! " But is it in your *instructions*, that you must lie with me ? "—" Yes, indeed," said she. " I am sorry for it," said I. " Why," said she, " I am wholesome, and cleanly too, I'll assure you."— " Yes," said I, " I don't doubt that ; but I love to lie by myself."—" How so ? " said she ; " was not Mrs. Jervis your bed-fellow at t'other house ? "

" Well," said I, quite sick of her and my condition ; " you must do as you are instructed, I think. I can't help myself, and am a most miserable creature." She repeated her insufferable nonsense.—" Mighty miserable indeed, to be well beloved by one of the finest gentlemen in England ! "

I AM NOW COME DOWN IN MY WRITING TO THIS PRESENT SATURDAY, AND A DEAL I HAVE WRITTEN.

My wicked bed-fellow has very punctual orders ; for she locks me and herself in, and ties the two keys (for there is a double door to the room) about her wrist when she goes to bed. She talks of the house having been attempted to be broken open two or three times ; whether to frighten me, I cannot tell ; but it makes me fearful : though not so much as I should be, if I had not other and much greater fears.

I slept but little last night. I got up and pretended to sit by the window which leads into the spacious garden ; but was writing all the time, from break of day, to her getting up, and after, when she was absent.

At breakfast she presented the two maids to me, the cook and housemaid, poor awkward souls, that I can see no hopes from them, as they seem devoted to her and ignorance. Yet I am resolved, if possible, to find some way to escape, before this wicked master comes.

There are, besides, of servants, the coachman Robert, a groom, helper, and footman : all but Robert (who is accessory to my ruin) strange creatures, that promise nothing ; and all equally devoted to this woman. The gardener looks like a good honest man ; but he is kept at a distance, and seems reserved.

I wondered I saw not Mr. Williams, the clergyman, but would not ask after him, apprehending it might give her some jealousy ;

but when I had beheld the rest, he was the only one I had hopes of; for I thought his cloth would set him above assisting in my ruin. But in the afternoon he came; for it seems he has a little Latin school in the neighbouring village, which he attends; and this brings him a little matter additional to my master's favour, till something better falls, of which he has hopes.

He is a sensible, sober young gentleman; and when I saw him, I confirmed myself in my hopes of him; for he seemed to take great notice of my distress and grief (for I could not hide it), though he appeared fearful of Mrs. Jewkes, who watched all our motions and words. He has an apartment in the house; but is mostly at a lodging in the town, for conveniency of his little school, only on Saturday afternoons and Sundays; he preaches sometimes for the minister of the village, which is about three miles off.

I hope to go to church with him to-morrow; sure it is not in her instructions to deny me! He can't have thought of *every* thing! And something may strike out for me there.

I have asked her, for a feint (because she shan't think I am so well provided), to indulge me with pen and ink, though I have been using my own so freely, during her absence; for I begged to be left to myself as much as possible. She says she will let me have it; but then I must promise not to send any writing out of the house, without her seeing it. I said it was only to divert my grief, when by myself; for I loved writing as well as reading: but I had nobody to send to, she knew well enough.—" No, not at *present*, may-be," said she; " but I am told you are a great writer, and it is in my instructions to see all you write: so, look you here," said she; " I will let you have a pen, ink, and two sheets of paper; for this employment will keep you out of worse thoughts: but I must see them always when I ask, written or not written."—" That's very hard," said I; " but may I not have to myself the closet in the room where we lie, with the key to lock up my things? " " I believe I may consent to that," said she; " and I will set it in order for you, and leave the key in the door. And there is a spinnet too," said she: " if it be in tune, you may play to divert you now and then; for I know my old lady learnt you; and below is my master's library; you may take out what books you will."

And indeed these and my writing will be all my amusement: for I have no work given me to do; and the spinnet, if in tune, will not find my mind, I am sure, in tune to play upon it. But I went directly and picked out some books from the library, with which I filled a shelf in the closet she gave me possession of; and from these I hope to receive improvement, as well as amusement. But no sooner was her back turned, than I set about hiding a pen of my own here, and another there, and a little of my ink in a broken china cup, and a little in another cup; and a sheet of paper here and there among my linen; with a little wax and a few papers in several places, lest I should be searched; and something, I thought, might happen to open a way for my deliverance, by these or some other means. O the pride, thought I, I shall have, if I can secure my innocence, and escape the artful wiles of this wicked master! If he comes hither, I am undone to be sure! for this naughty woman will assist him, rather than fail, in the worst of his attempts; and he'll have no occasion to send her out of the way, as he would have done Mrs. Jervis once. So I must set all my little wits at work.

It is a grief to me to write, and not to be able to send to you what I write; but now it is all the diversion I have, and if God will favour my escape with my innocence, as I trust he graciously will, for all these black prospects, with what pleasure shall I read them afterwards!

I was going to say, "Pray for your dutiful daughter," as I used; but, alas! you cannot know my distress, though I am sure I have your prayers: and I will write on, as things happen, that if a way should open, my scribble may be ready to be sent: for what I do must be at a jerk, to be sure.

O how I want such an obliging, honest-hearted man as John!

I AM NOW COME TO SUNDAY.

Well, here is a sad thing! I am denied by this barbarous woman to go to church, as I had built upon I might: and she has huffed poor Mr. Williams all to pieces, for pleading for me. I find he is to be forbid the house if she pleases. Poor gentleman! all his dependence is upon my master, who has a very good living for him if the incumbent die, who has kept his bed these four months, of old age and dropsy.

He pays me great respect, and I see pities me; and would, perhaps, assist my escape from these dangers: but I have nobody to plead for me; and why should I wish to ruin a poor gentleman, by engaging him against his interest? Yet one would do any thing to preserve one's innocence; and Providence, would, perhaps, make it up to *him!*

O judge (but how shall you see what I write?) of my dis-

96

tracted condition, to be reduced to such a pass as to desire to lay traps for mankind !—But he wants sadly to say something to me, as he whisperingly hinted.

The wretch (I think I will always call her the *wretch* henceforth) abuses me more and more. I was but talking to one of the maids just now, indeed a little to tamper with her by degrees, and she popt upon us, and said, " Nay, Madam, don't offer to tempt poor innocent country maids from doing their duty. You wanted her to take a walk with you. But I charge you, Nan, never stir with her, nor obey her, without letting me know it, in the smallest trifles.—I say walk with you ! and where would you go, I tro'? "—" Why, barbarous Mrs. Jewkes," said I, " only to look a little up the elm-walk, since you would not let me go to church."

" Nan," said she, to shew me how much they were all in her power, " pull off Madam's shoes, and bring them to me. I have taken care of her others."—" Indeed she shan't," said I. " Nay," said Nan, " but I must if my mistress bids me : so pray, Madam, don't hinder me." And so, indeed, (would you believe it?) she took my shoes off, and left me barefoot ; and, for my share, I have been so frighted at this, that I have not power even to relieve my mind by my tears. I am quite stupefied !—Here I was forced to leave off.

Now I will give you a picture of this wretch. She is a broad, squat, pursy, *fat thing*, quite ugly, if any thing human can be so called ; about forty years old. She has a huge hand, and an arm as thick as my waist, I believe. Her nose is flat and crooked, and her brows grow down over her eyes ; a dead, spiteful, grey, goggling eye, to be sure she has ; and her face flat and broad : and as to colour, looks as if it had been pickled a month in saltpetre : I dare say she drinks. She has a hoarse man-like voice, and is as thick as she's long : and yet looks so deadly strong, that I am afraid she would dash me at her foot in an instant, if I was to vex her. So that with a heart more ugly than her face, she frightens me sadly ; and I am undone, to be sure, if God does not protect me ; for she is very, very wicked—indeed she is.

This is poor helpless spite in me :—but the picture is too near the truth, notwithstanding. She sends me a message, just now, that I shall have my shoes again, if I will accept of her company to walk with me in the garden—To *waddle* with me rather, thought I.

Well, 'tis not my business to quarrel with her downright. I shall be watched the narrower if I do : and so I will go with the hated wretch. O for my dear Mrs. Jervis! or rather to be safe with my dear father and mother.

Oh! I am out of my wits for joy! Just as I have got my shoes on, I am told John, honest John, is come on horseback! —A blessing on his faithful heart! What joy is this! But I'll tell you more by-and-by. I must not let her know I am so glad to see this dear blessed John, to be sure!—Alas! but he looks sad, as I see him out of the window! What can be the matter? I hope my dear parents are well, and Mrs. Jervis, and Mr. Longman, and everybody, my naughty master not excepted—for I wish him to live, and repent of all his wickedness to poor me.

O dear heart! what a world do we live in!—I am now come to take up my pen again: but I am in a sad taking truly! Another puzzling trial, to be sure.

Here was John, as I said; and the poor man came to me, with Mrs. Jewkes, who whispered that I would say nothing about the shoes for my *own* sake, as she said. The poor man saw my distress, by my red eyes, and my haggard looks, I suppose; for I have had a sad time of it, you must needs think; and though he would have hid it, if he could, yet his own eyes ran over: "Oh, Mrs. Pamela!" said he; "Oh, Mrs. Pamela!" —"Well, honest fellow-servant," said I, "I cannot help it at present: I am obliged to your honesty and kindness, to be sure," and then he wept more. Said I (for my heart was ready to break to see his grief; for it is a touching thing to see a man cry), "Tell me the worst! Is my master coming?"—"No, no," said he, and sobbed. "Well," said I, "is there any news of my poor father and mother? How do they do?"—"I hope well," said he; "I know nothing to the contrary."— "There's no mishap, I hope, to Mrs. Jervis or to Mr. Longman, or my fellow-servants!"—"No—" said the poor man; with a long N—o, as if his heart would burst. "Well, thank God, then!" said I.

"The man's a fool," said Mrs. Jewkes, "I think: what ado is here! why sure thou'rt in love, John. Dost thou not see young Madam is well! What ails thee, man?"—"Nothing at all," said he: "but I am such a fool as to cry for joy to see good Mrs. Pamela: but I have a letter for you."

I took it, and saw it was from my master, so I put it in my pocket. "Mrs. Jewkes," said I, "you need not, I hope, see this."—"No, no," said she, "I see whose it is, well enough; or else, may-be, I must have insisted on reading it."—"And here is one for you, Mrs. Jewkes," said he; "but yours," said he to me, "requires an answer, which I must carry back early in the morning or to-night if I can."—"You have no more, John," said Mrs. Jewkes, "for Mrs. Pamela, have you?"—"No," said he, "I have not; but every body's kind love and service."—"Aye, to us both to be sure," said she. "John," said I, "I will read the letter, and pray take care of yourself; for you are a good man, God bless you! and I rejoice to see you, and hear from you all." But I longed to say more; only that nasty Mrs. Jewkes.—

So I went up and locked myself in my closet, and opened the letter; and this is a copy of it.

"MY DEAREST PAMELA,

"I send purposely to you on an affair that concerns you very much, and me somewhat, but chiefly for your sake. I am conscious that I have proceeded by you in such a manner as may justly alarm your fears, and give concern to your honest friends: all my pleasure is, that I *can* and *will* make you amends for the disturbance I have given you. As I promised, I sent to your father the day after your departure, that he might not be too much concerned for you, and assured him of my honour to you; and made an excuse, such an one as ought to have satisfied him, for you not coming to him. But this was not sufficient, it seems; for he, poor man! came to me next morning, and set my family almost in an uproar about you.

"Oh, my dear girl! what trouble has not your obstinacy given me, and yourself too! I had no way to pacify him, but to promise that he should see a letter written from you to Mrs. Jervis, to satisfy him you are well.

"Now all my care in this case is for your aged parents, lest they should be touched with too fatal a grief for you, whose duty and affection for them I know to be so strong and laudable: for this reason I beg you will write a few lines to them, and let me prescribe the form; which I have done, putting myself as near as I can in your place, and expressing your sense with a warmth that I doubt will have too much possessed you.

"After what is done, and which cannot now be helped, but which I assure you, shall turn out honourably, I expect not to be refused; because I cannot possibly have any view in it, but to satisfy your parents, which is more *your* concern than *mine;* and so I beg you will not alter one tittle of the underneath. If you do, it will be impossible for me to send it, or that it should answer the good end I propose by it.

"I have promised, that I will not approach you without your

leave; if I find you easy, and not attempting to dispute or avoid your present lot, I will keep to my word, although 'tis a difficulty upon me. Nor shall your restraint last long: for I will assure you, that I am resolved very soon to convince you of my good intentions, and with what ardour I am *yours*, &c."

The letter he prescribed for me was this:

"DEAR MRS. JERVIS,

"I have, instead of being driven, by Robin, to my dear father's, been carried off, to where I have no liberty to tell. However, at present, I am not used hardly; and I write to beg you to let my dear father and mother, whose hearts must be well nigh broken, know that I am well; and that I am, and, by the grace of God, ever will be, their honest, as well as dutiful daughter, and *your obliged friend*.

"I must neither send date nor place; but have most solemn assurances of honourable usage."

I knew not what to do on this most strange request and occasion. But my heart bled so much for you, my dear father, who had taken the pains to go yourself, and enquire after your poor daughter, as well as for my dear mother, that I resolved to write, and pretty much in the above form,[1] that it might be sent to pacify you, till I could let you, some how or other, know the true state of the matter. And I wrote this to my strange wicked master himself:

"SIR,

"If you knew but the anguish of my mind, and how much I suffer by your dreadful usage of me, you would surely pity me, and consent to my deliverance. What have I done, that I should be the *only* mark of your cruelty? I can have no hope, no desire of living left me, because I cannot have the least dependence upon your solemn assurances, after what has passed. It is impossible they should be consistent with the dishonourable methods you take.

"Nothing but your promise of not seeing me here in deplorable bondage, can give me the least ray of hope.

"Don't, I beseech you, drive the poor distressed Pamela upon a rock, that may be the destruction both of her soul and body! You don't know, Sir, how dreadfully I *dare*, weak as I am of mind and intellect, when my virtue is in danger. And, O!

---

[1] See p. 81; her alterations are in a different character.

hasten my deliverance, that a poor unworthy creature, below the notice of such a gentleman as you, may not be made the sport of a high condition, for no reason in the world, but because she is not able to defend herself, nor has a friend that can right her.

"I have, Sir, in part to shew my obedience to you, but, I own, more to give ease to the minds of my poor distressed parents, whose poverty, one would think, should screen them from violences of this sort, as well as their poor daughter, followed nearly the form you prescribed for me, in the letter to Mrs. Jervis: the alterations I have made (for I could not help a few) are of such a nature, as though they shew my concern a little, yet must answer the end you are pleased to say you propose by this letter.

"For God's sake, good Sir, pity my lowly condition, and my present great misery; and *let* me join with all the rest of your servants to bless that goodness, which you have extended to every one, but the poor afflicted, heart-broken

"PAMELA."

I thought when I had written this letter, and that which he had prescribed, it would look like placing a confidence in Mrs. Jewkes, to shew them to her; and I shewed her, at the same time, my master's letter to me; for I believed the value he expressed for me, would give me credit with one who professed in every thing to serve him, right or wrong; though I had so little reason to pride myself in it. I was not mistaken; for it has influenced her a little; she is, at present, very obliging, and runs over in my praises: but is the less to be minded, because she praises as much the author of my miseries, and his *honourable* intentions, as she calls them; for I see that she is capable of thinking, as I fear *he* does, that every thing which makes for his wicked will is honourable, though to the ruin of the innocent. Pray God I may find it otherwise! Though, I hope, whatever the wicked gentleman may intend, that I shall be at last rid of her impertinent bold way of talk, when she thinks, from his letter, that he means honourably.

I AM NOW COME TO MONDAY, THE FIFTH DAY OF MY BONDAGE
AND MISERY.

I was in hope to have an opportunity to see John, and have a little private talk with him, before he went away; but it could not be. The poor man's excessive sorrow made Mrs. Jewkes take it into her head to think he loved me; so she brought up a message to me from him this morning, that he was going. I desired he might come up to *my* closet, as I called it; but she came with him. The honest man, as I thought him, was as full of concern as before, at taking leave. I gave him two letters, the one for Mrs. Jervis, inclosed in another for my master: but Mrs. Jewkes would see me seal them up, lest I should inclose any thing else. I was surprised, at the man's going away, to see him drop a bit of paper, just at the head of the stairs, which I took up without being observed by Mrs. Jewkes: but I was a thousand times more surprised, when I returned to my closet, and opening it, read as follows:

" Good Mrs. Pamela,

" I am grieved to tell you how much you have been deceived and betrayed, and that by such a vile dog as I. Little did I think it would come to this. But I must say, if ever there was a rogue in the world, it is me.—I have all along shewed your letters to my master: he employed me for that purpose; he saw every one, before I carried them to your father and mother; and then sealed them up, and sent me with them. I had some business that way, but not half so often as I pretended: and as soon as I heard how it was, I was ready to hang myself. You may well think I could not stand in your presence. O vile, vile wretch, to bring you to this! If you are ruined, I am the rogue that caused it. All the justice I can do you is to tell you, you are in vile hands; and I am afraid will be undone, in spite of all your sweet innocence; I believe I shall never live, after I know it. If you can forgive me, you are exceeding good; but I shall never forgive myself, that's certain. Howsoever, it will do you no good to make this known; and mayhap I may live to do you service. If I can, I will. I am sure I ought.—Master kept your last two or three letters, and did not send them at all. I am the most abandoned wretch of wretches.   J. Arnold.

" You see your undoing has been long hatching. Pray take care of yourself. Mrs. Jewkes is a devil: but in master's t'other house you have not one false heart but myself. Out upon me for a villain! "

My dear father and mother, when you come to this place, I make no doubt your hair will stand on end as mine does!—O the deceitfulness of the heart of men!—This John, that I took to be the honestest of men; that you took for the same; that was always praising you to me, and me to you, and for nothing so much as for our *honest* hearts; this *very* fellow was all the while a vile hypocrite, and a perfidious wretch, and helping to carry on my ruin.

But he says so much of himself, that I will only sit down with this sad reflection, That power and riches never want tools to promote their vilest ends; there is nothing so hard to be known as the heart of man :—I can but pity the poor wretch, since he seems to have great remorse; I believe it best to keep his wickedness secret. If it lies in my way, I will encourage his penitence; for I may possibly make some discoveries by it.

One thing I should mention in this place; he brought down, in a portmanteau, all the clothes and things my lady and master had given me, and moreover two velvet hoods, and a velvet scarf, that used to be worn by my lady; but I have no comfort in them, or any thing else.

Mrs. Jewkes had the portmanteau brought into my closet, and she shewed me what was in it; but then locked it up, and said, she would let me have what I would out of it, when I asked; but if I had the key, it might make we want to go abroad, may-be; and so the confident woman put it in her pocket.

I gave myself over to sad reflections upon this strange and surprising discovery of John's, and wept much for him, and for myself too; for now I see, as he says, my ruin has been long hatching, that I can make no doubt what my master's *honourable* professions will end in—What a heap of hard names does the poor fellow call himself! But what must they deserve who set him to work! O what has this wicked master to answer for, to be so corrupt himself, and to corrupt others, who would have been innocent; and to carry on a plot, to ruin a poor creature, who never did him harm, nor wished him any; and who can still pray for his happiness, and his repentance?

I can't but wonder what these *gentlemen*, as they are called, can think of themselves for these vile doings! John had *some* inducement; for he hoped to please his master, who rewarded him; and the same may be said, bad as she is, for the odious Mrs. Jewkes. But what inducement has my *master*, for taking so much pains to do the devil's work?—If he loves me, as it's falsely called, must he therefore lay traps for me, to ruin me, and make me as bad as himself? I cannot imagine what good the undoing of such a poor creature as I can procure him.— To be sure I am a very worthless body. People say I am handsome; but if I was so, should not a gentleman prefer an honest

103

servant to a guilty harlot? And must he be *more* earnest to seduce me, because I dread to be seduced, and would rather lose my life than my honesty.

Well, these are strange things! I cannot account for them; but surely nobody will say that these fine gentlemen have any tempter but their own wicked wills!—This naughty master could run away from me, when he apprehended his servants might discover his vile attempts in that sad closet affair; but is it not strange, that he should not be afraid of the All-seeing Eye, from which even that base, plotting heart of his, in its most secret motions, could not be hid!—But what avail these sorrowful reflections? He is and will be wicked, and designs me a victim to his lawless attempts, if the God in whom I trust, and to whom I hourly pray, prevent it not.

TUESDAY AND WEDNESDAY.

I have been hindered from writing on Tuesday, by this wicked woman's watching me so close: I will therefore put both these days together. I have taken an airing in the chariot, and walked several times in the garden; but have always her at my heels.

Mr. Williams came, and took a walk with us, and while Mrs. Jewkes's back was turned (encouraged by the hint he had before given me), I said, " Sir, I see two tiles upon that parsley-bed; might not one cover them with mould, with a note between them, on occasion?"—" A good hint," said he; " let that sun-flower by the back-door of the garden, be the place; I have a key to the door; for it is my nearest way to the town."

O what inventions will necessity put us upon! I hugged myself at the thought; and she coming to us, he said, as if he was continuing a discourse we were in, " No, not extraordinary pleasant."—" What's that? what's that?" said Mrs. Jewkes. " Only," said he, " the town, I'm saying, is not very pleasant." —" No, indeed," said she, " 'tis not; 'tis a poor town to my thinking."—" Are there any gentry in it?" said I. So we chatted on about the town, to deceive her. But my deceit intended no hurt to any body.

We then talked of the garden, how large and pleasant it was, and sat down on the tufted slope of a fish-pond, to see the fishes play upon the surface of the water: she said, I should angle if I would.

" I wish," said I, " you'd be so kind as to fetch me a rod and baits."—" Pretty mistress!" said she, " I know better than that, I'll assure you, at this time."—" I mean no harm," said

104

I, "indeed."—"Let me tell you," said she, "I know none who have their thoughts more about them than you. A body ought to look to it where you are. But we'll angle a little to-morrow." Mr. Williams, who is much afraid of her, turned the discourse to a general subject. I sauntered in, and left them to talk by themselves; he went away to town, and she was soon after me.

I had got to my pen and ink; and I said, "I want some paper, Mrs. Jewkes" (putting what I was about in my bosom): "you know I have written two letters, and sent them by John." (O how his name, poor guilty fellow, grieves me!) "Well," said she, "you have some left; one sheet did for those two letters."—"Yes," said I; "but I used half another for a cover, you know; and see how I have scribbled the other half:" so I shewed her a parcel of broken scraps of verses, which I had tried to recollect, and had written purposely that she might see, and think me usually employed to such idle purposes. "Aye," said she, "so you have: well, I'll give you two sheets more; but let me see how you dispose of them, either written or blank."—"Well," thought I, "I hope yet, Argus, to be too hard for thee." Now Argus, the poets say, had a hundred eyes, and was set to watch with them all, as she does.

She brought me the paper, and said, "Now, Madam, let me see you write something."—"I will," said I, and took the pen and wrote, "I wish Mrs. Jewkes would be so good to me, as I would be to her, if I had it in my power."—"That's pretty now," said she, "well, I hope I am; but what then?"—"Why then (*wrote I*) she would do me the favour to let me know what I have done to be made her prisoner; and what she thinks is to become of me."—"Well, and what then?" said she. "Why then of consequence (*scribbled I*) she would let me see her instructions, that I may know how far to blame or acquit her."

Thus I fooled on to shew her my fondness for scribbling (for I had no expectations of any good from her), that she might suppose I employed myself, as I said, to no better purpose at other times; for she will have it that I am upon some plot, I am so silent, and love so much to be by myself. She would have made me write on a little farther. "No," said I; "you have not answered me."—"Why," said she, "what can you doubt, when my master himself assures you of his honour?"—"Aye," said I, "but lay your hand to your heart, Mrs. Jewkes, and tell me, if you yourself believe him."—"Yes," said she, "to be sure I do."—"But," said I, "what do *you* call honour?"— "Why," said she, "what does *he* call honour, think you?"— "Ruin! shame! disgrace!" said I, "I fear."—"Pho! pho!"

said she, " if you have any doubt about it, he can best explain his own meaning : I'll send him word to come and satisfy you, if you will."— " Horrid creature ! " said I, all in a fright, " canst thou not stab me to the heart? I'd rather thou wouldst, than say such another word ! But I hope there's no thought of his coming."

She had the wickedness to say, " No, no ; he don't intend to come, as I know of—but if I was he, I would not be long away." —" What means the woman ? " said I.—" Mean ! " said she (turning it off), " why I mean I would come, if I was he, and put an end to all your fears—by making you as happy as you wish." —" 'Tis out of his power," said I, " to make *me* happy, great and rich as he is ; but by leaving me innocent, and giving me liberty to go to my dear father and mother."

She went away soon after, and I ended my letter, in hopes to have an opportunity to lay it in the appointed place. So I went to her, and said, " I suppose, as it is not quite dark, I may take another turn in the garden."—" 'Tis too late," said she ; " but if you will go, don't stay :—and, Nan, see and attend Madam," as she called me.

So I went towards the pond, the maid following me, and dropped purposely my hussey : when I came near the tiles, I said, " Mrs. Anne, I have dropt my hussey ; be so kind as to look for it : I had it by the pond-side." She went back to look, and I slipped the note between the tiles, and covered them as quick as I could with the light mould, quite unperceived ; the maid finding the hussey, I took it, sauntered in again, and met Mrs. Jewkes coming to see after me. What I wrote was this :

" Reverend Sir,

" The want of an opportunity to speak my mind to you, I am sure, will excuse this boldness in a poor creature that is betrayed hither, I have reason to think, for the worst of purposes. You know something of my story, my native poverty, which I am not ashamed of, my late lady's goodness, and my master's designs upon me. 'Tis true, he promises honour, and all that ; but the honour of the wicked is disgrace and shame to the virtuous : and he may think he keeps his promises, according to the notions he holds, and yet, according to mine and every good body's, basely ruin me.

" I am so wretched and ill-treated by this Mrs. Jewkes, and she is so ill-principled a woman, that as I may soon want the opportunity which the happy hint of this day affords to my hopes, I throw myself at once upon your goodness, without the least reserve; for I cannot be worse than I am, should that fail me; which I dare say, to your power, it will not: for I see it, Sir, in your looks, I hope it from your cloth, and I doubt it not from your inclination, in a case circumstanced as my unhappy one is. For, Sir, in helping me out of my present distress, you perform all the acts of religion in one; and the highest mercy and charity, both to the body and soul of a poor wretch, that, believe me, Sir, has at present, not so much as in thought, swerved from her innocence.

"Is there not some way to be found out for my escape, without danger to yourself? Is there no gentleman or lady of virtue in this neighbourhood, to whom I may fly, only till I can find a way to get to my poor father and mother? Cannot Lady Davers be made acquainted with my sad story, by your conveying a letter to her? My poor parents are so low in the world, they can do nothing but break their hearts for me; and that, I fear, will be the end of it.

"My master promises, if I will be easy, as he calls it, in my present lot, he will not come down without my consent. Alas! Sir, this is nothing: for what's the promise of a person who thinks himself at liberty to act as he has done by me? If he comes, it must be to ruin me; and come to be sure he will, when he thinks he has silenced the clamours of my friends, and lulled me, as no doubt he hopes, into a fatal security.

"Now, Sir, is all the time I have to work and struggle for the preservation of my honesty. If I stay till he comes, I am undone. You have a key to the back garden-door; I have great hopes from that. Study, good Sir, and contrive for me. I will faithfully keep your secrets—Yet I should be loth to have you suffer for me!

"I say no more, but commit this to the happy tiles, in the bosom of that earth, where I hope my deliverance will take root, and bring forth such fruit, as may turn to my inexpressible joy, and your eternal reward, both here and hereafter: as shall ever pray,

"Your oppressed humble servant."

THURSDAY.

This completes a terrible week since my setting out, as I hoped to see you, my dear father and mother. O how different were my hopes then, from what they are now! Yet who knows what these happy tiles may produce? But I must tell you, first, how I have been beaten by Mrs. Jewkes! 'Tis very true! —and thus it came about:

My impatience was great to walk in the garden, to see if any thing had offered, answerable to my hopes. But this wicked Mrs. Jewkes would not let me go without her; and said, she was not at leisure. We had a great many words about it; I told her, it was very hard I could not be trusted to walk by myself in the garden for a little air; but must be dogged and watched worse than a thief.

She still pleaded her instructions, and said she was not to trust me out of her sight. "You had better," said she, "be easy and contented, I'll assure you: for I have worse orders than you have yet found. I remember," added she, "your asking Mr. Williams if there were any gentry in the neighbourhood? This makes me suspect you want to get away to them, to tell your sad dismal story, as you call it."

My heart was at my mouth; for I feared, by that hint, she had seen my letter under the tiles: O how uneasy I was! At last she said—"Well, since you take on so, you may take a turn, and I will be with you in a minute."

When I was out of sight of her window, I went towards the hopeful place: but was soon forced to slacken my pace by her odious voice: "Hey-dey, why so nimble, and whither so fast?" said she, "what! are you upon a wager?" I stopt for her till her pursy sides were waddled up to me; she held by my arm, half out of breath; so I was forced to pass by the dear place, without daring to look at it.

The gardener was at work a little farther, and I began to talk about his art; but she said, "Softly, my instructions are, not to let you be so familiar with the servants."—"Why," said I, "are you afraid I should confederate with them to commit a robbery upon my master?"—"May-be I am," said the odious wretch; "for to rob him of yourself, would be the worst that could happen to him, in his opinion."

"And pray," said I, walking on, "how came I to be his property? What right has he in me, but such as a thief may plead to stolen goods?"—"Why, was ever the like heard?" says she. "This is downright rebellion, I protest!—Well, well, lambkin" (which the foolish woman often calls me), "if I was in his place, he should not have his property in you long questionable."—"Why, what would you do," said I, "if you were he?"—"Not stand shill-I shall-I, as he does, but put you and himself both out of your pain."—"Why, Jezebel," said I (I could not help it), "would you ruin me by force?" Upon this she gave me a deadly slap upon the shoulder: "Take that," said she; "whom do you call Jezebel?"

I was so surprised (for you never beat me, my dear father and mother, in your lives), that I was like one thunderstruck; and looked round, as if I wanted somebody to help me: but, alas! I had nobody; and said, rubbing my shoulder, "Is this also in your instructions?—Alas! for me! am I to be beaten too?" And so fell a crying, and threw myself upon the grass-walk we were upon. Said she, in a great pet, "I won't be called such names, I'll assure you. Marry, come up! I see you have a spirit: you must and shall be kept under. I'll manage such little provoking things as you, I warrant ye! Come, come, we'll go in a'doors, and I'll lock you up; you shall have no shoes, nor any thing else, if this be the case."

I did not know what to do. This was a cruel thing to me; I blamed myself for my free speech; for now I had given her some pretence of severity, and had, by my pertness, ruined the only project I had left. The gardener saw this scene: but she called to him, "Well, Jacob, what do you stare at? Pray mind what you are upon." And away he walked to another quarter, out of sight.

Well, thought I, I must put on the dissembler a little, I see. She took my hand roughly, "Come, get up," said she, "and come in a'doors.—I'll Jezebel you, I will!"—"Why, dear Mrs. Jewkes," said I. "None of your dears and your coaxing!" said she, "why not Jezebel again?" She was in a passion, I saw, and I was out of my wits. I have often heard women blamed for their tongues; I wish mine had been shorter. "But I can't go in," said I, "indeed I can't!"—"Why," said she, "can't you? I'll warrant I can take such a thin body as you under my arm, and carry you in, if you won't walk. You don't know my strength."—"Yes, but I do," said I, "too well; and will you not use me worse, when I come in?" So I arose; and she muttered to herself all the way, she to be a Jezebel with me, that had used me so well! and such like.

When I came near the house, I said, sitting down upon the bench—"Well, I will *not* go in, till you say you forgive me, Mrs. Jewkes. If you will forgive my calling you that name, I will forgive your beating me." She sat down by me, and seemed in a great pucker, and said, "Well, come, I will forgive you this time;" and so kissed me as a mark of reconciliation. "But pray," said I, "tell me where I am to walk or go, and give me what liberty you can; and when I know the most you can favour me with, you shall see I will be as content as I can, and not ask you for more."

"Aye," said she, "this is something like; I wish I could

give you all the liberty you desire; for you must think it is no pleasure to me to tie you to my petticoat, as it were, and not to let you stir without me.—But people that will do their duties must have some trouble; and what I do is to serve as good a master as lives."—" Yes," said I, " to every body but me ! "— " He loves you too well, to be sure," returned she, " and that's the reason; so you *ought* to bear it."—" I say *love !* " replied I. " Come," said she, " don't let the servant see you have been crying, nor tell her any tales; for you won't tell them fairly, I am sure. I'll send her to you, and you shall take another walk in the garden, if you will : may-be it will get you a stomach to your dinner, for you don't eat enough to keep life and soul together. You are beauty to the bone, or you could not look so well as you do, with so little stomach, so little, rest, and so much pining and whining for nothing at all." Well thought I, say what thou wilt, so I can be rid of thy bad tongue and company : and I hope to find some opportunity now, to come to my sun-flower. But I walked the other way to take that in my return, to avoid suspicion.

I forced my discourse to the maid; but it was all upon general things; for I find she is asked after every thing I say and do. When I came near the place, as I had been devising, I said, " Pray step to the gardener, and ask him to gather a salad for me to dinner." She called out, " Jacob ! " Said I, " He can't hear you so far off; and pray tell him, I should like a cucumber too, if he has one." When she had stept about a bow-shot from me, I popt down, and whipt my fingers under the upper tile, and pulled out a letter without direction, and thrust it into my bosom, trembling for joy. She was with me before I could well secure it; and I was in such a taking, that I feared I should discover myself. " You seem frighted, Madam," said she. " Why," said I, with a lucky thought, (alas ! your poor daughter will make an intriguer by-and-by; but I hope an innocent one !) " I stopped to smell at the sun-flower, and a great nasty worm ran into the ground, that startled me; for I can't abide worms." Said she, " Sun-flowers don't smell."—So I find," replied I. And then we walked in. Mrs. Jewkes said, " Well, you have made haste now. You shall go another time."

I went up to my closet, locked myself in, and, opening my letter, found in it these words :

" I am infinitely concerned for your distress. I most heartily wish it may be in my power to serve and save so much innocence, beauty, and merit. My whole dependence is upon Mr. B. and I have a near view of being provided for by his favour to me. But yet I would sooner forfeit all my hopes in him (trusting to God for the rest) than not assist you, if possible. I never looked upon Mr. B. in the light he now appears in. I am entirely of opinion, you should, if possible, get out of his hands, and especially as you are in very bad ones in Mrs. Jewkes's.

" We have here the widow Lady Jones, mistress of a good fortune, and a woman of virtue, I believe. We have also old Sir Simon Darnford, and his lady, who is a good woman; and they have two daughters, virtuous young ladies. All the rest are but middling people, and traders, at best. I will try, if you please, either Lady Jones or Lady Darnford, if they'll permit you to take refuge with them. I see no probability of keeping myself concealed in this matter; but will, as I said, risque all things to serve you; for I never saw sweetness and innocence like yours; your hard case has attached me entirely to you; for I well know, as you so happily express, if I can serve you in this case, I shall thereby perform all the acts of religion in one.

" As to Lady Davers, I will convey a letter, if you please, to her; but it must not be from our post-house, I give you caution; for the man owes all his bread to Mr. B. and his place too; and I believe, by something that dropt from him over a can of ale, has his instructions. You don't know how you are surrounded; all which confirms me in your opinion, that no honour is meant you, let what will be professed; and I am glad you want no caution on that head.

" Give me leave to say, that I had heard much in your praise, but, I think, greatly short of what you deserve, both as to person and mind : my eyes convince me of the one, your letter of the other. For fear of losing the present lucky opportunity, I am longer than otherwise I should be. But I will not enlarge any farther than to assure you that I am, to the best of my power, *your faithful friend and servant,*

" ARTHUR WILLIAMS.

" I will come once every morning, and once every evening, after school-time, to look for your letters.—I'll come in, and return without going into the house, if I see the coast clear : otherwise, to avoid suspicion, I'll come in."

I instantly, in answer to this pleasing letter, wrote as follows :

III

" REVEREND SIR,

"O how suited to your function and your character is your kind letter! God bless you for it! I now think I am beginning to be happy. I should be sorry to have you suffer on my account; but I hope it will be made up to you an hundred-fold, by that God whom you so faithfully serve. I should be too happy could I ever have it in my power to contribute in the least to it.—But, alas! to serve me, must be for God's sake only; for I am poor and lowly in fortune; though in mind, I hope, too high to do a mean or unworthy deed to gain a kingdom.

"Any way you think best I shall be pleased with: for I know not the persons, nor in what manner to apply to them. I am glad of the hint you gave me of the man at the post-house. I was thinking of opening a way for myself by letter, when I could have opportunity; but I see more and more that I am surrounded with dangers: and that there is no dependence to be placed on my master's honour.

"I should think, Sir, if either of those ladies would give leave, I might get out by favour of your key. As it is impossible, watched as I am, to know when it can be, suppose, Sir, you could get one made by it, and put it, the next opportunity, under the sun-flower. I am sure no time should be lost: it is rather wonderful she is not thoughtful about this key, for she forgets not the minutest thing. But, Sir, if I had this key I could, if these ladies would not shelter me, run away any where: and if I was once out of the house, they could have no pretence to force me in again; for I have done no harm, and hope to make my story good to any compassionate body: by this way *you* need not to be known. Torture should not wring it from me, I assure you.

"One thing more, good Sir. Have you no correspondence with my master's Bedfordshire family? By that means, may-be, I could be informed of his intentions of coming hither, and when. I inclose you a latter of a deceitful wretch (for I can trust you with any thing), poor John Arnold. Its contents will tell why I inclose it. Perhaps, by this means, something may be discovered; for he seems willing to atone for his treachery to me by the intimation of future service. I leave the hint to you to improve upon, and am, Reverend Sir, *your for ever obliged and thankful servant.*

"I hope, Sir, by your favour, I could send a little packet now-and-then to my poor father and mother. I have about five or six guineas: shall I put half in your hands, to defray the charge of a man and horse, or any other incidents?"

I had but just time to transcribe this before I was called to dinner; I put that for Mr. Williams in my bosom, to get an opportunity to lay it in the dear place.

Of all the flowers in the garden, the sun-flower, sure, is the loveliest!—It is a propitious one to me! How nobly my plot succeeds! But I begin to be afraid my writings may be discovered; for they grow large: I stitch them hitherto in my under coat, next my linen. If this brute should search me! but I must try to please her and then she won't.

I am but just come off from a walk in the garden, and have deposited my letter; we took a turn in the garden to angle, as Mrs. Jewkes had promised me. She baited the hook, I held it, and soon hooked a lovely carp. "Play it, play it," said she. I did, and brought it to the bank. A sad thought just then came into my head; and I threw it in again. What pleasure it seemed to have, to flounce, when at liberty! "Why throw it in?" said she. "O Mrs. Jewkes!" said I, "I was thinking this poor carp was the unhappy Pamela. I was comparing you and myself to my naughty master. As we hooked and deceived the poor carp, so was I betrayed by false baits; and when you said, 'Play it, play it,' it went to my heart to think I should sport with the destruction of the poor fish I had betrayed; I could not but fling it in again: and did you not see the joy with which the happy carp flounced from us? O," said I, "may some good merciful body procure me my liberty in the same manner; for I think my danger equal!"

"Lord bless thee!" said she, "what a thought is there!"— "I can angle no more," added I. "I'll try *my* fortune," said she, and took the rod. "Do," answered I; "and I will plant life, if I can, while you are destroying it. I have some horse-beans, and will go and stick them in one of the borders, to see how long they will be coming; and I will call them my garden."

So you see, dear father and mother, that this furnishes me with a good excuse to look after my garden another time; and if the mould should look a little freshish, it won't be so much suspected. She mistrusted nothing of this; and I went and stuck in here-and-there my beans, for about the length of five ells, of each side of the sun-flower, and easily deposited the letter. And not a little proud am I of this contrivance. Surely something will do at last!

FRIDAY, SATURDAY.

I have just now told a trick of mine; now I'll tell you a trick of this wicked woman's. She comes up to me. Says she,

" I have a bill I cannot change till to-morrow; and a tradesman wants his money most sadly; I don't love to turn poor
tradesmen away without their money: have you any about
you?"—" I have a little," replied I, " how much will do?"—
" Oh!" said she, " I want eight pounds."—" Alack!" said I,
" I have but between five and six."—" Lend me that," said
she, " till to-morrow." I did so; and she went down stairs;
and when she came up, she laughed, and said, " Well, I have
paid the tradesman."—" I hope," said I, " you'll give it me
again to-morrow." At this she, laughing, said, " Why, what
occasion have you for money? To tell you the truth, lambkin,
I didn't want it. I only feared you might make a bad use of
it; and *now* I can trust Nan with you a little oftener, especially
as I have got the key of your portmanteau; so that you can
neither corrupt her with money, nor fine things." Never did
any body look more silly than I.—O how I fretted to be so
foolishly outwitted!—and the more, as I had hinted to Mr.
Williams, that I would put some in his hands to defray the
charges of my sending to you. I cried for vexation.—And now
I have not five shillings left to support me, if I *can* get away.—
Was ever such a fool as me!—I must be priding myself in my
contrivances, indeed. Said I, " Was this in your instructions,
wolfkin?" (for she called me *lambkin*.) " *Jezebel*, you mean,
child!" said she. " Well, now I forgive you heartily; let's
buss and be friends."—" Out upon you!" said I; " I cannot
bear you." But I durst not call her names again; for I dread
her huge paw most sadly. The more I think of this the more
I regret it, and blame myself.

This night the man from the post-house brought a letter for
Mrs. Jewkes, in which was one inclosed to me: she brought it
me up. Said she, " Well, my good master don't forget us.
He has sent you a letter, and see what he writes to me." So
she read, that he hoped her fair charge was well, happy, and contented. " Aye, to be sure," said I, " I can't but choose!"
That he did not doubt her care and kindness to me; that I
was very dear to him, and she could not use me too well: and
the like. " There's a master for you!" said she: " sure you
will love and pray for him." I desired her to read the rest.
" No, no," said she, " but I won't." Said I, " Are there any
orders for taking my shoes away, and for beating me?"—" No,"
said she, " nor about Jezebel neither."—" Well," returned I,
" I cry truce: for I have no mind to be beat again."—" I
thought," said she, " we had forgiven one another."

My letter is as follows:

"MY DEAR PAMELA,

"I begin to repent already, that I have bound myself by promise not to see you till you give me leave! for I think the time very tedious. Can you place so much confidence in me as to *invite* me down? Assure yourself, that your generosity shall not be thrown away upon me. I would press this, as I am uneasy for your uneasiness; for Mrs. Jewkes acquaints me that you take your restraint very heavily, and neither eat, drink, nor rest well; I have too great an interest in your health not to wish to shorten the time of this trial, which will be the consequence of my coming down to you. John, too, has intimated to me your concern, with a grief that hardly gave him leave for utterance; a grief that a little alarmed my tenderness for you. Not that I fear any thing, but that your disregard to me, which yet my proud heart will hardly permit me to own, may throw you upon some rashness that might encourage a daring hope: but how poorly do I descend, to be anxious about such a menial as he! I will only say one thing, that if you will give me leave to attend you at the hall (consider *who* it is that requests this from you as a *favour*), I solemnly declare that you shall have cause to be pleased with this obliging mark of your confidence and consideration for me. If I find Mrs. Jewkes has not behaved to you with the respect due to one I so dearly love, I will put it entirely in your power to discharge her the house, if you think proper; and Mrs. Jervis, or who else you please, shall attend you in her place. This I say on a hint John gave me, as if you resented something from that quarter. Dearest Pamela, answer favourably this earnest request of one that cannot live without you, and on whose honour to you, you may absolutely depend; and so much the more, as you place a confidence in it. I am, and assuredly ever will be, *your faithful and affectionate*, &c.

"You will be glad, I know, to hear your father and mother are well, and easy upon your last letter. That gave me a pleasure that I am resolved you shall not repent. Mrs. Jewkes will convey to me your answer."

I but slightly read this letter for the present, to give way to one I had hopes of finding, by this time, from Mr. Williams. I took an evening turn, as I called it, in Mrs. Jewkes's company; and walking by the place, I said, "Do you think, Mrs. Jewkes, any of my beans can have struck since yesterday?" She laughed, and said, "You are a poor gardener, but I love to see you divert yourself." She passing on, I found my good friend had provided for me; and, slipping it in my bosom (for her back was towards me)—"Here," said I, (having a bean in my hand) "is one of them; but it has not stirred."—"No, to be sure," said she, and turned upon me a most wicked jest, unbecoming the mouth of a woman, about planting, &c. When I came in, I went to my closet, and read as follows:

"I am sorry to tell you that I have had a repulse from Lady Jones. She is concerned at your case, she says, but don't care to make herself enemies. I applied to Lady Darnford, and told her, in the most pathetic manner, your sad story, and shewed her your more pathetic letter. I found her well-disposed; but she would advise with Sir Simon, who is not a man of an extra-ordinary character for virtue; but he said to his lady, in my presence, 'Why, what is all this, my dear, but that our neigh-bour has a mind to his mother's waiting-maid! And if he takes care she wants for nothing, I don't see any great injury will be done her. He hurts no *family* by this.'" (So, my dear father and mother, it seems that poor people's honesty is to go for nothing.) "'And I think, Mr. Williams, you, of all men, should not engage in this affair, against your friend and patron.' He spoke this in so determined a manner, that the lady said no more, and I had only to beg that no notice should be taken of the matter, as from *me*.

"I have hinted your case to Mr. Peters, the minister of this parish; but I am concerned to say, that he imputed selfish views to me, as if I would make an interest in your affections by my zeal. And when I represented the duties of our function, and the like, and protested my disinterestedness, he coldly said, I was very good; but was a young man, and knew little of the world. And though it was a thing to be lamented, yet when he and I should set about to reform mankind in this respect, we should have enough upon our hands; for he said, it was too common and fashionable a case to be withstood by a private clergyman or two: and then uttered some reflections upon the conduct of the present fathers of the church, in regard to the first personages of the realm, as a justification of his coldness on this score.

"I represented the different circumstances of your affair; that other women lived evilly by their own consent; but to serve you, was to save an innocence that had but few examples; I then shewed him your letter.

"He said it was prettily written: he was sorry for you; and that your good intentions ought to be encouraged: 'But what,'

116

said he, 'would you have *me* do, Mr. Williams?' 'Why, suppose, Sir,' said I, ' you give her shelter in your house with your spouse and niece, till she can get to her friends?'—'What, and embroil myself with a man of Mr. B.'s power and fortune ! No, not I, I'll assure you !—and I would have you consider what you are about. Besides, she owns,' continued he, 'that he promises to do honourably by her; and her shyness will procure her good terms enough; for he is no covetous nor wicked gentleman, except in this case; and 'tis what all young gentlemen will do.'

" I am greatly concerned for him, I assure you; but am not discouraged by this ill success, let what will come of it, if I can serve you.

" I don't hear as yet that Mr. B. is coming. I am glad of your hint as to that unhappy fellow, John Arnold. Something, perhaps, will strike out from that, which may be useful. As to your packets, if you seal them up, and lay them in the usual place, if you find it not suspected, I will watch an opportunity to convey them; but if they are large, you had best be very cautious. This evil woman, I find, mistrusts me much.

" I just hear, that the gentleman is dying whose living Mr. B. has promised me. I have almost a scruple to take it, as I am acting so contrary to his desires; but I hope he'll one day thank me for it. As to money, don't think of it at present. Be assured you may command all in my power without reserve.

" I believe, when we hear he is coming, it will be best to make use of the key, which I shall soon procure you : I can borrow a horse for you, to wait within half a mile of the back-door, over the pasture; and will contrive by myself, or somebody, to have you conducted some miles distant, to one of the villages thereabouts; so don't be discomforted, I beseech you. I am, Mrs. Pamela, *your faithful friend*, &c."

I made a thousand sad reflections upon the former part of this honest gentleman's kind letter; and but for the hope he gave me at last, should have given up my case as quite desperate. I then wrote to thank him most gratefully for his kind endeavours; to lament the little concern the gentry had for my deplorable case : the wickedness of the world, first to give way to such iniquitous fashions, and then plead the frequency of them, against the attempt to amend them; and how unaffected people were with the distress of others. I recalled my former hint as to writing to Lady Davers, which I feared would only serve to apprise her brother that she knew his wicked scheme, and make him come down the sooner, and render him more determined on my ruin; besides, it might make Mr. Williams guessed at as a means of conveying my letter: and being very fearful, that if that good lady *would* interest herself in my behalf (which was a doubt, because she both loved and feared her brother), it would have no effect upon him; and that therefore I would wait the happy event I might hope for from his kind assistance in the key and the horse. I intimated my master's letter, begging to be permitted to come down: was fearful it might be sudden; and that I was of opinion no time was to be lost; for we might let slip all our opportunities; telling him the money-trick of this vile woman, &c.

I had not time to take a copy of this letter, I was so watched. But when I had it in my bosom, I was easy. And so I went to seek out Mrs. Jewkes, and told her I would have her advice upon the letter I had received from my master; which point of confidence in her pleased her not a little. " Aye," says she, " now this is something like: and we'll take a turn in the garden, or where you please." I pretended it was indifferent to me; and so we walked into the garden. I began to talk to her of the letter; but was far from acquainting her with all the contents; only that he wanted my consent to come down, and hoped she used me kindly, and the like. And I said, " Now, Mrs. Jewkes, let me have your advice as to this."— " Why then," said she, " I will give it you freely: e'en send to him to come down. It will highly oblige him, and I dare say you'll fare the better for it."—" How the *better ?* " said I. " I dare say, you think yourself he intends my ruin."—" I hate," said she, " that foolish word. Your *ruin !*—Why, ne'er a lady in the land may live happier than you, if you will, or be more honourably used."

" Well, Mrs. Jewkes," said I, " I shall not at this time dispute with you about the words *ruin* and *honourable ;* for I find we have quite different notions of both: but I will speak plainer than ever I did. Do you think he intends to make proposals to me as a kept mistress, or rather a kept slave ? "—" Why, lambkin," said she, " what dost thou think thyself ? "—" I fear," said I, " he does."—" Well," said she, " but if he does (for I know nothing of the matter, I assure you), you may have your own terms—I see that; for you may do any thing with him."

I could not bear this to be spoken, though it was all I feared of a long time, and began to exclaim most sadly. " Nay," said she, " he may marry you, as far as I know."—" No, no," said I, " that cannot be. I neither desire nor expect it. His condition don't permit me to have such a thought : the whole series of his conduct convinces me of the contrary : you would have me invite him to come down, would you? Is not this to invite my ruin? "

" 'Tis what *I* would do," said she, " in your place; and if it was to be as you *think*, I should rather be out of my pain than live in continual frights and apprehensions, as you do."—" No," replied I, " an *hour* of innocence is worth an *age* of guilt; and were my life to be made ever so miserable by it, I should never forgive myself if I were not to lengthen out to the longest minute my happy time of honesty. Who knows what Providence may do for me? "

" Why, may-be," said she, " as he loves you so well, you may prevail upon him by your prayers and tears; and for that reason I should think you'd better let him come down."—" Well," said I, " I will write him a letter, because he expects an answer, or may-be he will make a pretence to come down.—How can it go? "—" I'll take care of that," said she, " it is in my instructions."—" Aye," thought I, " so I doubt, by the hint Mr. Williams gave me about the post-house."

The gardener coming by, I said, " Mr. Jacob, I have planted a few beans, and I call the place my garden. It is just by the door out yonder : I'll shew it you; pray don't dig them up." So I went with him, and when we had turned the alley, out of her sight, and were near the place, I said, " Pray step to Mrs. Jewkes, and ask her if she has any more beans for me to plant." He smiled at my foolishness; and I popped the letter under the mould, and stepped back, as if waiting for his return : which, being near, was immediate, and she followed him. " What should *I* do with beans?" she said, and sadly scared me, for she whispered me, " I am afraid of some fetch. You send me on such simple errands."—" What fetch? " said I : " it is hard I can neither stir nor speak, but I must be suspected."—" Why," said she, " my master writes, that I must have all my eyes about me; for though you are as innocent as a dove, yet you're as cunning as a serpent. But I'll forgive you, if you cheat *me*."

Then I thought of my money, and could have called her names, had I dared. I said, " Pray, Mrs. Jewkes, now you talk of forgiving me, if I cheat you, be so kind as to pay me my money : for though I have no occasion for it, yet I know you was but in jest, and intended to give it me again."—" You shall have it in a proper time," said she; " but, indeed, I was in earnest to get it out of your hands, for fear you should make an ill use of it."—So we cavilled upon this subject as we walked in, and I went up to write my letter to my master. As I intended to shew it her, I resolved to write accordingly as to her part of it : for I made little account of his offer of Mrs. Jervis to me, instead of this wicked woman (though the most agreeable thing that could have befallen me, except my escape from hence), nor indeed any thing he said. For to be honourable in the just sense of the word, he need not have caused me to be run away with, and confined as I am. I wrote as follows :

" HONOURED SIR,

"When I consider how easily you might make me happy, since all I desire is to be permitted to go to my poor mother and father; when I reflect upon your former proposal to me, in relation to a certain person, not one word of which is now mentioned; and upon my being in that strange manner run away with, and still kept here a miserable prisoner; do you think, Sir (pardon your poor servant's freedom; my fears make me bold; do you think, I say), that your general assurances of honour to me can have the effect they ought to have? O good Sir ! I too much apprehend that *your* notions of honour and *mine* are very different from one another : I have no other hope but in your continued absence. If you have any proposals to make me that are consistent with your honourable professions, in my *humble* sense of the word, a few lines will communicate them to me, and I will return such an answer as befits me. But what proposals can one in your high station have to make to one in my low degree ! I know what belongs to your exalted station too well, to imagine that any thing can be expected but sad temptations, and utter distress, if you come down : you know not, Sir, when I am made desperate what the wretched Pamela *dares do !*

"Whatever rashness you may impute to me, I cannot help it ; but I wish I may not be forced upon any that otherwise would never enter my thoughts. Forgive me, Sir, my plainness; I should be loth to behave to my master unbecomingly : but I must say, Sir, my innocence is so dear to me, that my observations must be dispensed with. If you mean honourably, why, Sir, should you not let me know it plainly? Why is it necessary to imprison me to convince me of it? Why must I be close watched, attended, and hindered from stirring out, from speaking to any body, or from going so much as to church to pray for you, who have been, till of late, so generous a benefactor to me? Why, Sir, I humbly ask, why all this, if you mean honourably? It is not for me to expostulate so freely with you, Sir, so greatly my superior. Pardon me, I hope you will: but as to *seeing you*, I cannot bear the dreadful apprehension. Whatever you have to propose, whatever you intend by me, let my assent be that of a free person, and not of a sordid slave, who is to be threatened and frightened into a compliance with measures, which your conduct seems to imply. My restraint is hard upon me; I am very uneasy under it. Shorten it, I beseech you, or—But I will not dare say more, than that I am *your greatly oppressed, unhappy servant.*"

After I had taken a copy of this, I folded it up, and Mrs. Jewkes, coming just as I had done, sat down by me, and said, when she saw me direct it, " I wish you would tell me if you have taken my advice, and consented to my master's coming down."—" If it will oblige you," said I, " I will read it to you."—" That's good," said she; " then I'll love you dearly." Said I, " Then you must not offer to alter one word."—" I won't," replied she. So I read it to her; she praised me much for my wording it, but said, she thought I pushed the matter very close; and it would better bear *talking* of, than *writing* about. She wanted an explanation or two as about the proposal to a *certain person;* but I said she must take it as she heard it. " Well, well," said she, " I make no doubt you understand one another, and will do so more and more." I sealed up the letter, and she undertook to convey it.

SUNDAY.

For my part, I knew it in vain to expect leave to go to church now; so I did not ask: I was the more indifferent, because if I might have had permission, the sight of the neighbouring gentry, who had despised my sufferings, would have given me great regret and sorrow; and it was impossible I should have edified under any doctrine preached by Mr. Peters: so I applied myself to my private devotions.

Mr. Williams came yesterday, and this day, as usual, and took my letter; but, having no good opportunity, we avoided one another's conversation, and kept at a distance; but I was concerned I had not the key; for I would not have lost a moment in that case.

When I was at my devotion, Mrs. Jewkes came up, and wanted me to sing her a psalm, as she had often, on common days, importuned me for a song upon the spinnet: but I declined it, because my spirits were so low I could hardly speak, nor cared to be spoken to : but when she was gone, I, remembering the 137th psalm to be a little touching, turned to it, and took the liberty to alter it, somewhat nearer to my case. I hope I did not sin in it; but thus I turned it.

> When sad I sat in B——n Hall,
>   All guarded round about,
> And thought of every absent friend,
>   The tears for grief burst out.
> My joys and hopes all overthrown,
>   My heart-strings almost broke.
> Unfit my mind for melody,
>   Much more to hear a joke;
> Then she to whom I prisoner was,
>   Said to me tauntingly——
> " Now cheer your heart, and sing a song,
>   And tune your mind to joy."——
> " Alas ! " said I, " how can I frame
>   My heavy heart to sing,
> Or tune my mind while thus enthrall'd
>   By such a wicked thing ?
> But yet, if from my innocence
>   I e'en in thought should slide,
> Then let my fingers quite forget
>   The sweet spinnet to guide.
> And let my tongue within my mouth
>   Be locked for ever fast,
> If I rejoice, before I see
>   My full deliv'rance past."
> And thou, Almighty, recompence
>   The evils I endure
> From those that seek my sad disgrace,
>   So causeless to procure.
> Remember, Lord, this Mrs. Jewkes,
>   When, with a mighty sound,
> She cries, " down with her chastity,
>   Down to the very ground."
> E'en so shalt thou, O wicked one,
>   At length to shame be brought :
> And happy shall all those be call'd
>   That my deliv'rance wrought.
> Yes, blessed shall the man be call'd
>   That shames thee of thy evil,
> And save me from thy vile attempts,
>   And thee, too, from the d——l.

MONDAY, TUESDAY, WEDNESDAY.

I write now with a little more liking, though less opportunity, because Mr. Williams has got a large parcel of my papers safe in his hands to send them to you, as he has opportunity; so that I am not quite uselessly employed; I am, besides, delivered from the fear of their being found, if I should be searched. I have been permitted to take an airing, five or six miles, with Mrs. Jewkes: but though I know not the reason, she watches me more closely than ever; so that we have discontinued, by consent, for these three days, the sun-flower correspondence.

The poor cook-maid has had a bad mischance; for she has been hurt much by a bull in the pasture, by the side of the garden, not far from the back-door. This pasture I am to cross, which is about half a mile, and then is a common, and near that a private horse-road, where I hope to find an opportunity for escaping, as soon as Mr. Williams can get me a horse, and has made all ready for me: he has got me the key, which he put under the mould, just by the door.

He just now has signified that the gentleman is dead, whose living he has had hope of, he came pretendedly to tell Mrs. Jewkes of it. She wished him joy. See what the world is! one man's death is another man's joy. Thus we thrust out one another! My hard case makes me serious. He found means to slide a letter into my hands, and is gone away: he looked at me with such respect and solemnness at parting, that Mrs. Jewkes said, "Why, Madam, I believe our young parson is half in love with you."—"Ah! Mrs. Jewkes," said I, "he knows better." Said she (I believe to sound me), "Why, I can't see you can, either of you, do better; and I have lately been so touched for you, seeing how heavily you apprehended dishonour from my master, that I think it is pity you should not have Mr. Williams."

I knew this must be a fetch of her's, because instead of being troubled for me, as she pretended, she watched me closer, and him too: so I said, "There is not the man living that I desire to marry. If I can but keep myself honest, it is all my desire: and to be a comfort and assistance to my poor parents: if this should be my happy lot, it is the very top of my ambition."—"Well, but," said she, "I have been thinking very seriously that Mr. Williams would make you a good husband; and as he will owe all his fortune to my master, he will be very glad to be obliged to him for a wife of his choosing; especially," said she, "such a pretty one, and one so ingenious, and genteely educated."

This gave me a doubt whether she knew of my master's intimation of that sort formerly: I asked her if she had reason to surmise that *that* was in view? "No," she said; "it was only her own thought:" but it was very likely that my master had either that in view, or something better for me. But if I approved of it, she would propose such a thing to her master directly : and gave a detestable hint, that I might take resolutions upon it, of bringing such an affair to effect. I told her, I abhorred her vile insinuation : and as to Mr. Williams, I thought him a civil good sort of man; but as, on one side, he was above me, so, on the other, I said, of all things, I did not love a parson. Finding she could make nothing of me, she quitted the subject.

I will open this letter by-and-by, and give you the contents of it; for she is up and down so much that I am afraid of her surprising me.

Well, I see Providence has not abandoned me : I shall be under no necessity to make advances to Mr. Williams, if I was (as I am sure I am not) disposed to it. This is his letter :

" I know not how to express myself, lest I should appear to you to have a selfish view in the service I would do you. But I really know but one effectual and honourable way to disengage yourself from the dangerous situation you are in. It is that of marriage with some person that you can make happy in your approbation. As for my own part, it would be, as things stand, my apparent ruin ! and worse still, I should involve you in misery too. But yet, so great is my veneration for you, so entire my reliance on Providence, upon so just an occasion, that I should think myself but too happy if I might be accepted. I would, in this case, forego all my expectations, and be your conductor to some safe distance. But why do I say *in this case ?* That I will do whether you think fit to reward me so eminently or not : and I will, the moment I hear of Mr. B——'s setting out (and I think now I have settled a very good method of intelligence of all his motions), get a horse ready, and myself to conduct you. I refer myself wholly to your goodness and direction, and am, with the highest respect, *your most humble faithful servant.*

" Don't think this a sudden resolution. I always admired your hearsay character; and the moment I saw you, wished to serve so much excellence."

What shall I say, my dear father and mother, to this unexpected declaration ? I want, more than ever, your blessing and direction. But, after all, I have no mind to marry; I had rather live with you. But yet, I would marry a man who begs from door to door, and has no home, rather than endanger my honesty. Yet I cannot, methinks, hear of being a wife. After a thousand different thoughts, I wrote as follows :

" REVEREND SIR,

"I am greatly confused at the contents of your last. You are much too generous; I can't bear you should risk all your future prospects for so unworthy a creature. I cannot think of your offer without equal concern and gratitude; for nothing but to avoid my utter ruin can make me think of changing my condition; and so, Sir, you ought not to accept of such an involuntary compliance, as mine would be, was I, upon the last necessity, to yield to your very generous proposal. I will rely wholly upon your goodness to me, in assisting my escape; but shall not, on your account principally, *think* of the honour you propose for me, at present; and never shall, but at the pleasure of my parents, who, poor as they are, in such a weighty point are as much entitled to my obedience and duty as if they were ever so rich. I beg you, therefore, Sir, not to think of any thing from me but everlasting gratitude, which will always bind me to be *your most obliged servant.*"

THURSDAY, FRIDAY, SATURDAY, THE 14TH, 15TH, AND 16TH, OF MY BONDAGE.

Mrs. Jewkes has received a letter, and is much civiller to me, and Mr. Williams too, than she used to be. I wonder I have not one in answer to mine from my master. I suppose I put the matter too home to him; and he is angry. I am not the more pleased with her civility; for she is horrid cunning, and is not a whit less watchful. I laid a trap to get her instructions, which she carries in the bosom of her stays; but it has not yet succeeded.

My last letter is come safe to Mr. Williams by the old conveyance, so that he is not suspected. He has intimated, that though I have not come so readily as he hoped into his scheme, yet his diligence shall not be slackened, and he will leave it to Providence and myself to dispose of him as he shall be found to deserve. He has signified to me, that he shall soon send a special messenger with the packet to you; I have added to it what has occurred since.

SUNDAY.

I am just now quite astonished!—I hope all is right—but I have a strange turn to acquaint you with. Mr. Williams and Mrs. Jewkes came to me both together; he in ecstacies, she with a strange fluttering sort of air. " Well," said she, " Mrs. Pamela, I give you joy! I give you joy! Let nobody speak but me!" Then she sat down, as out of breath, puffing and blowing.

" Why, every thing turns as I said it would ! " said she : " why there is to be a match between you and Mr. Williams. Well, I always thought it. Never was so good a master !—Go to, go to, naughty mistrustful Mrs. Pamela, nay, Mrs. Williams," said the forward creature, " I may as well call you so : you ought on your knees to beg his pardon a thousand times for mistrusting him."

She was going on; but I said, " Don't torture me thus, I beseech you, Mrs. Jewkes. Let me know all !—Ah ! Mr. Williams," said I, " take care, take care ! "—" Mistrustful again ! " said she; " do, Mr. Williams, shew her your letter : and I will shew her mine : they were brought by the same hand."

I trembled at the thoughts of what this might mean; and said, " You have so surprised me, that I cannot stand, hear, or read !—Why did you come up in such a manner to attack such weak spirits ? " Said he to Mrs. Jewkes, " Shall we leave our letters with Mrs. Pamela, and let her recover from her surprise ? "—" Aye," said she, " with all my heart; here is nothing but flaming honour and good-will ! " And so saying, they left me their letters, and withdrew.

My heart was quite sick with the surprise; so that I could not directly read them, notwithstanding my impatience; but, after awhile, recovering, I found the contents thus strange and unexpected :

" MR. WILLIAMS,

" The death of Mr. Fownes has now given me the opportunity I have long wanted, to make you happy, and that in a double respect : for I shall soon put you in possession of his living, and, if you have the art of making yourself well received, of one of the loveliest wives in England. She has not been used (as she has reason to think) according to her merit; but when she finds herself under the protection of a man of virtue and probity, and a happy competency to support life in the manner to which she has been of late years accustomed, I am persuaded she will forgive these seeming hardships which have paved the way to so happy a lot, as I hope it will be to you both. I have only to account for the odd conduct I have been guilty of, which I shall do when I see you : but, as I shall soon set out for London, I believe it will not be yet this month. Meantime, if you can prevail with Pamela, you need not suspend your mutual happiness : only let me have notice of it first, and that she approves of it; which ought to be, in so material a point, entirely at her option; as I assure you, on the other

126

hand, I would have it at yours, that nothing may be wanting to complete your happiness. I am *your humble servant.*"

Was ever the like heard?—Lie still, my throbbing heart, divided as thou art, between thy hopes and thy fears!—But this is the letter Mrs. Jewkes left with me.

"MRS. JEWKES,
        "You have been very careful and diligent in the task which, for reasons I shall hereafter explain, I had imposed upon you. Your trouble is now almost at an end; for I have written my intentions to Mr. Williams so particularly, that I need say the less here, because he will not scruple, I believe, to let you know the contents of my letter. I have only one thing to mention, that if you find what I have hinted to him in the least measure disagreeable to either, you assure them both, that they are at entire liberty to pursue their own inclinations. I hope you continue your civilities to the mistrustful, uneasy Pamela, who will now begin to think better of hers and *your friend,* &c."

I had hardly time to transcribe these letters, though, writing so much, I write pretty fast, before they both came up again in high spirits; and Mr. Williams said, "I am glad, Madam, I was *beforehand* in my declarations to you; this generous letter has made me the happiest man on earth; and, Mrs. Jewkes, if I can procure this fair one's consent, I shall think myself——"
I interrupted the good man, and said, "Ah! Mr. Williams, take care, take care; don't let——" There I stopt, and Mrs. Jewkes said, "Still mistrustful! I never saw the like in my life! But I see," said she, "I was not wrong, while my old orders lasted, to be wary of you both—*I* should have had a hard task to prevent you, I find; for as the saying is, *Nought can strain consent of twain.*"
I doubted not her taking hold of his joyful indiscretion. I took her letter, and said, "Here, Mrs. Jewkes, is yours; I thank you for it; but I have been so long in a maze, that I can say nothing to this for the present. Time will bring all to light.—Sir," said I, "here is yours; may every thing turn to your happiness! I give you joy of my master's goodness in the living."—"It will be *dying,*" said he, "not a *living,* without you."—"Forbear, Sir," said I; "while I have a father and mother, I am not my own mistress, poor as they are: and I'll see myself quite at liberty before I shall think myself fit to make a choice."
Mrs. Jewkes lifted up her eyes and hands, and said, "Such

art, such caution, such cunning, for thy years!"—"Well!—Why," said I, (that he might be on his guard, though I hope there cannot be deceit in this; it would be strange villainy if there should!) "I have been so used to be made a fool of by fortune, that I hardly can tell how to govern myself; and am almost an infidel as to mankind. But I hope I may be wrong; henceforth, Mrs. Jewkes, you shall regulate my opinions as you please, I will consult you in every thing—that I think proper," said I to myself; for though I may forgive her, I can never love her.

She left Mr. Williams and me a few minutes together; I said, "Consider, Sir, what you have done."—"'Tis impossible," said he, "there can be deceit."—"I hope so," said I; "but what necessity was there for you to talk of your *former* declaration? Let *this* be as it will, *that* could do no good, especially before this woman. Forgive me, Sir; they talk of women's promptness of speech; but I see an honest heart is not always to be trusted with itself in bad company."

He was going to reply, but though her task is said to be ALMOST (I took notice of that word) at an end, she came up to us again, and said, "Well, I had a good mind to shew you the way to church to-morrow." I was glad of this, because, though in my present doubtful situation I should not have chosen it, yet I would have encouraged her proposal, to be able to judge of her being in earnest or otherwise, whether one might depend upon the rest. But Mr. Williams again indiscreetly helped her to an excuse, by saying, that it was now best to defer it one Sunday, and till matters were riper for my appearance: she readily took hold of it, and confirmed his opinion.

After all, I hope the best; but if this should turn out to be a plot, I fear nothing but a miracle can save me. But sure the heart of man is not capable of such deceit. Besides, Mr. Williams has it under his own hand, he dare not but be in earnest; and then again, though, to be sure, he has been very wrong to me, yet his education, and parents' example, have neither of them taught him such very black contrivances. So I will hope for the best!

Mr. Williams, Mrs. Jewkes, and I, have been all three walking together in the garden; she pulled out her key, and we walked a little in the pasture to look at the bull, an ugly, grim, surly creature, that hurt the poor cook-maid, who is got pretty well again. Mr. Williams pointed at the sun-flower, but I was forced to be very reserved to him; for the poor gentleman has no guard, no caution at all.

We have just supped together, all three; and I cannot yet think but all must be right. Only I am resolved not to marry, if I can help it; and I will give no encouragement, I am resolved, at least, till I am with you.

Mr. Williams said, before Mrs. Jewkes, he would send a messenger with a letter to my father and mother. I think the man has no discretion: but I desire you will send no answer till I have the pleasure and happiness, which now I hope for soon, of seeing you. He will, in sending my packet, send a most tedious parcel of stuff, of my *oppressions, distresses,* and *fears;* so I will send this with it (for Mrs. Jewkes gives me leave to send a letter to my father, which looks well): I am glad I can conclude, after all my sufferings, with my *hopes,* to be soon with you, which I know will give you comfort; and so I rest, begging the continuance of your prayers and blessings, *your ever dutiful daughter.*

My dear Father and Mother,

I have so much time upon my hands, that I must write to employ myself. The *Sunday evening,* where I left off, Mrs. Jewkes asked me, if I chose to lie by myself? I said, " Yes, with *all* my heart, if she pleased."—" Well," said she, " after to-night you shall." I asked her for more paper, and she gave me a bottle of ink, eight sheets of paper, which she said was all her store (for now she would get me to write for her to our master, if she had occasion), and six pens, with a piece of sealing-wax. This looks mighty well. She pleased me, when she came to bed, very much to give encouragement to Mr. Williams, and said many things in his behalf; and blamed my shyness to him. I told her, I was resolved to give no encouragement, till I had talked to my father and mother. She said, she fancied I thought of somebody else, or I could never be so insensible. I assured her, as I could do very safely, that there was not a man on earth I wished to have; and as to Mr. Williams, he might do better by far; and I had proposed so much happiness in living with my poor father and mother, that I could not think of any scheme of life with pleasure, till I had tried that. I asked her for my money; and she said it was above in her strong box, but that I should have it to-morrow. All these things look well.

Mr. Williams would go home this night, though late, because he would dispatch a messenger to you with a letter he had proposed from himself, and my packet. But pray don't encourage him, as I said; for he is much too precipitate in this matter;

though he is a very good man, and I am much obliged to him.

Alas-a-day! we have had bad news from poor Mr. Williams. He has had a sad mischance; fallen among rogues in his way home last night; but, by good chance, has saved my papers. This is the account he gives of it to Mrs. Jewkes.

"GOOD MRS. JEWKES,
        "I have had a sad misfortune in going from you. When I had got as near the town as the dam, and was going to cross the wooden bridge, two fellows got hold of me, and swore they would kill me, if I did not give them what I had. They rummaged my pockets, and took from me my snuff-box, my seal-ring, half a guinea, some silver, and halfpence; also my handkerchief, and two or three letters I had in my pockets. By good fortune, the letter Mrs. Pamela gave me was in my bosom, so that escaped; but they bruised my head and face, and cursing me for having no more money, tipped me into the dam, crying, 'Lie there, parson, till to-morrow!' My shins and knees were bruised in the fall against one of the stumps; and I had like to have been suffocated in water and mud. I shan't be able to stir out this day or two: for I am a frightful spectacle! My hat and wig I was forced to leave behind me, and go home a mile and a half without: but they were found next morning, and brought me, with my snuff-box, which the rogues must have dropped. My cassock is sadly torn, as is my band. I was much frighted; for a robbery in these parts has not been known many years. Diligent search is making after the rogues. My humble respects to good Mrs. Pamela; if *she* pities my misfortunes I shall be the sooner well, and fit to wait on her. This did not hinder me writing a letter, though with great pain, as I do this," [*To be sure this good man can keep no secret!*] "and sending it away by a man and horse, this morning. I am, good Mrs. Jewkes, *your most obliged humble servant.*

        "God be praised, it is no worse! and I find I have got no cold, though miserably wet from top to toe. My fright, I believe, prevented me from catching cold; for I was not myself for some hours, and know not how I got home. I will write a letter of thanks this night, if I am able, to my kind patron, for his inestimable goodness to me. I wish I was enabled to say all I hope with regard to the *better part* of his bounty to me, incomparable Mrs. Pamela."

The wicked brute fell a laughing when she read this letter, till her fat sides shook : said she, " I can't but think how the poor parson looked, after parting with his pretty mistress in such high spirits, when he found himself at the bottom of the dam ! And what a figure he must have cut in his tattered band and cassock, and without a hat and wig, when he got home ! I warrant," added she, " he was in a sweet pickle ! " I said I thought it was very barbarous to laugh at such a misfortune ; but she replied, as he was safe, she laughed ; otherwise she should have been sorry : she was glad to see me concerned for him— It looked *promising*, she said.

I heeded not her reflection ; but as I have been used to causes for mistrusts, I cannot help saying, that I don't like this thing : and their taking his letters most alarms me. How happy it was they missed my packet ! I know not what to think of it : but why should I let every accident break my peace ? Yet it *will* do so, while I stay here.

Mrs. Jewkes is mightily at me to go with her in the chariot to visit Mr. Williams. She is so officious to bring on the affair between us, that, being a cunning, artful woman, I know not what to make of it ; I have refused her absolutely ; urging, that except I intended to encourage his suit, I ought not to do it. And she is gone without me.

I have strange temptations to get away in her absence, for all these fine appearances. 'Tis sad to have nobody to advise with :—I know not what to do. But, alas for me ! I have no money to buy any-body's civilities, or to pay for necessaries or lodging. But I'll go into the garden, and resolve afterwards.—

I have been in the garden and to the back-door, and there I stood, my heart up at my mouth. I could not see I was watched ; so this looks well. But if any thing should go bad afterwards, I should never forgive myself for not taking this opportunity. Well, I will go down again, and see if all is clear, and how it looks out at the back-door in the pasture.

To be sure there is witchcraft in this house ; and I believe Lucifer is bribed, as well as all about me, and is got into the shape of that nasty grim bull, to watch me ! For I have been down again, and ventured to open the door, and went out about a bow-shot into the pasture ; but there stood that horrid bull, staring me full in the face, with fiery saucer eyes, as I thought. So I got in again, for fear he should come at me. Nobody saw me, however. Do you think there are such things as witches and spirits ? If there be, I believe in my heart Mrs. Jewkes has got this bull of her side. But what could I do without money or a friend? O this wicked woman to trick me so! Every thing, man, woman, and beast, is in a plot against your poor Pamela, I think!—Then I knew not one step of the way, nor how far to any house or cottage; and whether I could gain protection, if I got to a house; and now the robbers are abroad too, I may run into as great danger as I want to escape; nay, much greater, if these promising appearances hold: and sure my master cannot be so black as that they should not!—What can I do?—I have a good mind to try for it once more; but then I may be pursued and taken: it will be worse for me; this wicked woman will beat me, take my shoes away, and lock me up.

But after all, if my master should mean *well*, he can't be angry at my fears, if I should escape; and nobody can blame me: I can more easily be induced, with you, when all my apprehensions are over, to consider his proposal of Mr. Williams, than I could here; he pretends, as you have read in his letter, he will leave me to my choice; why then, should I be afraid? I will go down again, I think! But yet my heart misgives me, because the difficulties in escaping; and being so poor and so friendless!—O good God! the preserver of the innocent! direct me what to do!

I have just now a sort of strange persuasion upon me, that I ought to try to get away, and leave the issue to Providence. So, once more—I'll see, at least if this bull be still there.

Alack-a-day! what a fate is this! I have not the courage to go, neither can I think to stay. But I must resolve. The gardener was in sight last time; so made me come up again. But I'll contrive to send him out of the way, if I can:—For if I never should have such another opportunity, I could not forgive myself. Once more I'll venture. God direct my foot-steps, and make smooth my path, and my way to safety!

Well, here I am, come back again! frighted, like a fool, out of all my purposes. O how terrible every thing appears to me! I had got twice as far as I was before, out of the back-door: I looked and saw the bull, as I thought, between me and the door: and another bull coming towards me the other way. Well, thought I, here is a double witchcraft to be sure! Here is the spirit of my master in one bull, and Mrs. Jewkes's in the other: now I am gone, to be sure! O help! cried I, like a fool, and ran back to the door, as swift as if I flew. When I had got the door in my hand, I ventured to look back, to see if these supposed bulls were coming; when I saw they were only two cows grazing in distant places, that my fears had made all this rout about.

But as everything is so frightful to me, I find I am not fit to think of my escape; for I shall be equally frighted at the first strange man that I meet with : I am persuaded, that fear brings one into more dangers, than the caution which goes along with it delivers one from.

I then locked the door, and put the key in my pocket, and was in a sad quandary; but I was soon determined; for the maid Nan came in sight, and asked if any thing was the matter, that I was so often up and down stairs ! God forgive me ! but I had a sad lie at my tongue's end : said I, " Though Mrs. Jewkes is sometimes a little hard upon me, yet I know not where I am without her, I go up, and I come down to walk about in the garden; and, not having her, know scarcely what to do with myself."—" Aye," said the idiot, " she is main good company, Madam; no wonder you miss her."

So here I am again, and likely to be; for I have no courage to help myself any where else. O why are poor foolish maidens tried with such dangers, when they have such weak minds to grapple with them ? I will, since it is so, hope the best : but yet I cannot but observe how grievously every thing makes against me : for here are the robbers; though I fell not into their hands, yet they gave me as much terror, and had as great an effect upon my fears, as if I had : and here is the bull; it has as effectually frightened me, as if I had been hurt by it instead of the cook-maid ; and so these join together to make a very dastard of me. But my folly was worst of all, because that deprived me of my money; for had I *that*, I believe I should have ventured both the bull and the robbers.

MONDAY AFTERNOON.

So, Mrs. Jewkes is returned from her visit : " Well," said she, " I would have you set your heart at rest; for Mr. Williams will do very well again. He is not half so bad as he fancied. O these scholars," said she, " they have not the hearts of mice ! He has only a few scratches on his face, which," said she, " I suppose he got by grappling among the gravel at the bottom of the dam, to try to find a hole in the ground, to hide himself from the robbers. His shin and his knee hardly ail any thing. He says in his letter, he was a frightful spectacle : he might be so when he first came in doors; but he looks well enough now : and, only for a few groans now-and-then, when he thinks of his danger, I see nothing the matter with him. So, Mrs. Pamela," said she, " I would have you be very easy about it."—" I am glad of it," said I, " for all your jokes, Mrs. Jewkes."

133

" Well," said she, " he talks of nothing but you; and when I told him I would fain have persuaded you to come with me, the man was out of his wits with his gratitude to me : and has laid open all his heart to me, told me all that has passed, and what was contriving between you." This alarmed me prodigiously, as I saw by two or three instances, that his honest heart could keep nothing, believing every one as undesigning as himself. I said, but with a heavy heart, " Ah ! Mrs. Jewkes, Mrs. Jewkes, this might have done with me had he any thing he could have told you of. But you know well enough that had we been disposed, we had no opportunity for it, from your watchful care and circumspection."—" No," said she, " that's very true, Mrs. Pamela; not so much as for that declaration that he owned before me he had found opportunity to make for all my watchfulness. Come, come," said she, " no more of these shams with me ! You have an excellent headpiece for your years : but may-be I am as cunning as you. However," said she, " all is well now; because my *watchments* are now over, by my master's directions. How have you employed yourself in my absence ? "

I was so troubled at what might have passed between Mr. Williams and her, that I could not hide it; and she said, " Well, Mrs. Pamela, since all matters are likely to be so soon and so happily ended, let me advise you to be a little less concerned at his discoveries; and make me your confident, as *he* has done, and I shall think you have some regard for me, and reliance upon me; and perhaps you might not repent it."

She was so earnest, that I mistrusted she did this to pump me : I knew how to account for her kindness to Mr. Williams in her visit to him; which was only to get out of him what she could. " Why, Mrs. Jewkes," said I, " is all this fishing about for something, where there is nothing, if there is now an end to your *watchments* as you call them ? "—" Nothing," said she, " but womanish curiosity, I'll assure you; for one is naturally led to find out matters where there is such privacy intended."—" Well," said I, " pray let me know what he has said; and then I'll give you an answer to your curiosity."—" I don't care," said she, " whether you do or not; for I have as much as I wanted from him; and I despair of getting out of you any thing you ha'n't a mind I should know, my little cunning dear."—" Well," said I, " let him have said what he would, I care not : for I am sure he can say no harm of me; and so let us change the talk."

I was the easier, because, for all her pumps, she gave no hints of the key and the door, &c., which, had he communicated to her, she would not have forborne giving me a touch of. So we gave up one another, as despairing to gain our ends. But I am sure he must have said more than he should. And I am the more apprehensive all is not right, because she has been actually, these two hours, shut up a writing; though she pretended she had given me up all her stores of paper, &c., and that I should write for her. I begin to wish I had ventured every thing, and gone off, when I might. O when will this state of doubt and uneasiness end?

She has just been with me, and says she shall send a messenger to Bedfordshire; and he shall carry a letter of thanks for me, if I will write it, for my master's favour to me. "Indeed," said I, "I have no thanks to give, till I am with my father and mother : and besides, I sent a letter, as you know, but have had no answer to it." She said, she thought that his letter to Mr. Williams was sufficient, and the least I could do was to thank him. "No need of it," said I, "for I don't intend to have Mr. Williams : what then is that letter to me?"—"Well," said she, "I see thou art quite unfathomable!"

I don't like this. O my foolish fears of bulls and robbers! For now all my uneasiness begins to double upon me. O what has this incautious man said! it, no doubt, is the subject of her long letter.

I will close this day's writing with just saying, that she is very silent and reserved to what she was, and says nothing but "No," or "Yes," to what I ask. Something must be hatching, I doubt!—I rather think so, because I find she does not keep her word with me, about lying by myself, and my money; to both which points she returned suspicious answers, saying as to the one, "Why, you are very earnest for your money; I shan't run away with it:" and to the other, "Good luck! you need not be so willing, as I know of, to part with me for a bed-fellow till you are sure of one you *like better.*" This cut me to the heart! And, at the same time, stopped my mouth.

TUESDAY, WEDNESDAY.

Mr. Williams has been here, but we have had no opportunity to talk together : he seemed confounded at Mrs. Jewkes's change of temper and reservedness after her kind visit, and their freedom with one another, and much more at what I am going to tell you. He asked if I would take a turn in the garden with Mrs. Jewkes and him. "No," said she, "I can't go." Said he, "May not Mrs. Pamela take a walk?"—"No," said she, "I desire she

135

won't."—" Why, Mrs. Jewkes," said he, " I am afraid I have disobliged you."—" Not at all," replied she : " but I suppose you will soon be at liberty to walk together as much as you please : I have sent a messenger for my last instructions about *this* and *more* weighty matters ; when they come, I shall leave you to do as you both will ; but, till then, it is no matter how little you are together." This alarmed us both : and he seemed quite struck of a heap ; and put on, as I thought, a self-accusing countenance. So I went behind her back, and held my two hands together, flat, with a bit of paper I had between them, and looked at him : he seemed to take me as I intended ; intimating the renewing of the correspondence by the tiles. I left them both together, and retired to my closet, to write a letter for the tiles ; but having no time for a copy, I will give the substance only.

I expostulated with him on his too great openness and easiness to fall into Mrs. Jewkes's snares ; told him my apprehensions of foul play ; and gave briefly the reasons which moved me : begged to know what he had said, and intimated that I thought there was the highest reason to resume our project of the escape by the back-door. I put this in the usual place in the evening, and now wait with impatience for an answer.

THURSDAY.

I have the following answer :

" DEAR MADAM,

    " I am utterly confounded, and must plead guilty to all your just reproaches. I wish I were master of but half your caution and discretion ! I hope, after all, this is only a touch of this ill woman's temper, to shew her power and importance : for I think Mr. B. neither can, nor dare deceive me in so black a manner. I would expose him all the world over, if he did. But it is not, *cannot* be in him. I have received a letter from John Arnold, in which he tells me, that his master is preparing for his London journey ; and believes, afterwards, he will come into these parts ; but he says, Lady Davers is at their house, and is to accompany her brother to London, or meet him there. He professes great zeal and affection to your service : and I find he refers to a letter he sent me before, but which is not come to my hand. I *think* there can be no treachery ; for it is a particular friend at Gainsborough that I have ordered him to direct to : and this is come safe to my hands by this means ; for well I know, I durst trust nothing to Brett, at the post-house here. This gives me a little pain ; but I hope all will end well,

136

and we shall soon hear, if it be necessary to pursue our former intentions. If it be, I will lose no time to provide a horse for you, and another for myself; for I can never do either God or myself a better service, though I were to forego all my expectations for it here. I am *your most faithful humble servant.*

" I was too free with Mrs. Jewkes; I was led to it by her dissimulation and by her pretended concern to make me happy with you. I hinted that I would not have scrupled to have procured your deliverance by any means; and that I had proposed to you, as the only honourable one, marriage with me. But I assured her, though she would hardly believe me, that you discouraged my application, which is too true ! But not a word of the back-door, key, &c."

Mrs. Jewkes continues still sullen and ill-natured, and I am almost afraid to speak to her. She watches me as close as ever, and pretends to wonder why I shun her company as I do.

I have just put under the tiles these lines, inspired by my fears, which are, indeed, very strong; and, I doubt, not without reason.

" SIR,

" Every thing gives me additional disturbances. The missed letter of John Arnold's makes me suspect a plot. Yet I am loth to think myself of so much importance, as to suppose every one in a plot against me. Are you sure, however, the London journey is not to be a Lincolnshire one? May not John, who has been once a traitor, be so again? Why *need* I be thus in doubt? If I could have this horse, I would turn the reins on his neck, and trust to Providence to guide him for my safeguard ! For I would not endanger you, now just upon the edge of your preferment. Yet, Sir, I fear your fatal openness will make you suspected as accessary, let us be ever so cautious.

" Were my *life* in question, instead of my *honesty*, I would not wish to involve you, or any body, in the least difficulty, for so worthless a poor creature. But, O Sir ! my *soul* is of equal importance with the soul of a princess, though my quality is inferior to that of the meanest slave.

" Save, then, my innocence, good Heaven ! and preserve my mind spotless : and happy shall I be to lay down my worthless life, and see an end to all my troubles and anxieties.

" Forgive my impatience : but my presaging mind bodes horrid mischiefs !—Everything looks dark around me : and this woman's impenetrable sullenness and silence, without any apparent reason, from a conduct so very *contrary*, bid me fear the worst. Blame me, Sir, if you think me wrong; and let me have your advice what to do; which will oblige *your most afflicted servant.*"

FRIDAY.

I have this half-angry answer; but, what is more to me than all the letters in the world could be, yours, dear father, inclosed.

" MADAM,

"I think you are too apprehensive by much; I am sorry for your uneasiness. You may depend upon me, and all I can do. But I make no doubt of the London journey, nor of John's contrition and fidelity. I have just received, from my Gains-borough friend, this letter, as I suppose, from your good father, in a cover directed for me, as I had desired. I hope it contains nothing to add to your uneasiness. Pray, dearest Madam, lay aside your fears, and wait a few days for the issue of Mrs. Jewkes's letter, and mine of thanks to Mr. B. Things, I hope, *must* be better than you expect. Providence will not desert such piety and innocence; and be this your comfort and reliance : which is the best advice that can be given by *your most faithful humble servant.*"

The father's letter was as follows :

" MY DEAREST DAUGHTER,

"Our prayers are at length heard, and we are over-whelmed with joy. O what sufferings, what trials, hast thou gone through ! Blessed be the Divine Goodness, which has enabled thee to withstand so many temptations ! We have not yet had leisure to read through your long accounts of all your hardships. I say *long*, because I wonder how you could find time and opportunity for them; but otherwise they are the delight of our spare hours : we shall read them over and over, as long as we live, with thankfulness to God, who has given us so virtuous and so discreet a daughter. How happy is our lot, in the midst of our poverty ! O let none ever think children a burden to them; when the poorest circumstances can produce so much riches in a Pamela ! Persist, my dear daughter, in the same excellent course; and we shall not envy the highest estate, but defy them to produce such a daughter as ours.

"I said we had not read through all yours. We are too impatient, so turned to the end; where we find your virtue within view of its reward, and your master's heart turned to see the folly of his ways, and the injury he had intended to our dear child : for he *would* have ruined you if he could. But seeing your virtue, his heart is touched, and he has, no doubt, been awakened by your good example.

" We don't see that you can do any way so well, as to come into the present proposal, and make Mr. Williams, the worthy Mr. Williams ! God bless him ! happy. And though we are poor, and can add no merit, reputation, or fortune, to our dear child, but rather must be a disgrace to her, as the world will think : yet I hope I do not sin in my pride, to say, that there is no good man, of a common degree, but may think himself happy in you. But, as you say you had rather *not* marry at present, far be it from us to offer violence to your inclination ! So much prudence as you have shewn in all your conduct, would make it very wrong in us to mistrust it in this, or to offer to direct you to your choice. But, alas ! my child, what can *we* do for you ?—To partake our hard lot, and to involve yourself into as hard a life, would not help *us ;* but *add* to our afflictions. It will be time enough to talk of these things, when we have the pleasure you now put us in hope of, of seeing you with us; which God grant. *Amen, Amen,* say *your most indulgent parents,* Amen !

" Our humble service and thanks to the worthy Mr. Williams. Again we say, God bless him for ever !

" O what a deal we have to say to you ! God give us a happy meeting ! We understand the squire is setting out for London. He is a fine gentleman, and has wit at will. I wish he was as good. But I hope he will now reform."

O what inexpressible comfort, my dear father, has your letter given me ?—You ask, *what* can you do for me !—What is it you *cannot do* for your child?—You can give her the advice she *has so much wanted* and *still* wants, and will *always* want : you can confirm her in the paths of virtue, into which you first initiated her ; and you can pray for her with hearts so sincere and pure, that are not to be met with in palaces !—Oh ! how I long to throw myself at your feet, and receive the blessings of such good parents ! But, alas ! how are my prospects again overclouded, to what they were when I closed my last parcel ! More trials, more dangers, I fear, must your poor Pamela be engaged in ; but, through the Divine Goodness, and your prayers, I hope, at last, to get well out of all my difficulties ; as they are not the effect of my vanity or presumption.

139

But I will proceed with my hopeless story. I saw Mr. Williams was a little nettled at my impatience; so I wrote to assure him I would be as easy as I could, and wholly directed by him; especially as my father, whose respects I mentioned, had assured me my master was setting out for London, which he must have known, or he would not have written me word of it.

SATURDAY, SUNDAY.

Mr. Williams has been here both these days, as usual; but is very indifferently received by Mrs. Jewkes; and, to avoid suspicion, I left them together, and went up to my closet most of the time he was here. They had a quarrel, and she seems quite out of humour with him; but I thought it best not to say any thing; and he said he would seldom trouble the house, till he had an answer to his letter from Mr. B. "The less the better," she replied. Poor man! he has got but little by his openness and making Mrs. Jewkes his confidant.

I am more and more satisfied there is mischief brewing: I shall begin to hide my papers, and be circumspect. She seems impatient for an answer to her letter to my master.

MONDAY, TUESDAY, THE 25TH AND 26TH DAYS OF MY HEAVY RESTRAINT.

Still more and more strange things to write! A messenger is returned, and now all is out! O wretched, wretched Pamela! what at last will become of me?—Such strange turns and trials sure never poor creature of my years experienced. He brought two letters, one to Mrs. Jewkes, and one to me: but as the greatest wits may be sometimes mistaken, they being folded and sealed alike, that for *me* was directed to Mrs. Jewkes, and that for *her* was directed to me. But *both* are abominably bad! She brought me up that directed for me, and said, "Here's a letter for you: long-looked-for is come at last. I will ask the messenger a few questions, and then I will read mine." So she went down, and I broke it open in my closet and found it directed—"*To Mrs.* PAMELA ANDREWS." But when I opened it, it began, "Mrs. Jewkes." I was quite confounded; "But," thought I, "this may be a lucky mistake." So I read on these horrid contents.

"MRS. JEWKES,

"What you write me, has given me no small disturbance. This wretched *fool's plaything*, no doubt, is ready to leap at *any*

140

thing that offers, rather than express the least sense of gratitude for all the benefits she has received from my family, and which I was determined more and more to heap upon her. I reserve her for my future resentment; I charge you double your diligence in watching her, to prevent her escape. I send this by an honest Swiss, who attended me in my travels, a man I can trust: and so let him be your assistant; for the artful *creature* is enough to corrupt a nation by her seeming innocence and simplicity; and she may have got a party, perhaps, among my servants with you, as she has here. Even John Arnold, whom I confided in, and favoured more than any, has proved an execrable villain, and shall meet his reward for it.

" As to that *college novice*, Williams, I need not bid you take care he sees not this *painted bauble;* for I have ordered Mr. Shorter, my attorney, to throw him instantly into gaol, on an action of debt, for money he has had of me, which I had intended never to carry to account against him; for I know all his rascally practices, besides what you write me of his perfidious intrigue with that girl, and his acknowledged contrivance for her escape, when he knew not that I designed her any mischief; and when, if he had been guided by a sense of piety, or compassion for injured innocence, as he pretends, he would have expostulated with me, as his function, and my friendship for him, might have allowed him. But to enter into a vile intrigue with the *amiable gewgaw*, to favour her escape in so base a manner (to say nothing of his disgraceful practices against me in Sir Simon Darnford's family, of which Sir Simon has informed me), is a conduct, that, instead of promoting the ungrateful wretch, as I intended, shall pull down upon him utter ruin. Monsieur Colbrand, my trusty Swiss, will obey you without reserve, should my other servants refuse. As for her denying that she encouraged his declaration, I believe it not. 'Tis certain the *speaking picture*, with all that pretended innocence and bashfulness, would have run away with him. Yes, she would have run away with a fellow that she had been acquainted with but a few days: at a time when she had the strongest assurances of my honour to her.

" I think I now hate her perfectly; and, though I will do nothing to her *myself*, yet I can bear, for the sake of my revenge, *injured honour*, and *slighted love*, to see any thing, even what *she most fears*, be *done to her;* and then she may be turned loose to her evil destiny, and echo to the woods and groves her piteous lamentations for the loss of her fantastical innocence, which the romantic idiot makes such a work about. I shall go to London with my sister Davers; and the moment I can disengage myself, which perhaps may be in three weeks from this time, I will be with you, and decide *her fate*, and put an end to your trouble. Meantime, be doubly careful; for this innocent, as I have warned you, is full of contrivances. I am *your friend*."

I had but just read this dreadful letter through, when Mrs. Jewkes came up, in a great fright, guessing at the mistake, and that I had her letter: she found me with it open in my hand, just sinking away. "What business," said she, "had you to read my letter?" and snatched it from me. "You see," said she, looking upon it, "it says Mrs. Jewkes, at top: you ought, in manners, to have read no further."—" O add not," said I, "to my afflictions! I shall be soon out of all your ways! This is too much! I never can support this——" and threw myself upon the couch, in my closet, and wept most bitterly. She read it in the next room, and came in again afterwards: "Why this," said she, "is a sad letter indeed; I am sorry for it; but I feared you would carry your niceties too far!"—"Leave me, Mrs. Jewkes," said I, "for a while; I cannot speak nor talk."—"Poor heart!" said she; "well, I'll come up again presently, and hope to find you better. But here, take your own letter; I wish you well: but this is a sad mistake!" So she put down the letter which was intended for me: but I have no spirit to read it at present. "O man! hard-hearted, cruel man; what mischiefs art thou not capable of, unrelenting persecutor as thou art!" I sat ruminating, when I had a little come to myself, upon the terms of this wicked letter: and had no inclination to look into my own. The bad names, *fool's plaything, artful creature, painted bauble, gewgaw, speaking picture*, are hard words for your poor Pamela; and I began to think whether I was not a very naughty body, and had not done vile things: but when I thought of his having discovered poor John, and of Sir Simon's base officiousness, in telling him of Mr. Williams, with what he had resolved against him, in revenge for his goodness to me, I was quite dispirited; and yet still more, about that fearful Colbrand, and what he could *see done to me;* for then I was ready to gasp for breath, and my heart quite failed me. Then how dreadful are the words, he will *decide my fate* in three weeks! "Gracious heaven!" said I, "strike me dead before that time with a thunderbolt, or provide some way for my escaping these threatened mischiefs!" God forgive me if I sinned.

At last I took up the letter directed for Mrs. Jewkes, but

designed for me; and I find *that* little better than the other. These are the hard terms it contains:

"Well have you done, perverse, forward, artful, yet foolish Pamela, to convince me, before it is too late, how ill I had done to place my affections on so unworthy an object: I had vowed honour and love to your unworthiness, believing you a mirror of bashful modesty and unspotted innocence; and that no perfidious designs lurked in so fair a bosom. But now I have found you out, you specious hypocrite! and see, that though you could not repose the least confidence in one you had known for years, and who, under my good mother's misplaced favour for you, had grown up in a manner with you; when my passion, in spite of my pride, and the difference of our condition, made me stoop to a meanness that now I despise myself for; yet you could enter into an intrigue with a man you never knew till within these few days past, and resolve to run away with a stranger, whom your fair face and insinuating arts had bewitched to break through all the ties of honour and gratitude to me, even at a time when the happiness of his future life depended upon my favour.

"Henceforth, for Pamela's sake, whenever I see a lovely face, will I mistrust a deceitful heart: and whenever I hear of the greatest pretences to innocence, will I suspect some deep-laid mischief. You were determined to place no confidence in me, though I have solemnly engaged my honour to you. What, though I had alarmed your fears by sending you one way when you hoped to go another; yet, had I not, to convince you of my resolution to do justly by you, engaged not to come near you without your consent? Was not this a voluntary demonstration of the generosity of my intention to you? Yet how have you requited me? The very first fellow that your charming face and insinuating address could influence, you have practised upon, corrupted too, I may say (and even ruined, as the ungrateful wretch shall find), and thrown your *forward* self upon him. As, therefore, you would place no confidence in me, my honour owes you nothing: and in a little time you shall find how much you have erred, in treating as you have done a man who was once *your affectionate and kind friend*.

"Mrs. Jewkes has directions concerning you: if your lot is now harder than you might wish, you will bear it the easier, because your own rash folly has brought it upon you."

Alas for me! what a fate is mine, to be thus thought artful, forward, and ungrateful! when all I intended was to preserve my innocence; and all my poor little shifts, which his superior wit and cunning have rendered ineffectual, were forced upon me in my own necessary defence.

When Mrs. Jewkes came up to me again, she found me bathed in tears. She seemed, as I thought, to be moved by compassion. Finding myself now entirely in her power, and that it was not for me to provoke her, I said, " It is now, I see, in vain for me to contend against my evil destiny, and the superior arts of my barbarous master. I will resign myself to the Divine Will, and prepare to expect the worst. But you see how poor Mr. Williams is drawn in and undone; I am sorry I am made the cause of *his* ruin :—Poor, poor man !—to be thus involved, for my sake !—But if you'll believe me," said I, " I gave no encouragement to what he proposed, as to marriage; nor would he have proposed it, I believe, but as the only honourable way he thought was left to save me; his principal motive was virtue and compassion to one in distress. What other view could he have ? You know I am poor and friendless. All I beg of you is, to let the poor gentleman have notice of my master's resentment, and let him fly the country, and not be thrown into gaol. This will answer my master's end as well; for it will as effectually hinder him from assisting me, as if he was in a prison."

" Ask me," said she, " to do any thing that is in my power, consistent with my duty and trust, I will do it. I am sorry for you both; but I shall keep no correspondence with him, nor let you." I offered to talk of a duty superior to that she mentioned, which would oblige her to help distressed innocence, and not permit her to go the length enjoined by lawless tyranny; but she plainly bid me be silent on that head; for it was in vain to attempt to persuade her to betray her trust :—" All I have to advise you," said she, " is to be easy; lay aside all your contrivances and arts to get away; make me your friend, by giving me no reason to suspect you; for I glory in my fidelity to my master : you have both practised some strange sly arts, to make such a progress as he owned there was between you. I must be more circumspect than I have been." This doubled my concern, for I now apprehended I should be much closer watched than before.

" Well," said I, " since I have, by this strange accident, discovered my hard destiny, let me read over again that fearful letter of yours, that I may get it by heart, and with it feed my distress, and make calamity familiar to me."—" Then," said she, " let me read yours again." I gave her mine, and she lent me

hers; I took a copy of it, with her leave; because I would prepare myself for the worst. And when I had done, I pinned it
on the head of the couch: "This," said I, "is the use I shall
make of this wretched copy of your letter; and here you shall
always find it wet with my tears."

She said she would go down to order supper, and insisted upon
my company. I would have excused myself; but she put on a
commanding air, that I durst not oppose. When I went down,
she took me by the hand, and presented me to the most hideous
monster I ever saw in my life. "Here, Monsieur Colbrand,"
said she, "here is *your* pretty ward and *mine*; let us try to make
her time with us easy." He bowed, put in his foreign grimaces,
and, in broken English, told me, "I was happy in de affections
of de vinest gentleman in de varld!" I was quite frightened,
and ready to drop down; I will describe him to you, my dear
father and mother, and you shall judge if I had not reason to
be alarmed, as I was apprised of his hated employment, to watch
me closer.

He is a giant of a man for stature; taller by a good deal than
Harry Mawlidge, in your neighbourhood, and large-boned,
scraggy, and has a hand!—I never saw such an one in my life.
He has great staring eyes, like the bull's that frightened me so;
vast jaw-bones sticking out; eyebrows hanging over his eyes;
two great scars upon his fore-head, and one on his left cheek;
two large whiskers, and a monstrous wide mouth; blubber lips,
long yellow teeth, and a hideous grin. He wears his own frightful
long hair, tied up in a great black bag; a black crape neckcloth,
about a long ugly neck; and his throat sticking out like a wen.
As to the rest, he was dressed well enough, and had a sword on,
with a nasty red knot to it; leather gaiters, buckled below his
knees; and a foot near as long as my arm, I verily think.

He said, he fright de lady, and offered to withdraw; but she
bid him not. I told Mrs. Jewkes, that, as she knew I had been
crying, she should not have called me to the gentleman, without
letting me know he was there. I soon went up to my closet,
for my heart ached all the time I was at table, not being able
to look upon him without horror; and this brute of a woman,
though she saw my distress, *before* this addition to it, no doubt
did it on purpose to strike more terror into me. And indeed
it had its effect; for when I went to bed, I could think of nothing
but this hideous person, and my master's more hideous actions;
and thought them well paired. When I dropped asleep, I
dreamed they were both coming to my bedside with the worst
designs: I jumped out of my bed in my sleep, and frighted

145

Mrs. Jewkes, till, waking with the terror, I told her my dream, the wicked creature only laughed, and said, all I feared was but a dream, as well as that.

Poor Mr. Williams is actually arrested, and carried away to Stamford : so there is an end of all my hopes from him. Poor gentleman ! his over security and openness have ruined us both. I was but too well convinced that we ought not have lost a moment's time : he was angry, and thought me too impatient. The detestable artifices of my master induced me to think, that he who had so cunningly, and so wickedly, contrived all his stratagems, so that it was impossible to avoid them, would stick at nothing to complete them. I fear I shall soon find it so.

But one stratagem I have just invented, though a very discouraging one to think of, because I have neither friends nor money, nor know one step of the way. But let bulls, bears, lions, tigers, and, what is worse, false, treacherous, deceitful men, stand in my way, I cannot be more in danger than I am ; I depend nothing upon his three weeks : for how do I know, now he is in such a passion, and has already begun his vengeance on poor Mr. Williams, that he will not change his mind, and come down to Lincolnshire before he goes to London ?

My stratagem is this : I will endeavour to get Mrs. Jewkes to go to bed without me, as she often does while I sit locked up in my closet ; and as she sleeps very sound in her first sleep, of which she never fails to give notice, by snoring, if I can but then get out between the two bars of the window (for you know I am very slender), then I can drop upon the leads underneath, which are little more than my height, and which leads are over a little summer parlour, that jets out towards the garden ; as I am light I can easily drop from them ; for they are not high from the ground : then I shall be in the garden : and as I have the key of the back-door, I will get out. But I have another piece of cunning still ; good heaven succeed to me my dangerous though innocent devices ! I have read of a great captain, who, being in danger, leaped overboard into the sea ; and his enemies, as he swam, shooting at him with bows and arrows, he unloosed his upper garment, and took another course ; by this means, while they stuck that with their darts and arrows, he escaped, and lived to triumph over them all. So I will strip off my upper petticoat, throw it into the pond, with my neck handkerchief ! When they miss me, they will go to the pond first, thinking I have drowned myself : and when they see some of my clothes floating there, they will be all employed in dragging the pond, which is a very large one; and as I shall not, perhaps, be missed till the morning, this will give me opportunity to get a great way off; and I am sure I will run for it, when I am out. So I trust that Providence will direct my steps to some good place of safety, and make *some* worthy body my friend; for if I suffer ever so, I cannot be in more danger, nor in worse hands, than where I am; and with such avowed bad designs.

O my dear parents ! don't be frightened when you come to read this !—But all will be over before you can see it; and so God direct me for the best !—My writings, for fear I should not escape, I will bury in the garden; for no doubt I shall be searched, and used dreadfully, if I can't get off. So I will close here, for the present, to prepare for my plot.—Prosper thou, O gracious Protector of oppressed innocence ! this last effort of thy poor handmaid ! that I may escape the crafty devices and snares to rob me of my virtue ! but by this one trial only, I see no way of escaping ! Whatever becomes of me, bless my dear parents, and protect poor Mr. Williams from ruin ! for he was happy before he knew me.

Just now I heard Mrs. Jewkes, who is in her cups, own to the horrid Colbrand, that the robbing of poor Mr. Williams was a contrivance of hers, and executed by the groom and a helper, in order to seize my letters, which they missed. They are now both laughing at the dismal story, which they little think I overheard.—O how my heart aches ! what are not such wretches capable of ? can you blame me for endeavouring to get out of such clutches ?

PAST ELEVEN O'CLOCK.

Mrs. Jewkes is come up, and gone to bed; and bids me not stay long in my closet, but come to bed.—O for a dead sleep for the treacherous brute ! I never saw her so tipsy; that gives me hopes. I have tried again, and find I can get my head through the iron bars. I am now all prepared, as soon as I hear her fast; and now I'll seal up these, and my other papers, my last work :—and to thy Providence, O my gracious God, commit the rest !—Once more, God bless you both ! and send us a happy meeting; if not here, in his heavenly kingdom.—Amen.

THURSDAY, FRIDAY, SATURDAY, SUNDAY, THE 28TH, 29TH, 30TH, AND 31ST DAYS OF MY DISTRESS.

And distress indeed; for here I am still; and every thing has been worse and worse ! Oh ! the poor unhappy Pamela !—

147

Without any hope left, and ruined in all my contrivances. But, oh! my dear parents, rejoice with me, even in this low plunge of my distress; for your poor Pamela has escaped from an enemy worse than any she ever met with; an enemy she never thought of before, and was hardly able to stand against; I mean the weakness and presumption of her own mind; which had well nigh, had not the Divine Grace interposed, sunk her into the lowest, last abyss of misery and perdition!

I will proceed, as I have opportunity, with my sad relation; for my pen is all I have to employ myself with: and I have been so weak, that, till yesterday evening, I have not been able to hold a pen.

I took with me but one shift, besides what I had on, two handkerchiefs, and two caps, which my pocket held (for it was not for me to encumber myself), and all my stock of money, which was but five or six shillings, to set out for I knew not where: and got out of the window, not without some difficulty, sticking a little at my hips; but I was resolved to get out if possible. It was farther from the leads than I thought. I was afraid I had sprained my ancle; and when I had dropped, it was still farther off from the leads to the ground: but I did pretty well there; at least, I got no hurt to hinder me from pursuing my intentions. So being now on the ground, I hid my papers under a rose-bush, and covered them with mould, and there they still lie, as I hope. Then I went away to the pond: the clock struck twelve just as I got out; it was a dark misty night, and very cold; but I felt it not then.

When I came to the pond-side, I flung in my upper-coat, as I had designed, my neck-handkerchief, and a round-eared cap, with a knot; and then, with great speed, ran to the door, and took the key out of my pocket, my heart beating all the time against my bosom, as if it would have forced its way through it. I found that I was most miserably disappointed; for the wicked woman had taken off that lock, and put another on; so that my key would not open it. I tried in vain, and feeling about, I found a padlock, besides, on another part of the door. O then how my heart sunk! I dropt down with grief and confusion, unable to stir or support myself, for a while. But my fears awakening my resolution, and knowing that my attempt would be as terrible for me as any other danger I could then encounter, I clambered up upon the ledges of the door, and upon the lock, which was a great wooden one, and reached the top of the door with my hands; then, little thinking I could climb so well, I made shift to hold on the top of the wall with my hands; but, alas for me ! nothing but ill luck !—no escape for poor Pamela ! —The wall being old, the bricks I held gave way, just as I was taking a spring to get up; down came I, and received such a blow upon my head, with one of the bricks, that it quite stunned me; I broke my shins and ancle besides, and beat off the heel of one of my shoes.

In this dreadful way, flat upon the ground, lay poor I, for I believe five or six minutes; and then trying to get up, I sunk down again two or three times; and my left hip and shoulder were very stiff, and full of pain, with bruises; besides, my head bled, and ached grievously, with the blow I had with the brick. Yet these hurts I valued not; but crept a good way, upon my feet and hands, in search of a ladder, I just recollected to have seen against the wall two days before, on which the gardener was nailing a nectarine branch, but no ladder could I find, and the wall was very high. " What now," thought I, " must become of the miserable Pamela !" Then I began to wish myself most heartily again in my closet, and to repent of my attempt, which I now censured as rash, because it did not succeed.

God forgive me ! but a sad thought came just then into my head !—I tremble to think of it ! My apprehensions of the usage I should meet with, had like to have made me miserable for ever ! O my dear, dear parents, forgive your poor child ; but being quite desperate, I crept along, till I could raise myself on my staggering feet; and away limped I !—What to do, but to throw myself into the pond, and put a period to all my griefs in this world !—But O ! to find them infinitely aggravated (had I not, by the Divine Grace, been withheld) in a miserable *eternity !* As I have escaped this temptation (blessed be God for it !), I will tell you my conflicts on this dreadful occasion, that the Divine Mercies may be magnified in my deliverance, that I am yet on this side of the dreadful gulf, from which there could have been no return.

It was well for me, as I have since thought, that I was so maimed, which made me the longer before I got to the water; this gave me time to consider, and abated the impetuosity of my passions, which possibly might otherwise have hurried me, in my first transport of grief (on my seeing no way to escape, and the hard usage I had reason to expect from my dreadful keepers), to throw myself in. But my weakness of body made me move so slowly, that it gave time for reflection, and for a ray of grace to dart upon my benighted mind. When I came to the pond side, I sat down on the sloping bank, and began to ponder my wretched condition; and thus I reasoned with myself:

"Pause here a little, Pamela, on what thou art about, before thou takest the dreadful leap; and consider whether there be no way yet left, no hope, if not to escape from this wicked house, yet from the mischief threatened thee in it." I then considered; and, after I had cast about in my mind every thing that could make me hope, and saw no probability; a wicked woman devoid of compassion! a horrid helper, just arrived in this dreadful Colbrand! an angry and resenting master, who now hated me, and threatened the most afflicting evils! and that I should, in all probability, be deprived of the opportunity I now had before me, to free myself from their persecutions! "What hast thou to do, distressed creature," said I to myself, "but throw thyself upon a merciful God (who knows how innocently I suffer) to avoid the merciless wickedness of those who are determined on my ruin?" And then, thought I, (Oh! that thought was surely of the devil's instigation; for it was very soothing and powerful with me)—"These wicked wretches, who now have no remorse, no pity on me, will then be moved to lament their misdoings; and when they see the dead corpse of the unhappy Pamela dragged out on these dewy banks, lying breathless at their feet, they will find that remorse to soften their obdurate hearts, which now has no place there!—My master, my angry master, will then forget his resentments, say, 'O this is the unhappy Pamela! that I have causelessly persecuted and destroyed. Now do I see she preferred her honesty to her life,' will he say, 'and is no hypocrite nor deceiver; but was the innocent creature she pretended to be!' Then," thought I, "will he, perhaps, shed a few tears over the poor corpse of his persecuted servant; and, though he may give out it was love and disappointment, in order to hide his own guilt, for the unfortunate Mr. Williams; yet will he be inwardly grieved, and order me a decent funeral, and save me from the dreadful stake, and the highway interment; the young men and maidens all around my poor father's will pity poor Pamela! But, O! I hope I shall not be the subject of their ballads and elegies: but that my memory, for the sake of my dear father and mother, may quickly slide into oblivion."

I was once rising, so indulgent was I to this sad way of thinking, to throw myself in; but my bruises made me slow, and I thought, "What art thou about to do, wretched Pamela! How knowest thou, though the prospect be all dark to thy short-sighted eye, what God may do for thee, even when all human means fail? God Almighty would not lay me under these sore afflictions, if he had not given me strength to grapple with them, if I will exert it as I ought: and who knows but that the presence I so very much dread of my angry and designing master, may be better for me than these persecuting emissaries of his, who, for his money, are true to their wicked trust, and are hardened by a long habit of wickedness against compunction of heart? God *can* touch his heart in an instant; and if this should *not* be done, I can *then* put an end to my life by some other means, if I am so resolved. How do I know but *these bruises* and *maims* that I have received, while I pursued the escape I had meditated, may not have furnished myself with the opportunity to precipitate myself, and of surrendering up myself, spotless and unguilty, to that Merciful Being who gave it. Then," thought I, " who gave thee, presumptuous as thou art, a power over thy life? Who authorised thee to put an end to it, when the weakness of thy mind suggests not to thee a way to preserve it with honour? How knowest thou what purpose God may have to serve, by the trials with which thou art now exercised? Art thou to put a bound to the Divine Will, and to say, ' Thus much will I bear, and no more ' ? And wilt thou *dare* to say, that if the trial be augmented, and continued, thou wilt sooner die than bear it?

"This act of despondency," thought I, " is a sin, that, if I pursue, admits no repentance, and can therefore hope no forgiveness. And wilt thou, to shorten thy transitory griefs, *heavy* as they are, and *weak* as thou fanciest thyself, plunge both body and soul into everlasting misery? Hitherto," thought I, " thou art the innocent, the suffering Pamela; and wilt thou, to avoid thy sufferings, be the guilty aggressor? And, because wicked men persecute thee, wilt thou fly in the face of the Almighty, and distrust his grace and goodness, who can *still* turn all these sufferings into benefits? And how do I know but that God, who sees all the lurking vileness of my heart, may have permitted these sufferings on that very score, and to make me rely solely on his grace and assistance, who, perhaps, have too much prided myself in a vain dependence on my own foolish contrivances?

"Then, again," thought I, " wilt thou suffer in *one* moment all the good lessons of thy poor honest parents, and the benefits of their example (who have persisted in doing their duty with resignation to the Divine Will, amidst the extreme degrees of disappointment, poverty and distress, and the persecutions of an ungrateful world and merciless creditors), to be thrown away upon thee; and bring down, as in all probability this thy rashness will, their gray hairs with sorrow to the grave, when they shall understand, that their beloved daughter, slighting the tenders of Divine Grace, despairing of the mercies of a protecting God, has blemished, in this *last act*, a *whole* life which they had hitherto approved and delighted in?

"What, then, presumptuous Pamela, dost thou *here*?" thought I: "quit with speed these perilous banks, and fly from these curling waters, that seem, in their meaning murmurs, to reproach thy rashness! Tempt not God's goodness on the mossy banks, that have been witnesses of thy guilty purpose; and while thou hast power left thee, avoid the tempting evil, lest thy grand enemy, now repulsed by Divine Grace, and due reflection, return to the assault with a force that thy weakness may not be able to resist! and let one rash moment destroy all the convictions which now have awed thy rebellious mind into duty and resignation to the Divine Will!"

And so saying, I arose; but was so stiff with my hurts, so cold with the moist dews of the night, and the wet grass on which I had sat, as also with the damps arising from so large a piece of water, that with great pain I got from this pond, which now I think of with terror; and bending my limping steps toward the house, took refuge in the corner of an out-house, where wood and coals are laid up for family use, till I should be found by my cruel keepers, and consigned to a more wretched confinement, and worse usage, than I had hitherto experienced! And there behind a pile of fire-wood I crept, and lay down, as you may imagine, with a mind just broken, and a heart sensible to nothing but the extremest woe and dejection.

This, my dear father and mother, is the issue of your poor Pamela's fruitless enterprise; and who knows, if I had got out at the back-door, whether I had been at all in a better case, moneyless, friendless, as I am, and in a strange place! But blame not your poor daughter too much: nay, if ever you see this miserable scribble, all bathed and blotted with my tears, let your pity get the better of your reprehension. But I know it will. And I must leave off for the present. For, oh! my strength and my will are at this time very far unequal to one another. But yet I will add, that though I should have praised God for my deliverance, had I been freed from my wicked keepers, and my designing master, yet I have more abundant reason to praise him, that I have been delivered from a worse enemy, *myself*.

I will conclude my sad relation.

It seems Mrs. Jewkes awaked not till day-break; and not

finding me in bed, she called me; and, no answer being returned, she relates, that she got out of bed, ran to my closet; and, missing me, searched under the bed, and in another closet, finding the chamber door, as she had left it, quite fast, and the key, as usual, about her wrist. For if I could have got out of the chamber door, there were two or three passages and doors to them all, double-locked and barred, to go through into the great garden : so that, to escape, there was no way, but out of the window I had passed, because the other windows are a great way from the ground.

Mrs. Jewkes was excessively frightened; she instantly raised the Swiss, and the two maids, who lay not far off; and finding every door fast, she said, "I must be carried away, as Peter was out of prison, by some angel." It is a wonder she had no worse thought.

She says, she wept and wrung her hands, and took on sadly, running about like a mad woman, little thinking I could have got out of the closet window, between the iron bars; and indeed I don't know whether I could do so again. But at last finding that casement open, they concluded it must be so; and ran out into the garden, and found my footsteps in the mould of the bed which I dropt down upon from the leads : immediately Mrs. Jewkes, Colbrand, and Nan, went towards the back-door, to see if that was fast; while the cook was sent to the out-offices, to raise the men, and make them get horses ready, to take each a different way to pursue me.

Finding that door double-locked, and padlocked, the heel of my shoe, and the broken bricks, they concluded I was got away by some means over the wall; and then, they say, Mrs. Jewkes seemed like a distracted woman : till at last Nan had the thought to go towards the pond; and there seeing my coat, cap, and handkerchief, in the water, cast almost to the banks by the agitation of the waves, she thought it was me; and, screaming out, ran to Mrs. Jewkes, and said, "O Madam, Madam ! here's a piteous thing !—Mrs. Pamela lies drowned in the pond."—Thither they all ran; and, finding my clothes, doubted not I was at the bottom : they all, Swiss among the rest, beat their breasts, and made most dismal lamentations : Mrs. Jewkes sent Nan to the men, to bid them get the drag-net ready, and leave the horses, and come to try to find the poor innocent ! as she, it seems, *then* called me, beating her breast, and lamenting my hard fate, but most what would become of them, and what account they should give to my master.

While every one was thus differently employed, some weeping

and wailing, some running here and there, Nan came into the wood-house; and there lay poor I, so weak, so low and dejected, and so stiff with my bruises, that I could not stir, or get upon my feet. I said, with a low voice (for I could hardly speak), "Mrs. Ann, Mrs. Ann!"—The creature was sadly frighted, and was taking up a billet to knock me on the head, believing I was some thief, but I cried out, "Mrs. Ann, help me, for pity's sake! for I cannot get up!"—"Bless me," said she, "what! you, Madam! Why, our hearts are almost broken, and we are going to drag the pond for you, believing you had drowned yourself. Now," said she, "you'll make us all alive again!"

And, without helping me, she ran away to the pond, and brought all the servants to the wood-house. The wicked woman, as she entered said, "Where is she? Plague of her spells and witchcrafts! She shall dearly repent of this trick, if my name be Jewkes;" and coming to me, took hold of my arm so roughly, and gave me such a pull, as made me squeal out (my shoulder being bruised on that side), and drew me on my face. "O, cruel creature," said I, "if you knew what I have suffered, it would move you to pity me!"

Even Colbrand seemed to be concerned, and said, "Fie, Madam, fie, you see she is almost dead! You must not be so rough with her." The coachman, Robin, seemed to be sorry for me too, and said with sobs, "What a scene is here! Don't you see she's all bloody in her head, and cannot stir?"—"Curse of her contrivances!" said the horrid creature, "she has frightened *me* out of my wits, I'm sure. How the d—l came you here?"—"O!" said I, "ask me no questions, but let the maids carry me up to my prison; and there let me die decently and in peace!" For indeed I thought I could not live two hours. The still more inhuman tigress said, "I suppose you want Mr. Williams to pray by you, don't you? Well, I'll send for my master this minute; let him come and watch you himself for me; for there's no such thing as holding you, I'm sure."

So the maids took me up between them, and carried me to my chamber; and when the wretch saw how bad I was, she began a little to relent—while every one wondered (at which I had neither strength nor inclination to tell them) how all this came to pass, which they imputed to sorcery or witchcraft.

I was so weak, when I got up stairs, that I fainted away with dejection, pain, and fatigue; and they undressed me, and got me to bed; and Mrs. Jewkes ordered Nan to bathe my shoulder, arm, and ancle, with some old rum, warmed; they cut my hair a little from the back part of my head, and washed it; for it was clotted with blood, from a pretty long, but not a deep gash; and put a family plaister upon it; for, if this woman has any good quality, it is, it seems, in a readiness and skill to manage in cases where sudden misfortunes happen in a family.

After this, I fell into a pretty sound and refreshing sleep, and lay till twelve o'clock tolerably easy, considering I was very feverish, and aguishly inclined. She took a deal of care to fit me to undergo more trials, which I had hoped would have been happily ended : but Providence did not see fit.

She would make me rise about twelve; but I was so weak, I could only sit up till the bed was made, and went into it again; and was, as they said, delirous some part of the afternoon. Having a tolerable night on Thursday, I was a good deal better on Friday, and on Saturday got up and ate a little spoon-meat, and my feverishness seemed to be gone; and I was so mended by evening, that I begged her indulgence in my closet, to be left to myself; which she consented to, it being double-barred the day before, and I assuring her, that all my contrivances, as she called them, were at an end. But first she made me tell the whole story of my enterprize; which I did very faithfully, knowing now that nothing could stand me in any stead, or contribute to my safety or escape : and she seemed full of wonder at my resolution; but told me frankly, that I should have found it a hard matter to get quite off; for she was provided with a warrant from my master (who is a justice of peace in this county, as well as in the other), to get me apprehended, if I *had* got away, on suspicion of wronging him, let me have been where I would.

O how deep-laid are the mischiefs designed to fall on my devoted head !—Surely, surely, I cannot be worthy of all this contrivance !—This too well shews me the truth of what was hinted to me formerly at the other house, that my master swore he would *have* me ! O preserve me, Heaven ! from being *his* in his own wicked sense of the abjuration !

I must add, that now the woman sees me recover so fast, she uses me worse, and has abridged me of paper, all but one sheet, which I am to shew her, written or unwritten, on demand : and has reduced me to one pen : yet my hidden stores stand me in stead. But she is more and more snappish and cross ; and tauntingly calls me Mrs. Williams, and any thing she thinks will vex me.

SUNDAY AFTERNOON.

Mrs. Jewkes has thought fit to give me an airing, for three or four hours this afternoon. I am a good deal better; and should be much more so, if I knew for what I was reserved. But health is a blessing hardly to be coveted in my circumstances, since that but exposes me to the calamity I am in continual apprehension of; whereas a weak and sickly state might possibly move compassion for me. O how I dread the coming of this angry and incensed master; though I am sure I have done him no harm.

Just now we heard that he had like to have been drowned in crossing the stream, a few days ago, in pursuing his game. What is the matter, that, with all his ill usage of me, I cannot hate him? To be sure, I am not like other people! He has certainly done enough to make me hate him; but yet, when I heard his danger, which was very great, I could not in my heart forbear rejoicing for his safety; though his death would have ended my afflictions. Ungenerous master! if you knew this, you surely would not be so much my persecutor! but for my good lady's sake I must wish him well; and oh what an angel would he be in my eyes yet, if he would cease his attempts and reform!

Well, I hear, by Mrs. Jewkes, that John Arnold is turned away, being detected in writing to Mr. Williams; and that Mr. Longman and Mr. Jonathan, the butler, have incurred his displeasure, for offering to speak in my behalf. Mrs. Jervis too is in danger; for all these three probably went together to beg in my favour; for now it is known where I am.

Mrs. Jewkes has, with the news about my master, received a letter; but she says the contents are too bad for me to know. They must be bad indeed, if they be worse than what I have already known.

Just now the horrid creature tells me, as a secret, that she has reason to think he has found out a way to satisfy my scruples: it is, by marrying me to this dreadful Colbrand, and buying me of him on the wedding-day, for a sum of money!—Was ever the like heard?—She says it will be my duty to obey my husband: and that Mr. Williams will be forced, as a punishment, to marry us; and that when my master has paid for me, and I am surrendered up, the Swiss is to go home again, with the money, to his former wife and children; for she says, it is the custom of those people to have a wife in every nation.

But this, to be sure, is horrid romancing! Yet, abominable as it is, it may possibly serve to introduce some plot now hatching!—With what strange perplexities is my poor mind agitated! Perchance, some sham-marriage may be designed on purpose to ruin me: but can a husband sell his wife against her own consent? And will such a bargain stand good in law?

Nothing offers these days but squabblings between Mrs. Jewkes and me. She grows worse and worse to me. I vexed her yesterday, because she talked nastily; and told her she talked more like a vile London prostitute, than a gentleman's house-keeper; and she thinks she cannot use me bad enough for it. She curses and storms at me like a trooper, and can hardly keep her hands off me. You may believe she must talk sadly, to make me say such harsh words: indeed it cannot be repeated: as she is a disgrace to her sex. And then she ridicules me, and laughs at my notions of honesty; and tells me, impudent creature as she is! what a fine bed-fellow I shall make for my master (and such like), " with such whimsical notions about me !"— Do you think this is to be borne? And yet she talks worse than this, if possible! Quite filthily! O what vile hands am I put into!

THURSDAY.

I have now every reason to apprehend my master will be here soon; for the servants are busy in setting the house to rights; and a stable and coach-house are cleaning out, that have not been used some time. I asked Mrs. Jewkes; but she tells me nothing, nor will hardly answer me when I ask her a question. Sometimes I think she puts on these strange wicked airs to me, purposely to make me wish for, what I dread most of all things, my master's coming down. *He* talk of love!—If he had the least notion of regard for me, he would not give this naughty body such power over me:—and if he *does* come, where is his promise of not seeing me without I consent to it? But it seems, *his honour owes me nothing.* So he tells me in his letter. And why? Because I am willing to keep mine. But, indeed, he says, *he hates me perfectly ;* and it is plain he does, or I should not be left to the mercy of this woman; and, what is worse, to my woeful apprehensions.

FRIDAY, THE 36TH DAY OF MY IMPRISONMENT.

I took the liberty yesterday afternoon, finding the gates open, to walk out before the house; and, before I was aware, had got to the bottom of the long row of elms; and there I sat myself down upon the steps of a broad stile, which leads into the road, and goes toward the town. And as I sat musing about what always busies my mind, I saw several people running towards me from the house, men and women, as in a fright. At first I wondered what was the matter, till they came nearer: I found they were all alarmed, thinking I had attempted to get off. There was first the horrible Colbrand, running with his long legs, well nigh two yards at a stride: then there was one of the grooms, poor Mr. Williams's robber; then I spied Nan half out of breath, and the cook-maid after her; and lastly came waddling as fast as she could, Mrs. Jewkes, exclaiming most bitterly, as I found, against me. Colbrand said, "O how have you frighted us all!"—And went behind me, lest I should run away, as I suppose.

I sat still, to let them see I had no view to get away; for, besides the improbability of succeeding, my last sad attempt had cured me of enterprising again. And when Mrs. Jewkes came within hearing, I found her terribly incensed, and raving about my contrivances. "Why," said I, "should you be so concerned? Here I have sat a few minutes, and had not the least thought of getting away, or going farther; but to return as soon as it was duskish." She would not believe me; and the barbarous creature struck at me with her horrid fist, and, I believe would have felled me, had not Colbrand interposed and said, he saw me sitting still, looking about me, and not seeming to have the least inclination to stir. But this would not serve: she ordered the two maids to take me each by an arm, and lead me back into the house, and up stairs; and there have I been locked up ever since, without shoes. In vain have I pleaded, that I had no design, as indeed I had not. Last night I was forced to lie between her and Nan; and I find she is resolved to make a handle of this against me, in her own behalf. Indeed, what with her usage, and my own apprehensions of still worse, I am quite weary of my life.

Just now she has been with me, and given me my shoes, and has laid her imperious commands upon me, to dress myself in a suit of clothes out of the portmanteau, which I have not seen lately, against three or four o'clock; for, she says, she is to have a visit from Lady Darnford's two daughters, who come purposely to see me; and so she gave me the key of the portmanteau. But I did not obey her; and I told her, I would not be made a shew of, nor see the ladies. She left me, saying, it should be worse for me if I did not. But how can that be?

FIVE O'CLOCK IS COME.

And no young ladies!—So that I fancy—But hold! I hear their coach, I believe. I'll step to the window. I won't go down to them, I am resolved.

Good Sirs! good Sirs! What will become of me? Here is my master come in his fine chariot! Indeed he is!—What shall I do? Where shall I hide myself?—O! what shall I do? Pray for me! But O! you will not see this!—Now, good God of Heaven, preserve me! if it is thy blessed will!

Though I dread to see him, yet I wonder I have not. No doubt something is resolving against me, as he stays to hear all her stories. I can hardly write; yet, as I can do nothing else, I know not how to forbear!—I cannot hold my pen—How crooked and trembling the lines!—I must leave off till I can get quieter fingers!—Why should the guiltless tremble so, when the guilty can possess their minds in peace?

Now let me give you an account of what passed last night; for I had no power to write, nor yet opportunity, till now.

This vile woman held my master till half an hour after seven; and he came hither about five in the afternoon. And then I heard his voice on the stairs, as he was coming up to me. It was about his supper; for he said, "I shall choose a boiled chicken with butter and parsley." And up he came.

He put on a stern and majestic air; and he can look very majestic when he pleases. "Well, perverse Pamela, ungrateful runaway," said he, for my first salutation: "You do well, don't you, to give me all this trouble and vexation?" I could not speak; but throwing myself on the floor, hid my face, and was ready to die with grief and apprehension.—He said, "Well may you hide your face! well may you be ashamed to see me, vile forward one as you are!" I sobbed, and wept, but could not speak. And he let me lie, and went to the door, and called Mrs. Jewkes. "There," said he, "take up that fallen angel! —Once I thought her as innocent as an angel: but I have now no patience with her. The little hypocrite prostrates herself thus, in hopes to move my weakness in her favour, and that I'll raise her from the floor myself. But I shall not touch her. No," said he, "let such fellows as Williams be taken in by her artful wiles! I know her now, and she is for any fool's turn that will be caught by her."

I sighed as if my heart would break!—And Mrs. Jewkes lifted me up upon my knees; for I trembled so I could not stand. "Come," said she, "Mrs. Pamela, learn to know your best friend ! Confess your unworthy behaviour, and beg his honour's forgiveness of all your faults." I was ready to faint; and he said, "She is mistress of arts, I'll assure you; and will mimic a fit, ten to one, in a minute."

I was struck to the heart at this, but could not speak presently; only lifted my eyes up to Heaven !—And at last said, "God forgive you, Sir !"—He seemed in a great passion, and walked up and down the room, casting sometimes an eye upon me, and seeming as if he would have spoken, but checked himself.—And at last he said, "When she has *acted* this her *first part* over, perhaps I will see her again, and she shall *soon* know what she has to trust to."

And so he went out of the room; and I was quite sick at heart. "Surely," said I, "I am the wickedest creature that ever breathed !"—"Well," said the impertinent, "not so wicked as *that* neither; but I am glad you begin to see your faults. Nothing like being humble !—Come, I'll stand your friend, and plead for you, if you'll promise to be more dutiful for the future. Come, come," added the wretch, "this may be all made up by to-morrow morning, if you are not a fool."—"Be gone, hideous woman !" said I, "and let not my afflictions be added to by thy inexorable cruelty, and unwomanly wickedness."

She gave me a push, and went away in a violent passion. It seems she made a story of this; and said, I had such a spirit, there was no bearing it.

I laid down on the floor, and had no power to stir, till the clock struck nine; and then the wicked woman came up again. "You must come down stairs," said she, "to my master; that is, if you please, spirit !"—Said I, "I believe I cannot stand."—"Then," said she, "I'll send Monsieur Colbrand to carry you down."

I got up as well as I could, and trembled all the way down stairs; she went before me into the parlour; and a new servant that he had waiting on him, instead of John, withdrew as soon as I came in: and, by the way, he had a new coachman too; which looked as if Bedfordshire Robin was turned away.

"I thought," said he, when I came down, "you should have sat at table with me, when I had not company; but when I find you cannot forget your original, but must prefer my menials to me, I call you down to wait on me while I sup, that I may have some talk with you, and throw away as little time as possible upon you."

"Sir," said I, "you do me honour to wait upon you: and I

never shall, I hope, forget my original." But I was forced to stand behind his chair, that I might hold by it. "Fill me," said he, "a glass of that Burgundy." I went to do it; but my hand shook so, that I could not hold the plate with the glass in it, and spilt some of the wine. So Mrs. Jewkes poured it for me, and I carried it as well as I could, and made a low curtsey. He took it, and said, "Stand behind me, out of my sight!"

"Why, Mrs. Jewkes," said he, "you tell me, she remains very sullen still, and eats nothing."—"No," said she, "not so much as will keep life and soul together."—"And is always crying, you say, too?"—"Yes, Sir," answered she, "I think she is, for one thing or another."—"Aye," said he, "your young wenches will feed upon their tears; and their obstinacy will serve them for meat and drink. I think I never saw her look better in my life.—But, I suppose, she lives upon love. The sweet Mr. Williams, and her little villainous plots together, have kept her alive and well, for mischief, love, and contradiction, are the natural ailments of a woman."

I was forced to hear all this, and be silent; and indeed my heart was too full to speak.

"And so you say," said he, "that she had *another* project, but yesterday, to get away?"—"She denies it herself," said she; "but it had all the appearance of one. I'm sure she made me in a fearful pucher about it. I'm glad your honour is come; and, I hope, whatever be your honour's intention concerning her, you will not be long about it; for you'll find her as slippery as an eel, I'll assure you."

"Sir," said I, clasping his knees with my arms, not knowing what I did, and falling on my knees, "have mercy on me, and hear me, concerning that wicked woman's usage of me."

He cruelly interrupted me, and said, "I am satisfied she has done her duty; it signifies nothing what you say against Mrs. Jewkes. That you are here, little hypocrite as you are, pleading your cause before me, is owing to her care of you; else you had been with the parson.—Wicked girl!" said he, "to tempt a man to undo himself, as you have done him, at a time I was on the point of making him happy for his life!"

I rose; but said, with a deep sigh, "I have done, Sir!—I have done!—I have a strange tribunal to plead before. The poor sheep, in the fable, had such an one; when it was tried before the vulture, on the accusation of the wolf!"

"So, Mrs. Jewkes," said he, "you are the wolf, I the vulture, and this the poor innocent lamb on her trial before us!—Oh!

161

you don't know how well this innocent is read in reflection. She has wit at will, when she has a mind to display her innocence, at the price of other people's character."

"Well," said the aggravating creature, "this is nothing to what she has called me; I have been a Jezebel, a London prostitute, and what not!—But I am content with her ill names, now I see it is her fashion, and she can call your honour a vulture."

Said I, "I had no thought of comparing my master."—And was going to say more; but he said, "Don't prate, girl!"—"No," said she, "it don't become you, I am sure."

"Well," said I, "since I must not speak, I will hold my peace; but there is a righteous Judge, who knows the secrets of all hearts; and to him I appeal."

"See there!" said he: "now this meek, good creature is praying for fire from Heaven upon us! O she can curse most heartily, in the spirit of Christian meekness, I'll assure you.—Come, saucy-face, give me another glass of wine."

So I did, as well as I could; but wept so, that he said, "I suppose I shall have some of your tears in my wine!"

When he had supped, he stood up, and said, "O how happy for you it is, that you can, at will, make your speaking eyes overflow in this manner, without losing any of their brilliancy! You have been told, I suppose, that you are *most* beautiful in your tears!—Did you ever," said he to *her* (who all this while was standing in one corner of the parlour), "see a more charming creature than this? Is it to be wondered at, that I demean myself thus to take notice of her?—See," said he, and took the glass with one hand, and turned me round with the other, "what a shape, what a neck! what a hand! and what a bloom on that lovely face! But who can describe the tricks and artifices that lie lurking in her little, plotting, guileful heart! 'Tis no wonder the poor parson was infatuated with her. I blame him less than I do her; for who could expect such artifice in so young a sorceress?"

I went to the further part of the room, and held my face against the wainscot; and, in spite of all I could do to refrain crying, sobbed as if my heart would break. He said, "I am surprised, Mrs. Jewkes, at the mistake of the letters you tell me of! But, you see, I am not afraid any body should read what I write. I don't carry on private correspondences, and reveal every secret that comes to my knowledge, and then corrupt people to carry my letters against their duty, and all good conscience."

"Come hither, hussy," said he, "you and I have a dreadful reckoning to make.—Why don't you come, when I bid you?"—"Fie upon it, Mrs. Pamela," said she; "what, not stir, when his honour commands you to come to him? Who knows but his goodness will forgive you?"

He came to me (for I had not power to stir), and put his arm about my neck, and would kiss me; and said, "Well, Mrs. Jewkes, if it were not for the thought of this cursed parson, I believe in my heart, so great is my weakness, that I could *yet* forgive this intriguing little slut, and take her to my bosom."

"O," said the sycophant, "you are very good, Sir, very forgiving, indeed!—But come," added the profligate wretch, "I hope you will be so good as to take her to your bosom; and that, by to-morrow morning, you'll bring her to a better sense of her duty!"

Could any thing in womanhood be so vile? I had no patience, but yet grief and indignation choked up the passage of my words; and I could only stammer out a passionate exclamation to Heaven, to protect my innocence. But the word was the subject of their ridicule. Was ever poor creature worse beset!

He said, as if he had been considering whether he could forgive me or not.—"No, I cannot yet forgive her neither. She has given me great disturbance; has brought great discredit upon me, both abroad and at home; has corrupted all my servants at the other house; has despised my honourable views and intentions to her, and sought to run away with this ungrateful parson. And surely I ought not to forgive all this!" Yet, with all this wretched grimace, he kissed me again, and would have put his hand into my bosom; but I struggled, and said, I would die before I would be used thus. "Consider, Pamela," said he, in a threatening tone, "consider where you are! and don't play the fool: if you do, a more dreadful fate awaits you than you expect.—But, take her up stairs, Mrs. Jewkes, and I'll send a few lines to her to consider of;—and let me have your answer Pamela, in the morning. Till then you have to resolve: and after that your doom is fixed." So I went up stairs, and gave myself up to grief, and expectation of what he would send; but yet I was glad of this night's reprieve.

He sent me, however, nothing at all. And about twelve o'clock, Mrs. Jewkes and Nan came up, as the night before, to be my bed-fellows; and I would go to bed with some of my clothes on: which they muttered at sadly; and Mrs. Jewkes railed at me particularly; indeed I would have sat up all night, for fear, if she would have let me. For I had but very little rest that night, apprehending this woman would let my master in. She did nothing but praise him and blame me; but I answered her as little as I could.

He has Sir Simon Tell-tale, alias Darnford, to dine with him to-day, whose family sent to welcome him into the country; and it seems, the old knight wants to see me; so I suppose I shall be sent for, as Samson was, to make sport for him. Here I am, and must bear it all.

TWELVE O'CLOCK, SATURDAY NOON.

Just now he has sent me up, by Mrs. Jewkes, the following proposals. So here are the honourable intentions all at once laid open. They are, my dear parents, to make me a vile kept mistress; which I hope, I shall always detest the thoughts of. But you'll see how they are accommodated to what I should have most desired, could I have honestly promoted it, your welfare and happiness. I have answered them as I am sure you'll approve, and I am prepared for the worst; for though I fear there will be nothing omitted to ruin me, and though my poor strength will not be able to defend me, yet I will be innocent of crime in my intention, and in the sight of God; and to him leave the avenging of all my wrongs. I shall write to you my answer against his articles, and hope the best, though I fear the worst. But if I should come home to you ruined and undone, and may not be able to look you in the face, yet pity and inspirit the poor Pamela, to make her little remnant of life easy; for long I shall not survive my disgrace : and you may be assured it shall not be my fault, if it be my misfortune.

" TO MRS. PAMELA ANDREWS.

" *The following* ARTICLES *are proposed to your serious consideration ; and let me have an answer, in writing, to them ; that I may take my resolutions accordingly. Only remember that I will not be trifled with ; and what you give for an answer, will absolutely decide your fate, without expostulation, or further trouble.*"

THIS IS MY ANSWER.

" *Forgive, Sir, the spirit your poor servant is about to shew in her answer to your Articles. Not to be warm, and in earnest, on such an occasion as the present, would shew a degree of guilt that, I hope, my soul abhors. I will not trifle with you, nor act like a person doubtful of her own mind, for it wants not one moment's consideration with me, and I therefore return the* ANSWER *following, let what will be the consequence."*

" *Article* I. If you can convince me that the hated parson has had no encouragement from you in his addresses, and that you have no inclination for him, in preference to me, then I will offer the following proposals to you, which I will punctually make good."

" *Answer.* As to the first Article, Sir, it may behove me (that I may not deserve, in your opinion, the opprobrious terms of *forward* and *artful*, and such like) to declare solemnly, that Mr. Williams never had the least encouragement from me, as to what you hint; and I believe his principal motive was the duty of his function, quite contrary to his apparent interest, to assist a person he thought in distress. You may, Sir, the rather believe me, when I declare, that I know not the man breathing I would wish to marry; and that the only one I could honour more than another, is the gentleman, who, of all others, seeks my everlasting dishonour."

" *Art.* II. I will directly make you a present of five hundred guineas, for your own use, which you may dispose of to any purpose you please : and I will give it absolutely into the hands of any person you shall appoint to receive it; and expect no favour in return, till you are satisfied in the possession of it."

" *Answer.* As to your second proposal, let the consequence be what it will, I reject it with all my soul. Money, Sir, is not my chief good; may God Almighty desert me whenever it is; and whenever, for the sake of that, I can give up my title to that blessed hope which will stand me in stead, at a time when millions of gold will not purchase one happy moment of reflection on a past mis-spent life."

" *Art.* III. I will likewise directly make over to you a purchase I lately made in Kent, which brings in two hundred and fifty pounds per annum, clear of all deductions. This shall be made over to you in full property for your life, and for the lives of any children to perpetuity that you may happen to have : and your father shall be immediately put into possession of it, in trust for these purposes : and the management of it will yield a comfortable subsistence to him and your mother for life; and I will make up any deficiencies, if such should happen, to that clear sum, and allow him fifty pounds per annum besides, for his life, and that of your mother, for his care and management of this your estate."

" *Answer.* Your third proposal, Sir, I reject for the same reason; and am sorry you could think my poor honest parents would enter into their part of it, and be concerned for the management of an estate, which would be owing to the prostitution of their poor daughter. Forgive, Sir, my warmth on this occasion; but you know not the poor man, and the poor woman, my ever dear father and mother, if you think that they would not much rather choose to starve in a ditch, or rot in a noisome dungeon, than accept of the fortune of a monarch upon such wicked terms. I dare not say all that my full mind suggests to me on this grievous occasion.—But, Sir, you know them not; nor shall the terrors of death, in its most frightful form, I hope, through God's assisting grace, ever make me act unworthy of such poor honest parents."

"*Art*. IV. I will, moreover, extend my favour to any other of your relations, that you may think worthy of it, or that are valued by you."

"*Answer*. Your fourth proposal I take upon me, Sir, to answer as the third. If I have any friends that want the favour of the great, may they *ever* want it, if they are capable of desiring it on unworthy terms!"

"*Art*. V. I will besides, order patterns to be sent you for choosing four complete suits of rich clothes, that you may appear with reputation as if you were my wife. And I will give you the two diamond rings, and two pairs of ear-rings, and diamond necklace, that were bought by my mother, to present to Miss Tomlins, if the match that was proposed between her and me had been brought to effect : and I will confer upon you still *other* gratuities, as I shall find myself obliged by your good behaviour and affection."

"*Answer*. Fine clothes, Sir, become not me; nor have I any ambition to wear them. I have greater pride in my poverty and meanness, than I should have in dress and finery. Believe me, Sir, I think such things less become the humble-born Pamela than the rags your good mother raised me from. Your rings, Sir, your necklace, and your ear-rings, will better befit ladies of degree than me : and to lose the best jewel, my virtue, would be poorly recompensed by those you propose to give me, What should I think, when I looked upon my finger, or saw, in the glass, those diamonds on my neck, and in my ears, but that they were the price of my honesty, and that I wore those jewels outwardly, because I had none inwardly?"

"*Art*. VI. Now, Pamela, you will see, by this, what a value I set upon the free-will of a person *already* in my power; and who, if these proposals are not accepted, shall find that I have not taken all these pains, and risqued my reputation, without

166

resolving to gratify my passion for you, at all adventures; and if you refuse, I will accomplish my purpose without making any terms at all."

"*Answer.* I know, Sir, by woeful experience, that I am in your power: I know all the resistance I can make will be poor and weak, and perhaps stand me in little stead: I dread your *will* to ruin me is as great as your *power*: yet, Sir, will I dare to tell you, that I will make no free-will offering of my virtue. All that I *can* do, poor as it is, I *will* do, to convince you that your offers shall have no part in my choice: and if I cannot escape the violence of man, I hope, by God's grace, I shall have nothing to reproach myself, for not doing all in my power to avoid my disgrace; and then I can safely appeal to the great God, my only refuge and protector, with this consolation, that my will bore no part in the violation."

"*Art.* VII. You shall be mistress of my person and fortune, as much as if the foolish ceremony had passed. All my servants shall be yours: and you shall choose any two persons to attend yourself, either male or female, without any control of mine; and if your conduct be such, that I have reason to be satisfied with it, I know not (but will not engage for this) that I may, after a twelvemonth's cohabitation, marry you; for if my love increase for you, as it has done for many months past, it will be impossible for me to deny you any thing.

"And now, Pamela, consider well, it is in your power to oblige me on such terms as will make yourself, and all your friends, happy; but this will be over this very day, irrevocably over; and you shall meet with all you fear, without the least benefit arising from it to yourself.

"I beg you will well weigh the matter, and comply with my proposals: and I will instantly set about securing to you the full effect of them: and let me, if you value yourself, experience a grateful return on this occasion, and I'll forgive all that's past."

"*Answer.* I have not once dared to look so high as to such a proposal as your seventh article contains. Hence have proceeded all my little abortive artifices to escape from the confinement you have put me in; although you promised to be honourable to me. Your honour, well I know, would not let you stoop to so mean and unworthy a slave as the poor Pamela: all I desire is, to be permitted to return to my native meanness unviolated. What have I done, Sir, to deserve it should be otherwise? For the obtaining of this, though I would not have *married* your chaplain, yet would I have *ran away* with your meanest servant, if I had thought I could have got safe to my beloved poverty. I heard you once say, Sir, that a certain great commander, who could live upon lentils, might well refuse the bribes of the greatest monarch : and I hope, as I contentedly live at the meanest rate, and think not myself above the lowest condition, that I am also above making an exchange of my honesty for all the riches of the Indies. When I come to be proud and vain of gaudy apparel, and outside finery; then (which I hope will never be) may I rest my principal good in such vain trinkets, and despise for them the more solid ornaments of a good fame, and a chastity inviolate.

" Give me leave to say, Sir, in an answer to what you hint, that you may, in a twelvemonth's time, marry me, on the continuance of my good behaviour; that *this* weighs less with me, if possible, than any thing else you have said ; for, in the first place, there is an end of all merit, and all good behaviour on my side, if I have *now* any, the moment I consent to your proposals : and I should be so far from *expecting* such a honour, that I will pronounce, that I should be most *unworthy* of it. What, Sir, would the world say, were you to marry your harlot?—That a gentleman of your rank in life should stoop, not only to the base-born Pamela, but to a base-born prostitute !—Little, Sir, as I know of the world, I am not to be caught by a bait so poorly covered as this !

" Yet, after all, dreadful is the thought, that I, a poor, weak, friendless, unhappy creature, am too fully in your power ! But permit me, Sir, to pray, as I now write, on my bended knees, that before you resolve upon my ruin, you will weigh well the matter. Hitherto, Sir, though you have taken large strides to this crying sin, yet are you on *this* side the commission of it. When once it is done, nothing can recall it ! And where will be your triumph?—What glory will the spoils of such a weak enemy yield you? Let me but enjoy my poverty with honesty, is all my prayer; and I will *bless* you, and *pray for* you, every moment of my life ! Think, O think ! before it is yet too late, what stings, what remorse, will attend your dying hour, when you come to reflect, that you have ruined, perhaps soul and body, a wretched creature, whose only pride was her virtue ! And how pleased you will be, on the contrary, if, in that tremendous moment, you shall be able to acquit yourself of this foul crime, and to plead, in your own behalf, that you suffered the earnest supplications of an unhappy wretch to prevail with you to be innocent yourself, and let her remain so ! May God Almighty, whose mercy so lately saved you from the peril of perishing in deep waters, (on which I hope you will give me cause to congratulate you !) touch your heart in my favour, and save *you* from this *sin*, and *me* from this *ruin !* —And to him do I commit my cause; and to him will I give the glory, and night and day pray for you, if I may be permitted to escape this great evil ! *Your poor oppressed, broken-spirited servant.*"

I took a copy of this for your perusal, my dear parents, if I shall ever be so happy to see you again, (for I hope my conduct will be approved of by you;) and at night when Sir Simon was gone, he sent for me. "Well," said he, "have you considered my proposals?"—"Yes, Sir," said I, "I have; and there is my answer : but pray let me not see you read it."—"Is it your bashfulness," said he, "or your obstinacy, that makes you not choose I should read it before you?"

I offered to go away; and he said, "Don't run from me; I won't read it till you are gone. But," said he, "tell me, Pamela, whether you comply with my proposals, or not?"—"Sir," said I, "you will see presently; pray don't hold me;" for he took my hand. Said he, "Did you well consider, before you answered?"—"I did, Sir," said I. "If it be not what you think will please me," said he, "dear girl, take it back again, and reconsider it; for if I have this as your absolute answer, and I don't like it, you are undone; for I will not sue meanly where I can command. I fear," said he, "it is not what I like, by your manner : and let me tell you, that I cannot bear denial. If the terms I have offered are not sufficient, I will augment them to two-thirds of my estate; for," said he, and swore a dreadful oath, "I cannot live without you : and, since the thing is gone so far, *I will not !*" And so he clasped me in his arms, in such a manner as quite frightened me; and kissed me two or three times.

I got from him and ran up stairs, and went to the closet, and was quite uneasy and fearful.

In an hour's time he called Mrs. Jewkes down to him ! And I heard him very high in passion : and all about poor me ! I heard her say it was his own fault; there would be an end of all my complaining and perverseness, if he was once resolved; and other most impudent aggravations. I am resolved not to go to bed this night, if I can help it Lie still, lie still, my poor fluttering heart !—What will become of me?

ALMOST TWELVE O'CLOCK, SATURDAY NIGHT.

He sent Mrs. Jewkes about ten o'clock, to tell me to come to him. "Where?" said I. "I'll shew you," said she. I went down three or four steps, and saw her making to his chamber, the door of which was open : so I said, " I cannot go there ! "— " Don't be foolish," said she; " but come; no harm will be done to you."—" Well," said I, " if I die, I cannot go there." I heard him say, " Let her come, or it shall be worse for her. I can't bear," said he, " to speak to her myself ! "—" Well," said I, " I cannot come, indeed I cannot;" and so I went up again into my closet, expecting to be fetched by force.

But she came up soon after, and bid me make haste to bed : said I, " I will not go to bed this night, that's certain ! "— " Then," said she, " you shall be *made* to come to bed; and Nan and I will undress you." I knew neither prayers nor tears would move this wicked woman : so I said, " I am sure you will let my master in, and I shall be undone ! "—" Mighty piece of undone," she said : but he was too much exasperated against me, to be so familiar with me, she would assure me ! " Aye," said she, " you'll be disposed of another way soon, I can tell you for comfort : and I hope your *husband* will have your obedience, though nobody else can have it."—" No husband in the world," said I, " shall make me do an unjust or base thing." She said that would be soon tried; and Nan coming in, " What ! " said I, " am I to have *two* bed-fellows again, these warm nights ? "—" Yes," said she, " slippery one, you are, till you can have *one good one* instead of us." Said I, " Mrs. Jewkes, don't talk nastily to me. I see you are beginning again; and I shall affront you, may-be; for next to bad actions are bad words; for they could not be spoken, if they were not in the heart."—" Come to bed, Purity ! " said she. " You are a non-such, I suppose."—" Indeed," said I, " I can't come to bed; and it will do you no harm to let me stay all night in the great chair ! "—" Nan," said she, " undress my young lady. If she won't let you, I'll help you; and, if neither of us can do it quietly, we'll call my master to do it for us; though," said she, " I think it an office worthier of Monsieur Colbrand ! " —" You are very wicked," said I.—" I know it," said she; " I am a Jezebel, and a London prostitute, you know."—" You did great feats," said I, " to tell my master all this poor stuff; but you did not tell him how you beat me."—" No, lambkin," said she (a word I had not heard a good while), " that I left for you to tell; and you was going to do it, if the *vulture* had not taken the *wolf's* part, and bid the poor innocent *lamb* be silent ! "— " Aye," said I, " no matter for your fleers, Mrs. Jewkes; though I can have neither justice nor mercy here, and cannot be heard in my defence, yet a time will come, may-be, when I *shall* be heard, and when your guilt will strike you dumb!"—"Aye, spirit!" said she, "and the *vulture* too! Must we be both dumb? Why that, lambkin, will be pretty!—Then," said the wicked one, "you'll have all the talk to yourself!—Then how will the tongue of the pretty lambkin bleat out *innocence*, and *virtue*, and *honesty*, till the whole trial be at an end!"—"You're a wicked woman, that's certain," said I; "and if you thought any thing of another world, could not talk thus. But no wonder!—It shows what hands I'm got into!"—"Aye, so it does," said she; but I beg you'll undress and come to bed, or I believe your innocence won't keep you from *still worse* hands."—"I will come to bed," said I, "if you will let me have the keys in my own hand; not else, if I can help it."—"Yes," said she, "and then for another contrivance, another escape!"—"No, no," said I, "all my contrivances are over, I'll assure you! Pray let me have the keys, and I will come to bed." She came to me, and took me in her huge arms, as if I was a feather. Said she, "I do this to shew you what a poor resistance you can make against me, if I please to exert myself; and so, lambkin, don't say to your wolf, 'I *won't* come to bed!'" And set me down and tapped me on the neck: "Ah!" said she, "thou art a pretty creature, it's true; but so obstinate! so full of spirit! if thy strength was but answerable to that, thou wouldest run away with us all, and this great house too, on thy back!—But undress, undress, I tell you."

"Well," said I, "I see my misfortunes make you very merry, and witty too: but I will *love* you, if you will humour me with the keys of the chamber-doors."—"Are you *sure* you will love me?" said she: "now speak your conscience!"—"Why," said I, "you must not put it so close; neither would you, if you thought you had not given reason to doubt it!—But I will love you as well as I can! I would not tell a wilful lie; if I did, you would not believe me, after your hard usage."—"Well," said she, "that's all fair, I own!—But, Nan, pray pull off my young lady's shoes and stockings."—"No, pray don't," said I, "I will come to bed presently, since I must." And so I went to the closet, and scribbled a little about this idle chit-chat. And she being importunate I was forced to go to bed; but with some of my clothes on, as the former night: she let me hold the two keys; for there are two locks, there being a double door, and so I got a little sleep that night, having had none for two or three nights before.

I can't imagine what she means; but Nan offered to talk a little once or twice, but she snubbed her, and said, "I charge you, wench, don't open your lips before me : and if you are asked any questions by Mrs. Pamela, don't answer her one word, while I am here!" But she is a lordly woman to the maid-servants; and that has always been her character. O how unlike good Mrs. Jervis in every thing!

SUNDAY MORNING.

A thought came into my head; I meant no harm; but it was a little bold. For, seeing my master dressing to go to church, and his chariot getting ready, I went to my closet, and I writ :

" The prayers of this congregation are earnestly desired for a gentleman of great worth and honour, who labours under a temptation to exert his great power to ruin a poor, distressed, worthless maiden. And also,

" The prayers of this congregation are earnestly desired, by a poor distressed creature, for the preservation of her virtue and innocence."

Mrs. Jewkes came up : "Always writing," said she, and would see it; and straight, all that ever I could say, carried it down to my master. He looked upon it, and said, "Tell her she shall soon see how her prayers are answered. She is very bold : but as she has rejected all my favours, her reckoning for all is not far off." I looked after him out of the window; and he was charmingly dressed. He is a handsome, fine gentleman! —What a pity his heart is not as good as his appearance!— Why can't I hate him?—But don't be uneasy if you should see this; for it is impossible I should love him; for his vices all *ugly* him over, as I may say.

My master sends word, that he shall not come home to dinner : I suppose he dines with Sir Simon Darnford. I am much concerned for poor Mr. Williams. Mrs. Jewkes says he is confined still, and takes on much. All his trouble is brought upon him for my sake : this grieves me much. My master, it seems, will have his money from him : this is very hard; for it is three fifty pounds he gave him, as he thought, as salary for three years that he had been with him : but there was no agreement between them, and he absolutely depended on my master's favour. It was the more generous of him to run these risks for the sake of oppressed innocence! and I hope he will meet with his reward in due time. Alas for me! I dare not plead for him : that would raise my oppressor's jealousy more : and I have not interest to save myself.

172

Mrs. Jewkes has received a line from my master; I wonder what it is, for his chariot is come home without him. But she will tell me nothing; so it is in vain to ask her. I am so fearful of plots and tricks, I know not what to do!—Every thing I suspect; for now my disgrace is avowed, what can I think? To be sure, the worst will be attempted. I can only pour out my soul in prayer to God, for his blessed protection; but, if I must suffer, let me not be long a mournful survivor! Only let me not shorten my own time sinfully!

This woman left upon the table, in the chamber, this letter of my master's to her, and I bolted myself in till I had transcribed it: you'll see how tremblingly, by the lines. I wish poor Mr. Williams's release; but this letter makes my heart ache. Yet I have another day's reprieve, thank God.

" MRS. JEWKES,

" I have been so pressed on Williams's affair, that I shall set out this afternoon, in Sir Simon's chariot, and with Parson Peters, who is his intercessor, for Stamford; and shall not be back till to-morrow evening, if then. As to your ward, I am thoroughly incensed against her: she has withstood her time, and now, would she sign and seal to my articles, it is too late. I shall discover something, perhaps, by him; and will, on my return, let her know, that all her ensnaring loveliness shall not save her from the fate that awaits her. But let her know nothing of this, lest it put her frightful mind upon plots and artifices. Be sure trust her not without another with you at night, lest she venture the window in her foolish rashness: for I shall require her at your hands. *Yours*, &c."

I had but just finished taking a copy of this, and laid the letter where I had it, and unbolted the door, when she came up, in a great fright, for fear I should have seen it: but I being in my closet, and that laying as she left it, she did not mistrust. " O," said she, " I was afraid you had seen my master's letter here, which I carelessly left on the table."—" I wish," said I, " I had known that."—" Why sure," said she, " if you had, you would not have offered to read my letters."—" Indeed," said I, " I should, at this time, if it had been in my way. Do let me see it."—" Well," said she, " I wish poor Mr. Williams well off: I understand my master is gone to make up matters with him, which is very good. To be sure," added she, " he is a very good gentleman, and very forgiving !"—" Why," said I, as if I had known nothing of the matter, " how can he make matters up with him ? Is not Mr. Williams at Stamford ? "— " Yes," said she, " I believe so : but Parson Peters pleads for him, and he is gone with him to Stamford, and will not be back to-night : so we have nothing to do, but to eat our suppers betimes, and get to bed."—" Aye, that's pure," said I ; " and I shall have good rest this night, I hope."—" So," said she, " you might every night, but for your idle fears. You are afraid of your friends when none are near you."—" Aye, that's true," said I ; " for I have not one near me."

So have I one more good honest night before me ; what the next may be I know not : so I'll try to take a good sleep, while I can be a little easy. Therefore, here I say, " Good night, my dear parents ; " for I have no more to write about this night ; and though his letter shocks me, yet I will be as brisk as I can, that she mayn't suspect I have seen it.

TUESDAY NIGHT.

For the future I will always mistrust most, when appearances look fairest. O your poor daughter ! what has she not suffered since what I wrote on Sunday night ! My worst trial, and my fearfullest danger ! O how I shudder to write you an account of this wicked interval of time ! For, my dear parents, will you not be too much frightened and affected with my distress, when I tell you that his journey to Stamford was all abominable pretence ; for he came home privately, and had nigh effected all his vile purposes, and the ruin of your poor daughter ; and that by such a plot as I was not in the least apprehensive of ; and oh ! what a vile and unwomanly part that wicked wretch, Mrs. Jewkes, acted in it.

I left off with informing you how much I was pleased that I had one night's reprieve added to my honesty. But I had less occasion to rejoice than ever, as you will judge, by what I have said already. Take, then, the dreadful story, as well as I can relate it.

The maid Nan is a little apt to drink, if she can get at liquor : and Mrs. Jewkes happened, or designed, as is probable, to leave a bottle of cherry-brandy in her way, and the wench drank some of it more than she should : and when she came in to lay the cloth, Mrs. Jewkes perceived it, and scolded her sadly ; for she has too many faults of her own, to suffer any of the like sort in any body else, if she can help it ; and she bid her get out of her sight, when we had supped, and go to bed, to sleep off her liquor before we came to bed. So the poor maid went muttering upstairs.

About two hours after, which was near eleven o'clock, Mrs. Jewkes and I went up to bed; I pleasing myself with what a charming night I should have. We locked both doors, and saw poor Nan, as I thought (but, oh! it was my abominable master, as you shall hear by-and-by), sitting fast asleep, in an elbow chair, in a dark corner of the room, with her apron thrown over her head and neck. Mrs. Jewkes said, " There is that beast of a wench, fast asleep, instead of being a bed! I knew," said she, " she had taken a fine dose."—" I'll wake her," said I. " No, don't," said she; " let her sleep on; we shall lie better without her."—" Aye," said I, " so we shall; but won't she get cold ? "

Said she, " I hope you have no writing to-night."—" No," replied I, " I will go to bed with you, Mrs. Jewkes." Said she, " I wonder what you can find to write about so much; and am sure you have better conveniences of that kind, and more paper than I am aware of; and I had intended to rummage you, if my master had not come down; for I spied a broken tea-cup with ink, which gave me suspicion! but as he is come, let him look after you, if he will; and if you deceive him, it will be his own fault."

All this time we were undressing ourselves. And I fetched a deep sigh. " What do you sigh for ? " said she. " I am thinking, Mrs. Jewkes," answered I, " what a sad life I live, and how hard is my lot. I am sure, the thief that has robbed is much better off than I, bating the guilt; I should, I think, take it for a mercy to be hanged out of the way, rather than live in these cruel apprehensions." Being not sleepy, and in a prattling vein, I began to give a little history of myself, as I did, once before, to Mrs. Jervis; in this manner:

" Here," said I, " were my poor honest parents; they took care to instil good principles into my mind, till I was almost twelve years of age; and taught me to prefer goodness and poverty to the highest condition of life; and they confirmed their lessons by their own practice; for they were, of late years, remarkably poor, and always as remarkably honest, even to a proverb: for, *As honest as Goodman Andrews*, was a bye-word.

" Well, then," said I, " comes my late dear good lady and takes a fancy to me, and said she would be the making of me, if I was a good girl: she put me to sing, to dance, to play on the spinnet, in order to divert her melancholy hours; and also taught me all manner of fine needle-work; but still this was her lesson—*My good* Pamela, *be virtuous, and keep the men at a distance.*—So I was, I hope, and so I did; and yet, though I say it, they all loved me, and respected me, and would do any thing for me, as if I was a gentlewoman.

" But then, what comes next? Why, it pleases God to take my good lady; and then comes my master: and what says he? Why, in effect it is: ' *Be not virtuous*, Pamela.'

" So I have lived about sixteen years in virtue and reputation; and all at once, when I come to know what is good, and what is evil, I must renounce all the good, all the whole sixteen years' innocence, which, next to God's grace, I owed chiefly to my parents, and my lady's good lessons and examples, and choose the evil; so, in a moment's time, become the vilest of creatures! All this for what, I pray? Why, truly, for a pair of diamond ear-rings, a necklace, and a diamond ring for my finger, which would not become me: for a few paltry fine clothes which, when I wore them, would make but my former poverty more ridiculous to every body that saw me, especially when they knew the base terms I wore them upon. But, indeed I was to have a great parcel of guineas besides; I forget how many; for, had they been ten times more, they would not have been so much to me as the honest six guineas you tricked me out of, Mrs. Jewkes.

" Well! but then I was to have I know not how many pounds a year for life; and my poor father (there was the jest of it!) was to be the manager for the abandoned prostitute his daughter; and then (there was the jest again!), my kind, forgiving, virtuous master would pardon me all my misdeeds!

" Yes, thank him for nothing, truly. And what, pray, are all these violent misdeeds? Why, they are for daring to adhere to the good lessons that were taught me, and not learning a new one, that would have reversed all my former; for not being contented when I was run away with, in order to be ruined, but contriving, if my poor wits had been able, to get out of danger, and preserve myself honest.

" Then was he once jealous of poor John, though he knew John was his own creature, and helped to deceive me.

" Then was he outrageous against poor parson Williams; and him has this good merciful master thrown into gaol; and for what? Why, truly, for that being a divine, and a good man, he had the fear of God before his eyes, and was willing to forgo all his expectations of interest, and assist an oppressed poor creature.

" But, to be sure, I must be forward, bold, saucy, and what not, to dare to run away from certain ruin, and to strive to escape from an unjust confinement; and I must be married to the parson, nothing so sure!

"He would have had but a poor catch of me, had I consented; but he, and *you* too, know I did not want to marry *any body*. I only wanted to go to my poor parents, to have my liberty, and not to be confined by such an unlawful restraint; which would not have been inflicted upon me, but only that I am a poor, destitute, young body, and have no friend that is able to right me.

"So, Mrs. Jewkes," said I, "here is my history in brief. I am a very unhappy young creature! And why am I so? Why because my master sees something in my person that takes his present fancy, and because I would not be undone. I, therefore, must, and shall be undone! and this is all the reason that can be given."

She heard me run on all this time, while I was undressing, without any interruption; and I said, "Well, I must go to the two closets, ever since an affair of the closet at the other house, though he is so far off. And I have a good mind to wake this poor maid."—"No, don't," said she, "I charge you. I am very angry with her, and she'll get no harm there: and if she wakes, she may come to bed well enough, as long as there is a candle in the chimney."

So I looked into the closets, and kneeled down in my own, as I used to do, to say my prayers, and this with my underclothes in my hand, all undressed; and passed by the poor sleeping wench, as I thought, in my return. But, O! little did I think it was my wicked, wicked master, in a gown and petticoat of hers, and her apron over his face and shoulders. What meanness will not Lucifer make his votaries stoop to, to gain their abominable ends!

Mrs. Jewkes, by this time, was got to bed, on the farther side, as she used to be; and, to make room for the maid, when she should awake. I got into bed, and lay close to her. I said, "Where are the keys! Though," said I, "I am not so much afraid to-night."—"Here," said the wicked woman, "put your arm under mine, and you shall find them about my wrist, as they used to be." So I did, and the abominable designer held my hand with her right hand, as my right arm was under her left.

In less than a quarter of an hour, I said, "There's poor Nan awake; I hear her stir."—"Let us go to sleep," said she, "and not mind her: she'll come to bed when she's quite awake."— "Poor soul," said I, "I'll warrant she'll have the head-ache to-morrow for this ! "—" Be silent," said she, " and go to sleep ; you keep me awake : I never found you in so talkative a humour in my life."—" Don't chide me," said I, " I will but say one thing more : Do you think Nan could hear me talk of my master's offers ? "—" No, no," said she, " she was dead asleep."—" I'm glad of that," said I, " because I would not expose my master to his common servants; and I knew *you* were no stranger to his *fine* articles." Said she, " I think they were *fine* articles, and you were bewitched you did not close with them : but let us go to sleep." So I was silent, and the pretended Nan (O wicked, base, villainous designer ! what an unexpected plot was this !) seemed to be awaking; and Mrs. Jewkes, abhorred creature ! said, " Come, Nan ! what, are you awake at last ? Pr'ythee come to bed ; for Mrs. Pamela is in a talking fit, and won't go to sleep one while."

At that, the pretended she came to the bed-side, and sitting down in a chair, where the curtain hid her, began to undress. Said I, " Poor Mrs. Anne, I warrant your head aches most sadly ! How do you do ?" She answered not a word. Said the superlatively wicked woman, " You know I have ordered her not to answer you." And this plot, to be sure, was laid when she gave her these orders, the night before.

I heard her, as I thought, breathe quick and short : " Indeed," said I, " Mrs. Jewkes, the poor maid is not well. What ails you, Mrs. Anne ? " And still no answer was made.

I tremble to relate it ! the pretended she came into bed, but trembled like an aspen-leaf ; and I, poor fool that I was ! pitied her much.—But well might the barbarous deceiver tremble at his vile dissimulation, and base designs.

What words shall I find, my dear mother (for my father should not see this shocking part), to describe the rest, and my confusion, when the guilty wretch took my left arm, and laid it under his neck, and the vile procuress held my right ; and then he clasped me round the waist !

Said I, " Is the wench mad ! Why, how now, Confidence ? " thinking still it had been Nan. But he kissed me with frightful vehemence ; and then his voice broke upon me like a clap of thunder, " Now, Pamela," said he, " is the dreadful time of reckoning come, that I have threatened." I screamed out in such a manner, as never any body heard the like. But there was nobody to help me ; and both my hands were secured, as I said. Sure never poor soul was in such agonies as I. " Wicked man !" said I, " wicked abominable woman !—O God ! my God ! this *time !* this *one time !* deliver me from this distress !

or strike me dead this moment." And then I screamed again and again.

Said he, " One word with you, Pamela; hear me but one word; and hitherto you see I offer nothing to you."—" Is this *nothing*," said I, " to be in bed here? To hold my hands between you! I will hear, if you will instantly leave the bed, and take this villainous woman from me!"

Said she (O disgrace of woman kind!)—" What you do, Sir, do: don't stand, dilly dallying. She cannot exclaim worse than she has done: and she'll be quieter, when she knows the worst."

" Silence!" said he to her; " I must say one word to you, Pamela! You see, now you are in my power! You cannot get from me, nor help yourself: yet have I not offered any thing amiss to you. But if you resolve not to comply with my proposals, I will not lose this opportunity: if you do, I will yet leave you."

" O Sir," said I, " leave me, and I will do any thing I ought to do."—" Swear then, to me," said he, " that you will accept my proposals!" and then (for this was all detestable grimace) he put his hand in my bosom. With struggling and terror I fainted away, and did not come to myself soon; so that they both, from the cold sweats that I was in, thought me dying. And I remember no more than that, when with great difficulty they brought me to myself, she was sitting on one side of the bed with her clothes on: and he on the other with his, and in his gown and slippers.

Your poor Pamela cannot answer for the liberties taken with her in her deplorable state. And when I saw them, I sat up in my bed, without any regard to what appearance I made, and nothing about my neck; and he soothing me, with an aspect of pity and concern. I put my hand to his mouth, and said, " O tell me, yet tell me not, what have I suffered in this distress?" I talked quite wild, and knew not what; for, to be sure, I was on the point of distraction.

He most solemnly, and with a bitter imprecation, vowed he had not offered the least indecency; that he was frightened at the terrible manner I was taken in the fit; that he should desist from his attempt; and begged but to see me easy and quiet, and he would leave me and go to his own bed. " O, then," said I, " take with you this most wicked woman, this vile Mrs. Jewkes, as an earnest, that I may believe you."

" And will you, Sir," said the wicked wretch, " for a fit or two, give up such an opportunity as this?—I thought you had known the sex better. She is now, you see, quite well again!"

This I heard; more she might say; but I fainted away once more, at those words, and at his clasping his arms about me again. When I came a little to myself, I saw him sit there, and the maid Nan, holding a smelling-bottle to my nose, and no Mrs. Jewkes.

He said, taking my hand, "I vow to you, my dear Pamela, that I will leave you the moment I see you better, and pacified. Here's Nan knows and will tell you my concern for you. I vow to God, I have not offered any indecency to you: and, since I found Mrs. Jewkes so offensive to you, I have sent her to the maid's bed, and the maid shall lie with you to-night. But promise me, that you will compose yourself, and I will leave you."—"But," said I, "will not Nan also hold my hand! Will not she let you come in again to me?" He said, "By heaven! I will not come in again to-night. Nan, undress yourself, go to bed, and do all you can to comfort the dear creature—and now, Pamela," said he, "give me your hand, and say you forgive me, and I will leave you to your repose." I held out my trembling hand, which he kissed: and I said, "God forgive you, Sir, as you *have been* just in my distress; and as you *will be* just to what you promise!" He withdrew with a countenance of remorse: Nan shut the doors, and at my request, brought the keys to bed.

This, O my dear parents, was a most dreadful trial. I tremble still to think of it; and dare not recall all the horrid circumstances. I hope, as he assures me, he was not guilty of indecency; but have reason to bless God, who, by disabling my faculties, empowered me to preserve my innocence; and, when all my strength would have signified nothing, magnified himself in my weakness.

I was so weak all day on Monday that I could not get out of my bed. My master shewed great tenderness for me; and I hope he is really sorry, and that this will be his last attempt: but he does not say so.

He came in the morning, as soon as he heard the door open, and I began to be fearful. He stopped short of the bed, and said, "Rather than give you apprehension, I will come no farther." I said, "Your honour, Sir, and your mercy is all I have to beg." He sat himself on the side of the bed, and asked kindly how I did; begged me to be composed; and said, I still looked a little wild. I said, "Pray, good Sir, let me not see this infamous Mrs. Jewkes: I cannot bear her sight."—"She shan't come near you all this day, if you'll promise to compose yourself."—" Then, Sir, I will try." He pressed my hand very tenderly, and went out. What a change does this shew ! O may it be lasting !—But, alas! he seems only to have altered his method of proceeding; and retains, I doubt, his wicked purpose.

On Tuesday, about ten o'clock, when my master heard I was up, he sent for me down into the parlour. As soon as he saw me, he said, " Come nearer to me, Pamela." I did so, and he took my hand, and said, " You begin to look well again : I am glad of it. You little slut, how did you frighten me on Sunday night ! "—" Sir," said I, " pray name not that night ; " and my eyes overflowed at the remembrance, and I turned my head aside.

Said he, " Place some little confidence in me : I know what those charming eyes mean, you need not explain yourself : for I assure you, that as soon as I saw you change, and a cold sweat bedew your pretty face, and you fainted away, I quitted the bed, and Mrs. Jewkes did so too. I put on my gown, and she fetched her smelling-bottle, and we both did all we could to restore you : and my passion for you was all swallowed up in the concern I had for your recovery; for I never saw a fit so strong and violent in my life; and feared we should not bring you to life again ; for what I saw you in once before was nothing to it. This," said he, " might be my ignorance of what passion your sex *can* shew when they are in earnest. But this I repeat to you, that your mind may be entirely comforted—Whatever I offered to you, was before you fainted, and that, I am sure, was innocent."

" Sir," said I, " that was very bad : and it was too plain you had the worst designs."—" When," said he, " I tell you the truth in one instance, you may believe me in the other. I know not, I declare (beyond this lovely bosom), your sex ; but that I did intend what you call the *worst* is most certain : though I would not too much alarm you now, I could curse my weakness and folly, which makes me own that I love you beyond all your sex, and cannot live without you. But, if I am master of myself, and my own resolution, I will not attempt to force you to any thing again."—" Sir," said I, " you may easily keep your resolution, if you'll send me out of your way, to my poor parents ; that is all I beg."

" 'Tis a folly to talk of it," said he. " You must not, shall not go ! And if I could be assured you would not attempt it, you should have better usage, and your confinement should be

181

made easier to you."—" But to what end, Sir, am I to stay?" said I: " you yourself seem not sure you can keep your own present good resolutions; and do you think, if I was to stay, when I *could* get away, and be safe, it would not look as if either I confided too much in my own strength, or would tempt my ruin? and as if I was not in earnest to wish myself safe, and out of danger? And then, how long am I to stay? and to what purpose? and in what light must I appear to the world? Would not *that* censure me, although I might be innocent? You will allow, Sir, that, if there be any thing valuable or exemplary in a good name, or fair reputation, one must not despise the world's censure, if one can avoid it."

" Well," said he, " I sent not for you on this account, just now: but for two reasons: the first is, that you promise me, that for a fortnight to come you will not offer to go away without my express consent: and this I expect for *your own* sake, that I may give you a little more liberty. And the second is, that you will see and forgive Mrs. Jewkes; she thinks that as all her fault was her obedience to me, it would be very hard to sacrifice her to your resentment."

" As to the first, Sir," said I, " it is a hard injunction, for the reasons I have mentioned. And as to the second, considering her vile unwomanly wickedness, and her endeavours to instigate you more to ruin me, when your returning goodness seemed to have some compassion upon me, it is still harder. But, to shew my obedience to your commands " (for you know, my dear parents, I might as well make a merit of my compliance, when my refusal will stand me in no stead), " I will consent to both; and to every thing else that you shall be pleased to enjoin, which I can do with innocence."

" That's my good girl!" said he, and kissed me: " that is quite prudent, and shews me that you don't take insolent advantage of my favour for you; and will, perhaps, stand you in more stead than you are aware of."

So he rung the bell, and said, " Call down Mrs. Jewkes." She came down, and he took my hand, and put it into hers; and said, " Mrs. Jewkes, I am obliged to you for all your diligence and fidelity to me; but Pamela, I must own, is not so; because the service I employed you in was offensive to her; and you were not to favour her, but obey me. But yet I'll assure you, she has this *once* obliged me by consenting to be friends with you; and if she gives me no great cause, I shall not put you on such disagreeable service again. Now be once more bed-fellows and companions for some days longer; see that Pamela

sends no letter nor messages out of the house, nor keeps a correspondence unknown to me, especially with that Williams; and,
as for the rest, shew the dear girl all the respect that is due to
one I must love, if she will deserve it, as I hope she will yet;
and let her be under no unnecessary or harsh restraints. But
your watchful care is not to cease; and remember, you are
not to disoblige me, to oblige her; and I will not, cannot, yet
part with her."

Mrs. Jewkes looked very sullen, and as if she would be glad
still to do me a good turn, if it lay in her power. I took courage
then to drop a word or two for poor Mr. Williams; but he was
angry, and said he could not endure to hear his name in *my*
mouth; so I was forced to have done, for that time.

All this time my papers that I had buried under the rose-bush
lay there still: I begged leave to send a letter to you. So I
should, he said, if he might read it first. But this did not
answer my design: and yet I would have sent you such a letter
as he might see, if I had been sure my danger was over. But
that I cannot; for he now seems to take another method, and
what I am more afraid of, because he may watch an opportunity, and join force with it, when I am least prepared: for
now he seems to abound with kindness, and talks of love without reserve, and makes nothing of allowing himself in the
liberty of kissing me, which he calls innocent: but which I do
not like, and especially in the manner he does it: but for a
master to do it at all to a servant, has meaning too much in it
not to harm an honest body.

WEDNESDAY MORNING.

I find I am watched and suspected still very close: I wish
I was with you; but that must not be this fortnight. I don't
like this fortnight, it will be a tedious and a dangerous one to
me, I doubt.

My master just now sent for me down to take a walk with
him in the garden; but I like him not at all, nor his ways; for
he would have his arm about my waist, and said abundance of
fond things, enough to make me proud, if his design had not
been apparent. After walking about, he led me into a little
alcove, on the farther part of the garden; and really made me
afraid of myself; for he began to be very teazing, and made
me sit on his knee; and was so often kissing me, that I said,
" Sir, I don't like to be here at all, I assure you. Indeed you
make me afraid ! " And what made me more so, was what he
once said to Mrs. Jewkes, when he did not think I heard him,

and which, though always uppermost with me, I did not mention before, because I did not know how to bring it in, in my writing.

She, I suppose, had been encouraging him in his wickedness; for it was before the last dreadful trial; and I only heard what he answered.

Said he, " I will try *once* more; but I have begun wrong: for I see terror does but add to her frost; she is a charming girl, and may be thawed by kindness; and I should have melted her by love, instead of freezing her by fear."

Is he not a sad wicked man for this? To be sure, I blush while I write it. But I trust, that that God, who has delivered me from the paw of the lion and the bear, that is, his and Mrs. Jewkes's violences, will soon deliver me from this *Philistine*, that I may not *defy the commands of the living God!*

But this expression coming into my thoughts, I was of opinion I could not be too much on my guard, at all times; more especially when he took such liberties: for he professed honour while his actions did not correspond. I begged and prayed he would let me go; and had I not appeared quite regardless of all he said, and resolved not to stay, if I could help it, I know not how far he would have proceeded: for I was forced to fall down upon my knees.

At last he walked out with me, still bragging of his honour and his love, " Yes, yes, Sir," said I, " your honour is to destroy mine; and your love is to ruin me, I see too plainly. I will not walk with you, Sir," said I, " any more."—" Do you know," said he, " whom you talk to, and where you are? "

You may believe I had reason to think him not so decent as he should be; for I said, " As to where I am, Sir, I know it too well, and that I have no creature to befriend me; and as to whom I talk to, Sir, let me ask you what you would have me answer? "

" Why, tell me," said he, " what answer you would make? " —" It will only make you angry," said I, " and so I shall fare worse, if possible."—" I won't be angry," said he. " Why, then, Sir," said I, " you cannot be my late good lady's son; for she loved me, and taught me virtue. You cannot be my master; for no master demeans himself so to his poor servant."

He put his arm round me, and his other hand on my neck; which made me more angry and bold; and he said, " What then am I? "—" Why," said I (struggling from him, and in a great passion), " to be sure you are Lucifer himself, in the *shape* of my master, or you could not use me thus."—" These are too

184

great liberties," said he, in anger; "I desire that you will not repeat them, for your own sake; for if you have no decency towards *me*, I'll have none towards *you*."

I was running from him; and he said, "Come back, when I bid you." Knowing every place was alike dangerous to me, and I had nobody to run to, I came back at his call; and seeing him look displeased, I held my hands together, wept, and said, "Pray, Sir, forgive me."—"No," said he, "rather say, 'Pray, Lucifer, forgive me:' and now, since you take me for the devil, how can you expect any good from me? How can you expect any thing but the worst treatment from me?—You have given me a character, Pamela; and blame me not that I act up to it."

"Sir," said I, "let me beg you to forgive me: I am really sorry for my boldness; but indeed you don't use me like a gentleman; and how can I express my resentment, if I mince the matter, while you are so indecent?"

"Precise fool!" said he, "what indecencies have I offered you? I was bewitched I had not gone through my purpose last Sunday night; and then your licentious tongue had not given the worst name to little puny freedoms, that shew my love and my folly at the same time. But, be gone," said he, taking my hand, and tossing it from him, "and learn another conduct, and more wit; and I will lay aside my foolish regard for you and assert myself. Be gone!" said he again, with an haughty air.

"Indeed, Sir," said I, "I cannot go, till you pardon me, which I beg on my bended knees. I am truly sorry for my boldness. But I see how you go on: you creep by little and little upon me; and now soothe me, and now threaten me; and if I should forbear to shew my resentment, when you offer incivilities to me, would not that be to be lost by degrees? Would it not shew, that I could bear any thing from you, if I did not express all the indignation I *could* express, at the first approaches you make to what I dread? And have you not as good as avowed my ruin? And have you once made me hope you will quit your purposes against me? How, then, Sir, can I act, but by shewing my abhorrence of every step that makes towards my undoing? And what is left me but words? And can these words be other than such strong ones, as shall shew the detestation, which from the bottom of my heart, I have for every attempt upon my virtue? Judge for me, Sir, and pardon me."

"Pardon you," said he, "when you don't repent! When

you have the boldness to justify yourself in your fault; why don't you say, you never will again offend me?"—"I will endeavour, Sir," said I, "always to preserve that decency towards you which becomes me. But really, Sir, I must beg your excuse for saying, that when you forget what belongs to decency in your actions, and when words are all that are left me, to shew my resentment of such actions, I will not promise to forbear the strongest expressions that my distressed mind shall suggest to me; nor shall your frowns deter me, when my honesty is in question."

"What then," said he, "do you beg pardon for? Where is the promise of amendment, for which I should forgive you?"—"Indeed, Sir," said I, "I own, that must absolutely depend on your usage of me: for I will bear any thing you can inflict upon me with patience, even to the laying down of my life to shew my obedience to you in other cases; but I cannot be patient, I cannot be passive, when my virtue is at stake;—it would be criminal in me if I was!"

He said, he never saw such a fool in his life! and he walked by the side of me some yards, without saying a word, and seemed vexed; and at last walked in, bidding me attend him in the garden after dinner. Having a little time, I went up and wrote thus far.

WEDNESDAY NIGHT.

If, my dear parents, I am not destined more surely than ever for ruin, I have now more comfort before me than ever I yet knew: and am either nearer my *happiness* or *misery*, than ever I was. God protect me from the latter, if it be his blessed will! I have now such a scene to open to you, that I know will alarm both your hopes and your fears, as it does mine. And this it is.

After my master had dined, he took a turn into the stables, to look at his stud of horses; and, when he came in, he opened the parlour-door, where Mrs. Jewkes and I sat at dinner; and, at his entrance, we both rose up; but he said, "Sit still, sit still, and let me see how you eat your victuals, Pamela."—"O," said Mrs. Jewkes, "very poorly, indeed, Sir."—"No," said I, "pretty well, Sir, *considering*."—"None of your *considerings!*" said he, "pretty face;" and tapped me on the cheek. I blushed, but was glad he was so good humoured; but I could not tell how to sit before him, nor to behave myself. So he said, "I know, Pamela, you are a nice carver: my mother used to say so."—"My lady, Sir," said I, "was very good to me in every thing, and would always make me do the honours of her table for her, when she was with her few select friends that she loved."—"Cut up," said he, "that chicken." I did so. "Now," said he, and took a knife and fork, and put a wing upon my plate, "let me see you eat that."—"O Sir!" said I, "I have eat a whole breast of chicken already, and cannot eat so much." But he said I must eat it for his sake, and he would teach me to eat heartily; so I did eat it; but was much confused at his so kind and unusual freedom and condescension. You can't imagine how Mrs. Jewkes looked and stared, and how respectful she seemed to me, and called me *good Madam*, I'll assure you, urging me to take a little bit of tart.

My master took two or three turns about the room, musing and thoughtful, as I had never before seen him; and at last he went out, saying, "I am going into the garden; you know, Pamela, what I said to you before dinner." I rose and curtsied, saying I would attend his honour. He said, "Do, good girl!"

"Well," said Mrs. Jewkes, "I see how things will go. *O Madam*," as she called me again, "I am sure you are to be our mistress! And then I know what will become of me."—"Ah! Mrs. Jewkes," said I, "if I can but keep myself virtuous, 'tis the most of my ambition: and I hope no temptation shall make me otherwise."

Notwithstanding I had no reason to be pleased with his treatment of me before dinner, yet I made haste to attend him. I found him walking by the side of that pond, which, for want of grace, and through a sinful despondence, had like to have been so fatal to me; and the sight of which, ever since, has been a trouble and reproach to me. And it was by the side of this pond, and not far from the place where I had that dreadful conflict, that my present hopes, if I am not to be deceived again, began to dawn; which I presume to flatter myself with being a happy omen for me, as if God Almighty would shew your sinful daughter how well I did to put my affiance in his goodness, and not to throw away myself, because my ruin seemed inevitable to my short-sighted apprehension.

So he was pleased to say, "Well, Pamela, I am glad you are come of your own accord: give me your hand." I did so: and he looked at me very steadily, and pressing my hand all the time, at last said, "I will now talk to you in a serious manner.

"You have a good deal of wit, a great deal of penetration, much beyond your *years*, and, as I thought, your *opportunities*.

187

You are possessed of an open, frank, and generous mind; and a person so lovely, that you excel all your sex, in my eyes.

"All these accomplishments have engaged my affections so deeply, that, as I have often said, I cannot live without you; and I would divide, with all my soul, my estate with you, to make you mine upon my own terms. These you have absolutely rejected; and that, though in saucy terms enough, yet in such a manner, as makes me admire you the more. Your pretty chit-chat to Mrs. Jewkes, the last Sunday night, so innocent, and so full of beautiful simplicity, half disarmed my resolution before I approached your bed : and I see you so watchful over your virtue, that, though I hoped to find it otherwise, I cannot but confess my passion for you is increased by it. But now, what shall I say further, Pamela? I will make you, though a party, my adviser in this matter, though not, perhaps, my definitive judge.

"You know I am not a very abandoned profligate : I have hitherto been guilty of no very enormous or vile actions. This of confining you thus, may, perhaps, be one of the worst. Had I been utterly given up to my passions, I should, before now, have gratified them, and not have shewn that remorse and compassion for you, which have reprieved you more than once, when absolutely in my power; and you are as inviolate a virgin as you were when you came into my house.

"But what can I do? Consider the pride of my condition. I cannot endure the thought of marriage, even with a person of equal or superior degree to myself; and have declined several proposals of that kind : how then, with the distance between us in the world's judgment, can I think of making you my wife? Yet I must have you; I cannot bear the thoughts of any other man supplanting me in your affections : the very apprehension has made me hate the name of Williams, and use him in a manner unworthy of my temper.

"Now, Pamela, judge for me; and since I have told you, thus candidly, my mind; and I see yours is big with some important meaning, by your eyes, your blushes, and that sweet confusion which I behold struggling in your bosom, tell me, with like openness and candour, what you think I ought to do, and what you would have me do."

It is impossible for me to express the agitations of my mind, on this unexpected declaration, so contrary to his former behaviour. His manner too had something so noble, and so sincere, as I thought, that, alas for me! I found I had need of all my poor discretion, to ward off the blow which this treatment gave to my most guarded thoughts. I threw myself at his feet; for I trembled, and could hardly stand : " O Sir," said I, " spare your poor servant's confusion ! O spare the poor Pamela ! "—" Speak out," said he, " and tell me what you think I ought to do."—" I cannot say what you *ought* to do," answered I : " but I only beg you will not ruin me ; and if you think me virtuous, if you think me sincerely honest, let me go to my poor parents. I will vow to you, that I will never suffer myself to be engaged without your approbation."

Still he insisted upon a more explicit answer to his question, of what I thought he ought to do. And I said, " As to *my* thoughts of what you ought to do, I must needs say, that I think you ought to regard the world's opinion, and avoid doing any thing disgraceful to your birth and fortune ; and, therefore, if you really honour the poor Pamela with your respect, a little time, absence, and the conversation of worthier persons of my sex, will effectually enable you to overcome a regard so unworthy your condition : and this, good Sir, is the best advice I can offer."

" Charming creature ! lovely Pamela ! " said he (with an ardour that was never before so agreeable to me), " this generous manner is of a piece with all the rest of your conduct. But tell me, still more explicitly, what you would advise me to in this case ? "

" O Sir," said I, " take not advantage of my credulity, and these my weak moments ; but were I the first lady in the land, instead of the poor abject Pamela, I would, I *could* tell you. But I can say no more——"

O my dear father and mother ! I know you will be concerned for me ; for now I am for myself. And now I begin to be afraid, I know too well the reason, why all his hard trials of me, and my black apprehensions, would not let me hate him.

But be assured still, by God's grace, that I shall do nothing unworthy of your Pamela ; and if I find that he is still capable of deceiving me, and that this conduct is only put on to delude me more, I shall think nothing in this world so vile, and so odious, and nothing so desperately guileful, as the heart of this man.

He generously said, " I will spare your confusion, Pamela. But I hope I may promise myself, that you can love me preferably to any other man ; and that no one in the world has had any share in your affections : for I am very jealous of what I love ; and if I thought you had a secret whispering in your soul, that had not yet come up to a wish, for any other man breathing, I should not forgive *myself* to persist in my affection for you; nor *you*, if you did not frankly acquaint me with it."

As I still continued on my knees, on the grass border by the pond side, he sat himself down on the grass by me, and took me in his arms: "Why hesitates my Pamela?" said he. "Can you not answer me with truth, as I wish? If you cannot, speak, and I will forgive you."

"O good Sir," said I, "it is not *that;* indeed it is not: but a frightful word or two that you said to Mrs. Jewkes, when you thought I was not in hearing, comes across my mind, and makes me dread that I am in more danger than ever I was in my life."

"You have never found me a common liar," said he, "too fearful and foolish Pamela! nor will I answer how long I may hold in my present mind: for my pride struggles hard within me, I'll assure you: and if you doubt me, I have no obligation to your confidence or opinion. But, at present, I am really sincere in what I say: and I expect you will be so too; and answer directly my questions."

"I find, Sir," said I, "I know not myself; and your question is of such a nature, that I only want to tell you what I heard, and have your kind answer to it; or else what I have to say to your question, may pave the way to my ruin, and shew a weakness that I did not believe was in me."

"Well," said he, "you may say what you have overheard; for, in not answering me directly, you put my soul upon the rack; and half the trouble I have had with *you* would have brought to my arms one of the finest ladies in England."

"O Sir," said I, "my virtue is as dear to me as if I was of the highest quality; and my doubts (for which you know I have had too much reason) have made me troublesome. But now, Sir, I will tell you what I heard, which has given me great uneasiness.

"You talked to Mrs. Jewkes of having begun wrong with me, in trying to subdue me with terror, and of frost, and such like; you remember it well: and that you would, for the future, change your conduct, and try to *melt* me, that was your word, by kindness.

"I fear not, Sir, the grace of God supporting me, that any acts of kindness would make me forget what I owe to my virtue; but, Sir, I may, I find, be made more miserable by such acts, than by terror; because my nature is too frank and open to make me wish to be ungrateful: and if I should be taught a

lesson I never yet learnt, with what regret should I descend
to the grave, to think that I could not hate my undoer; and
that, at the last great day, I must stand up as an accuser of the
poor unhappy soul that I could wish it in my power to save!"

"Exalted girl!" said he, "what a thought is that! Why,
now, Pamela, you excel yourself! You have given me a hint
that will hold me long. But, sweet creature," said he, "tell
me what is this lesson, which you never yet learnt, and which
you are afraid of learning?"

"If, Sir," said I, "you will again generously spare my confusion, I need not speak it: but this I will say, in answer to
the question you seem most solicitous about, that I know not
the man breathing that I would wish to be married to, or that
ever I thought of with such an idea. I had brought my mind
so to love poverty, that I hoped for nothing but to return to
the best, though the poorest of parents; and to employ myself
in serving God, and comforting them; and you know not, Sir,
how you disappointed those hopes, and my proposed honest
pleasures, when you sent me hither."

"Well, then," said he, "I may promise myself, that neither
the parson, nor any other man, is the secret motive to your
steadfast refusal of my offers?"—"Indeed, Sir," said I, "you
may; and, as you was pleased to ask, I answer, that I have
not the least shadow of a wish or thought for any man
living."

"But," said he, ("for I am foolishly jealous, and yet it shews
my fondness for you,) have you not encouraged Williams to
think you will have him?"—"Indeed, Sir," said I, "I have
not; but the very contrary."—"And would you not have had
him," said he, "if you had got away by his means?"—"I had
resolved, Sir," said I, "in my mind, otherwise; and he knew
it, and the poor man——"—"I charge you," said he, "say
not a word in his favour! You excite a whirlwind in my soul,
if you name him with kindness; and then you'll be borne away
with the tempest."

"Sir," said I, "I have done!"—"Nay," said he, "but do
not have done; let me know the whole. If you have any
regard for him, speak out; for it would end fearfully for *you*,
for *me*, and for *him*, if I found that you disguised any secret
of your soul from me in this nice particular.''

"Sir," said I, "if I have ever given you cause to think me
sincere——"—"Say then," said he, (interrupting me with great
vehemence, and taking both my hands between his,)—"say,
that you now, in the presence of God, declare, that you have

191

not any the most hidden regard for Williams, or any other man."

" Sir," said I, " I do. As God shall bless me, and preserve my innocence, I have not."—" Well," said he, " I will believe you, Pamela; and in time, perhaps, I may better bear that man's name. And if I am convinced that you are not prepossessed, my vanity makes me assured, that I need not to fear a place in your esteem, equal, if not preferable, to any man in England. But yet it stings my pride to the quick, that you was so easily brought, and at such a short acquaintance, to run away with that college novice ! "

" O good Sir," said I, " may I be heard one thing? And though it bring upon me your highest indignation, I will tell you perhaps the unnecessary and imprudent, but yet the whole truth.

" My honesty (I am poor and lowly, and am not entitled to call it *honour*) was in danger. I saw no means of securing myself from your avowed attempts. You had shewed you would not stick at little matters; and what, Sir, could any body have thought of my sincerity, in preferring that to all other considerations, if I had not escaped from those dangers, if I could have found any way for it? I am not going to say any thing for him; but, indeed, indeed Sir, I was the cause of putting him upon assisting me in my escape. I got him to acquaint me what gentry there were in the neighbourhood that I might fly to; and prevailed upon him—Don't frown at me, good Sir, for I must tell you the whole truth—to apply to one Lady Jones ; to Lady Darnford; and he was so good as to apply to Mr. Peters, the minister : but they all refused me; and then it was he let me know that there was no honourable way but marriage. That I declined; and he agreed to assist me for God's sake."

" Now," said he, " you are going——" I boldly put my hand before his mouth, hardly knowing the liberty I took ! " Pray, Sir," said I, " don't be angry; I have just done; I would only say, that rather than have staid to be ruined, I would have thrown myself upon the poorest beggar that ever the world saw, if I thought him honest. And I hope, when you duly weigh all matters, you will forgive me, and not think me so bold and so forward as you have been pleased to call me."

" Well," said he, " even in this your last speech, which, let me tell you, shews more your honesty of heart than your prudence; you have not over-much pleased me. But I *must* love you; and that vexes me. But tell me, Pamela, for now

192

the former question recurs; since you so much prize your honour and virtue; since all attempts against that are so odious to you; and since I have avowedly made several of these attempts; do you think it is possible for you to love me *preferably* to any other of my sex?"

"Ah! Sir," said I, "and here my doubt recurs that you may thus graciously use me, to take advantage of my credulity."

"*Still* perverse and doubting!" said he. "Cannot you take me as I am at present? and that, I have told you, is sincere and undesigning, whatever I may be hereafter."

"Ah! Sir," replied I, "what can I say? I have already said too much, if this dreadful *hereafter* should take place. Don't bid me say how well I can——" And then, my face glowing as the fire, I, all abashed, leaned upon his shoulder, to hide my confusion.

He clasped me to him with great ardour, and said, "Hide your dear face in my bosom, my beloved Pamela! your innocent freedoms charm me!—But then say, how well—what?"

"If you will be good," said I, "to your poor servant, and spare her, I cannot say too much!—But, if not, I am doubly undone! Undone indeed!"

Said he, "I hope my present temper will hold; for I tell you frankly, that I have known, in this agreeable hour, more sincere pleasure than I have experienced in all the guilty tumults that my desiring soul compelled me into, in the hopes of possessing you on my own terms. And, Pamela, you must pray for the continuance of this temper; and I hope your prayers will get the better of my temptations."

This sweet goodness overpowered all my reserves; I threw myself at his feet, and embraced his knees. "What pleasure, Sir, you give me at these gracious words is not lent your poor servant to express!—I shall be too much rewarded for all my sufferings if this goodness hold! God grant it may, for your own soul's sake, as well as mine. And, oh! how happy shall I be if——"

He stopt me, and said, "But, my dear girl, what must we do about the world, and the world's censure? Indeed, I cannot marry."

Now was I again struck all of a heap. However, soon recollecting myself—"Sir," said I, "I have not the presumption to hope such an honour. If I may be permitted to return in peace and safety to my poor parents, to pray for you there, it is all I at present request! This, Sir, after all my apprehensions and dangers, will be a great pleasure to me. And if I know my own poor heart, I shall wish you happy in a lady of a suitable degree, and rejoice most sincerely in every circumstance that shall make for the happiness of my late good lady's most beloved son."

"Well," said he, "this conversation, Pamela, is gone farther than I intended it. You need not be afraid of trusting yourself with *me;* I ought to be doubtful of myself when I am with *you :*—but before I say any thing further on this subject, I will take my proud heart to task; and, till then, let every thing be as if this conversation had never passed. Only let me tell you, that the more confidence you place in me, the more you'll oblige me : but your doubts will only beget *cause* of doubts." And with this ambiguous saying, he saluted me with a more formal manner than before, and lent me his hand; we walked toward the house, side-by-side, he seeming very thoughtful and pensive, as if he had already repented of his goodness.

What shall I do, what steps take, if all this be designing?— O the perplexities of these cruel doubtings !—To be sure, if he be false, I have gone too far ! I am, on the apprehension of this, ready to bite my forward tongue (or rather to beat my more forward heart that dictated to that poor machine), for what I have said. But surely he must be sincere for the *time !* —He could not be such a practical dissembler !—If he could, how desperately wicked is the heart of man ?—And where could he learn of all these barbarous arts? If so, it must be native surely to the sex !—But silent be my rash censuring; be hushed, ye stormy tumults of my disturbed mind; for have I not a father who is a man !—A man who knows no guile ! who would do no wrong !—who would not deceive or oppress to gain a kingdom !—How then can I think it is native to the sex? And I must also hope my good lady's son cannot be the *worst* of men !—If he is, hard the lot of the excellent woman that bore him !—But much harder the lot of your poor Pamela, who has fallen into such hands !—But I will trust in God and hope the best; and so lay down my pen for this time.

THURSDAY MORNING.

Somebody rapped at our chamber-door this morning, soon after it was light : Mrs. Jewkes asked who it was. My master said, "Open the door, Mrs. Jewkes."—"O," said I, "for God's sake, Mrs. Jewkes, don't."—"Indeed," said she, "but I must." —"Then," said I, and clung about her, "let me slip on my clothes first." But he rapped again, and she broke from me; and I was frighted, and folded myself in the bed-clothes. He

194

entered, and said—"What, Pamela, so fearful, after what passed yesterday between us?"—"O Sir, Sir," said I, "I fear my prayers have wanted their wished effect. Pray, good Sir, consider——" He sat down on the bed-side, and interrupted me, "No need of your foolish fears; I shall say but a word or two, and go away."

"After you went up stairs," said he, "I had an invitation to a ball, which is to be this night at Stamford, on occasion of a wedding; and I am going to call on Sir Simon, his lady and daughters; for the bride is a relation of theirs: I shall not be at home till Saturday—I come therefore to caution *you*, Mrs. Jewkes, before Pamela, (that she may not wonder at being closer confined than for these three or four days past,) that nobody sees her, nor delivers any letter to her, in that space; for a person has been seen lurking about, and enquiring after her; and I have been well informed, that either Mrs. Jervis or Mr. Longman has written a letter, with a design of having it conveyed to her:—and," said he, "you must know, Pamela, that I have ordered Mr. Longman to give up his accounts, and have dismissed Jonathan, and Mrs. Jervis, since I have been here; for their behaviour has been intolerable; they have made such a breach between my sister Davers and me, as we shall never, perhaps, make up. Now, Pamela, I shall take it kindly in you, if you will confine yourself to your chamber for the time I am absent, and not give Mrs. Jewkes cause of trouble or uneasiness; as, you know, she acts by my orders."

"Alas! Sir," said I, "I fear all these good people have suffered for my sake!"—"Why," said he, "I believe so too; and there never was a girl of your innocence, that set a large family in such an uproar, surely. But let that pass. You know both of you my mind, and, in part, the reason of it. I shall only say, that I have had such a letter from my sister as I could not have expected: and, Pamela," said he, "neither you nor I have reason to thank her, as you shall know, perhaps, at my return. I go in my coach, Mrs. Jewkes, because I take Lady Darnford and Mr. Peter's niece, and one of Lady Darnford's daughters, along with me; and Sir Simon and his other daughter go in his chariot; so let all the gates be fastened: and don't take any airing in either of the chariots, nor let any body go to the gate without you, Mrs. Jewkes."—"I'll be sure," said she, "to obey your honour."

"I will give Mrs. Jewkes no trouble, Sir," said I; "and will keep pretty much in my chamber, and not stir so much as into the garden without her; to show you I will obey every thing

I *can*. But I begin to fear——"—" Ay," said he, " more plots and contrivances, don't you? But, I'll assure you, you never had less reason; and I tell you the truth; for I am really going to Stamford, *this time*; and upon the occasion I tell you. And so, Pamela, give me your hand, and one kiss; and then I am gone."

I durst not refuse, and said, " God bless you, Sir, wherever you go! But I am sorry for what you tell me about your servants."

He and Mrs. Jewkes had a little talk without the door; and I heard her say, " You may depend, Sir, upon my care and vigilance."

He went in his coach, as he said he should, and very richly dressed, which looks as if what he said was likely: but really I have been used to so many tricks, plots, and surprises, that I know not what to think. But I mourn for poor Mrs. Jervis. So here is parson Williams, poor naughty John, good Mrs. Jervis, Mr. Longman, and Mr. Jonathan, turned away for me! Mr. Longman is rich, indeed, and so need the less matter it; but I know it will grieve him: and for poor Mr. Jonathan, I am sure it will cut that good old servant to the heart. Alas! for me! what mischiefs am I the occasion of! Or, rather, my master, whose actions towards me have made so many of my kind friends forfeit his favour for my sake!

I am very sad about these things: if he really loved me, methinks he should not be so angry that his servants loved me too. I know not what to think!

FRIDAY NIGHT.

I have removed my papers from under the rose-bush; for I saw the gardener begin to dig near the spot; and I was afraid he would find them.

Mrs. Jewkes and I were looking yesterday through the iron gate that fronts the elms; and a gypsey-like body made her way up to us, and said, " If, Madam, you will give me some broken victuals, I will tell you both your fortunes." I said, " Let us hear our fortunes, Mrs. Jewkes." She said, " I don't like these sort of people: but we will hear what she'll say to us, however. I shan't fetch you any victuals, woman; but I will give you some pence," said she.

But Nan coming out, she said, " Fetch some bread, and some of the cold meat, and you shall have your fortune told, Nan."

This you'll think, like some of my other matters, a very trifling thing to write about. But mark the discovery of a dreadful plot which I have made by it. O bless me! what can I think of this naughty, this very naughty gentleman? Now will I hate him most heartily. Thus it was:

Mrs. Jewkes had no suspicion of the woman, the iron gate being locked; she on the outside, and we on the inside: and so put her hand through. She said, muttering over a parcel of cramp words, "Why, Madam, you will marry soon, I can tell you." At that she seemed pleased, and said, "I am glad to hear that;" and shook her fat sides with laughing. The woman looked most earnestly at *me* all the time, and as if she had meaning. Then it came into my head, from my master's caution, that possibly this woman might be employed to try to get a letter into my hands; and I was resolved to watch all her motions. So Mrs. Jewkes said, "What sort of a man shall I have, pray?"—"Why," said she, "a man younger than yourself; and a very good husband he'll prove."—"I am glad of that," said she; and laughed again. "Come, Madam, let us hear *your* fortune."

The woman came to me, and took my hand. "O!" said she, "I cannot tell your fortune: your hand is so white and fine, I cannot see the lines: but," said she, pulling up a little tuft of grass, "I have a way for that;" and so rubbed my hand with the mould-part of the tuft: "Now," said she, "I can see the lines."

Mrs. Jewkes was very watchful of all her ways, and took the tuft, and looked upon it, lest any thing should be in that. And then the woman said, "Here is the line of Jupiter, crossing the line of life; and Mars—Odd! my pretty mistress," said she, "you had best take care of yourself: for you are hard beset, I'll assure you. You will never be married, I can see; and will die of your first child."—"Out upon thee, woman!" said I, "better thou hadst never come here."

Said Mrs. Jewkes, whispering, "I don't like this: it looks like a cheat: pray, Mrs. Pamela, go in this moment."—"So I will," said I; "for I have enough of fortune-telling." And in I went.

The woman wanted sadly to tell me more, which made Mrs. Jewkes threaten her, suspecting still the more; and away the woman went, having told Nan her fortune that she would be drowned.

This thing ran strongly in all our heads; and we went, an hour after, to see if the woman was lurking about, and took Mr. Colbrand for our guard. Looking through the iron gate, we saw a man sauntering about the middle of the walk, which filled Mrs. Jewkes with still more suspicions; and she said,

"Mr. Colbrand, you and I will walk towards this fellow, and see what he saunters there for; and, Nan, do you and Madam stay at the gate."

So, opening the iron gate, they walked down towards the man; and, guessing the woman, if employed, must mean something by the tuft of grass, I cast my eye that way, where she pulled it, and saw more grass seemingly pulled up: then I doubted not something was there for me; so I walked to it, and standing over it, said to Nan, "That's a pretty sort of wild flower, which grows yonder, near the elm, the fifth from us on the left; pray pull it for me." Said she, "It is a common weed."—"Well," said I, "but pull it for me; there are sometimes beautiful colours in a weed."

While she went on, I stooped, and pulled up a good handful of the grass, and in it a bit of paper, which I put instantly in my bosom, and dropped the grass; and my heart went pit-a-pat at the odd adventure. Said I, "Let's go in, Mrs. Anne."—"No," said she; "we must stay till Mrs. Jewkes comes."

I was all impatience to read this paper: and when Colbrand and she returned, I went in. Said she, "Certainly there is some reason for my master's caution: I can make nothing of this sauntering fellow: but, to be sure, there was some roguery in the gypsey."—"Well," said I, "if there was, she lost her aim, you see."—"Aye, very true," said she; "but that was owing to my watchfulness; and you was very good to go away when I spoke to you."

I hasted up stairs to my closet, and found the billet to contain, in a hand that seemed disguised, and bad spelling, the following words:

"Twenty contrivances have been thought of to let you know your danger; but all have proved in vain. Your friends hope it is not yet too late to give you this caution, if it reaches your hands. The squire is absolutely determined to ruin you; and because he despairs of any other way, he will pretend great love and kindness to you, and that he will marry you. You may expect a parson, for this purpose, in a few days; but it is a sly artful fellow of a broken attorney, that he has hired to personate a minister. The man has a broad face, pitted much with the small-pox, and is a very good companion. So take care of yourself. Doubt not this advice. Perhaps you'll have had but too much reason already to confirm you in the truth of it. From your zealous well-wisher,

"SOMEBODY."

198

Now, my dear father and mother, what shall we say of this truly diabolical master! O how shall I find words to paint my grief, and his deceit! I have as good as confessed I love him; but, indeed, it was on supposing him good. This, however, has given him too much advantage. But now I will break this wicked forward heart of mine, if it will not be taught to hate him! O what a black dismal heart must *he* have! So here is a plot to ruin me, and by my own consent too! No wonder he did not improve his wicked opportunities (which I thought owing to remorse for his sin, and compassion for me), when he had such a project as *this* in reserve!—Here should I have been deluded with the hopes of a happiness that my highest ambition could have aspired to!—But how dreadful must have been my lot, when I had found myself an undone creature, and a guilty harlot, instead of a lawful wife? Oh! this is indeed too much for your poor Pamela to support! I hoped all the worst was over; and that I had the pleasure of beholding a reclaimed man, and not an abandoned libertine. What must your poor daughter do? All her hopes now are dashed! And if this fails him, then comes my forced disgrace! for this shows he will never leave till he has ruined me!—O the wretched, wretched Pamela!

SATURDAY NOON, ONE O'CLOCK.

My master is come home, and, to be sure, has been where he said. So *once* he has told truth; and this matter seems to be gone off without a plot: no doubt he depends upon his sham wicked marriage! He has brought a gentleman with him to dinner; and so I have not seen him yet.

TWO O'CLOCK.

I am very sorrowful, and still have greater reason; for just now, as I was in my closet, opening the parcel I had hid under the rose-bush, to see if it was damaged by lying so long, Mrs. Jewkes came upon me by surprise, and laid her hands upon it; for she had been looking through the key-hole, it seems.

I know not what I shall do! For now he will see all my private thoughts of him, and all my secrets, as I may say! What a careless creature I am!—To be sure I deserve to be punished.

You know I had the good luck, by Mr. Williams's means, to send you all my papers, down to Sunday night, the 17th day of my imprisonment. But now these papers contain all my matters from that time to Wednesday the 27th day of my distress; and which, as you may now perhaps never see, I will briefly mention the contents to you.

In these papers, then, are included an account of Mrs. Jewkes's arts to draw me in to approve of Mr. Williams's proposal for marriage; and my refusing to do so; and desiring you not to encourage his suit to me. Mr. Williams's being wickedly robbed, and a visit of hers to him; whereby she discovered all his secrets. How I was inclined to get off, while she was gone, but was ridiculously prevented by my foolish fears, &c. My having the key of the back-door. Mrs. Jewkes's writing to my master all the secrets she had discovered of Mr. Williams : and her behaviour to me and him upon it. Continuance of my correspondence with Mr. Williams by the tiles; begun in the parcel you had. My reproaches to him for thus revealing himself to Mrs. Jewkes; and his letter to me in answer, threatening to expose my master, if he deceived him; mentioning in it John Arnold's correspondence with him; and a letter which John sent, and was intercepted, as it seems. Of the correspondence being carried on by a friend of his at Gainsborough : of the horse he was to provide for me, and one for himself. Of what Mr. Williams had owned to Mrs. Jewkes; and of my encouraging his proposals. It contained a pressing letter of mine to him, urging my escape before my master came; with his half-angry answer to me. Your good letter, my dear father, sent to me by Mr. Williams's conveyance; in which you would have me encourage Mr. Williams, but leave it to me; and in which fortunately you take notice of my being uninclined to marry. My earnest desire to be with you. The substance of my answer to Mr. Williams, expressing more patience, &c. A dreadful letter of my master to Mrs. Jewkes, which, by mistake, was directed to me; and one to me, directed by a like mistake to her; and very free reflections of mine upon both. The concern I expressed for Mr. Williams's being taken in, deceived, and ruined. An account of Mrs. Jewkes's glorying in her wicked fidelity. A sad description I gave of Monsieur Colbrand, a person he sent down to assist Mrs. Jewkes in watching me. How Mr. Williams was arrested, and thrown into gaol; and the concern I expressed upon it; and my free reflections on my master for it. A projected contrivance of mine, to get away out of the window, and by the back door; and throwing my petticoat and handkerchief into the pond to amuse them while I got off; an attempt that had like to have ended very dreadfully for me ! My further concern for Mr. Williams's ruin on my account : and, lastly, my overhearing

Mrs. Jewkes brag of her contrivance to rob Mr. Williams, in order to get at my papers, which, however, he preserved, and sent safe to you.

These, down to the execution of my unfortunate plot to escape, are, to the best of my remembrance, the contents of the papers which this merciless woman seized : for, how badly I came off, and what followed, I still have safe, as I hope, sewed in my under-coat, about my hips.

In vain were all my prayers and tears to her, to get her not to show them to my master. She said, it had now come out why I affected to be so much alone, and why I was always writing. And she thought herself happy, she said, she had found these ; and often had she searched every place she could think of for writings to no purpose before. And she hoped, she said, there was nothing in them but what *any body* might see ; " For," said she, " you know you are all *innocence !* "—" Insolent creature ! " said I, " I am sure you are *all guilt !* And so you must do your worst ; for now I can't help myself, and I see there is no mercy to be expected from you."

Just now my master being come up, she went to him upon the stairs, and gave him my papers. " There, Sir," said she : " you always said Mrs. Pamela was a great writer ; but I never could get at anything of hers before." He took them, and, without coming to me, went down to the parlour again. And, what with the gypsey affair, and what with this, I could not think of going down to dinner ; and she told him that too ; and so I suppose I shall have him up stairs, as soon as his company is gone.

SATURDAY, SIX O'CLOCK.

My master came up, and in a pleasanter manner than I expected, said, " So, Pamela, we have seized your treasonable papers ? "—" Treasonable ! " said I, very sullenly. " Aye," said he, " I suppose so ; for you are a great plotter ; but I have not read them yet."

" Then, Sir," said I, very gravely, " it will be truly honourable in you *not* to read them ; but to give them to me again." —" To whom," says he, " are they written ? "—" To my father, Sir ; but I suppose you *see* to whom."—" Indeed," returned he, " I have not read three lines yet."—" Then, pray Sir, *don't* read them, but give them to me again."—" That I will not," said he, " till I *have* read them."—" Sir," said I, " you served me not well in the letters I wrote formerly : I think it was not worthy your character to contrive to get them into your

201

hands by that false John Arnold; for should such a gentleman as you mind what your poor servant writes?"

"Yes," said he, "by all means, mind what such a servant as *my* Pamela writes."

"*Your* Pamela!" thought I. Then the sham marriage came into my head; and indeed it has not been out of it, since the gypsey affair. "But," said he, "have you any thing in these papers you would not have me see?"—"To be sure, sir," said I, "there is; for what one writes to one's father and mother, is not for every body to see."—"Nor," said he, "am I every body."

"Those letters," added he, "that I did see, by John's means, were not to your disadvantage, I'll assure you; for they gave me a very high opinion of your wit and innocence: and if I had not loved you, do you think I would have troubled myself about your letters?"

"Alas! Sir," said I, "great pride to me *that!* For they gave you such an opinion of my innocence, that you was resolved to ruin me. And what advantage have they brought *me*, who have been made a prisoner, and used as I have been between you and your housekeeper?"

"Why, Pamela," said he, a little seriously, "why this behaviour for my goodness to you in the garden? This is not of a piece with your conduct and softness there; that quite charmed me in your favour: and you must not give me cause to think you will be more insolent, as you find me kinder."—"Ah! Sir," said I, "you know best your own heart and designs! But I fear I was too open-hearted then; and that you still keep your resolution to undo me, and have only changed the form of your proceedings."

"When I tell you once again," said he, a little sternly, "that you cannot oblige me more than by placing some confidence in me, I will let you know that these foolish and perverse doubts are the worst things you can be guilty of. But," said he, "I shall possibly account for the *cause* of them, in these particulars of yours; for I doubt not you have been sincere to your *father* and *mother*, though you begin to make *me* suspect you: for I tell you, perverse girl, that it is impossible you should be thus cold and insensible, after what last passed in the garden, if you were not prepossessed on some *other* person's favour: and let me add, that if I find it so, it shall be attended with such effects as will make every vein in your heart bleed."

He was going away in wrath; and I said, "One word, good Sir, one word before you read them, since you *will* read them:

pray make allowances for all the harsh reflections that you will find in them on your own conduct to me : and remember only that they were not written for your sight; and were penned by a poor creature hardly used, and who was in constant apprehension of receiving from you the worst treatment that you could inflict upon her."

"If that be all," said he, "and there be nothing of *another* nature that I *cannot* forgive, you have no cause for uneasiness; for I had as many instances of your saucy reflections upon me in your former letters as there were lines; and yet I never upbraided you on that score; though, perhaps, I wished you had been more sparing of your epithets and your freedoms."

"Well, Sir," said I, "since you *will*, you *must* read them : I think I have no reason to be afraid of being found insincere, or having, in any respect, told you a falsehood : because, though I don't remember all I wrote, yet I know I wrote my heart, and that is not deceitful. Remember, Sir, another thing, that I always declared I thought myself right to endeavour to make my escape from this forced and illegal restraint : so you must not be angry that I would have done so if I could."—"I'll judge you, never fear," said he, "as favourably as you deserve; for you have too powerful a pleader within me." And so went down stairs.

About nine o'clock he sent for me down into the parlour. I went a little fearfully, and he held the papers in his hand, and said, "Now, Pamela, you come upon your trial." Said I, "I hope I have a *just* judge to hear my cause."—"Aye," said he, "and you may hope for a *merciful* one too, or else I know not what will become of you."

"I expect," continued he, "that you will answer me directly, and plainly, to every question I shall ask you. In the first place, here are several love-letters between you and Williams." — "Love-letters? Sir," said I.—"Well, call them what you will," said he, "I don't entirely like them, I'll assure you, with all the allowances you desired me to make for you."—"Do you find, Sir," said I, "that I encouraged his proposals?"—"Why," said he, "you discourage his address in appearance; but no otherwise than all your cunning sex do to ours, to make us more eager in pursuing you."

"Well, Sir," said I, "that is your comment; but it does not appear so in the text."—"Smartly said!" says he : "where a d—l gottest thou, at these years, all this knowledge? And then thou hast a memory, as I see by your papers, that nothing escapes."—" Alas ! Sir," said I, " what poor abilities I have serve only to make me more miserable ! I have no pleasure in my memory which impresses things upon me, that I could be glad never *were*, or everlastingly to *forget*."

" Well," said he, " but where are the accounts (since you have kept so exact a journal of all that has befallen you) *previous* to these in my hand ? "—" My father has them, Sir," said I. " By whose means ? " said he. " By Mr. Williams's," said I. " Well answered," said he. " But cannot you contrive to get me a sight of them ? "—" That would be pretty ! " said I. " I wish I could have contrived to have kept those you have from your sight." Said he, " I *must* see them, Pamela, or I shall never be easy ; for I must know how this correspondence between you and Williams began : and if I *can* see them it shall be better for you, if they answer what these give me hope they will."

" I can tell you, Sir, very faithfully," said I, " what the beginning was ; for I was bold enough to be the *beginner*."— " That won't do," said he ; " for though this may appear a punctilio to *you*, to *me* it is of high importance."—" Sir," said I, " if you please to let me go to my father, I will send them to you by any messenger you shall send for them."—" Will you so ? But I dare say, if you will write for them, they will send them to you, without the trouble of such a journey to yourself : and I beg you will."

" I think Sir," said I, " as you have seen all my *former* letters through John's baseness, and now *these*, through your faithful housekeeper's officious watchfulness, you *might* see *all the rest ;* but I hope you will not desire it, till I can see how much my pleasing you in this particular will be of use to myself."

" You must trust to my honour for that. But tell me, Pamela," said the sly gentleman, " since I have seen *these* would you have voluntarily shown me *those*, had they been in your possession ? "

I was not aware of this inference, and said, " Yes, truly, Sir, I think I should, if you commanded it."—" Well, then, Pamela," said he, " as I am sure you have found means to continue your journal, I desire, till the *former part* can come, that you will show me the *succeeding*."—" O Sir," said I, " have you caught me so ? But indeed you must excuse me there."

" Why," said he, " tell me truly, have you not continued your account till now ? "—" Don't ask me, Sir," said I.—" But I insist upon your answer," replied he.—" Why, then, Sir, I will not tell an untruth ; I have."—" That's my good girl ! " said he; "I love sincerity at my heart"—"In *another*, Sir," said I, "I presume you mean!"—"Well," said he, "I'll allow you to be a little witty upon me; because it is *in you*, and you cannot help it; but you will greatly oblige me, to show me voluntarily what you have written. I long to see the particulars of your plot, and your disappointment, where your papers leave off: for you have so beautiful a manner that it is partly that, and partly my love for you, that has made me desirous of reading all you write; though a great deal of it is against myself; for which you must expect to suffer a little; and as I have furnished you with the subject, I have a title to see the fruit of your pen. Besides," said he, "there is such a pretty air of romance in *your* plots, and *my* plots, that I shall be better directed in what manner to wind up the catastrophe of the pretty novel."

"If I was your equal, Sir," said I, "I should say, this is a very provoking way of jeering at the misfortunes you have brought upon me."

"O," said he, "the liberties you have taken with my character in your letters set us upon a par, at least, in that respect."—"Sir, I could not have taken those liberties if you had not given me the cause: and the *cause*, Sir, you know, is before the *effect*."

"True, Pamela," said he; "you chop logic very prettily. What the deuce do we men go to school for? If our wits were equal to women's we might spare much time and pains in our education, for nature teaches your sex what, in a long course of nature and study, ours can hardly attain to. But indeed every lady is not a Pamela."

"You delight to banter your poor servant," said I.—"Nay," continued he, "I believe I must assume to myself half the merit of your wit too; for the innocent exercises you have had for it from me have certainly sharpened your invention."

"Sir," said I, "could I have been without those *innocent* exercises, as you are pleased to call them, I should have been glad to have been as dull as a beetle."—"But then, Pamela," said he, "I should not have loved you so well."—"But then, Sir, I should have been safe, easy, and happy."—"Aye, may-be so, and may-be not; and the wife too of some clouterly plough-boy."—"But then, Sir, I should have been content and innocent; and that's better than being a princess, and not so."—"May-be not," said he; "for with that pretty face, some of us keen fox-hunters should have found you out; and, in spite of your romantic notions (which then, perhaps, would not have had so strong a place in your mind), might have been more happy with the ploughman's wife, than I have been with my mother's Pamela."—" I hope, Sir," said I, " God would have given me more grace."

" Well, but," resumed he, " as to these writings of yours, that follow your fine plot, I *must* see them."—" Indeed, Sir, you *must not*, if I can help it."—" Nothing," said he, " pleases me better than that in all your arts and stratagems, you have a great regard to truth; and, in all your little pieces of deceit, told very few *wilful* fibs. Now I expect you'll continue this laudable rule in your conversation with me. Let me know where you have found supplies of pen, ink, and paper, when Mrs. Jewkes was so vigilant, and gave you but two sheets at a time? —Tell me the truth."

" Why, Sir, little did I think I should have such occasion for them; but when I went away from your house I begged some of each of good Mr. Longman, who gave me plenty."—" Yes, yes," said he, " it must be *good* Mr. Longman ! All your confederates are good, every one of them; but such of my servants as have done their duty, and obeyed my orders, are painted by you as black as devils; so am I too, I dare say."

" Sir," said I, " I hope you won't be angry; but, saving yourself, do you think they are painted worse than they deserve? "

" You say, saving myself, Pamela ; but is not that saving a mere compliment to me because I am present, and you are in my hands? "—" Good Sir, excuse me ; but I fancy I might ask you, why you should think so, if there was not a little bit of conscience that told you there was but too much reason for it? "

He kissed me, and said—" I must either do this, or be angry with you ; for you are very saucy, Pamela. But with your bewitching chit-chat, and pretty impertinence, I will not lose my question. Where did you hide your paper, pens, and ink? "

" Some, Sir, in one place, some in another; that I might have some left, if others should be found."—" That's a good girl ! " said he, " I love you for your sweet veracity. Now tell me where it is you hide your written papers, your saucy journal ! " —" I must beg your excuse for that, Sir," said I.—" But," answered he, " you will not have it : for I *will* know, and *see* them."—" That is very hard, Sir," said I ; " but I must say you shall not, if I can help it."

We were standing most of the time, but he then sat down, and took me by both my hands, and said,—" Well said, my pretty Pamela, *if you can help it!* But I will not let you help it. Tell me, are they in your pocket?"—"No, Sir," said I; my heart up at my mouth. Said he—"I know you won't tell a downright *fib* for the world; but for *equivocation!* no Jesuit ever went beyond you. Answer me, are they in neither of your pockets?"—"No, Sir," said I.—"Are they not," said he, "about your stays?"—"No, Sir," replied I: "but pray, no more questions; for ask me ever so much, I will not tell you."

"O," said he, "I have a way for that. I can do as they do abroad, when the criminals won't confess; torture them till they do."—"But pray, Sir," said I, "is this fair or honest? I am no criminal; and I won't confess."

"O, my girl!" said he, "many an innocent person has been put to the torture. But let me know where they are, and you shall escape the *question,* as they call it abroad."

"Sir," said I, "the torture is not used in England; and I hope you won't bring it up."—"Admirably said!" replied he. "But I can tell you of as good a punishment. If a criminal won't plead with us here in England, we *press* him to death, or till he does plead. And so, Pamela, that is a punishment that shall certainly be yours, if you won't tell without."

Tears stood in my eyes, and I said, "This, Sir, is very cruel and barbarous."—"No matter," said he; "it is but like your *Lucifer,* you know, in my shape! And after I have done so many heinous things by you, as *you* think, you have no great reason to judge so hardly of this; or, at least, it must be of a piece with the rest."

"But, Sir," said I (dreadfully afraid he had some notion they were about me), "if you will be obeyed in this unreasonable manner—though it is sad tyranny, to be sure—let me go up to them, and read them over again, and you shall see so far as to the end of the sad story that follows those you have."

"I'll see them all," said he, "down to this time, if you have written so far, or, at least, till within this week."—"Then let me go up to see them," said I, "and see what I have written, and to what day, to show them to you, for you won't desire to see every thing."—"But I will," replied he. "But say, Pamela, tell me truth, are they *above?*" I was much affrighted. He saw my confusion. "Tell me truth," said he. "Why, Sir," answered I, "I have sometimes hid them under the dry mould in the garden; sometimes in one place, sometimes in another; and those in your hand were several days under a rose-bush in the garden."—"Artful slut!" said he, "what's this to my question? Are they not *about* you?"—"If," said I, "I must pluck them from my hiding-place behind the wainscot, won't you see me?"—"Still more and more artful," said he. "Is this an answer to my question? I have searched every place above, and in your closet for them, and cannot find them; so I *will* know where they are. Now," said he, "it is my opinion they are about you; and I never undressed a girl in my life; but I will now begin to strip my pretty Pamela; and I hope I shall not go far before I find them."

I fell a crying, and said—"I will not be used in this manner. Pray, Sir," said I (for he began to unpin my handkerchief), "consider! Pray, Sir, do!"—"Pray," said he, "do *you* consider; for I will see these papers. But, may-be," said he, "they are tied about your knees with your garters;" and stooped. Was ever any thing so vile and wicked? I fell on my knees, and said, "What *can* I do? If you'll let me go up, I'll fetch them."—"Will you," said he, "on your honour, let me see them all, and not offer to conceal a single paper?"— "I will, Sir."—"On your honour?"—"Yes, Sir."—And so he let me go up stairs, crying sadly for vexation to be so used. Sure nobody was ever so served as I am!

I went to my closet, and sat down. I could not bear the thoughts of giving up my papers. Besides I must almost undress me to untack them.—So I writ thus:

"SIR,—
        "To expostulate with such an arbitrary gentleman, I know will signify nothing; most hardly do you use the power you so wickedly have got over me. I have heart enough, Sir, to do a deed that would make you regret using me thus: I can hardly bear it, and what I am further to undergo. But a superior consideration withholds me; thank God it does! I will, however, keep my word, if you insist upon it when you have read this; but, Sir, let me beg of you to give me time till to-morrow morning, that I may just run them over, and see what I put into your hands against me: I will then give my papers to you, without the least alteration; but I should beg still to be excused, if you please; but if not, spare them to me till to-morrow morning: and this, so hardly am I used, shall be thought a favour, which I shall be very thankful for."

I guessed it would not be long before I heard from him: and he accordingly sent up Mrs. Jewkes for what I had promised. So I gave her this note to carry to him. He sent word that I must keep my promise, and he would give me till morning : but that I must bring them to him without his asking again.

So I took off my under-coat, and with great trouble unsewed them. There is a vast quantity. I will slightly touch upon the subjects, because I may not, perhaps, get them again for you to see.

They begin with an account of my attempting to get away out of the window first, and then throwing my petticoat and handkerchief into the pond. How sadly I was disappointed, the lock of the back-door being changed. In trying to climb over the door, I tumbled down, and was piteously bruised; the bricks giving way, and tumbling upon me. Finding I could not get off, and dreading the hard usage I should receive, I was so wicked as to think of throwing myself into the water. My sad reflections upon this matter.—How Mrs. Jewkes used me upon this occasion. How my master had like to have been drowned in hunting; and my concern for his danger, notwithstanding his usage of me. Mrs. Jewkes's wicked reports to frighten me, that I was to be married to the ugly Swiss, who was to sell me, on the wedding-day, to my master. Her vile way of talking to me, like a London prostitute. My apprehensions on seeing preparations made for my master's coming. Her causeless fears that I was trying to get away again, when I had no thoughts of it; and my bad usage upon it.—My master's dreadful arrival, and his hard, very hard treatment of me; and Mrs. Jewkes insulting me. His jealousy of Mr. Williams and me. How Mrs. Jewkes vilely instigated him to wickedness. And down to here I put into one parcel, hoping it would content him. But, for fear it should not, I put into another parcel the following : viz.

A copy of his proposals to me, of a great parcel of gold, fine clothes, and rings, and an estate of I can't tell what a-year : and fifty pounds a-year for the life of both you, my dear parents, to be his mistress; with an insinuation that he would marry me at a year's end : all sadly vile : threatening, if I did not comply, to ruin me without allowing me any thing. A copy of my answer, refusing all, with just abhorrence : but begging at last his goodness and mercy towards me, in the most moving manner I could think of. An account of his angry behaviour, and Mrs. Jewkes's wicked advice hereupon. His trying to get me to his chamber; and my refusal to go. A deal of stuff and chit-chat between me and the odious Mrs. Jewkes, in which she was very wicked and insulting. Two notes I wrote, as if to be carried to church, to pray for his reclaiming, and my safety, which Mrs. Jewkes seized, and officiously showed him. A confession of mine, that, notwithstanding his bad usage, I could not hate him. My concern for Mr. Williams. A horrid contrivance of my master's to ruin me; being in my room, disguised in the maid's clothes, who lay with me and Mrs. Jewkes. How narrowly I escaped, (it makes my heart ache to think of it!) by falling into fits. Mrs. Jewkes's detestable part in this affair. How he seemed moved at my danger, forbore his abominable designs, and assured me he had offered no indecency. How ill I was for a day or two after, and how kind he seemed. How he made me forgive Mrs. Jewkes. How, after this, and great kindness pretended, he made rude offers to me in the garden, which I escaped. How I resented them. Then I had written, how kind he was to me, praised me, and gave me great hopes of his being good at last. Of the too tender impressions this made upon me; and how I began to be afraid of my own weakness and consideration for him, though he had used me so ill. How sadly jealous he was of Mr. Williams; and how I, as I justly could, cleared myself as to his doubts on that score. How, when he had raised me up to the highest hope of his goodness, he again deceived me, and went off more coldly. My free reflections upon this trying occasion.

This brought down matters from Thursday, the 20th day of my imprisonment, to Wednesday the 41st. Here I was resolved to end, let what would come; for only Thursday, Friday, and Saturday, remains to give an account of. Thursday he set out to a ball at Stamford; Friday was the gypsey story; and this is Saturday, his return from Stamford. Truly, I shall have but little heart to write, if he is to see all.

These two parcels of papers I have got ready for him against to-morrow morning. I have always used him very freely in my writings, and showed him no mercy; but he must thank himself for it; as I have only written truth; and I wish he had deserved a better character at my hands, as well for his own sake as mine. I don't know whether you'll ever see what I write, yet I must say, that I will go to bed, remembering you in my prayers, as I always do, and as I know you do me: so, my dear parents, good night.

SUNDAY MORNING.

I remembered what he said, of not being obliged to ask again for my papers; and what I should be forced to do, I thought I would do in such a manner as might show I would not disoblige on purpose: though I stomached this matter very heavily. I therefore got in readiness my two parcels; and he, not going to church in the morning, bid Mrs. Jewkes tell me he was gone into the garden.

I knew that was for me to go to him; and so I went: for how can I help being at his beck? which grieves me not a little, though he is my master. I am wholly in his power, and it would do me no good to incense him; if I refused to obey in little matters, my refusal in greater would have the less weight. So I went down to the garden; but as he walked in one walk, I took another, that I might not seem too forward.

He soon 'spied me, and said—" Do you expect to be courted to come to me?"—" Sir," said I, crossing the walk to attend him, "I did not know but I should interrupt you in your meditations this good day."

"Was that the case," said he, "truly, and from your heart?" —" Why, Sir," said I, "I don't doubt but you have very good thoughts sometimes; though not towards me."—"I wish," said he, "I could avoid thinking so well of you as I do. But where are the papers?—I dare say you had them about you yesterday: for you say in those I have, that you will bury your writings in the garden, lest you should be *searched*, if you did not escape. This," added he, "gave me a glorious pretence to search you; and I have been vexing myself all night, that I did not strip you garment by garment, till I had found them." —" O fie, Sir," said I, "let me not be scared, with hearing that you had such a thought in earnest."

"Well," said he, "I hope you have not now the papers to give me: for I had rather find them myself, I'll assure you."

I did not like this way of talk at all; and thinking it best not to dwell upon it, said—" Well, but, Sir, you will excuse me, I hope, giving up my papers."

"Don't trifle with me," said he: "where are they?—I think I was very good last night, to humour you as I did. If you have either added or diminished, and not strictly kept your promise, woe be to you!"—" Indeed, Sir," said I, "I have neither added nor diminished. Here is the parcel that goes on with my sad attempt to escape, and the terrible consequences which might have followed. It goes down to the naughty articles you sent me; and as you know all that has happened since, I hope these will satisfy you."

He was going to speak; but I said, to drive him from thinking of any more—" I must beg you, Sir, to read the matter favourably, if I have exceeded in any liberties of my pen."

"I think," said he, half-smiling, "you may wonder at my

patience, that I can be so easy to read myself abused as I am by such a saucy slut."—"Sir," said I, "I have wondered you should be so desirous to see my bold stuff; and, for that very reason, I have thought it a very *good* or a very *bad* sign."— "What," said he, "is your *good* sign?"—"That it may have an effect upon your temper, at last, in my favour, when you see me so sincere."—"Your *bad* sign?"—"Why, that if you can read my reflections and observations upon your treatment of me, with tranquillity, and not be moved, it is a sign of a very cruel and determined heart. Now, pray, Sir, don't be angry at my boldness, in telling you so freely my thoughts."—"You may, perhaps," said he, "be least mistaken, when you think of your bad sign."—"God forbid!" said I.

So I took out my papers, and said—"Here, Sir, they are. But if you please to return them, without breaking the seal, it will be very generous: and I will take it as a great favour, and a good omen."

He broke the seal instantly, and opened them: "So much for your *omen!*" replied he. "I am sorry for it," said I, very seriously; and was walking away. "Whither now?" said he. "I was going in, Sir, that you might have time to read them, if you thought fit." He put them into his pocket, and said—"You have *more* than these."—"Yes, Sir; but all they contain, *you* know as well as I."—"But I don't know," said he, "the light you put things in: so give them me, if you have not a mind to be searched."

"Sir," said I, "I can't stay, if you won't forbear that ugly word"—"Give me then no reason for it. Where are the other papers?"—"Why, unkind Sir, if it must be so, here they are;" and I gave him, out of my pocket, the second parcel, sealed up, as the former, with this superscription: "*From the naughty articles, down through sad attempts, to Thursday the 42nd day of my imprisonment.*"—"This is last Thursday, is it?"—"Yes, Sir; but now you *will* see what I write, I shall find some other way to employ my time; for how can I write with any face, what must be for your perusal, and not for those I intended to read my melancholy stories?"

"Yes," said he, "I would have you continue your writing, by all means; and I will not ask you for any after these; except any thing very extraordinary occurs. I have another thing to tell you," added he, "that if you send for those from your father, and let me read them, I may, very probably, give all back again to you."

This a little encourages me to continue my scribbling; but,

for fear of the worst, I will, when they come to any bulk, contrive to hide them, if I can, that I may protest I have them not about me, which before I could not, and that made him so resolutely bent to try to find them upon me; for which I might have suffered frightful indecencies.

He then led me to the side of the pond: and, sitting down on the slope, made me sit by him. " Come," said he, " this being the scene of part of your project, where you so artfully threw in some of your clothes, I will just look upon that part of your relation."—" Sir," said I, " let me, then, walk about at a little distance; for I cannot bear the thought of it."—" Don't go far," said he.

When he came, as I suppose, to the place where I mentioned the bricks falling upon me, he got up, and walked to the door, and looked upon the broken part of the wall: for it had not been mended; then came back, reading on to himself, towards me; took my hand, and put it under his arm.

" Why this," said he, " my girl, is a very moving tale. It was a desperate attempt, and, had you got out, you might have been in great danger; for you had a very bad and lonely way; and I had taken such measures, been where you would, I should have had you."

" You may see, Sir," said I, " what I ventured, rather than be ruined; and you will be so good as hence to judge of the sincerity of my profession, that my honesty is dearer to me than my life."—" Romantic girl ! " said he, and read on.

He was very serious at my reflections, on what God had enabled me to escape. And when he came to my reasonings about throwing myself into the water, he said, " Walk gently before : " and seemed so moved, that he turned his face from me; and I blessed this good sign, nor did so much repent at his seeing this mournful part of my story.

He put the papers in his pocket, when he had read my reflections, and thanks for escaping from *myself;* and said, taking me about the waist—" O my dear girl ! you have touched me sensibly with your mournful relation, and sweet reflections upon it. I should truly have been miserable, had it taken effect. I see you have been used too roughly; and it is a mercy you stood proof in that fatal moment."

Then he most kindly folded me in his arms: " Let us, my Pamela, walk from this accursed piece of water; for I shall not with pleasure look upon it again, to think how near it was fatal to my fair one. I thought," added he, " of terrifying you to my will, since I could not move you by love; and Mrs. Jewkes too well obeyed me, when the terrors of your return, after your disappointment, were so great, that you had hardly courage to withstand them; but had like to have made so fatal a choice, to escape the treatment you apprehended."

"Sir," said I, "I have reason to bless my dear parents, and my good lady, your mother, for giving me a religious education; but for that, and God's grace, I should, more than upon one occasion, have attempted a desperate act: I the less wonder how poor creatures, who have not the fear of God before their eyes, and give way to despondency, cast themselves into perdition."

"Come, kiss me," said he, "and tell me you forgive me, for exposing you to so much danger and distress. If I can see those former papers of yours, and these in my pocket give me no cause to alter my opinion, I will endeavour to defy the world and its censures, and make my Pamela amends, if in the power of my whole life, for all the hardships I have made her undergo."

All this looked well; but you shall see how strangely it turned. For this sham marriage came into my head again; and I said—"Your poor servant is far unworthy of this great honour: what will it be but to create envy to herself, and discredit to you? Therefore, Sir, permit me to return to my poor parents; that is all I ask."

He was in a fearful passion then. "And is it *thus*," said he, "in my fond conceding moments, but I am to be answered and despised? Perverse, unreasonable Pamela! be gone from my sight, and know as well how to behave in a hopeful prospect, as in a distressful state; then, and not till then, shalt thou attract my notice."

I was startled, and going to speak, but he stamped with his foot, and said, "Be gone, I tell you, I cannot bear this stupid romantic folly."

"One word," said I; "but one word. I beseech you, Sir."

He turned from me in great wrath, and took down another alley, and I went in, with a very heavy heart. I fear I was too unseasonable, just at a time when he was so condescending; but if it was a piece of art on his side, as I apprehended, to introduce the sham wedding (for he is full of stratagem and art), I think I was less to blame.

So I went up to my closet; and wrote thus far, while he walked about till dinner was ready; he is now sat down to it, as I hear by Mrs. Jewkes, very sullen, thoughtful, and out of humour : and she asks, what I have done to him. Now, again, I dread to see him ! When will my fears be over ?

Well, he continues exceeding wrathful. He has ordered his travelling chariot to be got ready with all speed. What is to come next, I wonder !

Sure I did not say *so much !* But see the lordliness of a high condition !—A poor body must not put in a word, when they take it in their heads to be angry ! What a fine time a person of an equal condition would have of it, if she were even to marry such a one : his poor dear mother spoiled him at first. Nobody must speak to, or contradict him, as I have heard, when he was a child; and so he has not been used to be controlled, and cannot bear the least thing to cross his violent will. This is one of the blessings attending men of high condition ! Much good may it do them with their pride of birth, and pride of fortune ! say I : all that it serves for, as far as I can see, is, to multiply their disquiets, and every body's else who has to do with them.

So, so ! where will this end ? Mrs. Jewkes has been with me from him, and says, I must get out of the house this moment. " Well," said I; " but whither am I to be carried next ? "— " Why, home," said she, " to your father and mother."—" And can it be ? " said I : " no, no, I doubt I shall not be so happy as that !—To be sure some bad design is on foot again !—Sure," said I, " Mrs. Jewkes, he has not found out some other house-keeper *worse than you !* " She was very angry, you may well think. But I know she can't be made worse than she is.

She came up again. " Are you ready ? " said she. " Bless me ! " said I, " you are very hasty : I have heard of this not a quarter of an hour ago. But I shall be soon ready; for I have but little to take with me, and no kind friends in this house to take leave of to delay me. Yet, like a fool, I can't help crying. Pray," said I, " just step down, and ask if I may not have my papers."

I am quite ready now, against she comes up with an answer; and I will put up these few writings in my bosom that I have left.

I don't know what to think—nor how to judge; but I shall ne'er believe I am with you, till I am on my knees before you, begging both your blessings. Yet I am sorry he is so *angry* with me. I thought I did not say *so much.*

There is, I see, the chariot drawn out, the horses too, and

215

the grim Colbrand going to get on horseback. What will be the end of all this?

Well, where this will end, I cannot say. But here I am, at a little poor village, almost such a one as yours! I shall learn the name of it by-and-by: and Robin assures me he has orders to carry me to you, my dear father and mother. O that he may not deceive me again! But, having nothing else to do, and I am sure I shall not sleep a wink to-night, if I was to go to bed, I will write my time away, and take up my story where I left off, on Sunday afternoon.

Mrs. Jewkes came up to me, with this answer about my papers: "My master says he will not read them yet, lest he should be moved by any thing in them to alter his resolution. But if he should read them, he will send them to you afterwards to your father's. But," said she, "here are your guineas I borrowed: for all is over with you, I find."

She saw me cry, and said, "Do you repent?"—"Of what?" said I. "Nay, I can't tell," replied she; "but to be sure he has had a taste of your satirical flings, or he would not be so angry. So," continued she, and held up her hand, "thou hast a spirit!—But I hope it will now be brought down."—"I hope so too," said I.

"Well," added I, "I am ready." She lifted up the window, and said, "I'll call Robin to take your portmanteau; bag and baggage!" proceeded she, "I'm glad you're going."—"I have no words," said I, "to throw away upon *you*, Mrs. Jewkes: but," making her a very low curtsey, "I most heartily thank you for all your *virtuous* civilities to me, and so adieu; for I'll have no portmanteau, I'll assure you, nor any thing, but these few things I have brought with me in my handkerchief, besides what I have on." For I had all this time worn my own bought clothes, though my master would have had it otherwise; however, I put up paper, ink, and pens.

As I passed by the parlour, she stepped in, and said, "Sir, you have nothing to say to this girl, before she goes?" I heard him reply, though I did not see him, "Who bid you say, *the girl*, Mrs. Jewkes, in that manner? She has offended only me."

"I beg your honour's pardon," said the wretch; "but if I was your honour, she should not, for all the trouble she has cost you, go away scot-free."—"No more of this, as I *told you before*," said he: "what! when I have such proof that her

216

virtue is all her pride, shall I rob her of that?—No," added he, "let her go, perverse and foolish as she is; but she *deserves* to go honest, and she *shall* go so!"

I was so transported with this unexpected goodness, that I opened the door before I knew what I did; and said, falling on my knees, with my hands folded and lifted up, "O thank your honour a million of times! May God bless you, for this instance of your goodness to me! I will pray for you as long as I live, and so shall my dear father and mother. And Mrs. Jewkes," said I, "I will pray for *you* too, poor wicked wretch that you are."

He turned from me, went into his closet, and shut the door. He need not have done so; for I would not have gone nearer to him.

Surely I did not say *so much*, to incur all this displeasure.

I think I was loth to leave the house. Can you believe it?—What could be the matter with me, I wonder? I felt something so strange at my heart! I wonder what ailed me! But this was so *unexpected!*—I believe that was all. Yet I am very strange still. Surely I cannot be like the old murmuring Israelites, to long after the onions and garlic of Egypt, when they had suffered there such heavy bondage?—I'll take thee, O contradictory, ungovernable heart, to severe task, for this thy strange impulse, when I get to my dear father and mother's; and I find any thing in thee that should not be, depend upon it, thou shalt be humbled, if strict abstinence, prayer, and mortification will do it.

But yet, after all, this *last* goodness of his has touched me too sensibly. I almost wish I had not heard it; yet, methinks, I am glad I did; for I should rejoice to think the best of him, for his *own* sake.

Well, I went out to the chariot, the same that brought me down. "So, Mr. Robert," said I, "here I am again! a poor sporting-piece for the great! a mere tennis-ball of Fortune. You have your orders, I hope"—"Yes, Madam," said he. "Pray, now," said I, "don't *Madam* me, nor stand with your hat off to such a one as I."—"Had not my master," said he, "*ordered* me not to be wanting in respect to you, I would have shown you all I could."—"Well," said I, with my heart full, "that's very kind, Mr. Robert."

Mr. Colbrand, mounted on horseback, with pistols before him, came up to me, as soon as I got in, with *his* hat off too. "What, Monsieur!" said I, "are *you* to go with me?"—"Part of the way," he said, "to see you safe."—"I *hope* that's kind, too, in you, Mr. Colbrand," said I.

217

I had nobody to wave my handkerchief to, nor take leave of; and I resigned myself to my contemplations, with this strange wayward heart of mine, which I never found so ungovernable and awkward before.

So away drove the chariot! And when I had got out of the elm-walk, into the great road, I could hardly think but I was in a dream all the time. A few hours before, in my master's arms almost, with twenty kind things said to me, and a generous concern for the misfortunes he had brought upon me, and only by *one* rash half-word exasperated against me, and turned out of doors at an hour's warning; and all his kindness changed to hate! And I now, from three o'clock to five, several miles off! But if I am going to you, all will be well again, I hope.

Lack-a-day, what strange creatures are men!—*gentlemen*, I should say rather! For my dear deserving good mother, though poverty be both your lots, has had better hap, and you are, and have always been, blest in one another!—Yet this pleases me too; he was so good, he would not let Mrs. Jewkes speak ill of me, and scorned to take her odious unwomanly advice. O what a black heart has this poor wretch! So I need not rail against *men* so much; for my master, bad as I have thought him, is not half so bad as this woman. To be sure she must be an atheist! Do you think she is not?

We could not reach further than this little poor place and sad ale-house, rather than inn; for it began to be dark, and Robin did not make so much haste as he might have done; and he was forced to make hard shift for his horses.

Mr. Colbrand, and Robert too, are very civil. I see he has got my portmanteau lash'd behind the chariot. I did not desire it; but I shall not come quite destitute. A thorough riddance of me, I see—bag and baggage, as Mrs. Jewkes says. Well, my story, surely, would furnish out a surprising kind of novel, if well told.

Mr. Robert came just now, and begged me to eat something: I thanked him, but said I could not eat. I bid him ask Mr. Colbrand to walk up; and he came; but neither of them would sit; nor put their hats on. What mockado is this, to such a poor soul as I! I asked them, if they were at liberty to tell me the truth of what they were to do with me? If not, I would not desire it. They both said, Robin was ordered to carry me to my father's; and Mr. Colbrand was to leave me within ten miles, and then strike off for the other house, to wait my master's arrival. They both spoke so solemnly, I could not but believe them.

But when Robin went down, the other said, he had a letter to give me next day at noon, when we were to bait at Mrs. Jewkes's relation's. "May I not," said I, "beg the favour to see it to-night?" He seemed so loth to deny me, that I have hopes to prevail on him by-and-by.

Well, my dear father and mother, I have got the letter on great promises of secrecy, and making no use of it. I will try if I can open it without breaking the seal, and will take a copy of it by-and-by; for Robin is in and out, there being hardly any room, in this little house, to be long alone. Well, this is the letter:

"When these lines are delivered to you, you will be far on your way to your father and mother, where you have so long desired to be; and I hope, I shall forbear thinking of you with the least shadow of that fondness my foolish heart had entertained for you. I bear you no ill-will; but the end of my detaining you being over, I would not that you should tarry with me an hour after the ungenerous preference you gave, at a time I was inclined to pass over all other considerations, for an honourable address to you; for well I found the tables entirely turned upon me, and that I was in far more danger from *you*, than you were from *me ;* for I was just upon resolving to defy all the censures of the world, and to make you my wife.

"I will acknowledge another truth: That had I not parted with you as I did, but permitted you to stay till I had read your journal, reflecting, as I doubt not I shall find it, and heard your bewitching pleas in your own behalf, I feared I could not trust myself with my own resolution. And this is the reason, I frankly own, that determined me not to see you, nor hear you speak; for well I know my weakness in your favour.

"But I will get the better of this fond folly: nay, I hope I have already done it, since it was likely to cost me so dear. And I write this to tell you, that I wish you well with all my heart, though you have spread such mischief through my family. Yet I cannot but say that I could wish you not to think of marrying in haste; and particularly not to have this cursed Williams. But what is all this to me now? Only, my weakness makes me say, that as I had already looked upon you as *mine*, and you have so soon got rid of your first husband, you will not refuse to my *memory*, the decency every common person observes, to pay a twelvemonth's compliment, though but a *mere* compliment, to my ashes.

"Your papers shall be faithfully returned; and I have paid so dear for my curiosity, in the affection they have riveted upon me for you, that you would look upon yourself amply revenged, to know what they have cost me.

"I thought of writing only a few lines, but I have run into length. I will now try to recollect my scattered thoughts, and resume my reason: and shall find trouble enough to replace my affairs, and my own family, and to supply the chasms you have made in it: for let me tell you, though I can forgive *you*, I never can my *sister*, nor my domestics; for my vengeance must be wreaked somewhere.

"I doubt not your prudence in forbearing to expose me any more than is necessary for your own justification; and for *that* I will suffer myself to be accused by you; and will also accuse myself, if it be needful. For I am, and ever will be, *your affectionate well-wisher*."

This letter, when I expected some new plot, had affected me more than any thing of *that* sort could have done. His great value for me is here confessed, and his rigorous behaviour accounted for in such a manner, as tortures me much. This wicked gypsey story is a forgery on us both, and has quite ruined me. My dear parents, forgive me! but I found, before, to my grief, that my heart was too partial in his favour; but *now*, with so much openness, affection, and *honour* too (which was all I had doubted), I am quite overcome. This was a happiness, however, I had no reason to expect. But I must own to you, that I shall never be able to think of any body in the world but him. "Presumption!" you will say; and so it is; but love is not a voluntary thing—*Love*, did I say— But come, it is not, I hope, gone so far as to make me *very* uneasy: for I know not *how* it came, nor *when* it began; but it has crept, like a thief, upon me, before I knew what was the matter.

I wish, since it is too late, and my lot determined, that I had not had this letter, nor heard him take my part to the vile woman; for then I should have blessed myself, in having escaped, so happily, his designing arts upon my virtue; but *now*, my poor mind is all topsy-turvied, and I have made an escape, to be more a prisoner.

But I hope that all is for the best: and I shall, with your prudent advice and pious prayers, be able to overcome this weakness. But, my dear Sir, I will keep a longer time than a twelvemonth, as a *true* widow, for a compliment, and *more* than a compliment, to your ashes ! O the dear word !—How kind, how moving, how affectionate is the word ! Why was I not a duchess, to show my gratitude for it ? But must labour under the weight of an obligation, even had this happiness befallen me, that would have pressed me to death, and which I never could return by a whole life of faithful love, and cheerful obedience !

Forgive your poor daughter ! I am sorry to find this trial so sore upon me ; and that all the weakness of my sex and tender years is come upon me, and too mighty to be withstood by me. But time, prayer, and resignation to God's will, and the benefits of your good lessons and examples, I hope, will enable me to get over this heavy trial.

O my treacherous heart to serve me thus ! and give me no notice of the mischiefs thou wast about to bring upon me !— But thus foolishly to give thyself up to the proud invader, without consulting thy poor mistress in the least ? But thy punishment will be the *first* and the *greatest :* and well deservest thou to smart, perfidious traitor ! for giving up so weakly thy *whole self,* before a summons came, and to one who had used me so hardly ; and when, too, thou hadst so well maintained thy post against the most violent and avowed, and therefore, as I thought, more dangerous attacks !

After all, I must either not shew you this my weakness, or tear it out of my writing. *Memorandum,* to consider of this when I get home.

MONDAY MORNING, ELEVEN O'CLOCK.

We are just come to the inn kept here by Mrs. Jewkes's relation. The first compliment I had, was in a very impudent manner. How I liked the squire ! I could not help saying, " Bold, forward woman ! is it for *you,* who keep an inn, to treat passengers thus ? " She was but in jest, she said, and asked pardon : and she came and begged excuse again, very submissively, after Robin and Mr. Colbrand had talked to her a little.

The latter in great form now gave me, before Robin, the letter I had given him back for that purpose. I retired, as if to read it ; and so I did ; for I think I can't read it too often ; though, for my peace of mind's sake, I had better forget it. I am sorry I cannot bring you back a sound heart ; but it is an honest one to anybody but me, for it has deceived nobody else.

More and more surprising things still—Just as I had sat down

221

to eat a bit of victuals, to get ready for my journey, came in Mr. Colbrand, in a mighty hurry. "O Madam! Madam!" said he, "here be de groom from de Squire B. all over in a lather, man and horse!" O how my heart went pit-a-pat! "What now," thought I, "is to come next!" He went out, and presently returned with a letter for me, and another, inclosed, for Mr. Colbrand. This seemed odd, and put me all in a trembling. So I shut the door; and, never, sure, was the like known! found the following agreeable contents:

"In vain, my Pamela, do I struggle against my affection for you. I must needs, after you were gone, venture to entertain myself with your journal. When I found Mrs. Jewkes's bad usage of you, after your dreadful temptations and hurts; and particularly your generous concern on hearing how narrowly I escaped drowning (though my death would have been your *freedom*, and I had made it your *interest* to wish it); and your most agreeable confession in another place, that, notwithstanding all my hard usage, you could not *hate* me; expressed in so sweet, so soft, and innocent a manner, that I flatter myself you may be brought to *love* me, (together with the rest of your admirable journal :) I began to repent my parting with you; and, God is my witness! for no unlawful end, as *you* would call it; but the very contrary : as all this was improved in your favour by your behaviour at leaving my house; for O! that melodious voice praying for me at your departure, and thanking me for my rebuke to Mrs. Jewkes, still dwells upon my ears, and delights my memory. I went to bed, but could not rest; about two I arose, and made Thomas get one of the best horses ready, in order to overtake you, while I sat down to write.

"Now, my dear Pamela, let me beg of you, on receipt of this, to order Robin to drive you back again to my house. I would have set out myself, for the pleasure of bearing you company back in the chariot; but am really indisposed; I believe, with vexation that I parted thus with my soul's delight, as I now find you are, and must be, in spite of the pride of my own heart.

"You cannot imagine the obligation your return will lay me under to your goodness; and yet, if you will not so far favour me, you shall be under no restraint, as my letter inclosed to Colbrand will shew, which I have not sealed, that you may read it. But spare me, my dearest girl, the confusion of following you to your father's : which I must do, if you persist to go on; for I find I cannot live a day without you.

"If you are the generous Pamela I imagine you to be (for

222

hitherto you have been all goodness, where it has *not* been merited), let me then see the further excellence of your disposition, that you can forgive the man who loves you more than himself; let me see by it, that you are not prepossessed in any other person's favour : one instance more I would beg, and then I am all gratitude; which is, that you would dispatch Monsieur Colbrand with a letter to your father, assuring him that all will end happily; and to desire that he will send to you, at my house, the letters you conveyed to him by means of Williams. And when I have all my proud, and perhaps *punctilious* doubts answered, I shall have nothing to do but to make you happy, and be so myself. For I must be *yours, and only yours.*"

MONDAY MORNING, NEAR THREE O'CLOCK.

O my exulting heart ! how it throbs in my bosom, as if it would reproach me for so lately upbraiding it for giving way to the love of so dear a gentleman. " But take care thou art not too credulous, neither, O fond believer ! Things that we wish are apt to gain a too ready credence with us. This sham marriage is not yet cleared up : the vile Mrs. Jewkes may yet instigate the mind of this master : his pride of heart and condition may again take place; and a man that could, in so *little* a space, first love me, then hate, then banish me his house, and now send for me again, in such affectionate terms, may *still* waver, may *still* deceive thee. Therefore will I not acquit thee yet, O credulous, fluttering, throbbing mischief ! that art so ready to believe what thou wishest; I charge thee to keep better guard than thou hast lately done, and lead me not to follow too implicitly thy flattering and desirable impulses." Thus foolishly dialogued I with my heart; and yet, all the time, this heart is Pamela.

I opened the letter to Monsieur Colbrand; which was in these words :

" MONSIEUR,
          " I am sure you'll excuse the trouble I give you. I have, for good reasons, changed my mind; and I have besought it, as a favour, that Mrs. Andrews will return to me the moment Tom reaches you. I hope, for the reasons I have given her, that she will have the goodness to oblige me. But, if not, you are to order Robin to pursue his directions, and set her down at her father's door. If she *will* oblige me in her return, perhaps she'll give you a letter to her father, for some papers to be

223

delivered to you for her; which you'll be so good, in that case, to bring to her *here!* but if she will *not* give you such a letter, return with her to me, if she please to favour me so far, with all the expedition her health and safety will permit; for I am rather indisposed, but hope it will soon go off. I am *yours*, &c.

" On second thoughts, let Tom go forward with Mrs. Andrews's letter, if she pleases to give one; and you return with her, for her safety."

Now this is a dear generous manner of treating me. O how I love to be generously used!—Now, my dear parents, I could wish to consult you how to act. Should I go back, or should I not? I doubt he has too great hold in my heart, for me to be easy presently, if I should refuse: and yet the gypsey information makes me fearful.

Well, I will, I think, trust in his generosity! Yet is it not too great a trust?—especially considering how I have been used! —But that was while he avowed his bad designs; and now he gives great hope of his good ones. I *may* be the means of making many happy, as well as myself, by placing a generous confidence in him.

And then, I think, he might have sent to Colbrand, or to Robin, to carry me back, whether I would or not. And how different his behaviour to that! Would it not look as if I was *prepossessed,* as he calls it, if I don't oblige him: and a silly female piece of pride to make him follow me to my father's, and as if I would use him hardly in *my* turn, for having used me ill in *his!* Upon the whole, I resolved to obey him, and if he uses me ill afterwards, double will be his ungenerous guilt— Though hard my lot, to have my credulity so justly blameable, as it will then seem. For the world, the *wise* world, that never is wrong itself, judges always by events. And if he should use me ill, then I shall be blamed for trusting him: if well, O then I did right, to be sure!—But, how would my censurers act in my case, before the event justifies or condemns the action, is the question?

Then I have no notion of obliging by halves; but of doing things with a grace, where they are to be done; and so I wrote the desired letter to you, assuring you, that I had before me happier prospects than ever I yet had; and hoped all would end well: and begging you to send me, by the bearer, Mr. Thomas, my master's groom, those papers I conveyed to you by Mr. Williams; for that they would clear up a point in my conduct, that my master was desirous to know, before he resolved to favour me, as intended. But you will have *that* letter, before you can have *this;* which I would not send you, without the preceding, now in my master's hands.

Having given the letter to Mr. Thomas, to carry to you, when he had baited and rested, after his great fatigue, I sent for Monsieur Colbrand and Robin, and gave to the former his letter. When he had read it, I said, " You see how things stand. I am resolved to return to our master; and as he is not so well as were to be wished, the more haste you make the better : don't mind my fatigue; but consider only yourselves and the horses." Robin, who guessed the matter by his conversation with Thomas (as I suppose), said, " God bless you, Madam, and reward you, as your obligingness to my good master deserves; and may we all live to see you triumph over Mrs. Jewkes ! "

I wondered to hear him say so; for I was always careful of exposing my master, or even that naughty woman, before the common servants. Yet I question whether Robin would have said this, if he had not guessed, by Thomas's message, and my resolving to return, that I might stand well with his master. So selfish are the hearts of poor mortals, they are ready to change as favour goes.

They were not long getting ready; and I am just setting out, back again; and I hope, shall have no reason to repent it.

Robin put on very vehemently; and when we came to the little town where we lay on Sunday night, he gave his horses a bait, and said, he would push for his master's that night, as it would be moon-light, if I should not be too much fatigued : because there was no place between that and the town adjacent to his master's, fit to put up at, for the night. But Monsieur Colbrand's horse, beginning to give way, made a doubt between them; wherefore I said (hating to lie on the road), if it could be done, I should bear it well enough, I hoped; that Monsieur Colbrand might leave his horse, when it failed, at some house, and come into the chariot. This greatly pleased them both; and, about twelve miles short, he left the horse, took off his spurs, holsters, &c., and, with many ceremonial excuses, came into the chariot : I sat the easier for it; for my bones ached sadly with the jolting, so many miles travelling in so few hours, from Sunday night, five o'clock. But, for all this, it was eleven o'clock at night when we came to the village adjacent to my master's; and the horses began to be very much tired, and Robin too : but I said, it would be a pity to put up only three miles short of the house.

About one we reached the gate : and every body was a-bed.

But one of the helpers got the keys from Mrs. Jewkes, and opened the gates; the horses could hardly crawl into the stable. And I, when I went to get out of the chariot, fell down, and thought I had lost the use of my limbs.

Mrs. Jewkes came down with her clothes huddled on, and lifted up her hands and eyes at my return; but showed more care of the horses than of me. By that time the two maids came; and I made shift to creep in, as well as I could.

It seems my poor master was very ill indeed, and had been upon the bed most part of the day; and Abraham (who succeeded John) sat up with him. He was got into a fine sleep and heard not the coach come in, nor the noise we made; for his chamber lies towards the garden, on the other side the house. Mrs. Jewkes said he had a feverish complaint, and had been blooded; and very prudently ordered Abraham, when he awaked, not to tell him I was come, for fear of surprising him, and augmenting his fever; nor indeed to say any thing of me, till she herself broke it to him in the morning, as she should see how he was.

So I went to bed with Mrs. Jewkes, after she had caused me to drink almost half a pint of burnt wine, made very rich, and cordial, with spices, which I found very refreshing, and set me into a sleep I little hoped for.

TUESDAY MORNING.

Getting up pretty early, I have written thus far, while Mrs. Jewkes lies snoring in bed, fetching up her last night's disturbance. I long for her rising, to know how my poor master does. 'Tis well for *her* she can sleep so purely. No love, but for herself, will ever break her rest, I am sure. I am deadly sore all over, as if I had been soundly beaten. I did not think I could have lived under such fatigue.

Mrs. Jewkes, when she got up, went to know how my master did, and he had had a good night; and, having drank plentifully of sack-whey, had sweated much; so that his fever had abated considerably. She said that he must not be surprised, and she would tell him news. He asked what; and she said I was come. He raised himself up in his bed; " Can it be? " said he, " what, already? " She told him I came last night. Monsieur Colbrand coming to enquire of his health, he ordered him to draw near, and was highly pleased with his account of the journey, my readiness to come back, and to reach home that night. And he said, " Why, these tender fair ones, I think, bear fatigue better than we men. But she is very good, to give me such an instance of her readiness to oblige me.—Pray, Mrs. Jewkes," said he,

"take care of her health! and let her lie a-bed all day." She
told him, I had been up these two hours. "Ask her," said
he, "if she will be so good as to make me a visit: if she won't,
I'll rise and go to her."—"Indeed, Sir," said she, "you must
be still; and I'll go to her."—"But don't urge her too much,"
said he, "if she be unwilling."

She came and told me all the above; and I said, I would
most willingly wait upon him; and I longed to see him, and
was much grieved he was so ill. So I went down with her.
"Will she come?" said he, as I entered the room. "Yes,
Sir," said she; "and she said, at the first word, 'Most willingly.'"—"Sweet excellence!" he replied.

As soon as he saw me, he said, "O my beloved Pamela! you
have made me quite well. I'm concerned to return my acknowledgments to you in so unfit a place and manner; but will you
give me your hand?" I did, and he kissed it with great
eagerness. "Sir," said I, "you do me too much honour!—I
am sorry you are so ill."—"I can't be ill," said he, "while you
are with me. I am very well already;" and, said he, kissing
my hand again, "You shall not repent this goodness. My
heart is too full of it, to express myself as I ought. But I am
sorry you have had such fatigue. Life is not life without you!
had you refused me, and I had hardly hopes you would oblige
me, I should have had a severe fit of it, I believe; for I was
taken very oddly, and knew not what to make of myself, but
now I shall be well instantly. You need not, Mrs. Jewkes,"
added he, "send for the doctor from Stamford; this lovely
creature is my doctor, for her absence was my disease."

He begged me to sit down by his bed-side, and asked me, if
I had obliged him with sending for my former packet: I said
I had, and hoped it would be brought. He said it was doubly
kind.

I would not stay long, because of disturbing him. He got
up in the afternoon, and desired my company; and seemed quite
pleased, easy, and much better. He said, "Mrs. Jewkes, after
this instance of my good Pamela's obligingness in her return,
I am sure we ought to leave her entirely at her own liberty;
and if she pleases to take a turn in the chariot, or in the garden,
or to the town, or wherever she will, let her be left at liberty,
and asked no questions: and pray do all in your power to oblige
her." She said she would, to be sure.

He took my hand, and said, "One thing I will tell you,
Pamela, because I know you will be glad to hear it, and yet not
care to ask me: I had, before you went, taken Williams's bond

227

for the money: how the poor man had behaved, I can't tell; but he could get no bail; and if I have no fresh reason given me, perhaps, I shall not exact the payment; he has been some time at liberty, and now follows his school; but, methinks I could wish you not to see him at present."

"Sir," said I, "I will not do any thing to disoblige you wilfully; and I am glad he is at liberty, because I was the occasion of his misfortunes." I durst say no more, though I wanted to plead for the poor gentleman; which, in gratitude, I thought I ought, when I could do him a service. I said, "I am sorry, Sir, Lady Davers, who loves you so well, should have incurred your displeasure, and that there should be any variance between your honour and her: I hope it was not on my account." He took out of his waistcoat pocket, as he sat in his gown, his letter-case, and said, "Here, Pamela, read *that* when you go up stairs, and let me have your thoughts upon it; and that will let you into the affair."

He said, he was very heavy, of a sudden, and would lie down, to indulge for that day; and if he was better in the morning, would take an airing in the chariot. So I took my leave for the present, and went up to my closet, and read the letter he put into my hands as follows:

"BROTHER,

"I am very uneasy at what I hear of you; and must write, whether it please you, or not, my *full* mind. I have had some people with me, desiring me to interpose with you, who have a greater regard for your honour than, I am sorry to say, you have yourself. Could I think, that a brother of mine would so meanly run away with my late dear mother's waiting-maid, keep her a prisoner from all her friends, and to the disgrace of your own? But I thought, when you would not let the wench come to me, on my mother's death, that you meant no good.—I blush for you, I assure you. She was an innocent, good girl; but I suppose that's over with her now, or soon will. What can you mean by this, let me ask? You will have her either for a kept mistress or a wife. If the former, there are enough to be had without ruining a poor girl my mother loved, who really was a very good one; and of *this* you may be ashamed. As to the *other*, I dare say you don't think of it: but if you *should*, you would be utterly inexcusable. Consider, brother, that ours is no upstart family; but it is as ancient as the best in the kingdom! For several hundred years, the heirs of it have not been known to have disgraced themselves by

228

unequal matches; and you know you have been sought by some of the best families in the nation, for your alliance. It might be well enough if you were descended of a family of yesterday, or but a remove or two from the dirt you seem so fond of. But let me tell you, that I, and all mine, will renounce you for ever, if you can descend so meanly; and I shall be ashamed to be called your sister. Handsome as you are in your person; so happy in the gifts of your mind, that every body courts your company; possessed of such a noble and clear estate; and very rich in money besides, left you by the best of fathers and mothers, with such ancient blood in your veins, untainted! for *you* to throw away yourself thus, is intolerable; yet it would be very wicked in you to ruin the girl. So that I beg you will restore her to her parents, and give her one hundred pounds, or so, to make her happy in some honest fellow of her own degree; it will be doing something, and also oblige and pacify *your much grieved sister.*

" If I have written too sharply, consider it is my love for you, and the shame you are bringing upon yourself; I wish this may have the intended effect upon you."

This is a sad letter, my dear father and mother; one may see how poor people are despised by the proud and the rich! yet we were all on a footing originally: and many of those gentry, who brag of their ancient blood, would be glad to have it as wholesome and as *really* untainted as ours!—Surely these proud people never think what a short stage life is; and that, with all their vanity, a time is coming, when they must submit to be on a level with us. The philosopher said true, when he looked upon the skull of a king, and that of a poor man, that he saw no difference between them. Besides, do they not know, that the richest of princes, and the poorest of beggars, are to have one great and tremendous Judge, at the last day; who will not distinguish between them, according to their circumstances in life; on the contrary, may make their condemnations the greater, as their neglected opportunities were greater! Poor souls! how do I pity their pride!—O keep me, heaven, from *their* high condition, if my mind shall ever be tainted with *their* vice, or polluted with so cruel and inconsiderate a contempt of that humble estate they behold with so much scorn!

Besides, how do these gentry know, supposing they could trace back their ancestry for one, two, three, or even five hundred years, that then the original stems of these poor families, though they have not kept such elaborate records of their good-for-nothingness, as it often proves, were not deeper rooted?—How can they be assured, that one hundred years hence, or two, some of those now despised upstart families may not revel in their estates, while their descendants may be reduced to the other's dunghills?—And, perhaps, such is the vanity, as well as changeableness of human estates, in *their* turns set up for pride of family, and despise the others!

These reflections occurred to my thoughts, made serious by my master's indisposition, and this proud letter of the *lowly* Lady Davers, against the *high-minded* Pamela. *Lowly*, I say, because she could *stoop* to such vain *pride*; and *high-minded* I, because I hope I am too *proud* ever to do the like!—But, after all, poor wretches that we be! we scarce know what we *are*, much less what we *shall be!*—Again, I pray to be kept from the sinful pride of a high estate.

On this occasion I recall the following lines, which I have read; where the poet argues in a much better manner:

> ————————Wise Providence
> Does various parts for various minds dispense:
> The *meanest slaves*, or those who *hedge* and *ditch*,
> Are useful, by their sweat, to feed the *rich*.
> The *rich*, in due return, impart their store,
> Which comfortably feeds the lab'ring *poor*.
> Nor let the *rich* the *lowest slave* disdain:
> He's *equally* a *link* of Nature's *chain*;
> Labours to the *same end*, joins in *one view*;
> And *both alike* the Will Divine pursue;
> And, at the last, are levell'd, *king* and *slave*,
> Without distinction, in the silent grave.

WEDNESDAY MORNING.

My master sent me a message just now, he was so much better, that he would take a turn, after breakfast, in the chariot, and requested my company. I hope I shall know how to be humble, and comport myself under all these favours.

Mrs. Jewkes is one of the most obliging creatures in the world; I have respect shown me by every one, as if I was as great as Lady Davers—But now, if this should all end in the sham marriage!—It cannot be, I hope. Yet the pride of greatness and ancestry, and such like, is so strongly set out in Lady Davers's letter, that I cannot flatter myself to be so happy as all these desirable appearances make for me. Should I be now deceived, I shall be worse off than ever. I shall see what light this new honour will procure me!—So I'll get ready. But I won't, I think, change my garb, for it might look as if I would be nearer on a level with him: yet, should I not, it may be thought a disgrace to him; but I will, I think, open the portmanteau, and, for the first time since I came hither, put on my best silk nightgown. Yet that will be making myself a sort of right to the clothes I had renounced: and I am not sure I shall have no other crosses to encounter. So I will go as I am; for, though ordinary, I am as clean as a penny, though I say it. So I'll e'en go as I am, except he orders otherwise. Mrs. Jewkes says I ought to dress as fine as I can; but I say, I think not. As my master is at breakfast, I will venture down to ask him how he will have me be.

Well, he is kinder and kinder, and, thank God, purely recovered!—How charmingly he looks, to what he did yesterday! Blessed be God for it!

He arose, and came to me, took my hand, and would set me down to him; then said, " My charming girl seemed going to speak. What would you say?"—" Sir," said I (a little ashamed), " I think it is too great an honour to go into the chariot with you."—" No, my dear Pamela," said he; " the *pleasure* of your company will be greater than the *honour* of mine; and so say no more on that head."

" But, Sir," said I, " I shall disgrace you to go thus."—" You would grace a prince, my fair one," said the dear gentleman, " in that dress, or any you shall choose: you look so pretty that, if you will not catch cold in that round-ear'd cap, go just as you are."—" Sir," said I, " then you'll be pleased to go a byeway, that it mayn't be seen you do so much honour to your servant."—" My good girl," said he, " I doubt you are afraid of yourself being talked of, more than me: for I hope, by degrees, to take off the world's wonder, and teach it to expect that which is due to my Pamela."

There's for you, my dear father and mother!—Did I not do well to come back?—O could I get rid of my fears of this sham marriage (for all this is not inconsistent with that frightful scheme) I should be too happy!

So I came up, with great pleasure, for my gloves; and now wait his kind commands.—" Dear, dear Sir," said I to myself, as if speaking to him, " for God's sake let me have no more trials and reverses; I could not bear it now, I verily think."

At last the welcome message came, that my master was ready; I went down as fast as I could, and he, before all the servants, handed me in as if I was a lady. Mrs. Jewkes begged he would take care he did not catch cold, as he had been ill. And I had the pride to hear his new coachman say to one of

231

his fellow servants, " They are a charming pair, I am sure !
'tis pity they should be parted ! "—O my dear father and mother !
I fear your girl will grow as proud as any thing ! You will
think I have special reason to guard against it, when you read
the kind particulars I shall now relate.

He ordered dinner to be ready by two ; and Abraham, who
succeeds John, went behind the coach. He bid Robin drive
gently, and told me, he wanted to talk to me about his sister
Davers, and other matters. Indeed, at first setting out, he
kissed me a little too often ; and I was afraid of Robin's looking
back, through the fore glass, and people seeing us, as they passed ;
but he was exceedingly kind to me, in his words, as well. At
last, he said :

" You have, I doubt not, read over and over, my sister's
saucy letter ; and find, as I told you, that you are no more
obliged to her than I am. She intimates, that some people
have been with her ; and who should they be, but the officious
Mrs. Jervis, Mr. Longman, and Jonathan ! and for that I
dismissed them my service. I see," said he, " you are going
to speak in their behalf ; but your time is not come to do that,
if ever I shall permit it.

" My sister," says he, " I have been before-hand with : for
I have renounced her. I am sure I have been a kind brother
to her ; and gave her 3000*l.* more than her share came to by
my father's will, when I entered upon my estate. The woman,
surely, was beside herself with passion and insolence, when she
wrote me such a letter ; for well she knew I would not bear it.
But you must know, Pamela, she is much incensed, that I will
give no ear to a proposal of hers, of a daughter of my Lord——,
who," said he, " neither in person, mind, nor acquirements,
even with all her opportunities, is to be named in a day with my
Pamela. Yet you see the plea, my girl, which I made to you
before, of the pride of condition, and the world's censure,
which I own, sticks a little too close with me still : for a woman
shines not forth to the public as a man ; and the world sees not
your excellencies and perfections : if it did, I should entirely
stand acquitted by the severest censurers. But it will be said,
that here is Mr. B——, with such and such an estate, has
married his mother's waiting-maid : not considering that no
lady in the kingdom can outdo her, or better support the condition to which she will be raised. And," said he, putting his
arm round me, and again kissing me, " I pity my dear girl, too,
for *her* part in this censure ; for she will have to combat the
pride and slights of the neighbouring gentry. Sister Davers,

you see, will never be reconciled to you. The other ladies will not visit you; and you will, with a merit superior to all, be treated as if unworthy their notice. Should I now marry my Pamela, how will she relish all this? Won't these be cutting things to my fair one? For, as to me, I have nothing to do, but, with a good estate in possession, brazen out the matter of my former pleasantry on this subject, with my companions of the chace, the green, and the assemblée : stand their rude jests for once or twice, and my fortune will create me always respect enough, I warrant you. But what will my poor girl do, as to *her* part, with her own sex? For some company you must keep. My station will not admit it to be with my servants; the ladies will fly your acquaintance, and still, though my wife, will treat you as my mother's waiting-maid. What says my girl to this?"

You may well guess, my dear father and mother, how transporting these generous and condescending sentiments were to me?—I thought I had the harmony of the spheres all around me; and every word that dropped from his lips was as sweet as the honey of Hybla to me. "Oh, Sir!" said I, "how inexpressibly kind and good is all this! Your poor servant has a much greater struggle than this to go through, a more knotty difficulty to overcome."

"What is that?" said he, a little impatiently : "I will not forgive your doubts now."—"No, Sir," said I, "I cannot doubt; but it is, how I shall *support*, how I shall *deserve* your goodness to me?"—"Dear girl!" said he, and pressed me to his breast, "I was afraid you would have made me angry again; but that I would not be, because I see you have a grateful heart; and this your kind and cheerful return, after such cruel usage as you had experienced in my house, enough to make you detest the place, has made me resolve to bear any thing in you, but doubts of my honour, at a time when I am pouring out my soul, with a true and affectionate ardour, before you."

"But, good Sir," said I, "my greatest concern will be for the rude jests you will yourself encounter with, for thus stooping beneath yourself. For as to *me*, considering my lowly estate, and little merit, even the slights and reflections of the ladies will be an honour to me : and I shall have the pride to place more than half their ill-will to their envy at my happiness. And if I can, by the most cheerful duty, and resigned obedience, have the pleasure to be agreeable to you, I shall think myself but too happy, let the world say what it will."

He said, "You are very good, my dearest girl : but how will

you bestow your time, with no visits to receive or pay? No parties of pleasure to join in? No card tables to employ your winter evenings, and even, as the taste is, half the day, summer and winter? And you have often played with my mother too, and so know how to perform a part there, as well as in the other diversions : and I shall not desire you to live without such amusements, as *my wife* might expect, were I to marry a lady of the first quality."

" O, Sir," said I, " how shall I bear your goodness? But do you think, Sir, in such a family as yours a person whom you shall honour with the name of mistress of it, will not find useful employments for her time, without looking abroad for any others?

" In the first place, Sir, if you will give me leave, I will myself look into such parts of the family economy as may not be beneath the rank to which I shall have the honour of being exalted, if any such there can be; and this, I hope, without incurring the ill-will of any *honest* servant.

" Then, Sir, I will ease you of as much of your family accounts, as I possibly can, when I have convinced you that I am to be trusted with them; and, you know, Sir, my late good lady made me her treasurer, her almoner, and every thing.

" Then, Sir, if I must needs be visiting, or visited, and the ladies won't honour me so much, or even if they *would* now and then, I will visit, if your goodness will allow me so to do, the sick poor in the neighbourhood around you; and administer to their wants and necessities, in such matters as may not be hurtful to your estate, but comfortable to them, and entail upon you their blessings, and their prayers for your health and welfare.

" Then I will assist your housekeeper, as I used to do, in making jellies, comfits, sweetmeats, marmalades, and cordials; and to pot, candy, and preserve, for the uses of the family; and to make myself all the fine linen of it for yourself and me.

" Then, Sir, if you will sometimes indulge me with your company, I will take an airing in your chariot now and then : and when you shall return home from your diversions on the green, or from the chace, or where you shall please to go, I shall have the pleasure of receiving you with duty, and a cheerful delight; and, in your absence, count the moments till your return; and you will, may-be, fill up some part of my time, the sweetest by far ! with your agreeable conversation, for an hour or two now and then; and be indulgent to the impertinent overflowings of my grateful heart, for all your goodness to me.

" The breakfasting time, the preparations for dinner, and sometimes to entertain your chosen friends, and the company you shall bring home with you, *gentlemen*, if not *ladies*, and the supperings, will necessarily fill up a great part of the day.

" And may-be, Sir, now and then, a good-humoured lady will drop in : and I hope, if they do, I shall so behave myself, as not to *add* to the disgrace you will have brought upon yourself : for, indeed, I will be very circumspect, and as discreet as I can, and as humble too as shall be consistent with your honour.

" Cards, 'tis true, I can play at, in all the usual games that our sex delight in : but this I am not fond of, nor shall ever desire to play, unless to induce such ladies, as you may wish to see, not to abandon your house for want of an amusement they are accustomed to.

" Music, which our good lady taught me, will fill up some intervals, if I should have any. And, you know, I love reading and scribbling; and though all the latter will be employed in the family accounts, between the servants and me, and you and myself; yet reading, at proper times, will be a pleasure to me, which I shall be unwilling to give up for the best company in the world, except yours.—And, O Sir, that will help to polish my mind, and make me worthier of your company and conversation; and, with your explanations of what I shall not understand, will be a sweet employment and improvement too.

" But one thing, Sir, I ought not to forget, because it is the chief : my duty to God will, I hope, always employ some good portion of my time, with thanks for his superlative goodness to me, and to pray for *you* and *myself* : for *you*, Sir, for a blessing on you, for your great goodness to such an unworthy creature; for *myself*, that I may be enabled to discharge my duty to you, and be found grateful for all the blessings I shall receive at the hands of Providence, by means of your generosity and condescension.

" With all this, Sir," said I, " can you think I shall be at a loss to pass my time ? But, as I know that every slight to me will be, in some measure, a slight to you, I shall beg not to go very fine in dress, but only appear so, that you may not be ashamed of it after the honour I shall have of being called by your worthy name : for well I know, Sir, that nothing so much excites the envy of my own sex, as seeing a person above them, in appearance, and in dress. And that would bring down upon me an hundred *saucy things*, and *low-born brats*, and I can't tell what."

There I stopped; for I had prattled a great deal; and he said, clasping me to him, "Why stops my dear Pamela?—Why does she not proceed? I could dwell upon your words all the day long: you shall direct your own pleasures, and your own time, so sweetly do you choose to employ it: and thus shall I find some of my own bad actions atoned for by your exemplary goodness, and God will bless *me* for *your* sake.

"O," said he, "what pleasure you give me in this sweet foretaste of *my* happiness! I will now defy the saucy, busy censures of the world; and bid them know *your* excellence, and *my* happiness, before they, with unhallowed lips, presume to judge of *my* actions, and *your* merit!—Let me tell you, my Pamela, that I can add my hopes of a still more pleasing amusement, your bashful modesty would not permit you to hint, and which I will no otherwise touch upon, lest it should seem, to your nicety, to detract from the present purity of my good intention, than to say, I hope to have superadded to all these, such an employment, as will give me a view of perpetuating my happy prospects, and my family at the same time; of which I am almost the only male."

I blushed, I believe: yet could not be displeased at the decent and charming manner with which he insinuated this distant hope: and, Oh! judge for me, how my heart was affected with all these things!

He was pleased to add another charming reflection, which showed me the noble sincerity of his kind professions. "I do own to you, my Pamela," said he, "that I love you with a purer flame than ever I knew in my life; and which commenced for you in the garden; though you, unkindly, by your unseasonable doubts, nipped the opening bud, while too tender to bear the cold blasts of slight and negligence. I know more sincere joy and satisfaction in this sweet hour's conversation with you, than all the guilty tumults of my former passion ever did, or (had even my attempts succeeded) ever could have afforded me."

"O, Sir," said I, "expect not words from your poor servant, equal to these most generous professions. Both the means, and the will, I now see, are given to you, to lay me under an everlasting obligation. How happy shall I be, if, though I cannot be worthy of all this goodness and condescension, I can prove myself not entirely unworthy of it! But I can only answer for a grateful heart; and if ever I give you cause wilfully (and you will generously allow for *involuntary* imperfections) to be disgusted with me, may I be an out-cast from your house and favour, and as much repudiated, as if the law had divorced me from you !

"But, Sir," continued I, "though I was so unseasonable in the garden, you would, I trust, had you *then* heard me, have pardoned my imprudence, and owned I had some cause to fear, and to wish to be with my poor father and mother: I the rather say this, that you should not think me capable of returning insolence for your goodness; or appearing foolishly ungrateful, when you was so kind to me."

"Indeed, Pamela," said he, "you gave me great uneasiness; for I love you too well not to be jealous of the least appearance of your indifference to me, or preference of any other person, not excepting your parents themselves. This made me resolve not to hear you; for I had not got over my reluctance to marriage; and a little weight, you know, turns the scale, when it hangs in an equal balance. Still you see, that though I could part with you, while my anger held, yet the regard I had then newly professed for your virtue, made me resolve not to offer to violate it; and you have also seen, that the painful struggle I underwent when I began to reflect, and to read your moving journal, between my desire to recall you, and my doubt whether you would return (though I resolved not to force you to it), had like to have cost me a severe illness: but your kind and cheerful return has dispelled all my fears, and given me hope, that I am not indifferent to you; and you see how your presence has chased away my illness."

"I bless God for it," said I; "but since you are so good as to encourage me, and will not despise my weakness, I will acknowledge, that I suffered more than I could have imagined till I experienced it, in being banished your presence in so much anger: and I was the more affected, when you answered the wicked Mrs. Jewkes so generously in my favour, at my leaving your house. For this, Sir, awakened all my reverence for you: and you saw I could not forbear, not knowing what I did, to break boldly in upon you, and acknowledge your goodness on my knees."—"'Tis true, my dear Pamela," said he, "we have sufficiently tortured one another; the only comfort that can result from it, will be, reflecting upon the matter coolly and with pleasure, when all these storms are overblown (as I hope they now are), and we sit together secured in each other's good opinion, recounting the uncommon gradations, by which we have ascended to the summit of that felicity, which I hope we shall soon attain.

"Meantime," said he, "let me hear what my dear girl would

have said in her justification, could I have trusted myself with her, as to her fears, and the reason of wishing herself from me, when I had begun to show my fondness for her, in a manner I thought agreeable to her and virtue."

I pulled out of my pocket the gypsey-letter; but I said, before I shewed it to him, " I have this letter, Sir, to show you, what I think you will allow must have given me the greatest disturbance : but as I know not the writer, and the hand seems to be disguised, I would beg the favour, if you guess whose it is, it may not turn to their prejudice, as it was written probably with a view only to serve me."

He read it; and being signed *Somebody*, he said, " Yes, this is indeed from *Somebody ;* and, disguised as the hand is, I know the writer : don't you see, by the setness of some of these letters, and a little secretary cut here and there, especially in the *c*, and the *r*, it is the hand of a person bred in the law ? Why, Pamela," said he, " 'tis old Longman's : an officious rascal !— But I have done with him."—" O Sir," said I, " it would be too insolent in me to offer (so much I am overwhelmed with your goodness) to defend any body you are angry with : yet, Sir, so far as they have incurred your displeasure for my sake, and for no other want of duty or respect, I could wish—but I dare not say more."

" But," said he, " as to the letter, and the information it contains :—let me know, Pamela, when you received this ? "— " On the Friday, Sir," said I, " that you went to the wedding at Stamford."—" How could it be conveyed to you," said he, " unknown to Mrs. Jewkes, when I gave her such strict charge to attend you, and you promised me not to throw yourself in the way of such intelligence ? For," said he, " when I went to Stamford, I knew, from private intimation, that somebody would attempt to see you, or give you a letter, if not to get you away ; but was not certain from what quarter, whether from my sister Davers, Mrs. Jervis, Mr. Longman, or John Arnold, or your father ; and as I was then struggling with myself, whether to give way to my honourable inclinations, or to free you, and let you go to your father, to avoid the danger I found myself in of the former, (for I had absolutely resolved never to wound again even your ears with proposals of a contrary nature;) that was the reason I desired you to permit Mrs. Jewkes to be so much on her guard till I came back, when I thought I should have decided this disputed point within myself, between my pride and my inclinations."

" This, good Sir," said I, " explains to me your conduct in

that case, and what you said to me and Mrs. Jewkes on that occasion : and I see more and more how much I may depend upon your honour and goodness. But I will tell you all the truth." I then recounted the whole affair of the gypsey, and how the letter was put among the loose grass, &c. And he said, " The man who thinks a thousand dragons sufficient to watch a woman, when her inclination takes a contrary bent, will find all too little : she will engage the stones in the street, or the grass in the field, to act for her, and help on her correspondence. If the mind," said he, " be not engaged, I see there is hardly any confinement sufficient for the body : you have told a very pretty story ; and, as you never gave me any reason to question your veracity, even in your severest trials, I doubt not the truth of what you now mention. I will, in turn, give you such a proof of mine, as you shall find to carry conviction with it.

" You must know, then, my Pamela, I had actually formed such a project, so well informed was that old rascally *Somebody !* The time was fixed for the very person described in this letter to be here ; and I thought he should read some part of the ceremony (as little as was possible to deceive you) in my chamber : so I hoped to have you mine upon terms that *then* would have been much more agreeable to me than real matrimony. I did not in haste intend you the mortification of being undeceived ; so that we might have lived for years, perhaps, very lovingly together ; I being at liberty to confirm or abrogate it as I pleased."

" O Sir," said I, " I am out of breath with the thoughts of my danger. But what good angel prevented the execution of this deep-laid design ? "

" Why *your* good angel, Pamela," said he ; " for when I considered that it would make *you* miserable, and me not happy ; that if you should have a dear little one, it would be out of my own power to legitimate it, if I wished it to inherit my estate ; and that, as I am almost the last of my family, and most of what I possess must descend to a strange line, and disagreeable and unworthy persons ; notwithstanding that I might, in this case, have issue of my own body ; when I further considered your untainted virtue, what dangers, trials, and troubles, I had involved you in, only because you were beautiful and virtuous, which had excited all my passion for you ; and reflected also upon your tried prudence and truth ! I, though I doubted not effecting this my last plot, resolved to overcome myself ; and however I might suffer in struggling with my affection for you,

239

to part with you, rather than betray you under so black a veil. Besides," said he, " I remembered how much I had exclaimed against and censured an action of this kind, attributed to one of the first men of the law, and of the kingdom, as he afterwards became; and that it was but treading in a path another had marked out for me, and as I was assured, with no great satisfaction to himself, when he came to reflect; my foolish pride was a little piqued with this, because I loved to be, if I went out of the way, my own original, as I may call it; on all these considerations it was, that I rejected this project, and sent word to the person that I had better considered of the matter, and would not have him come, till he heard further from me; and, in this suspense, I suppose, some of your confederates, Pamela (for we have been a couple of plotters, though your virtue and merit have procured you faithful friends and partisans, which my money and promises could not), one way or other, got knowledge of it, and gave you this notice; but, perhaps, it would have come too late, had not your white angel got the better of my black one, and inspired me with resolutions to abandon the project, just as it was to have been put into execution. But I own that from these appearances, you were but too well justified in your fears, on this odd way of coming at this intelligence; and I have only one thing to blame you for, that though I was resolved not to *hear* you in your own defence, yet, having so ready a talent at your pen, you might have cleared your part of this matter up to me by a line or two; and when I had known what seeming good grounds you had for pouring cold water on a young flame, just rising to an honourable expansion, I should not have imputed it, as I was apt to do, to unseasonable insult for my tenderness to you, on one hand; to perverse nicety, on the other; or to (what most alarmed me) prepossession for some other person: and this would have saved us both much fatigue, I of mind, you of body."

" And, indeed, Sir," said I, " of *mind* too : and I could not better manifest this, than by the cheerfulness with which I obeyed your recalling me to your presence."

" Ay, that, my dear Pamela," said he, and clasped me in his arms, " was the kind, the inexpressibly kind action, which has riveted my affections to you, and obliges me, in this unreserved manner, to pour my whole soul into your bosom."

I said, " I had the less merit in this my return, being driven by an irresistible impulse to it; and could not help it, if I would."

" This," said he (and honoured me by kissing my hand), " is

engaging, indeed; if I may hope, that my Pamela's gentle inclination for her persecutor was the strongest motive for her return; and I so much value a voluntary love in the person I would wish for my wife, that I would have even prudence and interest hardly named in comparison with it; and can you return me sincerely the honest compliment I now make you?—In the *choice* I have made, it is impossible I should have any view to my *interest*. Love, *true* love, is the *only* motive by which *I* am induced. And were I not what I am, could you give me the *preference* to any other you know in the world, notwithstanding what has passed between us?"—"Why," said I, "should your so much obliged Pamela refuse to answer this kind question? Cruel as I have thought you, and dangerous as your views to my honesty have been; you, Sir, are the only person living that was ever more than indifferent to me; and before I knew this to be, what I blush now to call it, I could not hate you, or wish you ill, though, from my soul, the attempts you made were shocking, and most distasteful to me."

"I am satisfied, my Pamela," said he, "nor do I want to see the papers you have kindly written for to your father; though I wish to see them, for the sake of the sweet manner you relate what has passed, and to have before me the whole series of your sufferings, that I may learn the degree of kindness sufficient to recompense you."

Thus, my dear father and mother, did your happy daughter find herself blessed by her generous master ! An ample recompence for all her sufferings did I think this sweet conversation. A hundred tender things did he express besides, which, though they never can escape my memory, would be too tedious to write down. Oh, how I blessed God, and, I hope, ever shall, for all his gracious favours to his unworthy handmaid ! What a happy change ! And who knows but my generous master may put it in my power, without injuring him, to dispense around me, to many persons, the happy influences of the condition to which I shall be, by his kind favour, exalted? Doubly blest shall I be, in particular, if I can return the hundredth part of the obligations I owe to such honest good parents, to whose pious instructions and examples, under God, I owe all my present happiness, and future prospects.—O the joy that fills my mind on these proud hopes ! on these delightful prospects ! —It is too mighty for me; and I must sit down to ponder all these things, and to admire and bless the goodness of that Providence, which has, through so many intricate mazes, made me tread the path of innocence, and so amply rewarded me, for what it has enabled me to do ! All glory to God alone be ever given for it, by your poor enraptured daughter !—I will now continue my most pleasing relation.

As the chariot was returning home from this sweet airing, he said, "From all that has now passed between us, my Pamela will see, and believe, that the trials of her virtue are all over from me ; but, perhaps, there will be some few yet to come of her patience and humility. For, importuned by Lady Darnford and her daughters, I promised them a sight of my beloved girl : so I intend to have their whole family, and Lady Jones, and Mrs. Peters' family, to dine with me once in a few days. And, as I believe you would hardly choose to grace the table on the occasion, till you can do it in your own right, you will not refuse coming down to us if I desire it ; for I would preface our nuptials," said the dear gentleman—O what a sweet word was that !—"with their good opinion of your merit ; and to see you and your sweet manner, will be enough for that purpose ; and so by degrees, prepare my neighbours for what is to follow : they already have your character from me, and are disposed to admire you."

"Sir," said I, "after all that has passed I should be unworthy not to say, that I *can* have no will but yours : and however awkwardly I shall behave in such company, weighed down with the sense of your obligations on one side, and my own unworthiness with their observations on the other, I will not scruple to obey you."

"I am obliged to you, Pamela," said he ; "and pray be only dressed as you are ; for since they know your condition, and heard the story of your present dress, and how you came by it, one of the young ladies begs it as a favour to see you just as you are : and I am the rather pleased it should be so, because they will perceive you owe nothing to dress, but make a much better figure with your own native stock of loveliness, than the greatest ladies arrayed in the most splendid attire, and adorned with the most glittering jewels."

"O Sir," said I, "your goodness beholds your poor servant in a light greatly beyond her merit ! But it must not be expected that others, ladies especially, will look upon me with *your* favourable eyes : yet I should be best pleased to wear this humble garb, till you, for your own sake, shall order it otherwise : for," said I, "I hope it will be always my pride to glory most in your goodness : to show every one, that as to my happiness in this life, I am entirely the work of your bounty : and to let the world see from what a lowly original you have raised me to honour, that the greatest ladies would rejoice in."

"Admirable Pamela!" said he; "excellent girl!—Surely thy sentiments are superior to those of all thy sex!—I might have *addressed* a hundred fine ladies; but never could have had reason to *admire* one as I do you."

As, my dear father and mother, I repeat these generous sayings, only because they are the effect of my master's goodness, being far from presuming to think I deserve one of them; so I hope you will not attribute it to my vanity; for I do assure you, I think I ought rather to be more *humble*, as I am more *obliged*: for it must be always a sign of a poor condition, to receive obligations one cannot repay; as it is of a rich mind when it can confer them without accepting or *needing* a return. It is, on one side, the state of the human creature, compared, on the other to the Creator: and so, with due deference, may his beneficence be said to be god-like, and that is the highest that can be said.

The chariot brought us home about two; and, blessed be God, my master is pure well, and cheerful; it makes me hope he does not repent his late generous treatment of me. He handed me out of the chariot, with the same goodness as when he put me into it, before several of the servants. Mrs. Jewkes came to enquire how he did. "Quite well, Mrs. Jewkes," said he; "I thank God and this good girl for it!"—"I am glad of it," said she; "but I hope you are not the worse for my care and my doctoring of you!"—"No, but the better, Mrs. Jewkes," said he; "you have much obliged me by both."

Then he said, "Mrs. Jewkes, you and I have used this good girl very hardly."—"I was afraid, Sir," said she, "I should be the subject of her complaints."—"I assure you," said he, "we have had a quite different subject to talk of; I trust she will forgive us both: you especially, because you acted by my orders. I only mean, that the necessary consequence of those orders has been very grievous to my Pamela: and now we must make her amends, if we can."

"Sir," said she, "I always said to Madam (as she called me) that you was very good, and very forgiving."—"No," said he, "I have been stark naught, and it is she, I hope, will be very forgiving. But all this preamble is to tell you, Mrs. Jewkes, that now I desire you'll study to oblige her, as much as (to obey me) you was forced to disoblige her before. And you'll remember, that in every thing, she is to be her own mistress."—"Yes," said she, "and mine too, I suppose, Sir?"—"Aye," said the generous gentleman, " I believe it will be so in a little time."—" Then," said she, " I know how it will go with me ! " And so put her handkerchief to her eyes.—" Pamela," said my master, " comfort poor Mrs. Jewkes."

This was very generous already, to seem to put her in my power; and I took her by the hand, and said, " I shall never take upon me, Mrs. Jewkes, to abuse any opportunity put into my hand by my generous master; nor shall I ever wish to do you disservice, if I might; for I consider what you have done, was in obedience to a will I must also submit to; and so, if the *effects* of our obedience may be different, yet, as they proceed from *one* cause, *that* must be always reverenced by me."

" See there, Mrs. Jewkes," said my master, " we are both in generous hands; and if Pamela did not pardon you, I should think she but half forgave me, because you acted by my instructions."

" Well," said she, " God bless you both together, since it must be so; and I will double my diligence to oblige my lady, as I find she will soon be."

O my dear father and mother, now pray for me on another score; lest I should grow too proud, and be giddy with all these promising things, so soothing to the vanity of my years and sex. But even to this hour can I pray, that God would remove from me all these delightful prospects, if they were likely to corrupt my mind, so as to make me proud and vain, and not acknowledge, with thankful humility, the blessed Providence which has so visibly conducted me through the dangerous paths I have trod to this happy moment.

My master was pleased to say, that he thought I might as well dine with him, since he was alone; but I begged he would excuse me, for fear, as I said, such excess of goodness and condescension, all at once, should turn my head; and that he would by slower degrees bring on my happiness, lest I should not know how to bear it.

" Persons that doubt themselves," said he, " seldom do amiss : and if there was any fear of what you say, you could not have it in your thoughts: for none but the presumptuous, the conceited, and the thoughtless, err capitally. But nevertheless," said he, " I have such an opinion of your prudence, that I shall generally think what you do right, because it is *you* that do it."

" Sir," said I, " your kind expressions shall not be thrown away upon me, if I can help it; for they will task me with the care of endeavouring to deserve your good opinion, and your approbation, as the best rule of my conduct."

Being then about to go up stairs—" Permit me, Sir," said I (looking about me with some confusion, to see that nobody was there), " thus on my knees to thank you, as I often wanted to do in the chariot for all your goodness to me, which shall never, I hope, be cast away upon me." And so I had the boldness to kiss his hand.

I wonder since how I came to be so forward. But what could I do?—My poor grateful heart was like a too full river, which overflows its banks; and it carried away my fear and my shamefacedness, as that does all before it on the surface of its waters!

He clasped me in his arms with transport, and condescendingly kneeled by me, and kissing me, said, " O my dear obliging good girl, on my knees, as you on yours, I vow to you everlasting truth and fidelity : and may God but bless us both with half the pleasures that seem to lie before us, and we shall have no reason to envy the felicity of the greatest princes!"—" O Sir," said I, " how shall I support so much goodness?—I am poor indeed in *every thing*, compared to you! and how far, very far, do you, in every generous way, leave me behind you!"

He raised me, and, as I bent towards the door, led me to the stairs foot, and, saluting me there again, left me to go up to my closet, where I threw myself on my knees in raptures of joy, and blessed that gracious God who had thus changed my distress to happiness, and so abundantly rewarded me for all the sufferings I had passed through.—And oh, how light, how very light, do all those sufferings *now* appear, which *then* my repining mind made so grievous to me!—Hence, in every state of life, and in all the changes and chances of it, for the future, will I trust in Providence, who knows what is best for us, and frequently turns the very evils we most dread, to be the cause of our happiness, and of our deliverance from greater.—My experiences, young as I am, as to this great point of reliance on God, are strong, though my judgment in general may be weak and uninformed; but you'll excuse these reflections, because they are your beloved daughter's; and, so far as they are not amiss, derive themselves from the benefit of yours, and my late good lady's examples and instructions.

I have written a vast deal in a little time; and shall only say, to conclude this delightful Wednesday, that in the afternoon my good master was so well, that he rode out on horseback, and came home about nine at night; and then stepped up to me, and, seeing me with pen and ink before me in my closet, said, " I come only to tell you I am very well, my Pamela; and since I have a letter or two to write, I will leave you to proceed in yours, as I suppose that was your employment," (for I had put by my papers at his coming up;) and so he saluted me, bid me good night, and went down; and I finished up to this place before I went to bed. Mrs. Jewkes told me, if it was more agreeable to me, she would lie in another room; but I said— " No, thank you, Mrs. Jewkes; pray let me have your company." And she made a fine curtsey, and thanked me.—How times are altered!

This morning my master came up to me, and talked with me on various subjects, for a good while together, in the most kind manner. Among other things, he asked me if I chose to order any new clothes against my marriage. (O how my heart flutters when he mentions this subject so freely!) I said I left every thing to his good pleasure, requesting, as before, that I might not be too fine.

He said, " I think, my dear, it shall be very private: I hope you are not afraid of a sham marriage, and pray get the service by heart, that you may see nothing is omitted." I glowed between shame and delight. O how I felt my cheeks burn!

I said, I apprehended nothing, but my own unworthiness. Said he, " I think it shall be done within fourteen days at this house." O how I trembled! but not with grief, you may believe—" What says my girl? Have you to object against any day of the next fourteen? Because my affairs require me to go to my other house, and I think not to stir from this till I am happy with you."

" I have no will but yours," said I, (all glowing like the fire :) " But, Sir, did you say in the *house*?"—" Aye," said he; " for I care not how privately it be done; and it must be very public if we go to church."—" It is a *holy rite*, Sir," said I; " and would be better, methinks, in a *holy place*."

" I see " (said he most kindly), " my lovely maid's confusion; your trembling tenderness shows I ought to oblige you all I can. Therefore my own little chapel, which has not been used for two generations but for a lumber-room, because our family seldom resided here long together, shall be cleared, and cleaned, and got ready for the ceremony, if you dislike your own chamber or mine."

" Sir," said I, " that will be better than the chamber: and

246

I hope it will never be lumbered again, but kept to the use for which, as I *presume*, it has been consecrated."—" O yes," said he, " it was consecrated in my great great grandfather's time, who built that and the good old house together.

" But now, my good girl, if I do not too much add to your sweet confusion, shall it be in the *first* seven days, or the *second* of this fortnight?" I looked down, quite out of countenance. " Tell me," said he.—" In the second, if you please, Sir," said I.—" As *you* please," said he, most kindly : " but I should thank you, Pamela, if you would choose the first."—" I'd *rather*, Sir, if you please," said I, " have the second."—" Well," said he ; " be it so ; but don't defer it till the last day of the fourteen."

" Pray, Sir," said I, " since you embolden me to talk on this important subject, may I not send my dear father and mother word of my happiness ?"—" You may," said he, " but charge them to keep it secret, till you or I direct the contrary. I told you I would see no more of your papers ; but I meant, not without your consent : but if you will show them to me (and now I have no motive for my curiosity but pleasure in reading what you write) I shall acknowledge it as a favour."

" If, Sir," said I, " you will be pleased to let me write over again one sheet, I will ; though I had relied upon your word, and not written them for your perusal."—" What is that ?" said he ; " though I cannot consent to it beforehand : for I more desire to see them, as being your true sentiments at *the time*, and *not* written for my perusal."—" Sir," said I, " what I am loth you should see are very severe reflections on the letter I received by the gypsey, when I apprehended your design of the sham marriage ; there are other things too, but that is the worst."— " It cannot be worse," said he, " my dear Sauce-box, than I have seen already ; and I will allow your treating me in ever so black a manner on that occasion, because it must have had a very black appearance to you."—" Well, Sir," said I, " I think I will obey you before night."—" But don't alter a word," said he. " I won't, Sir," replied I, " since you order it."

While we were talking Mrs. Jewkes came up, and said Thomas was returned. " O," said my master, " let him bring up the papers :" for he hoped, and so did I, that you had sent them. But it was a great baulk, when he came up, and said, " Sir, Mr. Andrews did not care to deliver them ; and would have it, that his daughter was forced to write that letter to him : the old gentleman took on sadly, and said that his daughter was undone, or else she would not have turned back when on her way, (as I told him she did," said Thomas,) " instead of coming

247

to them." I began to fear now that all would be bad for me again.

"Well, Tom," said he, "don't mince the matter: tell me, before Mrs. Andrews, what they said."—"Why, Sir, both he and Goody Andrews, after conferring together upon your letter, Madam, came out, weeping bitterly, which grieved my very heart! They said, now all was over with their poor daughter; and either she had written that letter by compulsion, or yielded to your honour; and was, or would be, ruined!"

My master seemed vexed, as I feared. And I said, "Pray, Sir, be so good as to excuse the fears of my honest parents. They cannot know your goodness to me."

"And so" (said he, without answering me), "they refused to deliver the papers?"—"Yes, and please your honour," said Thomas; "though I told him, that you, Madam, of your own accord, on a letter I had brought you, very cheerfully wrote what I carried: but the old gentleman said—'Why, wife, there are in these papers twenty things nobody should see but ourselves, and especially not the squire. O, the poor girl has had so many stratagems to struggle with! but at last she has met with one too hard for her. Can it be possible to account for her setting out to come to us in such post-haste, and when above half-way, to send us this letter, and go back again of her own accord, as you say; when we know, that all her delight would have been to come to us, and to escape from the perils she has so long contended with?' And then, Sir, he said, he could not bear this; for his daughter was ruined, to be sure before now. And so," said Thomas, "the good old couple sat themselves down, hand-in-hand, leaning upon each other's shoulder, and did nothing but lament.—I was piteously grieved," said he; "but all I could say did not comfort them; nor would they give me the papers; though I said I should deliver them to Mrs. Andrews herself. And so, and please your honour, I came away without them."

My good master saw me all bathed in tears, at this description of your distress and fears for me; and he said, "I would not have you take on so. I am not angry with your father in the main; he is a good man; and I would have you write out of hand, and it shall be sent by the post to Mr. Atkins, who lives within two miles of your father, and I'll inclose it in a cover of mine, in which I'll desire Mr. Atkins, the moment it comes to his hand, to convey it safely to your father and mother: and say nothing of their sending the papers, that it may not make them uneasy; for I want not now to see them on any other score than that of mere curiosity; and that will do at any time." So saying, he saluted me before Thomas, and, with his handkerchief, wiped my eyes; and said to Thomas—"The good old folks are not to be blamed in the main. They don't know my honourable intentions by their dear daughter; who, Tom, will soon be your mistress: though I shall keep the matter private some days, and would not have it spoken of by my servants out of the house."

Thomas said, "God bless your honour! you know best." And I said, "O Sir, you are all goodness!—How kind is this, to forgive the disappointment, instead of being angry, as I feared you would!" Thomas then withdrew. And my master said, "I need not remind you of writing out of hand, to make the good folks easy: and I will leave you to yourself for that purpose; only send me down such of your papers as you are willing I should see, with which I shall entertain myself for an hour or two. But one thing," added he, "I forgot to tell you: the neighbouring gentry I mentioned will be here to-morrow, to dine with me, and I have ordered Mrs. Jewkes to prepare for them."—"And *must* I, Sir," said I, "be shown to them?" —"O yes," said he: "that's the chief reason of their coming. And you'll see nobody equal to yourself; don't be concerned."

I opened my papers when my master had gone, and laid out those beginning at the Thursday morning he set out for Stamford, with the morning visit he made me before I was up, and the injunctions of watchfulness, &c., to Mrs. Jewkes; the next day's gypsey affair, and my reflections, in which I called him *truly diabolical*, and was otherwise very severe, on the strong appearances then against him. His return on Saturday, with the dread he put me in, on offering to search me for my papers which followed those he had got by Mrs. Jewkes's means. My being forced to give them up. His carriage to me after he had read them, and questions to me. His great kindness on seeing the dangers I had escaped, and the troubles I had undergone. How I unseasonably, in the midst of his goodness, expressed my desire of being sent to you, having the intelligence of a sham marriage, from the gypsey, in my thoughts. How this enraged him, and made him turn me away that very Sunday, and send me to you. The particulars of my journey, and my grief at parting with him: and my free acknowledgment to you, that I found, unknown to myself, I had begun to love him and could not help it. His sending to beg my return: but yet generously leaving me at liberty, when he might have forced me to return, willing or not. My resolutions to oblige him, and fatiguing journey back. My concern for his illness on my return. His kind reception of me, and showing me his sister Davers's angry letter against his behaviour to me, desiring him to set me free, and threatening to renounce him as a brother, if he should degrade himself by marrying me. My serious reflections on this letter, &c. (all which, I hope, with the others you will see shortly). And this carried matters down to Thursday night last.

All that followed was so kind on his side, being our chariot conference, as above, on Wednesday morning, and how good he has been ever since, that I thought I would go no further; for I was ashamed to be so very open on that tender and most grateful subject : though his great goodness to me deserves all possible acknowledgment.

When I had looked these out, I carried them into the parlour; and said, putting them into his hands, " Your allowances, good Sir, as heretofore : if I have been too open and free in my reflections or declarations, let my fears on one side, and my sincerity on the other, be my excuse."—" You are very obliging, my good girl," said he. " You have nothing to apprehend from my thoughts, any more than from my actions."

So I went up, and wrote the letter to you, briefly stating my present happiness, and my master's goodness, expressing my gratitude of heart to the kindest gentleman in the world, and assuring you I should soon have the pleasure of sending back to you, not only those papers, but all that since succeeded them, as I know you delight, in your leisure hours, to read my scribble : and I said, taking it to my master before I sealed it, " Will you please, Sir, to peruse what I write to my dear parents ? "—" Thank you, Pamela," said he, and set me on his knee, while he read it, and seemed much pleased with it : and giving it me again, " You are very happy," said he, " my beloved girl, in your style and expressions : the affectionate things you say of me, are inexpressibly obliging; and again, with this kiss," said he, " do I confirm for truth all that you have promised for my intentions in this letter." O what halcyon days are these ! God continue them ! A change now would kill me quite.

He went out in his chariot in the afternoon; and in the evening returned, and sent me word, he would be glad of my company for a little walk in the garden; and down I went that very moment.

He came to meet me. " So," said he, " how does my girl do now ? Whom do you think I have seen since I went out ? "—" I don't know, Sir," said I. " Why," said he, " there is a turning in the road, about five miles off, round a meadow, that has a pleasant foot-way, by a little brook, and a double row of limes on each side, where, now-and-then, the gentry in the neighbourhood walk, and angle and divert themselves. I'll show it you next opportunity. I stept out of my chariot to walk across this meadow, and bid Robin meet me on the further part of it : and whom should I spy there, walking, with a book in his hand, reading, but your humble servant, Mr. Williams?—Don't blush, Pamela," said he. " As his back was towards me, I thought I would speak to the man : and before he saw me, I said, ' How do you, old acquaintance?' (for," said he, " you know we were of one college for a twelve-month.) I thought the man would have jumped into the brook, he gave such a start at hearing my voice, and seeing me."

" Poor man !" said I. " Ay," said he, " but not too much of your poor man, in that soft accent, neither, Pamela. ' I am sorry my voice is so startling to you, Mr. Williams. What are you reading ? '—' Sir,' said he, stammering with the surprise, ' it is the French Telemachus : for I am about perfecting myself in the French tongue.' Thought I, I had rather so, than perfecting my Pamela in it. ' You do well,' replied I. ' Don't you think that yonder cloud may give us a small shower?' And it began to wet. He said, he believed not much.

" ' If,' said I, ' you are for the village, I'll give you a cast; for I shall call at Sir Simon's on returning from my little round.' He asked if it was not too great a favour ? ' No,' said I, ' don't talk of that; let us walk on, and we shall soon meet my chariot.'

" So, Pamela," continued my master, " we fell into conversation as we walked. He said he was very sorry he had incurred my displeasure; and the more, as he was told, by Lady Jones, who had it from Sir Simon's family, that I had a more honourable view than at first was apprehended. I said, ' We fellows of fortune, Mr. Williams, sometimes take too much liberty with the world : wantoning, very probably, as you contemplative folks would say, in the sun-beams of a dangerous affluence, we cannot think of confining ourselves to the common paths, though the safest and most eligible. And, you may believe I could not bear to be supplanted in a view that lay next my heart; and that by an old acquaintance, whose good, before this affair, I was studious to promote.'

" ' I would only say, Sir,' said he, ' that my *first* motive was entirely such as became my function : ' " and very politely, said my master, he added, " ' And I am very sure, that however

251

inexcusable I might seem in the *progress* of the matter, yourself, Sir, would have been sorry to have it said, you had cast your thoughts on a person that nobody could have wished for but yourself.'

" ' Well, Mr. Williams,' said I, ' I see you are a man of gallantry, as well as religion : but what I took most amiss was, that if you thought me doing a wrong thing, you did not expostulate with me upon it, as your function might have allowed you to do ; but immediately determine to counter-plot me, and attempt to secure to yourself a prize you would have robbed me of, and that from my own house. But the matter is at an end, and I retain no malice, though you did not *know* but I might, at last, do honourably by her, as I actually intend.'

" ' I am sorry for *myself*, Sir,' said he, ' that I should so unhappily incur your displeasure ; but I rejoice for *her* sake in your honourable intentions : allow me to say, that if you make Mrs. Andrews your lady, she will do credit to your choice, with all who see her, or come to know her ; and, for person and mind, you may challenge the county.'

" In this manner," said my master, " did the parson and I confabulate ; and I set him down at his lodgings in the village. But he kept your secret, Pamela ; and would not own, that you gave any encouragement to his addresses."

" Indeed, Sir," said I, " he could not say that I did ; and I hope you believe me."—" I do," said he : " but it is still my opinion, that if, when I saw plots set up against my plots, I had not discovered the parson as I did the correspondence between you might have gone to a length that would have put our present situation out of both our powers."

" Sir," said I, " when you consider, that my utmost presumption could not make me hope for the honour you now seem to design me : that I was so hardly used, and had no prospect before me but dishonour, you will allow, that I should have seemed very little in earnest in my profession of honesty, not to endeavour to get away ; but yet I resolved not to think of marriage ; for I never saw the man I could love, till your goodness emboldened me to look up to you."

" I should, my dear Pamela," said he, " make a very ill compliment to my vanity, if I did not believe you : but justice calls upon me to say, that it is, some things considered, beyond my merit."

There was a sweet noble expression for your poor daughter, my dear father and mother ! And from my master too !

I was glad to hear this account of the interview between

Mr. Williams and himself; but I dared not to say so. I hope in time he will be reinstated in his good graces.

He was so good as to tell me, he had given orders for the chapel to be cleared. O how I look forward with inward joy, yet with fear and trembling!

FRIDAY.

About twelve o'clock came Sir Simon, his lady, and two daughters, and Lady Jones, and her sister-in-law, and Mr. Peters, with his spouse and niece. Mrs. Jewkes, who is more and more obliging, was much concerned I was not dressed in some of my best clothes, and made me many compliments.

They all walked into the garden before dinner; and, I understood, were so impatient to see me, that my master took them into the largest alcove, after they had walked two or three turns, and stept himself to me. " Come, my Pamela," said he, " the ladies can't be satisfied without seeing you, and I desire you'll come." I said, I was ashamed; but I would obey him. Said he, " The two young ladies are drest out in their best attire; but they make not such an appearance as my charming girl in this ordinary garb."—" Sir," said I, " shan't I follow you? For I can't bear you to do me so much honour."—" Well," said he, " I'll go before you." And he bid Mrs. Jewkes bring a bottle of sack, with some cake. So he went down to them.

This alcove fronts the longest gravel-walk in the garden, so that they saw me most of the way I came; and my master told me afterwards, with pleasure, all they said of me.

Will you forgive the little vain slut, your daughter, if I tell you all, as he was pleased to tell me? He said, 'spying me first, " There, ladies, comes my pretty rustic!"—They all, I saw, which abashed me, stood at the windows, and in the door-way, looking full at me.

My master told me, that Lady Jones said, " She is a charming creature, I see that at this distance." And Sir Simon, it seems, who had been a sad rake in his younger days, swore he never saw so easy an air, so fine a shape, and so graceful a presence. The Lady Darnford said, I was a sweet girl. And Mrs. Peters said very handsome things. Even the parson said, I should be the pride of the county. O dear Sirs! all this was owing to the light my good master's favour placed me in, which made me shine out in their eyes beyond my deserts. He said the young ladies blushed, and envied me.

When I came near, he saw me in a little confusion, and was so kind as to meet me : " Give me your hand," said he, " my good girl; you walk too fast." I did so, with a curtsey; and he, leading me up the steps of the alcove, in a most gentleman-like manner, presented me to the ladies, who all saluted me, and said they hoped to be better acquainted with me: and Lady Darnford was pleased to say, I should be the flower of their neighbourhood. Sir Simon said, "Good neighbour, by your leave;" and saluting me, added, "Now will I say, that I have kissed the loveliest maiden in England." But, for all this, methought I owed him a grudge for a tell-tale, though all had turned out so happily. Mr. Peters very gravely followed his example, and said, like a bishop, "God bless you, fair excellence!" Said Lady Jones, "Pray, dear Madam, sit down by me." They all sat down; but I said I would stand, if they pleased. "No, Pamela," said my master; "pray sit down with these good ladies, my neighbours :—They will indulge it to you, for *my* sake, till they know you better; and for *your own* when they are acquainted with you."—"Sir," said I, "I shall be proud to deserve their indulgence."

They all so gazed at me, I could not look up; for I think it one of the distinctions of persons of condition, and well-bred, to put bashful bodies out of countenance. "Well, Sir Simon," said my master, "what say you now to my pretty rustic?" He swore a great oath, that he should better know what to say, if he was as young as himself. Lady Darnford said, "You will never leave off, Sir Simon."

Said my master, "You are a little confused, my good girl, and out of *breath;* but I have told all my kind neighbours here a good deal of your story and your excellence."—"Yes," said Lady Darnford, "my dear neighbour, as I *will* call you; we that are here present have all heard of your uncommon story." —"Madam," said I, "you have then heard what must make your kind allowance for me very necessary."—"No," said Mrs. Peters, "we have heard what will always make you valued as an honour to our sex, and as a worthy pattern for all the young ladies in the county."—"You are very good, Madam," said I, "to make me able to look up, and to be thankful for this honour."

Mrs. Jewkes came in with the Canary, brought by Nan to the alcove, and some cake on a silver salver; and I said, "Mrs. Jewkes, let me assist you in serving the ladies with the cake."— I took the salver, and went round to the good company with it, ending with my master. The Lady Jones said, she never was served with such a grace, and it was giving me too much trouble. "O Madam," said I, "I hope my good master's favour will never

make me forget it is my duty to wait upon his friends."—
" *Master,* sweet one !" said Sir Simon, " I hope you won't
always call Mr. B. by that name, lest it should become a fashion
with all our ladies, through the county."—" I, Sir," said I,
" shall have many reasons to continue this style which cannot
affect your good ladies."

" Sir Simon," said Lady Jones, " you are very arch upon us :
but I see very well, that it will be the interest of all the gentlemen to bring their ladies into an intimacy with one, who can give
them such a good example."—" I am sure then, Madam," said I,
" it must be after I am polished and improved by the honour of
such an example as yours."

They were all very good and affable; and the young Lady
Darnford, who had wished to see me in this dress, said, " I beg
your pardon, dear Miss; but I had heard how sweetly this garb
became you, and was told the history of it; and begged that you
might favour us with your appearance in it."—" I am much
obliged to your Ladyship," said I, " that your kind prescription
was so agreeable to my choice."—" Why," said she, " *was* it
your choice then?—I am glad of that : though I am sure your
person must *give,* and not *take* ornament from any dress."

" You are very kind, Madam," said I : " but there will be the
less reason to fear I should forget my high obligations to the
kindest of gentlemen, when I can delight to show the humble
degree from which his goodness has raised me."—" My dear
Pamela," said he, " if you proceed at this rate, I must insist
upon your first seven days. You know what I mean."—" Sir,"
said I, " you are all goodness."

They drank a glass of sack each, and Sir Simon made me do so
too; saying, " It will be a reflection, I think, upon all the ladies,
if you do not as they do."—" No, Sir Simon," said I, " that
can't be, for the ladies' journey hither makes a glass of Canary
a proper cordial for them : but I won't refuse, because I will do
myself the honour of drinking good health to you, and all this
worthy company."

Said good Lady Darnford to my master, " I hope, Sir, we
shall have Mrs. Andrews's company at table." He said, very
obligingly, " Madam, it is her time now; and I will leave it to
her choice."—" If the good ladies, then, will forgive me, Sir,"
said I, " I had rather be excused." They all said, I must not
be excused. I begged I might. " Your reason for it, my dear
Pamela ? " said my master; " since the ladies request it, I
wish you would oblige them."—" Sir," replied I, " your goodness will make me, every day, worthier of the honour the ladies

do me; and when I can persuade myself that I am more worthy of it than at present, I shall with great joy embrace all the opportunities they will be pleased to give me."

Mrs. Peters whispered Lady Jones, as my master told me afterwards, "Did you ever see such excellence, prudence, and discretion?"—"Never in my life," said the other good lady. "She will adorn," she was pleased to say, "her distinction."—"Ay," says Mrs. Peters, "she would adorn any station in life."

My good master was highly delighted, generous gentleman as he is, with the favourable opinion of the ladies; and I took the more pleasure in it, because their favour seemed to lessen the disgrace of his stooping so much beneath himself.

Lady Darnford said, "We will not oppress you; though we could almost blame your too punctilious exactness; but if we excuse Mrs. Andrews from dinner, we must insist upon her company at the card-table, and at tea; for we shall pass the whole day with you, Sir, as we told you."—"What say you to that, Pamela?" said my master. "Sir," replied I; "whatever you and the ladies please, I will cheerfully do." They said I was very obliging. But Sir Simon rapt out an oath, and said, that *they* might dine together if they would; but *he* would dine with me, and nobody else. "For," said he, "I say, Sir, as Parson Williams said" (by which I found my master had told them the story), "you must not think you have chosen one that nobody can like but yourself."

The young ladies said, if I pleased, they would take a turn about the garden with me. I answered I would very gladly attend them; and so we three, and Lady Jones's sister-in-law, and Mr. Peters's niece, walked together. They were very affable, kind, and obliging; and we soon entered into a good deal of familiarity; and I found Miss Darnford a very agreeable person. Her sister was a little more on the reserve: and I afterwards heard, that, about a year before, she would fain have had my master make his addresses to her; but though Sir Simon is reckoned rich, she was not thought a sufficient fortune for him. And now, to have him look down so low as me, must be a sort of mortification to a poor young lady!—And I pitied her—Indeed I did!—I wish all young persons of my sex could be as happy as I am likely to be.

My master told me afterwards, that I left the other ladies, and Sir Simon and Mr. Peters, full of my praises; so that they could hardly talk of any thing else; one launching out upon my complexion, another upon my eyes, my hand, and in short (for you'll think me sadly proud), upon my whole person and behaviour; and they all magnified my readiness and obligingness in my answers, and the like: and I was glad of it, as I said, for my good master's sake, who seemed quite pleased and rejoiced. God bless him for his goodness to me!

Dinner not being ready, the young ladies proposed a tune upon the spinnet. I said, I believed it was not in tune. They said, they knew it was but a few months ago. "If it is," said I, "I wish I had known it.—Though indeed, ladies," added I, "since you know my story, I must own, that my mind has not been long in tune, to make use of it." So they would make me play upon it, and sing to it; which I did, a song my dear good lady made me learn, and used to be pleased with, and which she brought with her from Bath: and the ladies were much taken with the song, and were so kind as to approve my performance: and Miss Darn-ford was pleased to compliment me, that I had all the accomplish-ments of my sex. I said, I had had a good lady, in my master's mother, who had spared no pains nor cost to improve me. She said, she wished Mr. B. could be prevailed upon to give a ball on an approaching occasion, that we might have a dancing-match, &c. But I can't say I do, though I did not say so; for these occasions, I think, are too solemn for the *principals*, at least of our sex, to take part in, especially if they have the same thoughts of the solemnity that I have: for indeed, though I have before me a prospect of happiness, which may be envied by ladies of high rank, yet I must own to you, my dear parents, that I have some-thing very awful upon my mind, when I think of the matter; and shall more and more, as it draws nearer and nearer. This is the song:

Go, happy *paper*, gently steal,
　　And underneath her pillow lie;
There in *soft dreams*, my love reveal,
That love which I must still conceal,
　　And, wrapt in awful *silence*, die.

Should *flames* be doom'd thy hapless fate
　　To *atoms* Thou wouldst quickly turn,
My *pains* may bear a longer date;
For should I *live*, and should she *hate*,
　　In *endless* torments I should *burn*.

Tell fair Aurelia, she has charms
　　Might in a *Hermit* stir desire,
T' attain the heav'n that's in her arms,
I'd quit the *world's* alluring charms,
　　And to a *cell*, content, retire.

257

Of all that pleas'd my ravish'd eye,
  Her *beauty* should *supply* the place,
Bold *Raphael's strokes*, and *Titian's dye*,
Should but in vain presume to vie
  With her inimitable face.

No more I'd wish for Phoebus' *rays*,
  To gild the object of my *sight ;*
Much less the *taper's* fainting blaze,
Her *eyes* should measure out my *days ;*
  And when she *slept*, it should be night.

About four o'clock.—My master just came up to me, and said,
" If you should see Mr. Williams below, do you think, Pamela,
you should not be surprised ? "—" No, Sir," said I, " I hope not.
Why should I ? "—" Expect," said he, " a stranger, then, when
you come down to us in the parlour ; for the ladies are preparing themselves for the card-table, and they insist upon your
company."—" You have a mind, Sir," said I, " to try all my
courage."—" Why," said he, " does it want courage to see him ? "
—" No, Sir," said I, " not at all.   But I was grievously abashed
to see all those strange ladies and gentlemen ; and now to see Mr.
Williams before them, as some of them refused his application
for me, when I wanted to get away, it will a little shock me to see
them smile, in recollecting what has passed of that kind."—
" Well," said he, " guard your heart against surprises, though you
shall see, when you come down, a man that I can allow you to
love dearly, though hardly preferably to me."

This surprises me much.   I am afraid he begins to be jealous
of me.   What will become of me (for he looked very seriously)
if any turn should happen now ?—My heart aches ! I know not
what's the matter.   But I will go down as brisk as I can, that
nothing may be imputed to me.   Yet I wish this Mr. Williams
had not been there now, when they are all there ; because of their
fleers at him and me.   Otherwise I should be glad to see the poor
gentleman ; for indeed I think him a good man, and he has
suffered for my sake.

So I am sent for down to cards.   I'll go ; but wish I may
continue their good opinions of me ; for I shall be very awkward.
My master, by his serious question, and bidding me guard my
heart against surprises, though I should see, when I came down,
a man he can allow me to love dearly, though hardly better than
himself, has quite alarmed me, and made me sad !—I hope he
loves me !—But whether he does or not, I am in for it now, over
head and ears, I doubt, and can't help loving him ; 'tis a folly
to deny it.   I can't love any man preferably to him.   I shall soon
know what he means.

Now, my dear mother, I must write to *you*. Well might my good master say so mysteriously about guarding my heart against surprises. I never was so surprised; and never could see a man I loved so dearly! O, it was my dear, dear father, not Mr. Williams, who was below ready to receive and bless your daughter. Both my master and he enjoined me to write how the whole matter was, and my thoughts on this joyful occasion.

I will take the matter from the beginning that Providence directed his feet here, to this time, as I have had it from Mrs. Jewkes, my master, my father, the ladies, and my own heart and conduct, as far as I know of both; because they command it, and you will be pleased with my relation; and, as you know how I came by the connexion, will make one uniform relation of it.

It seems my dear father and you were so uneasy to know the truth of the story from Thomas, that, fearing I was betrayed and undone, he got leave of absence; and set out the day after Thomas was there; on Friday morning he got to the neighbouring town; and there he heard that the gentry in the neighbourhood were at my master's, at a great entertainment. He put on a clean shirt and neck-cloth he had in his pocket, at an alehouse there, and got shaved; and, after he had ate some bread and cheese, and drank a can of ale, he set out for my master's house, with a heavy heart, in fear of being brow-beaten. He had, it seems, asked at the alehouse what family the squire had down here, in hopes to hear something of me; they said, a housekeeper, two maids, and, at present, two coachmen, two grooms, a footman, and a helper. Was that all? he said. They told him, there was a young creature there, who *was*, or *was* to *be* his mistress, or somewhat of that nature; but had been his mother's waiting-maid. This, he said, grieved his heart, and confirmed his fears.

So he went on, and about three in the afternoon reached the gate; and, ringing there, Sir Simon's coachman came, when he asked for the housekeeper; though, from what I had written, in his heart he could not abide her. She sent for him, little thinking who he was, and asked him, in the hall, what was his business with her.—" Only, Madam," said he, " whether I cannot speak one word with the squire? "—" No, friend," said she, " he is engaged with several gentlemen and ladies." Said he,— " I have business with his honour of greater consequence to me than either life or death; " and tears stood in his eyes.

At which she went into the great parlour, where my master was talking very pleasantly with the ladies; and she said—" Sir, here is a good old man, who wants to see you on business of life and death, he says, and is very earnest."—"Aye," said he, " who can that be?—Let him stay in the little hall, and I'll soon come to him." They all stared; and Sir Simon said, " No more nor less, I dare say, my good friend, but a bastard child."—" If it is," said Lady Jones, " bring it in to us."—" I will," said he.

Mrs. Jewkes says, my master was much surprised when he saw who it was; and she much more, when my dear father said, " Good God! give me patience! but, great as you are, Sir, I must ask for my child!" and burst out into tears—(O what trouble have I given you both!)—My master said, taking him by the hand, " Don't be uneasy, Goodman Andrews: your daughter is in the way to be happy!" This alarmed my dear father, and he said, " What! then, is she dying!" And, trembling, could scarce stand. My master made him sit down by him, and said, " No, God be praised, she is very well: pray be comforted; I cannot bear to see you thus apprehensive; but she has written you a letter, to assure you that she has reason to be well satisfied and happy."

" Ah, Sir!" said he, " you told me once she was in London, waiting on a bishop's lady, but she was then a severe prisoner here."—" That's all over now, Goodman Andrews," said my master: " the times are altered: for now the sweet girl has taken me prisoner: and, in a few days, I shall put on the most agreeable fetters that ever man wore."

" O, Sir," said he, " you are too pleasant for my griefs. My heart's almost broken. But may I not see my poor child?"— " You shall presently," said he; " for she is coming down to us: and since you won't believe *me*, I hope you will *her*."

" I will ask you, good Sir," said he, " but one question, that I may know how to look upon her when I see her. Is she honest? Is she virtuous?"—" As the new-born babe, Mr. Andrews," said my good master; " and, in twelve days' time, I hope, will be my wife."

" O flatter me not, good your honour," said he, " it cannot be! it cannot be!—I fear you have deluded her with strange hopes; and would make me believe impossibilities!"—" Mrs. Jewkes," said he, " do you tell my dear Pamela's good father, when I go out, all you know of me, and your mistress that is to be. Make much of him, set out what you have, and make him drink a glass of what he likes best. If this be wine," added he, " fill me up a bumper."

She did so; and he took my father by the hand, and said, " Believe me, good man, and be easy; for I can't bear to see

260

you tortured in this cruel suspense : your dear daughter is the beloved of my soul. I am glad you are come ; for you'll see us all in the same story. Here's your dame's health ; and God bless you both for being the happy means of procuring for me so great a blessing ! " So he drank a bumper to this most obliging health.

" What do I hear ? It cannot surely be," said my father. " And your honour is too good, I hope, to mock a poor old man. This ugly story, Sir, of the bishop runs in my head.—But you say I shall see my dear child—and see her honest. If not, poor as I am, I would not own her."

My master bid Mrs. Jewkes not let me know yet that my father was come ; and went to the company, and said, " I have been agreeably surprised : here is honest old Goodman Andrews come full of grief to see his daughter : he fears she is seduced ; and tells me, good honest man, that, poor as he is, he will not own her if she be not virtuous."—" O," said they all with one voice almost, " Dear Sir ! shall we not see the good old man you have so praised for his plain good sense and honest heart ? "— " If," said he, " I thought Pamela would not be too much affected with the surprise, I would make you all witness to their first interview ; for never did daughter love a father, or father a daughter, as they two do one another." Miss Darnford, and all the ladies and gentlemen, begged it might be so. But was not this very cruel ? For well might they think I should not support myself in such an agreeable surprise.

He said kindly—" I only fear, that the dear girl may be too much affected."—" Oh," said Lady Darnford, " we'll all help to keep up her spirits." Says he, " I'll go up and prepare her ; but won't tell her of it." So he came up to me, as I have said, and amused me about Mr. Williams, to half prepare me for some surprise ; though that could not have been any thing to this ; and he left me, as I said, in that suspense, at his mysterious words, saying, he would send to me, when they were going to cards.

My master went from me to my father, and asked if he had eaten any thing. " No," said Mrs. Jewkes, " the good man's heart's so full, he cannot eat, nor do anything, till he has seen his dear daughter."—" That shall soon be," said my master. " I will have you come in with me ; for she is going to sit down with my guests, to a game at quadrille ! and I will send for her down."—" O, Sir," said my father, " don't, don't let me ; I am not fit to appear before your guests ; let me see my daughter by myself, I beseech you." Said he, " They all know your

261

honest character, Goodman Andrews, and long to see you, for Pamela's sake."

He took my father by the hand, and led him in, against his will, to the company. They were all very good. My master kindly said, " Ladies and gentlemen, I present to you one of the honestest men in England, my good Pamela's father." Mr. Peters went to him, and took him by the hand, and said, " We are all glad to see you, Sir; you are the happiest man in the world, in a daughter whom we never saw before to-day, but cannot enough admire."

Said my master, " This gentleman, Goodman Andrews, is the minister of the parish; but not young enough for Mr. Williams." This airy expression, my poor father said, made him fear that all was a jest. Sir Simon also took him by the hand and said, " Aye, you have a sweet daughter, Honesty; we are all in love with her." And the ladies came and said very fine things : Lady Darnford particularly, that he might think himself the happiest man in England, in such a daughter. " If and please you, Madam," said he, " she be but virtuous, 'tis all in all : for all the rest is accident. But I doubt his honour *has been too much upon the jest with me.*"—" No," said Mrs. Peters, " we are all witnesses that he intends very honourably by her."—" It's some comfort," said he, and wiped his eyes, " that such good ladies say so—But I wish I could see her."

They would have had him sit down by them, but he would only sit behind the door in the corner of the room, so that, entering, one could not see him; because the door opened against him, and almost hid him. The ladies all sat down; and my master said, " Desire Mrs. Jewkes to step up, and tell Mrs. Andrews the ladies wait for her." So down I came.

Miss Darnford rose, and met me at the door, and said, " Well, Miss Andrews, we long for your company." I did not see my dear father; and it seems his heart was too full to speak; and he got up, and sat down, three or four times successively, unable to come to me, or to say anything. The ladies looked that way; but I would not, supposing it was Mr. Williams. They made me sit down between Lady Darnford and Lady Jones; and asked me what I would play at. I said, " At what your ladyships please." I wondered to see them smile, and look upon me, and to that corner of the room; but I was afraid of looking, for fear of seeing Mr. Williams; though my face was that way too, and the table before me.

Said my master, " Did you send your letter away to the post-house, my good girl, for your father? "—" To be sure, Sir," said

I, "I did not forget that: I took the liberty to desire Mr. Thomas to carry it."—"What," said he, "I wonder will the good old couple say to it?"—"O Sir," said I, "your goodness will be a cordial to their dear honest hearts!" At that, my dear father, not able to contain himself, nor yet to stir from the place, gushed out into a flood of tears, which he, good soul, had been struggling with, it seems; and cried out, "Oh, my dear child!"

I knew the voice, and lifting up my eyes, saw my father. I gave a spring, and overturned the table, without regard to the company, and threw myself at his feet: "O my father! my father!" said I; "can it be? Is it you? Yes, it is!—O bless your happy"—daughter! I would have said, and down I sunk.

My master seemed concerned. "I feared," said he, "that the surprise would be too much for her spirits;" and all the ladies ran to me, and made me drink a glass of water; and I found myself encircled in the arms of my dearest father. "Oh, tell me," said I, "every thing. How long have you been here?—When did you come? How does my honoured mother?" And half a dozen questions more, before he could answer one.

They permitted me to retire with my father; and then I poured forth all my vows, and thanksgivings to God, for this additional blessing; and confirmed all my master's goodness to his scarce-believing amazement. We kneeled together, blessing God, and one another, for several ecstatic minutes; and my master coming in soon after, my dear father said, "O Sir, what a change in this! May God reward and bless you, both in this world and the next."

"May God bless us all!" said he; "but how does my sweet girl? I have been in pain for you.—I am sorry I did not apprise you beforehand."—"O Sir," said I, "it was you; and all you do must be good. But this was a blessing so unexpected!"

"Well," said he, "you have given pain to all the company. They will be glad to see you when you can; for you have spoiled all their diversion; and still painfully delighted them. Mr Andrews," added he, "do you make this house your own; and the longer you stay, the more welcome you'll be.—After you have a little composed yourself, my dear girl, step in to us again. I am glad to see you so well already." And so he left us.

"See you, my dear father," said I, "what goodness there is in this once naughty master? O pray for him! and for me that I may deserve it!"

"How long has this happy change been wrought, my dear

child ? "—" O," said I, " several days ! I have written down every thing ; and you'll see, from the depth of misery, what God has done for me."

" Blessed be his name ! " said he ; " but, do you say, he will marry you ? Can such a brave gentleman make a lady of the child of such a poor man as I ? O the Divine goodness ! How will your poor dear mother support these happy tidings ? I will set out to-morrow, to acquaint her with them ; for I am but half happy, till the dear good woman shares them with me !— To be sure, my child, we ought to go into some far country, to hide ourselves, that we may not disgrace you by our poverty."

" O my dear father," said I, " now you are unkind for the first time. Your poverty has been my glory, and my riches. I ever thought it an honour, rather than a disgrace, because you were always so honest, that your child might well boast of such a parentage ! "

In this manner, my dear mother, did we pass the happy moments, till Miss Darnford came to me and said, " How do you, dear Madam ? I rejoice to see you so well ! Pray let us have your company—and yours too, good Mr. Andrews," taking his hand. This was very obliging, I told her. We went to the great parlour ; and my master made my father sit down by him, and drink a glass of wine with him. Mean time, I made my excuses to the ladies, as well as I could, which they readily granted me. But Sir Simon, after his comical manner, put his hands on my shoulders : " Let me see," said he, " where your wings grow : for I never saw any body fly like you.—Why," said he, " you have broken Lady Jones's shins with the table. Shew her else, Madam."

His pleasantry made them laugh. I said, I was very sorry for my extravagancy ; and if it had not been my master's doings, I should have said, it was a fault to permit me to be surprised, and put out of myself before such good company. They said, all was very excusable ; and they were glad I suffered no more by it.

They were so kind as to excuse me at cards, and played by themselves ; and I went by my master's command, and sat on the other side, in the happiest place I ever was blest with, between two of the dearest men in the world to me, each holding one of my hands ;—my father, every now-and-then, with tears, lifting up his eyes, and saying, " Could I ever have hoped this ! "

I asked him, if he had been so kind as to bring the papers with him ? He said he had, and looked at me, as who should say, "Must I give them to you now?" I said, "Yes, if he pleased." Pulling them from his pocket, I stood up, and, with my best duty, gave them to my master.—"Thank you, Pamela," said he; "your father shall take all with him, to see what a sad fellow I have been, as well as the present happier alteration. But I must have all again, for the writer's sake."

The ladies and gentlemen would make me govern the tea-table, whatever I could do; and Abraham attended me, to serve the company. My master and my father sat together, and drank a glass or two of wine instead of tea, and Sir Simon joked with my master, saying, "I warrant you would not be such a woman's man, as to drink tea with the ladies. But your time's coming, and, I doubt not, you'll be made as comfortable as I."

My master was very urgent with them to stay supper; and at last they complied, on condition that I would grace the table, as they were pleased to call it. I begged to be excused. My master said, "Don't be excused, Pamela, since the ladies desire it: besides," said he, "we won't part with your father; so you may as well stay with us."

I hoped my father and I might sup by ourselves, or only with Mrs. Jewkes. But Miss Darnford, a most obliging young lady, said, "Indeed we will not part with you."

When supper was brought in, Lady Darnford took me by the hand, and said to my master, "Sir, by your leave;" and would have placed me at the upper end of the table. "Pray, Madam," said I, "excuse me; I cannot do it."—"Pamela," said my master, to the great delight of my father, as I saw by his looks, "oblige Lady Darnford, since she desires it. It is but a little before your time."

"Dear, good Sir," said I, "pray don't command it! Let me sit by my father, pray!"—"Why," said Sir Simon, "here's ado indeed! Sit down at the upper end, as you should do, and your father shall sit by you." This put my dear father upon difficulties. And my master said, "Come, I'll place you all:" and so put Lady Darnford at the upper end, Lady Jones at her right hand, and Mrs. Peters on the other; placing me between the two young ladies; but very genteely put Miss Darnford below her younger sister; saying, "Come, Miss, I put you here, because you shall edge in this little cuckow; for I notice, with pleasure, your goodness to her; besides, all you very young ladies should sit together." This pleased both sisters; for had the youngest been put there, it might have piqued her, as matters were once, to be placed below me; whereas Miss Darnford giving place to her youngest sister, made it less odd she should to me;

especially with that handsome turn of the dear man, as if I was a cuckow, and to be edged in.

My master kindly said, " Come, Mr. Andrews, you and I will sit together," taking his place at the bottom of the table, and setting my father on his right hand; and Sir Simon would sit on his left. " For," said he, " parson, I think the petticoats should be together: so do you sit down by that lady," (his sister.) A boiled turkey standing by me, my master said, " Cut up that turkey, Pamela, if not too strong work for you, that Lady Darnford may have less trouble." So I carved it in a trice, and helped the ladies. Miss Darnford said, " I would give something to be so dexterous a carver."—" O madam," said I, " my late good lady always made me do these things, when she entertained her female friends, on particular days."

" Aye," said my master, " I remember my poor mother would often say, if I or any body at table happened to be a little out in carving, ' I'll send up for my Pamela, to shew you how to carve.' " Said Lady Jones, " Mrs. Andrews has every accomplishment of her sex. She is quite wonderful for her years." Miss Darnford said, " I can tell you, Madam, she plays sweetly upon the spinnet, and as sweetly sings to it; for she has a fine voice."—" Foolish," said Sir Simon : " who, that hears her speak, knows not that ! And who, that sees her fingers, believes not that they were made to touch any key?—O parson ! " said he, " 'tis well you're by, or I should have had a blush from the ladies."—" I hope not, Sir Simon," said Lady Jones; " for a gentleman of your politeness would not say any thing that would make ladies blush."—" No, no," said he, " not for the world : but if I had, it would have been as the poet says :

" They blush, because they understand."

When the company went away, Lady Darnford, Lady Jones, and Mrs. Peters, severally invited my master, and me with him, to their houses; and begged he would permit me, at least, to come before we left those parts. And they said, " We hope when the happy knot is tied, you will induce Mr. B. to reside more among us."—" We were always glad," said Lady Darnford, " when he was here; but now we shall have double reason." O how grateful were these things to the ears of my good father !

When the company was gone, my master asked my father if he smoked. He answered, " No." He made us both sit down by him; and said, " I have been telling this sweet girl, that in fourteen days, and two of them are gone, she must fix on one to make me happy. I have left it to her to choose either one of the first or last seven." My father held up his hands and eyes; "God bless your honour," said he, "is all I can say!"—"Now, Pamela," said my master, taking my hand, "don't let a little wrong-timed bashfulness take place, without any other reason, because I should be glad to go to Bedfordshire as soon as I could; and I would not return till I carry my servants there a mistress, who should assist me to repair the mischiefs she has made in it."

I could not look up for confusion. And my father said, "My dear child, I need not, I am sure, prompt your obedience in whatever will most oblige so good a gentleman."—"What says my Pamela?" said my master: "she does not use to be at a loss for expression."—"Sir," said I, "were I too sudden, it would seem I doubted whether you would hold in your mind, and was not willing to give you time to reflect; yet, to be sure, I ought to resign myself implicitly to your will."

Said he, "I want not time for reflection; for I have often told you, and that long ago, I could not live without you: my pride of condition made me both tempt and terrify you to other terms; but your virtue was proof against all temptations, and was not to be awed by terrors: wherefore, as I could not conquer my passion for you, I corrected myself, and resolved, since you would not be mine, upon my terms, you should upon your own: and now I desire you not on any other, I assure you: and I think the sooner it is done the better.—What say you, Mr. Andrews?"—"Sir," said he, "there is so much goodness on your side, and, blessed be God! so much prudence on my daughter's, that I must be quite silent. But when it is done, I and my poor wife shall have nothing to do, but to pray for you both, and so look back with wonder and joy, on the ways of Providence."

"This," said my master, "is Friday night: and suppose, my girl, it be next Monday, Tuesday, Wednesday, or Thursday morning?—Say, my Pamela."

"Will you, Sir," said I, "excuse me till to-morrow for an answer?"—"I will," said he, and touched the bell, and called for Mrs. Jewkes. "Where," said he, "does Mr. Andrews lie to-night? You'll take care of him; he's a very good man; and will bring a blessing upon every house he sets his foot in."

My dear father wept for joy; and I could not refrain keeping company. My master, saluting me, bid us good night, and retired. I waited upon my dear father, and was so full of prattle, of my master's goodness, and my future prospects, that I believed afterwards I was turned all into tongue: but he indulged me, and was transported with joy; and went to bed, dreaming of

Jacob's ladder, and angels ascending and descending, to bless him and his daughter.

I arose early in the morning; but found my father was up, and gone to walk in the garden; I went to him, and with what delight and thankfulness did we go over every scene of it, which had before been so dreadful to me ! The fish-pond, the back-door, and every place : O what reason had we for thankfulness and gratitude !

About seven o'clock my good master joined us, in his morning gown and slippers; and looking a little heavy, I said, " Sir, I fear you had not good rest last night."—" That is your fault, Pamela," said he : " after leaving you, I must needs look into your papers, and could not but read them through; and so 'twas three o'clock before I went to sleep."—" I wish, Sir," said I, " you had had better entertainment."—" The worst part of it," said he, " was what I brought upon myself; and you have not spared me."—" Sir——," said I. He, interrupting me, said, " Well, I forgive you. You had too much reason for it. But I find, that had you got away, you would soon have been Williams's wife."—" Indeed, Sir," said I, " I had no notion of it, or of being any body's."—" I believe so," said he, " but it must have come as a thing of course; and I see your father was for it."—" Sir," said he, " I little thought of the honour your goodness would confer upon her; and that would have been a match far above what we could do for her. But when I found she was not for it, I resolved not to urge her; but to leave all to her own prudence."

" I see," said he, " all was sincere, honest, and open; I speak of it as a thing, if done, not well to be avoided; and I am satisfied. But," said he, " I must observe, as I have a hundred times, with admiration, what a prodigious memory, and easy and happy manner of narrative, this excellent girl has ! And though she is full of her pretty tricks and artifices, to escape the snares I laid for her, yet all is innocent, lovely, and uniformly beautiful. You are exceedingly happy in a daughter; and I hope I shall be so in a wife."—" Or," said my father, " may she not have that honour."—" I fear it not," said he; " and I hope I shall deserve it of her."

" But, Pamela," said my master, " I am sorry to find, in some parts of your journal, that Mrs. Jewkes carried her orders a little too far; and I the more take notice of it, because you have not complained of her behaviour, as she might expect for some parts of it; though a great deal was occasioned by my strict orders. But she had the insolence to strike my girl, I find."—" Sir," said I, " I was a little provoking, I believe; but as we forgave one another, I was the less entitled to complain of her."

" Well," said he, " you are very good; but if you have any particular resentment, I will indulge it so far as that she shall hereafter have nothing to do where you are."—" Sir," said I, " you are so kind that I ought to forgive every body; and when I see that my happiness is brought about by the very means I once thought my greatest grievance, I ought to bless those means, and forgive all that was disagreeable to me at the same time, for the great good that hath issued from it."—" That," said he, kissing me, " is sweetly considered; and it shall be my part to make you amends for what you have suffered, that you may still think lighter of the one, and have cause to rejoice in the other."

My dear father's heart was full; and he said, with his hands folded, and lifted up, " Pray, Sir, let me go—let me go—to my dear wife, and tell her all these blessed things, while my heart holds; for it is ready to burst with joy."—" Good man," said my master, " I love to hear this honest heart of yours speaking at your lips. I enjoin you, Pamela, to continue your relation, as you have opportunity; and though your father be here, write to your mother, that this wondrous story be perfect, and we, your friends, may read and admire you more and more."—" Aye, pray, pray do, my child," said my father. And this is the reason that I write on, my dear mother, when I thought not to do it, because my father could tell you all that passed while he was here.

My master took notice of my psalm, and was pleased to commend it: he said that I had very charitably turned the last verses, which, in the original, were full of heavy curses, to a wish that proved I was not of an implacable disposition; though my then usage might have excused it, if I had. " But," said he, " I think you shall sing it to me, to-morrow.

" After breakfast," added he, " if you have no objection, Pamela, we'll take an airing together; and it shall be in the coach, because we'll have your father's company." He would have excused himself; but my master would have it so; but he was much ashamed because of the meanness of his appearance.

My master would make us both breakfast with him on chocolate; and he said, " I would have you, Pamela, begin to dress as you used to do; for now, at least, you may call your *two other bundles* your own; and if you want any thing against the approaching occasion, private as I design it, I'll send to Lincoln for it, by a special messenger." I said, " My good lady's bounty, and his own, had set me much above my degree, and I had very good things of all sorts; and I did not desire any other, because I would not excite the censure of the ladies." That would be a different thing, he was pleased to say, when he publicly owned his nuptials, after we came to the other house. But, at present, if I were satisfied, he would not make words with me.

" I hope, Mr. Andrews," said he to my father, " you'll not leave us till you see the affair over, and then you'll be *sure* I mean honourably; besides, Pamela will be induced to set the day sooner."—" Oh, Sir," said he, " I bless God, I have no reason to doubt your meaning honourably; and I hope you'll excuse me if I set out on Monday morning very early, to my dear wife, to make her as happy as I am."

" Why, Pamela," says my good master, " may it not be performed on Tuesday? And then your father, may-be, will stay. I should have been glad to have had it to-morrow," added he, " but I have sent Monsieur Colbrand for a licence, that you may have no scruples unanswered; and he can't very well be back before to-morrow night, or Monday morning."

This was most agreeable news. I said, " Sir, I know my dear father will want to be at home; and as you was so good as to give me a fortnight from last Thursday, I should be glad if you would indulge me still to some day in the second seven."

" Well," said he, " I will not be too urgent; but the sooner you fix, the better.—Mr. Andrews, we must leave something to these Jephtha's daughters, in these cases. I suppose the little bashful folly, which, in the happiest circumstances, may give a kind of regret to quit the maiden state, and an awkwardness at the entrance into a new one, is a reason with Pamela : and so she shall name her day."—" Sir," said he, " you are all goodness."

I went up soon after, and new dressed myself, taking possession, in a happy moment, I hope, of my *two bundles*, as my master was pleased to call them (alluding to my former division of those good things my lady and himself bestowed upon me); and put on fine linen, silk shoes, and fine white cotton stockings, a fine quilted coat, a delicate green Mantua silk gown and coat, a French necklace, a laced cambric handkerchief, and clean gloves; and, taking my fan, I, like a little proud hussy, looked in the glass, and thought myself a gentlewoman once more;

but I forgot not to return due thanks, for being able to put on this dress with so much comfort.

Mrs. Jewkes would help to dress me; and complimented me highly, saying, that I now looked like her lady indeed; and as, she said, the little chapel was ready, and divine service would be read in it to-morrow, she wished the happy knot might then be tied. Said she, " Have you not seen the chapel, Madam, since it has been cleaned out? "—" No," said I : " but are we to have service in it to-morrow, do you say? I am glad of that; for I have been a sad heathen lately, sore against my will ! —But who is to officiate? "—" Somebody," replied she, " Mr. Peters will send."—" You tell me very good news," said I, " Mrs. Jewkes : I hope it will never be a lumber-room again."— " Aye," said she, " I can tell you more good news; for the two Miss Darnfords and Lady Jones, are to be here at the opening of it; and will stay and dine with you."—" My master," said I, " has not told me that."—" You must alter your style, Madam," said she; " it must not be *master* now sure ! "—" O," returned I, " that is a language I shall never forget : he shall always be my master; and I shall think myself more and more his servant."

My poor father did not know I went up to dress myself; and he said his heart misgave him, when he saw me first, for fear I was made a fool of, and that here was some fine lady who was to be my master's true wife. He stood in admiration, and said, " O my dear child, how well will you become your happy condition. Why you look like a lady already ! "—" I hope, my dear father," said I, " I shall always be your dutiful daughter, whatever my condition be."

My master sent me word he was ready; and, when he saw me, said, " Dress as you will, Pamela, you're a charming girl; " and so handed me to the coach, and would make my father and me sit both on the foreside, and sat himself over against me, and bid the coachman drive to the meadow; that is, where he once met Mr. Williams.

The conversation, as we went, was most agreeable to me and my dear father : and he more and more exceeded in goodness and generosity. While I was gone up to dress, he had presented my father with twenty guineas, desiring him to buy himself and my mother such apparel as they should think proper; but I knew not this till after we came home, my father having no opportunity to tell me of it.

He was pleased to inform me of the chapel being in tolerable order : and said, it looked very well, and against he came down next, it should be all new white-washed, painted, and lined; and a new pulpit-cloth, cushion, desk, &c., and be kept in order for the future. He told me the two Miss Darnfords and Lady Jones would dine with him on Sunday: "With their servants and mine," said he, "we shall make a tolerable congregation. And," added he, "have I not well contrived to shew you that the chapel is really a little house of God, and has been consecrated before we solemnize our nuptials in it?"—"O, Sir," replied I, "your goodness to me is 'inexpressible!'"—"Mr. Peters," said he, "offered to officiate in it, but would not stay dinner, because he has company at his own house; and so I intend that divine service shall be performed by one, to whom I shall make some yearly allowance, as a sort of chaplain. You look serious, Pamela," added he: "I know you think of your friend Williams." —"Indeed, Sir," said I, "if you won't be angry, I did, poor man! I am sorry I have been the cause of his disobliging you."

On coming to the meadow, where the gentry sometimes walk, the coach stopt, and my master alighting, led me to the brook-side, a very pretty summer walk. He asked my father, if he chose to walk out, or go on in the coach to the further end? He, poor man, chose to go on in it, for fear, he said, any gentry should be walking there; and he told me, he was most of the way upon his knees in the coach, thanking God for his gracious mercies; and begging a blessing upon my good master and me.

I was quite astonished, when we came into the shady walk, to see Mr. Williams. "See there," said my master, "poor Williams taking his solitary walk again, with his book." It seems, it was so contrived; for Mr. Peters had been, as I since find, desired to tell him to be in that walk at such an hour in the morning.

"So, old acquaintance," said my master, "again have I met you in this place? What book are you now reading?" He said, it was Boileau's Lutrin. Said my master, "You see I have brought with me my little fugitive, that would have been: while you are perfecting yourself in French, I am trying to learn English; and hope soon to be master of it."

"Mine, Sir," said he, "is a very beautiful piece of French: but your English has no equal."

"You are very polite, Mr. Williams," said my master; "and he that does not think as you do, deserves no share in her.— Pamela," added he, very generously, "why so strange, where you was once so familiar? I do assure you both, I meant not by this interview to insult Mr. Williams, or confound you." Then I said, "Mr. Williams, I am very glad to see you well;

272

and though the generous favour of my good master has happily changed the scene, since our last interview, I am very glad of an opportunity to acknowledge, with gratitude, your good intentions, not so much to serve me, as *me*, but as a person that then had great reason to believe herself in distress.—And I hope, Sir," added I to my master, " your goodness will permit me to say this."

" You, Pamela," said he, " may make what acknowledgments you please to Mr. Williams's good intentions; and I would have you speak as you think; but I do not apprehend myself to be quite so much obliged to those intentions."

" Sir," said Mr. Williams, " I beg leave to say, I knew that, by education, you was no libertine; nor had I reason to think you so by inclination : and when you came to reflect, I hoped you would not be displeased with me. And this was no small motive with me to do at first as I did."

" Aye, but, Mr. Williams," said my master, " could you think, I should have had reason to thank you, if, loving one person above all her sex, you had robbed me of her, and married her yourself?—And," said he, " you are to consider that she was an old acquaintance of mine, but quite a new one to you; that I had sent her down to my own house, for better securing her; and that you, who had access to my house, could not effect your purpose, without being guilty, in some sort, of a breach of the laws of hospitality and friendship. As to my designs upon her, I own they had not the best appearance : but still I was not answerable to Mr. Williams for these; much less could you be excused to invade a property so very dear to me, and to endeavour to gain an interest in her affections, when you could not be certain that matters would not turn out as they have actually done."

" I own," said he, " some parts of my conduct seem exceptionable, as you state it. But, Sir, I am but a young man. I meant no harm. I had no interest, I am sure, to incur your displeasure; and when you think of everything, the inimitable graces of person, and perfections of mind, that adorn this excellent lady (so he called me), your generosity will allow something as an extenuation of a fault which your anger would not permit as an excuse."

" I have done," said my master; " nor did I meet you here to be angry with you. Pamela knew not that she should see you; and, as you are both present, I would ask you, Mr. Williams, if, now you know my honourable designs towards this good girl, you could really be *almost*, I will not say *quite*, as well pleased with the friendship of my wife as with the favour of Mrs. Andrews?"

"Sir," said he, "I will answer you truly. I think I could have preferred with her, any condition that befel me, had I considered only *myself*. But, Sir, I was very far from having any encouragement to expect her *favour ;* and I had much more reason to believe, that, if she could have hoped for your goodness, her heart would have been too much pre-engaged to think of any body else. And give me leave further to say, Sir, that, though I tell you sincerely my thoughts, were I only to consider *myself :* yet when I consider *her good,* and *her merit,* I should be highly ungenerous, were it put to my *choice,* if I could not wish her in a condition so much superior to what I could raise her to, and so very answerable to her merit."

"Pamela," said my master, "you are obliged to Mr. Williams, and ought to thank him : he has distinguished well. But as for *me,* who might have lost you by his means, I am glad it was not left to his *choice.*—Mr. Williams," added he, "I give you Pamela's hand, because I know it will be pleasing to her, in token of her friendship and esteem for you; and I give you mine, that I will not be your enemy : but yet I must say, that I think I owe this proper manner of your thinking more to your disappointment, than to the generosity you talk of."

Mr. Williams kissed my hand; and my master said, "Sir, you will go home and dine with me, and I'll shew you my little chapel;—and, do you, Pamela, look upon yourself at liberty to number Mr. Williams in the list of your friends."

How generous, how noble, was this ! Mr. Williams had tears of pleasure in his eyes; I was silent : but Mr. Williams said, "Sir, I shall be taught by your generosity, to think myself inexcusably wrong, in all that could give you offence; and my future life shall shew my respectful gratitude."

We walked on till we came to the coach, where was my dear father. "Pamela," said my master, "tell Mr. Williams who that good man is."—"O, Mr. Williams !" said I, "it is my dear father : " and my master added, "one of the honestest men in England : Pamela owes every thing that she is to be, as well as her being, to him : for, I think, she would not have brought me to this; nor made so great resistance, but for the good lessons, and religious education, she had inbibed from him."

Mr. Williams said, taking my father's hand, "You see, good Mr. Andrews, with inexpressible pleasure, no doubt, the fruits of your pious care : and will, with your beloved daughter, soon reap its happy effects."—"I am overcome," said my dear

274

father, "with his honour's goodness: I can only say, I bless *God*, and bless *him*."

Mr. Williams and I being nearer the coach than my master, and he offering to draw back to give way to him, he kindly said, "Pray, Mr. Williams, oblige Pamela with your hand, and step in yourself." He bowed, and took my hand; and my master made him step in, and sit next me, all that ever he could do; and sat himself over against him, next my father, who sat against me.

And he said, "Mr. Andrews, I told you yesterday, that the divine you saw was *not* Mr. Williams: I now tell you this gentleman *is;* and though I have been telling him, I think not *myself* obliged to his intentions, yet I will own that Pamela and *you* are; and though I won't promise to love him, I would have you."

"Sir," said Mr. Williams, "you have a way of overcoming, which all my reading scarcely affords an instance of; and it is the more noble, as it is on this side, as I presume, of the happy ceremony; which, great as your fortune is, will lay you under an obligation to so much virtue and beauty, when the lady becomes yours; for you will then have a treasure that princes might envy you."

Said my generous master, (God bless him!) "Mr. Williams, it is impossible that you and I should long live at variance, when our sentiments so well agree on subjects the most material."

I was quite confounded; and my master seeing it, took my hand, and said, "Look up, my good girl, and collect yourself. Don't injure Mr. Williams and me so much, as to think we are capping compliments, as we used to do verses at school. I dare answer for us both, that we say not a syllable we don't think."

"O, Sir," said I, "how unequal am I to all this goodness! Every moment that passes adds to the weight of the obligations you oppress me with."

"Think not too much of that," said he, most generously. "Mr Williams's compliments to you have great advantage of mine: for though equally sincere, I have much to say, and to do, to compensate the sufferings I have made you undergo; and at last, must sit down dissatisfied, because those will never be balanced by all I can do for you."

He saw my dear father quite unable to support these affecting instances of his goodness and he let go my hand, to take his: and said, seeing his tears, "I wonder not, my dear Pamela's father, that your honest heart springs thus to your eyes, to

275

see all her trials at an end. I will not pretend to say, that I had formerly either power or will to act thus; but since I began to resolve on the change you see, I have reaped so much pleasure in it, that my own *interest* will keep me steady: for, till within these few days, I knew not what it was to be happy."

Poor Mr. Williams, with tears of joy in his eyes, said, " How happily, Sir, have you been touched by the Divine grace before you have been hurried into the commission of sins that the deepest penitence could hardly have atoned for! God has enabled you to stop short of the evil; and you have nothing to do but to rejoice in the good, which now will be doubly so, because you can receive it without the least inward reproach."

" You do well," said he, " to remind me, that I owe all this to the grace of God. I bless him for it; and I thank this good man for his excellent lessons to his daughter: and I hope, from *her* good example, and *your* friendship, Mr. Williams, in time to be half as good as my tutoress: and that," said he, " I believe you'll own, will make me, without disparagement to any man, the best fox-hunter in England." Mr. Williams was going to speak; and he said, " You put on so grave a look, Mr. Williams, that, I believe what I have said, with you practical good folks, is liable to exception: but I see we are become quite brave: and we must not be too serious neither."

What a happy creature, my dear mother, is your Pamela !— O may my thankful heart, and my good use of the blessings before me, continue this delightful prospect to a long date, for the sake of the dear good gentleman, who thus becomes the happy instrument in the hand of Providence to bless all he smiles upon ! To be sure, I shall never enough acknowledge the value he is pleased to express for my unworthiness, in that he has prevented my wishes, and, unasked, sought the occasion of being reconciled to a good man, who, for my sake, had incurred his displeasure ; and whose name he could not, a few days before, permit to pass through my lips !—But see the wonderful ways of Providence ! The very things I most dreaded his seeing or knowing, the contents of my papers, have, as I hope, satisfied all his scruples, and been a means to promote my happiness.

Henceforth let not us poor short-sighted mortals pretend to rely on our own wisdom; or vainly think, that we are absolutely to direct for ourselves. I have great reason to say, that, when I was most disappointed, I was nearer my happiness : for had I made my escape, which was so often my chief point in view, and what I placed my heart upon, I had escaped the blessings now before me, and fallen, perhaps, headlong into the miseries I would have avoided. And yet after all, it was necessary I should take the steps I did, to bring on this wonderful turn: O the unsearchable wisdom of God!—And how much ought I to adore the Divine goodness, and humble myself, who am made a poor instrument, as I hope, not only to magnify his graciousness to this gentleman and myself, but also to dispense benefits to others! Which God of his mercy grant!

In this agreeable manner did we pass the time in our second happy tour; and I thought Mrs. Jewkes would have sunk into the ground, when she saw Mr. Williams brought in the coach with us, and treated so kindly. We dined together, in a most pleasant, easy, and frank manner; and I found I needed not, from my master's generosity, to be under any restraint, as to my conduct to this good clergyman: for he, when he fancied me reserved, moved me to be free, and often called upon me to help my father and Mr. Williams: and seemed to take delight in seeing me carve, as he does in every thing I do.

After dinner we went and looked into the chapel, which is a very decent one; and when finished, as he designs it against his next coming down, will be a very pretty place. My heart, my dear mother, on first entering, throbbed with awful joy, at the thoughts of the solemnity, which I hope, will in a few days be performed here. When I came up towards the little pretty altar-piece, while they were admiring a communion-picture, I gently stept into a corner, out of sight, and poured out my soul to God, on my knees, in supplication and thankfulness, that, after having been so long absent from divine service, the first time I entered into a house dedicated to his honour, should be with such blessed prospects before me; and begging of God to continue me humble, and make me worthy of his mercies; and that he would be pleased to bless the *next* author of my happiness, my good master.

I heard my master say, "Where's Pamela?" So I broke off sooner than I would, and went up to him.

He said, "Mr. Williams, I hope I have not so offended you by my past conduct (for I ought to be ashamed of it) that you will refuse to officiate, and give us your instructions here to-morrow. Mr. Peters was so kind, for the first time to offer it; but I knew it would be inconvenient for him; and, besides, I was willing to make this request to you an introduction to our reconciliation."

"Sir," said he, "most willingly, and most gratefully, will I obey you: though if you expect a discourse, I am wholly unprepared for the occasion."—"I would not have it," replied he, " pointed to any particular occasion; but if you have one upon the text—*There is more joy in heaven over one sinner that repenteth, than over ninety-nine just persons that need no repentance,* and if it make me not such a sad fellow as to be pointed at by mine and the ladies' servants we shall have here, I shall be well content. 'Tis a general subject," added he, " makes me speak of that; but any one you please will do : for you cannot make a bad choice, I am sure."

" Sir," said he, " I have one upon that text : but I am ready to think that a thanksgiving one, which I made on a great mercy to myself, if I may be permitted to make my own acknowledgements of your favour the subject of a discourse, will be suitable to my grateful sentiments. It is on the text—*Now lettest thou thy servant depart in peace; for mine eyes have seen thy salvation.*"

" That text," said I, " will be a very suitable one for me."—" Not so, Pamela," said my master; " because I don't let you *depart in peace;* but I hope you will stay *here* with *content.*"

" O but, Sir," said I, " I have seen *God's salvation!* and if any body ever had reason, I have, to say, with the blessed Virgin —*My soul doth magnify the Lord; for he hath regarded the low estate of his handmaiden, and exalted one of low degree.*"

Said my good father, " I am sure, if there were time for it, the book of *Ruth* would afford a fine subject for the honour done my dear child."—" Why, good Mr. Andrews," said my master, " should you say so?—I know that story; and Mr. Williams will confirm what I say, that my good girl here will confer as much honour as she will receive."

" Sir," said I, " you are inexpressibly generous : but I shall never think so."—" Why, my Pamela," said he, " that's another thing : it will be best for me to think you *will;* and kind in you to think you *shan't;* and then we shall always have an excellent rule to regulate our conduct to one another."

Was not this nobly, wisely said?—O what a blessed thing to be matched to a man of sense and generosity!—How edifying! How!—But what shall I say?—I am at a loss for words.

Mr. Williams said, when we came out of the little chapel, he would look over his discourses, for one for the next day. My master said, " I have one thing to say, before you go—When my jealousy, on account of this good girl, put me upon such a vindictive conduct to you, I took a bond for the money I had caused you to be troubled for : I really am ashamed of the matter, as I never could intend, when I presented it to you, to have it again, but I knew not how far matters might have gone

278

between you; and so I was willing to have that in awe over you: I think it is no extraordinary present, therefore, to return you the bond cancelled." So he took it from his pocket, and gave it him. "I think," added he, "all the charges attending it, and the trouble you had, were defrayed by my attorney; I ordered that they should."—"They were, Sir," said he; "and ten thousand thanks to you for this goodness, and the kind manner in which you do it!"—"If you will go, Mr. Williams," said he, "shall my chariot carry you home?"—"No, Sir," answered he, "I thank you. My time will be so well employed all the way, in thinking of your favours, that I chose to meditate upon them, as I walk home."

My dear father was a little uneasy about his habit, for appearing at chapel next day, because of the Miss Darnfords, and the servants, for fear, poor man, he should disgrace my master; and he told me, when he was mentioning this, of my master's kind present of twenty guineas for clothes for you both; which made my heart truly joyful. But oh, to be sure I can never deserve the hundredth part of his goodness! It is almost a hard thing to lie under the weight of such deep obligations on one side, and such a sense of one's own unworthiness on the other. O! what a godlike power is that of doing good! I envy the rich and the great for nothing else.

My master coming to us just then, I said, "Oh, Sir, will your bounty know no limits? My dear father has told me what you have given him."—"A trifle, Pamela," said he, "a little earnest only of my kindness. Say no more of it. But did I not hear the good man expressing a sort of concern for somewhat? Hide nothing from me, Pamela."—"Only, Sir," said I, "he knew not how to absent himself from divine service, and yet is afraid of disgracing you by appearing."

"Fie, Mr. Andrews," said he; "I thought you knew that the outward appearance was nothing. I wish I had as good a habit *inwardly*, as you have. But I'll tell you, Pamela, your father is not much thinner than I am, nor much shorter; he and I will walk up together to my wardrobe; though it is not so well stored here, as in Bedfordshire.

"And so," said he pleasantly, "don't you pretend to come near us, till I call you; for you must not yet see how men dress and undress themselves."—"O Sir," said my father, "I beg to be excused. I am sorry you were told."—"So am not I," said my master: "pray come along with me."

He carried him up stairs, and shewed him several suits, and would have had him take his choice. My poor father was quite confounded : for my master saw not any he thought too good, and my father none that he thought bad enough. And my good master, at last (he fixing his eyes upon a fine drab, which he thought looked the plainest) would help him to try the coat and waistcoat on himself; and, indeed, one would not have thought it because my master is taller, and rather plumper, as I thought; but, as I saw afterwards, they fitted him very well : and being plain, and lined with the same colour, and made for travelling in a coach, pleased my poor father much. He gave him the whole suit, and, calling up Mrs. Jewkes, said, " Let these clothes be well aired against to-morrow morning. Mr. Andrews brought only with him his common apparel, not thinking to stay Sunday with us. And pray see for some of my stockings, and whether any of my shoes will fit him : and see also for some of my linen; for we have put the good man quite out of his course, by keeping him Sunday over." He was then pleased to give him the silver buckles out of his own shoes. So, my good mother, you must expect to see my dear father a great beau. " Wig," said my master, " he wants none; for his own venerable white locks are better than all the perukes in England. But I am sure I have hats enow somewhere."— " I'll take care of every thing, Sir," said Mrs. Jewkes. And my poor father, when he came to me, could not refrain tears. " I know not how," said he, " to comport myself under these great favours. O my child ! it is all owing to the Divine goodness, and your virtue."

SUNDAY.

This blessed day all the family seemed to take delight to equip themselves for the celebration of the Sabbath, in the little chapel; and Lady Jones and Mr. Williams came in her chariot, and the two Miss Darnfords in their own. And we breakfasted together in a most agreeable manner. My dear father appeared quite spruce and neat, and was greatly caressed by the three ladies. As we were at breakfast, my master told Mr. Williams, we must let the Psalms alone, he doubted, for want of a clerk; but Mr. Williams said, " No, nothing should be wanting that he could supply." My father said, if it might be permitted him, he would, as well as he was able, perform that office; for it was always what he had taken delight in. And as I knew he had learned psalmody formerly, in his youth, and had constantly practised it in private, at home, on Sunday evenings (as well as endeavoured to teach it in the little school he so unsuccessfully set up, at the beginning of his misfortunes,

280

before he took to hard labour), I was in no pain for his under-taking it in this little congregation. They seemed much pleased with this; and so we went to chapel, and made a pretty tolerable appearance; Mrs. Jewkes, and all the servants, attending, but the cook: and I never saw divine service performed with more solemnity, nor assisted at with greater devotion, and decency; my master, Lady Jones, and the two Misses, setting a lovely example.

My good father performed his part with great applause, making the responses, as if he had been a practised parish-clerk; and giving the xxiiid psalm,[1] which consisting of but three staves, we had it all; he read the line, and began the tune with a heart so entirely affected with the duty, that he went through it distinctly, calmly, and fervently at the same time; so that Lady Jones whispered me, that good men were fit for all companies, and present to every laudable occasion: and Miss Darnford said, " God bless the dear good man!" You must think how I rejoiced in my mind.

I know, my dear mother, you can say most of the shortest psalms by heart; so I need not transcribe it, especially as your chief treasure is a Bible, of which I know nobody makes more, or better use.

[1] The Lord is only my support
    And he that doth me feed:
How can I then lack any thing,
    Whereof I stand in need?
In pastures green he feedeth me,
    Where I do safely lie;
And after leads me to the streams
    Which run most pleasantly.

And when I find myself near lost,
    Then home he doth me take;
Conducting me in his right paths,
    E'en for his own name's sake.
And though I were e'en at death's door,
    Yet would I fear no ill;
For both thy rod and shepherd's crook,
    Afford me comfort still.

Thou hast my table richly spread
    In presence of my foe;
Thou hast my head with balm refresh'd
    My cup doth overflow.
And, finally, while breath doth last,
    Thy grace shall me defend,
And in the house of God will I
    My life for ever spend.

Mr. Williams gave an excellent discourse on liberality and generosity, and the blessings attending the right use of riches, from the xith chapter of Proverbs, vers. 24, 25. "*There is that scattereth, and yet increaseth; and there is that withholdeth more than is meet; but it tendeth to poverty. The liberal soul shall be made fat: and he that watereth, shall be watered also himself.*" And he treated the subject so handsomely, that my master's delicacy, who at first feared some personal compliments, was not offended, Mr. Williams judiciously keeping to generals; and it was an elegant and sensible discourse, as my master said.

My father was in the clerk's place, just under the desk: and Lady Jones, by her footman, whispered him to favour us with another psalm, when the sermon ended. He thinking that the former was rather of the longest chose the shortest in the book, which, you know, is the cxviith.[1]

My master and the ladies thanked Mr. Williams for his excellent discourse, and so did I, most heartily: he was pleased to take my dear father by the hand, as did also Mr. Williams, and thanked him. The ladies likewise made him their compliments: and the servants all looked upon him with countenances of respect and pleasure.

At dinner, do what I could, I was forced to take the upper end of the table, my master sat at the lower end, between Mr. Williams and my father. Said he, "Pamela, you are so dexterous, I think you may help the ladies yourself; and I will help my two good friends." I had dressed myself in a flowered satin, which was my lady's, and looked quite fresh and good, and was given me, at first, by my master; the ladies, who had not seen me out of my homespun before, made me abundance of fine compliments.

Talking of the psalms just after dinner, my master said to my father, "Mr. Andrews, I think in the afternoon, as we shall have only prayers, we may have one longer psalm; what think you of the cxxxviith?"—"O good Sir," said I, "pray, pray not a word more!"—"Say what you will, Pamela," said he, "you shall sing it to us, according to your own version, before these

---

[1] O all ye nations of the world,
    Praise ye the Lord always;
And all ye people every where,
    Set forth his noble praise.

For great his kindness is to us;
    His truth doth not decay;
Wherefore praise ye the Lord our God,
    Praise ye the Lord alway.

good ladies go away." My father smiled, but was half concerned for me, and said, "Will it bear, and please your honour?"—
"O ay," said he, "never fear it; so long as Mrs. Jewkes is not in the hearing."

This excited all the ladies' curiosity; and Lady Jones said, she would be loth to desire to hear any thing that would give me concern, but should be glad if I would give leave for it. "Madam," said I, "I must beg you won't insist upon it. I cannot bear it."—"You shall see it, indeed, ladies," said my master; "and pray, Pamela, not always as *you* please, neither." —"Then, Sir," said I, "not in my hearing, I hope."—"Sure, Pamela," returned he, "you would not write what is not fit to be heard."—"Sir," said I, "there are particular cases and occasions that may make a thing passable at one time, but not tolerable at another."—"O," said he, "let me judge of that as well as you, Pamela. These ladies know much of your story; and what they do know is more to your credit than mine; so if I am not averse to revive the occasion, you may very well bear it." Said he, "I will put you out of your pain, Pamela: here it is:" and took it out of his pocket.

I stood up, and said, "Really, Sir, I can't bear it! I hope you'll allow me to leave the room a minute, if you will read it."—
"Indeed, but I won't," answered he. Lady Jones said, "Pray, good Sir, don't let us hear it, if Mrs. Andrews be so unwilling."—
"Well, Pamela," said my master, "I will put it to your choice, whether I shall read it now, or you will sing it by-and-by."—
"That's very hard, Sir," said I. "It must be one, I assure you," said he. "Why then, Sir," replied I, "you must do as you please; for I cannot sing it."

"Well, then," said my master, "I find I must read it; and yet," added he, "after all, I had as well not, for it is no great reputation to myself."—"O then," said Miss Darnford, "pray let us hear it, to choose."

"Why then," proceeded he, "the case was this: Pamela, I find, during her confinement (that is," added he, "when she was taken prisoner, in order to make me one; for that is the upshot of the matter), in the journal she kept, and intended for nobody's perusal, but her parents, tells them, that she was importuned, one Sunday, by Mrs. Jewkes, to sing a psalm; but her spirits not permitting, she declined it. After Mrs. Jewkes was gone down, she says, she recollected, that the cxxxviith Psalm was applicable to her own case; and Mrs. Jewkes having often, on other days, in vain, besought her to sing a song, she turned it more to her own supposed case; and, believing she had a design against her honour, and looking upon her as her gaoler, she thus gives her version of this psalm. Pray, Mr. Williams, do you read one verse of the common translation, and I will read one of Pamela's." Then Mr. Williams, pulling out his little common prayer-book, read the two first stanzas:

I

When we did sit in Babylon,
    The rivers round about,
Then in remembrance of Sion,
    The tears for grief burst out.

II

We hang'd our harps and instruments
    The willow trees upon;
For in that place, men, for that use,
    Had planted many a one.

My master then read:

I

When sad I sat in B——n hall,
    All guarded round about,
And thought of ev'ry absent friend,
    The tears for grief burst out.

II

My joys and hopes all overthrown,
    My heart-strings almost broke,
Unfit my mind for melody,
    Much more to bear a joke.

The ladies said it was pretty: and Miss Darnford, that somebody else had more need to be concerned than the versifier.

"I knew," said my master, "I should get no credit by shewing this. But read on, Mr. Williams."

III

Then they to whom we pris'ners were,
    Said to us tauntingly,
" Now let us hear your Hebrew songs,
    And pleasant melody."

" Now, this," said my master, " is very near: " and read:

III

Then she to whom I pris'ner was,
    Said to me tauntingly,
" Now cheer your heart, and sing a song,
    And tune your mind to joy."

"Mighty sweet," said Mr. Williams. "But let us see how the next verse is turned. It is this:

IV

> "Alas!" said we, "who can once frame
> His heavy heart to sing
> The praises of our living God,
> Thus under a strange king?"

"Why," said my master, "it is turned with beautiful simplicity, thus:

IV

> "Alas," said I, "how can I frame
> My heavy heart to sing,
> Or tune my mind, while thus enthrall'd
> By such a wicked thing!"

"Very pretty," said Mr. Williams. Lady Jones said, "O dear Madam, could you wish that we should be deprived of this new instance of your genius and accomplishments?"

"O!" said my dear father, "you will make my good child proud."—"No," said my master, very generously, "Pamela can't be proud. For no one is proud to hear themselves praised but those who are not used to it.—But proceed, Mr. Williams." He read:

V

> But yet, if I Jerusalem
> Out of my heart let slide,
> Then let my fingers quite forget
> The warbling harp to guide.

"Now," said my master, "for Pamela's version.

V

> But yet, if from my innocence
> I, e'en in thought, should slide,
> Then let my fingers quite forget
> The sweet spinnet to guide."

Mr. Williams read:

VI

> And let my tongue within my mouth
> Be tied for ever fast,
> If I rejoice before I see
> Thy full deliv'rance past.

"This also," said my master, "is very near:

VI

> And let my tongue within my mouth
> Be locked for ever fast,
> If I rejoice, before I see
> My full deliv'rance past."

285

"Now, good Sir," said I, "oblige me; don't read any further."
—"O pray, Madam," said Mr. Williams, "let me beg to have
the rest read; for I long to know whom you make the sons
of Edom, and how you turn the Psalmist's execrations against
the insulting Babylonians."

"Well, Mr. Williams," replied I, "*you* should not have said
so." "O," said my master, "that is one of the best things of
all. Poor Mrs. Jewkes stands for Edom's sons; and we must
not lose this, because I think it one of my Pamela's excellencies,
that though thus oppressed, she prays for no harm upon the
oppressor.—Read, Mr. Williams, the next stanza." So he read:

VII

Therefore, O Lord, remember now
The cursed noise and cry,
That Edom's sons against us made,
When they rais'd our city.

VIII

Remember, Lord, their cruel words,
When, with a mighty sound,
They cried—" Down, yea, down with it,
Unto the very ground."

"Here seems," said my master, "in what I am going to read,
a little bit of a curse, but I think it makes no ill figure in the
comparison.

VII

And thou, Almighty, recompence
The evils I endure
From those that seek my sad disgrace,
So causeless to procure."

"And now," said he, "for Edom's sons: though a little
severe in the imputation.

VIII

Remember, Lord, this Mrs. Jewkes,
When, with a mighty sound,
She cried, ' Down with her chastity,
Down to the very ground.' "

"Sure, Sir," said I, "this might have been spared!" But
the ladies and Mr. Williams said, "No, by no means!" And
I see the poor wicked woman has no favourers among them.

"Now," said my master, "read the Psalmist's heavy curses."
And Mr. Williams read:

E'en so shalt thou, O Babylon,
  At length to dust be brought:
And happy shall that man be call'd,
  That our revenge has wrought.

X

Yea, blessed shall that man be call'd,
  That takes thy little ones,
And dashes them in pieces small
  Against the very stones.

" Thus," said he, very kindly, " has *my* Pamela turned these lines :

IX

E'en so shalt thou, O wicked one,
  At length to shame be brought:
And happy shall all those be call'd
  That my deliv'rance wrought.

X

Yea, blessed shall the man be call'd
  That shames thee of thy evil,
And saves me from thy vile attempts,
  And thee, too, from the d—l."

" I fancy this blessed man," said my master, smiling, " was, at that time, hoped to be you, Mr. Williams, if the truth was known."—" Sir," said he, " whoever it was intended for *then*, it can be nobody but your good self *now*."

I could hardly hold up my head for the praises the kind ladies were pleased to heap upon me. I am sure, by this, they are very partial in my favour; all because my master is so good to me, and loves to hear me praised; but I see no such excellence in these lines as they would make me believe, but what is borrowed from the Psalmist.

We all, as before, and the cook-maid too, attended the prayers of the church in the afternoon; and my dear father concluded with the following stanzas of the cxlvth Psalm; suitably magnifying the holy name of God for all mercies; but did not observe altogether the method in which they stand; which was the less necessary, he thought, as he gave out the lines:

The Lord is just in all his ways:
  His works are holy all:
And he is near all those that do
  In truth upon him call.

He the desires of all of them
 That fear him will fulfil;
And he will hear them when they cry
 And save them all he will.

The eyes of all who wait on thee
 Thou dost them all relieve:
And thou to each sufficient food
 In season due dost give.

Thou openest thy plenteous hand,
 And bounteously dost fill
All things whatever, that do live,
 With gifts of thy good-will.

My thankful mouth shall gladly speak
 The praises of the Lord:
All flesh, to praise his holy name,
 For ever shall accord.

We walked in the garden till tea was ready; and as he went by the back-door, my master said to me, "*Of all the flowers in the garden, the sun-flower is the fairest!*"—"O, Sir," said I, "let that now be forgot!" Mr. Williams heard him say so, and seemed a little out of countenance: whereupon my master said, "I mean not to make you serious, Mr. Williams; but we see how strangely things are brought about. I see other scenes hereabouts that, in my Pamela's dangers, give me more cause of concern, than any thing you ever did should give you."— "Sir," said he, "you are very generous."

My master and Mr. Williams afterwards walked together for a quarter of an hour, and talked about general things, and some scholastic subjects; and joined us, very well pleased with one another's conversation.

Lady Jones said, putting herself on one side me, as my master was on the other, "But pray, Sir, when is the happy time to be? We want it over, that we may have you with us as long afterwards as you can." Said my master, "I would have it to-morrow, or next day at farthest, if Pamela will: for I have sent for a licence, and the messenger will be here to-night, or early in the morning, I hope. But," added he, "pray, Pamela, do not take beyond Thursday." She was pleased to say, "Sure it will not be delayed by you, Madam, more than needs!"— "Well," said he, "now you are on my side, I will leave you with her to settle it: and I hope she will not let little bashful niceties be important with her;" and so he joined the two Misses.

Lady Jones told me I was to blame, she would take upon her

288

to say, if I delayed it a moment; because she understood Lady
Davers was very uneasy at the prospect that it would be so;
and if any thing should happen, it would be a sad thing!—
"Madam," said I, "when he was pleased first to mention it,
he said it should be in fourteen days; and afterwards asked me
if I would have it in the first or the second seven. I answered,
(for how could I do otherwise?) 'In the second.' He desired
it might not be the last day of the second seven. And as he was
then pleased to speak his mind, no doubt, I would not, for any
thing, seem too forward."

"Well, but," said she, "as he now urges you in so gentlemanly
a manner for a shorter day, I think, if I was in your place, I
would agree to it." She saw me hesitate and blush, and said,
"Well, you know best; but I say only what I would do."
I said, I would consider of it; and if I saw he was very earnest, I
should think I ought to oblige him.

Miss Darnfords were begging to be at the wedding, and to
have a ball; and they said, "Pray, Mrs. Andrews, second our
requests, and we shall be greatly obliged to you."—"I cannot,"
said I, "promise that, if I might."—"Why so?" said they.
"Because," answered I, "I know not what! But I think one
may with pleasure celebrate an *anniversary* of one's nuptials,
but the *day itself*—Indeed, ladies, I think it too solemn a matter
for the *parties* of our sex to be very gay upon; it is a serious
and awful affair; and I am sure, in your own cases, you would
be of my mind."—"Why, then," said Miss Darnford, "the more
need one has to be light-hearted and merry."

"I told you," said my master, "what sort of an answer you'd
have from Pamela." The younger Miss said she never heard of
such grave folks in her life on such an occasion: "Why, Sir,"
said she, "I hope you'll sing psalms all day, and Miss will fast
and pray! Such sackcloth and ashes doings, for a wedding,
I never heard of!" She spoke a little spitefully, I thought,
and I returned no answer. I shall have enough to do, I reckon
in a while, if I am to answer every one that will envy me.

We went into tea, and all the ladies could prevail upon my
master for, was a dancing-match before he left this country;
but Miss Darnford said, it should then be at her house; for
truly if she might not be at the wedding she would be affronted,
and come no more hither, till we had been there.

When they were gone, my master would have had my father
stay till the affair was over; but he begged to set out as soon
as it was light in the morning; for, he said, my mother would
be doubly uneasy at his stay, and he burned with impatience

to let her know all the happy things that had befallen her daughter. When my master found him so desirous to go, he called Mr. Thomas, and ordered him to get a particular bay horse ready early in the morning for my father, and a portmanteau to put his things in, and to attend him a day's journey. " If," said he, " Mr. Andrews chooses it, see him safe to his own home :—and," added he, " since that horse will serve you, Mr. Andrews, to ride backwards and forwards to see us, when we go into Bedfordshire, I make you a present of it, with the accoutrements." Seeing my father going to speak, he added, " I won't be said nay." O how good was this !

He also said many kind things at supper-time, and gave him all my papers ; but desired, when he and my mother had read them that he would return them to him again. And then he said, " So affectionate a father and daughter may perhaps be glad to be alone together ; therefore remember me to your good wife, and tell her I hope, before long, to see you together on a visit to your daughter at my other house : so I wish you good night, and a good journey, if you go before I see you." Then he shook hands, and left my dear father almost unable to speak, through the sense of his favours and goodness.

You may believe, my dear mother, how loth I was to part with my father ; who was also unwilling to part with me ; but he was so impatient to see you, and tell you the blessings with which his heart overflowed, that I could not detain him.

Mrs. Jewkes brought two bottles of cherry-brandy, two of cinnamon-water, and some cake ; they were put up in the portmanteau with my father's newly-presented clothes ; for he said he would not, for any thing, be seen in them in his neighbourhood till I was publicly known to be married ; nor would he lay out any part of the twenty guineas till then, for fear of reflexions, and would consult me as to what he should say. " Well," said I, " as you please, my dear father ; and I hope now we shall often have the pleasure of hearing from one another without needing any art or contrivance."

He said he would go to bed betimes, that he might be up as soon as it was light ; and so he took leave of me, and said he would not love me, if I got up in the morning to see him go, which would but make us the more loath to part, and grieve us both all day.

Mr. Thomas brought him a pair of boots, and told him he would call him up at peep of day, and put up every thing at night ; and so I received his blessing, and his prayers, and his kind promises of procuring the same from you, my dear mother, and went up to my closet with a heavy heart, yet a half pleased one, if I may so say; for that, as he must go, he was going to the best of wives, and with the best of tidings. But I begged he would not work so hard as he had done; for I was sure my master would not have given him twenty guineas for clothes, if he had not designed to do something else for him; and that he should be the less concerned at receiving benefits from my good master, because he, who had so many persons to employ in his large possessions, could make him serviceable to a degree equivalent, without hurting any body else.

He promised me fair; and pray, dear mother, see he performs. I hope my master will not see this: for I will not send it you, till I can send you the best of news: and the rather, as my dear father can supply the greatest part of what I have written *since* the papers he carries you, by his own observation. So good night, my dear mother: and God send my father a safe journey, and a happy meeting to you both.

MONDAY.

Mr. Colbrand being returned, my master came up to my closet, and brought me the licence. O how my heart fluttered at the sight of it! "Now, Pamela," said he, "tell me, if you can oblige me with the day. Your word is all that's wanting." I made bold to kiss his dear hand: and, though unable to look up, said, "I know not what to say, Sir, to all your goodness: I would not, for any consideration, that you should believe me capable of receiving negligently an honour, that all the duty of a long life, were it to be lent me, will not be sufficient to enable me to be grateful for. I ought to resign myself, in every thing I may or can implicitly to your will."—"But what?" said he, with a kind impatience. "Why, Sir," said I, "when from last Thursday you mentioned fourteen days, I had reason to think that term your choice; and my heart is so wholly yours, that I am afraid of nothing, but being forwarder than you wish."—"Impossible, my dear creature!" said he, folding me in his arms: "impossible! If this be all, it shall be set about this moment, and this happy day shall make you mine!—I'll send away instantly," said the dear gentleman; and was going.

I said, "No, pray, Sir, pray, Sir, hear me! Indeed it cannot be to-day!"—"Cannot!" said he. "No, indeed, Sir!" said I; and was ready to sink, to see his generous impatience! "Why flattered you then my fond heart," replied he, "with the hope that it might?"—"Sir!" said I, "I will tell you what I

291

had thought, if you'll vouchsafe me your attention."—" Do, then," said he.—" I have, Sir, a great desire, that whenever the day is, it may be on a Thursday. On a Thursday my dear father and mother were married, and, though poor, they are a very happy pair : on a Thursday your poor Pamela was born ; on a Thursday my dear good lady took me from my parents into her protection : on a Thursday, Sir, you caused me to be carried away to this place, to which I now, by God's goodness, and your favour, owe so amazingly all my present prospects : and on a Thursday it was you named to me that fourteen days from that you would confirm my happiness. Now, Sir, if you please to indulge my superstitious folly, you will greatly oblige me ; I was sorry, Sir, for this reason, when you bid me not defer till the last day of the fourteen, that Thursday in next week was that last day."

" This, Pamela, is a little superstitious, I must needs say ; and I thlnk you should begin now to make another day in the week a happy one : as, for example, on a Monday, may you say, my father and mother concluded to be married on the Thursday following. On a Monday so many years ago, my mother was preparing all her matters to be brought to bed on the Thursday following. On a Monday seven weeks ago, it was that you had but two days more to stay, till you was carried away on Thursday. On a Monday, I myself," said he, " well remember it was that I wrote you the letter which prevailed on you so kindly to return to me ; and on the same day, you *did* return to my house here ; which, I hope, my girl, will be as propitious an æra as any you have named ! and now, lastly, will you say, which will crown the work ; and, on a Monday, I was married. Come, come, my dear," added he, " Thursday has reigned long enough o'conscience ; let us now set Monday in its place, or, at least, on equality with it, since you see it has a very good title and as we now stand in the week before us, claims propriety ; then, I hope, we shall make Tuesday, Wednesday, Friday, Saturday, and Sunday, as happy days as Monday and Thursday ; and so, by God's blessing, move round, as the days move, in a delightful circle, till we are at a loss what day to prefer to the rest."

O how charming was this said !—And how sweetly kind !

" Indeed, Sir," said I, " you rally my folly very agreeably ; but don't let a little matter stand in the way, when you are so generously obliging in greater ; indeed I like Thursday best, if I may choose."

" Well, then," said he, " if you can say you have a better

292

reason than this, I will oblige you : else I'll send away for the parson this moment."

And so, I protest, he was going ! Dear Sirs, how I trembled ! " Stay, stay, Sir," said I : " we have a great deal to say first ; I have a deal of silly prate to trouble you with ! "—" Well, say then, in a minute," replied he, " the most material ; for all, we have to say may be talked of while the parson is coming."— " O but indeed," said I, " it cannot be to-day ! "—" Well, then, shall it be to-morrow ? " said he. " Why, Sir, if it must not be on a Thursday, you have given so many pleasant distinctions for a Monday, let it then be next Monday ? "—" What, a week still ! " said he. " Sir," answered I, " if you please, for that will be as you enjoined within the second seven days."—" Why, girl," said he, " 'twill be seven months till next Monday. Let it," said he, " if not to-morrow, be on Wednesday ; I protest I will stay no longer."

" Then, Sir," returned I, " please to defer it for *one* day more, and it will be my beloved Thursday."—" If I consent to defer it till then, may I hope, my Pamela," said he, " that next Thursday shall *certainly* be the happy day ? "—" *Yes, Sir,*" said I ; and I am sure I looked very foolishly. Yet, my dear father and mother, why should I, with such a fine gentleman, whom I so dearly love, and so much to my honour too ? But there is something greatly awful upon my mind, in the solemn circumstance, and a change of condition never to be recalled, though all the prospects are so desirable. And I can but wonder at the thoughtless precipitancy with which most young folks run into this important change of life !

So now, my dear parents, have I been brought to fix so near a day as next Thursday ; and this is Monday. O dear, it makes me out of breath almost, to think of it. This was a great cut off ; a whole week out of ten days. I hope I am not too forward ! Yet, if it obliges my dear master, I am justified ; for he deserves of me all things in my power.

After this he rode out on horseback, attended by Abraham, and did not return till night. How, by degrees, things steal upon one. I thought even this small absence tedious, and the more as we expected him to dinner. I wish I may not be too fond, and make him indifferent : but you, my dear father and mother, were always fond of one another, and never indifferent, let the world run as it would.

When he returned, he said he had a pleasant ride, and was led out to a greater distance than he intended. At supper he told me, that he had a great mind Mr. Williams should marry us ;

because, he said, it would shew a thorough reconciliation on his part.

"But," said he, most generously, "I am apprehensive, from what passed between you, the poor man would take it hardly, and as a sort of insult, which I am not capable of. What says my girl: Do you think he would?"—"I hope not, Sir," said I: "as to what he *may* think, I can't answer; but as to any reason for his thoughts, I can: for indeed, Sir," said I, "you have been already so generous, that he cannot, I think, mistake your goodness." He then spoke with resentment of Lady Davers's behaviour, and I asked if any thing new had occurred. "Yes," said he, "I have had a letter from her impertinent husband, professedly at her instigation, that amounted to little less than a piece of insolent bravery, on supposing I was about to marry you. I was so provoked," added he, "that, after I had read it, I tore it in a hundred pieces, scattered them in the air, and bid the man who brought it let his master know what I had done with his letter, and would not permit him to speak to me, as he would fain have done.—I think the fellow talked somewhat of his lady coming hither: but she shall not set a foot within my doors; and I suppose this treatment will hinder her."

I was much concerned at this: and he said, "Had I a hundred sisters, Pamela, their opposition should have no weight with me: I did not intend you should know it; but you must expect a little difficulty from the pride of my sister, who has suffered so much from that of her brother; and we are too nearly allied in mind, as well as blood, I find. But this is not *her* business: and if she would have it so, she should have done it with more *decency*. Little occasion had *she* to boast of her birth, that knows not what belongs to good manners."

I said, "I am very sorry, Sir, to be the unhappy occasion of a misunderstanding between so good a brother and so worthy a sister."—"Don't say so, Pamela, because this is an unavoidable consequence of the happy prospect before us. Only bear it well yourself, because she is my sister; and leave it to me to make her sensible of her own rashness."

"If, Sir," said I, "the most lowly behaviour, and humble deportment, and in every thing shewing a dutiful regard to good Lady Davers, will have any weight with her ladyship, assure yourself of all in my power to mollify her."—"No, Pamela," returned he, "don't imagine, when you are my wife, I will suffer you to do any thing unworthy of that character. I know the duty of a husband, and will protect your gentleness to the utmost, as much as if you were a princess by descent."

"You are inexpressibly good, Sir," said I, "but I am far from taking a gentle disposition to shew a meanness of spirit: this is a trial I ought to expect; and well may I bear it, that have so many benefits to set against it which all spring from the same cause."—"Well," said he, "all the matter shall be this: we will talk of our marriage as a thing to be done next week. I find I have spies upon me wherever I go, and whatever I do: but now I am on so laudable a pursuit, that I value them not, nor those who employ them. I have already ordered my servants to have no conference with any body for ten or twelve days to come. And Mrs. Jewkes tells me every one names Thursday come sevennight for our nuptials. So I will get Mr. Peters, who wants to see my little chapel, to assist Mr. Williams, under the notion of breakfasting with me next Thursday morning, since you won't have it sooner; and there will nobody else be wanting; and I will beg of Mr. Peters to keep it private, even from his own family, for a few days. Has my girl any objection?"

"Oh Sir," answered I, "you are so generous in all your ways, I *can* have no objection! But I hope Lady Davers and you will not proceed to irreconcileable lengths, and when her ladyship comes to see you, and to tarry with you two or three weeks, as she used to do, I will keep close up, so as not to disgust her with the sight of me."—"Well," said he, "we will talk of that afterwards. You must do then as I shall think fit: and I shall be able to judge what both you and I ought to do. But what still aggravates the matter is, that she should instigate the titled ape, her husband, to write to me, after she had so little succeeded herself. I wish I had kept his letter, that I might have shewn you how a man, that generally *acts* like a fool, can take upon him to *write* like a lord. But I suppose it is of my sister's penning, and he, poor man! is the humble copier."

TUESDAY.

Mr. Thomas is returned from you, my dear father, with the good news of your health, and your proceeding in your journey to my dear mother. My master has just now been making me play upon the spinnet, and sing to it; and commended me for both. But he does so in all I do, so partial does his goodness make him to me.

ONE O'CLOCK.

We are just returned from an airing; and I have been delighted with his conversation upon English authors, poets particularly.

He entertained me also with a description of some of the curiosities he had seen in Italy and France, when he made what the polite world call the grand tour. He said he wanted to be at his other seat; for he knew not well how to employ himself here, having not purposed to stay half the time. "Pamela," said he, "you will hardly be troubled with so much of my company after we are settled there; for I have many things to adjust: and I must go to London: having accounts run on longer than ordinary with my banker. I don't know," added he, "but the ensuing winter I may give you a taste of the diversions of the town for a month or so." I said his will and pleasure should determine mine; and I never could have a desire after those or any other entertainments that were not in his own choice.

He was pleased to say, "I make no doubt of being very happy in you; and hope you will be so in me: for," said he, "I have no very enormous vices to gratify, though I pretend not to the greatest purity neither."—"Sir," said I, "if you can account to your own mind, I shall always be easy in whatever you do. Our greatest happiness here, Sir, is of very short duration; and this life, at the longest, is a poor transitory one; and I hope we shall be so happy as to be enabled to look forward, with comfort, to another, where our pleasures will be everlasting."

"You say well, Pamela; and I shall, by degrees, be more habituated to this way of thinking, as I more and more converse with you; but you must not be over-serious with me, all at once: though I charge you never forbear to mingle your sweet divinity in our conversation, whenever it can be brought in à propos, and with such a cheerfulness of temper as shall not throw a gloomy cloud over our innocent enjoyments."

I was abashed at this, and silent, fearing I had offended: but he said, "If you attend rightly to what I said, I need not tell you again, Pamela, not to be discouraged from suggesting to me, on every proper occasion, the pious impulses of your own amiable mind."—"Sir," said I, "you will be always indulgent, I make no doubt, to my imperfections, so long as I mean well."

My master made me dine with him, and would eat nothing but what I helped him to; my heart is, every hour, more enlarged with his goodness and condescension. But, still—what ails me, I wonder; a strange sort of weight hangs upon my mind, as Thursday draws on, which makes me often sigh involuntarily, and damps the pleasures of my delightful prospects! I hope this is not ominous, but only the foolish weakness of an over-thoughtful mind, on an occasion the most solemn and important of one's life, next to the last scene, which shuts up all.

I could be very serious! But I will commit all my ways to that blessed Providence, which hitherto has so wonderfully conducted me, through real evils, to this hopeful situation. I only fear that I shall be too unworthy to hold the affections of so dear a gentleman!—God teach me humility, and to know my own demerit: And this will be, next to his grace, my surest guide in the state of life to which, though most unworthy, I am going to be exalted. Don't cease your prayers for me, my dear parents; for, perhaps, this new condition may be subject to still worse hazards than those I have escaped; should conceitedness, vanity, and pride, take hold of my frail heart; and if I was, for my sins, to be left to my own conduct, a frail bark in a tempestuous ocean, without ballast, or other pilot than my own inconsiderate will. But my master said, on another occasion, that those who doubted most, always erred least; and I hope I shall always doubt my own strength, my own unworthiness.

I will not trouble you with twenty sweet agreeable things that passed in conversation with my excellent benefactor; nor with the civilities of Mr. Colbrand, Mrs. Jewkes, and all the servants, who seem to be highly pleased with my conduct to them: and as my master, hitherto, finds no fault that I go too low, nor they that I carry it too high, I hope I shall continue to have everybody's good will. Yet I will not seek to gain any one's by little meannesses or debasements; but aim at an uniform and regular conduct, willing to conceal involuntary errors, as I would have my own forgiven; and not too industrious to discover real ones, or to hide such, if any appear, as might encourage bad hearts, or unclean hands, in cases, where my master should receive damage, or the morals of the transgressors seem wilfully and habitually corrupt. In short, I will endeavour, all I can, that good servants shall find in me a kind encourager; indifferent ones be made better, by inspiring them with a laudable emulation; and bad ones, if not too bad in nature, and quite irreclaimable, reformed by kindness, expostulation, and even proper menaces, if necessary, but most by a good example: all this, if God pleases.

WEDNESDAY.

Now, my dear parents; I have but this *one* day, between me and the most solemn rite that can be performed. My heart cannot yet shake off this heavy weight. Sure I am ungrateful to the Divine goodness, and the favour of the best of benefactors! Yet I hope I am not!—For at times, my mind is all exultation, with the prospect of what good to-morrow's happy solemnity may, by the leave of my generous master, put it into my power to do. O how shall I find words to express, as I ought, my thankfulness, for all the mercies before me !

My dear master is all love and tenderness ! He sees my weakness, and generously pities and comforts me ! I begged to be excused supper; but he brought me down himself from my closet, and placed me by him, bidding Abraham not wait. I could not eat, and yet I tried, lest he should be angry. He kindly forbore to hint any thing of the dreadful, yet delightful to-morrow ! and put, now and then, a little bit on my plate, and guided it to my mouth. I was concerned to receive his goodness with so ill a grace. " Well," said he, " if you won't eat, drink at least with me." I drank two glasses, by his over-persuasions, and said, " I am really ashamed of myself."—" Why, indeed," said he, " my dear girl, I am not a very dreadful enemy, I hope ! I cannot bear anything that is the least concerning to you."—" Oh ! Sir," said I, " all is owing to my sense of my own unworthiness ! To be sure, it cannot be any thing else."

He rang for the things to be taken away, and then reaching a chair, sat down, and with his arms about me, said the most generous and affecting things that ever dropt from the honey-flowing mouth of Love. All I have not time to repeat : some I will.—And oh ! indulge your foolish daughter, who troubles you with her weak nonsense; because what she has to say, is so affecting to her; and if she went to bed, instead of scribbling, she could not sleep.

" This sweet confusion and thoughtfulness in my beloved Pamela," said he, " on the near approach of our happy union, when I hope all doubts are cleared up, and nothing of dishonour apprehended, shew me plainly, what a wretch I was to attempt such purity with a worse intention :—no wonder that one so virtuous should find herself deserted of life itself on a violence so dreadful to her honour, and seek a refuge in the shadow of death. But now, my dearest Pamela, that you have seen a purity on my side, as nearly imitating your own, as our sex can shew to yours; and since I have, all this day, suppressed even the least intimation of the coming day, that I might not alarm your tender mind; why all this concern? why all this affecting, yet sweet confusion? You have a generous friend, my dear girl, in me; a protector now, not a violator of your innocence :

why then, once more I ask, this strange perplexity, this sweet confusion ? "

" O Sir," said I, and hid my face in his arms, " expect not reason from a foolish creature : you should have still indulged me in my closet : I am ready to beat myself for this ungrateful return to your goodness. But I know not what !—I am, to be sure, a silly creature.—O had you but suffered me to stay by myself above, I should have made myself ashamed of so culpable a behaviour !—But goodness added to goodness every moment, and the sense of my own unworthiness, quite overcome my spirits."

" Now," said the generous man, " will I, though reluctantly, make a proposal to my sweet girl.—If I have been too pressing for the day; if another will still be more obliging; if you have fears that will not then be, say but the word, and I'll submit. Yes, my Pamela; for though I have these three days past, thought every tedious hour a day, till Thursday comes, if you earnestly desire it, I will postpone it. Say, my dear girl, *freely* say; but accept not my proposal without great reason, which yet I will not ask for."

" Sir," said I, " I can expect nothing but superlative goodness from you. This is a most generous instance of it : but I fear—yes, I fear it will be too much the same thing, some days hence, when the happy, yet fool that I am ! dreaded time shall be equally near."—" Kind, lovely charmer ! " said he, " now do I see you are to be trusted with power, from the generous use you make of it :—not one offensive word or look, from me, shall wound your nicest thoughts; but pray try to subdue this over-scrupulousness, and unseasonable timidity, I persuade myself you will if you can."

" Indeed, Sir, I will," said I; " for I am quite ashamed of myself, with all these lovely views before me !—The honour you do me, the kindness you shew me !—I cannot forgive myself !—For oh ! if I know the least of this idle foolish heart of mine, it has not a misgiving thought of your goodness; and I should abhor it if it were capable of the least affectation.—But, dear good Sir, leave me a little to myself, and I will take myself to a severer task than your goodness will let *you* do : and present my heart before you, a worthier offering than its way-ward follies will now let it seem to be.—But one thing is, having no kind friend, of one's own sex, to communicate my foolish thoughts to, and to be strengthened by their comfortings, I am left to myself : and, oh ! what a weak silly thing I am ! "

He kindly withdrew, for me to recollect myself, and in about half an hour, returned; and then, that he might not begin at once upon the subject, but say something agreeable to me, said, " Your father and mother have had a great deal of talk by this time about you, Pamela."—" O Sir," returned I, " your goodness has made them quite happy. But I can't help being concerned about Lady Davers."

He said, " I am vexed I did not hear the footman out, because it runs in my head he talked somewhat about her coming hither. She will meet with but an indifferent reception from me, unless she comes resolved to behave better than she writes."

" Pray, Sir," said I, " be pleased to bear with my good lady, for two reasons."—" What are *they* ? " said he. " Why, first, Sir," answered I, " because she is your sister; and may very well think, what all the world will, that you have much under-valued yourself in making me happy. Next, because, if her ladyship finds you out of temper with her, it will aggravate her still more against me; and every time that any warm words used between you, come into her mind, she will disdain me more."

" Don't concern yourself about it," said he; " for we have more proud ladies than she in our other neighbourhood, who, perhaps, have still less reason to be punctilious about their descent, and yet will form themselves upon her example, and say, ' Why, his own sister will not forgive him, nor visit him ! ' If I can subdue her spirit, which is more than her husband ever could, or indeed any body else, it is a great point gained; and if she gives me reason, I'll try for it, I assure you.

" Well, but my dear girl," continued he, " since the subject is so important, may I not say one word about to-morrow ? "— " Sir," said I, " I hope I shall be less a fool : I have talked as harshly to my heart as Lady Davers can do; and it suggests to me a better and more grateful behaviour."

He smiled, and kissing me, said, " I took notice, Pamela, of what you observed, that you have none of your own sex with you : I think it is a little hard; and I should like you to have had Miss Darnford; but then her sister must have been asked; and I might as well make a public wedding, which, you know, would require clothes, and other preparations. Besides," added he, " a foolish proposal was once made me of that second sister, who has two or three thousand pounds more than the other, left her by her grandmother, and she can't help being a little piqued : though," said he, " they could not expect it to succeed; for there is nothing in her person nor mind : and her fortune, the only inducement, would not do by any means; so I discouraged it at once."

"I am thinking, Sir," said I, "of another mortifying thing too; that were you to marry a lady of birth and fortune answerable to your own, all the eve to the day would be taken up in reading, singing, and sealing settlements, and portions, and such like: but now the poor Pamela brings you nothing at all; and the very clothes she wears are entirely the effects of your bounty, and that of your good mother: this makes me a little sad; for, alas! Sir, I am so much oppressed by your favours, and a sense of my obligations, that I cannot look up with the confidence I otherwise should on this awful occasion."

"There is, my dear Pamela," said he, "where the power is wanting, as much generosity in the will as in the action. To all that know your story, and your merit, it will appear that I cannot recompense you for what I made you suffer. You have had too many hard struggles and exercises; and have nobly overcome; and who shall grudge you the reward of the hard-bought victory?—This affair is so much the act of my own will, that I glory in being capable of distinguishing so much excellence, and my fortune is the more pleasurable to me, as I hope to make you some satisfaction for the past."

"This, Sir," said I, "is all goodness, unmerited on my side; and makes my obligations the greater! I can but wish for more worthiness!—But how poor is it to offer words only for such generous deeds! And to say, I *wish*—For what is a wish but the acknowledged want of power to oblige, and a demonstration of one's poverty in every thing but *will*."

"And that, my dear girl," said he, "is every thing: 'tis all I want: 'tis all that heaven itself requires of us: but no more of these little doubts, though they are the natural impulses of a generous and grateful heart. I want not to be employed in settlements. Those are for such to regard, who make convenience and fortune the prime considerations. I have possessions ample enough for us both; you deserve to share them with me: and you shall do it, with as little reserve as if you had brought me what the world reckons an equivalent: for you bring me what is infinitely more valuable—an experienced truth and well-tried virtue, and a wit and behaviour more than equal to the station you will be placed in: to say nothing of this sweet person, that itself might captivate a monarch; and of the meekness of temper, and sweetness of disposition, which makes you superior to all the women I ever saw."

Thus kind and soothing, and honourably affectionate, was the dear gentleman, to the unworthy, doubting, yet assured Pamela; and thus patiently did he indulge, and generously pardon, my impertinent weakness. He offered to go himself to Lady Jones, in the morning, and reveal the matter to her, and desire her secresy and presence; but I said that would disoblige the young Lady Darnfords. "No, Sir," said I, "I will cast myself upon your generous kindness; for why should I fear the kind protector of my weakness, and the guide and director of my future steps?"—"You cannot," said he, "forgive Mrs. Jewkes, for *she* must know it, and suffer her to be with you?"—"Yes, Sir," said I, "I can: she is very civil to me now; and her former wickedness I will forgive, for the sake of the happy fruits that have attended it, and because *you* mention her."

"Well," said he, "I will call her in, if you please."—"As you please, Sir," said I. And he rang for her: and when she came in, he said, "Mrs. Jewkes, I am going to entrust you with a secret."—"Sir," answered she, "I will be sure to keep it as such."—"Why," said he, "we intend to-morrow, privately as possible, for our wedding day, and Mr. Peters, and Mr. Williams are to be here, as to breakfast with me, and to shew Mr. Peters my little chapel. When the ceremony is over, we will take a little airing in the chariot, as we have done before; so it will not be wondered that we are dressed. The two parsons have promised secresy, and will go home. I believe you cannot well avoid letting one of the maids into the secret; but that I'll leave to you."

"Sir," replied she, "we all concluded it would be in a few days; and I doubt it won't be long a secret."—"No," said he, "I don't desire it should; but you know we are not provided for a public wedding, and I shall declare it when we go to Bedfordshire, which won't be long. But the men, who lie in the outhouses, need not know it; for, by some means or other, my sister Davers is acquainted with all that passes."—"Do you know, Sir," said she, "that her ladyship intends to be down here with you, in a few days? Her servant told me so, who brought you the letter you was angry at."—"I hope," said he, "we shall be set out for t'other house first; and shall be pleased she loses her labour."—"Sir," continued she, "her ladyship proposes to be here time enough to hinder your nuptials, which she takes, as we did, will be the latter end of next week."—"Well," said he, "let her come; but yet I desire not to see her."

Mrs. Jewkes said to me, "Give me leave, Madam, to wish you all manner of happiness; but I am afraid I have too well obeyed his honour to be forgiven by you."—"Indeed, Mrs. Jewkes," returned I, "you will be more your own enemy than I. I shall not presume, so much as by a whisper, to set my good

302

master against any one he pleases to approve of: and as to his old servants, I shall always value them, and never offer to dictate to his choice, or influence it by my own caprices."

" Mrs. Jewkes," said my master, " you find you need to apprehend nothing. My Pamela is very placable; and as we have both been sinners together, we must both be included in one act of grace."

" Such an example of condescension as I have before me, Mrs. Jewkes," said I, " may make you very easy; for I must be highly unworthy not to forgo all my little resentments if I had any, for the sake of so much goodness to myself."

" You are very kind, Madam," said she; " and depend upon it, I will atone for all my faults by my duty and respect to you as well as to my master."

" That's well said on both sides," said he; " but, Mrs. Jewkes, to assure you that my good girl here has no malice, she chooses you to attend her in the morning at the ceremony, and you must keep up her spirits."—" I shall," replied she, " be very proud of the honour: yet I cannot but wonder, Madam, to have seen you so very low-spirited, these two or three days past, with so much happiness before you."

" Why, Mrs. Jewkes," answered I, " there can be only one reason; which is, that I am a sad fool! I am not ungrateful neither; nor would I put on a foolish affectation: but my heart at times sinks within me; I know not why, except at my own unworthiness, and because this honour is too high for me to support myself under, as I should do—It is an honour, Mrs. Jewkes," added I, " I was not born to; and no wonder, then, I behave so awkwardly." She made me a fine compliment upon it, and withdrew, repeating her promises of care, secresy, &c.

He parted from me very tenderly; and I came up, and, to amuse my thoughts, wrote thus far. Mrs. Jewkes is come up, and it being past twelve, I will go to bed; but not one wink, I fear, shall I get this night—I could beat myself with anger. Sure there is nothing ominous in this strange folly!—But I suppose all young maidens are the same, so near so great a change of condition, though they carry it off more discreetly than I.

THURSDAY, SIX O'CLOCK IN THE MORNING.

I might as well have not gone to bed last night, for what sleep I had. Mrs. Jewkes said several things that would have been well enough from any body else of our sex; but the poor woman has so little purity of heart, that it is all *say* from her, and goes no further than the ear.

303

I fancy my master has not slept much neither: for I heard him up, and walking about his chamber, ever since break of day. He must have some concern, as well as I; for he is going to marry a poor foolish unworthy girl, brought up on the charity, as one may say (at least bounty), of his worthy family! And this foolish girl must be, to all intents and purposes, after twelve o'clock this day, as much his wife, as if he were to marry a duchess —And here he must stand the shocks of common reflection: "The great Mr. B. has done finely! he has married his poor servant *wench!*" will some say. The ridicule, and rude jests of his equals, and companions too, he must stand: and the disdain of his relations, and indignation of Lady Davers, his lofty sister. Dear good gentleman, he will have enough to do!—O how shall I merit all these things at his hands? I can only do the best I can, and pray to God to reward him; resolve to love him with a pure heart, and serve him with a sincere obedience. I hope he will continue to love me for *this ;* for, alas! I have nothing else to offer! But, as I can hardly expect so great a blessing, if I can be secure from his contempt, I shall not be unfortunate; and must bear his indifference, if his rich freinds should inspire him with it, and proceed in my duty with cheerfulness.

HALF AN HOUR PAST EIGHT O'CLOCK.

My good dear master, my kind friend, my generous benefactor, my worthy protector, and oh! all the good words in one, my affectionate husband, that is soon to be, (be curbed in, my proud heart, know thyself, and be conscious of thy unworthiness!) has just left me, with the kindest, tenderest expressions, and gentlest behaviour that ever blest a happy maiden. He approached me with a sort of reined-in rapture. "My Pamela," said he, "may I just ask after your employment?—Don't let me chide my dear girl this day, however. The two parsons will be here to breakfast with us at nine; and yet you are not a bit dressed! Why this absence of mind, and sweet irresolution?"

"Sir," said I, "I will set about a reformation this instant." He saw the Common Prayer-Book lying in the window. "I hope," said he, "my lovely maiden has been conning the lesson she is by-and-by to repeat. Have you not, Pamela?" and kissed me. "Indeed, Sir," said I, "I have been reading over the solemn service."—"And what thinks my fairest (for so he called me) of it?"—"Oh, Sir, 'tis very awful, and makes one shudder, to reflect upon it."—"No wonder," said he, "it should affect my sweet Pamela: I have been looking into it this morning, and I can't say but I think it a solemn, but very suitable service.

304

This I tell my dear love," continued he, and again clasped me to him, " there is not a tittle in it I cannot joyfully subscribe to : and *that*, my dear Pamela, should make you easy, and join cheerfully in it with me." I kissed his dear hand; " O my generous, kind protector," said I, " how gracious is it to confirm thus the doubting mind of your poor servant, which apprehends nothing so much as her own unworthiness of the honour and blessing that await her ! "—He was pleased to say, " I know well, my dearest creature, that, according to the liberties we people of fortune generally give ourselves, I have promised a great deal, when I say so. But I would not have said it, if deliberately I could not with all my heart. So banish from your mind all doubt and uneasiness; let a generous confidence in me take place; and let me *see* it does, by your cheerfulness in this day's solemn business; and then I will love you for ever."

" May God Almighty, Sir," said I, " reward all your goodness to me ! Oh, how kind it is in you, to supply the want of the presence and comfortings of a dear mother, of a living sister, or of the kind companions of my own sex, which most maidens have, to soothe their anxieties on the near approach of so awful a solemnity !—You, Sir, are all these tender relations in one to me ! Your kindness shall, if possible, embolden me to look up to you without that sweet terror that must confound poor bashful maidens on such an occasion, when surrendered up to a more doubtful happiness, and to half-strange men, whose good faith and good usage of them, must be less experienced, and is all involved in the dark bosom of futurity, and only to be proved by the trial."

" This, my dear Pamela," said he, " is very kindly said ! It shews that you enter gratefully into my intention. For I would, by my conduct, supply all these dear relations to you; and I voluntarily promise from my heart, to you, what I think I could not with such assured resolutions of performance to the highest-born lady in the kingdom; for, let me tell my sweet girl, that, after having been long tossed by the boisterous winds of a more culpable passion, I have now conquered it, and am not so much the victim of your beauty, all charming as you are, as of your virtue : and therefore may more boldly promise for myself, having so stable a foundation for my affection, which, should this outward beauty fail, will increase with your virtue, and shine forth the brighter, as that is more illustriously displayed by the augmented opportunities your future condition will afford you."—O the dear charming man, how nobly, how encouragingly kind was all this !

I could not suitably express myself, and he said, " I see my girl is at a loss for words ! I doubt not your good acceptance of my declarations. And when I have acted too much the part of a libertine formerly, for you to look back without some anxiety, I ought not, being now happily convicted, to say less. But why loses my girl her time? I will now only add, that I hope for many happy years, to make good, by my conduct, what so willingly flows from my lips."

He kissed me again, and said, " But whatever you do, Pamela, be cheerful; for else, may-be, of the small company we shall have, some one, not knowing how to account for your too nice modesty, will think there is *some other* person in the world, whose addresses would be still *more* agreeable to you."

This he said with an air of sweetness and pleasantry; but it alarmed me exceedingly, and made me resolve to appear as calm and as cheerful as possible; for this was, indeed, a most affecting expression, and enough to make me, if any thing can, behave as I ought, and to force my idle fears to give way to hopes so much better grounded. I began almost, on this occasion, to wish Mr. Williams were not to marry me, lest I should behave like a fool, and so be liable to an imputation I should be most unworthy to deserve.

I set about dressing instantly, and he sent Mrs. Jewkes to assist me. But I am never long dressing; and my master has now given me a hint, that will, for half an hour more, at least, keep my spirits brisk. Yet it concerns me a little, lest he should have any the least shadow of a doubt, that I am not, mind and person, entirely his.

Being now ready, and not called to breakfast, I sat down and writ thus far.

I dressed myself in a rich white satin night-gown that was my good lady's, and my best head-clothes, &c. I have got such a knack of writing, that when by myself, I cannot sit without a pen in my hand.—But I am now called to breakfast, I suppose the gentlemen are come !—Now courage, Pamela: remember thou art upon thy good behaviour.—Fie upon it ! my heart begins to flutter again ! " Foolish heart ! lie still !" Never, surely, was any maiden's perverse heart under so little command as mine !—It gave itself away, at first, without my leave; it has been, for weeks, pressing me with its wishes; yet now, when it should be happy itself, and make me so, it is throb, throb, throb, like a little fool; and filling me with such unseasonable misgivings, as abate the rising comforts of all my better prospects.

I thought I should have found no time nor heart to write again this day; but here are three gentlemen come, unexpectedly, to dine with my master; and so I shall not appear. He has done all he could, civilly, to send them away; but they still stay. And so I have nothing to do but to write till I go to dinner myself with Mrs. Jewkes: for my master was not prepared for this company, and it will be a little latish to-day. So I will begin with my happy story where I left off.

When I came down to breakfast, Mr. Peters and Mr. Williams were both there: and as soon as my master heard me coming, he met me at the door; and led me in with great tenderness. He had kindly spoken to them, as he told me afterwards, to mention no more of the matter to me than needs must. I paid my respects to them, I believe a little awkwardly, and was almost out of breath: but said, I had come down a little too fast.

When Abraham came in to wait, my master said (that the servants should not mistrust), " 'Tis well, gentlemen, you came as you did; for my good girl and I were going to take an airing till dinner-time. I hope you'll stay, and dine with me."—" Sir," said Mr. Peters, " we won't hinder your airing. I only came to see your chapel; but must be home to dinner; and Mr. Williams will dine with me."—" Then," said my master, " we will pursue our intentions, and ride out for an hour or two, as soon as I have shewed Mr. Peters my little chapel. Will you, Pamela, after breakfast, walk with us to it?"—" *If, If,*" said I, and had like to have stammered, foolish that I was!—" *If* you please, Sir." I could look none of them in the face. Abraham looking at me—" Why, child," said my master, " you have hardly recovered your fright yet: how came your foot to slip! 'Tis well you did not hurt yourself." Said Mr. Peters, improving the hint, " You ha'n't sprained your ankle, Madam, I hope."— " No, Sir," said I, " I believe not; but 'tis a little *painful* to me." And so it was, for I meant my foolishness! " Abraham," said my master, " bid Robin put the horses to the coach, instead of the chariot; and if these gentlemen *will* go, we can set them down."—" I had as leave walk," said Mr. Peters, " if Mr. Williams chooses it."—" Well, then," said my master, " let it be the chariot, as I told him."

I could eat nothing, though I attempted it; and my hand shook so, I spilled some of my chocolate, and so put it down again; they were all very good, and looked another way. My master said, when Abraham was out, " I have a quite plain ring here, Mr. Peters : and I hope the ceremony will dignify the ring; and that I shall give my girl reason to think it, for that cause, the most valuable one that can be presented her." Mr. Peters said, he was sure I should value it more than the richest diamond in the world.

I had bid Mrs. Jewkes not to dress herself, lest she should give cause of mistrust; and she took my advice. When breakfast was over, my master said, before Abraham, " Well, gentlemen, we will step into the chapel; and you must advise me as to the alterations I design. I am in the more haste, as the survey you are going to take of it, for the alterations, will take up a little time; and we shall not have much between that and dinner, for my little tour.—Pamela, you'll give us your opinion, won't you ? "—" Yes, Sir," said I; " I'll come after you."

So they went out, and I sat down in the chair again, and fanned myself : " I am sick at heart," said I, " Mrs. Jewkes." Said she, " Shall I fetch you a little cordial ? "—" No," said I. " I am a sad fool ! I want spirits, that's all." She took her smelling-bottle, and would have given it me; but I said, " Keep it in your hand : may-be, I shall want it; but I hope not."

She gave me very good words, and begged me to go : I got up : but my knees beat so against one another, I was forced to sit down again. At last I held by her arm, and, passing by Abraham, I said, " This ugly slip, coming down stairs, has made me limp; so I must hold by you, Mrs. Jewkes. Do you know what alterations there are to be in the chapel, that we must give our opinions on them ? "

Nan, she said, was let into the secret, and she had ordered her to stay at the chapel-door, to see that nobody came in. My dear master came to me, at entering the chapel, and took my hand, and led me up to the altar. " Remember, my dear girl," whispered he, " and be cheerful."—" I am, I will, Sir," said I; but hardly knew what I said; and so you may believe, when I said to Mrs. Jewkes, " Pray, Mrs. Jewkes, don't leave me; " as if I had all confidence in her, and none where it was most due. God forgive me ! but I never was so absent in my life, as at first : even till Mr. Williams had gone on his service, so far as to the awful words about " *requiring us, as we shall answer at the dreadful day of judgment;* " and then the solemn words, and my master's whispering, " Mind this, my dear," made me start. Said he, still whispering, " Know *you* any impediment ? " I blushed, and said, softly, " None, Sir, but my great unworthiness."

308

Then followed the sweet words, *Wilt thou have this woman to thy wedded wife*, &c. and I began to take heart a little, when my dearest master answered audibly to this question, "*I will.*" But I could only make a curtsey, when they asked me; though I am sure, my *heart* was readier than my *speech*, and answered to every article of *obey, serve, love*, and *honour*.

Mr. Peters gave me away, and I said after Mr. Williams, as well as I could, as my dear master did, with a much better grace, the words of betrothment; and the ceremony of the ring passing next, I received the dear favour at his worthy hands, with a most grateful heart; and he told me afterwards, that when he had done saying, *With this ring I thee wed*, &c. I curtsied, and said, "Thank you, Sir." May-be I did; for it was a most grateful part of the service, and my heart was overwhelmed with his goodness, and the tender grace wherewith he performed it. I was very glad the next part was the prayer, and kneeling; for I trembled so, I could hardly stand, betwixt fear and joy.

The joining of our hands, and declaration of our being married, to the few witnesses present; for, reckoning Nan, whose curiosity would not let her stay at the door, there were but Mr. Peters, and Mrs. Jewkes, and she; the blessing, the psalm, and prayers, and the concluding exhortation, were so many beautiful, welcome, and lovely parts of this divine office, that my heart was delighted with them, and my spirits a little freer.

Thus, my dearest parents, is your happy, thrice happy Pamela, at last married; and to whom?—Why to her beloved, gracious master! the lord of her wishes! and thus the once naughty assailer of her innocence, by a blessed turn of Providence, is become the kind, the gracious protector and rewarder of it. God be evermore blessed and praised! and make me not wholly unworthy of such transcendent honour! and bless and reward the dear good gentleman: who has thus exalted his unworthy servant, unto a place which the greatest ladies would think themselves happy in!

My master saluted me most ardently, and said, "God give you, my dear love, as much joy on this occasion as I have. He presented me to Mr. Peters, who saluted me; and said, "You may excuse *me*, dear Madam; for I gave you away, and you are my daughter." And Mr. Williams modestly withdrawing a little way, "Mr. Williams," said my master, "pray accept my thanks, and wish your *sister* joy." So he saluted me too; and said, "Most heartily, Madam, I do. And I will say, that to see so much innocence and virtue so eminently rewarded, is one of the greatest pleasures I have ever known." This my master took very kindly.

Mrs. Jewkes would have kissed my hand at the chapel-door; but I had got a new recruit of spirits just then; and kissed her and said, " Thank you, Mrs. Jewkes, for accompanying me. I have behaved sadly."—" No, Madam," said she, " pretty well, pretty well ! "

Mr. Peters walked out with me : Mr. Williams and my master came out after us, talking together.

Mr. Peters, when he came into the parlour, said, " I once more, Madam, must wish you joy on this happy occasion. I wish every day may add to your comforts; and may you very long rejoice in one another ! for you are the loveliest couple I ever saw joined." I told him, I was highly obliged to his kind opinion, and good wishes; and hoped my future conduct would not make me unworthy of them.

My good benefactor came in with Mr. Williams : " So, my dear life," said he, " how do you do? A little more composed, I hope ! Well, you see this is not so dreadful an affair as you apprehended."

" Sir," said Mr. Peters, very kindly, " 'tis a very solemn circumstance; and I love to see it so reverently and awfully entered upon. It is a most excellent sign : for the most *thoughtful* beginnings make the most *prudent* proceedings."

Mrs. Jewkes, of her own accord, came in with a large silver tumbler, filled with sack, and a toast, nutmeg, and sugar; and my master said, " That's well thought of, Mrs. Jewkes, for we have made but sorry breakfastings." And he would make me take some of the toast; as they all did, and drank pretty heartily; and I drank a little, and it cheered my heart, I thought, for an hour after.

My master took a fine diamond ring from his finger, and presented it to Mr. Peters, who received it very kindly. To Mr. Williams he said, " My old acquaintance, I have reserved for you, against a variety of solicitations, the living I always designed for you; and I beg you'll prepare to take possession of it; and as the doing it may be attended with some expence, pray accept of this towards it : " so he gave him (as he told me afterwards) a bank note of 5*ol.*

Thus did this generous good gentleman bless us all, and me in particular; for whose sake he was as bounteous as if he had married one of the noblest fortunes.

So he took his leave of the gentlemen, recommending secresy again, for a few days, and they left him; and none of the servants

310

suspected anything, as Mrs. Jewkes believes. Then I threw myself at his feet, blessed God, and blessed *him* for his goodness; and he overwhelmed me with kindness, calling me his sweet bride, and twenty lovely epithets, that swell my grateful heart beyond the power of utterance.

He afterwards led me to the chariot; and we took a delightful tour round the neighbouring villages; he did all he could, to dissipate those still perverse anxieties that dwell upon my mind, and, do what I can, spread too thoughtful an air, as he tells me, over my countenance.

We came home by half-past one; and he was pleasing himself with thinking, not to be an hour out of my company this blessed day, that (as he was so good as to say) he might inspire me with a familiarity which should improve my confidence in him, when he was told a footman of Sir Charles Hargrave had been here, to say that his master and two other gentlemen were on the road to take a dinner with him, in their way to Nottingham.

He was heartily vexed at this, and said to me, he should have been glad of their companies at any other time; but it was a barbarous intrusion now; and he wished they had been told he would not be at home at dinner: " Besides," said he, " they are horrid drinkers; and I mayn't be able to get them away to-night; for they do nothing but travel round the country, and beat up their friends' quarters all the way; and 'tis all one to them, whether they stay a night or a month at a place. But," added he, " I'll find some way, if I can, to turn them off, after dinner. Confound them," said he, in a violent pet, " that they should come this day, of all the days in the year ! "

We had hardly alighted, and got in, before they came; three mad rakes they seemed to be, setting up a hunting-note, as soon as they came to the gate, that made the court-yard echo again : and smacking their whips in concert.

So I went up to my chamber, and saw (what made my heart throb) Mrs. Jewkes's officious pains to put the room in order for a guest, that, however welcome, as now my duty teaches me to say, is yet dreadful to me to think of. So I took refuge in my closet, and had recourse to pen and ink, to divert my anxiety of mind. If one's heart is so sad, and one's apprehensions so great, where one so extremely loves, and is so extremely obliged; what must be the case of those poor maidens who are forced, for sordid views, by their tyrannical parents or guardians, to marry the man they almost hate, and, perhaps, to the loss of the man they most love? O that is a sad thing, indeed !—And what have not such cruel parents to answer for? And what do not such poor innocent victims suffer !—But, blessed be God, this lot is so far from being mine !

My good master (for I cannot yet have the presumption to call him by a more tender name) came up to me, and said, " I came to ask my dear bride," (O the charming word !) " how she does ? I see you are writing, my dear," said he. " These confounded rakes are half mad, I think, and will make me so ! However," said he, " I have ordered my chariot to be got ready, as if under an engagement five miles off, and will see them out of the house, if possible ; then ride round, and return as soon as I can get rid of them. I find," said he, " Lady Davers is full of our affairs. She has taken great freedoms with me, before Sir Charles : and they have all been at me, without mercy ; and I was forced to be very serious, or else they would have come up to have seen you, since I would not call you down." He kissed me, and said, " I shall quarrel with them, if I can't get them away ; for I have lost two or three precious hours with my soul's delight : " and so he went down.

Mrs. Jewkes asked me to dinner in the little parlour. I went down, and she was so complaisant as to offer to wait upon me : and was with difficulty persuaded to sit down with me. But I insisted she should : " For," said I, " it would be very extra-ordinary, if one should so soon go into such distance, Mrs. Jewkes. Whatever my new station may require of me," added I, " I hope I shall always conduct myself, so that pride and insolence shall bear no part in my character."

" You are very good, Madam," said she ; " but I will always know my duty to my master's lady."—" Why then," replied I, " if I must take state upon me so early, Mrs. Jewkes, let me exact from you what you call your duty ; and sit down with me when I desire you."

This prevailed upon her ; and I made a shift to get down a bit of apple-pie, and a little custard ; but that was all.

My good master came in again, and said, " Well, thank my stars, these rakes are going now ; but I must set out with them ; I choose my chariot, for if I took horse, I should have difficulty to part with them ; for they are like a snow-ball, and intend to gather company as they go, to make a merry tour of it for some days together."

We both got up, when he came in ; " Fie, Pamela ! " said he ; " why this ceremony now ?—Sit still, Mrs. Jewkes."—" Nay, Sir," said she, " I was loth to sit down ; but my lady would have me."—" She is very right, Mrs. Jewkes," said my master, and tapped me on the cheek ; " for we are yet but half married ; so she is not above half your lady yet !—Don't look so down, don't be so silent, my dearest," said he; "why, you hardly spoke twenty words to me all the time we were out together. Something I will allow for your bashful sweetness; but not too much.—Mrs. Jewkes, have you no pleasant tales to tell my Pamela, to make her smile, till I return ? "—" Yes, Sir," said she, " I could tell twenty pleasant stories; but my lady is too nice to hear them."—" Ah ! poor woman ! " thought I : " thy chastest stories will make a modest person blush, if I know thee; and I desire to hear none of them."

My master said, " Tell her one of the shortest you have, in my hearing."—" Why, Sir," said she, " I knew a bashful young lady, as Madam may be, married to——"—" Dear Mrs. Jewkes," interrupted I, " no more of your story, I beseech you; I don't like the beginning of it."—" Go on, Mrs. Jewkes," said my master. " No, pray, Sir, don't require it," said I.—" Then we'll have it another time, Mrs. Jewkes," said he.

Abraham coming in to tell him the gentlemen were going, and that his chariot was ready—" I am glad of that," said he, and went and set out with them. I took a turn in the garden with Mrs. Jewkes, after they were gone; and, having walked awhile, I said, I should be glad of her company down the elm-walk, to meet the chariot; for, oh ! I know not how to look up at him, when he is with me, nor how to bear his absence, when I have reason to expect him ; what a strange contradiction is there in this unaccountable passion !

What a different aspect every thing in and about this house bears now, to my thinking, to what it once had ! The garden, the pond, the alcove, the elm-walk. But, O ! my prison is become my palace ! and no wonder everything wears another face ! We sat down upon the broad stile, leading towards the road : and Mrs. Jewkes was quite another person to me, to what she was the last time I sat there.

At last my best beloved returned, and alighted there. " What, my Pamela," (and Mrs. Jewkes then left me) " what," (said he, and kissed me) " brings you this way ? I hope to meet me."—" Yes, Sir," said I. " That's kind, indeed," said he; " but why that averted eye ?—that downcast countenance, as if you was afraid of me ? "—" You must not think so, Sir," said I. " Revive my heart then," said he, " with a more cheerful aspect; and let that over-anxious solicitude which appears in the most charming face in the world, be chased from it.—Have you, my dear girl, any fears that I can dissipate ; any doubts that I can obviate ; any hopes that I can encourage ; any request that I can gratify?—Speak, my dear Pamela; and if I have power, *but* speak, and to purchase one smile, it shall be done!"

"I cannot, Sir," said I, "have any fears, any doubts, but that I shall never be able to deserve all your goodness. I have no hopes, but that my future conduct may be agreeable to you, and my determined duty well accepted. Nor have I any request to make, but that you will forgive all my imperfections; and among the rest, this foolish weakness, that makes me seem to you, after all that has passed, to want this further condescension, and these kind assurances. But, Sir, I am oppressed by your bounty; my spirits sink under the weight of it: and the oppression is still the greater, as I see not how, possibly, in my whole future life, by all I can do, to merit the least of your favours."

"I know your grateful heart," said he; "but remember, my dear, what the lawyers tell us, that marriage is the highest consideration which the law knows. This, my sweet bride, has made you mine, and me yours; and you have the best claim in the world to share my fortune with me. But, set that consideration aside, what is the obligation you have to me? Your mind is pure as that of an angel, and as much transcends mine. Your wit, and your judgment, to make you no compliment, are more than equal to mine: you have all the graces that education can give a woman, improved by a genius which makes those graces natural to you, you have a sweetness of temper, and a noble sincerity, beyond all comparison; and in the beauty of your person, you excel all the ladies I ever saw. Where, then, is the obligation, if not on my side, to you?—But let us talk of nothing henceforth but equality; although, if the riches of your mind, and your unblemished virtue, be set against *my* fortune (which is but an accidental good, and all I have to boast of), the condescension will be yours; and I shall not think I can possibly deserve you, till, after your sweet example, my future life shall become nearly as blameless as yours."—"O Sir," said I, "what comfort do you give me, that, instead of the danger of being ensnared by the high condition to which your goodness has exalted me, you make me hope, that I shall be confirmed and approved by you; and that we may have a prospect of perpetuating each other's happiness, till time shall be no more!—But, Sir, I will not, as you once cautioned me, be too serious. I will resolve, with these sweet encouragements, to be every thing you would have me: and I hope I shall, more and more, shew you that I have no will but yours." He kissed me very tenderly, and thanked me for this kind assurance, as he called it.

And so we entered the house together.

Now these sweet assurances, my dear father and mother, you will say, must be very consolatory to me; and being voluntary on his side, were all that could be wished for on mine; and I was resolved, if possible, to subdue my idle fears and apprehensions.

TEN O'CLOCK AT NIGHT.

As we sat at supper he was generously kind to me, as well in his actions as expressions. He took notice, in the most delicate manner, of my endeavour to conquer my foibles; and said, " I see with pleasure, my dear girl strives to comport herself suitably to my wishes. I see, even through the sweet tender struggles of your over-nice modesty, how much I owe to your intentions of obliging me. As I have once told you, that I am the conquest more of your virtue than your beauty, so not one alarming word or look shall my beloved Pamela hear or see, to give her reason to suspect the truth of what I aver. You may the rather believe me," continued he, " as you may see the pain I have to behold any thing that concerns you, even though your concern be causeless. Yet I will indulge my dear girl's bashful weakness so far, as to own, that so pure a mind may suffer from apprehension, on so important a change as this: and I can therefore be only displeased with such part of your conduct, as may make your sufferings greater than my own; when I am resolved, through every stage of my future life, in all events to study to make them less."

After supper, of which, with all his sweet persuasions, I could hardly taste, I drank two glasses of champagne, and afterwards a glass of sack; which he kindly forced upon me, by naming your healths: and as the time of retiring drew on, he noticed, but in a very delicate manner, how my colour went and came, and how foolishly I trembled. Nobody, surely, in such delightful circumstances, ever behaved so silly! And he said, " My dearest girl, I fear you have had too much of my company for so many hours together; and would better recollect yourself, if you retired for half an hour to your closet."

I wished for this, but durst not say so much, lest he should be angry; for as the hours grew on, I found my apprehensions increase, and my silly heart was the unquieter, every time I could lift up my eyes to his dear face; so sweetly terrible did he appear to my apprehensions. I said, " You are all goodness, dear Sir : " and I boldly kissed his dear hand, and pressed it to my lips with both mine. And saluting me very fervently he gave me his hand, seeing me hardly able to stand, and led me to my chamber door, and then most generously withdrew.

I went to my closet and on my knees thanked God for the blessing of the day; and besought his Divine goodness to conduct my future life in such a manner, as should make me a happy instrument of his glory. After this, being now left to my own recollection, I grew a little more assured and lightsome; and the pen and my paper being before me, amused myself with writing thus far.

ELEVEN O'CLOCK, THURSDAY NIGHT.

Mrs. Jewkes being come up with a message, desiring to know, whether her master may attend upon me in my *closet;* and hinting to me, that however, he did not expect to find me *there;* I have sent word, that I beg he would indulge me one quarter of an hour.—So, committing myself to the mercies of the Almighty, who has led me through so many strange scenes of terror and affrightment, to this happy, yet awful moment, I will wish you, my dear parents, a good night; and though you will not see this in time, yet I know I have your hourly prayers, and therefore cannot fail of them now. So good night; God bless you and me. Amen, if it be his blessed will, subscribes *your ever dutiful daughter!*

FRIDAY EVENING.

O how this dear excellent man indulges me in every thing! Every hour he makes me happier, by his sweet condescension, than the former.

He pities my weakness of mind, allows for all my little foibles, and endeavours to dissipate my fears; his words are so pure, his ideas so chaste, and his whole behaviour so sweetly decent, that never, surely, was so happy a creature as your Pamela! I never could have hoped such a husband could have fallen to my lot: and much less, that a gentleman, who had allowed himself in attempts, that I now will endeavour to forget for ever, should have behaved with so very delicate and unexceptionable a demeanour. No light frothy jests drop from his lips; no alarming railleries: no offensive expressions, nor insulting airs, reproach or wound the ears of your happy, thrice happy daughter; in short, he says everything that may embolden me to look up with pleasure, upon the generous author of my happiness.

At breakfast, when I knew not how to see him, he emboldened me by talking of *you,* my dear parents: a subject, he generously

316

knew, I *could* talk of : and gave me assurances that he would make you both happy. He begged I would send you a letter, to acquaint you with my nuptials : and, as he could make business that way, Thomas should carry it purposely, as to-morrow. "Nor will I," said he, "my dear Pamela, desire to see your writings, because I told you I would not; for now I will, in everything, religiously keep my word with my dear spouse, (O the dear delightful word !) and you may send all your papers to them, from those they have, down to this happy moment; only let me beg they will preserve them for me when they have read them; as also those I have not seen; which, however, I desire not to see till then, but then I shall take it as a favour, if you will grant it."

"It will be my pleasure, as well as my duty, Sir," said I, "to obey you in every thing; and I will write up to the conclusion of this day, that they may see how happy you have made me."

I know you will both join with me to bless God for his wonderful mercies and goodness to you, as well as to me : for he was pleased to ask particularly after your circumstances, and said, he had perceived from some of my first letters, that you owed money in the world : and he gave me fifty guineas, and bid me send them to you in my packet, to pay your debts, as far as they would go; and that you would quit your present business, and put yourself, and my dear mother, into a creditable appearance; and he would find a better place of abode for you than that you had, when he returned to Bedfordshire. O how shall I bear all these exceeding great and generous favours?—I send them, wrapt up, five guineas in a parcel, in double papers.

To me he gave no less than one hundred guineas more : and said, "I would have you, my dear, give Mrs. Jewkes, when you go from hence, what you think fit out of these, as from yourself." —"Dear Sir," said I, "let that be what you please."—"Give her, then," said he, "twenty guineas, as a compliment on your nuptials. Give Colbrand ten guineas; give the two coachmen five guineas each; to the two maids, at this house, five guineas each; give Abraham five guineas; give Thomas five guineas; and give the gardeners, grooms, and helpers, twenty guineas among them. And when I return with you to the other house, I will make you a suitable present, to buy such ornaments as are fit for my beloved wife to appear in. For now, my Pamela, you are not to mind, as you once proposed, what other ladies will say, but to appear as my wife ought to do : else it will look as if what you thought of, as a means to avoid the envy of others of your sex, was a wilful slight in me, which I hope I never shall be guilty of : I will shew the world that I value you as I ought, and as if I had married the first fortune in the kingdom : and why should it not be so, when I know none of the first quality that matches you in excellence ? "

He saw I was at a loss for words, and said, " I see, my dearest bride ! my spouse ! my wife ! my Pamela ! your grateful confusion."—And kissing me as I was going to speak, " I will stop your dear mouth," said he : " you shall not so much as thank me ; for when I have done ten times more than this, I shall but poorly express my love for so much beauty of mind, and loveliness of person ; which thus," said he, and clasped me to his generous bosom, " I can proudly now call my own ! " O how, my dear parents, can I think of anything, but redoubled love, joy, and gratitude ? Thus generously did he banish from my mind those painful reflections, and bashful apprehensions, that made me dread to see him for the first time this day, when I was called to attend him at breakfast ; and made me all ease, composure, and tranquillity.

He then, thinking I seemed somewhat thoughtful, proposed a little turn in the chariot till dinner-time ; and this was another sweet relief : he diverted me with twenty agreeable relations, of what observations he had made in his travels ; and gave me the characters of the ladies and gentlemen in his other neighbourhood ; telling me whose acquaintance he would have me most cultivate. When I mentioned Lady Davers with apprehension, he said, " To be sure, I love my sister dearly, notwithstanding her violent spirit, and I know she loves me ; and I can allow a little for her pride, as I know what my own so lately was ; and because she knows not my Pamela, and her excellencies, as I do. But you must not, my dear, forget what belongs to your character, as my wife, nor meanly stoop to her ; though I know you will choose by softness, to try to move her to a proper behaviour. But it will be my part to see that you do not yield too much.

" However," continued he, " as I would not publicly declare my marriage here, I hope she won't come near us till we are in Bedfordshire ; and then, when she knows we are married, she will keep away, if not willing to be reconciled ; for she dares not, surely, come to quarrel with me, knowing it is done, for that would have a hateful and wicked appearance, as if to try to make differences between man and wife. But we will have no more of this subject, nor talk of any thing," added he, " that shall give concern to my dearest." So he changed the talk to a

318

more pleasing subject, and said the kindest and most soothing things.

When we came home, which was about dinner-time, he was the same obliging kind gentleman; and in short, is studious to shew, on every occasion, his generous affection to me. After dinner, he told me he had already written to his draper in town, to provide him new liveries; and to his late mother's mercer, to send him patterns of the most fashionable silks, for my choice. I said, I was unable to express my gratitude for his favour and generosity; and as he knew best what befitted his own rank and condition, I would wholly leave myself to his good pleasure. But, by all his repeated bounties, of so extraordinary a nature, I could not but look forward with awe upon the condition to which he had exalted me; and now I feared I should hardly be able to act up to it, as to justify the choice he had condescended to make: yet I hoped I should have not only his general allowance for my imperfections, which I could only assure him should not be wilful ones, but his kind instructions; and that, as often as he observed any part of my conduct such as he could not entirely approve, he would let me know it; and I would think his reproofs of beginning faults most kind and most affectionate; for they would keep me from committing greater, and be a means to continue me the blessing of his good opinion.

He assured me, in the kindest manner, that nothing should ever lie upon his mind, which he would not reveal, and give me an opportunity, either of convincing him, or being convinced myself.

He then asked when I should be willing to go to the Bedford-shire house, I said, whenever he pleased. "We will come down hither again before the winter," said he, "if you please, in order to cultivate your acquaintance with Lady Jones, and Sir Simon's family; and, if it please God to spare us to one another, in the winter I will give you, as I promised, for two or three months, the diversions of London. I think," added he, "if my dear pleases, we will set out next week, about Tuesday, for t'other house."—"I can have no objection, Sir," said I, "to anything you propose; but how will you avoid Miss Darn-ford's solicitation for an evening to dance?"—"Why," said he, "we can make Monday evening do for that purpose, if they won't excuse us. But, if you please," said he, "I will invite Lady Jones, Mr. Peters and his family, and Sir Simon and his family, to my little chapel, on Sunday morning, and to stay dinner with me; and then I will declare my marriage to them, because my dear life shall not leave this country with the least

reason for a possibility of any body's doubting that it is so."
O! how good was this! But his conduct is all of a piece,
noble, kind, and considerate! What a happy creature am I!—
"And then may-be," said he, "they will excuse us till we return
into this country again, as to the ball. Is there any thing,"
added he, "that my beloved Pamela has *still* to wish? If you
have, freely speak."

"Hitherto, my dearest Sir," replied I, "you have not only
prevented my wishes, but my hopes, and even my thoughts.
And yet I must own, since your kind command of speaking my
mind seems to shew, that you expect me to say something;
that I have only one or two things to wish more, and then I
shall be too happy."—"Say," said he, "what they are."—
"Sir," proceeded I, "I am indeed ashamed to ask any thing,
lest it should not be agreeable to you, and lest it should seem
I was taking advantage of your kind condescensions to me, and
knew not when to be satisfied."

"I will only tell you, Pamela," said he, "that you are not
to imagine that these things, which I have done in hopes of
obliging you, are the sudden impulses of a new passion for you:
but, if I can answer for my own mind, they proceed from a
regular and uniform desire of obliging you; which, I hope, will
last as long as your merit lasts; and that, I make no doubt,
will last as long as I live. I can the rather answer for this,
because I really find so much delight in myself in my present
way of thinking and acting, as infinitely over-pays me, and
which, for that reason, I am likely to continue for *both* our sakes.
My beloved *wife*, therefore," said he, "for methinks I am grown
fond of a name I once despised, may venture to speak her mind;
and I will promise, that so far as it is agreeable to me, and I
cheerfully can, I will comply; and you will not insist upon it,
if that should not be the case."

"To be sure, Sir," said I, "I ought not, neither will I. And
now you embolden me to become an humble petitioner, and that,
as I ought, upon my knees, for the reinstating such of your
servants as I have been the unhappy occasion of their disobliging
you." He raised me up, and said, "My beloved Pamela has too
often been in this suppliant posture to me, to permit it any more.
Rise, my fairest, and let me know whom, in particular, you would
reinstate;" and he kindly held me in his arms, and pressed me
to his beloved bosom. "Mrs. Jervis, Sir," said I, "in the first
place, for she is a good woman; and the misfortunes she has
had in the world make your displeasure most heavy to her."

"Well," said he, "who next?"—"Mr. Longman, Sir," said

I; "and I am sure, kind as they have been to me, yet would I not ask it, if I could not vouch for their integrity, and if I did not think it was my dear master's interest to have such good servants."

"Have you any thing further?" said he. "Sir," said I, "your good old butler, who has so long been in your family, before the day of your happy birth, I would, if I might, become an advocate for!"

"Well," said he, "I have only to say, that had not Mr. Longman, and Mrs. Jervis, and Jonathan too, joined in a bold appeal to Lady Davers, which has given her an insolent handle to intermeddle in my affairs, I could easily have forgiven all the rest of their conduct; though they have given their tongues no little licence about me; because I desire every body should admire you; and it is with pride I observe not only their opinion and love, but that of every body else who knows you, justify my own. Yet I will forgive even this, because my Pamela desires it; and I will send a letter myself, to tell Longman what he owes to your interposition, if the estate he has made in my family does not set him above the acceptance of it. As to Mrs. Jervis, do you, my dear, write a letter to her, with your commands, instantly on the receipt of it, to go and take possession of her former charge; for now, my dearest girl, she will be more immediately your servant: and I know you love her so well, that you'll go thither with the more pleasure to find her there. But don't think," added he, "that all this compliance is to be for nothing."—"Ah! Sir," said I, "tell me but what I can do, poor as I am, but rich in will, and I will not hesitate one moment."—"Why, then," said he, "of your own accord, reward me for my cheerful compliance, with one sweet kiss." I instantly said, "Thus, then, dear Sir, will I obey; and, oh! you have the most generous way in the world, to make that a condition, which gives me double honour, and adds to my obligations." So I clasped my arms about his neck, and was not ashamed to kiss him once, and twice, and three times, once for every forgiven person.

"Now, my dearest Pamela," said he, "what other things have you to ask? Mr. Williams is already taken care of; and, I hope, will be happy. Have you nothing to say for John Arnold?"

"Why, dear Sir," said I, "you have seen the poor fellow's penitence in my letters."—"Yes, my dear, so I have: but that is his penitence for his having served me, against you; and I think, when he would have betrayed me afterwards, he deserves nothing to be said or done for him by either."

"But, dear Sir," said I, "this is a day of jubilee; and the less he deserves, poor fellow, the more will be your goodness. And as he was divided in his inclinations between his duty to you, and good wishes to me, and knew not how to distinguish the one from the other, when he finds us so happily united by your great goodness to me, he will have no more puzzles in his duty; for he has not failed in any other part of it; but, I hope, will serve you faithfully for the future."

"Well, then, suppose I put Mrs. Jewkes in a good way of business, in some inn, and give her John for a husband? And then your gypsey story will be made out, that she will have a husband younger than herself."

"You are all goodness, Sir," said I. "I can freely forgive poor Mrs. Jewkes, and wish her happy. But permit me, Sir, to ask, Would not this look like a very heavy punishment to poor John? And as if you could not forgive him, when you are so generous to every body else?"

He smiled, and said, "O my Pamela, this, for a forgiving spirit, is very severe upon poor Jewkes: but I shall never, by the grace of God, have any more such trying services to put him or the rest upon: and if *you* can forgive him, I think I may; and so John shall be at your disposal. And now let me know what my Pamela has further to wish?"

"O my dearest Sir," said I, "not one single wish more has your grateful Pamela. My heart is overwhelmed with your goodness! Forgive these tears of joy," added I: "you have left me nothing to pray for, but that God will bless you with life, health, and honour, and continue to me the blessings of your esteem; I shall then be the happiest creature in the world."

He clasped me in his arms, and said, "You cannot, my dear life, be so happy in me, as I am in you. O how heartily I despise all my former pursuits, and headstrong appetites! What joys, what true joys, flow from virtuous love; joys which the narrow soul of the libertine cannot take in, nor his thought conceive!— And which I myself, whilst a libertine, had not the least notion of!

"But," said he, "I expected my dear Pamela had something to ask for herself: but since all her own good is absorbed in the delight her generous heart takes in promoting that of others, it shall be my study to prevent her wishes, and to make her care for herself unnecessary, by my anticipating kindness."

In this manner, my dear parents, is your happy daughter blessed in a husband! O how my exulting heart leaps at the dear, dear word !—And I have only to be humble, and look up with gratitude to the all-gracious Dispenser of these blessings.

So, with a thousand thanks, I afterwards retired to my closet, to write to you thus far. And having completed what I purpose for this packet, and put up the kind obliging present, I have nothing more to say, but that I hope soon to see you both and receive your blessings on this happy, thrice happy occasion. And so hoping for your prayers, that I may preserve an humble and upright mind to my gracious God, a dutiful gratitude to my dear master and husband, that I may long rejoice in the continuance of these blessings and favours, and preserve, at the same time, an obliging deportment to every one else, I conclude myself, *your ever dutiful, and most happy daughter,*

PAMELA B——

O think it not my pride, my dear parents, that sets me on glorying in my change of name. Yours will be always dear to me, and what I shall never be ashamed of, I am sure ! But yet —for *such* a husband !—What shall I say, since words are too faint to express my gratitude, and my joy !

I have taken copies of my master's letters to Mr. Longman, and mine to Mrs. Jervis, which I will send, with the further occurrences, when I go to the other house, or give you when I see you, as I now hope soon to do.

SATURDAY MORNING, THE THIRD OF MY HAPPY NUPTIALS.

I must write on, till I come to be settled in the duty of the station to which I am so generously exalted, and to let you participate, with me, the transporting pleasures that arise from my new condition, and the favours hourly heaped upon me by the best of husbands. When my packet for you was finished, I set about writing, as he had kindly directed me, to Mrs. Jervis, and had no difficulty till I came to sign my name : so I brought it down with me, when called to supper, unsigned.

My good master (for I delight, and always shall, to call him by that name) had been writing to Mr. Longman ; and he said, pleasantly, " See here, my dearest, what I have written to your *somebody*." I read as follows :

" MR. LONGMAN,
       " I have the pleasure to acquaint you, that last Thursday I was married to my beloved Pamela. I have had reason to be disobliged with you, and Mrs. Jervis, and Jonathan, not for

323

your kindness to, and regard for, my dear spouse, that now is, but to the manner in which you appealed to my sister Davers; which has made a very wide breach between her and me. But as it was one of her first requests, that I would overlook what had past, and reinstate you in all your former charges, I think myself obliged, without the least hesitation, to comply with it. So, if you please, you may enter again upon an office which you have always executed with unquestionable integrity, and to the satisfaction of *yours, &c.*

" Friday afternoon.

" I shall set out next Tuesday or Wednesday for Bedfordshire; and desire to find Jonathan, as well as you, in your former offices; in which, I dare say, you'll have the more pleasure, as you have such an early instance of the sentiments of my dear wife, from whose goodness you may expect every agreeable thing. She writes herself to Mrs. Jervis."

I thanked him most gratefully for his goodness; and afterwards took the above copy of it; and shewed him my letter to Mrs. Jervis, as follows:

" My dear Mrs. Jervis,
        " I have joyful tidings to communicate to you. For yesterday I was happily married to the best of gentlemen, *yours* and *my* beloved master. I have only now to tell you, that I am inexpressibly happy: that my generous benefactor denies me nothing, and even anticipates my wishes. You may be sure I could not forget my dear Mrs. Jervis, and I made it my request, and had it granted, as soon as asked, that you might return to the charge which you executed with so much advantage to our master's interest, and so much pleasure to all under your direction. All the power that is put into my hands, by the most generous of men, shall be exerted to make every thing easy and agreeable to you: and as I shall soon have the honour of attending my beloved to Bedfordshire, it will be a very considerable addition to my delight, and to my unspeakable obligations to the best of men, to see my dear Mrs. Jervis, and to be received by her with that pleasure, which I promise myself from her affection. For I am, my dear good friend, and always will be, *yours very affectionately and gratefully,*

                                " Pamela ———"

He read this letter, and said, " 'Tis yours, my dear, and must be good: but don't you put your name to it?"—" Sir," said

324

I, "your goodness has given me a right to a very honourable one : but as this is the first occasion of the kind, except that to my dear father and mother, I think I ought to shew it you unsigned, that I may not seem over-forward to take advantage of the honour you have done me."

"However sweetly humble and requisite," said he, "this may appear to my dear Pamela's niceness, it befits me to tell you, that I am every moment more pleased with the right you have to my name; and, my dear life," added he, "I have only to wish I may be half as worthy as you are of the happy knot so lately knit." He then took a pen himself, and wrote, after Pamela, his most worthy surname; and I under-wrote thus : "O rejoice with me, my dear Mrs. Jervis, that I am enabled, by God's graciousness, and my dear master's goodness, thus to write myself."

These letters, and the packet to you, were sent away, by Mr. Thomas, early this morning.

My dearest master is just gone to take a ride out, and intends to call upon Lady Jones, Mr. Peters, and Sir Simon Darnford, to invite them to chapel and dinner to-morrow; and says, he chooses to do it himself, because the time is so short, they will, perhaps, deny a servant.

I forgot to mention, that Mr. Williams was here yesterday, to ask leave to go to see his new living, and to provide for taking possession of it; and seemed so pleased with my master's kindness and fondness for me, as well as his generous deportment to himself, that he left us in such a disposition, as shewed he was quite happy. I am very glad of it; for it would rejoice me to be an humble means of making all mankind so; and, oh ! what returns ought I not to make to the Divine goodness ! and how ought I to strive to diffuse the blessings I experience, to all within my knowledge !—For else, what is it for such a worm as I to be exalted ? What is my *single* happiness if I suffer it, niggard-like, to extend no further than to myself ? But then, *indeed*, do God Almighty's creatures act worthy of the blessings they receive, when they make, or endeavour to make, the whole creation, so far as in the circle of their power, happy !

Great and good God, as thou hast enlarged my opportunities, enlarge also my will, and make me delight in dispensing to others a portion of that happiness which I have myself so plentifully received at the hands of thy gracious Providence ! Then shall I not be useless in my generation !—Then shall I not stand a *single* mark of thy goodness to a poor worthless creature, that, in herself, is of so small account in the scale of beings, a mere cypher on the wrong side of a figure, but shall be placed on the right side; and, though nothing worth in myself, shall give signification by my *place*, and multiply the blessings I owe to the goodness, which has distinguished me by so fair a lot!

This, as I conceive, is the indispensable duty of a high condition; and how great must be the condemnation of poor creatures, at the great day of account, when they shall be asked what uses they have made of the opportunities put into their hands; and are only able to say, "We have lived but to *ourselves ;* we have circumscribed all the power thou hast given us into one *narrow selfish* compass; we have heaped up treasures for those who came after us, though we know not whether they would not make a still wrose use of them than we ourselves did." And how can such foolish pleaders expect any other sentence than the dreadful—"*Depart, ye cursed !*" But sure, my dear parents, such persons can have no notion of the exalted pleasures that flow from doing good, were there to be no after-account at all!

There is something so satisfactory and pleasing to reflect on the being able to administer comfort and relief to those who stand in need of it, as infinitely, of itself, rewards the beneficent mind. How often have I experienced this in my good lady's time, though but the second-hand dispenser of her benefits to the poor and sickly, when she made me her almoner!—How have I been affected with the blessings which the miserable have heaped upon her for her goodness, and upon me for being but the humble conveyer of her bounty to them!—And how delighted have I been, when the moving reports I have made of a particular distress have augmented my good lady's first intentions in relief of it!

This I recall with pleasure; for it is now, by the Divine goodness, become my part to do those good things she was wont to do; and, oh! let me watch myself, that my prosperous state do not make me forget to look up with due thankfulness to him who has entrusted me with the *power*, that I may not incur a terrible woe by the abuse or neglect of it!

Forgive me these reflections, my dear parents; and let me have your prayers, that I may not find my present happiness a snare to me, but consider, that more and more will be expected from me, in proportion to my power; and that I may not so unworthily act, as if I believed I ought to set up my rest in my *mean self*, and think nothing further to be done, with the opportunities given me, by the Divine favour, and the best of men!

326

My master returned home to dinner, in compliment to me, though much pressed to dine with Lady Jones, as also by Sir Simon, to dine with him. Mr. Peters could not conveniently provide a preacher, for his own church, to-morrow morning, at so short a notice, Mr. Williams being gone to his new living, but believed he could for the afternoon; so he promised to give us his company to dinner, and to read afternoon service; this made my master invite all the rest, as well as him, to dinner, and not to church: he made them promise to come; and told Mr. Peters, he would send his coach for him and his family.

Miss Darnford told him pleasantly, she would not come, unless he would promise to let her be at his wedding; by which I find Mr. Peters has kept the secret as my master desired.

He was pleased to give me an airing after dinner in the chariot, and renewed his kind assurances, and, if possible, is kinder than ever. This is sweetly comfortable, because it shews he does not repent of his condescensions to me: and it encourages me to look up to him with more satisfaction of mind, and less doubtfulness.

I begged leave to send a guinea to a poor body in the town, who, I heard by Mrs. Jewkes, lay very ill, and was very destitute. He said, " Send two, my dear, if you please." Said I, " Sir, I will never do anything of this kind without letting you know." He most generously answered, " I shall then, perhaps, have you do less good than you would otherwise do, from a doubt of me; though, I hope, your discretion, and my own temper, which is not avaricious, will make such doubts causeless.

" Now, my dear," continued he, " I'll tell you how we will order this point, to avoid even the shadow of uneasiness on one side, or doubt on the other.

" As to your father and mother, in the first place, they shall be quite out of the question; for I have already determined about them :—they shall go down, if they and you think well of it, to my little Kentish estate: which I once mentioned to you in such a manner, as made you reject it with a nobleness of mind, that gave me pain then, but pleasure since. There is a pretty little farm and house, untenanted, upon that estate, and tolerably well stocked, and I will further stock it for them; for such industrious folks won't know how to live without some employment: and it shall be theirs for both their lives, without paying any rent; I will allow them 50*l.* per ann. besides, that they may keep up the stock, and be kind to any other of your relations without being beholden to you or me, for small matters; and for greater, where needful you shall always have it in your power to accommodate them; for I shall never question your prudence. We will, as long as God spares our lives, go down once a year to see them; and they shall come up, as often as they please, it cannot be too often, to see us; for I mean not this, my dear, to send them from us.—Before I proceed, does my Pamela like this?"

"O, Sir," said I, "the English tongue affords not words, or at least I have them not, to express, sufficiently my gratitude. Teach me, dear Sir," continued I, pressing his hands to my lips, "teach me some other language, if there be any, that abounds with more grateful terms; that I may not thus be choked with meanings, for which I can find no utterance."

"My charmer!" says he, "your language is all wonderful, as your sentiments: and you most abound, when you seem most to want!—All that I wish is, to find my proposals agreeable to you; and if my *first* are not, my *second* shall be, if I can but know what you wish."

Did I say too much, my dearest parents, when I said, he was, if *possible*, kinder and kinder? For my heart is overwhelmed with his goodness.

"Well," said he, "my dearest, let me desire you to mention it to *them*, to see if they approve it. But, if it be your choice, and theirs, to have them nearer to you, or even under the same roof with you, I will freely consent to it."

"O no, Sir," said I (and I fear almost sinned in my grateful flight), "I am sure they would not choose that; they could not, perhaps, serve God so well, if they lived with you; for, so constantly seeing the hand that blesses them, they might, as must be my care to avoid, be tempted to look no further in their gratitude, than to the dear dispenser of such innumerable benefits!"

"Excellent creature!" said he, "my beloved wants no language, nor sentiment neither; her charming thoughts, so sweetly expressed, would grace any language; and this is a blessing almost peculiar to my fairest.—Your so kind acceptance, my Pamela," added he, "repays the benefit with interest, and leaves me under obligation to your goodness.

"But now, I will tell you what we will do, with regard to points of your own private charity; for far be it from me, to put under that name, the subject we have been mentioning; because that, and more than that, is duty, to persons so worthy, and nearly related to my Pamela, and, as such, to myself."

328

O how the sweet man outdoes me, in thoughts, words, power, and every thing !

"And this," said he, "lies in very small compass : for I will allow you two hundred pounds a year, which Longman shall constantly pay you, at fifty pounds a quarter, for your own use, and of which I expect no account; to commence from the day you enter into my other house : I mean," said he, "that the first fifty pounds shall then be due ; because you shall have something to begin with. And," added the dear generous man, "if this be pleasing to you, let it, since you say you want words, be signified by such a sweet kiss as you gave me yesterday." I hesitated not a moment to comply with these obliging terms ; and threw my arms about his dear neck, though in the chariot, and blessed his goodness to me. "Sir," said I, "I cannot bear this generous treatment !" He was pleased to say, "Don't be uneasy, my dear, about these trifles : God has blessed me with a very good estate, and all of it in a prosperous condition, and generally well tenanted.

"I lay up money every year, and have besides, large sums in government and other securities ; so that you will find, what I have hitherto promised, is very short of that proportion of my substance, which, as my dearest wife, you have a right to."

Thus sweetly did we pass our time till evening, when the chariot brought us home, and our supper succeeded in the same agreeable manner. Thus, in a rapturous circle, the time moves on, every hour bringing with it something more delightful than the past !—Sure nobody was ever so blest as I !

SUNDAY, THE FOURTH DAY OF MY HAPPINESS.

Not going to chapel this morning, the reason of which I told you, I bestowed the time, from the hour of my beloved's rising to breakfast, in prayer and thanksgiving, in my closet. I now begin to be quite easy, cheerful, and free in my spirits ; and the rather, as I find myself encouraged by the tranquillity, and pleasing vivacity, in the temper and behaviour of my beloved, who thereby shews he does not repent of his goodness to me.

I attended him to breakfast with great pleasure and freedom, and he seemed quite pleased with me, and said, "Now does my dearest begin to look upon me with an air of serenity and satisfaction : it shall be always my delight to give you occasion for this sweet becoming aspect of confidence and pleasure in me."—"My heart, dear Sir," said I, "is quite easy, and has lost all its foolish tumults, which, combating with my gratitude, might

329

give an unacceptable appearance to my behaviour, but now your goodness, Sir, has enabled it to get the better of its uneasy apprehensions, and my heart is all of *one* piece, and devoted to you, and grateful tranquillity. And could I be so happy as to see you and my good Lady Davers reconciled, I have nothing in this world to wish for more, but the continuance of your favour."

He said, " I wish this reconciliation as well as you : and I do assure you, more for your sake than my own : and if she would behave tolerably, I would make the terms easier to her, for that reason."

He said, " I will lay down one rule for you, my Pamela, to observe in your dress; and I will tell you every thing I like or dislike, as it occurs to me : I would have you do the same, on your part; that nothing may lie upon either of our minds, that may occasion the least reservedness.

" I have often observed, in married folks, that the lady soon grows careless in her dress; which to me, looks as if she would take no pains to secure the affection she had gained; and shews a slight to her husband, that she had not to her lover. Now, you must know, this has always given me great offence; and I should not forgive it even in my Pamela, though she would have *this* excuse for herself, which thousands could not make, that she looks lovely in every thing. So, my dear, I shall expect of you always to be dressed by dinner-time, except something extraordinary happens : and this, whether you are to go abroad, or stay at home. For this, my love, will continue to you that sweet ease in your dress and behaviour, which you are so happy a mistress of; and whomsoever I bring home to my table, you'll be in readiness to receive : and will not want to make those foolish apologies to unexpected visitors, which carry with them a reflection on the conduct of those who make them; and, besides, will convince me, that you think yourself obliged to appear as graceful to your husband, as you would to persons less familiar to your sight."

" This, dear Sir," said I, " is a most obliging injunction; and I most heartily thank you for it, and will always take care to obey it."—" Why, my dear," said he, " you may better do this than half your sex; because they too generally act in such a manner, as if they seemed to think it the privilege of birth and fortune, to turn day into night, and night into day, and are seldom stirring till 'tis time to sit down to dinner; and so all the good old family rules are reversed : for they breakfast when they should dine; dine when they should sup; and sup when they should go to bed; and, by the help of dear quadrille, sometimes go to bed when they should rise.—In all things but these, my dear," continued he, " I expect you to be a lady. My good mother was one of the old-fashioned cut, and in all other respects, as worthy a lady as any in the kingdom. So you have not been used to the new way, and may the easier practise the other."

" Dear Sir," said I, " pray give me more of your sweet injunctions."—" Why, then," continued he, " I shall, in the usual course, and generally, if not hindered by company, like to go to bed with my dearest by eleven ; and if I don't, shan't hinder you. I ordinarily now rise by six in summer. I will allow you to lie half an hour after me, or so. Then you'll have some time you may call your own, till you give me your company to breakfast ; which may be always so, as that we may have done at a little after nine. And you will have several hours again, at your disposal, till two o'clock, when I should like to sit down at table.

" You will then have several useful hours more to employ yourself in, as you please ; I would generally go to supper by eight. And when we are resolved to stick to these old-fashioned rules, as near as we can, we shall make our visitors conform to them too, expect them from us, and suit themselves accordingly : for I have always observed, that it is in every one's power to prescribe rules to himself. It is only standing a few ridiculous jests at first, from such, generally, as are not the most worthy to be minded : and after a while they will say, ' It signifies nothing to ask him : he will have his own way. There is no putting him out of his bias. He is a regular piece of clockwork ! ' And, why, my dear, should we not be so ? For man is as frail a piece of machinery as any clock-work whatever : and, by irregularity, is as subject to be disordered.

" Then, my dear," continued the charming man, " when they see they are received at my *own* times, with an open countenance, and cheerful heart ; when they see plenty and variety at my board, and meet a kind and hearty welcome from us both ; they will not offer to break in upon my conditions, nor grudge me my regular hours : and as most of these people have nothing to do except to rise in a morning, they may as well come to breakfast with us at half an hour after eight in summer, as at ten or eleven ; to dinner at two, as at four, five, or six : and to supper at eight, as ten or eleven. Then our servants too will know, generally, the times of their business, and their hours of leisure ; and we, as well as they, shall reap the benefit of this regularity. And who knows, my dear, but we may revive the good old fashion in our neighbourhood by this means ? At

331

least it will be doing our part towards it; and answering the good lesson I learned at school—'*Every one mend one.*' And the worst that will happen will be, that when some of my brother rakes, such as those who broke in upon us so unwelcomely last Thursday, are gone out of the way, and begin to consider whom they shall go to dine with in their rambles, they will only say, 'We must not go to him, for his dinner-time is over;' and so they'll reserve me for another time, when they happen to suit it better; or, perhaps, they will take a supper and a bed with me instead of it.

"Now, my dearest," continued the kind man, "you see here are more of my injunctions, as you call them; and though I will not be so set as to quarrel if they are not always exactly complied with, yet as I know you won't think them unreasonable, I shall be glad they may, as often as they can; and you will give your orders accordingly, to *your* Mrs. Jervis, who is a good woman, and will take pleasure in obeying you."

"O dearest, dear Sir," said I, "have you nothing more to honour me with? You oblige and improve me at the same time. What a happy lot is mine!"

"Why, let me see, my dearest," said he—"but I think of no more at present : for it will be needless to say, how much I value you for your natural sweetness of temper, and that open cheerfulness of countenance which adorns you, when nothing has given my fairest apprehensions for her virtue; a sweetness and a cheerfulness, that prepossesses in your favour, at first sight the mind of every one that beholds you. I need not, I hope, say that I would have you diligently preserve this sweet appearance : let no thwarting accident, no cross fortune (for we must not expect to be exempt from such, happy as we now are in each other), deprive this sweet face of this its *principal* grace : and when any thing unpleasing happens, in a quarter of an hour, at farthest, begin to mistrust yourself, and apply to your glass; and if you see a gloom arising, or arisen, banish it instantly; smoothe your dear countenance; resume your former composure; and then my dearest, whose heart must always be seen in her face, and cannot be a hypocrite, will find this a means to smoothe her passions also; and if the occasion be too strong for so sudden a conquest, she will know how to do it more effectually, by repairing to her closet, and begging that gracious assistance which has never yet failed her; and so shall I, who, as you once justly observed, was too much indulged by my good mother, have an example from you, as well as a pleasure in you, which will never be palled.

" I have frequently observed at the house of many a gentleman, that when we have unexpectedly visited, or broken in upon the family order laid down by the lady, and especially if any of us have lain under the suspicion of having occasionally seduced our married companion into bad hours, or given indifferent examples, the poor *gentleman* has been oddly affected at our coming; though the good breeding of the lady has made her just keep up appearances. *He* has looked so conscious; has been so afraid, as it were, to disoblige; has made so many excuses for some of us, before we have been accused, as have always shewn me how unwelcome we have been, and how much he is obliged to compound with his lady for a tolerable reception of us; and perhaps she too, in proportion to the honest man's concern to court her smiles, has been more reserved, stiff, and formal, and has behaved with an indifference and slight, that has made me wish myself out of *her* house; for too plainly have I seen, that it was not *his*. This, my dear, you may judge, has afforded me subject for animadversion upon the married life : for a man may not (though he is willing to flatter himself that he is master of his house, and will assert his prerogative upon great occasions, when it is strongly invaded) be always willing to contend; and such women as I have described, are always ready to take the field, and are worse enemies than the old Parthians, who annoy most when they seem to retreat; and never fail to return to the charge again, and carry on the offensive war, till they have tired our resistance, and made the husband willing, like a vanquished enemy, to compound for small matters, in order to preserve something. At least, the poor man does not care to let his friends see his case; and so will not provoke a fire to break out, that he sees (and so do his friends too) the *meek* lady has much ado to smother; and which very possibly burns, with a most comfortable ardour, after we are gone.

" You smile, my Pamela," said he, " at this whimsical picture ; and, I am sure I never shall have reason to include you in these disagreeable outlines; but yet will I say, that I expect from you, whoever comes to my house, that you accustom yourself to one even, uniform complaisance; that no frown take place on your brow; that however ill or well provided we may be for their reception, you show no flutter or discomposure; that whoever you may have in your company at the time, you signify not, by the least reserved look, that the stranger is come upon you unseasonably, or at a time you wish he had not. But be facetious, kind, and obliging to all; and if to any one more than to another, to such as have the least reason to expect it

333

from you, or who are most inferior at the table; for thus will you, my Pamela, cheer the doubting mind, quiet the uneasy heart, and diffuse ease, pleasure, and tranquillity, around my board.

"And be sure, my dear," continued he, "let no little accident ruffle your temper. I shall never forget once, that I was at Lady Arthur's, and a footman happened to stumble with a fine China dish, and broke it all to pieces: it was grievous to see the uneasiness of the poor lady; and she was so sincere in it, that she suffered it to spread all over the company, and it was a pretty large one too; and not a person in it, but turned either her consoler, or fell into stories of the like misfortunes; so we all became, during the evening, nothing but blundering footmen, and careless servants, or were turned into broken jars, plates, glasses, tea-cups, and such like brittle substances. And it affected me so much, that when I came home, I went to bed and dreamt, that Robin, with the handle of his whip, broke the fore-glass of my chariot; and I was so solicitous, methought, to keep the good lady in countenance for *her* anger, that I broke his head in revenge, and stabbed one of my coach-horses. All the comfort I had when it was done, methought, was, that I had not exposed myself before company; and there were no sufferers but guilty Robin, and one innocent coach-horse."

I was exceedingly diverted with these facetious hints, and the pleasant manner in which he gave them, and I promised to improve by the excellent lessons contained in them.

I then went up and dressed myself, like a bride, in my best clothes; and, on enquiry, hearing my dearest master was gone to walk in the garden, I went to him. He was reading in the little alcove; and I said, "Sir, am I licensed to intrude upon you?"—"No, my dear," said he, "because you cannot *intrude*. I am so wholly yours, that wherever I am, you have not only a right to join me, but you do me a very acceptable favour at the same time."

"I have, Sir," said I, "obeyed your first kind injunctions, as to dressing myself before dinner. But, may-be, you are busy, Sir?" He put up the papers he was reading, and said, "I can have no business or pleasure of equal value to your company, my dear. What were you going to say?"—"Only, Sir, to know if you have any more kind injunctions to give me? I could hear you talk a whole day together."—"You are very obliging, Pamela," said he; "but you are so perfectly what I wish, that I might have spared those I gave you; but I was willing you should have a taste of my freedom with you, to put you upon the like with me : for I am confident there can be no friendship lasting without freedom, and communicating to one another even the little caprices, if my Pamela can have any such, which may occasion uneasiness to either.

"Now, my dear," said he, "be so good as to find some fault with me, and say what you would wish me to do, to appear more agreeable to you."—"O, Sir," said I, and I could have kissed him, but for shame, (to be sure I shall grow a sad fond hussy !) "I have not one single thing to wish for ; no, not one !" He saluted me very kindly, and said, he should be sorry if I had, and forbore to speak it. "Do you think, my dear Sir," said I, "that your Pamela has no conscience ? Do you think that, because you kindly oblige her, and delight in obliging her, that she must rack her invention for trials of your goodness, and knows not when she's happy ? O, my dearest Sir," added I, "less than one half of the favours you have so generously conferred upon me, would have exceeded my utmost wishes."

"My dear angel," said he, and kissed me again, "I shall be troublesome to you with my kisses, if you continue thus sweetly obliging in your actions and expressions."—"O Sir," said I, "I have been thinking, as I was dressing myself, what excellent lessons you teach me.

"When you command me, at your table, to cheer the doubting mind, comfort the uneasy heart, and behave most kindly to those who have least reason to expect it, and are most inferior ; how sweetly, in every instance that could possibly occur, have you done this yourself, by your poor, unworthy Pamela, till you have diffused, in your own dear words, ease, pleasure, and tranquillity, around my glad heart !

"Then again, Sir, when you bid me not be disturbed by little accidents, or by strangers coming in upon me unexpectedly, how noble an instance did you give me of this, when on our happy wedding-day, the coming of Sir Charles Hargrave, and the other two gentlemen (for which you was quite unprovided, and which hindered our happiness of dining together on that chosen day), did not so disturb you, but that you entertained the gentlemen pleasantly, and parted with them civilly and kindly ! What charming instances are these, I recollect with pleasure, of your pursuing the doctrine you deliver !"

"My dear," said he, "these observations are very kind in you, and much to my advantage ; but if I do not always (for I fear these were too much accidents) so well pursue the doctrines I lay down, my Pamela must not expect my imperfections to be a plea for her non-observance of my lessons, as you call them ;

for, I doubt, I shall never be half so perfect as you; so I cannot permit you to recede in your goodness, though I may find myself unable to advance, as I ought, in my duty."

"I hope, Sir," said I, "by God's grace, I never shall."—"I believe it," said he; "but I only mention this, knowing my own defects, lest my future lessons should not be so well warranted by my practice, as in the instances you have kindly recollected."

He was pleased to take notice of my dress, and spanning my waist with his hands, said, "What a sweet shape is here! It would make one regret to lose it; and yet, my beloved Pamela, I shall think nothing but that loss wanting to complete my happiness." I put my bold hand before his mouth, and said, "Hush, hush! O fie, Sir! The freest thing you have ever yet said, since I have been yours!" He kissed my hand, and said, "Such an innocent wish, my dearest, may be permitted me, because it is the end of the institution. But say, would such a case be unwelcome to my Pamela?"—"I will say, Sir," said I, and hid my blushing face on his bosom, "that your wishes in every thing shall be mine: but, pray, Sir, say no more." He kindly saluted me, and thanked me, and changed the subject. I was not too free, I hope.

Thus we talked till we heard the coaches: and then he said, "Stay here in the garden, my dear, and I'll bring the company to you." When he was gone, I passed by the back-door, kneeled down against it, and blessed God for not permitting my then so much desired escape. I went to the pond, and kneeled down on the mossy bank, and again blessed God there, for his mercy in my escape from myself, my then worst enemy; though I thought I had none but enemies, and no friend near me. And so I ought to do in almost every step of this garden, and every room in this house! I was bending my steps to the dear little chapel, to make my acknowledgment there; but I saw the company approaching.

Miss Darnford said, "So, Miss Andrews, how do you now? O, you look so easy, so sweetly, so pleased, that I know you'll let me dance at your wedding, for I shall long to be there." Lady Jones was pleased to say I looked like an angel: and Mrs. Peters said, I improved upon them every time they saw me. Lady Darnford also made me a fine compliment, and said I looked freer and easier every time she saw me. "Dear heart! I wish," thought I, "you will spare these compliments! for I shall have some joke, I doubt, passed on me by-and-by, that will make me suffer for all these fine things."

Mr. Peters said softly, "God bless you, dear daughter, but

not so much as my wife knows it." Sir Simon came in last and took me by the hand, and said, " Mr. B., by your leave ; " and kissed my hand five or six times as if he was mad ; and held it with both his, and made a very free jest by way of compliment, in his way. Well, I think a *young rake* is hardly tolerable ; but an *old rake*, and an *old beau*, are two very sad things ! All this before daughters women grown ! I whispered my dearest, a little after, and said, " I fear I shall suffer much from Sir Simon's rude jokes by-and-by, when you reveal the matter."—" 'Tis his way, my dear," said he ; " you must now grow above these things." Miss Nanny Darnford said, with a sort of half grave, ironical air—" Well, Miss Andrews, if I may judge by your easy deportment now, to what it was when I saw you last, I hope you will let my sister, if you won't me, see the happy knot tied ; for she is quite wild about it." I curtseyed, and only said, " You are all very good to me, ladies." Mr. Peters's niece said, " Well, Miss Andrews, I hope, before we part, we shall be told the happy day." My good master heard her ; and said, " You shall, you shall, Madam."—" That's pure," said Miss Darnford.

He took me aside, and said softly, " Shall I lead them to the alcove, and tell them there, or stay till we go in to dinner ? "—" Neither, Sir, I think," said I, " I fear I shan't stand it."—" Nay," said he, " they must know it ; I would not have invited them else."—" Why, then, Sir," said I, " let it alone till they are going away."—" Then," replied he, " you must pull off your ring."—" No, no, Sir," said I, " that I must not."—" Well," said he, " do you tell Miss Darnford of it yourself."—" Indeed, Sir," answered I, " I cannot."

Mrs. Jewkes came officiously to ask my master, just then, if she should bring a glass of Rhenish and sugar before dinner, for the gentlemen and ladies : and he said, " That's well thought of ; bring it, Mrs. Jewkes."

And she came, a man attending her, with two bottles and glasses, and a salver ; and must needs, making a low curtsey, offer first to me, saying, " Will your ladyship begin ? " I coloured like scarlet, and said, " No ; my master, to be sure."

But they all took the hint, and Miss Darnford said, " I'll be hanged if they have not stolen a wedding."—Said Mr. Peters, " It must certainly be so ! "—" Ah ! Mr. Peters," said Sir Simon. " I'll assure you," said he, " I have not married them."— " Where were you," said she, " and Mr. Williams, last Thursday morning ? " Said Sir Simon, " Let me alone, let me alone ; if any thing has been stolen, I'll find it out ; I am a justice of the

337

peace, you know." And so he took me by the hand, and said, "Come, Madam, answer me, by the oath you have taken: Are you married or not?"

My master smiled to see me look so like a fool; and I said, "Pray, Sir Simon!"—"Ay, ay," said he, "I thought you did not look so smirking upon us for nothing."—"Well, then, Pamela," said my master, "since your blushes discover you, don't be ashamed, but confess the truth."

"Now," said Miss Darnford, "I am quite angry;" and said Lady Darnford, "I am quite pleased;—let me give you joy, dear Madam, if it be so." And so they all said, and saluted me round. I was vexed it was before Mrs. Jewkes; for she shook her fat sides, and seemed highly pleased to be a means of discovering it.

"Nobody," said my master, "wishes me joy."—"No," said Lady Jones, very obligingly, "nobody need; for, with such a peerless spouse, you want no good wishes!" And he saluted them; and when he came last to me, said, before them all, "Now, my sweet bride, my Pamela, let me conclude with you, for here I begin to love, and here I desire to end loving, but not till my life ends."

This was sweetly said, and taken great notice of, and it was doing credit to his own generous choice, and vastly more than I merited.

But I was forced to stand many more jokes afterwards: for Sir Simon said, several times, "Come, come, Madam, now you are become one of us, I shall be a little less scrupulous than I have been, I'll assure you."

When we came in to dinner, I made no difficulty of what all offered me, the upper end of the table; and performed the honours of it with pretty tolerable presence of mind, considering. And, with much ado, my good benefactor promising to be down again before winter, we got off the ball; but appointed Tuesday evening, at Lady Darnford's, to take leave of all this good company, who promised to be there, my master designing to set out on Wednesday morning for Bedfordshire.

We had prayers in the little chapel, in the afternoon; but they all wished for the good clerk again, with great encomiums upon you, my dear father; and the company staid supper also, and departed exceedingly well satisfied, and with abundance of wishes for the continuance of our mutual happiness; and my master desired Mr. Peters to answer for him to the ringers, at the town, if they should hear of it till our return into this country; and that then he would be bountiful to them, because he would not publicly declare it till he had first done so in Bedfordshire.

I have had very little of my dear friend's company this day; for he only staid breakfast, and rode out to see a sick gentleman, about eighteen miles off, who begged (by a man and horse on purpose) to speak with him, believing he should not recover, and upon part of whose estate my master has a mortgage. He said, " My dearest, I shall be very uneasy, if obliged to tarry all night from you; but lest you should be alarmed, if I don't come home by ten, don't expect me : for poor Mr. Carlton and I have pretty large concerns together; and if he should be very ill, and would be comforted by my presence (as I know he loves me, and his family will be more in my power, if he dies, than I wish for), charity will not let me refuse."

It is now ten o'clock at night, and I fear he will not return. I *fear* for the sake of his poor sick friend, who I doubt is worse. Though I know not the gentleman, I am sorry for his own sake, for his family's sake, and for my dear master's sake, who, by his kind expressions, I find, loves him : and methinks, I should be sorry any grief should touch his generous heart; yet there is no living in this world, without too many occasions for concern, even in the most prosperous state. And it is fit it should be so; or else, poor wretches as we are ! we should look no further, but be like sensual travellers on a journey homeward, who, meeting with good entertainment at some inn in the way, rest there, and never think of pursuing their journey to their proper home.— This, I remember, was often a reflection of my good lady's, to whom I owe it.

Mrs. Jewkes has been with me, and asked if I will have her for a bed-fellow, in want of a better ? I thanked her; but I said I would see how it was to lie by myself one night.

I might have mentioned, that I made Mrs. Jewkes dine and sup with me : and she was much pleased with it, and my behaviour to her. I could see by her manner, that she was a little struck inwardly at some of her former conduct to me. But, poor wretch ! it is much, I fear, because I am what I am; for she has otherwise very little remorse, I doubt. Her talk and actions are entirely different from what they used to be, quite circumspect and decent; and I should have thought her virtuous, and even pious, had I never known her in another light.

By this we may see, my dear father and mother, of what force example is; and what is in the power of the heads of families to do: and this shews that evil examples in superiors are doubly pernicious, and doubly culpable, because such persons are bad *themselves*, and not only do no good, but much *harm* to others; and the condemnation of such must, to be sure, be so much the greater. And how much the greater still must my condemnation be, who have had such a religious education under you, and been so well nurtured by my good lady, if I should forget, with all these mercies, what belongs to my station! O how I long to be doing some good! For all that is past yet is my dear master's; God bless him! and return him safe to my wishes! for methinks, already, 'tis a week since I saw him: if my love would not be troublesome and impertinent, I should be nothing else: for I have a true grateful spirit; and I had need to have such a one, for I am poor in every thing but will.

TUESDAY MORNING ELEVEN O'CLOCK.

My dear, dear—master (I am sure I should still say; but I will learn to rise to a softer epithet, now-and-then) is not yet come. I hope he is safe and well! So Mrs. Jewkes and I went to breakfast. But I can do nothing but talk and think of him, and all his kindness to me, and to you, which is still *me* more intimately! I have just received a letter from him, which he wrote overnight, as I find by it, and sent early this morning. This is a copy of it.

" TO MRS. ANDREWS.

" *Monday Night.*

" MY DEAREST PAMELA,

" I hope my not coming home this night will not frighten you. You may believe I cannot help it. My poor friend is so very ill, that I doubt he can't recover. His desires to have me stay with him are so strong, that I shall sit up all night with him, as it is now near one o'clock in the morning; for he can't bear me out of his sight: and I have made him and his distressed wife and children so easy, in the kindest assurances I could give him of my consideration for him and them, that I am looked upon (as the poor disconsolate widow, as she I doubt, will soon be, tells me) as their good angel. I could have wished we had not engaged to the good neighbourhood at Sir Simon's for to-morrow night; but I am so desirous to set out on Wednesday for the other house, that, as well as in return for the civilities of so many good friends, who will be there on purpose, I would not put it off. What I beg of you, therefore, my dear, is, that

340

you would go in the chariot to Sir Simon's, the sooner in the day the better, because you will be diverted with the company, who also much admire you; and I hope to join you there by your tea-time in the afternoon, which will be better than going home, and returning with you, as it will be six miles difference to me, and I know the good company will excuse my dress for the occasion. I count every hour of this little absence for a day: for I am, with the utmost sincerity, *my dearest love, for ever yours, &c.*

"If you could go to dine with them, it will be a freedom that would be very pleasing to them; and the more as they don't expect it."

I began to have a little concern, lest his fatigue should be too great, and for the poor sick gentleman and family; but told Mrs. Jewkes, that the least intimation of his choice should be a command to me, and so I would go to dinner there; and ordered the chariot to be got ready to carry me: when a messenger came up, just as I was dressed, to tell her, she must come down immediately. I see at the window, that visitors are come; for there is a chariot and six horses, the company gone out of it, and three footmen on horseback; and I think the chariot has coronets. Who can it be, I wonder!—But here I will stop; for I suppose I shall soon know.

Good Sirs! how unlucky this is! what shall I do? Here is Lady Davers come, and my kind protector a great many miles off.—Mrs. Jewkes, out of breath, comes to tell me this, and says she is enquiring for my master and me. She asked her, naughty lady as she is, if I was whor'd yet? There's a word for a lady's mouth! Mrs. Jewkes says, she knew not what to answer. And my lady said, " She is not married, I hope."—And said she, " I said, ' No;' because you have not owned it yet publicly." My lady said, "That was well enough." Said I, " I will run away, Mrs. Jewkes; and let the chariot go to the bottom of the elm-walk, and I will steal out of the door unperceived."—" But she is enquiring for you, Madam," replied she, " and I said you was within, but going out; and she said she would see you presently, as soon as she could have patience."—" What did she call me?" said I. " The creature, Madam, ' I will see the creature,' said she, ' as soon as I can have patience.' "—" Ay, but," said I, " *the creature* won't let her, if she can help it.

" Pray, Mrs. Jewkes, favour my escape, for this once; for I am sadly frightened."—Said she, " I'll bid the chariot go down, as you order, and wait till you come; and I'll step down

and shut the hall-door, that you may pass unobserved : for she
sits cooling herself in the parlour, over against the stair-case."—
" That's a good Mrs. Jewkes," said I : " but who has she with
her ? "—" Her woman," answered she, " and her nephew ; but
he is gone into the stables, and they have three footmen."—
" I wish," said I, " they were all three hundred miles off.—What
shall I do ? " So I wrote thus far, and wait impatiently to hear
the coast is clear.

Mrs. Jewkes tells me, I must come down or she will come up.
" What does she call me now ? " said I. " *Wench*, Madam.
' *Bid the wench come down to me*.' Her nephew and woman are
with her."

Said I, " I can't go, and that's enough !—You might contrive
it that I might get out, if you would."—" Indeed, Madam," said
she, " I cannot, for I went to shut the door, and she bid me let it
stand open ; and there she sits over against the stair-case."—
" Then," said I, " I'll get out of the window, I think ; " (and
fanned myself ;) " for I am sadly frighted."—" Laud, Madam,"
said she, " I wonder you so much disturb yourself.—You're on
the right side the hedge, I'm sure ; I would not be so discomposed for any body."—" Aye," said I, " but who can help
constitution ? I dare say, you would no more be so discomposed,
than I can help it." Said she, " Indeed, Madam, if it was to me,
I would put on an air as mistress of the house, as you *are*, go
and salute her ladyship, and bid her welcome."—" Ay, ay,"
replied I, " fine talking ! But how unlucky this is, your good
master is not at home."

" What answer shall I give her," said she, " to her desiring to
see you ? "—" Tell her," said I, " I am sick a-bed ; I'm dying,
and must not be disturbed ; I'm gone out—or any thing."

But her woman came up to me, just as I had uttered this, and
said, " How do you do, Mrs. Pamela ! My lady desires to speak
with you." So I must go. Sure she won't beat me.—O that
my dear protector was at home !

Well, now I will tell you all that happened in this frightful
interview.—And very bad it was.

I went down, dressed as I was, and my gloves on, and my fan
in my hand, to be just ready to get into the chariot, when I could
get away ; and I thought all my trembling fits had been over
now ; but I was mistaken ; for I trembled sadly : yet resolved
to put on as good an air as I could.

So I went to the parlour, and said, making a very low curtsey,
" Your servant, my good lady."—" And your servant, again,"
said she, " *my lady* ; for I think you are dressed out like one."

342

" A charming girl though," said her rakish nephew, and swore a great oath; "dear aunt, forgive me, but I must kiss her:" and was coming to me. I said, " Forbear, uncivil gentleman! I won't be used freely."—" Jackey," said my lady, " sit down, and don't touch the creature: she's proud enough already. There's a great difference in her air, I'll assure you, since I saw her last."

" Well, child," said she, sneeringly, " how dost find thyself? —Thou'rt mightily come on, of late!—I hear strange reports about thee!—Thou'rt almost got into fool's paradise, I doubt! —And wilt find thyself terribly mistaken in a little while, if thou thinkest my brother will disgrace his family to humour thy baby-face!"

" I see," said I, sadly vexed (her woman and nephew smiling by), " her ladyship has no very important commands for me; and I beg to withdraw."—" Beck," said she to her woman, " shut the door; my young lady and I must not have done so soon."

" Where's your well-mannered deceiver gone, child?" says she. Said I, " When your ladyship is pleased to speak intelligibly, I shall know how to answer."

" Well, but, my dear child," said she, in drollery, " don't be too pert, neither, I beseech thee. Thou wilt not find thy master's sister half so ready to take thy freedoms, as he is!—So, a little of that modesty and humility that my mother's waiting-maid used to shew, will become thee better than the airs thou givest thyself, since my mother's son has taught thee to forget thyself."

" I would beg," said I, " one favour of your ladyship, that if you would have me keep my distance, you will not forget your own degree."—" Why, suppose, Miss Pert, I should forget my degree, wouldst thou not keep thy distance then?"

" If you, Madam," said I, " lessen the distance yourself, you will descend to my level, and make an equality which I don't presume to think of; for I can't descend lower than I am—at least in your ladyship's esteem."

" Did I not tell you, Jackey," said she, " that I should have a wit to talk to?" He, who swears like a fine gentleman at every word, rapping out an oath, said, drolling, " I think, Mrs. Pamela, if I may be so bold as to say so, you should know you are speaking to Lady Davers."—" Sir," said I, " I hope there was no need of your information, so I can't thank you for it; and am sorry you seem to think it wants an oath to convince me of the truth of it."

He looked more foolish than I, at this, if possible, not expecting

343

such a reprimand :—and said, at last, " Why, Mrs. Pamela, you
put me half out of countenance with your witty reproof."—
" Sir," said I, " you seem quite a fine gentleman ; and it will
not be easily done, I dare say."

" How now, pert one," said my lady, " do you know whom
you talk to ? "—" I think I do not, Madam," replied I : " and,
for fear I should forget myself more, I'll withdraw. Your ladyship's servant ! " said I ; and was going : but she rose, and gave
me a push, and pulled a chair, and setting the back against the
door, sat down in it.

" Well," said I, " I can bear any thing at your ladyship's
hands ; " but I was ready to cry, though. And I went, and sat
down, and fanned myself at the other end of the room.

Her woman, who stood all the time, said softly, " Mrs. Pamela,
you should not sit in my lady's presence." And my lady,
though she did not hear *her*, said, " You shall sit down, child,
in the room where I am, when I give you leave."

So I stood up, and said, " When your ladyship will hardly
permit me to stand, one might be indulged to sit down."—" But
I asked you," said she, " whither your master is gone ! "—" To
one Mr. Carlton, Madam, about eighteen miles off, who is very
sick."—" And when does he come home ? "—" This evening,
Madam."—" And where are you going ? "—" To a gentleman's
house in the town, Madam."—" And how was you to go ? "—
" In the chariot."—" Why, you must be a lady in time, to be
sure !—I believe you'd become a chariot mighty well, child !—
Was you ever out in it with your master ? "

" Pray, your ladyship," said I, a little too pertly, perhaps,
" be pleased to ask half a dozen such questions together ; as
one answer may do for all."—" Why, Boldface," said she,
" you'll forget your distance, and bring me to your level before
my time."

I could no longer refrain tears, but said, " Pray, your ladyship,
let me ask, what I have done to be thus severely treated ? I
never did your ladyship any harm. And if you think I am
deceived, as you was pleased to hint, I should be more entitled
to your pity than your anger."

She arose, and led me to her chair ; then sat down ; and still
holding my hand, said, " Why, Pamela, I did indeed pity you,
while I thought you innocent ; and when my brother seized
you, and brought you down hither, without your consent, I
was concerned for you ; and was still more concerned for you,
and loved you, when I heard of your virtue and resistance, and
your laudable efforts to get away from him. But when, as I

fear, you have suffered yourself to be prevailed upon, and have lost your innocence, and added another to the number of the fools he has ruined " (*this shocked me a little*), " I cannot help shewing my displeasure to you."

" Madam," replied I, " I must beg no hasty judgment : I have *not* lost my innocence."—" Take care, take care, Pamela ! " said she : " don't lose your veracity, as well as your honour ! Why are you here when at full liberty to go whither you please ? —I will make one proposal ; and, if you are innocent, I'm sure you'll accept it. Will you go and live with me ?—I will instantly set out with you in my chariot, and not stay half an hour longer in this house, if you'll go with me.—Now, if you are innocent, and willing to keep so, deny me, if you can."

" I am innocent. Madam," replied I, " and willing to *keep* so ; and yet I cannot consent to this."—" Then," said she, very mannerly, " thou liest, child, that's all ; and I give thee up ! "

And so she arose, and walked about the room in great wrath. Her nephew and her woman said, " Your ladyship is very good ; 'tis a plain case, a very plain case ! "

I would have removed the chair to have gone out ; but her nephew came and sat in it. This provoked me, for I thought I should be unworthy of the honour I was raised to, though I was afraid to own it, if I did not shew some spirit : and I said, " What, Sir, is *your* pretence, in this house, to keep me a prisoner here ? "—" Because," said he, " I like it."—" Do you so, Sir ? " replied I : " if that is the answer of a gentleman to such a one as I, it would not, I dare say, be the answer of a gentleman to a gentleman."—" My lady ! my lady ! " said he, " a challenge, a challenge, by God ! "—" No, Sir," said I, " I am of a sex that gives no challenge ; and you think so too, or you would not give this occasion for the word."

Said my lady, " Don't be surprised, nephew ; the wench could not talk thus, if she had not been her master's bed-fellow. Pamela, Pamela," said she, and tapped me on the shoulder, two or three times, in anger, " thou hast lost thy innocence, girl ; and thou hast got some of thy bold master's assurance, and art fit to go any whither."—" Then, and please your ladyship," said I, " I am unworthy of your presence, and desire I may quit it."

" No," replied she ; " I will know first what reason you can give for not accepting my proposal, if you are innocent ! "— " I can give," said I, " a very good one ; but I beg to be ex- cused."—" I will hear it," said she. " Why, then," answered

345

I, " I should perhaps have less reason to like this gentleman, than where I am."

" Well, then," said she, " I'll put you to another trial. I'll set out this moment to your parents, and give you up safe to them. What say you to that?"—" Ay, Mrs. Pamela," said her nephew, " now what does your innocence say to that?—'Fore Gad, Madam, you have puzzled her now."

" Be pleased, Madam," said I, " to call off this fine gentleman. Your kindness in these proposals makes me think you would not have me baited."—" I'll be d——," said he, " if she does not make me a bull-dog! Why, she'll toss us all by-and-by!"— " Sir," said I, " you indeed behave as if you were in a bear-garden."

" Jackey, be quiet," said my lady. " You only give her a pretence to evade my questions. Come, answer me, Pamela."— " I will, Madam," said I; " and it is thus: I have no occasion to be beholden to your ladyship for this honour; for I am to set out to-morrow morning to my parents."—" Now again, thou liest, wench."—" I am not of quality," said I, " to answer such language."—" Once again," said she, " provoke me not, by these reflections, and this pertness; if thou dost, I shall do something by thee, unworthy of myself."—" That," thought I, " you have done already;" but I ventured not to say so. " But who is to carry you to them?" said she.—" Who my master pleases, Madam," said I.—" Ay," said she, " I doubt not, thou wilt do every thing he pleases, if thou hast not already. Now tell me, Pamela, from thy heart, hast thou not been in bed with thy master? Ha, wench?" I was quite shocked at this, and said, " I wonder how your ladyship can use me thus! I am sure you can expect no answer; my sex, and my tender years, might exempt me from such treatment, from a person of your ladyship's birth and quality, and who, be the distance ever so great, is of the same sex with me."

" Thou art a confident wench," said she, " I see!"—" Pray," said I, " let me beg you to permit me to go. I am waited for in town to dinner."—" No," replied she, " I can't spare you; and whomever you are to go to, will excuse you, when told 'tis *I* that command you not to go; and *you* may excuse it too, young Lady Would-be, if you consider it is the unexpected coming of your late lady's daughter, and your master's sister, that *commands* your stay."

" But a pre-engagement, your ladyship will consider, is some-thing?"—" Ay, so it is; but I know not why waiting-maids should assume these airs of *pre-engagements!* Oh, Pamela,

346

I am sorry for thy thus aping thy betters, and giving thyself such airs; I see thou'rt quite spoiled! A modest, innocent girl thou wast, and humble too, but now art fit for only what I fear thou art."

"Why, please your ladyship," said her kinsman, "what signifies all you say? The matter is over with her, no doubt, and she likes it; she is in a fairy dream, and 'tis pity to awaken her before it is out."—"Bad as you take me to be, Madam," said I, "I am not used to such language or reflections as this gentleman bestows upon me; and I won't bear it."

"Well, Jackey," said she, "be silent," and shaking her head, "Poor girl!" said she; "what a sweet innocent is here destroyed!—A thousand pities! I could cry over her, if that would do her good! But she is quite lost, quite undone: and then has assumed a carriage upon it, that all those creatures are distinguished by."

I cried sadly for vexation; and said, "Say what you please, Madam: if I can help it, I will not answer another word."

Mrs. Jewkes came in and asked, if her ladyship was ready for dinner? She said, "Yes." I would have gone out with her; but my lady said, taking my hand, she could not spare me. "Miss," said she, "you may pull off your gloves, and lay your fan by, for you *shan't* go; and if you behave well, you shall wait upon me at dinner, and then I shall have a little further talk with you."

Mrs. Jewkes said to me, "Madam, may I speak one word with you?"—"I can't tell, Mrs. Jewkes," said I: "for my lady holds my hand, and you see I am a kind of prisoner."

"What you have to say, Mrs. Jewkes," said she, "you may speak before me." But she went out, and seemed vexed for me; and she says, I looked like the very scarlet.

The cloth was laid in another parlour, and for *three* persons. "Come, my little dear," said she, with a sneer, "I'll hand you in; and I would have you think it as well as if it was my brother."

"What a sad case," thought I, "should I be in, if I were as naughty as she thinks me!" It was bad enough as it was.

"Jackey," said my lady, "let us go to dinner." She said to her woman, "Do you, Beck, help Pamela to 'tend us; we will have no men-fellows. Come, my young lady, shall I help you off with your white gloves?"—"I have not, Madam," said I, "deserved this at your ladyship's hands."

Mrs. Jewkes coming in with the first dish, she said, "Do you expect any body else, Mrs. Jewkes, that you lay the cloth for *three*?" Said she, "I hoped your ladyship and Madam would

347

have been reconciled."—" What means the clownish woman?" said my lady, in great disdain : " could you think the creature should sit down with me? "—" She does, please your ladyship, with my master."—" I doubt it not, good woman," said she, " and lies with him too, does she not? Answer me, Fat-face!" How these ladies are privileged!

" If she does, Madam," said she, " there may be a *reason* for it, perhaps!" and went out. " So!" said she, " has the wench got thee over, too! Come, my little dear, pull off thy gloves;" and off she pulled my left glove herself, and spied my ring. " O my dear God," said she, " if the wench has not got a ring! Well, this is a pretty piece of foolery, indeed! Dost know, my friend, that thou art miserably tricked? And so, poor innocent, thou hast made a fine exchange, hast thou not? Thy honesty for this bauble : and I'll warrant, my little dear has topped her part, and paraded like any real wife; and so mimics still the condition! Why," said she, and turned me round, " thou art as mincing as any bride! No wonder thou talkest of thy *pre-engagement!* Pr'ythee, child, walk before me to that glass; survey thyself, and come back, that I may see how finely thou canst act thy theatrical part!"

I was then resolved to try to be silent; although most sadly vexed. So I sat me down in the window, and she took her place at the upper end of the table, and her saucy Jackey, fleering at me most provokingly, sat down by her. Said he, " Shall not the bride sit down by us, Madam? "—" Ay, well thought of!" said my lady : " Pray, Mrs. Bride, your pardon for taking your place!" I said nothing.

Said she, with a poor pun, " Thou hast some modesty, how-ever, child! for thou canst not *stand it*, so must *sit down*, though in my presence!" I still kept my seat, and said nothing. Thought I, " This is a sad thing, that I am hindered too from showing my duty where most due, and shall have anger there too, may-be, if my dear master arrive before me!" So she ate some soup, as did her kinsman : and then, cutting up a fowl, said, " If thou *long'st*, my little dear, I will help thee to a pinion, or breast, or anything."—" But, may-be, child," said he, " thou likest the rump; shall I bring it thee? " and then laughed like an idiot, for all he is a lord's son, and may be a lord himself : for he is the son of Lord ——; and his mother, who was Lord Davers's sister, being dead, he received his education from Lord Davers's direction. Poor wretch! for all his great-ness! he'll never die for a plot—at least of his own hatching. If I could then have got up, I would have given you his picture.

But for one of twenty-five or twenty-six years of age, much about the age of my dear master, he is a most odd mortal.

"Pamela," said my lady, "help me to a glass of wine.—No, Beck," said she, "*you* shan't : " for she was offering to do it. " I will have my Lady Bride confer that honour upon me; and then I shall see if she can *stand up*." I was silent, and never stirred.

"Dost hear, *Chastity ?* " said she; "help me to a glass of wine, when I bid thee. What! not stir! Then I'll come and help *thee* to one." Still I stirred not, and fanning myself, continued silent. Said she, "When I have asked thee, meek one, half a dozen questions together, I suppose thou wilt answer them all at once!—Pretty creature, is not that ? "

I was so vexed, I bit a piece of my fan out, not knowing what I did; but still I said nothing, and did nothing but flutter it, and fan myself.

"I believe," said she, "my next question will make up half a dozen; and then, modest one, I shall be entitled to an answer."

He arose, and brought the bottle and glass, "Come," said he, "Mrs. Bride, be pleased to help my lady, and I will be your deputy."—"Sir," replied I, "it is in a good hand; help my lady yourself."—"Why, creature," said she, "dost thou think thyself above it ? " and then flew into a passion. "Insolence! " continued she, "this moment, when I bid you, know your duty, and give me a glass of wine, or——"

So I took a little spirit then—Thought I, I can but be beat. "If," said I, "to attend your ladyship at table, or even to kneel at your feet, was required of me, I would most gladly do it, were I only the person you think me; but, if it be to triumph over one who has received honours, that she thinks require her to act another part, not to be utterly unworthy of them, I must say I *cannot* do it."

She seemed quite surprised, and looked now upon her kinsman, and then upon her woman. "I'm astonished! quite astonished! —Well, then, I suppose you would have me conclude you my brother's wife; would you not ? "

"Your ladyship," said I, "*compels* me to say this ! "—"Well," returned she, "but dost thou *thyself* think thou art so ? "—"Silence," said her kinsman, "gives consent. 'Tis plain enough she does. Shall I rise, Madam, and pay my duty to my new aunt ? "

"Tell me," said my lady, "what, in the name of impudence, possesses thee to *dare* to look upon thyself as *my* sister ? "—"Madam," replied I, "that is a question will better become your most worthy brother to answer, than me."

She was rising in great wrath; but her woman said, " Good your ladyship, you'll do yourself more harm than her; and if the poor girl has been deluded so as you have heard, with the sham marriage, she'll deserve more your ladyship's pity than anger."—" True, Beck," said she; " but there's no bearing the impudence of the creature, in the mean time."

I would have gone out at the door, but her kinsman ran and set his back against it. I feared bad treatment from her pride, and violent temper; but this was worse than I expected. I said to him, " Sir, when my master comes to know your rude behaviour, you may have cause to repent it; " and went and sat down in the window again.

" Another challenge, by Gad," said he; " but I am glad she says her *master!* You see, Madam, she herself does not believe she is married, and is not *so much* deluded as you think for; " and coming to me with a most barbarous air of insult, he said, kneeling on one knee before me, " My new aunt, your *blessing* or your *curse,* I care not which; but quickly give me one or other, that I may not lose my dinner."

I gave him a most contemptuous look. " Tinsell'd boy! " said I (for he was laced all over), " twenty or thirty years hence, when you are *at age,* I shall know how to answer you better; mean time, sport with your footman, and not me! " so I re-moved to another window, nearer the door, and he look'd like a sad fool, as he is.

" Beck, Beck," said my lady, " this is not to be borne! Was ever the like heard? Is my kinsman and Lord Davers's, to be thus used by such a slut? " She was coming to me; and indeed I began to be afraid; for I have but a poor heart after all. But Mrs. Jewkes, hearing high words, came in again, with the second course, and said, " Pray, your ladyship, don't so discompose yourself. I am afraid this day's business will make matters wider than ever between your good ladyship and your brother: for my master doats upon Madam."

" Woman," said she, " do you be silent! Sure, I that was born in this house, may have some privilege in it, without being talked to by the saucy servants in it! "

" I beg pardon, Madam," replied Mrs. Jewkes; and, turning to me, said, " Madam, my master will take it very ill, to make him wait for you thus." So I rose to go out; but my lady said, " If it was only for *that* reason she shan't go." And went to the door and shut it, and said to Mrs. Jewkes, " Woman, don't come again till I call you; " and, coming to me, took my hand, and said, " Find your legs, Miss, if you please."

350

I stood up, and she tapped my cheek! "O," says she, " that scarlet glow shews what a rancorous little heart thou hast, if thou durst shew it;" and led me to her chair: "Stand there," said she, "and answer me a few questions while I dine, and I'll dismiss thee, till I call thy impudent master to account; then I'll have you face to face, and all this mystery of iniquity shall be unravell'd; for, between you, I will come to the bottom of it."

When she had sat down, I moved to the window on the other side, looking into the private garden; and her woman said, "Mrs. Pamela, don't make my lady angry. Stand by her ladyship, as she bids you." Said I, "Pray let it suffice *you* to attend your *lady's* commands, and don't lay *yours* upon *me*."—"Your pardon, sweet Mrs. Pamela," said she. "Times are much alter'd with you, I'll assure you!" Said I, "Her ladyship has a very good plea to be free in the house she was *born* in: but you may as well confine your freedom to the house in which you had your *breeding*."—"Why, how now, Mrs. Pamela," said she: "since you provoke me to it, I'll tell you a piece of my mind."—"Hush, hush, *good woman*," said I, alluding to my lady's language to Mrs. Jewkes, "my lady wants not your assistance:—besides, I can't scold."

The woman was ready to flutter with vexation; and Lord Jackey laughed, as if he would burst his sides; "G—d d—n me, Beck," said he, "you'd better let her alone to my lady here; for she'll be too many for twenty such as you and I." And then repeated, "I can't *scold*, quoth-a!—but, by Gad, Miss, you can speak d—d spiteful words, I can tell you that! Poor Beck, poor Beck!—'Fore Gad, she's quite dumb-foundered!"

"Well, but, Pamela," said my lady, "come hither, and tell me truly, dost thou think thyself really married?" Said I, and approached her chair, "My good lady, I'll answer all your commands, if you'll have patience with me, and not be so angry as you are; but I can't bear to be used thus by this gentleman, and your ladyship's woman."—"Child," said she, "thou art very impertinent to my kinsman: thou can'st not be civil to me; and my *ladyship's woman* is much thy betters. But that's not the thing!—Dost thou think thyself really married?"

"I see, Madam," said I, "you are resolved not to be pleased with *any* answer I shall return: if I should say, I am not, then you will call me hard names, and perhaps I shall tell a fib. If I should say, I am, your ladyship will ask, how I have the impudence to be so?—and will call it a sham marriage."—"I will be," said she, "answered more directly."—"Why, what,

351

Madam, does it signify what I think? Your ladyship will believe as you please."

"But can'st thou have the vanity, the pride, the folly," said she, "to think thyself actually married to *my* brother? He is no fool, child; and libertine enough of conscience; and thou art not the first in the list of his credulous harlots."—"Well, well," said I (and was in a sad flutter); "as I am easy and pleased with my lot, pray, Madam, let me continue so, as long as I can. It will be time enough for me to know the worst, when the worst comes. And if it be so bad, your ladyship should pity, rather than thus torment me before my time."

"Well," said she, "but dost not think I am concerned, that a young wench, whom my poor dear mother loved so well, should thus suffer herself to be deluded and undone, after such a noble stand as thou mad'st for so long a time!"

"I think myself far from being deluded and undone; and am as innocent and virtuous as ever I was in my life."—"Thou liest, child," said she.

"So your ladyship told me twice before."

She gave me a slap on the hand for this: I made a low curtsey, and said, "I humbly thank your ladyship;" but I could not refrain tears: and added, "Your dear brother, Madam, however, won't thank your ladyship for this usage of me, though I do."—"Come a little nearer me, my dear," said she, "and thou shalt have a little more than *that* to tell him of, if thou think'st thou hast not made mischief enough already between a sister and brother. But, child, if he was here, I would serve thee worse, and him too."—"I wish he was," said I.—"Dost thou threaten me, mischief-maker, and insolent as thou art?"

"Now, pray, Madam," said I (but got to a little distance), "be pleased to reflect upon all that you have said to me, since I had the *honour*, or rather *misfortune*, to come into your presence; whether you have said one thing befitting your ladyship's degree, even supposing I was the wench and the creature you imagine me to be?"—"Come hither, my pert dear," replied she; "come but within my reach for *one* moment, and I'll answer thee as thou deservest."

To be sure, she meant to box my ears. But I should be unworthy of my happy lot, if I could not shew some spirit.

When the cloth was taken away, I said, "I suppose I may now depart your presence, Madam."—"I suppose not," said she. "Why, I'll lay thee a wager, child, thy stomach's too full to eat, and so thou may'st fast, till thy mannerly master comes home."

"Pray your ladyship," said her woman, "let the poor girl

sit down at table with Mrs. Jewkes and *me*." Said I, "You are very kind, Mrs. Worden; but times, as you said, are much altered with me; and I have been of late so much honoured by better company, that I can't stoop to yours."

"Was ever such confidence?" said my lady.—"Poor Beck," said her kinsman; "why she beats you quite out of the pit!"—"Will your ladyship," said I, "be so good as to tell me how long I am to tarry? For you'll please to see by that letter, that I am obliged to attend my master's commands." So I gave her the dear gentleman's letter from Mr. Carlton's, which I thought would make her use me better, as she might judge by it of the honour done me by him. "Ay," said she, "this is my worthy brother's hand. It is directed to Mrs. Andrews—that's to you, I suppose, child!" And so she read on, making remarks, as she went along, in this manner:

"*My dearest Pamela.*"—Mighty well!—"*I hope my not coming home this night will not frighten you!*" Vastly tender, indeed. And did it frighten you, child?—"*You may believe I can't help it.*"—No, be sure! A person in thy way of life, is more tenderly used than an honest wife. But mark the end of it—"*I could have wished*"—Pr'ythee, Jackey, mind this—"*we*"—mind the significant *we*—"*had not engaged to the good neighbourhood, at Sir Simon's, for to-morrow night.*"—Why, does the good neighbourhood, and does Sir Simon, permit thy visits, child? They shall have none of mine, then—"*But I am so desirous to set out on Wednesday for the other house*"—So, Jackey, we but just nicked it, I find—"*that, as well as in return for the civilities of so many good friends, who will be there on purpose, I would not put it off.*"—Now mind, Jackey.—"*What I beg of you*"—Mind the wretch that could use me and your uncle as he has done; he is turned beggar to this creature!—"*I beg of you, therefore, my dear*"—My dear! there's for you! I wish I may not be quite sick before I get through—"*What I beg of you therefore, my dear,*" (and then she looked me full in the face), "*is, that you will go in the chariot to Sir Simon's, the sooner in the day the better,*"—Dear heart! and why so, when WE were not expected till night? why, pray observe the reason—Hem! (said she)—"*because you will be diverted with the company;*"—Mighty kind, indeed!—"*who all*"—Jackey, mind this—"*who all so much admire you.*"—"Now he'd ha' been hang'd before he would have said so complaisant a thing, had he been married, I'm sure!"—"Very true, aunt," said he: "a plain case that!"—(Thought I, "That's hard upon poor matrimony, though I hope my lady don't find it so." But I durst not speak out).—

"*Who all so much admire you,*" (said she) I must repeat that—
Pretty Miss !—I wish thou wast as *admirable* for thy virtue, as
for that baby-face of thine !—"*And I hope to join you there, by
your tea-time, in the afternoon,*"—So you're in very good time,
child, an hour or two hence, to answer all your important pre-
engagements !—"*which will be better than going home, and
returning with you ; as it will be six miles difference to me ; and
I know the good company will excuse my dress on the occasion.*"
Very true, any dress is good enough, I am sure, for such company
as *admire* thee, child, for a companion in thy ruined state !—
Jackey, mind again ! more fine things still !—"*I count every
hour of this little absence for a day !*"—There's for you ! Let
me repeat it—"*I count every hour of this little absence for a day !*"
Mind too the wit of the good man ! One may see love is a new
thing to him. Here is a very tedious time gone since he saw his
deary; no less than, according to *his* amorous calculation, a
dozen days and nights, at least ! and yet, TEDIOUS as it is, it is
but a LITTLE ABSENCE. Well said, my good, accurate, and
consistent brother ! But wise men in love are always the
greatest simpletons ! But now comes the reason *why* this
LITTLE absence, which, at the same time, is so GREAT AN ABSENCE,
is so *tedious :* for "*I am,*" ay, now for it ! "*with the* UTMOST
sincerity, my dearest love"—Out upon DEAREST love ! I shall
never love the word again ! Pray bid your uncle never call me
Dearest Love, Jackey !—"*For ever yours !*"—But, brother,
thou knowest thou liest. And so, my good Lady Andrews, or
what shall I call you ? your *dearest love* will be "*for ever yours !*"
And hast thou the vanity to believe this?—But stay, here is a
postscript. The poor man knew not when to have done to his
dearest love. He's sadly in for't, truly ! Why, his *dearest love,*
you are mighty happy in such a lover ! "*If you could go to
dine with them,*"—Cry your mercy, my *dearest love,* now comes the
pre-engagement—"*it will be a freedom that will be very pleasing
to them, and the more as they don't expect it.*"

"Well, so much for this kind letter ! But you see you cannot
honour this admiring company with this little-expected, and,
but in complaisance to his folly, I dare say, little-desired freedom.
I *admire* you so much, my *dearest love,* that I will not spare you
at all, this whole evening ! for 'tis a little hard, if thy master's
sister may not be blest a while with thy charming company."

So I found I had shewed her my letter to very little purpose,
and repented it several times, as she read on. "Well, then,"
said I, "I hope your ladyship will allow me to send my excuses
to your good brother, and say, that you are come, and are so

354

fond of me, that you will not let me go."—"Pretty creature," said she : "and wantest thou thy good master to come and quarrel with his sister on thy account? But thou shalt not leave me ; and I would now ask what it is thou meanest by shewing me this letter? "—"Why, Madam," said I, "to shew your ladyship how I was engaged for this day and evening."—"And for nothing else? " said she. "Why, I can't tell, Madam," said I : "but if you can collect from it any other circumstances, I might hope I should not be the *worse* treated."

I saw her eyes sparkling with passion ; and she took my hand, and said, grasping it very hard, "I know, confident creature, that you shewed it to insult me ! To let me see that he could be civiller to a beggar-born, than to me, or to my good Lord Davers ! You shewed it me, as if you'd have me be as credulous a fool as yourself, to believe your marriage true, when I know the whole trick of it, and have reason to believe *you* do too ; and you shewed it me, to upbraid me with his stooping to such painted dirt, to the disgrace of a family, ancient and untainted beyond most in the kingdom. And now will I give thee one hundred guineas for one bold word, that I may fell thee at my foot."

Was not this very dreadful? To be sure, I had better have kept the letter from her. I was quite frightened ; and this fearful menace, and her fiery eyes, and rageful countenance, made me lose all my courage. So I said, weeping, "Good your ladyship, pity me ! Indeed I am honest : indeed I am virtuous : indeed I would not do a bad thing for the world."

"Though I know," said she, "the whole trick of thy pretended marriage, and thy foolish ring here, and all the rest of the wicked nonsense : yet I should not have patience with thee if thou shouldst but offer to let me know thy vanity prompts thee to *believe* thou art married to *my* brother ! I could not bear the thought ! So take care, Pamela ; take care, beggarly brat ; take care."

"Good Madam," said I, "spare my dear parents. They are honest and industrious ; they were once in a very creditable way, and never were beggars. Misfortunes may attend any body : and I can bear the cruellest imputations on myself, because I know my innocence ! but upon such honest, industrious parents, who went through the greatest trials, beholden to nothing but God's blessings, and their own hard labour, I cannot bear reflection."

"What ! art thou setting up for a family, creature as thou art ! God give me patience with thee ! I suppose my brother's folly, and his wickedness, will soon occasion a search at the Herald's office, to set out thy wretched obscurity. Provoke me, I desire thou wilt. One hundred guineas will I give thee, to say but thou *thinkest* thou art married to my brother."

"Your ladyship, I hope, won't kill me : and since nothing I can say will please you, but your ladyship is resolved to quarrel with me; since I must not say what I think, on one hand, nor on another; whatever your ladyship designs by me, be pleased to do, and let me depart your presence."

She gave me a slap on the hand, and reached to box my ear; but Mrs. Jewkes hearkening without, and her woman too, they both came in at that instant; and Mrs. Jewkes said, pushing herself in between us, "Your ladyship knows not what you do : indeed you don't. My master would never forgive me, if I suffered, in his house, one he so dearly loves, to be so used; and it must *not* be, though you are Lady Davers." Her woman too interposed, and told her I was not worth her ladyship's anger. But she was like a person beside herself.

I offered to go, and Mrs. Jewkes would have led me out; but her kinsman set his back to the door, and put his hand to his sword, and said, I should not go, till his aunt permitted it. He drew it half-way, and I was so terrified, that I cried out, "Oh the sword ! the sword !" and, not knowing what I did, I ran to my lady herself, and clasped my arms about her, forgetting just then how much she was my enemy, and said, sinking on my knees, "Defend me, good your ladyship ! The sword ! the sword !" Mrs. Jewkes said, "Oh ! my lady will fall into fits ;" but Lady Davers was herself so startled at the matter being carried so far that she did not mind her words, and said, "Jackey, don't draw your sword ! You see, as great as her spirit is, she can't bear that."

"Come," said she, "be comforted : he shan't fright you ! I'll try to overcome my anger, and will pity you. So, wench, rise up, and don't be foolish." Mrs. Jewkes held her salts to my nose, and I did not faint. And my lady said, "Mrs. Jewkes, if *you* would be forgiven, leave Pamela and me by ourselves !— And Jackey, do you withdraw;—only you, Beck, stay."

So I sat down in the window, all in a fluster : for, to be sure, I was sadly frighted. Said her woman, "You should not sit in my lady's presence, Mrs. Pamela."—"Yes, let her sit till she is a little recovered of her fright," said my lady; "and do you set my chair by her." So she sat over-against me, and said, "To be sure, Pamela, you have been very provoking with your tongue; to be sure you have, as well upon my nephew (who is

356

a man of quality too) as me." And palliating her cruel usage, and beginning, I suppose, to think herself, she had carried it further than she could answer it to her brother, she wanted to lay the fault upon me. " Own," said she, " that you have been very saucy ; and beg mine, and Jackey's pardon, and I will try to pity you. For you are a sweet girl, after all ; if you had but held out, and been honest."

" 'Tis injurious to me, Madam," said I, " to imagine I am not honest ! "—Said she, " Have you not been a-bed with my brother ? tell me that."—" Your ladyship," replied I, " asks your questions in a strange way, and in strange words."

" Oh ! your delicacy is wounded, I suppose, by my plain question ! This niceness will soon leave you, wench ; it will, indeed. But answer me directly."—" Then your ladyship's next question," said I, " will be, am I married ? and you won't bear my answer to that, and will beat me again."

" I ha'n't beat you yet ;—have I, Beck ? " said she. " So you want to make out a story, do you ? But, indeed, I can't bear thou should'st so much as *think* thou art *my* sister. I know the whole trick of it ; and so, 'tis my opinion, thou dost. It is only thy little cunning, that it might look like a cloak to thy yielding, and get better terms from him. Thou see'st I know the world a little ; almost as much at thirty-two, as thou dost at sixteen. Remember that ! "

I rose from the window, and walking to the other end of the room—" Beat me again, if you please," said I, " but I must tell your ladyship, I scorn your words, and am as much married as your ladyship ! "

At that she ran to me ; but her woman interposed again, " Let the vain wicked creature go from your presence, Madam," said she. " She is not worthy to be in it. She will but vex your ladyship."—" Stand away, Beck," said she. " That's an assertion that I would not take from my brother. As much married as I ! Is that to be borne ? "—" But if the creature believes she is, Madam," said her woman, " she is to be as much pitied for her credulity, as despised for her vanity."

I was in hopes to have slipt out of the door ; but she pulled me back. " Pray, your ladyship," said I, " don't kill me ! I have done no harm." But locking the door, she put the key in her pocket. So seeing Mrs. Jewkes at the window, I lifted up the sash, and said, " Mrs. Jewkes, I believe the chariot had better go to your master, that he may know Lady Davers is here, and I cannot leave her ladyship."

She was resolved to be displeased, let me say what I would.

Said she, "No, no; he'll then think I make the creature my companion, and know not how to part with her."—" I thought your ladyship," replied I, " could not have taken exception at this message."—" Thou knowest nothing, wench," said she, " of what belongs to people of condition; how should'st thou?" —" Nor," thought I, " do I desire it at this rate."

"What shall I say, Madam?" said I. "Nothing at all," replied she; " let him expect his *dearest love*, and be disappointed: it is but adding a few more *hours*, and he will make every one *a day* in his amorous account." Mrs. Jewkes coming nearer me, and my lady walking about the room, being then at the end, I whispered, " Let Robert stay at the Elms: I'll have a struggle for't by-and-by."

"As much married as I!" repeated she. "The insolence of the creature!" So she walked about, talking to herself, to her woman, and now-and-then to me: but seeing I could not please her, I thought I had better be silent. And then it was, " Am I not worthy an answer?"—" If I speak," said I, " your ladyship is angry at me though ever so respectfully; if I do not, I cannot please. Would your ladyship tell me but how I shall oblige you, and I would do it with all my heart."

"Confess the truth," said she, " that thou art an undone creature; hast been in bed with thy master, and art sorry for it, and for the mischief thou hast occasioned between him and me; then I'll pity thee, and persuade him to pack thee off, with a hundred or two of guineas: some honest farmer may take pity of thee, and patch up thy shame, for the sake of the money; and if nobody will have thee, thou must vow penitence, and be as humble as I once thought thee."

I was quite sick at heart, at all this passionate extravagance, and to be hindered from being where was the desire of my soul, afraid too of incurring my dear master's displeasure: and, as I sat, I saw it was no hard matter to get out of the window, the parlour being even with the yard, and so have a fair run for it; and after I had seen my lady at the other end of the room again, having not pulled down the sash, when I spoke to Mrs. Jewkes, I got upon the seat, was out in a minute, and ran away as fast as I could, my lady calling after me to return, and her woman at the other window; but two of her servants appearing at her crying out, and she bidding them stop me, I said, " Touch me at your peril, fellows; " but their lady's commands would have prevailed, had not Mr. Colbrand, who, it seems, was kindly ordered by Mrs. Jewkes to be within call, when she saw how I was treated, came up, and put on one of his deadly fierce looks, the only time I thought it ever became him, and said, he would *chine* the man (that was his word) who offered to touch his lady; so he ran along-side of me; and I heard my lady say, " The creature flies like a bird ! " Mr. Colbrand, with his huge strides, could hardly keep pace with me. I never stopped till I reached the chariot, and Robert, seeing me at a distance, had got down, and held the door in his hand, with the step ready; but in I jumped, without touching it, saying, " Drive me, drive me, as fast as you can, out of my lady's reach ! " He mounted, and Colbrand said, " Don't be frightened, Madam : nobody shall hurt you." And shutting the door, away Robert drove; but I was quite out of breath, and did not recover it and my fright all the way.

Mr. Colbrand was so kind, but I did not know it till the chariot stopt at Sir Simon's, to step up behind, lest, as he said, my lady should send after me; and he told Mrs. Jewkes, when he got home, that he never saw such a runner as me, in his life.

When the chariot stopt, which was not till six o'clock, so long did this cruel lady keep me, Miss Darnford ran out to me : " O Madam," said she, " ten times welcome ! But you'll be beat, I can tell you; for Mr. B. has been come these two hours, and is very angry at you."

" That's hard, indeed," said I ; " indeed I can't afford it ! " for I hardly knew what I said, having not recovered my fright. " Let me sit down, Miss, any where, for I have been sadly off." So I sat down, and was quite sick with the hurry of my spirits, and leaned upon her arm.

She said, " Your lord and master came in very moody; and when he had staid an hour, and you not come, he began to fret, and said he did not expect so little complaisance from you. And he is now sit down with great persuasions to a game at loo. Come, you must make your appearance, lady-fair; for he is too sullen to attend you, I doubt."

" You have no strangers, have you, Madam ? " said I. " Only two women relations from Stamford," replied she, " and an humble servant of one of them."—" Only all the world, Miss," said I. " What shall I do, if he be angry ? I can't bear that."

Just as I had said so, came in Lady Darnford and Lady Jones to chide me, as they said, for not coming sooner. And before I could speak, came in my dear master. I ran to him. " How d'ye, Pamela ? " said he, saluting me with a little more formality than I could well bear. " I expected half a word from me, when I was so complaisant to your choice, would have determined you,

359

and that you'd have been here to dinner! and the rather, as I made my request a reasonable one, and what I thought would be agreeable to you."—"O dear Sir," said I, "pray hear me, and you'll pity me, and not be displeased: Mrs. Jewkes will tell you, that as soon as I had your kind commands, I said I would obey you, and come to dinner with these good ladies; and so prepared myself instantly, with all the pleasure in the world." Lady Darnford and Miss said, I was their dear! "Look you," said Miss, "did I not tell you, stately one, that something must have happened? But O these tyrants! these men!"

"Why, what hindered it, my dear?" said he: "give yourself time: you seem out of breath!"—"O Sir," said I, "out of breath! well I may! For just as I was ready to come away, who should drive into the court-yard, but Lady Davers!"—"Lady Davers! nay, then, my sweet dear," said he, and kissed me more tenderly, "hast thou had a worse trial than I wish thee, from one of the haughtiest women in England, though my sister! For she too, my Pamela, was spoiled by my good mother! But have you seen her?"

"Yes, Sir," said I, "and *more* than seen her!"—"Why sure," said he, "she has not had the insolence to strike my girl!"—"Sir," said I, "but tell me you forgive me; for I could not come sooner; and these good laides but excuse me, and I'll tell you all another time; for to take up the good company's attention now, will spoil their pleasantry, and be to them, though more important to me, like the lady's broken china you cautioned me about."

"That's a dear girl!" said he: "I see my hints are not thrown away upon you: I beg pardon for being angry; and, for the future, will stay till I hear your defence before I judge you." Said Miss Darnford, "This is a little better! To own a fault is some reparation, and what every lordly husband will not do." He said, "But tell me, my dear, did Lady Davers offer you any incivility?"—"O Sir," replied I, "she is your sister, and I must not tell you all; but she has used me very severely."—"Did you tell her," said he, "you were married?"—"Yes, Sir, I did at last: but she will have it, 'tis a sham-marriage, and that I am a vile creature: and she was ready to beat me, when I said so; for she could not have patience, that I should be deemed her sister, as she said."

"How unlucky it was," replied he, "I was not at home! Why did you not send to me here?"—"Send, Sir! I was kept prisoner by force. They would not let me stir, or do you think I would have been hindered from obeying you? Nay, I told

360

them I had a pre-engagement : but she ridiculed me, and said,
" Waiting-maids talk of pre-engagements ! " And then I
shewed her your kind letter ; and she made a thousand remarks
upon it, and made me wish I had not. In short, whatever I
could do or say, there was no pleasing her ; and I was a *creature*,
and *wench*, and all that was naught. But you must not be
angry with her on my account."

" Well, but," said he, " I suppose she hardly asked you to
dine with her ; for she came before dinner, I presume, if it was
soon after you had received my letter ? "—" No, Sir, dine with
my *lady !* no indeed !—Why, she would make me wait at table
upon her, with her woman, because she would not expose herself
and me before the men-servants : which you know, Sir, was
very good of her ladyship."

" Well," said he, " but *did* you wait at table upon her ? "—
" Would you have had me, Sir ? " said I. " Only Pamela,"
replied he, " if you did, and knew not what belonged to your
character, as my wife, I shall be very angry with you."—" Sir,"
said I, " I did not ; but refused it, out of consideration of the
dignity you have raised me to ; else, Sir, I could have waited
on my knees upon your sister."

" Now," said he, " you confirm my opinion of your prudence
and judgment. She is an insolent woman, and shall dearly
repent it."—" But, Sir, she is to be excused, because she won't
believe I am married : so don't be too angry at her ladyship."

He said, " Ladies, pray don't let us keep you from the company : I'll only ask a question or two more, and attend you."
Said Lady Jones, " I so much long to hear the story of poor
Madame's persecution, that, if it was not improper, I should be
glad to stay." Miss Darnford would stay for the same reason ;
my master saying he had no secrets to ask, and that it was kind
of them to interest themselves in my grievances.

But Lady Darnford went into the company, and told them the
cause of my detention ; for it seems my dear master loved me too
well to conceal his disappointment at my not being here to
receive him ; and they had all given the two Miss Boroughs and
Mr. Perry, the Stamford guests, such a character of me, that they
said they were impatient to see me.

Said my master, " But, Pamela, you said ' *they*,' and ' *them* ' ;
who had my sister with her, besides her woman ? "—" Her
nephew, Sir, and three footmen on horseback ; and she and her
woman were in her chariot and six."

" That's a sad coxcomb," said he : " how did he behave to
you ? "—" Not extraordinarily, Sir : but I should not complain ;

for I was even with him; because I thought I ought not to bear with him as with my lady."

"By Heaven!" said he, "if I knew he behaved unhandsomely to my jewel, I'd send him home to his uncle without his ears."—"Indeed, Sir," returned I, "I was as hard upon him as he was upon me." Said he, "'Tis kind to say so: but I believe I shall make them dearly repent their visit, if I find their behaviour to call for my resentment.

"But sure, my dear, you might have got away when you went to your own dinner?"—"Indeed, Sir," said I, "her ladyship locked me in, and would not let me stir."—"So you ha'n't eat any dinner?"—"No, indeed, Sir, nor had a stomach for any."—"My poor dear," said he. "But then how got you away at last?" "O Sir," replied I, "I jumped out of the parlour window, and ran away to the chariot, which had waited for me several hours, by the Elm-walk, from the time of my lady's coming (for I was just going, as I said); and Mr. Colbrand saw me through her servants, whom she called to, to stop me; and was so kind to step behind the chariot, unknown to me, and saw me safe here."

"I am sure," said he, "these insolent creatures must have treated you vilely. But tell me, what part did Mrs. Jewkes act in this affair?"—"A very kind part, Sir," said I, "in my behalf; and I shall thank her for it."—"Sweet creature!" said he, "thou lovest to speak well of every body: but I hope she deserves it: for she knew you was married. But come, we'll now join the company, and try to forget all you have suffered, for two or three hours, that we may not tire the company with our concerns; and resume the subject as we go home; and you shall find, I will do you justice as I ought."—"But you forgive me, Sir," said I, "and are not angry!"—"Forgive you, my dear," returned he. "I hope you forgive me! I shall never make you satisfaction for what you have suffered *from* me, and *for* me!" And with these words he led me into the company.

He very kindly presented me to the two stranger ladies, and the gentleman, and them to me; Sir Simon, who was at cards, rose from table, and saluted me: "Adad, Madam," said he, "I'm glad to see you here. What, it seems, you have been a prisoner! 'Tis well you was, or your spouse and I should have sat in judgment upon you, and condemned you to a fearful punishment for your first crime of *læsæ majestatis*:" (I had this explained to me afterwards, as a sort of treason against my liege lord and husband): "for we husbands, hereabouts," said he, "are resolved to turn over a new leaf with our wives, and *your* lord and master shall shew us the way, I can tell you that. But I see by your eyes, my sweet culprit," added he, "and your complexion, you have had sour sauce to your sweet meat."

Miss Darnford said, "I think we are obliged to our sweet guest at last; for she was forced to jump out at a window to come to us."—"Indeed!" said Mrs. Peters; and my master's back being turned, says she, "Lady Davers, when a maiden, was always vastly passionate; but a very good lady when her passion was over. She'd make nothing of slapping her maids about, and begging their pardons afterwards, if they took it patiently; otherwise she used to say the *creatures* were even with her."

"Ay," said I, "I have been a many *creatures* and *wenches*, and I know not what; for these were the names she gave me. And I thought I ought to act up to the part her dear brother has given me; and so truly, I have but just escaped a good cuffing."

Miss Boroughs said to her sister, as I overheard, but she did not design I should, "What a sweet creature is this! and then she takes so little upon her, is so free, so easy, and owns the honour done her so obligingly!" Said Mr. Perry, softly, "The loveliest person I ever saw! Who could have the heart to be angry with her one moment?"

Says Miss Darnford, "Here, my dearest neighbour, these gentry are admiring you strangely; and Mr. Perry says, you are the loveliest lady he ever saw; and says it to his own mistress's face too, I'll assure you!"—"Or else," says Miss Boroughs, "I should think he much flattered me."

"O Madam, you are exceedingly obliging; but your kind opinion ought to teach me humility, and to reverence so generous a worth as can give a preference against yourself, where it is so little due."—"Indeed, Madam," says Miss Nancy Boroughs, "I love my sister well; but it would be a high compliment to any lady, to be deemed worthy of a second or third place after you."

"There is no answering such politeness," said I: "I am sure Lady Davers was very cruel to keep me from such company."—"'Twas our loss, Madam," said Miss Darnford.—"I'll allow it," said I, "in degree; for you have all been deprived, several hours, of an humble admirer."

Mr. Perry said, "I never before saw so young a lady shine forth with such graces of mind and person."—"Alas, Sir," said I, my master coming up, "mine is but a borrowed shine, like that of the moon. Here is the sun, to whose fervent glow of

363

generosity I owe all the faint lustre that your goodness is pleased to look upon with so much kind distinction."

Mr. Perry was pleased to hold up his hands; and the ladies looked upon one another. My master said, hearing part of the last sentence, "What's the pretty subject that my Pamela is displaying, so sweetly, her talents upon?"

"Oh, Sir!" said Mr. Perry, "I will pronounce you the happiest man in England;" and so said they all.

My master said, most generously, "Thank ye, thank ye, thank ye, all round, my dear friends. I know not your subject; but if you believe me so for a *single* instance of this dear girl's goodness, what must I think myself when blessed with a *thousand* instances, and experiencing it in every single act and word, I do assure you, my Pamela's *person*, all lovely as you see it, is far short of her *mind*: that indeed first attracted my admiration, and made me her *lover*: but they were the beauties of her mind that made me her *husband*: and proud, my sweet dear," said he, pressing my hand, "am I of that title."

"Well," said Mr. Perry, very kindly, and politely, "excellent as your lady is, I know not the gentleman that could deserve her, but that one who could say such just and such fine things."

I was all abashed, and took Miss Darnford's hand, and said, "Save me, dear Miss, by your sweet example, from my rising pride. But could I deserve half these kind things, what a happy creature should I be!"—Said Miss Darnford, "You deserve them all, indeed you do."

The greatest part of the company having sat down to loo, my master being pressed, said he would take one game at whist; but had rather be excused too, having been up all night; and I asked how his friend did. "We'll talk of that," said he, "another time;" which, and his seriousness, made me fear the poor gentleman was dead, as it proved.

We cast in, and Miss Boroughs and my master were together, and Mr. Perry and I: and I had all four honours the first time, and we were up at one deal. Said my master, "An honourable hand, Pamela, should go with an honourable heart; but you'd not have been up if a knave had not been one."—"Whist, Sir," said Mr. Perry, "you know was a court game originally; and the knave, I suppose, signified always the prime minister."

"'Tis well," said my master, "if now there be but one knave in a court out of four persons, take the court through."

"The king and queen, Sir," said Mr. Perry, "*can* do no wrong, you know. So there are two that *must* be good out of four, and the ace seems too plain a card to mean much hurt."

364

"We compliment the king," said my master, "in that manner; and 'tis well to do so, because there is something sacred in the character. But yet, if force of example be considered, it is going a great way; for certainly a good master makes a good servant, generally speaking."

"One thing," added he, "I will say in regard to the *ace*; I have always looked upon that plain and honest-looking card in the light you do: and have considered whist as an English game in its original; which has made me fonder of it than of any other. For, by the ace, I have always thought the laws of the land denoted; and as the ace is above the king and queen, and wins them, I think the law should be thought so, too; though, may-be, I shall be deemed a *whig* for my opinion."

"I shall never play at whist," said Mr. Perry, "without thinking of this, and shall love the game the better for the thought; though I am no party-man."—"Nor I," said my master; "for I think the distinction of *whig* and *tory* odious; and love the one or the other only as they are honest and worthy men: and have never (nor ever shall, I hope) given a vote but what I thought was for the public good, let either *whig* or *tory* propose it."

"I wish, Sir," replied Mr. Perry, "all gentlemen in your station would act so."—"If there was no undue influence," said my master, "I am willing to think so well of all mankind that I believe they generally would. But you see," said he, "by my Pamela's hand, when all the court-cards get together, and are acted by *one mind*, the game is usually turned accordingly; though now-and-then too, it may be so circumstanced, that *honours* will do them no good, and they are forced to depend altogether upon *tricks*."

I thought this way of talking prettier than the game itself. But I said, "Though I have won the game, I hope I am no *trickster*."—"No," said my master, "God forbid but *court-cards* should *sometimes* win with *honour!* But you see, for all that, your game is as much owing to the *knave* as the *king*; and you, my fair one, lost no advantage, when it was put into your power."

"Else, Sir," said I, "I should not have done justice to my partner."—"You are certainly right, Pamela," replied he; "though you thereby beat your husband."—"Sir," said I, "you may be my partner next, and I must do justice, you know."—"Well," said he, "always choose so worthy a friend as chance has given you for a partner, and I shall never find fault with you, do what you will."

Mr. Perry said, " You are very good to me, Sir : " and Miss Boroughs, I observed, seemed pleased with the compliment to her humble servant; by which I saw she esteemed him, as he appears to deserve. " Dear Sir," said I, " how much better is this than to be locked in by Lady Davers."

The supper was brought in sooner on my account, because I had had no dinner; and there passed very agreeable compliments on the occasion. Lady Darnford would help me first, as I had so long fasted, she said. Sir Simon would have placed himself next me : and my master said he thought it was best, where there was an equal number of ladies and gentlemen, that they should sit intermingled, that the gentlemen might be employed in helping and serving the ladies. Lady Darnford said, she hoped Sir Simon would not sit above any ladies, at his own table especially. " Well," said he, " I shall sit over against her, however, and that's as well."

My dearest Sir could not keep his eye off me, and seemed generously to be delighted with all I did, and all I said; and every one was pleased to see his kind and affectionate behaviour to me.

Lady Jones resumed the discourse about Lady Davers again; and my master said, " I fear, Pamela, you have been hardly used, more than you'll say. I know my sister's passionate temper too well, to believe she could be over civil, especially as it happened so unluckily that I was out. If," added he, " she had no pique to you, my dear, yet what passed between her and me has so exasperated her, that she would quarrel with my *horse*, if she had thought I valued it, and nobody else was in her way."—" Dear Sir," said I, " don't say so of good Lady Davers."

" Why, my dear," said he, " I know she came on purpose to quarrel; and had she not found herself under a very violent uneasiness, after what had passed between us, and my treatment of her lord's letter, she would not have offered to come near me. What sort of language had she for me, Pamela ? "—" O, Sir, very good, only her *well-mannered brother*, and such as that."

" Only," said he, " 'tis taking up the attention of the company disagreeably, or I could tell you almost every word she said." Lady Jones wished to hear a further account of my lady's conduct, and most of the company joined with her, particularly Mrs. Peters; who said, that, as they knew the story, and Lady Davers's temper, though she was very good in the main, they could wish to be so agreeably entertained, if he and I pleased; because they imagined I should have no difficulties after this.

" Tell me, then, Pamela," said he, " did she lift up her hand

366

at you? Did she strike you? But I hope not."—"A little slap of the hand," said I, "or so."—"Insolent woman! She did not, I hope, offer to strike your face?"—"Why," said I, "I was a little saucy once or twice; and she would have given me a cuff on the ear, if her woman and Mrs. Jewkes had not interposed."—"Why did you not come out at the door?"—"Because," said I, "her ladyship sat in her chair against it one while, and another while locked it; else I offered several times to get away."

"She knew I expected you here: you say you shewed her my letter?"—"Yes, Sir," said I: "but I had better not; for she was then more exasperated, and made strange comments upon it."—"I doubt it not," said he; "but did she not see, by the kind epithets in it, that there was no room to doubt of our being married?"—"O, Sir," replied I, and made the company smile, "she said, for that very reason, she was sure I was not married!"

"That's like my sister!" said he, "exactly like her; and yet she lives very happily herself; for her poor lord never contradicts her. Indeed he *dares* not."

"You were a great many *wenches*, were you not, my dear? for that's a great word with her."—"Yes, Sir," said I, "*wenches* and *creatures* out of number: and worse than all that."—"What? tell me, my dear."—"Sir," said I, "I must not have you angry with my Lady Davers, while you are so good to me. 'Tis all nothing: only the trouble I have that I cannot be suffered to shew how much I honour her ladyship, as your sister."

"Well," said he, "you need not be afraid to tell *me:* I must love her after all, though I shall not be pleased with her on this occasion. It is her love for me, though thus oddly expressed, that makes her so uneasy: and after all, she comes, I'm sure, to be reconciled to me; though it must be through a good hearty quarrel first: for she can show a good deal of sun-shine, but it must always be after a storm: and I'll love her dearly, if she has not been, and will not be, too hard upon my dearest."

Mr. Peters said, "Sir, I love to see this complaisance to your sister, though she be in fault, so long as you can shew it with so much justice to the sweetest innocence and merit in the world." —"By all that's good, Mr. Peters," said he, "I'd present my sister with a thousand pounds, if she would kindly take my dear Pamela by the hand, wish her joy, and call her sister. And yet I should be unworthy of the dear creature that smiles upon me there, if it was not principally for her sake, and the pleasure it would give her, that I say this: for I will never be thoroughly

367

reconciled to my sister till she does; for I most sincerely think, as to myself, that my dear wife, there she sits, does me more honour in her new relation, than she receives from me."

"Sir," said I, "I am overwhelmed with your goodness!" My eyes were filled with tears of joy and gratitude: and all the company, with one voice, blessed him. Lady Jones was pleased to say, "The behaviour of you two happy ones, to each other, is most edifying. I am always improved when I see you. How happy would every good lady be with such a gentleman, and every good gentleman with such a lady. In short, you seem made for one another."

"O Madam," said I, "you are so kind, so good to me, I know not how to thank you enough." Said she, "You deserve more than I can express; for, to all who know your story, you are a matchless person.—You are an ornament to our sex; and your virtue, though Mr. B. is so generous as he is, has met with no more than its due reward. God long bless you together!"

"You are," said my dearest Sir, "very kind to me, Madam, I am sure. I have taken liberties in my former life, that deserved not so much excellence. I have offended extremely, by trials glorious to my Pamela, but disgraceful to me, against a virtue that I now consider as almost sacred; and I shall not think I deserve her, till I can bring my manners, sentiments, and actions, to a conformity with her own. In short, my Pamela, I want you to be nothing but what you are, and have been. You cannot be better; and if you could, it would be but filling me with despair to attain the awful heights of virtue, at which you are arrived. Perhaps," added the dear gentleman, "the scene I have beheld within these twelve hours, has made me more serious than otherwise I should have been; but I'll assure you, before all this good company, I speak the sentiments of my heart, and those not of this day only."

What a happy daughter is yours, O, my dear father and mother! I owe it all to God's grace, and to yours and my good lady's instructions; and to these let me always look back with grateful acknowledgments, that I may not impute to myself, and be proud, my inexpressible happiness.

The company were so kindly pleased with our concern, and my dear master's goodness, that he, observing their indulgence, and curious to know the further particulars as to my lady and me, repeated his question, what she had called me besides *wench* and *creature?* And I said, "My lady, supposing I was wicked, lamented over me, very kindly, my depravity and fall, and said what a thousand pities it was, so much virtue, as she

368

was pleased to say, was so destroyed; and that I had yielded, after so noble a stand!

"Excuse me, gentleman and ladies," said I; "you know my story, it seems, and I am commanded, by one who has a title to all my obedience, to proceed."

They gave bows of approbation, that they might not interrupt me; and I continued my story—the men-servants withdrawing at a motion of Mr. B. on my looking towards them: and then, a tight lass or two, at Lady Darnford's coming in, I proceeded.

"I told her ladyship, that I was still innocent, and would be so, and it was injurious to suppose me otherwise: 'Why, tell me, wench,' said she—But I think I must not tell you what she said."—"Yes, do," said my master, "to clear my sister; we shall think it very bad else."

I held my hand before my face—"Why, she said, 'Tell me wench, hast thou not been'"—hesitating—"'a very free creature with thy master?' or to that effect. When I said, she asked strange questions, and in strange words, she ridiculed my delicacy as she called it; and said, my niceness would not last long. I must know I was not really married, and that my ring was only a sham, and all was my cunning to cloak my yielding, and get better terms; she said, she knew the world as much at thirty-two, as I did at sixteen; and bid me remember that.

"I took the liberty to say (but I got a good way off) that I scorned her ladyship's words, and was as much married as her ladyship. And then I had certainly been cuffed, if her woman had not interposed, and told her I was not worthy her anger; and that I was as much to be pitied for my credulity, as despised for my vanity."

"My poor Pamela," said my master, "this was too, too hard upon you!"—

"O Sir," said I, "how much easier it was to me, than if it had been so!—That would have broken my heart quite! For than I should have deserved it all, and worse; and these reproaches, added to my own guilt, would have made me truly wretched."

Lady Darnford, at whose right hand I sat, kissed me with a kind of rapture, and called me a sweet exampler for all my sex. Mr. Peters said very handsome things; so did Mr. Perry: and Sir Simon, with tears in his eyes, said to my master, "Why, neighbour, this is excellent, by troth. I believe there is something in virtue, that we had not well considered. On my soul, there has been but one angel come down for this thousand years, and you have got her."

369

"Well, my dearest," said my master, "pray proceed with your story till we have done supper, since the ladies seem pleased with it."—"Why, Sir," said I, "her ladyship went on in the same manner; but said one time (and held me by the hand) she would give me a hundred guineas for one provoking word, or if I would but say I *believed* myself married, that she might fell me at her foot; but, Sir, you must not be angry with her. She called me *painted dirt, baby-face, waiting-maid, beggar's-brat,* and *beggar-born;* but I said, as long as I knew my innocence, I was easy in every thing but to have my dear parents abused. They were never beggars, nor beholden to any body, nor to any thing but God's grace and their own labour; that they once lived in credit; that misfortunes might befall any body; and that I could not bear they should be treated so undeservedly.

"Then her ladyship said, Ay, she supposed my master's folly would make us set up for a family, and that the Herald's office would shortly be searched to make it out."

"Exactly my sister again!" said he. "So you could not please her any way?"

"No, indeed, Sir. When she commanded me to fill her a glass of wine, and would not let her woman do it, she asked, if I was above it? I then said, 'If to attend your ladyship at table, or even kneel at your feet, was required of me, I would most gladly do it, were I only the person you think me. But, if it be to triumph over one, who has received honours she thinks require from her another part, that she may not be utterly unworthy of them, I must say, I *cannot* do it.' This quite astonished her ladyship; and a little before, her kinsman brought me the bottle and glass, and required me to fill it for my lady at her command, calling himself my deputy: and I said, ''Tis in a good hand, help my lady yourself.' So, Sir," added I, "you see I could be a little saucy upon occasion."

"You please me well, my Pamela," said he. "This was quite right. But proceed."

"Her ladyship said, she was astonished: adding, she supposed I would have her look upon me as her brother's wife: and, asked me, what in the name of impudence possessed me, to *dare* to look upon myself as her sister? I said, that was a question better became her most worthy brother to answer, than me. And then I thought I should have had her ladyship upon me, but her woman interposed. I afterwards told Mrs. Jewkes at the window, that since I was detained, I believed it was best to let Robert go with the chariot, and say, Lady Davers was come, and I could not leave her ladyship. But this did not please, though I thought it would : for she said, ' No, no, he'll think I make the creature my companion, and know not how to part with her.' "

" Exactly," said he, " my sister again ! "

" She said, I knew nothing what belonged to people of condition ; how should I ? ' What *shall* I say, Madam ? ' said I. ' Nothing at all,' answered she ; ' let him expect his *dearest love*,' alluding to your kind letter, ' and be disappointed ; it is but adding a few more hours to this heavy absence, and every one will become a day in his amorous account.'

" So, to be short, I saw nothing was to be done ; and I feared, Sir, you would wonder at my stay, and be angry ; I watched my opportunity, until my lady was at the further end of the room ; and the parlour being a ground floor, I jumped out of the window, and ran for it.

" Her ladyship called after me, so did her woman ; I heard her say, I flew like a bird ; and she called to two of her servants to stop me ; but I said, ' Touch me at your peril, fellows.' Mr. Colbrand, having been planted at hand by Mrs. Jewkes (who incurred her ladyship's displeasure, once or twice, by taking my part in the affair), seeing how I was used, put on a fierce look, cocked his hat with one hand, and put t'other on his sword, and said, he would chine the man who offered to touch his lady. So he ran alongside, and could hardly keep pace with me : And here, my dear Sir," concluded I, " I am, at your's and the good company's service."

They seemed highly pleased ; and my master said, he was glad Mrs. Jewkes behaved so well, as also Mr. Colbrand. " Yes, Sir," said I ; " when Mrs. Jewkes interposed once, her ladyship said, it was hard, she, who was born in that house, could not have some privilege in it, without being talked to by the saucy servants. She called her another time *fat face*, and *woman'd* her most violently."

" Well," said my master, " I am glad, my dear, you have had such an escape. My sister was always passionate, as Mrs. Peters knows ; and my poor mother had enough to do with us both ; for we neither of us wanted spirit. When I was a boy, I never came home from school or college for a few days, though we longed to see one another before, but on the first day we had a quarrel ; for she, being seven years older than I, would domineer over me, and I could not bear it. And I used, on her frequently quarrelling with the maids, being always at a word and a blow, to call her Captain Bab ; for her name is Barbara. When my Lord Davers courted her, my poor mother has made up quarrels between them three times in a day; and I used to tell her, she would certainly beat her husband, marry whom she would, if he did not beat her first, and break her spirit. Yet has she very good qualities. She was a dutiful daughter, is a good wife; she is bountiful to her servants, firm in her friend-ships, charitable to the poor, and, I believe, never any sister better loved a brother, than she me : and yet she always loved to vex and tease me; and as I would bear a resentment longer than she, she'd be one moment the most provoking creature in the world, and the next would do any thing to be forgiven; and I have made her, when she was the aggressor, follow me all over the house and garden to be upon good terms with me.

" But this case piques her more, because she had found out a match for me in the family of a person of quality and had set her heart upon bringing it to effect, and had even proceeded far in it, without my knowledge, and brought me into the lady's company, unknowing of her design : but I was then averse to matrimony upon any terms; and was angry at her proceeding in it so far without my privity or encouragement; and she cannot, for this reason, bear the thoughts of my being now married, and to her mother's waiting-maid too, as she reminds my dear Pamela, when I had declined her proposal with the daughter of a noble earl.

" This is the whole case," said he; " and allowing for the pride and violence of her spirit, and that she knows not, as I do, the transcendent excellencies of my dear Pamela, and that all her view, in her own conception, is mine and the family honour, she is a little to be allowed for : though never fear, my Pamela, but that I, who never had a struggle with her wherein I did not get the better, will do you justice and myself too."

This account of Lady Davers pleased every body, and was far from being to her ladyship's disadvantage in the main; and I would do any thing in the world to have the honour to be in her good graces; yet I fear it will not be easily, if at all, effected. But I will proceed.

After supper, nothing would serve Miss Darnford and Miss Boroughs, but we must have a dance; and Mr. Peters, who plays a good fiddle, urged it forward. My dear master though in a riding dress, took out Miss Boroughs. Sir Simon, for a man of his years, danced well, and took me out; but put on one of his free jokes, that I was fitter to dance with a younger man, he would have it (though I had not danced since my dear lady's death but once or twice, to please Mrs. Jervis, and, indeed, believed all my dancing days over) that as my master and I were the best dancers, we should dance once together *before* folks, as the old gentleman said; my dear Sir was pleased to oblige him: and afterwards danced with Miss Darnford, who has much more skill and judgment than I; though they complimented me with an easier shape and air.

We left the company with great difficulty, at about eleven, my dear master having been up all night before, and we being at the greatest distance from home; they seemed inclined not to break up so soon, as they were neighbours; and the ladies said, they longed to hear the end of Lady Davers's interview with her brother.

My master said, he feared we must not now think of going next day to Bedfordshire, as intended; and perhaps might see them again. So we took leave, and set out for home; where we arrived not till twelve o'clock, and found Lady Davers had gone to bed about eleven, wanting much that we should come home first; but so did not I.

Mrs. Jewkes told us, that my lady was sadly fretted that I had got away so; and seemed a little apprehensive of what I would say of her usage of me. She asked Mrs. Jewkes, if she thought I was really married? Mrs. Jewkes telling her, Yes, she fell into a passion, and said, " Begone, bold woman, I cannot bear thee. See not my face till I send for thee. Thou hast been very impudent to me once or twice to-day already, and art now worse than ever." She said, she would not have told her ladyship, if she had not asked her; and was sorry she had offended. She sent for her at supper-time: said she, " I have another question to ask thee, woman, and tell me, Yes, if thou darest." Was ever anything so odd? " Why, then," said Mrs. Jewkes, " I will say No, before your ladyship speaks." My master laughed: " Poor woman!" said he. She called her *insolent*, and *assurance;* and said, " Begone, bold woman as thou art !— but come hither, Dost thou know if that young harlot is to lie with my brother to-night? "

She knew not what to answer, because she had threatened her if she said Yes. But at last, my lady said, " I will know the bottom of this iniquity. I suppose they won't have so much impudence to lie together while I'm in the house: but I dare say they have been bed-fellows."

Said she, " I will lie to-night in the room I was born in; so get that bed ready." That room being our bed-chamber. Mrs. Jewkes, after some hesitation, replied, " Madam, my master lies there, and has the key."—" I believe, woman," said she, " thou tellest me a story."—" Indeed, Madam, he does, and has some papers there he will let nobody see;" for Mrs. Jewkes said she feared she would beat her if she went up, and found by my clothes, and some of my master's, how it was.

"So," she said, "I will then lie in the best room, as it is called; and Jackey shall lie in the little green room adjoining. Has thy master got the keys of those?"—"No, Madam," said Mrs. Jewkes; "I will have them made ready for your ladyship."

"And where dost thou lay thy pursy sides?" said she. "Up two pair of stairs, Madam, next the garden."—"And where lies the young harlotry?"—"Sometimes with me, Madam," said she.—"And sometimes with thy virtuous master, I suppose. Ha, woman! what say'st thou?"—"I must not speak," said Mrs. Jewkes.—"Well, thou may'st go," said she; "but thou hast the air of a secret keeper of that sort; I dare say thou'lt set the good work forward most cordially."—"Poor Mrs. Jewkes!" said my master, and laughed most heartily. This talk we had whilst we were undressing. So she and her woman lay together in the room my master lay in before I was happy. I said, "Dear Sir, pray, in the morning, let me lock myself up when you rise; and not be called down for ever so much; as I am afraid to see her ladyship; and I will employ myself about my journal, while these things are in my head."— "Don't be afraid, my dear," said he; "am not I with you?"

Mrs. Jewkes pitied me for what I underwent in the day; and I said, "We won't make the worst of it to my dear master, as we won't exasperate where we would reconcile: but," added I, "I am much obliged to you, Mrs. Jewkes, and thank you." Said my master, "I hope she did not beat your lady, Mrs. Jewkes!"—"Not much, Sir," said she; "but I believe I saved her once: yet I was most vexed at the young lord."— "Ay, Mrs. Jewkes," said my master, "let me know *his* behaviour, I can chastise him, though not my sister who is a woman; so let me know the part he acted."

"Nothing, my dear Sir," said I, "but impertinence, if I may so say, and foolishness, that was very provoking; but I spared him not, and so there is no room, Sir, for your anger."—"No, Sir," said Mrs. Jewkes, "nothing else indeed."

"How was her woman?" said my master. "Pretty impertinent," replied Mrs. Jewkes, "as ladies' women will be."— "But," said I, "you know she saved me once or twice."— "Very true, Madam," returned Mrs. Jewkes. "She said to me at table, that you were a sweet creature: she never saw your equal; but that you had a spirit; and she was sorry you answered her lady so, who never bore such contradiction before.

I told her," added Mrs. Jewkes, " that if I was in your place, I should have taken much more upon me, and that you are all sweetness. She said, I was got over, she saw."

My master told Mrs. Jewkes, he should not rise till eight or nine, as he had sat up all the night before; but it seems my lady, knowing he usually rose about six, got up soon after that hour; raised her woman, and her nephew; having a whimsical scheme in her head, to try to find whether we were in bed together: and about half an hour after six, she rapt at our chamber-door.

My master was waked at the noise, and asked who was there? " Open the door," said she; " open it this minute ! " I said, clinging about his neck, " Dear, dear Sir, pray, pray, don't ! O save me ! "—" Don't fear, Pamela," said he, " the woman's mad, I believe."

But he called out, " Who are you? What do you want? "— " You know my voice well enough," said she : " I *will* come in." —" Pray, Sir," said I, " don't let her ladyship in."—" Don't be frighted, my dear," said he; " she thinks we are not married, and are afraid to be found a-bed together, *I'll* let her in; but she shan't come near you."

So he slipt out of bed, and putting on some of his clothes, and gown and slippers, he said, " What bold body dare disturb my repose thus? " and opened the door. In rushed she; " I'll see your wickedness," said she, " I will : in vain shall you think to hide it from me."—" What should I hide? " said he. " How dare you set a foot in my house, after your usage of me? " I had covered myself over head and ears, and trembled every joint. He 'spied her woman and kinsman in the room, she crying out, " Bear witness, Jackey; bear witness, Beck; the creature is *now* in his bed." Not seeing the young gentleman before, who was at the feet of the bed, he said, " How now, Sir ! What is your business in this apartment? Begone this moment." And he went away directly.

" Beck," said my lady, " you see the creature is in his bed."— " I do, Madam," answered she. My master came to me, and said, " Ay, look Beck, and bear witness : here is my Pamela : my dear Angel, my lovely creature, don't be afraid; look up, and see how franticly this woman of quality behaves." At which, I just peeped, and saw my lady, who could not bear this, coming to me; and she said, " Wicked, abandoned wretch ! vile brother, to brave me thus ! I'll tear the creature out of bed before your face, and expose you both as you deserve."

At that he took her in his arms, as if she had been nothing; and carrying her out of the room, she cried out, "Beck, Beck! help me, Beck; the wretch is going to throw me down stairs." Her woman ran to him, and said, "Good Sir, for Heaven's sake, do no violence to my lady; her ladyship has been ill all night."

He set her down in the chamber she lay in, and she could not speak for passion. "Take care of your lady," said he, "and when she has rendered herself more worthy of my attention, I'll see her; till then, at her peril, and yours too, come not near my apartment." So he came to me, and with the sweetest soothing words, pacified my fears, gave me leave to write in my closet when my fright was over, and to stay there till things were more calm. Then he dressed himself, and went out of the chamber, permitting me to fasten the door after him.

At breakfast-time, my master tapped at the door, and I said, "Who's there?"—"I, my dearest," said he. "Oh then," replied I, "I will open it with pleasure." I had written on a good deal, but I put it by, when I ran to the door. I would have locked it again, when he was in; but he said, "Am not I here? Don't be afraid." Said he, "Will you come down to breakfast, my love?"—"O no, dear Sir," said I: "be pleased to excuse me." Said he, "I cannot bear the look of it, that the mistress of my house should breakfast in her closet, as if she durst not come down, and I at home!"—"O dearest Sir," replied I, "pray pass that over for my sake; and don't let my presence aggravate your sister for a kind punctilio."—"Then, my dear," said he, "I will breakfast with *you* here."—"No, pray, dear Sir," answered I, "breakfast with your sister."—"That, my dear," replied he, "will too much gratify her pride, and look like a slight to you."—"Dear Sir," said I, "your goodness is too great for me to want punctilious proofs of it. Pray oblige her ladyship. She is your guest; surely, Sir, you may be freest with your dutiful wife!"

"She is a strange woman," said he: "how I pity her! She has thrown herself into a violent fit of the colic, through passion; and is but now, her woman says, a little easier."—"I hope, Sir," said I, "when you carried her ladyship out, you did not hurt her."—"No," replied he, "I love her too well. I sat her down in the apartment she had chosen; and she but now desires to see me, and that I will breakfast with her, or refuses to touch any thing. But, if my dearest please, I will insist it shall be with you at the same time."

"O, no, no, dear Sir," said I: "I should never forgive myself if I did, I would on my knees beg her ladyship's goodness to me

376

now I am in your presence; though I thought I ought to carry it a little stiff when you were absent, for the sake of the honour you have done me. And, dear Sir, if my deepest humility will please, permit me to shew it."

"You shall do nothing," returned he, "unworthy of my wife, to please the proud woman! But I will, however, permit you to breakfast by yourself this once, as I have not seen her since I used her in so barbarous a manner, as I understood she exclaims I have; and as she will not eat any thing unless I give her my company." So he saluted me, and withdrew; and I locked the door after him again for fear.

Mrs. Jewkes soon after, rapp'd at the door. "Who's there?" said I. "Only I, Madam." So I opened the door. "'Tis a sad thing, Madam," said she, "you should be so much afraid in your own house." She brought me some chocolate and toast; and I asked her about my lady's behaviour: she said, she would not suffer any body to attend but her woman, because she would not be heard what she had to say; but she believed, she said, her master was very angry with the young lord, as she called her kinsman: for, as she passed by the door, she heard him say, in a high tone, "I hope, Sir, you did not forget what belongs to the character you assume;" or to that effect.

About one o'clock my master came up again; and he said, "Will you come down to dinner, Pamela, when I send for you?" —"Whatever you command, Sir, I must do; but my lady won't desire to see me."—"No matter whether she will or not. But I will not suffer, that she shall prescribe her insolent will to my wife, and in your own house too. I will, by my tenderness to you, mortify her pride; and it cannot be done so well as to her face."

"Dearest Sir," said I, "pray indulge me, and let me dine here by myself. It will make my lady but more inveterate." Said he, "I have told her we are married. She is out of all patience about it, and yet pretends *not* to believe it. Upon that I tell her then she shall have it her own way, and that I am *not*. And what has she to do with it either way? She has scolded and begged, commanded and prayed, blessed me, and cursed me by turns, twenty times, in these few hours. And I have sometimes soothed her, sometimes raged; and at last left her, and took a turn in the garden for an hour to compose myself, because you should not see how the foolish woman had ruffled me; and just now I came out, seeing her coming in."

Just as he had said so, I cried, "Oh! my lady, my lady!" for I heard her voice in the chamber, saying, "Brother, brother, one word with you——" stopping in sight of the closet where I was. He stept out, and she went up to the window, that looks towards the garden, and said, " Mean fool that I am, to follow you up and down the house in this manner, though I am ashamed and avoided by you ! You a brother !—you a barbarian ! is it possible we could be born of one mother ? "

" Why," said he, " do you charge me with a conduct to you, that you bring upon yourself ? Is it not surprising that you should take the liberty with me, that the dear mother you have named never gave you an example for to any of her relations ? Was it not sufficient that I was insolently taken to task by you in your letters, but my retirements must be invaded; my house insulted ? And, if I have one person dearer to me than another, that person must be singled out for an object of your violence."

" Ay," said she, " that one person is the thing ! But though I come with a resolution to be temperate, and to expostulate with you on your avoiding me so unkindly, yet cannot I have patience to look upon that bed in which I was born, and to be made the guilty scene of your wickedness with such a——"
—" Hush ! " said he, " I charge you, call not the dear girl by any name unworthy of her. You know not, as I told you, her excellence ; and I desire you'll not repeat the freedoms you have taken below."

She stamped with her foot, and said, " God give me patience ! So much contempt to a sister that loves you so well; and so much tenderness to a vile——"

He put his hand before her mouth : " Be silent," said he, " once more I charge you. You know not the innocence you abuse so freely. I ought not, neither will I bear it."

She sat down and fanned herself, and burst into tears, and such sobs of grief, or rather passion, that grieved me to hear; and I sat and trembled sadly.

He walked about the room in great anger; and at last said, " Let me ask you, Lady Davers, why am I thus insolently to be called to account by you ? Am I not independent ? Am I not of age ? Am not I at liberty to please myself ? Would to God, that instead of a woman, and my sister, any man breathing had dared, whatever were his relation, under that of a father, to give himself half the airs you have done ! Why did you not send on this accursed errand your lord, who could write me such a letter as no gentleman should write, nor any gentleman tamely receive ? He should have seen the difference."

" We all know," said she, " that since your Italian duel, you have commenced a bravo; and all your airs breathe as strongly

378

of the man-slayer as of the libertine."—" This," said he, " I will bear; for I have no reason to be ashamed of that duel, nor the cause of it; since it was to save a friend, and because 'tis levelled at myself only ! but suffer not your tongue to take too great a liberty with my Pamela."

She interrupted him in a violent burst of passion. " If I bear this," said she, " I can bear any thing !—O the little strumpet ! " He interrupted her then, and said wrathfully, " Be gone, rageful woman, this moment from my presence ! Leave my house this instant ! I renounce you, and all relations to you; and never more let me see your face, or call me a brother." And took her by the hand to lead her out. She laid hold of the curtains of the window, and said, " I will not go ! you shall not force me from you thus ignominiously in the wretch's hearing, and suffer *her* to triumph over me in your barbarous treatment of me."

Not considering any thing, I ran out of the closet, and threw myself at my dear master's feet, and said, " Dearest Sir, let me beg, that no act of unkindness, for my sake, pass between so worthy and so near relations.—Dear, dear Madam," said I, and clasped her knees, " pardon the unhappy cause of all this evil; on my knees I beg your ladyship to receive me to your grace and favour, and you shall find me incapable of any triumph but in your goodness to me."

" Creature," said she, " art *thou* to beg an excuse for me?—Art *thou* to implore my forgiveness? Is it to *thee* I am to owe the favour, that I am not cast headlong from my brother's presence? Be gone to thy corner, wench; be gone, I say, lest thy paramour kill me for trampling thee under my foot."

" Rise, my dear Pamela," said my master, " rise, dear life of my life ! and expose not so much worthiness to the ungrateful scorn of so violent a spirit." So he led me to my closet, and there I sat and wept.

Her woman came up, just as he had led me to my closet, and was returning to her lady; and she very humbly said, " Excuse my intrusion, good Sir ! I hope I may come to my lady."—" Yes, Mrs. Worden," said he, " you may come in, and pray take your lady down stairs with you, for fear I should too much forget what belongs either to my sister, or myself ! "

I began to think (seeing her ladyship so outrageous with her brother) what a happy escape I had the day before, though hardly enough used in conscience too, as I thought.

Her woman begged her ladyship to walk down : and she said, " Beck, seest thou that bed? That is the bed I was born in,

379

yet, thou sawest, as well as I, the wicked Pamela in it, this morning, and this brother of mine just risen from her!"

"True," said he, "you both saw it, and 'tis my pride that you could see it. 'Tis my bridal bed; and 'tis abominable, that the happiness I knew before you came, should be so barbarously interrupted."

"Swear to me but, thou bold wretch," said she, "that Pamela Andrews is really and truly thy lawful wife, without sham, deceit, or double meaning; and I know what I have to say."

"I'll humour you for once," said he, and then swore a solemn oath, that I was. "And," said he, "did I not tell you so at first?"

"I cannot *yet* believe you," said she, "because in this particular, I had rather have called you *knave* than *fool*."—"Provoke me not too much," said he; "for, if I should as much forget myself as you have done, you'd have no more of a brother in me, than I have a sister in you."

"Who married you?" said she; "tell me that: was it not a broken attorney in a parson's habit? Tell me truly, in the wench's hearing. When she's undeceived, she'll know how to behave herself better!"—"Thank God," thought I, "it is not so."

"No," said he, "and I'll tell you, that I blessed God, I abhorred that project, before it was brought to bear: and Mr. Williams married us."—"Nay, then," said she, "but answer me another question or two, I beseech you: who gave her away?"—"Parson Peters," said he. "Where was the ceremony performed?"—"In my own little chapel, which you may see, as it was put in order on purpose."

"Now," said she, "I begin to fear there is something in it. But who was present?" said she. "Methinks," replied he, "I look like a fine puppy, to suffer myself to be thus interrogated by an insolent sister: but, if you must know, Mrs. Jewkes was present."—"O, the procuress," said she: "but nobody else?"—"Yes," said he, "all my heart and soul!"

"Wretch!" said she; "and what would thy father and mother have said, had they lived to this day?"—"Their consents," replied he, "I should have thought it my duty to ask; but not yours, Madam."

"Suppose," said she, "I had married my father's groom! what would you have said to that?"—"I could not have behaved worse," replied he, "than you have done."—"And would you not have thought," said she, "I had deserved it?"

Said he, "Does your pride let you see no difference, in the

case you put?"—"None at all," said she. "Where can the difference be between a beggar's son married to a lady, or a beggar's daughter made a gentleman's wife?"

"Then, I'll tell you; the difference is, a man ennobles the woman he takes, be she *who* she will; and adopts her into his *own* rank, be it *what* it will : but a woman, though ever so nobly born, debases herself by a mean marriage, and descends from her *own* rank to *his* she stoops to.

"When the royal family of Stuart allied itself into the low family of Hyde (comparatively low, I mean), did any body scruple to call the lady Royal Highness, and Duchess of York? Did any one think her daughters, the late Queen Mary and Queen Anne, less royal for that?

"When the broken-fortuned peer goes into the city to marry a rich tradesman's daughter, be he duke or earl, does not his consort immediately become ennobled by his choice? and who scruples to call her lady, duchess, or countess?

"But when a duchess or countess dowager descends to mingle with a person of obscure birth, does she not then degrade herself, and is she not effectually degraded? And will any duchess or countess rank with her?

"Now, Lady Davers, see you not a difference between my marrying my dear mother's beloved and deserving waiting-maid, with a million of excellencies, and such graces of mind and person as would adorn any distinction; and your marrying a sordid groom, whose constant train of education, conversation, and opportunities, could possibly give him no other merit, than what must proceed from the vilest, lowest taste, in his sordid dignifier?"

"O, the wretch!" said she, "how he finds excuses to palliate his meanness!"

"Again," said he, "let me observe to you, Lady Davers, when a Duke marries a private person, is he not still her *head*, by virtue of being her husband? But when a lady descends to marry a groom, is not that groom her *head*, being her husband? Does not that difference strike you? For what lady of quality ought to respect another, who has made so sordid a choice, and set a groom above her? For, would it not be to put that groom upon a par with themselves? Call this palliation, or what you will; but if you see not the difference, you are blind, and a very unfit judge for yourself, much more unfit to be a censurer of me."

"Publish your fine reasons," said she, "and they will be sweet encouragement to all the young gentlemen that read them, to cast themselves away on the servant wenches in their families."

"Not at all, Lady Davers," replied he : "for if any young gentleman stays till he finds such a person as my Pamela, so enriched with the beauties of person and mind, so well fitted to adorn the degree she is raised to, he will stand as easily acquitted as I shall be, to all the world that sees her, except there be many more Lady Davers's than I apprehend can possibly be met with."

"And so," returned she, "you say you are actually and really married, honestly, or rather foolishly, married to this *slut ?* "

"I am indeed," said he, "if you presume to call her so ! And why should I not, if I please ? Who is there ought to contradict me ? Whom have I hurt by it ? Have I not an estate, free and independent ? Am I likely to be beholden to you, or any of my relations ? And why, when I have a sufficiency in my own single hands, should I scruple to make a woman equally happy, who has all I want ? For beauty, virtue, prudence, and generosity, too, I will tell you, she has more than any lady I ever saw. Yes, Lady Davers, she has all these *naturally ;* they are *born* with her ; and a few years' education, with her genius, has done more for her, than a whole life has done for others."

"No more, no more, I beseech you ; thou surfeitest me, honest man ! with thy weak folly. Thou art more than an idolator ; thou hast made a graven image, and fallest down to worship the works of thine own hands ; and, Jeroboam-like, wouldst have everybody else bow down before thy calf ! "

"Well said, Lady Davers ! Whenever your passion suffers you to descend to witticism, 'tis almost over with you. But let me tell you, though I myself worship this sweet creature, that you call such names, I want nobody else to do it ; and should be glad you had not intruded upon me, to interrupt me in the course of our mutual happiness."

"Well said, well said, my kind, my well-mannered brother ! " said she. "I shall, after this, very little interrupt your mutual happiness, I'll assure you. I thought you a gentleman once, and prided myself in my brother : but I'll say now, with the burial service, ' *Ashes to ashes, and dirt to dirt !* ' "

"Ay," said he, "Lady Davers, and there we must all end ; you with your pride, and I with my plentiful fortune, must come to it ; and then, where will be your distinction ? Let me tell you, except you and I mend our manners, though you have been no duellist, no libertine, as you call me, this amiable girl, whom your vanity and folly so much despise, will infinitely out-soar

382

us both; and he who judges best, will give the preference where due, without regard to birth or fortune."

"Egregious preacher!" said she: "what, my brother already turned Puritan!—See what marriage, and repentance may bring a man to! I heartily congratulate this change!—Well," said she (and came towards me; and I trembled to see her coming: but her brother followed to observe, and I stood up at her approach, and she said), "give me thy hand, Mrs. Pamela, Mrs. Andrews, Mrs. ——. What shall I call thee?—Thou hast done wonders in a little time: not only made a rake a husband; but thou hast made a rake a preacher! Take care," added she, "after all," in ironical anger, tapping me on the neck, "that thy vanity begins not where his ends; and that thou callest not thyself my sister."

"She shall, I hope, Lady Davers," said he, "when she can make as great a convert of you from pride, as she has of me from libertinism."

Mrs. Jewkes just then came up, and said dinner was ready. "Come, my Pamela," said my dear master; "you desired to be excused from breakfasting with us; but I hope you'll give Lady Davers and me your company to dinner."

"How dare you insult me thus?" said my lady.—"How dare you," said he, "insult me by your conduct, in my own house, after I have told you I am married? Or think of staying here one moment, and refuse my wife the honours that belong to her as such?"

"Merciful God!" said she, "give me patience!" and held her hand to her forehead.

"Pray, dear Sir," said I, "excuse me; don't vex my lady."—"Be silent, my dear love," said he: "you see already what you have got by your condescension. You have thrown yourself at her feet, and, insolent as she is, she has threatened to trample upon you. She'll ask you presently, if she is to owe her excuse to your interposition? And yet nothing else can make her forgiven."

Poor lady, she could not bear this; and, as if discomposed, she ran to her poor grieved woman, took hold of her hand, and said, "Lead me down, lead me down, Beck! Let us instantly quit this house, this cursed house, that once I took pleasure in: order the fellows to get ready, and I will never see it, nor its owner, more." And away she went down stairs in a great hurry. And the servants were ordered to make ready for their departure.

I saw my master was troubled, and I went to him, and said,

" Pray, dear Sir, follow my lady down, and pacify her. 'Tis her love to you."—" Poor woman ! " said he, " I am concerned for her ! But I insist upon your coming down, since things are gone so far. Her pride will get new strength else, and we shall be all to begin again."

" Dearest Sir," said I, " excuse my going down this once ! " —" Indeed, my dear, I won't," replied he. " What, shall it be said, that my sister should scare my wife from table, and I present ? No, I have borne too much already ; and so have you : and I charge you come down, when I send for you."

He departed, saying these words, and I durst not dispute, for I saw he was determined. And there is as much majesty as goodness in him ; as I have often observed, though never more than on the present occasion with his sister. Her ladyship instantly put on her hood and gloves, and her woman tied up a handkerchief full of things ; for her principal matters were not unpacked ; and the coachman got her chariot ready, and her footmen their horses ; and she appeared resolved to go. But her kinsman and Mr. Colbrand had taken a turn together somewhere ; and she would not come in, but sat fretting on a seat in the fore-yard, with her woman by her ; and at last said to one of the footmen, " Do you, James, stay to attend my nephew ; and we'll take the road we came."

Mrs. Jewkes went to her ladyship, and said, " Your ladyship will be pleased to stay dinner, 'tis just coming upon table."— " No," said she, " I have indeed enough of this house ! But give my service to your master, and I wish him happier than he has made me."

He had sent for me down, and I came, though unwillingly, and the cloth was laid in the parlour I had jumped out of ; my master walking about it. Mrs. Jewkes came in and asked, if he pleased to have dinner brought in ? for my lady would not come in, but desired her service, and wished him happier than he had made her. He, seeing at the window, when he went to that side of the room, all ready to go, stept out, and said, " Lady Davers, if I thought you would not be hardened rather than softened by my civility, I would ask you to walk in, and at least, let your kinsman and servants dine before they go." She wept, and turned her face from him, to hide it. He took her hand, and said, " Come, sister, let me prevail upon you ; walk in."—" No ! " said she, " don't ask me. I wish I could hate you as much as you hate me ? "—" You do," said he, " and a great deal more, I'll assure you, or else you'd not vex me as you do. Come, pray walk in."—" Don't ask me," said she.

Her kinsman just then returned: "Why, Madam," said he, "your ladyship won't go till you have din'd, I hope?"—"No, Jackey," said she, "I can't stay: I'm an *intruder* here, it seems!"—"Think," said my master, "of the occasion you gave for that word. Your violent passions are the only *intruders!* Lay them aside, and never sister was dearer to a brother."—"Don't say such another word," said she, "I beseech you; for I am too easy to forgive you any thing, for one kind word!"—"You shall have one hundred," said he, "nay, ten thousand, if they will do, my dear sister." And, kissing her, he added, "Pray give me your hand. John," said he, "put up your horses: you are all as welcome here, for all your lady's angry with me, as at any inn you can put up at. Come, Mr. H.," said he, "lead your aunt in; for she won't permit that honour to me."

This quite overcame her, and she said, giving her brother her hand, "Yes, I will, and you shall lead me any whither!" and kissed him. "But don't think," said she, "I can forgive you neither." So he led her into the parlour where I was. Said she, "Why do you lead me to this wench?"—"'Tis my wife, my dear sister; and if you will not love her, yet don't forget common civilities to her, for your own sake."

"Pray, Madam," said her kinsman, "since your brother is pleased to own his marriage, we must not forget common civilities, as Mr. B. says. And, Sir," added he, "permit me to wish you joy."—"Thank you, Sir," said he. "And may I?" said he, looking at me. "Yes, Sir," replied my master. So he saluted me, very complaisantly; and said, "I vow to God, Madam, I did not know this yesterday; and if I was guilty of a fault, I beg your pardon."

My lady said, "Thou'rt a good-natured, foolish fellow; thou might'st have saved this nonsensical parade, till I had given thee leave."—"Why, aunt," said he, "if they are actually married, there's no help for't; and we must not make mischief between man and wife."

"But, brother, do you think I'll sit at table with the creature?"—"No contemptuous names, I beseech you, Lady Davers! I tell you she is really my wife; and I must be a villain to suffer her to be ill used. She has no protector but me; and, if you will permit her, she will always love and honour you."—"Indeed, Madam, I will," said I.

"I cannot, I won't sit down to table with her," said she. "Pamela, I hope thou dost not think I will!"—"Indeed, Madam," said I, "if your good brother will permit it, I will

385

attend your chair while you dine, to shew my veneration for your ladyship, as the sister of my kind protector."—" See," said he, " her condition has not altered her ; but I cannot permit in her a conduct unworthy of my wife ; and I hope my sister will not expect it neither."

" Let her leave the room," replied she, " if I must stay."— " Indeed, you're out of the way, aunt," said her kinsman ; " that is not right, as things stand." Said my master, " No, Madam, that must not be : or, if so, we'll have two tables ; you and your nephew shall sit at one, and my wife and I at the other ; and then see what a figure your unreasonable punctilio will make you cut." She seemed irresolute, and he placed her at the table, the first course, which was fish, being brought in. " Where," said she to me, " would'st thou presume to sit ? Would'st have me give *place* to thee *too*, wench ? "—" Come," said my master, " I'll put that out of dispute ; " and so sat himself down by her, at the upper end of the table, and placed me at his left hand. " Excuse me, my dear," said he, " this once."—" Oh ! your cursed complaisance," said she, " to such a ———"—" Hush, sister ! " said he : " I will not bear to hear her spoke slightingly of ! 'Tis enough, that, to oblige your violent and indecent caprice, you make me compromise with you thus."

" Come, Sir," added he, " pray take your place next your gentle aunt,"—" Beck," said she, " do you sit down by Pamela, there, since it must be so ; we'll be hail-fellow all ! "—" With all my heart,"replied my master ; " I have so much honour for all the sex, that I would not have the meanest person of it stand, while I sit, had I been to have made the custom. Mrs. Worden, pray sit down."—" Sir," said she, " I hope I shall know my place better."

My lady sat considering ; and then, lifting up her hands, said, " Lord, what will this world come to ? "—" To nothing but what's very good," replied my master, " if such spirits as Lady Davers's do but take the rule of it. Shall I help you, sister, to some carp ? "—" Help your beloved ! " said she. " That's kind ! " said he : " now that's my good Lady Davers ! Here, my love, let me help you, since my sister desires it."—" Mighty well," returned she, " mighty well ! " but sat on one side, turning from me, as it were.

" Dear aunt," said her kinsman, " let's see you buss, and be friends ; since 'tis so, what signifies it ? "—" Hold thy fool's tongue ! is thy tone so soon turned since yesterday ? " Said my master, " I hope no affront was offered to my wife in her own house." She hit him a smart slap on the shoulder; "Take that, impudent brother," said she. "I'll *wife* you and in *her own* house!" She seemed half afraid; but he, in very good humour, kissed her, and said, "Sister, I thank you. But I have not had a blow from you before for some time!"

"'Fore Gad, Sir," said her kinsman, "'tis very kind of you to take it so well. Her ladyship is as good a woman as ever lived; but I have had many a cuff from her myself."

"I won't put it up neither," said my master, "except you'll assure me, you have seen her serve her lord so."

I pressed my foot to his, and said, softly, "Don't, dear Sir!" —"What!" said she, "is the creature begging me off from insult? If *his* manners won't keep him from outraging me, I won't owe his forbearance to *thee*, wench."

Said my master, and put some fish on my lady's plate, "Well does Lady Davers use the word *insult*. But let me see you eat one mouthful, and I'll forgive you;" he put the knife in one hand, and the fork in the other. "As I hope to live," said he, "I cannot bear this silly childishness, for nothing at all. I am quite ashamed of it."

She put a little bit to her mouth, but laid it down again: "I cannot eat," said she; "I cannot swallow, I am sure. It will certainly choke me." He had forbidden his men-servants to come in, that they might not behold the scene he expected: and rose from table himself, and filled a glass of wine, her woman offering, and her kinsman rising, to do it. Meantime, his seat between us being vacant, she turned to me—"How now, confidence," said she, "darest thou sit next *me*? Why dost thou not rise, and take the glass from thy property?"

"Sit still, my dear," said he; "I'll help you both." But I arose; for I was afraid of a good cuff; and said, "Pray, Sir, let me help my lady!"—"So you shall," replied he, "when she's in a humour to receive it as she ought."—"Sister," said he, with a glass in his hand, "pray drink; you'll then perhaps eat something."—"Is this to insult me?" said she. "No, really," returned he; "but to incite you to eat: for you'll be sick for want of it."

She took the glass, and said, "God forgive you, wicked wretch, for your usage of me this day! This is a little as it used to be! I once had your love, and now it is changed; and for whom? that vexes me!" and wept so, she was forced to set down the glass.

"You don't do well," said he. "You neither treat me like your brother, nor a gentleman; and if you would suffer

387

me, I would love you as well as ever. But for a woman of sense and understanding, and a fine bred woman, as I once thought my sister, you act quite a childish part. Come," added he, and held the glass to her lips, " let the brother you once loved prevail on you to drink this glass of wine." She then drank it. He kissed her, and said, " Oh ! how passion deforms the noblest minds ! You have lost much of that loveliness that used to adorn my sister. Let me persuade you to compose yourself, and be my sister again ! " For Lady Davers is a fine woman ; and has a presence as majestic for a lady, as her dear brother has for a gentleman.

He then sat between us, and said, when the second course came in, " Let Abraham come in, and wait ; " I touched his toe again ; but he minded it not ; and I saw he was right ; for her ladyship began to recollect herself, and did not behave half so ill before the servants, as she had done, and helped herself with some little freedom ; but she could not forbear a strong sigh and sob now and then. She called for a glass of the same wine she drank before. Said he, " Shall I help you again, Lady Davers ? " and rising, went to the side-board, and filled her a glass. " Indeed," said she, " I love to be soothed by my brother. Your health, Sir ! "

Said my master to me, with great sweetness, " My dear, now I'm up, I'll fill for you ! I must serve *both* sisters alike ! " She looked at the servant as a little check upon her, and said to my master, " How now, Sir !—Not that you know of." He whispered, " Don't shew any contempt before my servants, to one I have so deservedly made their mistress. Consider 'tis done."—" Ay," said she, " that's the thing that kills me."

He gave me a glass : " My good lady's health, Sir," said I. " That won't do ! " said she, leaning towards me, softly ; and was going to say, Wench or Creature, or some such word. And my master, seeing Abraham look towards her, her eyes being red and swelled, said, " Indeed, sister, I would not vex myself about it, if I was you."—" About what ? " said she. " Why," replied he, " about your lord's not coming down, as he had promised." He sat down, and she tapped him on the shoulder : " Ah, wicked one ! " said she, " nor will that do either ! "— " Why, to be sure," added he, " it would vex a lady of your sense and merit to be slighted, if it *was* so : but I am sure my lord loves you, as well as you love him ; and you know not what may have happened."

She shook her head, and said, " That's like your art. This makes one amazed you should be so caught."—" Who, my *lord* caught!" said he; "no, no; he'll have more wit. But I never heard you were jealous before."—"Nor," said she, "have you any reason to think so now. Honest friend, you need not wait," said she; "my woman will help us to what we want."—"Yes, let him," replied he. "Abraham, fill me a glass. Come," said my master, "Lord Davers to you, Madam: I hope he'll take care he is not found out."—"You're very provoking, brother. I wish you were as good as Lord Davers. But don't carry your jest too far."—"Well," said he, "'tis a tender point, I own. I've done."

By these kind managements the dinner passed over better than I expected. When the servants were withdrawn, my master said, still sitting between us, "I have a question to ask you, Lady Davers; and that is, if you'll bear me company to Bedfordshire? I was intending to set out thither to-morrow. But I'll tarry your pleasure, if you'll go with me."

"Is thy wife, as thou callest her, to go along with thee, friend?" said she. "Yes, to be sure," answered he, "my dear Quaker sister;" and took her hand, and smiled.—"And wouldst have me parade it with her on the road? Hey! And make one to grace her retinue? Hey! Tell me how thou wouldst chalk it out, if I would do as thou wouldst have me, honest friend?"

He clasped his arms about her, and kissed her. "You are a dear saucy sister," said he: "but I must love you. Why, I'll tell you how I'd have it. Here shall you and my Pamela."—"Leave out *my*, I desire you, if you'd have me sit patiently."—"No," said he, "I can't do that. Here shall you and my Pamela go together in your chariot, if you please; and she will then appear as one of your retinue; and your nephew and I will sometimes ride, and sometimes go into my chariot, to your woman."

"Shouldst thou like this, creature?" said she to me. "If your ladyship think it not too great an honour for me, Madam," said I. "Yes," replied she, "but my ladyship does think it would be too great an honour."

"Now I think of it," said he, "this must not be neither; for without you'd give her the hand, in your own chariot, my wife would be thought your woman, and that must not be."—"Why, that would, may-be," said she, "be the only inducement for me to bear her near me, in my chariot. But how then?"—"Why, then, when we came home, we'd get Lord Davers to come to us, and stay a month or two."

"And what if he was to come?"—"Why, I would have you,

as I know you have a good fancy, give Pamela your judgment on some patterns I expect from London, for clothes."—" Provoking wretch !" said she; "now I wish I may keep my hands to myself."—"I don't say it to provoke you," said he, "nor ought it to do so. But when I tell you I am married, is it not of consequence, that we must have new clothes ?"

"Hast thou any more of these obliging things to say to me, friend ?" said she. "I will make you a present," returned he, "worth your acceptance, if you will grace us with your company at church, when we make our appearance."—"Take that," said she, "if I die for't; wretch that thou art !" and was going to hit him a great slap; but he held her hand. Her kinsman said, "Dear aunt, I wonder at you; why, all these are things of course."

I begged to withdraw, and, as I went out, my good master said, "There's a person ! There's a shape ! There's a sweetness ! O, Lady Davers, were you a man, you would doat on her as I do."—"Yes," said the naughty lady, "so I should, for my harlot, but not for my wife." I turned on this, and said, "Your ladyship is cruel; and well may gentlemen take liberties, when ladies of honour say such things." I wept, and added, "Your ladyship's inference, if your good brother were not the most generous of men, would make me very unhappy."

"No fear, wench; no fear," said she : "thou'lt hold him as long as any body can, I see that !—Poor Sally Godfrey never had half the interest in him, I'll assure you."

"Stay, my Pamela," said he, in a passion; "stay when I bid you. You have now heard two vile charges upon me. I love you with such a true affection, that I ought to say something before this malicious accuser, that you may not think your consummate virtue linked to so black a villain."

Her nephew, who seemed uneasy, blamed her much : and I came back, but trembled as I stood : and he said, taking my hand, "I have been accused, my dear, as a dueller, and now as a profligate, in another sense : and there was a time I should not have received these imputations with so much concern as I do now, when I would wish, by degrees, by a conformity of my manners to your virtue, to shew every one the force of your example. But this briefly is the case of the first.

"I had a friend who had been basely attempted to be assassinated by bravoes, hired by a man of title in Italy, who, like many other persons of title, had no honour ! and, at Padua, I had the fortune to disarm one of these bravoes, in my friend's defence, and made him confess his employer; and him, I own, I challenged. At Sienna we met, and he died in a month after, of a fever; but I hope, not occasioned by the slight wounds he had received from me; though I was obliged to leave Italy upon it, sooner than I intended, because of his numerous relations, who looked upon me as the cause of his death; though I pacified them by a letter I wrote from Inspruck, acquainting them with the business of the deceased; and they followed me not to Munich as they intended.

"This is one of the good-natured hints, that might shock your sweetness, on reflecting that you are yoked with a murderer. The other——"—"Nay, brother," said she, "say no more. 'Tis your own fault if you go further."—"She shall know it all," said he; "and I defy the utmost stretch of your malice.

"When I was at the college, I was well received by a widow lady, who had several daughters, and but small fortunes to give them : the old lady set one of them, a deserving good girl she was, to draw me into marriage, for the sake of the fortune I was heir to; and contrived many opportunities to bring us and leave us together. I was not then of age : and the young lady, not half so artful as her mother, yielded to my addresses before the mother's plot could be ripened, and so utterly disappointed it. This, my Pamela, is the Sally Godfrey this malicious woman, with the worst intentions, has informed you of. And whatever other liberties I may have taken (for perhaps some more I have, which, had she known, you had heard of as well as this), I desire Heaven will only forgive me, till I revive its vengeance by the like offences, in injury to my Pamela.

"And now, my dear, you may withdraw : for this worthy sister of mine has said all the bad she knows of me; and what, at a proper opportunity, when I could have convinced you, that they were not my *boast*, but my *concern*, I should have acquainted you with myself : for I am not fond of being thought better than I am : though I hope from the hour I devoted myself to so much virtue, to that of my death, my conduct shall be irreproachable."

She was greatly moved at this, and the noble manner in which the dear gentleman owned and repented of his faults; and gushed out into tears, and said, "No, don't yet go, Pamela, I beseech you. My passion has carried me too far a great deal : " and, coming to me, she took my hand, and said, "You must stay to hear me beg his pardon ! " and so took his hand. But to my concern (for I was grieved for her ladyship's grief), he burst from her; and went out of the parlour into the garden, in a violent rage, that made me tremble. Her ladyship sat down, and leaned her head against my bosom, and made my neck wet with her tears; and I wept for company. Her kinsman was in a sad fret; and going out afterwards, he came in, and said, " Mr. B. has ordered his chariot to be got ready, and won't be spoken to by any body."—" Where is he ? " said she. " Walking in the garden till it is ready," replied he.

" Well," said she, " I have indeed gone too far. I was bewitched ! And now," said she, " malicious as he calls me, will he not forgive me for a twelvemonth : for I tell you, Pamela, if ever you offend, he will not easily forgive." I was all delighted, though sad, to see her ladyship so good to me. " Will you venture," said she, " to accompany me to him?—Dare you follow a lion in his retreats ? "—" I'll attend your ladyship," said I, " wherever you command."—" Well, wench,"said she, " Pamela, I mean, thou art very good in the main ! I should have loved thee as well as my mother did—if—but 'tis all over now ! Indeed you should not have married my brother ! But come, I must love him ! Let's find him out. Yet will he use me worse than a dog. I should not," added she, " have exasperated him, for I always have the worst of it. He knows I love him ! "

In this manner her ladyship talked, leaning on my arm, and walking into the garden. I saw he was still in a tumult, as it were; and he took another walk to avoid us. She called after him, and said, " Brother, brother, let me speak to you !— One word with you ! " And as we made haste towards him, and came near to him, " I desire," said he, " that you'll not oppress me more with your follies, and your violence. I have borne too much with you; and I will vow, for a twelvemonth from this day——"—" Hush," said she, " don't vow, I beg you; for too well you keep it, I know by experience, if you do. You see," said she, " I stoop to ask Pamela to be my advocate. Sure that will pacify you."

" Indeed," said he, " I desire to see neither of you, on such an occasion : let me be left to myself, for I will not be intruded upon thus ! " and was going away. But she said, " One word first, I desire. If you'll forgive *me*, I will forgive *you !* "— " What," said the dear man, haughtily, " will you forgive *me ?* " —" Why," said she, for she saw him too angry to mention his marriage, as a subject that required her pardon. " I will forgive you all your bad usage of me this day."

" I will be serious with you, sister : I wish you most sincerely well; but let us, from this time, study so much one another's quiet, as never to come near one another more."—" Never ! " said she. " And can you desire this, barbarous brother, can you?"—"I do," said he; "and have nothing to do, but to hide from you, not a brother, but a murderer, and a profligate, unworthy of your relation; and let me be consigned to penitence for my past evils; a penitence, however, that shall not be broken in upon by so violent an accuser.

"Pamela," said he, and made me tremble, "how dare you approach me, without leave, when you see me thus disturbed! Never for the future come near me, when I am in these tumults, unless I send for you."

"Dear Sir!" said I.—"Leave me," interrupted he. "I will set out for Bedfordshire this moment."—"What, Sir!" said I, "without me? What have I done?"—"You have too meanly," said he, "for my wife, stooped to this furious sister of mine; and, till I can recollect, I am not pleased with you: but Colbrand shall attend you, with two other servants: and Mrs. Jewkes shall wait upon you part of the way: and I hope you'll find me in a better disposition to receive you there, than I am at parting with you here."

Had I not hoped, that this was partly put on to intimidate my lady, I believe I could not have borne it: but it was grievous to me; for I saw he was most sincerely in a passion.

"I was afraid," said she, "he would be angry at you, as well as me; for well do I know his unreasonable violence, when he is moved. But one word, Sir," said she: "pardon Pamela, if you won't me; for she has committed no offence but that of good-nature, at my request. I will go directly, as I was about to do, had you not prevented me."

"I prevented you," said he, "through love; but you have stung me for it through hatred. As for my Pamela, I know, besides the present moment, I cannot be angry with her; and therefore I desire her never to see me, on such occasions, till in the temper I ought to be in, when so much sweetness approaches me. 'Tis therefore, I say, my dearest, leave me now."

"But, Sir," said I, "must I leave you, and let you go to Bedford without me? O dear Sir, how can I?" Said my lady, "You may go to-morrow, both of you, as you had designed; and I will go away this afternoon: and, since I cannot be forgiven, will try to forget I have a brother."

"May I, Sir," said I, "beg all your anger on myself, and to be reconciled to your good sister?"—"Presuming Pamela," replied he, and made me start, "art thou then so hardy, so well able to sustain my displeasure, which of all things, I expected from thy affection, and thy tenderness, thou wouldst have wished to avoid? Now," said he, taking my hand, and, as it were, tossing it from him, " begone from me, and reflect upon what you have said ! "

I was so frighted (for then I saw he took amiss what I said, that I took hold of his knee, as he was turning from me ; and I said, " Forgive me, good Sir ; you see I am *not* so hardy ! I cannot bear your displeasure ! " and was ready to sink.

His sister said, " Only forgive Pamela, 'tis all I ask. You'll break *her* spirit quite !—You'll carry your passion as much too far as I have done ! "—" I need not say," said he, " how well I love her ; but she must not intrude upon me at such times as these. I intended, as soon as I had quelled, by my reason, the tumults you had caused by your violence, to have taken such a leave of you both, as might become a husband and a brother ; but she has, unbidden, broken in upon me, and must take the consequence of a passion which, when raised, is as uncontrollable as your own."

Said she, " Did I not love you so well, as sister never loved a brother, I should not have given you all this trouble."—" And did I not," said he, " love you better than you are resolved to deserve, I should be indifferent to all you say. But this last instance, after the duelling story (which you would not have mentioned had you not known it is always a matter of concern for me to think upon), of poor Sally Godfrey, is a piece of spite and meanness, that I can renounce you my blood for."

" Well," said she, " I am convinced it was wrong. I am ashamed of it myself. 'Twas poor, 'twas mean, 'twas unworthy of your sister : and 'tis for this reason I stoop to follow you, to beg your pardon, and even to procure one for my advocate, who I thought had some interest in you, if I might have believed your own profession to her ; which now I shall begin to think made purposely to insult me."

" I care not what you think !—After the meanness you have been guilty of, I can only look upon you with pity ; for, indeed, you have fallen very low with me."

" 'Tis plain I have," said she. " But I'll begone. And so, brother, let me call you for this *once !* God bless you !—And Pamela," said her ladyship, " God bless you ! " and kissed me and wept.

I durst say no more ; and my lady turning from him, he said, " Your sex is the d—l ; how strangely can you discompose, calm, and turn, as you please, us poor weathercocks of men ! Your last kind blessing to my Pamela, I cannot stand. Kiss but each other again." And he then took both our hands, and joined them ; and my lady saluting me again, with tears on both

394

sides, he put his kind arms about each of our waists, and saluted us with great affection, saying, " Now, God bless you both, the two dearest creatures I have in the world."

" Well," said she, " you will quite forget my fault about Miss——" He stopt her before she could speak the name, and said, " For ever forget it !—And, Pamela, I'll forgive you too, if you don't again make my displeasure so light a thing to you, as you did just now."

Said my lady, " She did not make your displeasure a light thing to her; but the heavier it was, the higher compliment she made me, that she would bear it all, rather than not see you and me reconciled."—" No matter for that," said he : " it was either an absence of thought, or a slight by implication at least, that my niceness could not bear from her tenderness : for looked it not presuming that she could stand my displeasure, or was sure of making her terms when she pleased ? which, fond as I am of her, will not always, in wilful faults, be in her power."

" Nay," said my lady, " I can tell you, Pamela, you have a gentleman here in my brother; and you may expect such treatment from him, as that character, and his known good sense, and breeding, will always oblige him to show : but if you offend, the Lord have mercy upon you !—You see how it is by poor me !—And yet I never knew him forgive so soon."

" I am sure," said I, " I will take care, as much as I can; for I have been frightened out of my wits, and had offended before I knew where I was."

So happily did this storm blow over; and my lady was quite subdued and pacified.

When we came out of the garden, his chariot was ready; and he said, " Well, sister, I had most assuredly set off to my other house, had not things taken this happy turn; and, if you please, instead of it, you and I will take an airing :—and pray, my dear," said he to me, " bid Mrs. Jewkes order supper by eight o'clock, and we shall then join you."

" Sir," added he, to her nephew, " will you take your horse, and escort us? "—" I will," said he; " and am glad at my soul to see you all so good friends."

So my dear lord and master handed my lady into his chariot : her kinsman and his servants rode after them; and I went up to my closet to ruminate on these things. Foolish thing that I am, this poor Miss Sally Godfrey runs in my head !—How soon the name and quality of a wife give one privileges, in one's own account !—Yet, methinks I want to know more about her; for, is it not strange, that I, who lived years in the family, should hear nothing of this? But I was so constantly with my lady, that I might the less hear of it; for she, I dare say, never knew it, or she would have told me."

But I dare not ask him about the poor lady. Yet I wonder what became of her! Whether she be living? and whether any thing came of it?—May-be I shall hear full soon enough :— but I hope not to any bad purpose.

As to the other unhappy case, I know it was talked of, that in his travels, before I was taken into the family, he had one or two broils; and, from a youth, was always remarkable for courage, and is reckoned a great master of his sword. God grant he may never be put to use it, and that he may be always preserved in honour and safety !

About seven o'clock my master sent word, that he would have me not expect him to supper; for that he, and my lady his sister, and nephew, were prevailed upon to stay with Lady Jones; and that Lady Darnford, and Mr. Peter's family, had promised to meet them there. I was glad they did not send for me; and the rather, as I hoped these good families being my friends, would confirm my lady a little in my favour; and so I followed my writing closely.

About eleven o'clock they returned. I had but just come down, having tired myself with my pen, and was talking with Mrs. Jewkes and Mrs. Worden, whom I would, though unwillingly on their sides, make sit down, which they did over against me. Mrs. Worden asked me pardon, in a good deal of confusion, for the part she had acted against me, saying, that things had been very differently represented to her; and that she little thought I was married, and that she was behaving so rudely to the lady of the house.

I said, I took nothing amiss; and very freely forgave her; and hoped my new condition would not make me forget how to behave properly to every one; but that I must endeavour to act not unworthy of it, for the honour of the gentleman who had so generously raised me to it.

Mrs. Jewkes said, that my situation gave me great opportunities of shewing the excellency of my nature, that I could forgive offences against me so readily, as she, for her own part, must always acknowledge, with confusion of face.

" People," said I, " Mrs. Jewkes, don't know how they shall act, when their wills are in the power of their superiors; and I always thought one should distinguish between acts of malice, and of implicit obedience; though, at the same time, a person

396

should know how to judge between lawful and unlawful. And even the great, if at present angry they are not obeyed, will afterwards have no ill opinion of a person for withstanding them in their unlawful command."

Mrs. Jewkes seemed a little concerned at this; and I said I spoke chiefly from my own experience. For I could say, as they both knew my story, that I had not wanted for menaces and temptations; and had I complied with the one, or been intimidated by the other, I should not have been what I was.

"Ah! Madam," replied Mrs. Jewkes, "I never knew any body like you: and I think your temper sweeter, since the happy day, than before; and that, if possible, you take less upon you."

"Why, a good reason," said I, "may be assigned for that: I thought myself in danger: I looked upon every one as my enemy; and I could not but be fretful, uneasy, jealous. Yet when my dearest friend had taken from me the ground of my uneasiness, and made me quite happy, I should have been very blameable, if I had not shewn a satisfied and easy mind, and a temper that should engage every one's respect and love at the same time, if possible: and the more so, as it was but justifying, in some sort, the honour I had received: for the fewer enemies I made myself, the more I engaged every one to think, that my good benefactor had been less to blame in descending as he has done."

This way of talking pleased them both very much; and they made me many compliments upon it, and wished me to be always happy, as they said I so well deserved.

We were thus engaged, when my master, his sister, and her nephew came in: they made me quite alive; in the happy humour in which they all returned. The two women would have withdrawn; but my master said, "Don't go, Mrs. Worden: —Mrs. Jewkes, pray stay; I shall speak to you presently." And then saluting me, said, "Well, my dear love, I hope I have not trespassed upon your patience, by an absence longer than we designed. But it has not been to your disadvantage: for though we had not your company, we have talked of nobody else but you."

My lady came up to me, and said, "Ay, child, you have been all our subject. I don't know how it is, but you have made two or three good families, in this neighbourhood, as much your admirers, as your friend here."

"My sister," said he, "has been hearing your praises, Pamela, from half a score of mouths, with more pleasure than her heart will easily let her express."

"My good Lady Davers's favour," said I, "and the continuance of yours, Sir, would give me more pride than that of all the rest of the world put together."

"Well, child," said she, "proud hearts don't come down all at once; though my brother, here, has this day set mine a good many pegs lower than I ever knew it : but I will say, I wish you joy with my brother; " and so kissed me.

"My dear lady," said I, "you for ever oblige me !—I shall now believe myself quite happy. This was all I wanted to make me so. And I hope, I shall always, through my life, shew your ladyship, that I have the most grateful and respectful sense of your goodness."

"But, child," said she, "I shall not give you my company, when you make your appearance. Let your own merit make all your Bedfordshire neighbours your friends, as it has done here, by your Lincolnshire ones; and you'll have no need of my countenance, nor any body's else."

"Now," said her nephew, "'tis my turn. I wish you joy, with all my soul, Madam; and, by what I have seen, and by what I have heard, 'fore Gad, I think you have met with no more than you deserve; and so all the company says, where we have been : and pray forgive all my nonsense to you."

"Sir," said I, "I shall always, I hope, respect as I ought, so near a relation of my good Lord and Lady Davers; and I thank you for your kind compliments."—"Gad, Beck," said he, "I believe you've some forgiveness too to ask; for we were all to blame, to make Madam, here, fly the pit as she did : little did we think we made her quit her own house."

"Thou always," said my lady, "sayest too much, or too little."

Mrs. Worden said, "I have been treated with so much goodness and condescension, since you went, that I have been before-hand, Sir, in asking pardon for myself."

So my lady set down with me half an hour, and told me that her brother had carried her a fine airing, and had quite charmed her with his kind treatment of her; and had much confirmed her in the good opinion she had begun to entertain of my discreet and obliging behaviour :—"But," continued she, "when he would make me visit, without intending to stay, my old neighbours, (for," said she, "Lady Jones being nearest, we visited her first; and she scraped all the rest of the company together) they were all so full of your praises, that I was quite borne down; and, truly, it was Saul among the prophets!"

You may believe how much I was delighted with this: and I spared not my due acknowledgments.

When her ladyship took leave, to go to bed, she said, "Good night to you heartily, and to your good man. I kissed you when I came in, out of form, but I now kiss you out of *more* than form, I'll assure you."

Join with me, my dear parents, in my joy, for this happy turn: the contrary of which I so much dreaded, and was the only difficulty I had to labour with!—This poor Miss Sally Godfrey, I wonder what's become of her, poor soul; I wish he would, of his own head, mention her again.—Not that I am *very* uneasy, neither. You'll say, I must be a little saucy if I was.

My dear master gave me an account, when he went up, of the pains he had taken with his beloved sister, as he himself styled her; and of all the kind things the good families had said in my behalf; and that he observed she was not so much displeased with hearing them, as she was at first: when she would not permit any body to speak of me as his wife; and that my health, as his spouse, being put, when it came to her, she drank it; but said, "Come, brother, here's your Pamela to you:— but I shall not know how to stand this affair, when the Countess —— and the young ladies come to visit me." One of those young ladies was the person she was so fond of promoting a match for, with her brother. "Lady Betty, I know," said she, "will rally me smartly upon it; and you know, brother, she wants neither wit nor satire." He said, "I hope Lady Betty, whenever she marries, will meet with a better husband than I should have made her; for, in my conscience, I think I should have hardly made a tolerable one to any but Pamela."

He told me that they rallied him on the stateliness of his temper; and said they saw he would make an exceeding good husband where he was; but it must be owing to my meekness, more than his complaisance—"For," said Miss Darnford, "I could see well enough, when your ladyship detained her, though he had but hinted his desire of finding her at our house, he was so out of humour at her supposed non-compliance, that mine and my sister's pity for her was much more engaged, than our envy."

"Ay," said my lady, "he is too lordly a creature by much; and can't bear disappointment, nor ever could."

Said he, "Well, Lady Davers, you should not, of all persons,

399

find fault with me; for I bore a great deal from you, before I was at all angry."

"Yes," replied she; "but when I had gone a little too far, as I own I did, you made me pay for it severely enough! You know you did, sauce-box. And the poor thing too," added she, "that I took with me for my advocate, so low had he brought me! he treated her in such a manner as made my heart ache for her; but part was *art*, I know, to make me think the better of her."

"Indeed, sister," said he, "there was very little of that: for, at that time, I cared not what you thought, nor had complaisance enough to have given a shilling for your good or bad opinion of her or me. And, I own, I was displeased to be broken in upon, after your provocations, by either of you; and she must learn that lesson, never to come near me, when I am in those humours; which shall be as little as possible; for, after awhile, if let alone, I always come to myself, and am sorry for the violence of a temper, so like my dear sister's here; and, for this reason, think it is no matter how few witnesses I have of its intemperance, while it lasts; especially since every witness, whether they merit it or not, as you see in my Pamela's case, must be a sufferer by it, if unsent for they come in my way."

He repeated the same lesson to me again, and enforced it; and owned, that he was angry with me in earnest, just then; though more with himself afterwards, for being so: "But when, Pamela," said he, "you wanted to transfer all my displeasure upon yourself, it was so much *braving* me with your *merit*, as if I must *soon* end my anger, if placed *there*, or it was making it so *light* to you, that I was truly displeased: for," continued he, "I cannot bear that you should wish, on any occasion whatever, to have me angry with you, or not to value my displeasure as the heaviest misfortune that could befal you."

"But, Sir," said I, "you know that what I did was to try to reconcile my lady; and, as she herself observed, it was paying her a high regard."—"It was so," replied he; "but never think of making a compliment to *her* or *any* body living, at *my* expense. She had behaved herself so intolerably, that I began to think you had stooped much more than I ought to permit my wife to do: and acts of meanness are what I can't endure in any body, but especially where I love: and as she had been guilty of a very signal one, I had then much rather have renounced her, than have been reconciled to her."

"Sir," said I, "I hope I shall always comport myself so, as

400

not wilfully to disoblige you for the future; and the rather, as I am sure I shall want only to *know* your pleasure to *obey* it. But this instance shews me, that I may *much* offend, without designing it in the *least*."

"Now, Pamela," replied he, "don't be too serious: I hope I shan't be a very tyrannical husband: yet do I not pretend to be perfect or always governed by reason in my first transports; and I expect, from your affection, that you will bear with me, when you find me so. I have no ungrateful spirit, and can, when cool, enter as impartially into myself, as most men; and then I am always kind and acknowledging, in proportion as I have been wrong.

"But to convince you, my dear, of your fault (I mean, with regard to the impetuosity of my temper; for there was no fault in your intention, *that* I acknowledge), I'll observe only, that you met, when you came to me, while I was so out of humour, a reception you did not expect, and a harsh word or two that you did not deserve. Now, had you not broken in upon me while my anger lasted, but stayed till I had desired your company, you'd have seen none of this; but that affectionate behaviour, which, I doubt not, you'll always merit; and I shall always take pleasure in expressing; and in *this temper* shall you always find a proper influence over me: but you must not suppose, whenever I am out of humour, that, in opposing yourself to my passion, you oppose a proper butt to it; but when you are so good, like the slender reed, to *bend* to the hurricane, rather than, like the sturdy oak, to *resist* it, you will always stand firm in my kind opinion, while a contrary conduct would uproot you, with all your excellence, from my soul."

"Sir," said I, "I will endeavour to conform myself, in all things, to your will."—"I have no doubt of it; and I'll endeavour to make my will as conformable to reason as I can. And let me say, that this belief of you is one of the inducements I have had to marry at all: for nobody was more averse to this state than myself: and now we are upon this subject, I'll tell you why I was so averse.

"We people of fortune, or such as are born to large expectations, of both sexes, are generally educated wrong. You have occasionally touched upon this, Pamela, several times in your journal, so justly, that I need say the less to you. We are usually so headstrong, so violent in our wills, that we very little bear control.

"Humoured by our nurses, through the faults of our parents,

we practise first upon them; and shew the *gratitude* of our disposition, in an insolence that ought rather to be checked and restrained, than encouraged.

"Next, we are to be indulged in every thing at school; and our *masters* and *mistresses* are rewarded with further grateful instances of our boisterous behaviour.

"But in our *wise* parents' eyes, all looks well; all is forgiven and excused: and for no other reason, but because we are *theirs*.

"Our next progression is, we exercise our spirits, when brought home, to the torment and regret of our *parents themselves*, and torture their hearts by our undutiful and perverse behaviour, which, however ungrateful in us, is but the natural consequence of their culpable indulgence from our infancy upwards.

"Then, after we have, perhaps, half broken their hearts, a *wife* is looked out for: convenience, or birth, or fortune, are the first motives; affection the last (if it is at all consulted): and two people thus educated, trained up in a course of unnatural ingratitude, and who have been headstrong torments to all who had a share in their education, as well as those to whom they owe their being, are brought together; what can be expected, but that they should pursue, and carry on, the same comfortable conduct in matrimony, and join most heartily to plague one another? In some measure, this is right; because hereby they revenge the cause of all those whom they have aggrieved and insulted, upon one another.

"The gentleman has never been controlled: the lady has never been contradicted.

"*He* cannot bear it from one whose new relation, he thinks, should oblige her to shew a quite contrary conduct.

"*She* thinks it very barbarous, now, for the *first* time, to be opposed in her will, and that by a man from whom she expected nothing but tenderness.

"So great is the difference between what they both expected *from*, and what they find *in* each other, that no wonder misunderstandings happen, and ripen to quarrels; that acts of unkindness pass, which, even had the first motive to their union been *affection*, as usually it is not, would have effaced every tender impression on both sides.

"Appeals to parents and guardians often ensue! if, through friends, a reconciliation takes place, it hardly ever holds: for why? The fault is in the minds of *both*, and *neither* of them will think so: so that the wound (not permitted to be probed) is but skinned over; rankles still at the bottom, and at last breaks out with more pain and anguish than before. Separate beds are often the consequence; perhaps elopements; if not, an unconquerable indifference; possibly aversion. And whenever, for appearance sake, they are obliged to be together, every one sees, that the yawning husband, and the vapourish wife, are truly insupportable to each other; but separate, have freer spirits, and can be tolerable company.

" Now, my dear, I would have you think, and I hope you will have no other reason, that had I married the first lady in the land, I would not have treated her better than I will my Pamela : for my wife *is* my wife; and I was the longer in resolving on the state, because I knew its requisites, and doubted my conduct in it.

" I believe I am more nice than many gentlemen; having been a close observer of the behaviour of wedded folks, and hardly ever having seen it such as I could like in my own case. I may give you instances of a more particular nature of this, as we are *longer*, and, perhaps, I might say, *better* acquainted.

" Had I married with the views of most gentlemen, and with such as my good sister (supplying the place of my parents) would have recommended, I had wedded a fine lady, brought up in my own manner, and used to have her will in every thing.

" Some gentlemen can come into a compromise; and, after a few struggles, are tolerably contented. But, had I married a princess, I could not have done so. I must have loved her exceedingly well, before I had consented to knit the knot, and preferred her to all her sex : for without this, Pamela, indifferences, if not disgusts, will arise in every wedded life, that could not have made me happy at home; and there are fewer instances, I believe, of men loving better after matrimony than of women; the reasons of which 'tis not my present purpose to account for.

" Then I must have been morally sure that she preferred me to all men; and, to convince me of this, she must have lessened, not aggravated, my failings; she must have borne with my imperfections; she must have watched and studied my temper; and if ever she had any points to carry, any desire of overcoming, it must have been by sweetness and complaisance; and yet not such a slavish one, as should make her condescension seem to be rather the effect of her insensibility, than judgment or affection.

" She should not have caused any part of my conduct to wear the least aspect of compulsion or force. The word *command* on my side, or *obedience* on her's, I would have blotted from my vocabulary. For this reason I should have thought it my duty to have desired nothing of her, which was not significant, reasonable, or just; and then she should have shewn no reluctance, uneasiness, or doubt, to oblige me, even at half a word.

"I would not have excused her to let me twice enjoin the same thing, while I took so much care to make her compliance with me reasonable, and such as should not destroy her own free agency, in points that ought to be allowed her; and though I was not always right, yet she would bear with me, if she saw me set upon it; and expostulate with me on the right side of compliance : for it would shew (supposing *small points* in dispute, from which the greatest quarrels, among *friends*, generally arise), that she differed from me, not for *contradiction sake*, but desired to convince me for *my own ;* and that I should another time take better resolutions.

"This would be so obliging a conduct, that I should, in justice, double my esteem for one who, to humour me, gave up her own judgment; and I should see she had no other view in her expostulations, after her compliance, than to rectify my notions for the future; and then I could not but have paid the greater deference to her opinion and advice in more momentous matters.

"In all companies she must have shewn that she had, whether I deserved it altogether or not, a high regard and opinion of me; and this the rather, as such a conduct in her would be a reputation and security to herself : for if we rakes attempt a married lady, our first encouragement, exclusive of our own vanity, arises from the indifferent opinion, slight, or contempt, she expresses of her husband. I should expect her therefore, to draw a kind veil over my faults; such as she could not hide, to extenuate; to place my better actions in an advantageous light, and shew that I had *her* good opinion at least, whatever liberties the *world* took with my character.

"She must have valued my friends for *my* sake; been cheerful and easy, whomsoever I brought home; and, whatever faults she observed in me, have never blamed me before company, at least with such an air of superiority as to have shewn she had a better opinion of her own judgment than mine.

"Now, my Pamela, this is but a faint sketch of the conduct I must have expected from my wife, let her quality have been what it would : or, have lived with her on bad terms. Judge, then, if to me a lady of the modish taste could have been tolerable.

"The perverseness and contradiction I have too often seen,

in my visits, among people of sense, as well as condition, had prejudiced me to the married state; and, knowing I could not bear it, surely I was in the right to decline it: and you see, my dear, that I have not gone among this class of people for a wife; nor do I know where I could have found one suitable to my mind, if not you; for here is my misfortune: I could not have been contented to have been but *moderately happy* in a wife.

" Judge, you, from all this, if I could very well bear for you to think yourself so secured of my affection, as to take the faults of others upon yourself; and, by a supposed supererogatory merit, think your interposition sufficient to atone for the faults of others.

" Yet I am not perfect myself: no, I am greatly imperfect. But I will not allow, that my imperfections shall excuse those of my wife, or make her think I ought to bear faults in her which she can rectify, because she bears greater from me.

" Upon the whole, I may expect, that you will bear with me, and study my temper, *till*, and only *till*, you see I am capable of returning insult for obligation; and till you think, that I shall be of a gentler deportment, if I am roughly used, than otherwise. I should scorn myself, if there was one privilege of your sex a princess might expect, as my wife, to be indulged in, which I would not allow to my Pamela: for you are the wife of my affections; I never wished for one before you, nor ever do I hope to have another."

" I hope, Sir," said I, " my future conduct—"—" Pardon me," said he, " my dear, for interrupting you; but it is to say that I am so well convinced of your affectionate regard for me, I know I might have spared the greatest part of what I have said: and, indeed, it must be very bad for both of us, if I should have reason to think it *necessary* to say so much. But one thing has brought on another; and I have rather spoken what my niceness has made me *observe* in *other* families, than what I *fear* in *my own*. And, therefore, let me assure you, I am thoroughly satisfied with your conduct hitherto. You shall have no occasion to repent it; but find, though greatly imperfect, and passionate, on particular provocations (which yet I will try to overcome), that you have not a brutal or ungenerous husband, who is capable of offering insult for condescension, or returning evil for good."

I thanked him for these kind rules, and generous assurances; and said, they had made so much impression on my mind, that these, and his most agreeable injunctions before given me, and such as he might hereafter be pleased to give, should be so many rules for my future behaviour.

I am glad of the method I have taken of making a journal of all that passes in these first stages of my happiness, for it will sink the impression still deeper; and I shall turn to them for my better regulation, as often as I mistrust my memory.

Let me see—what are the rules I am to observe from this awful lecture? Why these:

1. That I must not, when he is in great wrath with any body, break in upon him without his leave.—*Well, I'll remember it, I warrant. But yet I think this rule is almost peculiar to himself.*

2. That I must think his displeasure the heaviest thing that can befal me.—*To be sure I shall.*

3. And so that I must not wish to incur it, to save any body else.—*I'll be further if I do.*

4. That I must never make a compliment to any body at his expense.

5. That I must not be guilty of any acts of wilful meanness.—*There is a great deal meant in this; and I'll endeavour to observe it all. To be sure, the occasion on which he mentions this, explains it; that I must say nothing, though in anger, that is spiteful or malicious, disrespectful or undutiful, and such like.*

6. That I must bear with him even when I find him in the wrong.—*This is a little hard, as the case may be.*

I wonder whether poor Miss Sally Godfrey be living or dead!

7. That I must be as flexible as the reed in the fable, lest, by resisting the tempest, like the oak, I be torn up by the roots.—*Well, I'll do the best I can!—There is no great likelihood, I hope, that I should be too perverse; yet, sure, the tempest will not lay me quite level with the ground, neither.*

8. That the education of young people of condition is generally wrong.—*Mem. That if any part of children's education fall to my lot, I never indulge and humour them in things they should be restrained in.*

9. That I accustom them to bear disappointments and control.

10. That I suffer them not to be too much indulged in their infancy.

11. Nor at school.

12. Nor spoil them when they come home.

13. For that children generally extend their perverseness from their nurse to the schoolmaster; from the schoolmaster to the parents.

14. And, in their next step, as a proper punishment for all, make their ownselves unhappy.

15. That undutiful and perverse children make bad husbands and wives; *and, collaterally, bad masters and mistresses.*

16. That, not being subject to be controlled early, they cannot, when married, bear one another.

17. That the fault lying deep, and in the minds of each other, neither will mend it.

18. Whence follow misunderstandings, quarrels, appeals, ineffectual reconciliations, separations, elopements, or, at best, indifference; perhaps, aversion.—*Mem. A good image of unhappy wedlock in the words* YAWNING HUSBAND, *and* VAPOURISH WIFE, *when together; but separate both quite alive.*

19. Few married persons behave as he likes.—*Let me ponder this with awe and improvement.*

20. Some gentlemen can compromise with their wives for quietness sake; but he can't.—*Indeed I believe that's true; I don't desire he should.*

21. That love before marriage is absolutely necessary.

22. That there are fewer instances of men than women loving better after marriage.—*But why so?—I wish he had given his reasons for this! I fancy they are not to the advantage of his own sex.*

23. That a woman give her husband reason to think she prefers him above all men.—*Well, to be sure, that should be so.*

24. That if she would overcome, it must be by sweetness, and complaisance : *that is, by yielding, he means, no doubt.*

25. Yet not such a slavish one, neither, as should rather seem the effect of her insensibility, than judgment or affection.

26. That the words COMMAND and OBEY shall be blotted out of his vocabulary.—*Very good!*

27. That a man should desire nothing of his wife, but what is significant, reasonable, just.—*To be sure that is right.*

28. But then, that she must not shew reluctance, uneasiness, or doubt, to oblige him; and that too at half a word; and must not be bid twice to do one thing.—*But may not this on some occasions be a little dispensed with? But he says afterwards, indeed,*

29. That this must not be only while he took care to make her compliance reasonable and consistent with her free agency, in points that ought to be allowed her.—*Come, this is pretty well, considering.*

30. That if the husband be set upon a wrong thing, she must not dispute with him, but do it, and expostulate afterwards.—

Good Sirs, I don't know what to say to this! It looks a little hard, methinks! This would bear a small debate, I fancy, in a parliament of women. But then he says,

31. Supposing they are only small points that are in dispute.—*Well, this mends a little. For small points, I think, should not be stood upon.*

32. That the greatest quarrels among friends (*and wives and husbands are, or should be, friends*) arise from small matters.—*This I believe; for I had like to have had anger here, when I intended very well.*

33. That a wife should not desire to convince her husband for CONTRADICTION sake, but for HIS OWN.—*As both will find their account in this, if one does, I believe 'tis very just.*

34. That in all companies a wife must shew respect and love to her husband.

35. And this for the sake of her own reputation and security; for,

36. That rakes cannot have a greater encouragement to attempt a married lady's virtue, than her slight opinion of her husband.—*To be sure, this stands to reason, and is a fine lesson.*

37. That a wife should therefore draw a kind veil over her husband's faults.

38. That such as she could not conceal, she should extenuate.

39. That his virtues she should place in an advantageous light:

40. And shew the world, that he had HER good opinion at least.

41. That she must value his friends for *his* sake.

42. That she must be cheerful and easy in her behaviour to whomsoever he brings home with him.

43. That whatever faults she sees in him, she never blame him before company.

44. At least, with such an air of superiority, as if she had a less opinion of his judgment, than her own.

45. That a man of nice observation cannot be contented to be only *moderately* happy in a wife.

46. That a wife take care how she ascribe supererogatory merit to herself; so as to take the faults of others upon her.—*Indeed, I think it is well if we can bear our own! This is of the same nature with the third: and touches upon me, on the present occasion for this wholesome lecture.*

47. That his imperfections must not be a plea for *hers*.—*To be sure, 'tis no matter how good the women are! but 'tis to be hoped men will allow a little. But indeed he says,*

48. That a husband who expects all this, is to be incapable of returning insult for obligation, or evil for good; and ought not to abridge her of any privilege of her sex.

Well, my dear parents, I think this last rule crowns the rest, and makes them all very tolerable; and a generous man, and a man of sense, cannot be too much obliged. And, as I have this happiness, I shall be very unworthy if I do not always so *think*, and so *act*.

Yet, after all, you see I have not the easiest task in the world. But I know my own intentions, that I shall not wilfully err; and so fear the less.

Not one hint did he give, that I durst lay hold of, about poor Miss Godfrey. I wish my lady had not spoken of it; for it has given me a curiosity that is not quite so pretty in me, especially so early in my nuptials, and in a case so long ago past. Yet he intimated too, to his sister, that he had other faults (of this sort, I suppose) that had not come to her knowledge !—But, I doubt not, he has seen his error, and will be very good for the future. I wish it, and pray it may be so, for his own dear sake !

WEDNESDAY, THE SEVENTH.

When I rose in the morning, I waited on Lady Davers, seeing her door open : she was in bed, but awake, and talking to her woman. I said, " I hope I don't disturb your ladyship."— " No, not at all," said she; " I am glad to see you. How do you do ?—Well," added she, " when do you set out for Bedfordshire ? " I said, " I can't tell, Madam; it was designed as to-day, but I have heard no more of it."

" Sit down," said she, " on the bedside. I find by the talk we had yesterday and last night, you have had but a poor time of it, Pamela (I must call you so yet," said she), " since you were brought to this house, till within these few days. And Mrs. Jewkes too has given Beck such an account as makes me pity you."

" Indeed, Madam," said I, " if your ladyship knew all, you *would* pity me; for never poor creature was so hard put to it. But I ought to forget it all now, and be thankful."

" Why," said she, " as far as I can find, 'tis a mercy you are here now. I am sadly moved with some part of your story; and you have really made a noble defence, and deserve the praises of all our sex."

" It was God enabled me, Madam," replied I. " Why," said she, " 'tis the more extraordinary, because I believe, if

409

the truth was known, you loved the wretch not a little."—
" While my trials lasted, Madam," said I, " I had not a *thought*
of *any thing*, but to preserve my innocence, much less of love."

" But tell me truly," said she, " did you not love him all the
time? "—" I had always, Madam," answered I, " a great reverence for my master, and thought all his good actions doubly
good; and for his naughty ones, though I abhorred his attempts
upon me, yet I could not hate him; and always wish'd him
well; but I did not know that it was love. Indeed I had not
the presumption."

" Sweet girl ! " said she, " that's prettily said; but when he
found he could not gain his ends, and began to be sorry for
your sufferings, and to admire your virtue, and to profess
honourable love to you, what did you think? "

" Think ! indeed, Madam, I did not know what to think;
I could neither hope nor believe so great an honour would fall
to my lot; and I fear'd more from his kindness, for some time,
than I had done from his unkindness; and, having had a
private intimation, from a kind friend, of a sham-marriage
intended, by means of a man who was to personate a minister,
it kept my mind in too much suspense, to be greatly overjoyed
by this kind declaration."

Said she, " I think he did make two or three attempts upon
you in Bedfordshire ! "—" Yes, Madam," said I, " he was very
naughty, to be sure."

" And *here*, he proposed articles to you, I understand? "—
" Yes, Madam," replied I; " but I abhorred so much the
thoughts of being a kept creature, that I rejected them with
great boldness; and was resolved to die before I would consent
to them."

" He afterwards attempted you, I think : did he not? "—
" O yes, Madam," said I, " a most sad attempt he made ! and
I had like to have been lost; for Mrs. Jewkes was not so good
as she should have been." So I told her ladyship that sad offer,
and how I fell into fits; and that they, believing me dying,
forbore.

" Any attempts after this base one ? " said she.

" He was not so good as he should have been," returned I,
" once in the garden, afterwards; but I was *so* watchful, and
so ready to take the alarm ! "

" But," said she, " did he not threaten you, at times, and put
on his stern airs, every now and then? "—" Threaten, Madam,"
replied I; " yes, I had enough of that !—I thought I should
have died for fear, several times."—" How could you bear

that ? " said she; " for he is a most daring and majestic mortal; he has none of your puny hearts; but as courageous as a lion : and, boy and man, never feared any thing. I myself," said she, " have a pretty good spirit; but, when I have made him truly angry, I have always been forced to make it up with him as well as I could; for, child, he is not one that is easily reconciled, I assure you.

" But after he had professed honourable love to you, did he never attempt you again ? "—" No, indeed, Madam, he did not. But he was a good while struggling with himself, and with his pride, as he was pleased to call it, before he could stoop so low; and considered again and again : and once, upon my saying but two or three words, to displease him, when very kind to me, he turned me out of doors, in a manner, at an hour's warning; for he sent me above a day's journey, towards my father's; and then sent a man and horse, post-haste, to fetch me back again; and has been exceedingly kind and gracious to me ever since, and made me happy."

" That sending you away," said she, " one hour, and sending after you the next, is exactly like my brother; and 'tis well if he don't turn you off twice or thrice before a year comes about, if you vex him : he would have done the same by the first lady in the land, if married to her. Yet he has his virtues, as well as his faults; for he is generous, nay, he is noble in his spirit; delights in doing good : but does not pass over a wilful fault easily. He is wise, prudent, and magnanimous; and will not tell a lie, nor disguise his faults; but you must not expect to have him all to yourself, I doubt.

" But I'll no more harp upon this string : you see how he was exasperated at me : and he seemed to be angry at you too : though something of it was art, I believe."

" Indeed, Madam," said I, " he has been pleased to give me a most noble lecture; and I find he was angry with me in earnest, and it will not be an easy task to behave unexceptionably to him; for he is very nice and delicate in his notions, I perceive; but yet, as your ladyship says, exceeding generous."

" Well," says she, " I am glad thou hadst a little of his anger; else I should have thought it art : and I don't love to be treated with low art, any more than he, and I should have been vexed if he had done it by me.

" But, I understand, child," says she, " that you keep a journal of all matters that pass, and he has several times found means to get at it : should you care I should see it ? It could not be to your disadvantage; for I find it had no small weight

411

with *him* in your favour; and I should delight to read all his stratagems, attempts, contrivances, menaces, and offers to you on one hand; and all your pretty counter-plottings, which he much praises, your resolute resistance, and the noble stand you have made to preserve your virtue, and the steps by which his pride was subdued, and his mind reduced to honourable love, till you were made what you now are: for it must be an uncommon story; and will not only give me great pleasure in reading, but will entirely reconcile me to the step he has taken: and that, let me tell you, is what I never thought to be; for I had gone far in bringing about a match with him and Lady Betty ——; and had said so much of it, that the earl, her father, approved of it; and so did the duke of ——, her uncle; and Lady Betty herself was not averse: and now I shall be hunted to death about it; and this has made me so outrageous upon the matter. But when I can find, by your writings, that your virtue is but suitably rewarded, it will be not only a good excuse for me, but for him, and make me love you."

"There is nothing I would not do," said I, "to oblige your ladyship; but my poor parents (who had rather have seen me buried quick in the earth, than to be seduced by the greatest of princes) have them in their hands at present: and your dear brother has bespoke them, when they have read them; but if he gives me leave, I will shew them to your ladyship, with all my heart: not doubting your generous allowances, as I have had his; though I have treated him very freely, while he had naughty views; and that your ladyship would consider them as the naked sentiments of my heart, from time to time, delivered to those, whose indulgence I was sure of and for whose sight only they were written."

"Give me a kiss now," said her ladyship, "for your cheerful compliance; for I doubt not my brother will consent I shall see them, because they must needs make for *your* honour; and I see he loves you better than any one in the world.

"I have heard," continued she, "a mighty good character of your parents, as industrious, honest, sensible, good folks, who know the world: and as *I* doubt not my brother's generosity, I am glad they will make no ill figure in the world's eye."

"Madam," said I, "they are the most honest, loving, and conscientious couple breathing. They once lived creditably, and brought up a great family, of which I am the youngest; but had misfortunes, by doing beyond their power for two unhappy brothers, who are both dead, and whose debts they stood bound for; and so became reduced, and, by harsh creditors (where most of the debts were not of their own contracting), turned out of all; in the midst of their poverty and disappointments, all their fear was, that I should be wicked, and yield to temptation, for the sake of worldly riches: and to God's grace, and their good lessons, and those I inbibed from my dear good lady, your ladyship's mother, it is that I owe the preservation of my innocence, and the happy station I am exalted to."

She was pleased to kiss me again, and said, "There is such a noble simplicity in thy story, such an honest artlessness in thy mind, and such a sweet humility in thy deportment, notwithstanding thy present station, that I believe I shall be forced to love thee, whether I will or not: and the sight of your papers, I dare say, will crown the work; will disarm my pride, banish my resentment on Lady Betty's account, and justify my brother's conduct; and redound to your own everlasting honour, so I make no doubt but my brother will let me see them.

"Worden," said my lady, "I can say any thing before you: and you will take no notice of our conversation: but I see you are much touched with it: did you ever hear any thing prettier, more unaffected, sincere, free, and easy?"—"Never, Madam," answered she, "in my life: and it is a great pleasure to see so happy a reconciliation, where there is so much merit."

I said, "I have discovered so much prudence in Mrs. Worden, that with the confidence your ladyship places in her, I have made no scruple of speaking my mind freely before her; and of blaming my dear master while blameworthy, as well as acknowledging his transcendent goodness to me since; which, I am sure, exceeds all I can ever deserve."—"May-be not," said my lady; "I hope you'll be very happy in each other; and I'll now rise and tell him my thoughts, and ask leave to read your papers: for I promise myself much pleasure in them; and shall not grudge a journey and a visit to you at the other house to fetch them."—"Your ladyship's favour," said I, "was all I had to wish for; and if I have that, and the continuance of your dear brother's goodness to me, I shall be easy under whatever else may happen."

So I took my leave, and withdrew; and she let me hear her say to Mrs. Worden, "'Tis a charming creature, Worden!— I know not which excels, her person or her mind!—Well may my brother love her."

I am afraid, my dear father and mother, I shall now be too proud indeed.

I had once a good mind to ask her ladyship about Miss Sally Godfrey; but I thought it was better let alone, since she did not mention it herself.

We breakfasted together with great good temper: my lady was very kind, and, asking my good master, he gave leave very readily, she should see all my papers, when you returned them to me; and he said, he was sure, on reading them, she would say, that I well deserved the fortune I had met with; and would be of opinion, that all the kindness of his future life would hardly be a sufficient reward for my virtue, and make me amends for my sufferings.

Her ladyship resolving to set out the next morning to return to her lord, my master ordered every thing to be made ready for his journey to Bedfordshire; and this evening our good neighbours will sup here, to take leave of my lady and us.

Nothing particular having passed at dinner or supper, but the most condescending goodness on my lady's side to me, and the highest civilities from Mr. Peter's family, Lady Jones, Sir Simon's family, &c., and reciprocal good wishes all round, and a promise obtained from my benefactor that he would endeavour to pass a fortnight or three weeks in these parts before the winter sets in; I shall conclude this day with observing, that I disposed of the money my master kindly gave me, in the method he directed; and I gave Mrs. Jewkes hers in such a manner as highly pleased her; and she wished me, with tears, all kind of happiness; and prayed me to forgive all her past wickedness to me, as she herself called it. I begged leave to present Mrs. Worden with five guineas for a pair of gloves; which he said was well thought of.

I should have mentioned, that Miss Darnford and I agreed upon a correspondence, which will be no small pleasure to me; for she is an admirable young lady, whom I prefer to every one I have seen; and I shall, I make no doubt, improve by her letters; for she is said to have a happy talent in writing, and is well read for so young a lady.

On Thursday morning my lady set out for her own seat; and my best friend and I, attended by Mr. Colbrand, Abraham, and Thomas, for this dear house. Her ladyship parted with her brother and me with great tenderness, and made me promise to send her my papers; which she intends to entertain Lady Betty with, and another lady or two, her intimates, as also her lord : and hopes to find, as I believe, some excuse in them for her brother's choice.

My dearest master has been all love and tenderness on the road, as he is in every place, and on every occasion. Oh, what a delightful change was this journey, to that which, so contrary to all my wishes, and so much to my apprehensions, carried me hence to the Lincolnshire house ! And how did I bless God at every turn, and at every stage !

We did not arrive here till yesterday noon. Abraham rode before, to let them know we were coming. And I had the satisfaction to find every body there I wished to see.

When the chariot entered the court-yard, I was so strongly impressed with the favours and mercies of God Almighty, on remembering how I was sent away from this house; the leave I took; the dangers I had encountered; a poor cast-off servant girl; and now returning a joyful wife, and the mistress, through his favour, of the noble house I was turned out of; I could hardly support my joy on the occasion. He saw how much I was moved, and tenderly asked me, why I seemed so affected ? Lifting his dear hand to my lips, I said, " O Sir ! God's mercies, and your goodness to me, on entering this dear, dear place, are above my expression; I can hardly bear the thoughts of them ! " He said, " Welcome, thrice welcome, joy of my life ! to your own house; " and kissed my hand in return. All the common servants stood at the windows, as unseen as they could, to observe us. With the most condescending goodness, and with great complaisance, he led me into the parlour, and kissed me with the greatest ardour. " Welcome again, my dearest life," said he, " a thousand times welcome to the possession of a house that is not more mine than yours."

I threw myself at his feet; " Permit me, dear Sir, thus to bless *God*, and thank *you*, for all *His* mercies, and *your* goodness. O may I so behave, as not to be *utterly unworthy ;* and then how happy shall I be ! "—" God give me, my dearest," said he, " life and health to reward all your sweetness ! and no man can then be so blest as I."

" Where," said he to Abraham, who passed by the door, " is Mrs. Jervis ? " She bolted in. " Here, good Sir," said she, " am I waiting impatiently, till called for, to congratulate you both." I ran to her, and clasped my arms about her neck, and kissed her. " O my dear Mrs. Jervis ! " said I, " my other dear mother ! receive your happy, happy Pamela; and join with me to bless God, and bless our master, for all these great things!" I was ready to sink in her arms, through excess of joy, to see the dear good woman, who was so often a mournful witness of my distress, as now of my triumph. "Dearest Madam," said she, "you do me too much honour. Let my whole life shew the joy I take in your deserved good fortune, and in my duty to you, for the early instance I received of your goodness in your kind letter."—"O Mrs. Jervis," replied I, "*there* all thanks are due, both from you and me; for our dear master granted me this blessing, as I may justly call it, the moment I begged it of him."—"Your goodness, Sir," said she, "I will for ever acknowledge; and I beg pardon for the wrong step I made in applying to my Lady Davers." He was so good as to salute her, and said, "All's over now, Mrs. Jervis; and I shall not remember you ever disobliged me. I always respected you, and shall now more and more value you, for the sake of that dear good creature, that, with joy unfeigned, I can call my wife."—"God bless your honour for ever!" said she; "and many, *many* happy years may ye live together, the envy and wonder of all who know you!"

"But where," said my dear master, "is honest Longman? and where is Jonathan?"—"Come, Mrs. Jervis," said I, "you shall shew me them, and all the good folks presently, and let me go up with you to behold the dear apartment which I have seen *before* with such different emotion to what I shall *now* do."

We went up; and in every room—the chamber I took refuge in when my master pursued me, my lady's chamber, her dressing-room, Mrs. Jervis's room, not forgetting her closet, my own little bed-chamber, the green-room, and in each of the other—I blessed God for my past escapes, and present happiness; and the good woman was quite affected with the zeal and pleasure with which I made my thankful acknowledgments to the Divine goodness. "O my excellent lady!" said she, "you are still the same good, pious, humble soul; and your marriage has added to your graces, as I hope it will to your blessings."

"Dear Mrs. Jervis," said I, "you know not what I have gone through! You know not what God has done for me! You know not what a happy creature I am now! I have a thousand things to tell you! and a whole week will be too little, every moment of it spent in relating what has befallen me, to acquaint you with it all. We shall be sweetly happy together, I make no doubt. But I charge you, my dear Mrs. Jervis, whatever you call me before strangers, that, when by ourselves, you call me nothing but *your* Pamela. For what an ungrateful creature

416

should I be, who have received so many mercies, if I attributed them not to the Divine goodness, but assumed to myself insolent airs upon them! No, I hope I shall be more and more thankful, as I am more and more blest; and more humble, as God, the author of all my happiness, shall more distinguish me."

We went down again into the parlour, to my dear master. Said he, "Call Longman in again; he longs to see you, my dear." He came in: "God bless you, my sweet lady!" said he, "as now, Heaven be praised, I may call you. Did I not say, Madam, that Providence would find you out?"—"O Mr. Longman," said I, "God be praised for all his mercies! I am rejoiced to see you;" and I laid my hands on his, and said, "Good Mr. Longman, how do you do?—I must always value you; and you don't know how much of my present happiness I owe to the paper, pens, and ink, you furnished me with. I hope my dear Sir and you are quite reconciled."—"O Madam," said he, "how good you are!—Why, I cannot contain myself for joy!" and then he wiped his eyes, good man!

Said my master, "Yes, I have been telling Longman, that I am obliged to him for his ready return to me; and that I will entirely forget his appeal to Lady Davers; and I hope he will be quite as easy and happy as he wishes. My partner here, Mr. Longman, I dare promise you, will do all *she* can to make you so."—"Heaven bless you both together," said he. "'Tis the pride of my heart to see this!—I returned with double delight, when I heard the blessed news; and I am sure, Sir," said he,—mark old Longman's words—"God will bless you for this every year more and more!—You don't know how many hearts you have made happy by this generous deed!"—"I am glad of it," said my dear master; "I am sure I have made my *own* happy; and, Longman, though I must think you SOMEBODY, yet, as you are not a young man, and so won't make me jealous, I can allow you to wish my dear wife joy in the tenderest manner."—"Adad! Sir," said he, "I am sure you rejoice me with your favour; 'tis what I long for, but durst not presume."—"My dear," said my master, "receive the compliment of one of the honestest hearts in England, that always revered your virtues!" And the good man saluted me with great respect, and said, "God in Heaven bless you both:" and kneeled on one knee, "I must quit your presence! indeed I must!" and away he went.

"Your goodness, Sir," said I, "knows no bounds: O may my gratitude never find any!"—"I saw," said my master, "when the good man approached you, that he did it with so

417

much awe and love mingled together, that I fancied he longed to salute my angel; and I could not but indulge his honest heart."—" How bless'd am I," said I, and kissed his hand. And indeed I make nothing now of kissing his dear hand, as if it was my own.

" When honest old Mr. Jonathan came in to attend at dinner, so clean, so sleek, and so neat, as he always is, with his silver hair, I said, " Well, Mr. Jonathan, how do you do? I am glad to see you. You look as well as ever, thank God ! "—" O dear Madam," said he, " better than ever, to have such a blessed sight ! God bless you, and my good master ! I hope, Sir," said he, " you'll excuse all my past failings."—" Ay, that I will, Jonathan," said he; " because you never had any, but what your regard for my dear wife was the occasion of. And now I can tell you, you can never err, because you cannot respect her too much."—" O, Sir," said he, " your honour is exceeding good. I'm sure I shall always pray for you both."

After dinner, Mr. Longman coming in, to talk of some affairs under his care, he said afterwards, " All your honour's servants are now happy; for Robert, who left you, had a pretty little fortune fallen to him, or he never would have quitted your service. He was here but yesterday, to inquire when you and my lady returned hither; and hoped he might have leave to pay his duty to you both."—" Ay," said my master, " I shall be glad to see honest Robin, for that's another of your favourites, Pamela. It was high time, I think, I should marry you, were it but to engage the respects of all my family to myself."— " There are, Sir," said I, " ten thousand reasons why I should rejoice in your goodness."

" But I was going to say," said Mr. Longman, " that all your honour's old servants are now happy, but one."—" You mean John Arnold," said my master. " I do, indeed," said he, " if you'll excuse me, Sir,"—" O," said I, " I have had my prayer for poor John answered as favourably as I could wish."— " Why," said Mr. Longman, " to be sure poor John has acted no very good part, take it altogether; but he so much honoured you, Sir, and so much respected you, Madam, that he wished to be obedient to both, and so was faithful to neither. But the poor fellow's heart is almost broken, and he won't look out for any other place; and says, he must live in your honour's service, or he must die wretched very shortly." Mrs. Jervis being present, " Indeed," says she, " the poor man has been here every day since he heard the joyful tidings; and he says, he hopes yet to be forgiven."—" Is he in the house now ? " said my master. " He is, Sir; and was here when your honour came in, and played at hide-and-seek to have one look at you both when you alighted; and was ready to go out of his wits for joy, when he saw your honour hand my lady in."—" Pamela," said my dear master, " you're to do with John as you please. You have full power."—" Then pray, Sir," said I, " let poor John come in."

The poor fellow came in, with so much confusion, that I have never seen a countenance that expressed so lively a consciousness of his faults, and mingled joy and shame. " How do you do, John? " said I; " I hope you are very well." The poor fellow could hardly speak, and looked with awe upon my master, and pleasure upon me. Said my master, " Well, John, nothing can be said to a man that has so much concern already : I am told you *will* serve me, whether I will or not; but I leave you altogether to my spouse here : and she is to do by you as she pleases."— " You see, John," said I, " your good master's indulgence. Well may I forgive that have so generous an example. I was always persuaded of your honest intentions, if you had known how to distinguish between your duty to your master, and your good will to me : you will have no more puzzles on that account, from the goodness of your dear master."—" I shall be but too happy ! " said the poor man. " God bless your honour !—God bless you, Madam !—I now have the joy of my soul in serving you both; and I will make the best of servants, to my power."— " Well, then, John," said I, " your wages will go on, as if you had not left your master :—May I not say so, Sir? " said I.— " Yes, surely, my dear; and augment them too, if you find his duty to you deserves it."—" A thousand million of thanks," said the poor man : " I am very well satisfied, and desire no augmentation." So he withdrew overjoyed; and Mrs. Jervis and Mr. Longman were highly pleased; for though incensed against him for his fault to me, when matters looked badly, yet they, and all his fellow-servants always loved John.

When Mr. Longman and Mrs. Jervis had dined, they came in again, to know if he had any commands : and my dear master, filling a glass of wine, said, " Longman, I am going to toast the happiest and honestest couple in England, my dear Pamela's father and mother."—" Thank you, dear Sir," said I.

" I think," continued he, " that little Kentish purchase wants a manager; and as it is a little out of your way, Longman, I have been purposing, if I thought Mr. Andrews would accept of it, that he should enter upon Hodge's farm that was, and so manage for me that whole little affair; and we will stock the farm for him, and make it comfortable; and I think if he will take that trouble upon him, it will be an ease to you, and a favour to me."

"Your honour," said he, "cannot do a better thing; and I have had some inkling given me, that you may, if you please, augment that estate, by a purchase, of equal amount, contiguous to it; and as you have so much money to spare, I can't see your honour can do better."—"Well," said he, "let me have the particulars another time, and we will consider about it. But, my dear," added he, "you'll mention this to your father, if you please.

"I have too much money, Longman, lies useless; though, upon this occasion, I shall not grudge laying out as much in liveries, and other things, as if I had married a lady of fortune equal, if possible, to my Pamela's merit; and I reckon you have a good deal in hand."—"Yes, Sir," said he, "more than I wish I had."

"I took with me, to Lincolnshire," said my master, "upwards of six hundred guineas, and thought to have laid most of them out there: ("Thank God," thought I, "you did not!" for he offered me five hundred of them, you know.)

"You have made some little presents, Pamela, to my servants there, on our nuptials; and these two hundred I have brought up, I will put into your disposal, that with some of them you shall do here as you did there."

"I am ashamed, good Sir," said I, "to be so costly, and so worthless!"—"Pray, my dear," replied he, "say not a word of that."

Said Mr. Longman, "Why, Madam, with money in stocks, and one thing or another, his honour could buy half the gentlemen round him. He wants not money, and lays up every year. And it would have been a pity but his honour should have wedded just as he has."—"Very true, Longman," said my master; and, pulling out his purse, said, "Tell out, my dear, two hundred guineas, and give me the rest."—I did so. "Now," said he, "take them yourself, for the purposes I mentioned. But, Mr. Longman, do you, before sun-set, bring my dear girl fifty pounds which is due to her this day, by my promise; and every three months, from this day, pay her fifty pounds, which will be two hundred pounds *per annum;* for her to lay out at her own discretion, and without account, in such a way as shall derive a blessing upon us all: for she was my mother's almoner, and shall be mine, and her own too."—"I'll go for it this instant," said Mr. Longman.

When he was gone, I looked upon my dear generous master

and on Mrs. Jervis; and he gave me a nod of assent; and I took twenty guineas, and said, "Dear Mrs. Jervis, accept of this, which is no more than my generous master ordered me to present to Mrs. Jewkes, for a pair of gloves, on my happy nuptials; and so you, who are much better entitled, by the love I bear you, must not refuse them."

Said she, "Mrs. Jewkes was on the spot, Madam, at the happy time."—"Yes," said my master, "but Pamela would have rejoiced to have had you there instead of her."—"That I should, Sir," replied I, "or instead of any body except my own mother." She gratefully accepted them, and thanked us both: but I don't know what she should thank *me* for; for I was not worth a fourth of them myself.

"I'd have you, my dear," said he, "in some handsome manner, as you know how, oblige Longman to accept of the like present."

Mr. Longman returned, and brought me the fifty pounds, saying, "I have entered this new article with great pleasure: '*To my lady——, fifty pounds: to be paid the same sum quarterly.*'" —"O Sir," said I, "what will become of me, to be so poor myself, and so rich in your bounty!—It is a shame to take all your profuse goodness would heap upon me thus: but indeed it shall not be without account."—"Make no words, my dear," said he; "are you not my wife? and have I not endowed you with my goods? and, hitherto, this is a very small part."

"Mr. Longman," said I, "and Mrs. Jervis, you both see how I am even oppressed with unreturnable obligations."—"God bless the donor, and the receiver too!" said Mr. Longman; "I am sure they'll bring back good interest; for, Madam, you had ever a bountiful heart; and I have seen the pleasure you used to take in dispensing of my late lady's alms and donations."

"Mr. Longman," said I, "though you are so willing to have me take large sums for nothing at all, I should affront you, if I ask'd you to accept from me a pair of gloves only, on account of my happy nuptials." He seemed not readily to know how to answer; and my master said, "If Longman refuse you, my dear, he may be said to refuse your first favour." On that I put twenty guineas in his hand; but he insisted upon it, that he would take but five. I said, "I must desire you to oblige me, Mr. Longman, or I shall think I have affronted you."—"Well, if I must," said he, "I know what I know."—"What is that, Mr. Longman?" said I. "Why, Madam," said he "I will not lay it out till my young master's birthday, which I hope will be within this year."

Not expecting this from the old gentleman, I looked at my

master, and then blushed so, I could not hold up my head. "Charmingly said, Longman!" said he, and clasped me in his arms: "O my dear life! God send it may be so! You have quite delighted me, Longman, though I durst not have said such a thing for the world."—"Madam," said the old gentleman, "I beg your pardon; I hope no offence: but I'd speak it ten times in a breath to have it so, take it as you please, while my good master bears it so well."—"Mrs. Jervis," said my master, "this is an over-nice dear creature; you don't know what a life I have had with her, even on this side matrimony." Said Mrs. Jervis, "I think Mr. Longman says very well; I am sure I shall hope for it too."

Mr. Longman, who had struck me of a heap, withdrawing soon after, my master said, "Why, my dear, you can't look up! The old man said nothing shocking."—"I did not expect it, though, from him," said I. "I was not aware but of some innocent pleasantry."—"Why, so it was," said he, "both innocent and pleasant: and I won't forgive you, if you don't say as he says. Come, speak before Mrs. Jervis."—"May every thing happen, Sir," said I, "that will give *you* delight!"—"That's my dearest love," said he, and kissed me with great tenderness.

When the servants had dined, I desired to see the maidens; and all four came up together. "You are welcome home, Madam," said Rachel; "we all rejoice to see you here, and more to see you our lady."—"O my good old acquaintances. I joy to see you!"—How do you do, Rachel?—How do you all do?" I took each by the hand, and could have kissed them. "For," said I to myself, "I kissed you all, last time I saw you, in sorrow; why should I not with joy?" But I forbore, in honour of their dear master's presence.

They seemed quite transported with me; and my good master was pleased with the scene. "See here, my lasses," said he, "your mistress! I need not bid you respect her, for you always loved her; and she'll have it as much in her power as inclination to be kind to the deserving."—"Indeed," said I, "I shall always be a kind friend to you: and your dear good master has ordered me to give each of you five guineas, that you may rejoice with me on my happiness." And I said, "God bless you every one! I am overjoyed to see you." And they withdrew with the greatest gratitude and pleasure, praying for us both.

I turned to my dear master: "'Tis to you, dear Sir," said I, "next to God, who put it into your generous heart, that all my happiness is owing! That my mind thus overflows with joy and gratitude!" And I would have kissed his hand, but he clasped me in his arms, and said, "My dear, you deserve it all." Mrs. Jervis came in: said she, "I have seen a very affecting sight; you have made your maidens quite happy, with your condescension and kindness. I saw them all four, as I came by the hall-door, just got up from their knees praising and praying for you both!"—"Dear good bodies!" said I; "and did Jane pray too? May their prayers be returned upon themselves, I say!"

My master sent for Jonathan, and I held up all the fingers of my two hands; and my master approving, I said, "Well, Mr. Jonathan, I could not be satisfied without seeing you in form, as it were, and thanking you for all your past good-will to me. You'll accept of *that* for a pair of gloves, on this happy occasion;" and I gave him ten guineas, and took his honest hand between both mine: "God bless you," said I, "with your silver hairs, so like my dear father!—I shall always value such a good old servant of the best of masters!" He said, "O such goodness! such kind words! It is a balm to my heart! Blessed be God I have lived to this day!" and his eyes swam with tears, and he withdrew. "My dear," said my master, "you make every one happy!"—"O Sir," said I, "'tis you, 'tis you; and let my grateful heart always spring to my lips, to acknowledge the blessings you heap upon me."

Then in came Harry, Isaac, Benjamin, and the two grooms of his house, and Arthur the gardener; for my dear master had ordered them by Mrs. Jervis thus to be marshall'd out; and he said, "Where's John?" Poor John was ashamed, and did not come in till he heard himself called for. I said to them, "How do you do, my old friends and fellow-servants? I am glad to see you all."

My master said, "I have given you a mistress, my lads, that is the joy of my heart: you see her goodness and condescension! Let your respect to her be but answerable, and she'll be proportionably as great a blessing to you all, as she is to me." Harry said, "In the names of all your servants, Sir, I bless your honour, and your good lady: we shall all study to deserve her ladyship's favour, as well as your honour's." So I gave every one five guineas to rejoice, as I said, in my happiness.

When I came to John, I said, "I saw you before, John: but I again tell you, I am glad to see you." He said, he was quite ashamed and confounded. "O forget every thing that's past, John: your dear good master will, and so will I. For God has wonderfully brought about all these things, by the very means I once thought most grievous. Let us therefore look forward, and

423

be only ashamed to commit faults for the time to come; for they may not always be attended with like consequences."

"Arthur," said my master, "I have brought you a mistress who is a great gardener. She'll shew you a new way to plant beans; and never any body had such a hand at improving a sun-flower, as she!"—"O, Sir," said I (but yet a little dashed), "my improvements in every thing are owing to you, I am sure!" They withdrew, blessing us both as the rest had done.

Then came in the postilion, and two helpers (for my master has, both here and at Lincolnshire, fine hunting horses; and it is the chief sport he takes delight in), as also the scullion-boy; and I said, "How do you all, and how dost do, Tommy? I hope you're very good. Your dear master has ordered you something apiece, in honour of me." And my master holding three fingers to me, I gave the postilion and helpers three guineas each, and the little boy two; and bid him let his poor mother lay it out for him, for he must not spend it idly. Mr. Colbrand, Abraham, and Thomas, I had before presented at t'other house.

When they were all gone but Mrs. Jervis, I said, "And now, dearest Sir, permit me, on my knees, thus to bless you, and pray for you. Oh! may God crown you with length of days, and increase of honour; may your happy, happy Pamela, by her grateful heart, appear always worthy in your dear eyes, though she cannot be so in her own, nor in those of any others!"

"Mrs. Jervis," said my master, "you see the excellency of this sweet creature! And when I tell you, that the charms of her person, all lovely as she is, bind me not so strongly to her, as the graces of her mind : congratulate me, that my happiness is built on so stable a basis."—"I do, most sincerely, Sir," said she : "this is a happy day to me!"

I stept into the library, while he was thus pouring out his kindness for me to Mrs. Jervis; and blessed God, on my knees, for the difference I now found to what I once knew in it. Mrs. Jervis had whispered him what I had done above, and he saw me upon my knees, unknown to me; but softly put to the door again, as he had opened it a little way. I said, not knowing he had seen me, "You have some charming pictures here, Sir."— "Yes, my dear life, so I have; but none equal to that which your piety affords me :—And may the God you delight to serve, bless more and more my dear angel!"—"Sir," said I, "you are all goodness!"—"I hope," replied he, "after your sweet example, I shall be better and better."

Do you think, my dear parents, there ever was so happy a creature as I? To be sure it would be very ungrateful to think with uneasiness, or any thing but compassion, of poor Miss Sally Godfrey.

He ordered Jonathan to let the evening be passed merrily, but wisely, as he said, with what every one liked, whether wine or October.

He was pleased to lead me up stairs, and gave me possession of my lady's dressing-room and cabinet, and her fine repeating watch and equipage; in short, of a complete set of diamonds, that were his good mother's; as also of the two pair of diamond ear-rings, the two diamond rings, and a diamond neck-lace, mentioned in his naughty articles, which her ladyship had intended for presents to Miss Tomlins, a rich heiress proposed for his wife, when he was just come from his travels; but which went off, after all was settled on both the friend's sides, because he approved not her conversation, and she had, as he told his mother, too masculine an air: and he never would see her but once, though the lady liked him very well.   He presented me also with her ladyship's books, pictures, linen, laces, &c. that were in her apartments; and bid me call those apartments mine.   O give me, my good God, humility and gratitude!

SUNDAY NIGHT.

This day, as matters could not be ready for our appearance at a better place, we staid at home; and my dear master employed himself in his library: and I was engaged pretty much, as I ought to be, in thankfulness, prayer, and meditation, in my newly presented closet: and I hope God will be pleased to give a blessing to me; for I have the pleasure to think I am not puffed up with great alteration; and yet am not wanting to look upon all these favours and blessings in the light wherein I ought to receive them, both at the hands of Heaven, and my dear benefactor.

We dined together with great pleasure, and I had, in every word and action, all the instances of kindness and affection, that the most indulged heart could wish.   He said he would return to his closet again; and at five o'clock would come and take a walk with me in the garden : and so retired as soon as he had dined, and I went up to mine.

About six, he came up to me, and said, "Now, my dear, I will attend you for a little walk in the garden :" and I gave him my hand with great pleasure.

This garden is much better cultivated than the Lincolnshire one ; but that is larger, and has nobler walks in it ; and yet there is a pretty canal in this, and a fountain and cascade.   We had

425

a deal of sweet conversation as we walked; and, after we had taken a turn round, I bent towards the little garden; and coming near the summer-house, took the opportunity to slip from him, and just whipt up the steps of this once frightful place, and kneeled down, and said, " I bless thee, O God, for my escapes, and for thy mercies! O let me always possess a grateful humble heart!" I went down again, joined him; and he hardly missed me.

Several of the neighbouring gentry sent their compliments to him on his return, but not a word about his marriage; particularly Mr. Arthur, Mr. Towers, Mr. Brooks, and Mr. Martin of the Grove.

MONDAY.

I had a good deal of employment in choosing patterns for my new clothes. He thought nothing too good; but I thought every thing I saw was; and he was so kind to pick out six of the richest, for me to choose three suits, saying we would furnish ourselves with more when in town. One was white flowered with silver most richly : and he was pleased to say, that, as I was a bride, I should appear in that the next Sunday. So we shall have, in two or three days, nothing but mantua-makers and tailors, at work. Bless me! what a chargeable, and what a worthless hussy I am to the dear gentleman!—But his fortune and station require a great deal of it; and his value for me will not let him do less, than if he had married a fortune equal to his own; and, as he says, it would be a reflection upon him if he did. So I doubt it will be as it is : for either way, the world will have something to say. He made me also choose some very fine laces, and linen : and has sent a message on purpose, with his orders, to hasten all down; what can be done in town, as the millinery matters, &c. to be completed there, and sent by particular messengers, as done. All to be here, and finished by Saturday afternoon, without fail.

I send John this morning, with some more papers, and with the few he will give you separate. My desire is, that you will send me all the papers done with, that I may keep my word with Lady Davers; to beg the continuance of your prayers and blessings; to give me your answer about my dear benefactor's proposal of the Kentish farm; to beg you to buy two suits of clothes, each, of the finest cloth for you, my dear father, and of a creditable silk for my dear mother; and good linen, and every thing answerable; and that you will, as my best friend bid me say, come as soon as possible; and he will send his chariot for you, when you tell John the day. Oh! how I long to see you, my dear parents, and to share with you my felicities!

You will have, I'm sure, the goodness to go to all your creditors which are chiefly those of my poor unhappy brothers, and get an account of all you are bound for; and every one shall be paid to the utmost farthing, and interest besides, though some have been cruel and unrelenting.—But they are all entitled to their own, and shall be thankfully paid.

Now I think of it, John shall take my papers down to this place; to amuse you, instead of those you part with: and I will continue writing till I am settled, and you are determined; and then I shall apply myself to the duties of the family, in order to become as useful to my dear benefactor, as my small abilities will let me.

If you think a couple of guineas will be of use to Mrs. Mumford, who I doubt has not much aforehand, pray give them to her, from me (and I will return them to you), as for a pair of gloves on my nuptials: and look through your poor acquaintance and neighbours, and let me have a list of such honest industrious poor, as are true objects of charity, and have no other assistance; particularly such as are blind, lame, or sickly; with their several cases; and also such poor families and housekeepers as are reduced by misfortunes, as ours was, and where a number of children may keep them from rising to a state of tolerable comfort, and I will choose as well as I can; for I long to begin with the quarterly benevolence my kind benefactor has bestowed upon me for such good purposes.

I shall keep account of all these matters; and Mr. Longman has furnished me with a vellum-book of white paper, some sides of which I hope soon to fill with the names of proper objects; and though my dear master has given me all this without account, yet shall he see (but nobody else) how I lay it out from quarter to quarter; and I will, if any be left, carry it on, like an accomptant, to the next quarter, and strike a balance four times a year, and a general balance at every year's end. I have written in it, *Humble* RETURNS *for* DIVINE MERCIES; and locked it up safe in my newly-presented cabinet.

I intend to let Lady Davers see no farther of my papers, than to her own angry letter to her brother; for I would not have her see my reflections upon it; and she'll know, down to that place, all that is necessary for her curiosity, as to my sufferings, the stratagems against me, and the honest part I have been enabled to act; when she has read them all, I hope she will be quite reconciled: for she will see it is all God Almighty's doings;

and that a gentleman of his parts and knowledge was not to be drawn in by such a poor young body as me.

I will detain John no longer. He will tell you to read this last part first, while he stays. And so, with my humble duty to you both, and my dear Mr. B.'s kind remembrance, I rest *your ever dutiful and gratefully happy daughter.*

HONOURED FATHER AND MOTHER,

I will now proceed with my journal. On Tuesday morning my dear Sir rode out, and brought with him to dinner, Mr. Martin of the Grove, Mr. Arthur, Mr. Brooks, and one Mr. Chambers; he told me, he had rode out too far to return to breakfast; but had brought some of his old acquaintance to dine with him. "Are you sorry for it, Pamela?" said he. I remembered his lessons, and said, "No, sure, Sir; I cannot be angry at any thing you are pleased to do!" Said he, "You know Mr. Martin's character, and have severely censured him in one of your letters, as one of my brother rakes, and for his three lyings-in."

He then told me how he came to bring them. Said he, "I met them all at Mr. Arthur's; and his lady asked me if I was *really* married? I said, 'Yes, *really*.'—'And to whom?' said Mr. Martin. 'Why,' replied I, bluntly, 'to my mother's waiting-maid.' They could not tell what to say to me, and looked upon one another. And I saw I had spoiled a jest, from each. Mrs. Arthur said, 'You have indeed, Sir, a charming creature, as ever I saw; and she has mighty good luck.'—'Ay,' said I, 'and so have I. But I shall say the less, because a man never did any thing of this nature, that he did not think he ought, if it were but in policy, to make the best of it.'—'Nay,' said Mr. Arthur, 'if you have sinned, it is with your eyes open; for you know the world as well as any gentleman of your years in it.'

"'Why really, gentlemen,' said I, 'I should be glad to please all my friends; but I can't expect, till they know my motives and inducements, that it will be so immediately. But I do assure you, I am exceedingly pleased *myself*; and that, you know, is most to the purpose.'

"Said Mr. Brooks, 'I have heard my wife praise your spouse, that is, so much for person and beauty, that I wanted to see her of all things.'—'Why,' replied I, 'if you'll all go and take a dinner with me, you shall see her with all my heart.—And, Mrs. Arthur, will you bear us company?'—'No, indeed, Sir,' said she. 'What, I'll warrant, my *wife* will not be able to recon-

428

cile you to my *mother's waiting-maid;* is not that it? Tell truth, Mrs. Arthur.'—' Nay,' said she, ' I shan't be backward to pay your spouse a visit, in company of the neighbouring ladies; but for one single woman to go, on such a sudden motion too, with so many gentlemen, is not right.—But that need not hinder you, gentlemen.' So," said he, "the rest sent, that they should not dine at home; and they and Mr. Chambers, a gentleman lately settled in these parts, one and all came with me; and so, my dear," concluded he, "when you make your appearance next Sunday, you're sure of a party in your favour: for all that see you must esteem you."

He went to them; and when I came down to dinner, he was pleased to take me by the hand, at my entrance into the parlour, and said, " My dear, I have brought some of my good neighbours to dine with you." I said, " You are very good, Sir."—"My dear, this gentleman is Mr. Chambers;" and so he presented every one to me; and they saluted me, and wished us both joy.

"I, for my part," said Mr. Brooks, "wish you joy most heartily. My wife told me of the beauties of your person; but I did not think we had such a flower in our county."—" Sir," said I, " your lady is very partial to me; and you are so polite a gentleman, that you will not contradict your good lady."

" I'll assure you, Madam," returned he, "you have not hit the matter at all; for we contradict one another twice or thrice a day. But the devil's in't if we are not agreed in so clear a case!" Said Mr. Martin, " Mr. Brooks says very true, Madam, in both respects " (meaning his wife's and his own contradiction to one another, as well as in my favour); " *for*," added he, " they have been married some years."

As I had not the best opinion of this gentleman, nor his jest, I said, " I am almost sorry, Sir, for the gentleman's jest upon himself and his lady; but I think it should have relieved him from a greater jest, your pleasant confirmation of it—But still the reason you give that it *may* be so, I hope may be given that it is *not so*;— to wit, that they have been married some years."

Said Mr. Arthur, " Mr. Martin, I think the lady has very handsomely reproved you."—" I think so too," said Mr. Chambers; " and it was but a very indifferent compliment to a bride." Said Mr. Martin, " Compliment or not, gentlemen, I have never seen a matrimony of long standing, that it was not so, little or much; but I dare say it will never be so here."

" To be sure, Sir," said I, " if it was, I must be the ungratefullest person in the world, because I am the most obliged person

429

in it."—" That notion," said Mr. Arthur, " is so excellent, that it gives a moral certainty it never can."

" Sir," said Mr. Brooks, to my dear master, softly, " You have a most accomplished lady, I do assure you, as well in her behaviour and wit, as in her person, call her what you please."— " Why, my dear friend," said my master, " I must tell you, as I have said before now, that her person made me her lover, but her mind made her my wife."

The first course coming in, my dear Sir led me to my place; and set Mr. Chambers, as the greatest stranger, at my right hand, and Mr. Brooks at my left. Mr. Arthur was pleased to observe, much to my advantage, on the ease and freedom with which I behaved myself, and helped them; and said he would bring his lady to be a witness, and a learner both, of my manner. I said, I should be proud of any honour Mrs. Arthur would vouchsafe to do me; and if once I could avail myself of his good lady's example, and those of the other gentlemen present, I should have the greater opinion of my fitness for the place I filled, at present, with much insufficiency.

Mr. Arthur drank to my health and happiness, and said, " My wife told your spouse, Madam, you had very good luck in such a husband; but I now see who has the best of it." Said Mr. Brooks, " Come, let's make no compliments; for the plain truth is, our good neighbour's generosity and judgment have met with so equal a match in his lady's beauty and merit, that I know not which has the best luck.—But may you be both long happy together, say I!" And so he drank a glass of wine.

My best friend, who always delights to have me praised, seemed much pleased with our conversation: and said the kindest, tenderest, and most respectful things to me. Insomuch that the rough Mr. Martin said, " Did you ever think our good friend here, who used to ridicule matrimony so much, would make so complaisant a husband?—How long do you intend, Sir, that this shall hold? "—" As long as my good girl deserves it," said he. " I hope for ever. But," continued the kind gentleman, " you need not wonder I have changed my mind as to wedlock; for I never expected to meet with one whose behaviour and sweetness of temper was so well adapted to make me happy."

After dinner, and having drank good healths to each of their ladies, I withdrew; and they sat and drank two bottles of claret a-piece, and were very merry; and went away full of my praises, and vowing to bring their ladies to see me.

John, having brought me your kind letter, my dear father, I told my good master, after his friends were gone, how grateful

430

you received his generous intentions as to the Kentish farm, and promised your best endeavours to serve him in that estate; and that you hoped for your industry and care to be very little troublesome to him, as to the liberal manner in which he intended to add to a provision, which of itself exceeded all you wished. He was very well pleased with your cheerful acceptance of it.

I am glad your engagements in the world lie in so small a compass; as soon as you have gotten an account of them exactly, you will be pleased to send it me, with the list of the poor folks you are so kind to promise to procure me.

I think, as my dear master is so generous, you should account nothing that is plain, too good. Pray don't be afraid of laying out upon yourselves. He intends that you shall not, when you come, return to your old abode; but stay with us, till you set out for Kent; so you must dispose of yourselves accordingly. And I hope, my dear father, you have quite left off all slavish business. As Farmer Jones has been kind to you, as I have heard you say, pray when you take leave of them, present them with three guineas worth of good books; such as a Family Bible, a Common Prayer, a Whole Duty of Man, or any other you think will be acceptable; for they live a great way from church; and in winter the ways from their farm thither are impassable.

He has brought me my papers safe; and I will send them to Lady Davers the first opportunity, down to the place I mentioned in my last.

My dear Mr. B. just now tells me, that he will carry me, in the morning, a little airing, about ten miles off, in his chariot and four, to breakfast at a farm-house, noted for a fine dairy, and where, now and then, the neighbouring gentry, of both sexes, resort for that purpose.

THURSDAY.

We set out soon after six, accordingly; and, driving pretty smartly, got at his truly neat house at half an hour after eight; and I was much pleased with the neatness of the good woman; and her daughter and maid; he was so good as to say he would now and then take a turn with me to the same place, and on the same occasion, as I seemed to like it : for it would be a pretty exercise, and procure us appetites to our breakfasts, as well as our return would to our dinners. But I find this was not, though a very good reason, the only one for which he gave me this agreeable airing; and I shall acquaint you.

We were prettily received and entertained here, and an elegancy ran through every thing, persons as well as furniture, yet all plain. And my master said to the good housewife, "Do your young boarding-school ladies still at times continue their visits to you, Mrs. Dobson?"—"Yes, Sir," said she, "I expect three or four of them every minute."

"There is, my dear," said he, "within three miles of this farm a very good boarding-school for ladies; the governess of it keeps a chaise and pair, which is to be made a double chaise at pleasure: in summer, when the Misses perform their task to satisfaction, she favours them with an airing to this place, three or four at a time: and after breakfasting, they are carried back: this serves both for a reward, and for exercise; and the Misses who have this favour are not a little proud of it; and it brings them forward in their respective tasks."

"A very good method, Sir," said I. And just as we were talking, the chaise came in with four Misses, all pretty much of a size, with a maid-servant. They passed by us into another little neat apartment through ours; and made their honours very prettily. I went into the room to them, and asked questions about their work, and their lessons: and what they had done to deserve such a fine airing and breakfasting; and they all answered me very prettily. "And pray, little ladies," said I, "what may I call your names?" One was called Miss Burduff, one Miss Nugent, one Miss Booth, and the fourth Miss Goodwin. "I don't know which," said I, "is the prettiest; but you are all best, my little dears; and you have a very good governess to indulge you with such a fine airing, and such delicate cream, and bread and butter. I hope you think so too."

My master came in, and I had no mistrust in the world; he kissed each of them: but looked more wistfully on Miss Goodwin, than on any of the others; but I thought nothing just then: had she been called Miss Godfrey, I had hit upon it in a trice.

When we went from them, he said, "Which do you think the prettiest of those Misses?"—"Really, Sir, it is hard to say: Miss Booth is a pretty brown girl, and has a fine eye; Miss Burduff has a great deal of sweetness in her countenance, but is not so regularly featured; Miss Nugent is very fair; and Miss Goodwin has a fine black eye, and is, besides, I think, the genteelest shaped child: but they are all pretty."

The maid led them into the garden, to shew them the bee-hives, and Miss Goodwin made a particular fine curtsey to my master: I said, "I believe Miss knows you, Sir?" and taking her by the hand, I said, "Do you know this gentleman, my pretty dear?"—"Yes, Madam," said she; "it is my own dear uncle." I clasped her in my arms: "O why did you not tell me, Sir," said I, " that you had a niece among these little ladies? " I kissed her, and away she tript after the others.

" But pray, Sir," said I, " how can this be?—You have no sister nor brother, but Lady Davers.—How can this be? "

He smiled : and then I said, " O my dearest Sir, tell me now the truth. Does not this pretty Miss stand in a nearer relation to you, than as a niece?—I know she does ! I know she does ! " And I embraced him as he stood.

" 'Tis even so, my dear ; and you remember my sister's good-natured hint of Miss Sally Godfrey ! "—" I do well, Sir. But this is Miss Goodwin."—" Her mother chose that name for her," said he, " because she should not be called by her own."

" Well," said I, " excuse me, Sir ; I must go and have a little prattle with her."—" I'll send for her in again," replied he ; and in she came in a moment. I took her in my arms, and said, " O, my charming dear ! will you love me?—Will you let me be your aunt? "—" Yes, Madam, with all my heart ; and I will love *you* dearly : but I mustn't love my uncle."— " Why so? " said he. " Because you would not speak to me at first ! And because you would not let me call you uncle," (for it seems she was bid not, that I might not guess at her presently), " and yet," said the pretty dear, " I had not seen you a great while, so I hadn't ! "

" Well, Pamela, now can you allow me to love this little innocent? "—" Allow you, Sir ! you would be very barbarous, if you did not ; and I should be more so, if I did not further it all I could, and love the little lamb myself, for your sake and for her own ; and in compassion to her poor mother, though unknown to me." And tears stood in my eyes.

" Why, my love, are your words so kind, and your countenance so sad ! "—I drew to the window from the child : and said, " Sad it is not, Sir ; but I have a strange grief and pleasure mingled at once in my breast, on this occasion ; it is indeed a twofold grief and a twofold pleasure."—" As how, my dear? " said he.—" Why, Sir, I cannot help being grieved for the poor mother of this sweet babe, to think, if she be living, she must call her chiefest delight her shame ; if she be no more, she must have had sad remorse on her poor mind, on leaving the world, and her poor babe : in the second place, I grieve, that it must be thought a kindness to the dear little soul, not to let her know how near her dearest relation in the world is to her. Forgive me, dear Sir, I say not this to reproach you in the least. And I have a twofold cause of joy : first, that I have had the grace

433

to escape the like unhappiness with this poor gentlewoman: and next, that this discovery has given me an opportunity to shew the sincerity of my grateful affections for you, Sir, in the love I will always express to this dear child."

Then I stept to her, and kissing her, said, "Join with me, my pretty love, to beg your dear uncle to let you come and live with your new aunt: indeed, my little precious, I'll love you dearly."

"Will you, Sir," said the little charmer, "will you let me go and live with my aunt?"

"You are very good, my Pamela. And I have not once been deceived in the hopes my fond heart had entertained of your prudence."—"But will you, Sir," said I, "grant me this favour? I shall most sincerely love the little charmer; and all I am capable of doing for her, both by example and affection, shall most cordially be done. My dearest Sir, oblige me in this thing! I think already, my heart is set upon it! What a sweet employment, and companionship shall I have!"

"We'll talk of this some other time," replied he; "but I must, in prudence, put some bounds to your amiable generosity. I had always intended to surprise you into this discovery; but my sister led the way to it, out of a poorness in her spite, I could not brook; and though you have pleased me beyond expression, in your behaviour on this occasion, yet you have not gone much beyond my expectations; for I have such an high opinion of you, I think nothing could have shaken it, but a contrary conduct on so tender a circumstance."

"Well, Sir," said the dear little Miss, "then you will not let me go home with my aunt, will you? I am sure she will love me."—"When you break up next, my dear, if you are a good girl, you shall pay your new aunt a visit."—She made a low curtsey.—"Thank you, Sir," answered she. "Yes, my dear," said I, "and I will get you some fine things against the time. I would have brought you some now, had I known I should have seen my pretty love."—"Thank you, Madam," returned she.

"How old, Sir," said I, "is Miss?"—"Between six and seven," answered he. "Was she ever, Sir, at your house?"—"My sister carried her thither once, as a little relation of her lord's."—"I remember, Sir," said I, "a little Miss; and Mrs. Jervis and I took her to be a relation of Lord Davers."

"My sister," said he, "knew the whole secret from the beginning; and it made her a great merit with me, that she kept it from the knowledge of my father, who was then living,

434

and of my mother to her dying-day; though she descended so low, in her rage, to hint the matter to you."

The little Misses took their leaves soon after; and I know not how, but I am strangely affected with this dear child. I wish I might have her home. It would be a great pleasure to have such a fine opportunity, obliged as I am, to shew my love for himself, in my fondness for this dear Miss.

As we came home together in the chariot, he gave me the following particulars of this affair, additional to what he had before mentioned:

That this lady was of a good family, and the flower of it: but that her mother was a person of great art and address, and not altogether so nice in the particular between himself and Miss, as she ought to have been: that especially, when she found him unsettled and wild, and her daughter in more danger from him than he was from her, yet she encouraged their privacies, and even when she had reason to apprehend, from their being surprised together in a way not so creditable to the lady, that she was far from forbidding their private meetings; on the contrary, that on a certain time, she had set one, formerly her footman, and a half-pay officer, her relation, to watch an opportunity, and to frighten him into a marriage with the lady: that accordingly, after surprising him in her chamber, when just let in, they drew their swords, and threatened instantly to kill him, if he did not promise marriage on the spot; and that they had a parson ready below stairs, as he found afterwards: he then suspected, from some strong circumstances, Miss was in the plot; which so enraged him, with their menaces together, that he drew, and stood upon his defence; and was so much in earnest, that the man he pushed into the arm, and disabled; and pressing pretty forward upon the other, as he retreated, he rushed in upon him near the top of the stairs, pushed him down one pair, and he was much hurt by the fall:—Not but that, he said, he might have paid for his rashness: the business of his antagonists was rather to frighten than to kill him: that, upon this, in the sight of the old lady, the parson she had provided and her other daughters, he went out of their house, with bitter execrations against them all.

That after this, designing to break off all correspondence with the whole family, and Miss too, she found means to engage him to give her a meeting at Woodstock, in order to clear herself: that, poor lady! she was there obliged, naughty creature as he was! to make herself quite guilty of a worse fault, in order to clear herself of a lighter: that they often met at Godstow,

Woodstock, and every neighbouring place to Oxford, where he was then studying, as it proved, guilty lessons, instead of improving ones; till, at last, the effect of their frequent interviews grew too obvious to be concealed; that the young lady then, not fit to be seen, for the credit of the family, was confined, and all manner of means were used, to induce him to marry her: that, finding nothing would do, they at last resolved to complain to his father and mother; but that he made his sister acquainted with the matter, who then happened to be at home; and by her management and spirit, their intentions of that sort were frustrated; and, seeing no hopes, they agreed to Lady Davers's proposals, and sent poor Miss down to Marlborough, where, at her expense, which he repaid her, she was provided for, and privately lay-in; that Lady Davers took upon herself the care of the little one, till fit to be put to the boarding-school, where it now is: and that he had settled upon the dear little Miss such a sum of money, as the interest of it would handsomely provide for her; and the principal would be a tolerable fortune, fit for a gentlewoman, when she came to be marriageable. "This, my dear," said he, "is the story in brief. And I do assure you, Pamela," added he, "I am far from making a boast of, or taking a pride in this affair: but since it has happened I can't say but I wish the poor child to live, and be happy: and I must endeavour to make her so."

"Sir," said I, "to be sure you should; and I shall take a very great pride to contribute to the dear little soul's felicity, if you will permit me to have her home. But does Miss know any thing who are her father and mother?" I wanted him to say if the poor lady was living or dead. "No," answered he. "Her governess has been told, by my sister, that she is the daughter of a gentleman, and his lady, who are related to Lord Davers, and now live in Jamaica; she calls me uncle, only because I am brother to Lady Davers, whom she calls aunt, and who is very fond of her, as is also my lord, who knows the whole matter; they have her, at all her little school recesses, at their house, and are very kind to her.—I believe the truth of the matter is little known or suspected; for as her mother *is* of no mean family, her friends try to keep it secret as much as I: and Lady Davers, till her wrath boiled over, t'other day, has managed the matter very dexterously and kindly."

The words, mother *is* of no mean family, gave me not to doubt the poor lady was living. And I said, "But how, Sir, can the dear Miss's poor mother be content to deny herself the enjoyment of so sweet a child!"—"Ah Pamela," replied he, "now *you*

436

come in; I see you want to know what's become of the poor mother.—'Tis natural enough : but I was willing to see how the little suspense would operate upon you."—" Dear Sir," said I—— " Nay," replied he, " 'tis very natural, my dear ! I think you have had great patience, and are come at this question so fairly, you deserve to be answered.

" You must know then, there is some foundation for saying, that her mother at least lives in Jamaica; for there she does live, and very happily too. For I must observe, that she suffered so much in child-bed, nobody expected her life; and this, when she was up, made such an impression upon her, that she dreaded nothing so much as the thoughts of returning to her former fault; and, to say the truth, I had intended to make her a visit as soon as her month was well up. So, unknown to me, she engaged herself to go to Jamaica, with two young ladies, born there, and returning to their friends, after having been four years in England for their education : and, recommending to me, by a very moving letter, her little baby, and that I would not suffer it to be called by her name, but Goodwin, that her shame might be the less known, for hers and her family's sake; she got her friends to assign her five hundred pounds in full of all demands upon her family, and went up to London, embarked with her companions, at Gravesend, and sailed to Jamaica; where she is since well and happily married, passing, to her husband, for a young widow, with one daughter, which her husband's friends take care of, and provide for. And so you see, Pamela, that, in the whole story, on both sides, the truth is as much preserved as possible."

" Poor lady ! " said I : " how her story moves me !—I am glad she is so *happy* at last."—" And, my dear," said he, " are you not glad she is so *far off* too ? "—" As to that, Sir, I cannot be sorry, to be sure, as she is so happy; which she could not have been *here*. For, Sir, I doubt you would have proceeded with your temptations, if she had not gone; and it showed her so much in earnest to be good, that she could leave her native country, her relations, you, whom she so well loved, her dear baby, and try a new fortune, in a new world, among strangers, and hazard the seas; and all to preserve herself from further guiltiness !—Indeed, Sir," said I, " I bleed for what her distresses must be, in this case; I am grieved for her poor mind's remorse, through her child-bed terrors, which could have so great an effect; and I honour her resolution. I should rank such a returning dear lady in the class of those who are most virtuous; and doubt not God Almighty's mercies to her, and that her present happiness is the result of his gracious Providence, blessing her penitence and reformation. But, Sir," said I, " did you not once see the poor lady, after her lying-in ? "

" I did not believe her so much in earnest, and I went down to Marlborough, and heard she was gone from thence to Balne. I went there, but she was gone to a relation's at Reading. Thither I went, and heard she was gone to Oxford. I followed : and there she was, but I could not see her.

" She at last received a letter from me, begging a meeting ; for I found her departure with the ladies resolved on, and that she was with her friends, only to take leave of them, and receive her agreed-on portion : she appointed the Saturday following, and that was Wednesday, to give me a meeting at the old place, at Woodstock.

" Then I thought I was sure of her, and doubted not I should spoil her intended voyage. I set out on Thursday to Gloucester, on a party of pleasure ; and on Saturday to Woodstock : but when I came thither, I found a letter instead of my lady ; it was to beg my pardon for deceiving me ; expressing her concern for her past fault, her affection to me, and the apprehension she had of being unable to keep her good resolves, if she met me ; that she had set out the Thursday for her embarkation, fearing nothing else could save her ; and had appointed this meeting on Saturday, at the place of her former guilt, that I might be suitably impressed upon the occasion, and pity and allow for her ; and that she might get three or four days start of me, and be quite out of my reach. She recommended again, as upon the spot where the poor little one owed its being, my tenderness to it for her sake ; that was all she had to request, she said ; but would not forget to pray for me in all her own dangers, and in every difficulty she was going to encounter."

I wept at this moving tale : " And did not this make a deep impression upon you, Sir ? " said I : " surely, such an affecting lesson as this must, on the very guilty spot too—(I admire the dear lady's pious contrivance !) One would have thought, Sir, it was enough to reclaim you for ever ! All your naughty purposes, I doubt not, were quite changed ! "

" Why, my dear, I was much moved, you may be sure, when I came to reflect : but at first, I was so assured of being a successful tempter, and spoiling her voyage, that I was vexed, and much out of humour ; but, on reflection, I was quite overcome with this instance of her prudence, penitence, and resolution ; and more admired her than I ever had done. Yet I could not bear she should so escape me neither ; so much overcome me, as it were, in an heroical bravery; and I hastened away, got a bill of credit of Lord Davers, upon his banker in London, for five hundred pounds; and set out thither, having called at Oxford, and got what light I could, as to where I might hear of her.

"On arriving in town, which was not till Monday morning, I went to Crosby Square, where the friends of the two ladies lived. She had set out, in the flying coach on Tuesday, got to the two ladies that very night, and on Saturday set out, with them, for Gravesend, near the time I expected her at Woodstock.

"You may suppose I was much affected with this. However, I got my bill of credit converted into money; and set out with my servant on Monday, and reached Gravesend that night; where I found that she and the two ladies had gone on board from the inn I put up at, in the morning: and the ship waited only for the wind, which then was turning about in its favour.

"I went directly on board, and asked for Mrs. Godfrey. But judge, my dear, her surprise and confusion, on seeing me. She had nearly fainted away. I offered any money to put off the sailing till next day, but it was not complied with; and fain would I have got her on shore, and promised to attend her, if she would go over land, to any part of England the ship might touch at. But she was immovable. Every one concluded me her humble servant, and were touched at the moving interview; the young ladies, and their female attendants especially. With great difficulty, upon my solemn assurances of honour, she trusted herself with me in one of the cabins; and there I entreated her to quit her purpose; but in vain: she said, I had made her quite unhappy by this interview! She had difficulties enough upon her mind before; but now I had embittered all her voyage, and given her the deepest distress.

"I could prevail upon her but for one favour, and that with the greatest reluctance; which was, to accept of the five hundred pounds as a present from me; and to draw upon me for a greater sum, as one who had her effects in my hands, when she arrived, if she found it convenient for her. But she would not promise even to correspond with me, and was determined on going; I believe, if I would have married her, which yet I had not in my head, she would not have been diverted from her purpose."

"But how, Sir," said I, "did you part?"—"I would have sailed with her, and been landed at the first port in England or Ireland, I cared not which, they put in at; but she was too full of apprehensions to admit it: and the rough fellow of a master, captain they called him, would not stay a moment, the wind and

439

tide being quite fair; and was very urgent with me to go ashore, or to go the voyage; and being impetuous in my temper, *spoilt, you know, my dear, by my mother,* and not used to control, I thought it very strange, that wind or tide, or any thing else, should be preferred to me and my money: but so it was; I was forced to go; and so took leave of the ladies, and the other passengers, wished them a good voyage; gave five guineas among the ship's crew, to be good to the ladies, and took such a leave as you may better imagine than I express. She recommended, once more to me, the dear Guest, as she called her, the ladies being present; and thanked me for all these instances of my regard, which, she said, would leave a strong impression on her mind; and, throwing her arms about my neck; we took such a leave, as affected every one present, men, as well as ladies.

"So with a truly heavy heart, I went down the ship's side, to my boat; and stood up in it, looking at her, as long as I could see her, and she at me, with her handkerchief at her eyes; and then I gazed at the ship, *till* and *after* I had landed, as long as I could discern the least appearance of it; for she was under sail in a manner, when I left her; and so I returned highly disturbed to my inn.

"I went to bed, but rested not; returned to London the next day, and set out again for the country. So much for poor Sally Godfrey. She sends, by all opportunities, with the knowledge of her husband, to learn how her child by her first husband does; and has the satisfaction to know she is happily provided for. Half a year ago, her spouse sent a little negro boy, about ten years old, as a present to wait upon her; but he was taken ill of the small pox, and died in a month after he was landed."

"Sure, Sir," said I, "your generous mind must have been long affected with this melancholy case, and all its circumstances."

"It hung upon me some time," said he; "but I was full of spirits and inconsideration. I went soon after to travel; a hundred new objects danced before my eyes, and kept reflection from me. And you see, I had five or six years afterwards, and even before that, so thoroughly lost all the impressions you talk of, that I doubted not to make my Pamela change her name, without either act of parliament, or wedlock, and be Sally Godfrey the Second."—"O you dear naughty man!" said I, "this seems but too true! But I bless God, that it is not so!—I bless God for your reformation, and that for your own dear sake as well as mine!"

"Well, my dear," said he, "and I bless God for it too!—I

do most sincerely !—'Tis my greater pleasure, because I have, as I hope, seen my error so early; and that with such a stock of youth, and apparent health on my side, I can truly abhor my past liberties, and pity poor Sally Godfrey, from the same motives that I admire my Pamela's virtues; and resolve to make myself as worthy of them as possible: and I will hope, my dear, your prayers for my pardon, and my perseverance, will be of no small efficacy on this occasion."

These agreeable reflections, on this melancholy, but instructive story, brought us in view of his own house; and we alighted, and walked in the garden till dinner was ready.

MONDAY MORNING.

Yesterday we set out, attended by John, Abraham, Benjamin, and Isaac, in fine new liveries, in the best chariot, which had been cleaned, lined, and new harnessed; so that it looked like a quite new one: but I had no arms to quarter with my dear lord and master's; though he jocularly, upon my noticing my obscurity, said, that he had a good mind to have the olive-branch, which would allude to his hopes, quartered for mine. I was dressed in the suit of white, flowered with silver, a rich head-dress, and the diamond necklace, ear-rings, &c. I mentioned before: and my dear Sir, in a fine laced silk waistcoat, of blue Paduasoy, and his coat a pearl-coloured fine cloth, with gold buttons and button-holes, and lined with white silk. I said, I was too fine, and would have laid aside some of the jewels; but he said, it would be thought a slight to me from him, as his wife: and though I apprehended that people might talk as it was, yet he had rather they should say any thing, than that I was not put upon an equal foot, as his wife, with any lady he might have married.

It seems, the neighbouring gentry had expected us; and there was a great congregation; for (against my wish) we were a little late; so that, as we walked up the church to his seat, we had many gazers and whisperers: but my dear master behaved with so intrepid an air, and was so cheerful and complaisant to me, that he did credit to his kind choice, instead of shewing as if he was ashamed of it; and I was resolved to busy my mind entirely with the duties of the day: my intentness on that occasion, and my thankfulness to God, for his unspeakable mercies to me, so took up my thoughts, I was much less concerned than I should otherwise have been, at the gazings and whisperings of the congregation, whose eyes were all turned to our seat.

441

When the sermon was ended, we staid the longer for the church to be pretty empty; but we found great numbers at the doors, and in the porch; and I had the pleasure of hearing many commendations, as well of my person as my dress and behaviour, and not one reflection, or mark of disrespect. Mr. Martin, who is single, Mr. Chambers, Mr. Arthur, and Mr. Brooks, with their families, were all there: and the four gentlemen came up to us, before we went into the chariot, and in a very kind and respectful manner, complimented us both; Mrs. Arthur and Mrs. Brooks were so kind as to wish me joy; and Mrs. Brooks said, " You sent Mr. Brooks, Madam, home t'other day, quite charmed, with a manner which you have convinced a thousand persons this day is natural to you."

" You do me great honour, Madam," replied I. " Such a good lady's approbation must make me too sensible of my happiness." My dear master handed me into the chariot, and stood talking to Sir Thomas Atkyns (who was making him abundance of compliments, and is a very ceremonious gentleman, a little to extreme that way), I believe to familiarize me to the gazers, which concerned me a little; for I was dashed to hear the praises of the country people, and see them crowd about the chariot. Several poor people begged my charity: and I beckoned John, and said, " Divide, in the further church-porch, that money to the poor, and let them come to-morrow morning to me, and I will give them something more, if they don't importune me now." So I gave them all the silver I had, between twenty and thirty shillings; and this drew away from me their clamorous prayers for charity.

Mr. Martin came up to me on the other side, and leaned on the very door, while my master was talking to Sir Thomas, whom he could not leave, and said, " By all that's good, you have charmed the whole congregation. Not a soul but is full of your praises. My neighbour knew, better than any body could tell him, how to choose for himself. Why," said he, " the dean himself looked more upon you, than his book."

" O, Sir," said I, " you are very encouraging to a weak mind ! " —" I vow," said he, " I say no more than is truth : I'd marry to-morrow, if I were sure of a person of but one-half of your merit.—You are, and 'tis not my way to praise too much, an ornament to your sex, an honour to your spouse, and a credit to religion.—Every body is saying so : for you have by your piety edified the whole church."

As he had done speaking, the dean himself complimented me, that the behaviour of so good a lady would be very edifying to this congregation, and encouraging to himself. " Sir," said I, " you are very kind : I hope I shall not behave unworthy of the good instructions I shall have the pleasure to receive from so worthy a divine."

Sir Thomas then applied to me, my master stepping into the chariot, and said, " I beg pardon, Madam, for detaining your good spouse : but I have been saying, he is the happiest man in the world." I bowed to him; but could have wished him further, to make me sit so in the notice of every one : which, for all I could do, dashed me not a little.

Mr. Martin said to my master, " If you'll come to church every Sunday, with your charming lady, I will never absent myself, and she'll give a good example to all the neighbourhood." —" O, my dear Sir," said I, " you know not how much I am obliged to Mr. Martin. He has, by his kind expressions, made me dare to look up with pleasure and gratitude."

Said my master, " My dear love, I am very much obliged, as well as you, to my good friend, Mr. Martin." And he said to him, " We will constantly go to church, and to every other place, where we can have the pleasure of seeing Mr. Martin."

Mr. Martin said, " Gad, Sir, you are a happy man, and I think your lady's example has made you more polite and handsome too, than I ever knew you before, though we never thought you unpolite neither." So he bowed and went to his own chariot; and as we drove away, the people kindly blessed us, and called us a charming pair. As I have no other pride, I hope, in repeating these things, than in the countenance the general approbation gives to my dear master, for his stooping so low, you will excuse me for it.

In the afternoon we went again to church, and a little early, at my request; but it was quite full, and soon after even crowded : so much does novelty (the more's the pity !) attract the eyes of mankind. Mr. Martin came in, after us, and made up to our seats; and said, " If you please, my dear friend, I will sit with you this afternoon."—" With all my heart," said my master. I was sorry for it; but was resolved my duty should not be made second to bashfulness, or any other consideration : and when divine service began, I withdrew to the further end of the pew, and left the gentlemen in the front; and they both behaved quite suitably to the occasion. I mention this the rather, because Mr. Martin was not very noted for coming to church, or attention when there.

The dean preached again, though not usual, out of compliment to us; and an excellent sermon he made on the relative duties of

443

Christianity: and took my particular attention, with his fine observations on the subject. Mr. Martin addressed himself twice or thrice to me, during the sermon; but I was so wholly engrossed with hearkening to the good preacher, that he forbore interrupting me; yet I, according to the lesson formerly given me, observed to him a cheerful and obliging behaviour, as one of his friends and intimates. My Master asked him to supper; and he said, " I am so taken with your lady, that you must not encourage me too much; for I shall be always with you, if you do." He was pleased to say, " You cannot favour us with too much of your company; and as I left you in the lurch in your single estate, I think you will do well to oblige us as much as you can; and who knows but my happiness may reform another rake !"—" *Who* knows? " said Mr. Martin, " why, I know—for I am more than half reformed already." At the chariot door, Mrs. Arthur, Mrs. Brooks, and Mrs. Chambers, were brought to me, by their respective spouses; and presently the witty Lady Towers joined them. Mrs. Arthur said, she wished me joy; and that all the good ladies, my neighbours, would meet and make me a visit. " This," said I, " will be an honour I can never enough acknowledge. It will be very kind so to countenance a person, who will always study to deserve your favours, by the most respectful behaviour." Lady Towers said, " My dear neighbour, you want no countenance, your own merit is sufficient. I had a slight cold, that kept me at home in the morning; but I heard you so much talked of, and praised, I resolved not to stay away in the afternoon : and I join in the joy every one gives you." She turned to my master, and said, " You are a sly thief, as I always thought you. Where have you stolen this lady? And now, how barbarous is it, thus unawares, in a manner, to bring her here upon us, to mortify and eclipse us all."—" You are very kind, Madam," said he, " that you and all my worthy neighbours see with my eyes. But had I not known she had so much excellency of mind and behaviour, as would strike every body in her favour at first sight, I should not have dared to class her with such of my worthy neighbours, as now so kindly congratulate us both."

" I own," said she softly, " I was one of your censurers; but I never liked you so well in my life, as for this action, now I see how capable your bride is of giving distinction to any condition." And coming to me, " My dear neighbour," said she, " excuse me for having but in my thoughts, the remembrance that I have *seen you formerly*, when, by your sweet air, and easy deportment, you so much surpass us all, and give credit to your present happy condition."

"Dear good Madam," said I, "how shall I suitably return my acknowledgements! But it will never be a pain to me to look back upon my *former days*, now I have the kind allowance and example of so many worthy ladies to support me in the honours to which the most generous of men hath raised me."

"Sweetly said!" she was pleased to say. "If I was in another place, I would kiss you for that answer. Oh! happy Mr. B!" said she to my master, "what reputation have you not brought upon your judgment! I won't be long before I see you, I'll assure you, if I come by myself."—"That shall be your own fault, Madam," said Mrs. Brooks, "if you do."

So they took leave; and I gave my hand to my dear master, and said, "How happy have you made me, generous Sir!" The dean, who was just come up, heard me, and said, "And how happy you have made your spouse, I'll venture to pronounce, is hard to say, from what I observe from you both." I curtseyed, and blushed, not thinking any body heard me. And my master telling him he should be glad of the honour of a visit from him, he said he would pay his respects to us soon, and bring his wife and daughter to attend me. I said that was doubly kind; and I should be very proud of cultivating so worthy an acquaintance. I thanked him for his fine discourse; and he thanked me for my attention, which he called exemplary : so my dear master handed me into the chariot; and we went home, *both* happy.

Mr. Martin came in the evening with his friend Mr. Dormer; and entertained us with the favourable opinion, he said, every one had of me, and of the choice my good benefactor had made.

This morning the poor came, according to my invitation, and I sent twenty-five away with glad hearts.

TUESDAY.

My generous master has given me a most considerate, but yet, from the nature of it, melancholy instance of his great regard for my unworthiness, which I never could have wished, hoped for, or even thought of. He took a walk with me, after breakfast, into the garden; and a shower falling, he led me, for shelter, into the little summer-house, in the private garden, where he formerly gave me apprehension; and, sitting down by me, he said, "I have now finished all that lies on my mind, my dear, and am very easy : for have you not wondered that I so much employed myself in my library? Been so much at home, and yet not in your company?"—"No, Sir," said I: "I have never been so impertinent as to wonder at anything you please to employ yourself about; nor would give way to a curiosity that should be troublesome to you; and, besides, I know your large possessions: and the method you take of looking yourself into your affairs, must needs take up so much of your time, that I ought to be very careful how I intrude upon you."

"Well," said he, "but I'll tell you what has been my last work: I have considered that, at present, my line is almost extinct: and that the chief part of my *maternal* estate, in case I die without issue, will go to another line, and great part of my *personal* will fall into such hands, as I shall not care my Pamela should lie at the mercy of. I have, therefore, as human life is uncertain, so disposed my affairs, as to make you absolutely independent and happy; to secure to you the power of doing much good, and living as a person ought to do who is my relict: and prevent any body from molesting your father and mother, in the provision I design them, for the remainder of their days: and I have finished all this very morning, except to naming trustees for you; and if you have any body you would confide in more than another, I would have you speak."

I was so touched with this mournful instance of his excessive goodness, that I was unable to speak; and at last relieved my mind by a violent fit of weeping: and could only say, clasping my arms around the dear generous man, "How shall I support this! So very cruel, yet so very kind!"

"Don't, my dear," said he, "be concerned at what gives *me* pleasure. I am not the nearer my end, for having made this disposition; but I think the putting off these material points, when accidents every day happen, and life so precarious, is a most inexcusable thing. There are many important points to be thought of, when life is drawing to its utmost verge; and the mind may be so agitated and unfit, that it is a most sad thing to defer, to that time, any of those concerns, which more especially require a considerate and composed frame of temper, and perfect health and vigour, to give directions about them. My poor friend, Mr. Charlton, who died in my arms so lately, and had a mind disturbed by worldly considerations on one side, a weakness of body, through the violence of *his distemper*, on another, and the concerns of still as much more moment, as the soul is to the body, on a third, made so great an impression upon me then, that I was the more impatient to come to this

446

house, where were most of my writings, in order to make the dispositions I have now perfected : and since it is grievous to my dear girl, I will think myself of such trustees as shall be most for her benefit. I have only therefore to assure you, my dear, that in this instance, as I will do in any other I can think of, I have studied to make you quite easy, free, and independent. And as I shall avoid all occasions for the future, which may discompose you, I have but one request to make : which is, that if it should please God, for my sins, to separate me from my dearest Pamela, you will only resolve not to marry one person; for I would not be such a Herod, as to restrain you from a change of condition with any other, however reluctantly I may think of any other person succeeding me in your esteem."

I could not answer, and thought my heart would have burst, And he continued : "To conclude at once a subject so grievous to you, I will tell you, my Pamela, that this person is Mr. Williams; and my motive for this request is wholly owing to my niceness, and to no dislike I have for him, or apprehension that it is likely to be so : but methinks, it would reflect a little upon my Pamela, to give way to such a conduct, as if she had married a man for his *estate*, when she had rather have had *another*, had it not been for *that;* and now, the world will say, she is at liberty to pursue her inclination, the parson is the man !—And I cannot bear even the most distant apprehension, that I had not the preference with you of any man living, let me have been what I would, as I have shewn my dear life, that I preferred her to all her sex, of whatever degree."

I could not speak, might I have had the world; and he took me in his arms, and said, "I have now spoken all my mind, and expect no answer; and I see you too much moved to give me one, only say you forgive me. And I hope I have no one discomposing thing to say to my dearest for the rest of my life, —which, I pray God, for both our sakes, to lengthen for many happy years."

Grief still choked up the passage of my words; and he said, "The shower is over, my dear : let us walk out again." He led me out, and I would have spoken, but he said, "I will not hear my dear creature say any thing !" He then most sweetly changed the discourse.

"Don't you with pleasure, my dear, take in the delightful fragrance that this sweet shower has given to these banks of flowers? Your *presence* is so enlivening to me, I could almost fancy what we owe to the shower is owing to *that*." And then, in a sweet and easy accent (with his dear arms about me as he

447

walked), he sung me the following verses; of which he has favoured me with a copy :

All Nature bloom when you appear,
The fields their richest liv'ries wear;
Oaks, elms, and pines, blest with you,
Shoot out fresh greens, and bud anew,
    The varying seasons you supply;
    And when you're gone, they fade and die.

Sweet Philomel, in mournful strains,
To you appeals, to you complains,
The tow'ring lark, on rising wing,
Warbles to you, your praise does sing;
    He cuts the yielding air and flies
    To Heav'n, to type your future joys.

The purple violet, damask rose,
Each to delight your senses, blows :
The lilies ope, as you appear,
And all the beauties of the year
    Diffuse their odours at your feet,
    Who giv'st to ev'ry flow'r its sweet.

For flow'rs and women are ally'd;
Both, Nature's glory and her pride !
Of every fragrant sweet possest
They bloom but for the fair one's breast;
    And to the swelling bosom borne,
    Each other mutually adorn.

Thus sweetly did he palliate the woes, which his generous actions, mixed with the solemness of the occasion, and his strange request, had occasioned. He would permit me only to say, that I was not displeased with him ! " Displeased with you, dearest Sir ! " said I : " let me thus testify my obligations, and the force all your commands shall have upon me." And I took the liberty to clasp my arms about his neck, and kissed him.

But yet my mind was pained at times, and has been to this hour. God grant that I may never see the dreadful moment, that shall shut up the precious life of this excellently generous benefactor of mine ! And—but I cannot bear to suppose—I cannot say more on such a deep subject.

Oh ! what a poor thing is human life in its best enjoyments ! subjected to *imaginary* evils, when it has no *real ones* to disturb it; and can be made as effectually unhappy by its apprehensions of remote contingencies, as if struggling with the pangs of a present distress ! This duly reflected upon, methinks, should convince every one, that this world is not a place for the immortal mind to be confined to; and that there must be an hereafter where the *whole* soul shall be satisfied; where is no mixture, no unsatisfiedness; and where all is joy, peace, and love, for evermore!

I said, at supper, "The charming taste, you gave me, Sir, of your poetical fancy, makes me sure you have more favours of this kind to delight me with; and may I beg to be indulged with them?"—"Hitherto," said he, "my life has been too much a life of gaiety and action, to be busied so innocently.— Some little essays I have now and then attempted; but very few completed. Perhaps I may occasionally shew you what I have essayed. But I never could please myself in this way."

FRIDAY.

We had yesterday the company of almost all the neighbouring gentlemen, and their ladies, who, by appointment with one another, met to congratulate our happiness. Nothing could be more obliging, than the ladies; nothing more polite than the gentlemen. All was performed (for they came to supper) with decency and order, and much to every one's satisfaction; which was principally owing to good Mrs. Jervis's care and skill; who is an excellent manager.

For my part, I was dress'd out, only to be admired, and truly, had I not known that I did not make *myself*, as you, my dear father once hinted to me, and if I had had the vanity to think as well of myself, as the good company did, I might possibly have been proud. But I know, as my Lady Davers said, though in anger, yet in truth, that I am but a *poor bit of painted dirt*. All that I value myself upon is that God has raised me to a condition to be useful, in my generation, to better persons than myself. This is, and I hope will be, all my pride. For what was I of myself? All the good I can do, is but a poor third-hand good; for my dearest master himself is but the second-hand. God, the All gracious, the All-good, the All-bountiful, the Almighty, the All-merciful God, is the first; to HIM, therefore, be all the glory!

As I expect the unspeakable happiness, my ever dear and honoured parents, of enjoying you both, under this roof so soon, I will not enter into the particulars of the last agreeable evening: for I shall have a thousand things, as well as that, to talk to you upon. I fear you will be tired with my prattle when I see you! I am to return these visits singly; and there were eight ladies here of different families. Dear heart! I shall find enough to do!—I doubt my time will not be so well filled up, as I once promised my dear master. But he is pleased, cheerful, kind, affectionate! O what a happy creature am I—May I be always thankful to God, and grateful to *him*!—

When all these tumultuous visitings are over, I shall have my mind, I hope, subside into a family calm, that I may make myself a little useful to the household of my dear master; or else I shall be an unprofitable servant indeed! Lady Davers has sent her compliments to us both, very affectionately: and her lord's good wishes and congratulations: she desired my writings *per* bearer: and says, she will herself return them to me, with thanks, when she has read them; and she and her lord will come and be *my* guests (that was her particular kind word) for a fortnight.

I have now but one thing to wish for, and then, methinks, I shall be all ecstacy, and that is, your presence, both of you, and your blessings; which I hope you will bestow upon me every morning and night, till you are settled in the happy manner my dear Mr. B. has intended.

I tell my dear spouse, I want another dairy-house visit. If he won't at present permit it, I shall, please God to spare us, teaze him like any over-indulged wife, if, as the dear charmer grows *older* he won't let me have the pleasure of forming her tender mind, as well as I am able, lest, poor little soul! she fall into such snares as her unhappy dear mother fell into. I am providing a power of pretty things for her, against I see her next, that I may make her love me, if I can.

Just now I have the blessed news, you will set out hither on Tuesday morning. The chariot shall be with you without fail. God give us a happy meeting! O how I long for it! Forgive your impatient daughter, who sends this to amuse you on your journey; and desires to be *ever most dutifully yours*.

Here end, at present, the letters of PAMELA, to her parents. They arrived at their daughter's house on the Tuesday evening, and were received by her with the utmost joy and duty; and with great goodness and complaisance by Mr. B. And having resided there till every thing was put in order at the Kentish estate, they were carried down thither, by himself, and their daughter, and put in possession of the pretty farm designed for them.

The reader will here indulge us in a few brief observations, which naturally result from the story and characters; and which will serve as so many applications of its most material incidents to the minds of YOUTH OF BOTH SEXES.

450

First, then, in the character of the GENTLEMAN may be seen that of a fashionable libertine, who allowed himself in the free indulgence of his passions, especially as to the fair sex; and found himself supported in his daring attempts, by an affluent fortune in possession, a personal bravery, as it is called, rather to *give* than *take* offence, and an imperious will; yet, as he betimes sees his errors, and reforms in the bloom of youth, an edifying lesson may be drawn from it, for the use of such as are born to large fortunes; and who may be taught, by his example, the inexpressible difference between the hazards and remorse attending a profligate life, and the pleasures flowing from virtuous love, and benevolent actions.

In the character of Lady DAVERS, let the proud and the high-born see the deformity of unreasonable passion, and how weak and ridiculous such persons must appear, who suffer themselves, as is usually the case, to be hurried from the height of violence to the most abject submission; and subject themselves to be outdone by the humble virtue they so much despise.

Let good clergymen, in Mr. WILLIAMS, see, that whatever displeasure the doing their duty may give, for a time, to their proud patrons, Providence will, at last, reward their piety, and turn their distresses to triumph : and make them even *more* valued for a conduct that gave offence while the violence of passion lasted, than if they had meanly stooped to flatter or soothe the vices of the great.

In the examples of good old ANDREWS and his WIFE, let those who are reduced to a low estate see, that Providence never fails to reward honesty and integrity : and that God will, in his own time, extricate them by means unforeseen, out of their present difficulties, and reward them with benefits unhoped for.

The UPPER SERVANTS of great families may, from the odious character of Mrs. Jewkes, and the amiableness of Mrs. Jervis, Mr. Longman, &c. learn what to avoid, and what to choose, to make themselves valued and esteemed by all who know them. And, from the double conduct of poor John, the LOWER SERVANTS may learn fidelity, and how to distinguish between the lawful and unlawful commands of a superior.

The poor deluded female, who, like the unhappy Miss GODFREY, has given up her honour, and yielded to the allurements of a designing lover, may learn, from her story, to stop at the *first fault ;* and, by resolving to repent and amend, see the pardon and blessing which await her penitence, and a kind Providence ready to extend its mercy to receive and reward her returning duty.

451

Let the *desponding heart* be comforted by the happy issue which the troubles and trials of PAMELA met with, when they see that no danger or distress, however inevitable or deep, to their apprehensions, is out of the power of Providence to obviate or relieve; and that, too, at a time when all human prospects seem to fail. Let the *rich*, and those who are *exalted* from a *low* to a *high estate*, learn that they are not promoted only for a *single good ;* but that Providence has raised them, that they should dispense to all within their reach, the blessings heaped upon them; and that the greater the power to which they are raised, the greater good will be expected from them. From the low opinion she every where shews of herself, and her attributing all her excellencies to pious education, and her lady's virtuous instructions and bounty, let persons even of *genius* and *piety*, learn not to arrogate to themselves those gifts and graces, which they owe least of all to themselves; since the beauties of person are frail, and it is not in our power to give them to ourselves, or to be either prudent, wise, or good, without the assistance of Divine Grace. From the same good example, let *children* see what a blessing awaits their duty to their parents, though ever so low in the world; and that the only disgrace is to be dishonest; but none at all to be poor. From the *economy* she purposes to observe, in her elevation, let even *ladies of condition* learn, that there are family employments, in which they may and ought to make themselves useful; and that their duty to God, charity to the poor and sick, and the different branches of household management, ought to take up the most considerable portions of their time.

From her signal *veracity*, which she never forfeited, in all the hardships she was tried with, though her answers, as she had reason to apprehend, would often make against her; and the innocence she preserved in all her stratagems and contrivances to save herself from violation; persons, even *sorely tempted*, may learn to preserve a sacred regard to *truth ;* which always begets a reverence for them, even in the corruptest minds.

In short, her obliging behaviour to her equals, before her exaltation; her kindness to them afterwards; her forgiving spirit, and her generosity;

Her meekness in every circumstance where her virtue was not concerned;

Her charitable allowances for others, as in the case of Miss Godfrey, for faults she would not have forgiven in herself;

Her kindness and prudence to the offspring of that melancholy adventure;

Her maiden and bridal purity, which extend as well to her thoughts, as to her words and actions;

Her signal affiance in God;

Her thankful spirit; her grateful heart;

Her diffusive charity to the poor, which made her blessed by them whenever she appeared abroad:

The cheerful ease and freedom of her deportment;

Her parental, conjugal, and maternal duty;

Her social virtues;

Are all so many signal instances of the excellency of her mind, which may make her character worthy of the imitation of her sex; and the editor of these sheets will have his end, if it inspires a laudable emulation in the minds of any worthy persons, who may thereby entitle themselves to the rewards, the praises and the blessings, by which PAMELA was so deservedly distinguished.

END OF THE FIRST PART.

EVERYMAN'S LIBRARY: A Selected List

BIOGRAPHY

Baxter, Richard (1615–91). THE AUTOBIOGRAPHY OF RICHARD BAXTER. 868
Brontë, Charlotte (1816–55). LIFE, 1857. By *Mrs Gaskell*. 318
Byron, Lord (1788–1824). LETTERS. Edited by *R. G. Howarth*, B.LITT. 931
Cellini, Benvenuto (1500–71). THE LIFE OF BENVENUTO CELLINI, written by himself. 51
Dickens, Charles (1812–70). LIFE, 1874. By *John Forster* (1812–76). 2 vols. 781–2
Evelyn, John (1620–1706). DIARY. Edited by *William Bray*, 1819. 220–1
Franklin, Benjamin (1706–90). AUTOBIOGRAPHY, 1817. 316
Goethe, Johann Wolfgang von (1749–1832). LIFE, 1855. By *G. H. Lewes* (1817–78). 269
Hudson, William Henry (1841–1922). FAR AWAY AND LONG AGO, 1918. 956
Johnson, Samuel (1709–84). LIVES OF THE ENGLISH POETS, 1781. 2 vols. 770–1.
  BOSWELL'S LIFE OF JOHNSON, 1791. A new edition (1949). 1–2
Keats, John (1795–1821). LIFE AND LETTERS, 1848. by *Lord Houghton* (1809–85) 801
Lamb, Charles (1775–1834). LETTERS. New edition (1945) arranged from the Complete
  Annotated Edition of the Letters. 2 vols. 342–3
Nelson, Horatio, Viscount (1758–1805). LIFE, 1813. By *Robert Southey* (1774–1843). 52
Pepys, Samuel (1633–1703). DIARY. Newly edited (1953), with modernized spelling.
  3 vols. 53–5
Plutarch (46?–120). LIVES OF THE NOBLE GREEKS AND ROMANS. Dryden's edition.
  3 vols. 407–9
Rousseau, Jean Jacques (1712–78). CONFESSIONS, 1782. 2 vols. Complete and un-
  abridged. 859–60
Scott, Sir Walter (1771–1832). LOCKHART'S LIFE OF SCOTT. An abridgement from the
  seven-volume work by *J. G. Lockhart* himself. 39
Swift, Jonathan (1667–1745). JOURNAL TO STELLA, 1710–13. 757
Vasari Giorgio (1511–74). LIVES OF THE PAINTERS, SCULPTORS AND ARCHITECTS.
  Newly edited by *William Gaunt*. 4 vols. 784–7
Walpole, Horace (1717–97). SELECTED LETTERS. Edited, with Introduction, by *W.
  Hadley*, M.A. 775
Wellington, Arthur Wellesley, Duke of (1769–1852). LIFE, 1862 By *G. R. Gleig* (1796–
  1888). 341

ESSAYS AND CRITICISM

Anthology of ENGLISH PROSE, FROM BEDE TO STEVENSON. 675
Bacon, Francis, Lord Verulam (1561–1626). ESSAYS, 1597–1626. 10
Bagehot, Walter (1826–77). LITERARY STUDIES, 1879. 2 vols. 520–1
Belloc, Hilaire (1870–1953). STORIES, ESSAYS AND POEMS. 948
Burke, Edmund (1729–97). REFLECTIONS ON THE FRENCH REVOLUTION (1790). 460
Carlyle, Thomas (1795–1881). ESSAYS. Introduction by *J. R. Lowell*. 2 vols. Essays on
  men and affairs. 703–4. PAST AND PRESENT, 1843. New Introduction by *Douglas
  Jerrold*. 608. SARTOR RESARTUS, 1838; and HEROES AND HERO-WORSHIP, 1841. 278
Castiglione, Baldassare (1478–1529). THE BOOK OF THE COURTIER, 1528. *Sir Thomas
  Hoby's* Translation, 1561. 807
Century. A CENTURY OF ENGLISH ESSAYS, FROM CAXTON TO BELLOC. 653
Chesterfield, Earl of (1694–1773). LETTERS TO HIS SON; AND OTHERS. 823
Chesterton, Gilbert Keith (1874–1936). STORIES, ESSAYS AND POEMS. 913
Coleridge, Samuel Taylor (1772–1834). BIOGRAPHIA LITERARIA, 1817. 11. SHAKE-
  SPEAREAN CRITICISM, 1849. Edited by *Prof. T. M. Raysor* (1960), 2 vols. 162, 183
De la Mare, Walter (1873–1956). STORIES, ESSAYS AND POEMS. 940
De Quincey, Thomas (1785–1859). CONFESSIONS OF AN ENGLISH OPIUM-EATER, 1822.
  Edited by *Prof. J. E. Jordan* (1960). 223. ENGLISH MAIL-COACH AND OTHER
  ESSAYS. Edited by *Prof. J. E. Jordan*. 609
Eckermann, Johann Peter (1792–1854). CONVERSATIONS WITH GOETHE, 1836–8. Trans-
  lated by *John Oxenford*. Edited by *J. K. Moorhead*. 851
Elyot, Sir Thomas (1490?–1546). THE GOVERNOR. Edited with Introduction by *S. E.
  Lehmberg*. 227
Emerson, Ralph Waldo (1803–82). ESSAYS, 1841–4. 12
Gilfillan, George (1813–78). A GALLERY OF LITERARY PORTRAITS, 1845–54. 348
Gray, Thomas (1716–71). ESSAYS. (*See* Poetry.)
Hamilton, Alexander (1757–1804), and Others. THE FEDERALIST, 1787–8. 519

Hazlitt, William (1778–1830). LECTURES ON THE ENGLISH COMIC WRITERS, 1819; and FUGITIVE WRITINGS 411. LECTURES ON THE ENGLISH POETS, 1818, etc., 1825. 459. THE ROUND TABLE and CHARACTERS OF SHAKESPEAR'S PLAYS, 1817–18. 65. TABLE TALK, 1821–2, 321

Holmes, Oliver Wendell (1809–94). THE AUTOCRAT OF THE BREAKFAST-TABLE, 1858. 66

Hunt, Leigh (1784–1859). SELECTED ESSAYS. 78 essays.   829

Huxley, Aldous Leonard (b. 1894). STORIES, ESSAYS AND POEMS.   935

Johnson, Samuel (1709–84). THE RAMBLER.   994

Lamb, Charles (1775–1834). ESSAYS OF ELIA AND LAST ESSAYS OF ELIA, 1823–33.   14

Landor, Walter Savage (1775–1864). IMAGINARY CONVERSATIONS, AND POEMS, 1824–9, 1853.   890

Lawrence, David Herbert (1885–1930). STORIES, ESSAYS AND POEMS.   958

Locke, John (1632–1704). AN ESSAY CONCERNING HUMAN UNDERSTANDING, 1690. 2 vols.   332, 984

Lynd, Robert (1879–1949). ESSAYS ON LIFE AND LITERATURE.   990

Macaulay, Thomas Babington, Lord (1800–59). CRITICAL AND HISTORICAL ESSAYS, 1843. 2 vols. 225–6.   MISCELLANEOUS ESSAYS, 1823–59; LAYS OF ANCIENT ROME, 1842; and MISCELLANEOUS POEMS, 1812–47. 439

Machiavelli, Niccolò (1469–1527). THE PRINCE, 1513.   280

Mazzini, Joseph (1805–72). THE DUTIES OF MAN.   224

Milton, John (1608–74). PROSE WRITINGS.   795

Mitford, Mary Russell (1787–1855). OUR VILLAGE, 1824–32. Edited by Sir John Squire.   927

Modern Humour. An Anthology in Prose and Verse from over sixty authors.   957

Napoleon Buonaparte (1769–1821). LETTERS. Some 300 letters.   995

Newman, John Henry (1801–90). ON THE SCOPE AND NATURE OF UNIVERSITY EDUCATION; and CHRISTIANITY AND SCIENTIFIC INVESTIGATION, 1852.   723

Quiller-Couch, Sir Arthur (1863–1944). CAMBRIDGE LECTURES.   974

Rousseau, Jean Jacques (1712–78). ÉMILE; OR, EDUCATION.   518

Ruskin, John (1819–1900). SESAME AND LILIES, 1864; THE TWO PATHS, 1859; and THE KING OF THE GOLDEN RIVER; or THE BLACK BROTHERS, 1851. 219. THE SEVEN LAMPS OF ARCHITECTURE, 1849. 207

Sévigné, Marie de Rabutin-Chantal, Marquise de (1626–96). SELECTED LETTERS.   98

Spectator, The, 1711–14. 4 vols.   164–7

Spencer, Herbert (1820–1903). ESSAYS ON EDUCATION, 1861.   504

Steele, Sir Richard (1672–1729). THE TATLER, 1709–11.   993

Stevenson, Robert Louis (1850–94). VIRGINIBUS PUERISQUE, 1881. etc.   765

Swift, Jonathan (1667–1745). A TALE OF A TUB, 1704; THE BATTLE OF THE BOOKS, 1704, etc.   347

Swinnerton, Frank (b. 1884). THE GEORGIAN LITERARY SCENE. Revised 1951.   943

Thackeray, William Makepeace (1811–63). THE ENGLISH HUMOURISTS, 1851; CHARITY AND HUMOUR, 1853; and THE FOUR GEORGES, 1855.   610

Thoreau, Henry David (1817–62). WALDEN, OR LIFE IN THE WOODS, 1854.   281

Trench, Richard Chevenix (1807–86). ON THE STUDY OF WORDS, 1851; and ENGLISH PAST AND PRESENT, 1855.   788

Tytler, Alexander Fraser (1747–1814). ESSAY ON THE PRINCIPLES OF TRANSLATION, 1791.   168

Walton, Izaak (1593–1683). THE COMPLETE ANGLER, 1653.   70

FICTION

Ainsworth, William Harrison (1805–82). ROOKWOOD, 1834. Dick Turpin's ride. 870. THE TOWER OF LONDON, 1840. Lady Jane Grey. 400.   WINDSOR CASTLE, 1843. Henry VIII and Ann Boleyn. 709

American Short Stories of the 19th Century.   840

Andersen, Hans Christian (1805–75). FAIRY TALES AND STORIES. Reginald Spink Translation.   4

Austen, Jane (1775–1817). EMMA, 1816. 24.   MANSFIELD PARK, 1814. 23.   PRIDE AND PREJUDICE, 1823. 22.   SENSE AND SENSIBILITY, 1811. 21.   NORTHANGER ABBEY, 1818; and PERSUASION, 1818. 25

Balzac, Honoré de (1799–1850). AT THE SIGN OF THE CAT AND RACKET, 1830; and OTHER STORIES. Translated by Clara Bell. 349.   THE COUNTRY DOCTOR, 1833, 530. EUGÉNIE GRANDET, 1834. Translated by Ellen Marriage. 169.   OLD GORIOT, 1835. Translated by Ellen Marriage. 170.   THE WILD ASS'S SKIN, 1831. 26

Barbusse, Henri (1874–1935). UNDER FIRE, THE STORY OF A SQUAD, 1916.   798

Beaconsfield, Benjamin Disraeli, Earl of (1804–81). CONINGSBY, 1844.   535

Bennett, Arnold (1867–1931). THE OLD WIVES' TALE, 1908.   919

Blackmore, Richard Doddridge (1825–1900). LORNA DOONE: A ROMANCE OF EXMOOR, 1869.   304

Boccaccio, Giovanni (1313–75). DECAMERON, 1471. The unabridged Rigg Translation. 2 vols.   845–6

Borrow, George (1803–81). THE ROMANY RYE, 1857. Practically a sequel to Lavengro. 120

Brontë, Anne (1820–49). THE TENANT OF WILDFELL HALL and AGNES GREY.   685

2

Brontë, Charlotte (1816–55). For Mrs Gaskell's 'Life' *see* Biography. JANE EYRE, 1847. 287. THE PROFESSOR, 1857. 417. SHIRLEY, 1849. 288. VILLETTE, 1853. 351
Brontë, Emily (1818–48). WUTHERING HEIGHTS, 1848; and POEMS.   243
Bunyan, John (1628–88). PILGRIM'S PROGRESS, Parts I and II, 1678–84. Reset edition.
                                                                                    204
Burney, Fanny (Madame Frances d'Arblay, 1753–1849). EVELINA, 1778.   352
Butler, Samuel (1835–1902). EREWHON, 1872 (revised 1901); and EREWHON REVISITED, 1901. 881. THE WAY OF ALL FLESH. 1903. 895
Cervantes Saavedra, Miguel de (1547–1616). DON QUIXOTE DE LA MANCHA. Translated by *P. A. Motteux*. 2 vols.   385–6
Collins, Wilkie (1824–89). THE MOONSTONE, 1868. 979. THE WOMAN IN WHITE, 1860.
                                                                                    464
Conrad, Joseph (1857–1924). LORD JIM, 1900. Typically set in the East Indies. 925. THE NIGGER OF THE 'NARCISSUS'; TYPHOON; and THE SHADOW LINE. 980. NOSTROMO, 1904. New edition of Conrad's greatest novel. 38. THE SECRET AGENT, 1907. 282
Cooper, James Fenimore (1789–1851). THE LAST OF THE MOHICANS, 1826, A NARRATIVE OF 1757.   79
Daudet, Alphonse (1840–97). TARTARIN OF TARASCON, 1872; and TARTARIN ON THE ALPS, 1885.   423
Defoe, Daniel (1661?–1731). THE FORTUNES AND MISFORTUNES OF MOLL FLANDERS, 1722. 837. JOURNAL OF THE PLAGUE YEAR, 1722. 289. LIFE, ADVENTURES OF THE FAMOUS CAPTAIN SINGLETON, 1720. 74. ROBINSON CRUSOE, 1719. Parts 1 and 2 complete. 59
De Rojas, Fernando (15th century). CELESTINA: OR THE TRAGI-COMEDY OF CALISTO AND MELIBEA. Translation by *Phyllis Hartnell*, M.A.   100
Dickens, Charles (1812–70). BARNABY RUDGE, 1841. 76. BLEAK HOUSE, 1852–3. 236. CHRISTMAS BOOKS, 1843–8. 239. CHRISTMAS STORIES, 1850–67. 414. DAVID COPPERFIELD, 1849–50. 242. DOMBEY AND SON, 1846–8. 240. GREAT EXPECTATIONS, 1861. 234. HARD TIMES, 1854. 292. LITTLE DORRIT, 1857. 293. MARTIN CHUZZLEWIT, 1843–4. 241. NICHOLAS NICKLEBY, 1838–9. 238. OLD CURIOSITY SHOP, 1841. 173. OLIVER TWIST, 1838. 233. OUR MUTUAL FRIEND, 1864–5. 294. PICKWICK PAPERS, 1836–7. 235. A TALE OF TWO CITIES, 1859. 102
                                                                (See also Biography.)
Dostoyevsky, Fyodor (1821–81). THE BROTHERS KARAMAZOV, 1879–80. Translated by *Cons'ance Garnett*. 2 vols. 802–3. CRIME AND PUNISHMENT, 1866. *Constance Garnett* Translation. 501. THE IDIOT, 1873. Translated by *Eva M. Martin*. 682. LETTERS FROM THE UNDERWORLD, 1864; and OTHER TALES. 654. POOR FOLK, 1845; and THE GAMBLER, 1867. 711. THE POSSESSED, 1871. Translated by *Constance Garnett*. 2 vols. 861–2
Dumas, Alexandre (1802–70). THE BLACK TULIP, 1850. The brothers De Witt in Holland, 1672–5. 174. COUNT OF MONTE CRISTO, 1844. 2 vols. Napoleon's later phase. 393–4. MARGUERITE DE VALOIS, 1845. The Eve of St Bartholomew. 326. THE THREE MUSKETEERS, 1844. The France of Cardinal Richelieu. 81
Du Maurier, George Louis Palmella Busson (1834–96). TRILBY, 1894.   863
Edgeworth, Maria (1767–1849). CASTLE RACKRENT, 1800; and THE ABSENTEE 1812.
                                                                                    410
Eliot, George. ADAM BEDE, 1859. 27. DANIEL DERONDA, 1876. 2 vols. 539–40. MIDDLEMARCH, 1872. 2 vols. 854–5. THE MILL ON THE FLOSS, 1860. 325. ROMOLA, 1863. The Florence of Savonarola. 231. SILAS MARNER, THE WEAVER OF RAVELOE, 1861. 121
English Short Stories. Thirty-six stories from Middle Ages to present time.   743
Fielding, Henry (1707–54). AMELIA, 1751. 2 vols. Amelia is drawn from Fielding's first wife. 852–3. JONATHAN WILD, 1743; and JOURNAL OF A VOYAGE TO LISBON, 1755. 877. JOSEPH ANDREWS, 1742. A skit on Richardson's *Pamela*. 467. TOM JONES, 1749. 2 vols. The first great English novel of humour. 355–6
Flaubert, Gustave (1821–80). MADAME BOVARY, 1857. Translated by *Eleanor Marx-Aveling*. 808. SALAMMBO, 1862. Translated by *J. C. Chartres*. 869. SENTIMENTAL EDUCATION, 1869. Translation by *Anthony Goldsmith*. 969
Forster, Edward Morgan (*b.* 1879). A PASSAGE TO INDIA, 1924.   972
Galsworthy, John (1867–1933). THE COUNTRY HOUSE.   917
Gaskell, Mrs Elizabeth (1810–65). CRANFORD, 1853.   83
Ghost Stories. Eighteen stories.   952
Gogol, Nikolay (1809–52). DEAD SOULS, 1842.   726
Goldsmith, Oliver (1728–74). THE VICAR OF WAKEFIELD, 1766.   295
Goncharov, Ivan (1812–91). OBLOMOV, 1857. Translated by *Natalie Duddington*.   878
Gorky, Maxim (1868–1936). THROUGH RUSSIA.   741
Grossmith, George (1847–1912), and **Weedon** (1853–1919). DIARY OF A NOBODY, 1894.
                                                                                    963
Hawthorne, Nathaniel (1804–64). THE HOUSE OF THE SEVEN GABLES, 1851. 176. THE SCARLET LETTER: 1850. 122. TWICE-TOLD TALES, 1837–42. 531
Hugo, Victor Marie (1802–85). LES MISÉRABLES, 1862. 2 vols. 363–4. NOTRE DAME DE PARIS ,1831. 422. TOILERS OF THE SEA, 1866. 509
James, Henry (1843–1916). THE AMBASSADORS, 1903. 987. THE TURN OF THE SCREW 1898; and THE ASPERN PAPERS, 1888. 912

Jefferies, Richard (1848–87). AFTER LONDON, 1884; and AMARYLLIS AT THE FAIR, 1886. 951

Jerome, Jerome K. (1859–1927). THREE MEN IN A BOAT and THREE MEN ON THE BUMMEL. 118

Kingsley, Charles (1819–75). HEREWARD THE WAKE, 1866. 296. WESTWARD HO!, 1855. 20

Lamb, Charles (1775–1834), and **Mary** (1764–1847). TALES FROM SHAKESPEARE, 1807. Illustrated by *Arthur Rackham.* 8

Lawrence, David Herbert (1885–1930). THE WHITE PEACOCK, 1911. 914

Loti, Pierre (1850–1923). ICELAND FISHERMAN, 1886. 920

Lover, Samuel (1797–1868). HANDY ANDY, 1842. 178

Lytton, Edward Bulwer, Baron (1803–73). THE LAST DAYS OF POMPEII, 1834. 80

Malory, Sir Thomas (fl. 1400 ?–70). LE MORTE D'ARTHUR. 45–6

Mann, Thomas (1875–1955). STORIES AND EPISODES. 962

Manzoni, Alessandro (1785–1873). THE BETROTHED (*I Promessi Sposi*, 1840, rev. ed.). Translated (1951) from the Italian by *Archibald Colquhoun.* 999

Marie de France (12th century), LAYS OF, AND OTHER FRENCH LEGENDS. 557

Marryat, Frederick (1792–1848). MR MIDSHIPMAN EASY. 82. THE SETTLERS IN CANADA, 1844. 370

Maugham, W. Somerset (b. 1874). CAKES AND ALE, 1930. 932

Maupassant, Guy de (1850–93). SHORT STORIES. Translated by *Marjorie Laurie.* 907

Melville, Herman (1819–91). MOBY DICK, 1851. 179. TYPEE, 1846; and BILLY BUDD (*published*) 1924). South Seas adventures. 180

Meredith, George (1828–1909). THE ORDEAL OF RICHARD FEVEREL, 1859. 916

Mickiewicz, Adam (1798–1855). PAN TADEUSZ, 1834. Translated by *Prof. G. R. Noyes.* Poland and Napoleon. 842

Modern Short Stories. Selected by *John Hadfield.* Twenty stories. 954

Moore, George (1852–1933). ESTHER WATERS, 1894. 933

Mulock [Mrs Craik], Maria (1826–87). JOHN HALIFAX, GENTLEMAN, 1856. 123

Pater, Walter (1839–94). MARIUS THE EPICUREAN, 1885. 903

Poe, Edgar Allan (1809–49). TALES OF MYSTERY AND IMAGINATION. 336

Priestley, J. B. (b. 1894). ANGEL PAVEMENT, 1931. A finely conceived London novel. 938

Quiller-Couch, Sir Arthur (1863–1944). HETTY WESLEY, 1903. 864

Rabelais, François (1494 ?–1553). THE HEROIC DEEDS OF GARGANTUA AND PANTAGRUEL, 1532–5. 2 vols. *Urquhart and Motteux's* unabridged Translation, 1653–94. 826–7

Radcliffe, Mrs Ann (1764–1823). THE MYSTERIES OF UDOLPHO, 1794. 2vols. 865–6

Reade, Charles (1814–84). THE CLOISTER AND THE HEARTH, 1861. 29

Richardson, Samuel (1689–1761). PAMELA, 1740. 2 vols. 683–4. CLARISSA, 1747–8. 4 vols. 882–5

Russian Short Stories. Translated by *Rochelle S. Townsend.* 758

Scott, Sir Walter (1771–1832). THE ANTIQUARY, 1816. 126. THE BRIDE OF LAMMERMOOR, 1819. A romance of life in East Lothian, 1695. 129. GUY MANNERING, 1815. A mystery story of the time of George III. 133. THE HEART OF MIDLOTHIAN, 1818. Period of the Porteous Riots, 1736. 134. IVANHOE, 1820. A romance of the days of Richard I. 16. KENILWORTH, 1821. The tragic story of Amy Robsart, in Elizabeth I's time. 135. OLD MORTALITY, 1817. Battle of Bothwell Bridge, 1679. 137. QUENTIN DURWARD, 1823. A tale of fifteenth-century France. 140. REDGAUNTLET, 1824. A tale of adventure in Cumberland, about 1763. 141. ROB ROY, 1818. A romance of the Rebellion of 1715. 142. THE TALISMAN. 1825. Richard Cœur-de-Lion and the Third Crusade, 1191. 144

Shchedrin (M. E. Saltykov, 1826–92). THE GOLOVLYOV FAMILY, Translated by *Natalie Duddington.* 908

Shelley, Mary Wollstonecraft (1797–1851). FRANKENSTEIN, 1818. 616

Shorter Novels. VOL. I: ELIZABETHAN. 824. VOL. II: SEVENTEENTH CENTURY. 841. VOL. III: EIGHTEENTH CENTURY. All 3 vols. are edited by *Philip Henderson.* 856

Sienkiewicz, Henryk (1846–1916). QUO VADIS ? 1896. Translated by *C. J. Hogarth.* 970. TALES. Edited by *Monica Gardner.* 871

Smollett, Tobias (1721–71). THE EXPEDITION OF HUMPHRY CLINKER, 1771. 975. PEREGRINE PICKLE, 1751. 2 vols. 838–9. RODERICK RANDOM, 1742. 790

Somerville, E. Œ. (1858–1949), and **Ross, Martin** (1862–1915). EXPERIENCES OF AN IRISH R.M., 1908. 978

Stendhal (pseudonym of Henri Beyle, 1783–1842). SCARLET AND BLACK, 1831. Translated by *C. K. Scott Moncrieff.* 2 vols. 945–6

Sterne, Laurence (1713–68). A SENTIMENTAL JOURNEY THROUGH FRANCE AND ITALY 1768: JOURNAL TO ELIZA, written in 1767; and LETTERS TO ELIZA, 1766–7. 796. TRISTRAM SHANDY, 1760–7. 617

Stevenson, Robert Louis (1850–94). DR JEKYLL AND MR HYDE, 1886; THE MERRY MEN, 1887; WILL O' THE MILL, 1878; MARKHEIM, 1886; THRAWN JANET, 1881; OLALLA. 1885; THE TREASURE OF FRANCHARD. 767. KIDNAPPED, 1886; and CATRONA, 1893. 762. THE MASTER OF BALLANTRAE, 1869; WEIR OF HERMISTON, 1896. 764. ST IVES, 1898. Completed by Sir Arthur Quiller-Couch. 904. TREASURE ISLAND, 1883; and NEW ARABIAN NIGHTS, 1886. 763

Story Book for Boys and Girls. Edited by *Guy Pocock* (1955). 934

Surtees, Robert Smith (1803–64). JORROCKS'S JAUNTS AND JOLLITIES, 1838. 817

Swift, Jonathan (1667–1745). GULLIVER'S TRAVELS, 1726. An unabridged edition. 60
Tales of Detection. Nineteen stories. 928
Thackeray, William Makepeace (1811–63). HENRY ESMOND, 1852. 73. THE NEWCOMES, 1853–5. 2 vols. 465–6. PENDENNIS, 1848–50. 2 vols. 425–6. VANITY FAIR, 1847–8. 298. THE VIRGINIANS, 1857–9. 2 vols. 507–8
Tolstoy, Count Leo (1828–1910). ANNA KARENINA, 1873–7. Translated by *Rochelle S. Townsend*. 2 vols. 612–13. MASTER AND MAN, 1895; and OTHER PARABLES AND TALES. 469. WAR AND PEACE, 1864–9. 3 vols. 525–7
Trollope, Anthony (1815–82). THE WARDEN, 1855. 182. BARCHESTER TOWERS, 1857. 30. DOCTOR THORNE, 1858. 360. FRAMLEY PARSONAGE, 1861. 181. THE SMALL HOUSE AT ALLINGTON, 1864. 361. THE LAST CHRONICLE OF BARSET, 1867. 2 vols. 391–2
Turgenev, Ivan (1818–83). FATHERS AND SONS, 1862. Translated by *Dr Avril Pyman*. 742. SMOKE, 1867. Translated by *Natalie Duddington*. 988. VIRGIN SOIL, 1877. Translated by *Rochelle S. Townsend*. 528
Twain, Mark (pseudonym of Samuel Langhorne Clemens, 1835–1910). TOM SAWYER, 1876; and HUCKLEBERRY FINN 1884. 976
Verne, Jules (1828–1905). FIVE WEEKS IN A BALLOON, 1862, translated by *Arthur Chambers*; and AROUND THE WORLD IN EIGHTY DAYS, translated by *P. Desages*. 779. TWENTY THOUSAND LEAGUES UNDER THE SEA, 1869. 319
Voltaire, François Marie Arouet de (1694–1778). CANDIDE, AND OTHER TALES. *Smollett's* Translation, edited by *J. C. Thornton*. 936
Walpole, Hugh Seymour (1884–1941). Mr PERRIN and Mr TRAILL, 1911. 918
Wells, Herbert George (1866–1946). ANN VERONICA, 1909. 977. THE WHEELS OF CHANCE, 1896; and THE TIME MACHINE, 1895. 915
Woolf, Virginia (1882–1941). TO THE LIGHTHOUSE, 1927. 949
Zola, Émile (1840–1902). GERMINAL, 1885. Translated by *Havelock Ellis*. 897

HISTORY

Anglo-Saxon Chronicle. Translated by *G. N. Garmonsway*, F.R.HIST.SOC. 624
Bede, the Venerable (673–735). THE ECCLESIASTICAL HISTORY OF THE ENGLISH NATION. Translated by *John Stevens*. 479
British Orations. 1960 edition. 714
Burke, Edmund (1729–97). SPEECHES AND LETTERS ON AMERICAN AFFAIRS. 340
Carlyle, Thomas (1795–1881). THE FRENCH REVOLUTION, 1837. 2 vols. 31–2
Caesar, Julius (102?–44 B.C.). WAR COMMENTARIES. 'The Gallic Wars' and 'The Civil War'. 702
Chesterton, Cecil (1879–1918). A HISTORY OF THE U.S.A., 1917. Edited by *Prof. D. W. Brogan*, M.A. 965
Creasy, Sir Edward (1812–78). FIFTEEN DECISIVE BATTLES OF THE WORLD, 1852. 300
Demosthenes (384–322 B.C.). PUBLIC ORATIONS. 546
Gibbon, Edward (1737–94). THE DECLINE AND FALL OF THE ROMAN EMPIRE, 1776–88. Complete text. 6 vols. 434–6, 474–6
Green, John Richard (1837–83). A SHORT HISTORY, 1874. 727–8
Holinshed, Raphael (d. 1580?). HOLINSHED'S CHRONICLE, 1578. 800
Lincoln, Abraham (1809–65). SPEECHES AND LETTERS, 1832–65. 206
Lützow, Count Franz von (1849–1916). BOHEMIA: AN HISTORICAL SKETCH, 1896. 432
Mabinogion, The. Translated by *Gwyn and Thomas Jones*. 97
Macaulay, Thomas Babington, Baron (1800–59). THE HISTORY OF ENGLAND. 34–7
Maine, Sir Henry (1822–88). ANCIENT LAW, 1861. 734
Motley, John (1814–77). THE RISE OF THE DUTCH REPUBLIC, 1856. 3 vols. 86–8
Paston Letters, The, 1418–1506. 2 vols. A selection. 752–3
Prescott, William Hickling (1796–1859). HISTORY OF THE CONQUEST OF MEXICO, 1843. 2 vols. 397–8. THE HISTORY OF THE CONQUEST OF PERU, 1847. 301
Thucydides (c. 460–401 B.C.). HISTORY OF THE PELOPONNESIAN WAR. Translation by *Richard Crawley*. 455
Villehardouin, Geoffrey de (1160?–1213?), and **Joinville, Jean, Sire de** (1224–1317). MEMOIRS OF THE CRUSADES. Translated by *Sir Frank T. Marzials*. 333
Voltaire, François Marie Arouet de (1694–1778). THE AGE OF LOUIS XIV, 1751. Translated by *Martyn P. Pollack*. 780

LEGENDS AND SAGAS

Chrétien de Troyes (fl. 12th cent.). ARTHURIAN ROMANCES. 698
Kalevala, or The Land of Heroes. Translated by *W. F. Kirby*. 2 vols. 259–60
Njal's Saga. THE STORY OF BURNT NJAL (written about 1280–90). Translated from the Icelandic by *Sir G. W. Dasent* (1862). 558
Sturluson (1178–1241). HEIMSKRINGLA: Volume One: The Olaf Sagas. 2 vols. 717, 722. Volume Two: Sagas of the Norse Kings. 847

POETRY AND DRAMA

Aeschylus (525–455 B.C.). PLAYS. Translated into English Verse by *G. M. Cookson.* 62
Anglo-Saxon Poetry. A.D. 650 to 1000. Translated by *Prof. R. K. Gordon,* M.A. 794
Arnold, Matthew (1822–88). COMPLETE POEMS. 334
Ballads, A Book of British. 572
Beaumont, Francis (1584–1616). and Fletcher, John (1579–1625). SELECT PLAYS. 506
Blake, William (1757–1827). POEMS AND PROPHECIES. Edited by *Max Plowman.* 792
Browning, Robert (1812–89). POEMS AND PLAYS, 1833–64. 2 vols. 41–2. POEMS,
  1871–90. 2 vols. 964, 966
Burns, Robert (1759–96). POEMS AND SONGS. An authoritative edition. 94
Byron, George Gordon Noel, Lord (1788–1824). THE POETICAL AND DRAMATIC WORKS.
  3 vols. Edited by *Guy Pocock.* 486–8
Century. A CENTURY OF HUMOROUS VERSE, 1850–1950. 813
Chaucer, Geoffrey (c. 1343–1400). CANTERBURY TALES. New standard text edited by
  A. C. Cawley, M.A., PH.D. 307. TROILUS AND CRISEYDE. 992
Coleridge, Samuel Taylor (1772–1834). POEMS. 43
Cowper, William (1731–1800). POEMS. 872
Dante Alighieri (1265–1321). THE DIVINE COMEDY. *H. F. Cary's* Translation. 308
Donne, John (1573–1631). COMPLETE POEMS. Edited, with a revised Intro., by *Hugh
  I'Anson Fausset.* 867
Dryden, John (1631–1700). POEMS. Edited by *Bonamy Dobrée,* O.B.E., M.A. 910
Eighteenth-century Plays. Edited by *John Hampden.* 818
English Galaxy of Shorter Poems, The. Chosen and Edited by *Gerald Bullett.* 959
English Religious Verse. Edited by *G. Lacey May.* 937
Euripides (484 ?–407 B.C.). PLAYS. Translated by *A. S. Way,* D.LITT. 2 vols. 63, 271
Everyman, and Medieval Miracle Plays. Edited by *A. C. Cawley,* M.A., PH.D. 381
Goethe, Johann Wolfgang von (1749–1832). FAUST. Both parts of the tragedy, in the
  re-edited translation of *Sir Theodore Martin.* 335
Golden Book of Modern English Poetry, The. Edited by *Thomas Caldwell* and *Philip
  Henderson.* 921
Golden Treasury of English Songs and Lyrics, The, 1861. Compiled by Francis Turner
  Palgrave (1824–97). Enlarged edition, containing 88-page supplement. 96
Golden Treasury of Longer Poems, The. Revised edition (1954). 746
Goldsmith, Oliver (1728–74). POEMS AND PLAYS. Edited by *Austin Dobson.* 415
Gray, Thomas (1716–71). POEMS: WITH A SELECTION OF LETTERS AND ESSAYS. 628
Heine, Heinrich (c. 1797–1856). PROSE AND POETRY. With Matthew Arnold's essay
  on Heine. 911
Homer (? ninth century B.C.). ILIAD. New verse translation by *S. O. Andrew* and
  Michael Oakley. 453. ODYSSEY. The new verse translation (first published 1953) by
  S. O. Andrew. 454
Ibsen, Henrik (1828–1906). BRAND, a poetic drama. 1866. Translated by *F. E. Garrett.*
  716. A DOLL'S HOUSE, 1879; THE WILD DUCK, 1884; and THE LADY FROM THE SEA,
  1888. Translated by *R. Farquharson Sharp* and *Eleanor Marx-Aveling.* 494.
  GHOSTS, 1881; THE WARRIORS AT HELGELAND, 1857; and AN ENEMY OF THE PEOPLE,
  1882. Translated by *R. Farquharson Sharp.* 552. PEER GYNT, 1867. Translated by
  R. Farquharson Sharp. 747. THE PRETENDERS. 1864; PILLARS OF SOCIETY, 1877;
  and ROSMERSHOLM, 1887. Translated by *R. Farquharson Sharp.* 659
Ingoldsby Legends. Edited by *D. C. Browning,* M.A., B.LITT. 185
International Modern Plays. 989
Jonson, Ben (1573–1637). PLAYS. 2 vols. Complete collection. 489–90
Juvenal (c. A.D. 50–c. 130). SATIRES: with THE SATIRES OF PERSIUS. Introduction by
  Prof. H. J. Rose, M.A., F.B.A. *William Gifford* Translation, 1802. Revised by *John
  Warrington.* 997
Keats, John (1795–1821). POEMS. Revised, reset edition (1944). Ed. by *Gerald Bullett.*
  101
Kingsley, Charles (1819–75). POEMS. 793
La Fontaine, Jean de (1621–95). FABLES, 1668. *Sir Edward Marsh* Translation. 991
'Langland, William' (1330 ?–1400 ?). PIERS PLOWMAN, 1362. 571
Lessing, Gotthold Ephraim (1729–81). LAOCOÖN, 1766, etc. 843
Longfellow, Henry Wadsworth (1807–82). POEMS, 1823–66. 382
Marlowe, Christopher (1564–93). PLAYS AND POEMS. New edition by *M. R. Ridley,* M.A.
  383
Milton, John (1608–74). POEMS. New edition by *Prof. B. A. Wright,* M.A. 384
Minor Elizabethan Drama. 2 vols. Vol. I. Tragedy. Vol. II. Comedy. 491–2
Minor Poets of the Seventeenth Century. Edited and revised by *R. G. Howarth,* B.A.,
  B.LITT., F.R.S.L. 873
Modern Plays. 942
Molière, Jean Baptiste de (1622–73). COMEDIES. 2 vols. 830–1
New Golden Treasury. 695
Ovid (43 B.C.–A.D. 18). SELECTED WORKS. Chosen by *J. C.* and *M. J. Thornton.* 955
Persian Poems. Selected and edited by *Prof. A. J. Arberry,* M.A., LITT.D., F.B.A. 996
Poe, Edgar Allan (1809–49). POEMS AND ESSAYS. 791
Poems of our Time. An Anthology edited by *Richard Church,* C.B.E., *M. M. Bozman*
  and *Edith Sitwell,* D.LITT., D.B.E. Nearly 400 poems by about 130 poets. 981

Pope, Alexander (1688–1744). COLLECTED POEMS. Edited (1956) by *Prof. Bonamy Dobrée*, O.B.E., M.A.   760
Restoration Plays.   604
Rossetti, Dante Gabriel (1828–82). POEMS.   627
Shakespeare, William (1564–1616). A Complete Edition. Cambridge Text. Glossary. 3 vols. Comedies, 153; Histories, Poems and Sonnets, 154; Tragedies, 155
Shelley, Percy Bysshe (1792–1822). POETICAL WORKS. 2 vols.   257–8
Sheridan, Richard Brinsley (1751–1816). COMPLETE PLAYS.   95
Silver Poets of the Sixteenth Century. Edited by *Gerald Bullett*.   985
Spenser, Edmund (1552–99). THE FAERIE QUEENE. Glossary. 2 vols. 443–4. THE SHEPHERD'S CALENDAR, 1579; and OTHER POEMS. 879
Sophocles (496 ?–406 B.C.). DRAMAS. This volume contains the seven surviving dramas.   114
Stevenson, Robert Louis (1850–94). POEMS. A CHILD'S GARDEN OF VERSES, 1885; UNDERWOODS, 1887; SONGS OF TRAVEL, 1896; and BALLADS, 1890.   768
Swinburne, Algernon Charles (1837–1909). POEMS AND PROSE. A selection, edited with an Intro. by *Richard Church*.   961
Synge, J. M. (1871–1909). PLAYS, POEMS AND PROSE.   968
Tchekhov, Anton (1860–1904). PLAYS AND STORIES.   941
Tennyson, Alfred, Lord (1809–92). POEMS. 2 vols.   44, 626
Twenty-four One-Act Plays.   947
Virgil (70–19 B.C.). AENEID. Verse translation by *Michael Oakley*. 161. ECLOGUES AND GEORGICS. Verse translation by *T. F. Royds*. 222
Webster, John (1580 ?–1625 ?), and Ford, John (1586–1639). SELECTED PLAYS.   899
Whitman, Walt (1819–92). LEAVES OF GRASS, 1855–92. New edition (1947).   573
Wilde, Oscar (1854–1900). PLAYS, PROSE WRITINGS AND POEMS.   858
Wordsworth, William (1770–1850). POEMS. Ed. *Philip Wayne*, M.A. 3 vols. 203, 311, 998

REFERENCE

Reader's Guide to Everyman's Library. Compiled by *A. J. Hoppé*. This volume is a new compilation and gives in one alphabetical sequence the names of all the authors, titles and subjects in Everyman's Library.   (An Everyman Paperback, 1889).
Many volumes formerly included in Everyman's Library reference section are now included in Everyman's Reference Library and are bound in larger format.

RELIGION AND PHILOSOPHY

Aristotle (384–322 B.C.). POLITICS, etc. Edited and translated by *John Warrington*. 605 METAPHYSICS. Edited and translated by *John Warrington*. 1000
Bacon, Francis (1561–1626). THE ADVANCEMENT OF LEARNING, 1605.   719
Berkeley, George (1685–1753). A NEW THEORY OF VISION, 1709.   483
Browne, Sir Thomas (1605–82). RELIGIO MEDICI, 1642.   92
Bunyan, John (1628–88). GRACE ABOUNDING, 1666; and THE LIFE AND DEATH OF MR BADMAN, 1658.   815
Burton, Robert (1577–1640). THE ANATOMY OF MELANCHOLY, 1621. 3 vols.   886–8
Chinese Philosophy in Classical Times. Covering the period 1500 B.C.–A.D. 100.   973
Cicero, Marcus Tullius (106–43 B.C.). THE OFFICES (translated by *Thomas Cockman*, 1699); LAELIUS, ON FRIENDSHIP; CATO, ON OLD AGE; AND SELECT LETTERS (translated by *W. Melmoth*, 1753). With Note on Cicero's Character by De Quincey. Introduction by *John Warrington*.   345
Descartes, René (1596–1650). A DISCOURSE ON METHOD, 1637; MEDITATIONS ON THE FIRST PHILOSOPHY, 1641; and PRINCIPLES OF PHILOSOPHY, 1644. Translated by *Prof. J. Veitch*.   570
Ellis, Havelock (1859–1939). SELECTED ESSAYS. Sixteen essays.   930
Epictetus (*b. c.* A.D. 60). MORAL DISCOURSES, etc. Translated by *Elizabeth Carter*.   404
Gore, Charles (1853–1932). THE PHILOSOPHY OF THE GOOD LIFE, 1930.   924
Hindu Scriptures. Edited by *Nicol Macnicol*, M.A., D.LITT., D.D.   944
Hobbes, Thomas (1588–1679). LEVIATHAN, 1651.   691
Hooker, Richard (1554–1600). OF THE LAWS OF ECCLESIASTICAL POLITY, 1597. 2 vols.   201–2
Hume, David (1711–76). A TREATISE OF HUMAN NATURE, 1739. 2 vols.   548–9
James, William (1842–1910). PAPERS ON PHILOSOPHY.   739
Kant, Immanuel (1724–1804). CRITIQUE OF PURE REASON, 1781. Translated by *J. M. D. Meiklejohn*.   909
King Edward VI (1537–53). THE FIRST (1549) AND SECOND (1552) PRAYER BOOKS. 448
Koran, The. Rodwell's Translation, 1861.   380
Law, William (1686–1761). A SERIOUS CALL TO A DEVOUT AND HOLY LIFE, 1728.   91
Leibniz, Gottfried Wilhelm (1646–1716). PHILOSOPHICAL WRITINGS. Selected and translated by *Mary Morris*.   905
Locke, John (1632–1704). TWO TREATISES OF CIVIL GOVERNMENT, 1690.   751
Malthus, Thomas Robert (1766–1834). AN ESSAY ON THE PRINCIPLE OF POPULATION, 1798. 2 vols.   692–3

Marcus Aurelius (121–80). MEDITATIONS. *A. S. L. Farquharson* Translation.   **9**
Mill, John Stuart (1806–73). UTILITARIANISM, 1863; LIBERTY, 1859; and REPRE-
   SENTATIVE GOVERNMENT, 1861.   **482**
More, Sir Thomas (1478–1535). UTOPIA, 1516; and DIALOGUE OF COMFORT AGAINST
   TRIBULATION, 1553.   **461**
New Testament, The.   **93**
Newman, John Henry, Cardinal (1801–90). APOLOGIA PRO VITA SUA, 1864.   **636**
Nietzsche, Fredrich Wilhelm (1844–1900). THUS SPAKE ZARATHUSTRA, 1883–91.   **892**
Paine, Thomas (1737–1809). RIGHTS OF MAN, 1792.   **718**
Pascal, Blaise (1623–62). PENSÉES, 1670. Translated by *John Warrington*.   **874**
Plato (427–347 B.C.). THE REPUBLIC. Translated by *A. D. Lindsay*, C.B.E., LL.D. 64.
   THE TRIAL AND DEATH OF SOCRATES. Newly translated by *John Warrington*. 457.
   THE LAWS. A. E. Taylor (1869–1945) Translation. 275
Ramayana and Mahabharata. Condensed into English verse by *Romesh Dutt*, C.I.E. 403
Rousseau, Jean Jacques (1712–78). THE SOCIAL CONTRACT, ETC., 1762.   **660**
Saint Augustine (353–430). CONFESSIONS. *Dr Pusey's* Translation, 1838. 200.   THE
   CITY OF GOD. Complete text. 2 vols. 982–3
Saint Francis (1182–1226). THE LITTLE FLOWERS; THE MIRROR OF PERFECTION (by
   Leo of Assisi); and THE LIFE OF ST FRANCIS (by St Bonaventura).   **485**
Spinoza, Benedictus de (1632–77). ETHICS, 1677, etc. Translated by *Andrew Boyle*. 481
Swedenborg, Emanuel (1688–1772). THE TRUE CHRISTIAN RELIGION, 1771.   **893**
Thomas à Kempis (1380 ?–1471). THE IMITATION OF CHRIST, 1471.   **484**
Thomas Aquinas (1225–74). SELECTED WRITINGS.   **953**

SCIENCE

Boyle, Robert (1627–91). THE SCEPTICAL CHYMIST, 1661.   **559**
Darwin, Charles (1809–82). THE ORIGIN OF SPECIES, 1859. Embodies Darwin's final
   additions.   **811**
Eddington, Arthur Stanley (1882–1944). THE NATURE OF THE PHYSICAL WORLD, 1928.
                                                                      922
Euclid (fl. *c.* 330–*c.*275 B.C.). THE ELEMENTS OF EUCLID. Ed. *Isaac Todhunter.* **891**
Faraday, Michael (1791–1867). EXPERIMENTAL RESEARCHES IN ELECTRICITY, 1839–55.
                                                                      576
Harvey, William (1578–1657). THE CIRCULATION OF THE BLOOD.   **262**
Howard, John (1726 ?–90). THE STATE OF THE PRISONS, 1777.   **835**
Marx, Karl (1818–83). CAPITAL, 1867. Translated by *Eden* and *Cedar Paul.* 2 vols.
                                                                     848–9
Owen, Robert (1771–1858). A NEW VIEW OF SOCIETY, 1813; and OTHER WRITINGS. **799**
Pearson, Karl (1857–1936). THE GRAMMAR OF SCIENCE, 1892.   **939**
Ricardo, David (1772–1823). THE PRINCIPLES OF POLITICAL ECONOMY, 1817.   **590**
Smith, Adam (1723–90). THE WEALTH OF NATIONS, 1766. 2 vols.   **412–13**
White, Gilbert (1720–93). A NATURAL HISTORY OF SELBORNE, 1789. New edition
   (1949).   **48**
Wollstonecraft, Mary (1759–97), THE RIGHTS OF WOMAN, 1792; and Mill, John Stuart
   (1806–73), THE SUBJECTION OF WOMEN, 1869.   **825**

TRAVEL AND TOPOGRAPHY

Borrow, George (1803–81). THE BIBLE IN SPAIN, 1842. 151.   WILD WALES, 1862. 49
Boswell, James (1740–95). JOURNAL OF A TOUR TO THE HEBRIDES WITH SAMUEL
   JOHNSON, 1786. 387
Calderón de la Barca, Mme (1804–82). LIFE IN MEXICO, 1843.   **664**
Cobbett, William (1762–1835). RURAL RIDES, 1830. 2 vols.   **638–9**
Cook, James (1728–79). VOYAGES OF DISCOVERY. Ed by *John Barrow*, F.R.S., F.S.A. 99
Crèvecœur, J. Hector St John de (1735–1813). LETTERS FROM AN AMERICAN FARMER,
   1782.   **640**
Darwin, Charles (1809–82). THE VOYAGE OF THE 'BEAGLE', 1839.   **104**
Defoe, Daniel (1661 ?–1731). A TOUR THROUGH ENGLAND AND WALES, 1724–6. 2 vols.
                                                                     820–1
Hakluyt, Richard (1552–1616). VOYAGES. 8 vols.   264–5; 313–14; 338–9; 388–9
Kinglake, Alexander (1809–91). EOTHEN, 1844.   **337**
Lane, Edward William (1801–76). MODERN EGYPTIANS, 1836.   **315**
Park, Mungo (1771–1806). TRAVELS.   **205**
Polo, Marco (1254–1324). TRAVELS.   **306**
Portuguese Voyages, 1498–1663. Edited by *Charles David Ley.*   **986**
Stevenson, Robert Louis (1850–94). AN INLAND VOYAGE, 1878; TRAVELS WITH A
   DONKEY, 1879; and THE SILVERADO SQUATTERS, 1883.   **765**
Stow, John (1525 ?–1605). THE SURVEY OF LONDON. Elizabethan London.   **589**
Wakefield, Edward Gibbon (1796–1862). A LETTER FROM SYDNEY, etc.   **826**
Waterton, Charles (1782–1865). WANDERINGS IN SOUTH AMERICA, 1825.   **772**